Theodore Roosevelt's Caribbean

Theodore Roosevelt's Caribbean

The Panama Canal, the Monroe Doctrine, and the Latin American Context

Richard H. Collin

Louisiana State University Press
Baton Rouge and London

First printing
99 98 97 96 95 94 93 92 91 90   5 4 3 2 1

Designer: Diane B. Didier
Typeface: Palatino
Typesetter: G&S Typesetters, Inc.
Printer and binder: Thomson-Shore, Inc.

Library of Congress Cataloging-in-Publication Data

Collin, Richard H.
    Theodore Roosevelt's Caribbean: the Panama Canal, the Monroe
Doctrine, and the Latin American context / Richard H. Collin.
        p.   cm.
    Includes bibliographical references.
    ISBN 0-8071-1507-X (alk. paper)
    1. United States—Foreign relations—1901–1909. 2. Roosevelt,
Theodore, 1858–1919—Views on the Caribbean Area. 3. United States—
Foreign relations—Caribbean Area. 4. Caribbean Area—Foreign
relations—United States. 5. Caribbean Area—History—1810–1945.
I. Title.
E756.C76   1990
327.7308'09'041—dc20   89-28161
                                                                CIP

For Esther, Barney, and Rima

Contents

Preface and Acknowledgments

This is a book about contexts. It is a serious attempt to shift the major context of early twentieth-century American diplomacy to its own time and away from its current position as an appendage to post–World War II American history, more concerned about the Cold War or America's role as a superpower than with Kaiser Wilhelm II's Germany. Theodore Roosevelt presided over a brief transition era before World War I transformed the world and America's place in it. Roosevelt's main purpose was the exclusion of Europe, not the subjugation of Latin America. Although it was not the object of Roosevelt's foreign policy, Latin American poets and intellectuals were right in being frightened by the change in the hemispheric balance of power. The old Caribbean order was built around a loose Spanish cultural hegemony, which, combined with enough varied European political and economic enclaves, allowed ambitious Latin American leaders to play the Europeans off against each other or the Americans. Latin America lacked a unifying political presence or single intellectual voice. José Martí, who could have served as the George Washington of Cuban independence and possibly made the freeing of Cuba the start of a realistic Latin American nationalism, died a martyr in 1895. Without Martí or a leader like the Dominican Republic's Gregorio Luperón, who died in 1896, Latin America remained divided. Experiments with European positivism, a continuing attachment to Iberian culture, and the success of the nearby United States with its attractive republicanism, prosperity, and democratic culture further impeded Latin American cultural unity. After Spain's ouster from the New World in 1898, a politically unified United States, freed from its Civil War division, threatened to dominate the fractionalized Latin American republics in politics, economics, and culture. Fear of the new colossus gave Latin American writers their only rallying cry, but their words of warning did not begin to address the fundamental problems that bedeviled Latin America—economic backwardness, political instability, and an increasing gulf between the elites and the other classes.

Between 1895 and 1905 the complex confluence of what we generally call modernism—transportation, communication, and industrial technology—transformed the world. In Europe new systems of diplomatic alliances replaced a world order that had been dominated by British imperial and naval supremacy. Japan's successful war with China in 1894–1895 signaled the arrival of the first Asian industrial and naval power. In the New World the United States' challenge to Britain, its ouster of Spain, and its decision to build an isthmian canal led to a complete reordering of Europe's relationships with the United States. President Theodore Roosevelt's Corollary to the Monroe Doctrine of 1905 made the United States the international protector of the bankrupt Dominican Republic. The Roosevelt Corollary marked a sea change in the perceived relationships between North and Latin America and Europe. At the time the Dominican Republic was under direct diplomatic or naval threat from Germany, Italy, France, and indirectly Belgium. Roosevelt's Corollary was not simply (or even mainly) an extension of American national power but rather an international naval undertaking encouraged and recognized by all of the European powers. The major European powers were more concerned with the Russo-Japanese War and their changing alliances in Europe.

Europe was central to Theodore Roosevelt's foreign policy. The Caribbean became the central stage in America's contest with Europe for control of an interoceanic canal. When Ferdinand de Lesseps, the French promoter who had built the Suez Canal, failed to repeat the miracle at Panama, it became evident that a Panama canal was beyond the capabilities of private capital and required the financial resources of a government. The United States was the logical choice. After the Spanish-American War a congressional and popular consensus to build a canal led to American negotiations with Britain, France, and Colombia to acquire the rights to an American-controlled isthmian canal. The same complex technology that led to the naval revolution which caused the contest in Europe between Britain and the Continental powers, made the Panama Canal a huge engine of modernist technology and change and a serious affront to Colombia's Conservative leader José Manuel Marroquín. Marroquín, who was engaged in a bloody religious war to defend fundamental Spanish Catholicism against positivist Liberals who favored world trade, development capitalism, and secular European philosophies, remained unenchanted by the claims of Theodore Roosevelt, French intellectuals, and world opinion that a Panama canal would serve world civilization (and the Colombian export economy) as much as the United States' strategic and economic interests.

The United States was not nearly as unified a colossus as it appeared. Congress represented a vast sea of separate American local interests, and until the 1890s the president was a relatively weak political figure who superintended the division of national party spoils in a nation that had little foreign policy and little interest in foreign affairs. But because it worked within a system of toleration, coalition, and legislative compromise, the United States could deal better than Latin America with the confounding changes in the world that made complete localism impossible to sustain. America's favorable geography gave it a further advantage over Latin America and Europe.

Colombia's War of the Thousand Days became the grand complication to Roosevelt's strategy to eliminate both Great Britain and Germany from Caribbean affairs. From 1899 to 1902 Colombia engaged in a bitter civil war, the last of its nineteenth-century religious conflicts between orthodox Spanish Catholicism and "enlightened" Europeanized Liberals. There were other issues in the War of the Thousand Days, but the government's unyielding Catholic orthodoxy, Colombia's geographically dictated tradition of regionalism, and a massive failure of political skill all made the Colombian civil war an ideological as well as a military stalemate.

In spite of the accepted views of American impatience and bullying, American proposals to Colombia for a Panama canal were reasonable, reasonably negotiated, and represented a fair consensus of Latin American, United States, and European views on how to build a technologically difficult international waterway in the isthmus. There were differences about whether the canal should be under international or American control, but such issues were resolvable through normal diplomatic negotiations. Colombia's problems, religious and ideological, were not. The canal became a victim of Colombia's War of the Thousand Days. Marroquín, Colombia's acting president, who led the government forces, was a fierce defender of orthodox nineteenth-century Catholic values and an outspoken foe of modernism, development, and Liberal thought. He opposed Liberal political representation in Colombia's government and remained either ambivalent or opposed to a canal in Panama.

Ever since the first news of Panama's revolution of November 3, 1903, reached the United States, Congress and the press have searched for the "untold story of Panama," the specific fact that would tie Theodore Roosevelt directly to the revolution, thereby conclusively proving American complicity. But the real untold story of Panama is the usually ignored Marroquín, who turned diplomacy on its head, delayed, manipulated, bargained, and lied in his opposition to any change in the cultural and geographic separation of nineteenth-century Colombia from the modern world. The Panama canal, to be built by foreign capital, encourage world trade, and bring Yankee influence to his own country, was the symbolic antithesis of Marroquín's worldview. As a onetime academic willing to fight a revolution that cost a hundred thousand Colombian lives, Marroquín's opposition to the idea of a Panama canal is not surprising. What may be surprising is the skill he used in defeating Roosevelt's diplomacy. When Marroquín was on the point of losing his civil war to the Liberals, who had won control of most of Panama, he used the United States to intervene at his behest to settle the war after assuring the Americans that once the war was settled, an agreement on the canal would soon follow. He then refused to support his own treaty, appointed a separatist governor for Panama, and confounded Theodore Roosevelt as thoroughly as he had confounded Colombia's own Liberal party, which first viewed Marroquín as a compromising moderate.

Marroquín did not defeat Roosevelt without help. But his odd ally, Senator John Tyler Morgan, an Alabama Democrat who was Colombia's bitterest foe, led the efforts for an American canal in Nicaragua. Morgan's implacable opposition to a canal in Panama blocked Roosevelt from buying off Marroquín or seriously negotiating Colombian demands for more money. Morgan could use the Nicaraguan price of about $7 million to defeat Colombia's demands for an additional $25 or $35 million, figures that may have represented Marroquín's delaying tactics rather than Colombian greed. Roosevelt, facing the opposition in Colombia of a committed religious ideologue and in the Senate of a regional Democratic foe who turned a Nicaragua canal into an ideology, had either to give up the idea of a canal in Panama, by far the best technological site, or achieve it by unorthodox means. Roosevelt chose to shift American support from Colombia to Panama, and the Congress, involved in a bitter struggle over the chief executive's new foreign policy powers, debated Roosevelt's new role as an activist president.

Lost in the standard context of Latin American dependency or North American imperialism is the enormous skill of Colombia's Marroquín, who may have instinctively understood that to allow a canal at Panama would be to sacrifice everything he held dear and who determined to fight for what he most valued—the sheltered, Catholic, genteel age of nineteenth-century Bogotá untrammeled by technology, modernism, Protestant capitalism, or positivist Europeanized Latin American Liberals. Roosevelt and Marroquín were equally adept at representing their cultures. Roosevelt never did boast that he took the canal (he was misquoted by the very newspaper that most often pilloried him). In Roosevelt's era the United States was not opposed to Latin America and did not consider annexing any part of it. Given American racial politics, with President Theodore Roosevelt excoriated by the southern press for eating dinner in the White House with Booker T. Washington, the idea that Roosevelt or most Americans would willingly annex largely Negro and/or Catholic Latin American states was unthinkable, except to the Latin Americans who feared the colossus but did not understand much about it except its threatening size.

The proper context for Panama and for America's Caribbean diplomacy lies not with later twentieth-century models but with the world of Martí, Marroquín, and Morgan, and also with President Roosevelt's struggle to prevent a strong Germany from replacing a weak Spain in the Caribbean. Roosevelt's big stick, a metaphor he used effectively even before he had a modern navy, was directed at Europe, not Latin America. President Grover Cleveland had thundered at Great Britain in 1895, threatening war if the British did not concede the United States hegemony even in a Venezuelan border dispute. After Britain conceded in Venezuela by agreeing to arbitration, and later gave up its right to a joint isthmian canal in the Hay-Pauncetote II Treaty, Germany became the focus of American attention. German opportunism could not be questioned. Admiral Alfred von Tirpitz's new navy program, the occupation of Kiaochow, the aggressiveness of Germany's Caribbean naval forces, and the kaiser's policies and rhetoric all made America's traditional geographic advantage seem less daunting. Steam technology shrank the oceans; even one large German naval base in the Caribbean could disrupt the Caribbean balance of power.

American fears were justified, not because Germany could conquer substantial parts of Latin America, but because the introduction of European national rivalries into the New World, combined with the growing instability of Central America—Latin America's Balkans— would destabilize the entire region. What Roosevelt sought was stability, not dominance. Roosevelt's efforts in Central America and the Caribbean combined American Progressive idealism with strategic concerns over maintaining control of a Panama canal. Dominating Central America in 1905 was absurd. There was nothing to dominate. Encouraging capitalist development was not ominous but a means of applying North American principles to other cultures as a way of ending the region's revolutions, wars, and instability. That sugar was not Cuba's cure and that imposing temporary economic controls in the Dominican Republic did not solve that country's political or economic problems are beside the point. Roosevelt could no more control what happened after the economic truce than he could prevent World War I after he stopped being president.

Roosevelt's main purpose in the Dominican Republic was to put the fire out, not to rebuild the house. His other purpose was to keep the fox out of the Caribbean henhouse, in short to keep out Germany, which would bring its European rivals with it and kill the neighborhood. That putting out the fire and keeping the house secure were not enough is clear. But presidents are limited by the givens at the time and their limited term in office. President William Howard Taft quickly changed Roosevelt's emphasis on power and responsibility to one that favored American economic interests. Woodrow Wilson rejected some of Taft's economic focus, introduced his own idealism, intervened more forcefully than either Taft or Roosevelt, and had to deal once again with Germany's ability to destabilize the world, including Mexico (though not the Caribbean, which Roosevelt had secured). After World War I came the deluge—increased American interventions and further economic dominance. It makes no historical sense to make Roosevelt's era part of Fidel Castro's Cuba, Daniel Ortega's Nicaragua, or Manuel Antonio Noriega's or Omar Torrijos' Panama. There is enough in the first decade of the century to contain our interest. We need to work more closely with events of that time, not of our own. History is not a straight line but a study of contexts. The context of Roosevelt's era includes emerging technology, new relationships in the Old and New Worlds, startling new dimensions in art, economics, architecture, and literature, changes in the relationships of president and Congress, all the world's encounter with modernism, the attempt to end wars—not only the big European wars but the little Central American ones—and the emergence of Japan as a major power able to startle a world convinced of European superiority by winning a war against giant Russia.

By putting Roosevelt's age in its own context we may be able to begin a more vital historiography. Roosevelt became the symbol of Latin American frustration; his politics of controversy drew criticism to him like a lightning rod; his willingness to wage rhetorical battles with his enemies compounded the image of bellicosity and made him a convenient devil in a complex transitional period. The historiography bogs down on simplistic for or against questions. It is important to argue as Frederick Marks III does in *Velvet on Iron: The Diplomacy of Theodore Roosevelt* that Roosevelt was a moral person. But this is not my argument. The question of what constitutes morality in a practicing politician is a difficult one. A leader who always tells the absolute truth is not much of a politician. Roosevelt's political morality, especially in the Panama Canal incidents, is difficult to judge, since he was not operating in a vacuum but in a world with Kaiser Wilhelm, John Tyler Morgan, José Marroquín, J. P. Morgan, and William Randolph Hearst, and he had poet John Hay as his secretary of state. Politics is what is possible, and what is possible is determined by the context of the times, not by any absolute moral standard. This is not a book about morality but about context. I am more interested in the Caribbean context than in judgments about Roosevelt. Once we get Roosevelt and early twentieth century America back into their own time and place, when we know more about its relationships with the pre–World War I ethos it was a vital part of, we may be better able to judge what was right or wrong. Or we may decide that contexts are more interesting than moral judgments.

This work has evolved over many years. I began my research with the Theodore Roosevelt Papers. I then read in the related manuscript collections at the Library of Congress supplemented by the National Archives' diplomatic records for the period (RG 59). I worked in the National Archives' extensive naval records (RG 24, 38, 45, and 313) as I wrote the book. I supplemented my American research with the diplomatic and naval records at the Public Records Office, Kew, London (FO, CAB, ADM). I also began research in the French diplomatic archives (AMAE, N.S.) at the Quai d'Orsay and in the French naval archives at the Château de Vincennes (esp. BB⁴). I still regret not having examined unpublished Spanish-language sources, especially for Colombia, even though I used the considerable Latin American sources translated in American diplomatic and naval papers, in the published works of Charles Bergquist and Helen Delpar, and in doctoral dissertations, especially those of Thomas Favell, J. Leon Helguera, Vincent B. Dunlap, William Sullivan, David MacMichael, and Joseph Arbena. Colombia's and Panama's discontent with the United States is well documented in printed sources in both Spanish and English (one might add in French newspapers as well.) Nonetheless, I still consider this book as research in progress. The amount of archival and printed material for the period is massive (Theodore Roosevelt's Papers fill 485 microfilm rolls; the State Department's Miscellaneous Letters collection for 1900 to 1906 alone fills 251 rolls of microfilm). I intend to continue my research in the period and to publish the additions and new insights, modifications, contexts, and nuances. I hope other scholars will be able to use my work in their research whether they support or challenge my conclusions.

I am grateful to the many persons who helped in the research and writing of this book. The University of New Orleans Graduate Research Council, the University of New Orleans College of Liberal Arts Organized Research Fund, and the American Philosophical Society all awarded me timely and helpful grants and I thank them. The librarians at the Earl K. Long Library, University of New Orleans, were especially helpful and patient. My thanks to Anthony Tassin and Connie Phelps in Interlibrary Loan, to Sybil Boudreaux, Robert Heriard, Greg Spano, Ed McDonald, and Ethel Llamas for their help and support. I also wish to thank the staffs at the Howard Tilton Library, Tulane University; the Manuscript Reading Room, Library of Congress, especially Charles Kelly; Dane Hartgrove, Ron Swerzig, Richard von Doenhof, and Rick Cox at the National Archives; Nicholas B. Scheetz, Special Collections Division, Georgetown University Library; Evelyn M. Cherpack, Naval War College Archives; Kathleen Rohr, U.S. Naval Historical Center; and William E. Worthington, Jr., National Museum of American History.

I am grateful for the careful reading and useful criticism of Professor Willard B. Gatewood, Jr., of the University of Arkansas. A word of gratitude for the presence and support of Gerald P. Bodet, chairman of the University of New Orleans History Department. My thanks to Trudie Calvert, an excellent copy editor and a pleasure to work with. I also wish to thank Margaret Fisher Dalrymple, Barry L. Blose, and Les Phillabaum of Louisiana State University Press for their support and for their dedication to handsomely produced books. To Rima Drell Reck, my wife and colleague, who helped in so many ways, my gratitude for her example, her intellect, and her critical eye for the right words even outside her own many areas of expertise.

To my readers, my gratitude in advance for their patience with a long book and with whatever errors it still contains.

Abbreviations

AHR   *American Historical Review*

AMAE Archives du Ministère des Affaires Étrangères, Quai d'Orsay, Paris, France.

AMB   Arthur M. Beaupré

AQ   *American Quarterly*

BVC   Philippe Bunau-Varilla, *Panama: The Creation, Destruction, and Resurrection.* London, 1913.

CHLA Leslie Bethel, ed., *The Cambridge History of Latin America.* 5 vols. Cambridge, Eng., 1984–86.

DH   *Diplomatic History*

ER   Elihu Root

FO   Foreign Office (Britain)

FRUS United States, Department of State, *Papers Relating to Foreign Relations of the United States,* 1861–. Washington, D.C., 1861–.

GP   Germany, Auswärtiques Amt. *Die grosse Politik der europäischen Kabinette,* 1871–1914, ed. Johannes Lepsius, Albrecht Mendelssohn Bartholdy, and Friedrich Thimme. 40 vols. Berlin, 1922–27.

GTBD Great Britain, Foreign Office, *British Documents on the Origins of the War,* 1898–1914, ed. George P. Gooch and Harold Temperly. 11 vols. London, 1926–38.

HAHR *Hispanic American Historical Review*

HCL   Henry Cabot Lodge

HR   Jacob Hollander, *Debit of Santo Domingo, Senate Documents,* 59th Cong., 1st Sess., Confidential Executive Document No. 1 (or 1A) (Hollander Report).

JAH   *Journal of American History*

JBM   John Bassett Moore

JBMS John Bassett Moore Scrapbooks, Library of Congress

JH   John Hay

LA   *Libro Azul, documentos diplomáticos sobre el canal y la rebellion del Istmo de Panamá.* Bogotá, 1904.

LC   Library of Congress

LD   *Literary Digest*

MAE   Ministère des Affaires Étrangères, Paris.

MRL   Elting Morison, ed. *The Letters of Theodore Roosevelt.* 8 vols. Cambridge, Mass., 1951–54.

MVHR *Mississippi Valley Historical Review*

NA   National Archives

N.S.   Nouvelle Série, Correspondance Politique et Commerciale, 1897 à 1918.

NAR   *North American Review*

PHR   *Pacific Historical Review*

PRO   Public Record Office, Kew, London

RG   Record Group (National Archives)

RP   Theodore Roosevelt Papers, Library of Congress

SDIC   San Domingo Improvement Company

SP   *Story of Panama: Hearings on the Rainey Resolution Before the Committee on Foreign Affairs of the House of Representatives.* Washington, D.C., 1913.

TBR   Taft-Bacon Report in *House Documents,* 59th Cong., 2nd Sess., No. 2, Serial 5105, pp. 444–542.

TD   Thomas Dawson

TR   Theodore Roosevelt

TRAJ   *Theodore Roosevelt Association Journal*

TRJR   Theodore Roosevelt, Jr.

TRWN Theodore Roosevelt. *The Works of Theodore Roosevelt.* National Edition. 20 vols. New York, 1926.

WHT   William Howard Taft

WP   William Powell

Theodore Roosevelt's Caribbean

Part I

Context

Coming

1 The Latin American Context

Poverty, poetry, and sugar eventually symbolized the troubled relationship between the two Americas at the turn of the twentieth century. Latin American poverty stood in stark contrast with North American prosperity, and Latin American writers openly attacked the North Americans for being materialistic and soulless. In 1904, Rubén Darío summed up the attitude of a generation of frustrated Latin Americans in his poem addressed to President Theodore Roosevelt: "And though you have everything, you are lacking one thing: God!" The sugar technology of the late nineteenth century destroyed the cultural balance of Caribbean Latin America; sugar turned small farmers into wage laborers, introduced foreign development capitalism into subsistence agricultural societies, and even displaced rural livestock. Cuban writer Fernando Ortiz protested, "Tobacco is a magic gift of a savage world, sugar a scientific gift of civilization." Before sugar displaced all other agriculture, a Dominican writer in 1884 ironically observed the farmers' change of status: "Although, poor and coarse, at least they were property owners, and today, poorer and made more brutish, they have become proletarian. What Progress does that show?" The new sugar agriculture marked the beginning of extractive and exploitive commercial relations between North and South America.[1]

1. "To Roosevelt," in Rubén Darío, *Selected Poems of Rubén Darío*, trans. Lysander Kemp (Austin, Tex., 1965), 69–70. For the effects of sugar technology on Cuba see Louis A. Pérez, Jr., "Vagrants, Beggars, and Bandits: Social Origins of Cuban Separatism, 1878–1895," *AHR*, XC (1985), 1092–1121. For the effect of sugar on the Dominican Republic see H. Hoetink, *The Dominican People, 1850–1900: Notes for a Historical Sociology*, trans. Stephen K. Ault (Baltimore, 1982), 12–14; Fernando Ortiz, *Cuban Counterpoint: Tobacco and Sugar* (New York, 1947) rpr. in Michael M. Horowitz, *Peoples and Cultures of the Caribbean* (Garden City, N.Y., 1971), 150; Pedro F. Bono to Gregorio Luperón, 1884, quoted in Hoetink, *Dominican People*, 12; H. Paul Muto, "The Illusory Promise: The Dominican Republic and the Process of Economic Development, 1900–1930" (Ph.D. dissertation, University of Washington, 1976), esp. 29–61.

The two Americas were strikingly different. North America was predominantly Protestant, wealthy, materialistic, politically unified, and lucky. South America tended to be Catholic, poor, spiritual, politically chaotic, and consistently unlucky. North America was settled by British and northern Europeans who became landowners, South America by European gentlemen entrepreneurs gifted in export commerce. Both Americas shared the constitutional rhetoric of John Locke, which reflected the cultural and political heritage of the European Enlightenment, a predilection for republican government over monarchical, and a sublime disregard for the native Indians. In the North the Indians were killed or removed; in the South they were exploited, converted, ignored, and eventually pauperized.[2]

In 1811 Francisco Arango y Parreño, a Cuban economist who specialized in New World agriculture and commerce, first warned that "in the North there was growing a colossus composed of all castes and languages that threatened to swallow, if not all of our Americas, at least the northern part of it." Although many Spanish Americans admired the United States, they feared it as well, and the image of the colossus to the north symbolized their view of the United States'

2. A. Owen Aldridge, "The Concept of the Ibero-American Enlightenment," in *The Ibero-American Enlightenment* (Urbana, 1971), 3–20; Arthur P. Whitaker, "Changing and Unchanging Interpretations of the Enlightenment in Spanish America," *ibid.*, 21–57; Russell P. Sebold, "Enlightenment Philosophy and the Emergence of Spanish Romanticism," *ibid.*, 111–40; D.H. Meyer, "Uniqueness of the American Enlightenment," *AQ*, XXVIII (1976), 165–86; Peter Gay, "The Enlightenment," in C. Vann Woodward (ed.), *The Comparative Approach to American History* (New York, 1968), 34–46; James T. Kloppenberg, "The Virtues of Liberalism: Christianity, Republicanism, and Ethics in Early American Political Discourse," *JAH*, LXXIV (1987), 9–33; John Patrick Diggins, "Comrades and Citizens: New Mythologies in American Historiography," *AHR*, XC (1985), 614–49; Henry May, *The American Enlightenment* (New York, 1976); see also two special *AQ* issues: Joseph Ellis (ed.), "An American Enlightenment," *AQ*, XXVIII (1976), 147–292; and Joyce Appleby (ed.), "Republicanism in the History and Historiography of the United States," *AQ*, XXXVII (1985), 461–631. For John Locke see Jean S. Yolton and John W. Yolton (eds.), *John Locke: A Reference Guide* (Boston, 1985), useful for information on the various editions; John Dunn, *The Political Thought of John Locke* (Cambridge, Eng., 1969); and Maurice Cranston, "Locke and Liberty," *Wilson Quarterly*, X (Winter, 1986), 82–93. On the treatment of Indians see Samuel Shapiro, "A Common History of the Americas," in Shapiro (ed.), *Cultural Factors in Inter-American Relations* (South Bend, Ind., 1968), 42–43; and John Lynch, "Origins of Spanish-American Independence," in *CHLA*, III, 3–50; James Axtell, "The Invasion Within: The Contest of Cultures in Colonial North America," in Howard Lamar and Leonard Thompson (eds.), *The Frontier in History: North America and Southern Africa Compared* (New Haven, 1981), 237–69; for a recent view that places the Indians at the center of the American imagination see Richard Slotkin, *Regeneration Through Violence: The Mythology of the American Frontier* (Middletown, Conn., 1973).

dual role as an economic rival as well as a republican ally. Even though the United States and the Latin American states dealt with each other individually, both the unified colossus and the independent Latin American states at various times encouraged the imagery of a unified Latin America or a unified Western Hemisphere. This illusion was severely compromised by Spain's retention of Cuba and Puerto Rico as slaveholding colonies and by the disparity in wealth between the two Americas. Economic competition in Latin America between the United States and Great Britain also complicated the notion of unity. In various guises, however, such as the Monroe Doctrine of 1823, Simón Bolívar's Panama Congress of 1826, and the modern Pan-American movements that began in 1889, the image endured though more as idealized metaphor than political reality. Neither North nor South America welcomed the shrinking of the world's boundaries that occurred when coal, steam, and steel replaced wood and sail in ocean transport. The United States, born of English capitalism and Protestant energy, was much better able to deal with the modern world than were the heirs of Iberian Europe. In 1588, in the dramatic confrontation that began the British settlement of the New World, Elizabethan England's navy had defeated the Spanish Armada. As the nineteenth century closed, the United States defeated another Spanish navy at Manila, ousted Spain from Asia and the Americas, and became a dominant world power.[3]

Latin Americans, deeply ambivalent toward Spain, their cultural progenitor and consistent oppressor, were shocked by the sudden and dramatic change in the Caribbean and the world that occurred in 1898. When the United States defeated Spain in a world war that involved not only Cuba and Puerto Rico in the Caribbean but the Philip-

---

3. Arango y Parreño quoted in Juan de Onis, *The United States as Seen by Spanish American Writers, 1776–1890* (New York, 1952), 48; see *ibid.*, 46–48; David M. Pletcher, "United States Relations with Latin America: Neighborliness and Exploitation," *AHR*, LXXXII (1977), 41; Arthur P. Whitaker, *The United States and the Independence of Latin America, 1800–1830* (Baltimore, 1941); and *The Western Hemisphere Idea: Its Rise and Decline* (Ithaca, N.Y., 1954). For the controversy about Herbert E. Bolton's thesis of a commonality between the two Americas see Lewis Hanke (ed.), *Do the Americas Have a Common History? A Critique of the Bolton Theory* (New York, 1964); also see Harry Bernstein, *Making an Inter-American Mind* (Gainesville, 1961); Bernstein, *Origins of Inter-American Interest, 1700–1812* (Washington, D.C., 1945); Shapiro, "A Common History of the Americas," 40–41, 50, 60; and Leopoldo Zea, *Latin America and the World*, trans. Frances K. Hendrichs and Beatrice Becker (Norman, Okla., 1969), esp. 3–32, 93–99; for the changes in naval technology see Bernard Brodie, *Sea Power in the Machine Age* (Princeton, 1943).

pines in Asia, Spain lost its dominant New World presence to a new, stronger, and much more threatening political entity. In forcibly displacing Catholic Spain, the United States made clear its intention to expel any other foreign—European—intrusions from both Americas.[4]

The aristocratic Theodore Roosevelt, leading one of history's most famous cavalry charges in the Spanish-American War, was the apotheosis of militant Protestantism. He had all but two of the virtues the Latin American elites admired. He wrote, he governed, he hated business and businessmen, and he could fight. Unfortunately he was neither Catholic nor Latin American. The freeing of Cuba should have been a moment of great celebration for the new and growing sense of Latin American unity. But if history had smiled on Latin America, the actual deed would have been accomplished by Cubans led by José Martí, certainly not by Theodore Roosevelt and his North American Rough Riders. Martí, the last great Latin American intellectual and political leader of the century (Simón Bolívar was the first), had sacrificed his life for the revolution in 1895. Martí became the martyr, Roosevelt the hero; Cuba was freed but at great cost to an already troubled Latin American pride. History remained cruel toward Latin America even when ridding Cuba of an onerous oppression.[5]

By Theodore Roosevelt's era, it had become increasingly clear that Latin America was in trouble. The Bolívarian revolutions that displaced Spain produced constitutional government but brought neither the prosperity nor the political unity North America enjoyed. Lockean rhetoric that had been put into practice in North America did not achieve the high hopes of the new Latin American republics. Sophisticated leaders like Bolívar did not expect words or ideals to trans-

4. See David F. Trask, *The War with Spain in 1898* (New York, 1981); for the effect of the war on Latin America see Martin S. Stabb, *In Quest of Identity: Patterns in the Spanish-American Essay of Ideas, 1890–1960* (Chapel Hill, 1967), 10–13; John T. Reid, *Spanish American Images of the United States* (Gainesville, 1977), 130–31; Jean Franco, *The Modern Culture of Latin America: Society and Artist* (New York, 1967), 40; also see Frank Reuter, *Catholic Influence on American Colonial Policies, 1898–1904* (Austin, 1967).

5. There is no adequate biography of Theodore Roosevelt. Henry Pringle, *Theodore Roosevelt: A Biography* (New York, 1931), is reliable for chronology; William Harbaugh, *The Life and Times of Theodore Roosevelt*, is the best historical synthesis; Carleton Putnam, *Theodore Roosevelt: The Formative Years* (New York, 1958), and Edmund Morris, *The Rise of Theodore Roosevelt* (New York, 1979), are first volumes of projected multivolume biographies. For Roosevelt's war service see TR, *The Rough Riders*, in TRWN, XI; and Gerald F. Lindeman, *The Mirror of War: American Society and the Spanish-American War* (Ann Arbor, 1974), 91–113. On the circumstances of Martí's death see Richard Butler Gray, *José Martí: Cuban Patriot* (Gainesville, 1962), 32–33.

form Latin America. In 1815 Bolívar complained that Spanish Americans had been kept "in a state of permanent childhood with regard to public affairs. If we could at least have managed our domestic affairs and our internal administration, we could have acquainted ourselves with the process and machinery of government." Unwilling to follow George Washington's example of relinquishing a successful revolutionary's power, and earnestly doubting the ability of the South American republics to copy North American democracy, Bolívar favored a government of liberal centralization—with himself as lifetime president—as an alternative to either European monarchial absolutism or the United States' system of representative federalism. He also envisioned a confederation of Latin American states acting as a balance of power between absolutist Europe and the unified United States—with Britain as a possible ally against either as the need arose. In praising the "magnificent federal system" of the United States, Bolívar cautioned the Congress at Angostura on February 15, 1819: "Our moral constitution does not have the consistency needful to enjoy the benefits of a government completely representative, and so sublime as to be suitable for a republic of saints." In 1815 Bolívar envisioned Panama as a capital of peace, "situated as it is in the center of the world, looking in one direction towards Africa and Europe, and equidistant from America's two extremities." A half-century later Martí, also writing defensively, hoped that "Spanish America" might be "the world's balance of power." Both Bolívar and Martí were *pensadores*, a class of politically active writers, who in their passion for intellectual engagement and large questions resembled the Enlightenment *philosophes*. Latin America *pensadores* struggled to accommodate their Spanish traditions (and souls) with their attraction to Anglo-Saxon political ideas.[6]

6. Angostura quoted in William R. Shephard, "Bolívar and the United States," *HAHR*, I (1918), 286–87; Víctor Andrés Belaúnde, *Bolívar and the Political Thought of the Spanish American Revolution* (Baltimore, 1938); also see David Bushnell (ed.), *The Liberator Símon Bolívar: Man and Image* (New York, 1970); Gerhard Masur, *Símon Bolívar* (Rev. ed.; Albuquerque, 1969), 243–45; the text of the "Jamaica letter," September 6, 1815, translated as "Letter to an English Gentleman," is in R. A. Humphreys and John Lynch (eds.), *The Origins of the Latin American Revolutions, 1808–1826* (New York, 1964), 261–66, "in a state . . . government" quoted, *ibid.*, 263; Joseph B. Lockey, "Bolívar, After a Century," in Lockey, *Essays in Pan-Americanism* (Berkeley, 1939), 135–42; John Lynch, "Bolívar and the Caudillos," *HAHR*, LXIII (1983), 3–35; Simon Collier, "Nationality, Nationalism, and Supranationalism in the Writings of Símon Bolívar," *HAHR*, LXIII (1983), 37–64; and David Bushnell, "The Last Dictatorship: Betrayal or Consummation?" *HAHR*, LXIII (1983), 65–105. See also Onis, *The United States as Seen by Spanish*

In the nineteenth century North America settled its interior, developed its cities, and by the end of the century had begun to produce an indigenous art and culture. In the same period Latin America became more discordant. Little wars and big wars alternated; elites battled with natives, first culturally, then politically and economically, and finally in war after futile civil war. Cuba fought against Spanish oppression, Colombia fought Venezuela and itself, Central America defeated every attempt at political unification, and at the start of the twentieth century there were few Latin American nations that were not engaged in almost constant national or civil war. Latin America was isolated from both the world and its own past. At the end of the nineteenth century Latin America, badly divided within itself and torn by the dilemmas of industrialization, development, and modernism, faced an overwhelming new threat—a unified and apparently aggressive United States, geographically dominant and politically, economically, and culturally threatening.[7]

The Latin American writers fought back. José Martí journeyed to New York in 1881 and wrote both lovingly and violently. In his last letter, left unfinished before his hero's death, Martí wrote, "I have lived in the monster and I know its entrails; my sling is David's." Martí had first warned his Latin readers of the new dangers from the north in 1889: "Because of geographical morality" the United States wanted "to rule the continent, and it announces, in the words of its politicians, via pulpit and press, banquet and Congress—while laying hands on one island and trying to purchase another—that everything in North America must be its." Martí's anti-Americanism after 1888 laid the foundation for the increasingly anti-American writing that ended the nineteenth century and rose to a crescendo during Theodore Roosevelt's presidency.[8]

American Writers, 19–88; Panama quote in Gordon K. Lewis, *Main Currents in Caribbean Thought* (Baltimore, 1983), 324–25; José Martí, "The Washington Pan-American Congress," *La Nación* (Buenos Aires), December, 19–20, 1889, rpr. in José Martí, *Inside the Monster: Writings on the United States and American Imperialism,* ed. Philip S. Foner, trans. Elinor Randall (New York, 1975), 367; W. Rex Crawford, *A Century of Latin American Thought* (Cambridge, Mass., 1961), 4–5.

7. Octavia Paz, "Prologue," in Darío, *Selected Poems,* 15; Crawford, *A Century of Latin American Thought;* Leopoldo Zea, *The Latin American Mind,* trans. James H. Abbott and Lowell Dunham (Norman, Okla., 1963); José Agustín Balseiro, *The Americas Look at Each Other,* trans. Muna Muñoz Lee (Coral Gables, Fla., 1969); and E. J. Hobsbawm, *The Age of Capital, 1848–1875* (New York, 1975), 118–21.

8. For Martí's writing in New York see Roberta Day Corbitt, "This Colossal Theater: The United States Interpreted by José Martí" (Ph.D. dissertation, University of Ken-

That many North Americans were outspoken expansionists is undeniable. But the United States was not responsible for all of Latin America's problems at the turn of the century. The technology that brought capitalism to Latin America also brought new ideas. Positivism swept through the European elites clustered in the capitals and urban areas of mostly rural Latin America. In Buenos Aires, Montevideo, Santiago de Chile, and to a lesser degree in Rio de Janeiro and Mexico City, the new stirrings of an international culture—partly Hispanic-American, mostly French European—had begun. The technology that brought Minor Keith to Central America to begin a banana empire also permitted José Martí to come north, where he wrote of life, letters, art, and politics in the United States—and Europe as well—for intellectuals who read his articles published in Latin America's most influential journals, Buenos Aires' *La Nación*, Mexico City's *El Partido Liberal*, Montevideo's *La Opinión Pública*, and Caracas' *La Opinión Nacional*. Martí made Latin Americans aware of the lure and the threat of the new United States.[9]

Modernism, not the United States cast as a convenient devil, was the chief protagonist of the Latin nations. Modernization occurred worldwide in the nineteenth century, fueled by capitalism and the new technology capitalism helped create. Although a vast literature links capitalist expansion into Latin America with theories of political and economic imperialism recently recast as dependency, modernization was a process of internationalism, as much cultural as economic or social. Imperial and dependency theorists favor a direct relationship between the maturity of capitalist industrialism in the United

---

tucky, 1955). For Martí's life see Manuel Pedro Gonzales, *José Martí: Epic Chronicler of the United States in the Eighties* (Chapel Hill, 1953); Gray, *José Martí*; John M. Kirk, *José Martí: Mentor of the Cuban Nation* (Tampa, 1983). For a bibliography on Martí scholarship, see Robert Roland Anderson, *Spanish American Modernism: A Selected Bibliography* (Tucson, 1970), 107–28; José Martí to Manuel Mercado, May 18, 1895, in José Martí, *Our America: Writings on Latin America and the Struggle for Cuban Independence*, ed. Philip S. Foner, trans. Elinor Randall (New York, 1977), 440; Jose Martí, "The Washington Pan-American Congress," in Martí, *Inside the Monster*, 440.

9. For the Latin American journals Martí contributed to and for his pen names see Corbitt, "This Colossal Theater," 29. For American expansion see David M. Pletcher, *The Diplomacy of Annexation: Texas, Oregon, and the Mexican War* (Columbia, Mo., 1973), esp. 64–66, 576–611. Comprehensive critical treatments of American expansion include Frederick Merk, *Manifest Destiny and Mission in American History: A Reinterpretation* (New York, 1963); Richard W. Van Alstyne, *The Rising American Empire* (New York, 1960); Charles Vevier, "American Continentalism: An Idea of Expansion, 1845–1910," *AHR*, LXXV (1960), 323–35; and Albert K. Weinberg, *Manifest Destiny: A Study of Nationalist Expansionism in American History* (Baltimore, 1935).

States and the expansion of American foreign relations at the turn of the century. Many see the Spanish-American War of 1898 not as a conflict between Spain and the United States but as part of a U.S. master plan to consolidate its influence and markets and subjugate nearby Latin America as well as colonizing far-off Asia. In this view, Americans coveted the China market and wished to replace Europe as the chief exploiter of Latin America, especially the nearby Caribbean. Modernization theorists are dismissed as apologists for development capitalism, who ignore the political implications of Western capitalist expansion into preindustrial societies. There are few arguments about what happened but violent disagreements about the context.[10]

Modernization and intense nationalism occurred simultaneously and frequently overlapped. But there is ample evidence that entrepre-

---

10. For a summary of modernization theory see Cyril E. Black (ed.), *Comparative Modernization: A Reader* (New York, 1976), esp. James O'Connell, "The Concept of Modernization," *ibid.*, 13–14; and Donald R. Headrick, *The Tools of Empire: Technology and European Imperialism in the Nineteenth Century* (New York, 1981). For a critical view of dependency theory see David Ray, "The Dependency Model of Latin American Underdevelopment: Three Basic Fallacies," *Journal of Inter-American Studies and World Affairs*, XV (1973), 4–20. For a synthesis of the historiographical debate see William Glade, "Latin America and the International Economy, 1870–1914," in *CHLA*, IV, 46–56; and Thomas F. O'Brien, "Dependency Revisited: A Review Essay," *Business History Review*, LIV (1985), 663–70. For imperialism see Richard Koebner and H. D. Schmidt, *Imperialism: The Story and Significance of a Political Word, 1840–1960* (Cambridge, Eng., 1964); David Healy, *Modern Imperialism: Changing Styles in Historical Interpretation* (Washington, D.C., 1967); and Hugh de Santis, "Imperialist Impulse and American Innocence," in Gerald K. Haines and J. Samuel Walker (eds.), *American Foreign Relations: A Historiographical Review* (Westport, Conn., 1981), 65–90. For the influence of positivism in Latin America see Ralph Lee Woodward, Jr. (ed.), *Positivism in Latin America: 1850–1900* (Lexington, Mass., 1971). For the effect of technology on writers see Gerald Martin, "Literature, Music, and Art of Latin America from Independence to c. 1870," in *CHLA*, III, 838. For the effect of the War of 1898 see Philip S. Foner, *The Spanish-Cuban-American War and the Birth of American Imperialism* (2 vols.; New York, 1972). For the Cuban legal name for the War of 1898 as *Guerra Hispano-Cuban-Americano* and a review of Cuban historiography see Duvon C. Corbitt, "Cuba's Struggle for Independence," *HAHR*, XLIII (1963), 400. See also Louis A. Pérez, Jr., "Intervention, Hegemony, and Dependency: The United States in the circum-Caribbean, 1898–1980," *PHR*, LI (1982), 165–82. For a critical review of the extensive historiography of American economic expansionism see J. A. Thompson, "William Appleman Williams and the 'American Empire,'" *Journal of American Studies* (Great Britain), VII (1973), 91–104; and David M. Pletcher, "1861–1898: Economic Growth and Diplomatic Adjustment," in William H. Becker and Samuel Wells, Jr. (eds.), *Economics and World Power: An Assessment of American Diplomacy Since 1789* (Westport, Conn., 1984), 125–31. For a critical description of recent social science models see Steven W. Hughes and Kenneth J. Mijeski, "Contemporary Paradigms in the Study of Inter-American Relations," in John D. Martz and Lars Schoulz (eds.), *Latin America, the United States and the Inter-American System* (Boulder, Colo., 1980).

neurs and states not only worked independently but frequently at cross-purposes. American State Department records are filled with official annoyance at American entreprenurial zeal in Latin America. The United States may have had its share of international capitalists, but the Roosevelt administration—President Theodore Roosevelt, Secretary of State John Hay, and most of the working under-secretaries— were upper-class American aristocrats who found any business demeaning and the marginal enterprise of Latin American adventurers especially sleazy. European governments as well as businessmen promoted the building of railroads in colonial nations but frequently differed on the purposes and the locations of the railroads. Not until the twentieth century did the major European governments support the attempts of their foreign bondholders to collect private debts in Latin American nations. Until then the bondholders were relegated to peripheral status and regarded with diffidence or as petty annoyances by statesmen who disdained commerce and commerical people. The displacement of Mexican peons from their land and the enormous dislocations that occurred when export agriculture and railroads began to dominate British India were not part of a giant Western conspiracy to make the poor even poorer. The upheavals and changes in established institutions produced not only new problems but new adaptations to the massive economic, political, and cultural changes in the world.[11]

Communication, the most significant of the new technologies, permitted knowledge to transcend local, regional, and eventually national borders. When the German novelist Thomas Mann wrote in 1933, "we get rid of our ideas by giving them form and sending them on their travels," he was describing cultural rather than the more familiar political or economic modernization. Modernization was not

11. For the rejection of the connection between business and government see William E. Becker, *The Dynamics of Business-Government Relations, 1893–1921* (Chicago, 1981), viii–ix; and Mira Wilkins, *The Emergence of Multinational Enterprise: American Business Abroad from the Colonial Era to 1914* (Cambridge, Mass., 1970), 74–75; Thompson, "William Appleman Williams and the 'American Empire,'" 91–104; and Paul S. Holbo, "Economics, Emotion, and Expansion: An Emerging Foreign Policy," in H. Wayne Morgan (ed.), *The Gilded Age* (Rev. ed.; Syracuse, N.Y., 1970), 199–221, 315–19; Henry Eder to JH, March 1, 1902, Naval Records Collection, Subject File VI, International Relations and Politics, Colombia, Box 664, in RG 45, NA; J. Bancroft Davis to Henry C. C. Astwood, December 7, 1882, in *Instructions to Consuls*, vol. 105, pp. 477–78, RG 59, NA; Joel Migdal, "Capitalist Penetration in the Nineteenth Century: Creating Conditions for Social Control," in Robert P. Weller and Scott E. Guggenheim (eds.), *Power and Protest in the Countryside* (Durham, N.C., 1982), 73.

simply Westernization; the United States did not consciously threaten the indigenous Latin Catholic culture. Modernism is no more Western than science is Greek. Nor was industrialism exclusively Western. Japan and Russia are striking examples of a universal phenomenon. Nor is wealth an invariable index. Saudi Arabia is wealthy and premodern; Ireland is poor and modern.[12]

The same improved communication technology that led to the proliferation of railroads in hinterlands also contributed to changes in knowledge. When telegraph poles arrived in the small town of Samaná in the Dominican Republic in 1898, the people "spontaneously" helped put them up. A telegraph connection with the equally small town of Sánchez was the beginning of the end of the isolation that existed before the advent of modern communication systems. Children in developed societies learn informally and at home what children in premodern societies must learn formally and imperfectly in schools. To see the modernization process of the late nineteenth century purely as an exploitation of undeveloped peoples by the economically advanced Western capital states misses the sense of chaos that engulfed the West as the changes developed. The many political, diplomatic, and social crises of the early twentieth century are testament to the universal confusion. Modernization is better understood as an interaction that affected all parts of the world.[13]

The new technology made the once distant Americas more accessible to Europe and its capitalism. Latin America was not wealthy by any standard, though Argentina and Chile at the end of the nineteenth century were among the world's most promising nations economically and culturally, if not politically. The Latin American interior had always been grindingly poor, but by the twentieth century the divergence of wealth and power between the native American Indians and former African slaves—the bulk of Latin America's agricultural subsistence class—and the new European elite immigrant class

12. Thomas Mann, *Past Masters and Other Papers* (New York, 1933), 254; O'Connell, "Concept of Modernization," 17–23; Martin, "Literature, Music, and Art of Latin America," *CHLA*, III, 838; L. W. Pye (ed.), *Communications and Political Development* (Princeton, 1963), 3–21, 149–51.

13. Hoetink, *Dominican People*, 56; O'Connell, "Concept of Modernization," 19; Black, *Modernization*, 10. For an example of successful modernization in 1880s Guatemala see J. Fred Rippy, "United States and Guatemala During the Epoch of Justo Rufino Barrios," *HAHR*, XXII (1942), 595–605; for an overview of the modernization process see Hobsbawm, *Age of Capital*. For the view that a similar modernization process explains the destabilization that preceded the French Revolution see Simon Schama, *Citizens: A Chronicle of the French Revolution* (New York, 1989), esp. xv.

that dominated Latin American cities (and increasingly the national governments) began to grow alarmingly. Unlike the United States, where European expansion created a new organic political and economic entity based on rapid westward expansion which developed the land and its resources, Latin American development was sporadic and limited to the coasts.[14]

In the United States the frontier West and the settled East complemented each other. No better example of the fluidity of North American society exists than Theodore Roosevelt, the New York aristocrat and Dakota Territory rancher and cowboy. Roosevelt bought his first western land in 1883 and moved freely between his native and his adopted region for many years. In 1886 Roosevelt had to make a political choice. He could become one of the first senators from the Dakotas when the territory was admitted to the Union or he could run for mayor of New York City. Roosevelt chose—and lost—the mayoralty race, but he remained a citizen of both regions. When he helped raise a volunteer regiment for the war in 1898 and when he became the vice-presidential candidate in 1900, his western sympathies and connections were vital. Such a divided allegiance was not possible in Latin America, where the barriers between interior and exterior, based on race, class, and wealth, deepened and became more rigid throughout the nineteenth century.[15]

The Latin American intellectual establishment was divided between city and country before custom and politics made such divisions permanent. The most influential early effort to define Latin American elitism occurred in Argentina, the most developed of the Latin American nations. A literary and intellectual movement known as the Generation of 1837 formalized the belief that whatever Argen-

14. See Tulio Halperín Donghi, "Economy and Society in Post-Independence Spanish America," in CHLA, III, 299–346; Ralph Lee Woodward, Jr., "The Rise and Decline of Liberalism in Central America: Historical Perspectives on the Contemporary Crisis," Journal of International Studies and World Affairs, XXVI (1984), 291–96; Charles A. Hale, "Political and Social Ideas in Latin America, 1870–1930," in CHLA, IV, 367–441; Frederick Pike, Chile and the United States, 1880–1962 (South Bend, Ind., 1963), 94–107; and Thomas F. McGann, Argentina, the United States, and the Inter-American System, 1880–1914 (Cambridge, Mass., 1957).

15. For Roosevelt in the West see Hermann Hagedorn, Roosevelt in the Bad Lands (Boston, 1921); TR, Hunting Trips of a Ranchman (1885) and Ranch Life and the Hunting Trail (1888), rpr. in TRWN, I; Putnam, Theodore Roosevelt, 313–64. For the 1886 mayoralty race, see Morris, Rise of Theodore Roosevelt, 342–58; Harbaugh, Life and Times of Theodore Roosevelt, 70–71. E. Bradford Burns, The Poverty of Progress: Latin America in the Nineteenth Century (Berkeley, 1980).

tine civilization existed in the nineteenth century was concentrated in the urban center of Buenos Aires. Although the superiority of urban over rural society was accepted in most cosmopolitan urban centers, Argentina was more vehement. The Generation of 1837 regarded the mass of mixed race or native stock rural peoples not merely as backward but as inherent and permanent barbarians. Basing their dichotomy on a skewed reading of St. Augustine, the new Eurocentric elite called Buenos Aires the City of God and the home of civilization, and the rural interior the City of Man and the center of barbarism. From this assumption sprang the ideology that assured that nineteenth-century Latin America would expend much of its energy in disunity and discord.[16]

The disparity between North and South America is nowhere more evident than in the relations of the metropolis to the hinterland. In prenational North America, the first discord with Britain came from Anglo-American insistence on protection from Indians in settlement of the trans-Appalachian West. When in 1763 the British barred further settlement as too expensive and frivolous, the North Americans began to develop their first sense of a separate national identity that eventually resulted in revolution and independence. All North Americans looked westward. Thomas Jefferson, who was basically a localist rooted in limited central government and Virginia state politics and opposed to Hamiltonian federalism, added the Louisiana Purchase to the already vast national lands. Only when the expansion of slavery into the territories became an overt issue were the goals of westward expansion and integration questioned, though not enough to prevent the absorption of Texas and California.[17]

Jefferson was as much of a cultural Europeanist as Domingo Faustino Sarmiento, the chief spokesman for the ideal of a Europeanized Latin America. Sarmiento, a prolific writer, educational philosopher, and intellectual, was president of Argentina from 1868 to 1874. Whereas Jefferson eventually rejected Europe, Sarmiento embraced European values. Sarmiento's seminal book *Civilization and Barbarism: The Life of Juan Facundo Quiroga* (1845) became the foundation for Latin America's continuing intellectual reliance on European ideas and cul-

16. Burns, *Poverty of Progress*, 21–23.
17. Roy Allen Billington, *Westward Expansion: A History of the American Frontier* (2nd ed.; New York, 1960); Thomas P. Abernathy, *Western Lands and the American Revolution* (New York, 1937); see George Miles, "A Comparative Frontier Bibliography," in Lamar and Thompson (eds.), *The Frontier in History*, 317–33.

ture. Sarmiento, a vivid writer and at times as much a promoter of North America as of Europe, contrasted the superior civilization of nineteenth-century European culture reflected in Buenos Aires with the backward and despised "twelfth century" reflected in Argentina's gaucho countryside. Sarmiento suggested repopulating Argentina with Europeans, making war on the backward natives in the interior, and recreating Europe in Latin America by wholesale importation of European institutions and increased immigration. No effort was made to adapt immigrants to Latin America's indigenous cultures. So intense was Sarmiento's portrayal of the hated gaucho that his description took on a literary life of its own, ironically making the indigenous gaucho an image synonymous with Argentine culture. In 1872, José Hernández in the first part of his epical poem *Martín Fierro* celebrated the gaucho while excoriating the social injustice of urban elitism. Hernández' folk epic, ignored by the literary establishment, became an enduring popular classic.[18]

Sarmiento and the other Latin Europhiles helped create the political, philosophical, and literary divisions that paralyzed nineteenth-century Latin development. Despised native populations turned to caudillos—folk leaders of the interior—while the elites in the cities uncritically accepted European intellectual styles and fashions and adopted Western capitalism without attempting to modify development theories or practices to Latin America's preindustrial agricultural peoples. One of the chief themes of Latin American literature was Europe versus the interior with Europe cast in the role of redeemer of barbaric Latin America. Latin American architecture made no effort to develop its own forms, copying European architecture, a pattern that persisted into the twentieth century. Guatemala posed as the Paris of Central America, Buenos Aires, the Paris of South America, while Porfirio Díaz made Mexico City Spanish America's first electrified city to mimic Paris as the city of light. The aristocratic Brazilian Eduardo Prado spoke for most of the Latin American elites when he observed that "without a doubt the world is Paris." Rio de Janeiro's Avenida Central built in 1904 was a direct imitation of Baron Georges

18. Howard C. Rice, Jr., *Thomas Jefferson's Paris* (Princeton, 1976); Allison Williams Bunkley, *The Life of Sarmiento* (Princeton, 1952), 205–22; Burns, *Poverty of Progress*, 22–23, 60, 61; Crawford, *A Century of Latin American Thought*, 37–51; John David Crow, *The Epic of Latin America* (3rd ed., Berkeley, 1980), 568–79. For a comprehensive recent history of the gaucho see Richard W. Slatta, *Gauchos and the Vanishing Frontier* (Lincoln, Neb., 1983). Sarmiento's book is commonly referred to as *Facundo*.

Eugène Haussmann's Paris boulevards of the 1870s. Indeed, by re-maining clustered in the coastal cities European immigrants coming to Latin America had no need to create an indigenous architecture, as did the North Americans. The cultural dependency of Latin America on Europe in the nineteenth century was demeaning as well as sterile.[19]

Although Sarmiento's influence did not cause the conflict, his ex-tremist views encouraged the political gulf between the natives and the European immigrants, which eventually produced two discrete Latin American political systems, the educated Europeanist elites of the cities in natural opposition to the folk leader caudillos of the inte-rior. Caudilloism is a complex phenomenon. Many of the caudillos were simply enterprising bandits, but others were shrewd and wise leaders occasionally well if self-educated. In some striking ways the Latin caudillo resembled the late nineteenth-century North American local politician, the city boss who took responsibility for the poor working-class immigrants in return for their political support. In pre-modern Latin America the caudillo was as much a social as a political leader. Caudilloism became a liability only after caudillos ceased being local figures of limited power and emerged as national authoritarian leaders. Although the art of the caudillo leader has been clearly iden-tified with Latin American culture, the model transcends any single culture. Mohammad and Robin Hood share some of the characteris-tics of a caudillo. The persistence of the tradition in Latin America en-couraged by the almost religious intensity of the urban-rural schism made caudilloism a uniquely Latin American institution.[20]

The Latin American caudillo was inspired by the Christian saints and even Christ, by democracy, and by the family. Before national politics transformed the caudillo from leader of the folk into corrupter of the national treasury, the rural leader fulfilled a valuable social function. The caudillo served as a secular leader, even a family leader, at a time when much of Latin America was in an almost continuous

19. Burns, *Progress of Poverty*, 10, 20, 37–38; Norma Evenson, *Two Brazilian Capitals: Architecture and Urbanism in Rio de Janeiro and Brasília* (New Haven, 1973), 38, 73; Stabb, *In Quest of Identity*, 7; Lewis, *Main Currents in Caribbean Thought*, 305. See also Jeffrey D. Needell, *A Tropical* Belle *Epoque: The Elite Culture of Turn-of-the-Century Rio de Janeiro* (New York, 1987).

20. R. A. Humphreys, "The Caudillo Tradition," in R. A. Humphreys, *Tradition and Revolt in Latin America and Other Essays* (New York, 1969), 216–28; Hoetink, *Dominican People*, 98–100, 110, 125, 144; Burns, *Poverty of Progress*, 86–92; Charles E. Chapman, "The Age of the Caudillos: A Chapter in Hispanic American Literature," *HAHR*, XII (1932), 281–300; Glen Caudill Dealy, *The Public Man: An Interpretation of Latin American and Other Catholic Countries* (Amherst, Mass., 1977).

state of war. Contemporary novelist Gabriel García Márquez' portrait of Colombia in *One Hundred Years of Solitude* captures the ebb and flow of revolution and war that resembled the whimsical and destructive patterns of extremes of weather. García Márquez' four years, eleven months, and two days of uninterrupted rain is no more terrible than the constant storms of war and revolution that eventually destroyed the novel's stable society. Magic realism describes not only the literature of modern Latin America but its actual history.[21]

When Antonio Guzmán Blanco assumed national power in Venezuela in 1870, he not only made Venezuela a national state, but he defined the art and the role of the modern national caudillo. Guzmán Blanco was a brilliant intuitive national leader who established the major precedents of Latin America friction with the world. Guzmán used foreign relations to secure his domestic political control, institutionalized the use of foreign debt and investment as an economic and political tool, and developed a national consensus in Venezuela that enabled him to defy foreign powers. In his brilliant political innovations Guzmán Blanco broke the practice and the principle of Latin America's unwavering dependence on Europe. Together with José Martí, Guzmán Blanco began a tradition of Latin American cultural and political independence that eventually put Latin America in conflict with both Europe and the United States, a conflict that reflected reality much more accurately than Latin America's artificial cultural subservience to Western values in the earlier nineteenth century. Guzmán was an exceptionally gifted leader who intuitively balanced the intricacies of Venezuela's international and national relations as he shifted his nation's center of gravity from scattered independent regions to a single center in Caracas. Guzmán remained an individual caudillo. He was the system, and the new Venezuela could not survive beyond his rule. When Cipriano Castro, his successor, tried to follow Guzmán's precedents and examples, he did not have the proper sense of timing or the genius, and Venezuela was faced with crisis after monumental crisis.[22]

21. Hoetink, *Dominican People*, 125, 101; Gabriel García Márquez, *One Hundred Years of Solitude*, trans. Gregory Rabassa (New York, 1971), 291.
22. Julian Nava, "The Illustrious American: The Development of Nationalism in Venezuela Under Antonio Guzmán Blanco," *HAHR*, XLV (1965), 527–43; Malcolm Deas, "Colombia, Ecuador, and Venezuela, c. 1880–1930," in *CHLA*, IV, 670–74; John V. Lombardi, *Venezuela: The Search for Order, the Dream of Progress* (Oxford, 1982), 191–205; Miriam Hood, *Gunboat Diplomacy: Great Power Pressure in Venezuela, 1895–1905* (London, 1975); Judith Ewell, *Venezuela: A Century of Change* (Stanford, 1984).

Guzmán Blanco's success encouraged imitators throughout Latin America. His policies also encouraged his practice of misusing foreign debt, an institution with a life span limited to the gullibility of European investors and the realities of Latin American economies. Ulíses Heureaux, who ruled the Dominican Republic from 1883 until his assassination in 1899, was neither as gifted nor as successful as Guzmán Blanco, who served as his model and inspiration. But though Heureaux defines the highest state of caudillo corruption, he remains a complex political and social leader. Heureaux kept a copy of Machiavelli's *Prince* conspicuously displayed on his desk and clearly followed its precepts. His notable achievement was his self-conscious awareness of the role of the caudillo. "Before everything, I am an opportunist," Heureaux boasted. But like Guzmán Blanco, Heureaux encouraged not only Dominican nationalism but a new Latin American sense of political unity and cultural affinity. When a local businessman was reluctant to accept a government post, citing his lack of experience, Heureaux bellowed at him, "Do you think I have just come from France? We have all been brought up together and in our country, in service we are all good for anything." [23]

Guzmán Blanco and Ulíses Heureaux were leaders during a transition, the first effective break from Latin America's total reliance on European values and virtues. Unfortunately, the caudillo was as easily corrupted by European capital as the elites had been corrupted by European philosophy. Only Paraguay experimented successfully with indigenous development economics and a political system that favored the natives rather than the foreigners. But Paraguay was crushed in 1870 by Argentina, Brazil, and Uruguay in a triple alliance designed specifically to bring civilization to barbarian Paraguay. Life imitated art in fine magic realism style with the deaths of Guzmán Blanco and Heureaux. On July 26, 1899, Heureaux was assassinated; on July 29 a monstrous cyclone struck Santo Domingo; on July 31 Guzmán Blanco died in Paris. The era of the nineteenth-century caudillo on horseback ended in 1904, when Aparicio Saravia was killed in his battle against elitist President José Batlle of Uruguay. The caudillo soon passed into the mythology of Latin America, a synonym for *bandit* in North American eyes and an epical character for Latin America. The virtues of the heretofore despised inhabitants of the interior were recognized and celebrated in Euclides da Cunha's *Os sertões* (*Rebellion in the Backlands*),

---

23. Hoetink, *Dominican People*, 131, 132.

a historical account that transformed the 1896–1897 war in the Brazilian interior into literature and epic. Published in 1902, *Os sertões* remains one of the masterpieces of world literature.[24]

José Martí, an extraordinary Cuban intellectual, poet, educator, and journalist, defined the problem of Latin American nationalism and became the catalyst who helped transform Latin American culture from nineteenth-century derivative sterility to a unique internationalism that produced a dynamic and innovative Latin American literature. Seldom has a single writer had so profound or immediate an effect as Martí, an influence that preceded his unfortunate martyrdom in battle in 1895. Martí was born in Havana on January 28, 1853, the son of a Spanish army sergeant assigned to Cuba as part of Spain's increasingly burdensome colonial administration. Young Martí's intellectual capacities were evident from the start, and his early education was supported by Rafael Mendive, a well-known Cuban poet and schoolmaster.[25]

At the age of fifteen Martí played a significant political and intellectual part in Cuba's Ten Years' War with Spain (1868–1878), the first important Cuban-Spanish conflict. Martí was arrested for openly supporting and writing for a new revolutionary journal, *La Patria Libre*, convicted of treason, and sentenced to six years in prison. After he had served a year and a half of confinement at hard labor, Martí's sentence was commuted to exile in Spain in January, 1871. Undaunted, Martí wrote about his experiences, converting his personal revolutionary hardships into political literature. His *Political Prison in Cuba*, published in Havana as Martí left for his Spanish exile, marked the beginning of his remarkable new life as involuntary world traveler and one of the most cosmopolitan of the New World's writers. Martí was able to complete his education at the Universities of Madrid and

24. *Ibid.*, 135; Paul H. Lewis, "Paraguay from the War of the Triple Alliance to the Chaco War, 1870–1932," in *CHLA*, IV, 475–76; Burns, *Poverty of Progress*, 128–31. For da Cunha's political writings and his admiration of TR as a role model for Brazil, see Crawford, *A Century of Latin American Thought*, 194–98; Euclides da Cunha, *Rebellion in the Backlands*, trans. Samuel Putnam (Chicago, 1944). TR, unaware of da Cunha's work and fascinated by the Brazilian interior, which he explored in 1913, urged R. B. Cunningham-Graham to write about it; see Michael Wood, "The Backlands Rebellion," *New York Review of Books*, February 28, 1985, p. 7; R. B. Cunningham-Graham, *A Brazilian Mystic: Being the Life and Miracles of Antônio Conselherio* (London, 1920).

25. For Martí's life see Gonzales, *José Martí*; Gray, *José Martí*; and Corbitt, "This Colossal Theater." For a basic bibliography see Anderson, *Spanish American Modernism*, 1–15, 107–28. A handy chronology is in José Martí, *On Art and Literature: Critical Writings*, ed. Philip S. Foner, trans. Elinor Randall (New York, 1982), 345–52.

Zaragoza and received degrees of philosophy and law in 1874 while continuing as an active Cuban nationalist and revolutionary in Europe. After visiting France and England, Martí settled in Mexico City in 1875, in permanent political exile from his troubled homeland.[26]

Because of his almost constant exile, Martí's intellectual growth and his writing remained rooted in Cuba's revolutionary struggle. Although he was exposed to a wide variety of sophisticated world cultural influences, his new cosmopolitanism remained tempered by his intense Cuban and Latin American nationalism. Martí's two years in Mexico in the period just before the Porfirio Díaz era introduced him to Mexico City's active literary community, a Latin American intelligentsia that first suggested to Martí the potential of Pan-Hispanicism as an alternative to both European and North American cultural and political influence. Revolution once more made Martí an involuntary exile. When Porfirio Díaz swept to power in Mexico, displacing the ruling Liberal administration, Martí was forced to leave. After visiting Cuba under a general truce and amnesty, the twenty-four-year-old writer began another exile in 1877 as professor of French, English, Italian, and German literature and history of philosophy at the Central School of Guatemala.[27]

With the end of the Ten Years' War in Cuba, Martí returned to his homeland and began a family and a career as a lawyer. When his presence was discovered by the unfriendly Cuban colonial government, Martí was again deported to Spain. Refusing to concede to life as a Spanish exile, Martí escaped to Paris and then proceeded to New York in January, 1880. He made his last attempt to find a haven in Latin America as a professor in Caracas, Venezuela, where he founded and edited the journal *Revista Venezuela*. Martí was temperamentally and intellectually unable to adapt to life in an authoritarian state. At the death of Cecilio Acosta—one of the few remaining Venezuelan intellectuals who had not compromised under President Antonio Guzmán Blanco's new national regime—Martí published a celebratory essay that offended the Venezuelan government. Although Antonio Guzmán Blanco and José Martí were both seminal figures in the emergence of a new Latin America, neither could accommodate to the genius of the other. Guzmán Blanco wanted no part of free

26. Corbitt, "This Colossal Theater," 8; Gonzales, *José Martí*, 27–55; Crawford, *A Century of Latin American Thought*, 28–29.

27. Gray, *José Martí*, 6–20; Lewis, *Main Currents in Caribbean Thought*, 294–96; Corbitt, "This Colossal Theater," 10–14.

speech, revolutionary intellectuals, or José Martí. Once more Martí was banished. Rather than return to Europe, Martí took up residence in New York City, learned English, and began his new work as intellectual bridge between the two Americas and the world.[28]

Martí's enormous literary productivity—his complete works fill seventy volumes—obscures the chronic ill health that troubled him his entire life. Many of his more serious medical problems were consequences of his year and a half as a political prisoner. A weak heart and consumptive lungs frequently invalided him, and even at the height of his literary and political activity he was often bedridden. Initially, he found the United States exhilarating. Free of censorship, exposed to yet another new culture and society, Martí consciously set out to share his experiences of intellectual growth and cultural interaction with a North American society that like himself was at a stage of exciting growth. Martí was influential because of the timing—the cultural confluence of revolutionary Latin America troubled by its own political turmoil and the North American cultural as well as economic transformation—and his own developing literary ability.[29]

His earliest work, when he was struggling to perfect his English, was published in the New York *Sun* and in the Caracas *La Opinión Nacional*. Latin America's most influential journal, Buenos Aires' *La Nación*, invited Martí to become a regular contributor. Montevideo's *La Opinión Pública* and Mexico City's *El Partido Liberal* followed. Soon more than twenty Latin American journals were publishing his articles regularly. The articles varied in length and in subject material. Martí, who worked to "conceive newspaper articles as if they were books," regarded everything he wrote not as a newspaper fragment but as a major work. Martí wrote essays on such American literary figures as Ralph Waldo Emerson and Walt Whitman and pieces on Mark Twain, Henry Wadsworth Longfellow, Louisa May Alcott, and Helen Hunt Jackson, whose *Ramona* he lovingly translated into Spanish. His historical essays on General Ulysses S. Grant, Roscoe Conkling, Jesse James, and Buffalo Bill are filled with insight. For nearly a decade Martí revealed to an eager readership in Spanish America the great and the minute details of North American life. He described baseball, Coney Island, Fourth of July celebrations, eating at Delmonico's New

28. Corbitt, "This Colossal Theater," 27–28; Crawford, *A Century of Latin American Thought*, 228–30; Balseiro, *Americas Look at Each Other*, 116–17.
29. Gonzales, *José Martí*, 9, 27; Lewis, *Main Currents in Caribbean Thought*, 294–303.

York restaurant, searching for Easter eggs, and Thanksgiving turkeys with passion and style. Martí's prolific prose told Latin Americans more of life in the United States than they knew about their neighboring nations.[30]

Emerson and Whitman were major influences on Martí and through him on the new Latin American literary movements of the late nineteenth century that marked the first significant break from the older Spanish influence and the newer French vogue. Martí valued Emerson and Whitman not only for their literary skills but for their symbolic affirmation of cultural independence. He admired Emerson's "celestial sentences" and his universality that raised him above the provinciality of his culturally primitive New England. At times Martí so identified with Emerson's example that his writing took on the sound of Emerson's prose—in Spanish.[31]

Martí's role as cultural catalyst changed in the late 1880s to that of political critic as he saw the growth that he had earlier admired in the United States threaten Cuba and Latin America. Martí was equally effective as a literary critic, revolutionary writer, and political writer, but his political writings are the most dramatic. When newly elected President Benjamin Harrison appointed James G. Blaine his secretary of state, Martí's "anguished winter" began as the "fearsome eagle" became an ominous threat to Latin America. Martí withdrew his earlier Pan-Americanism and sharply distinguished between the two Americas, *Nuestra America*—our America—and North America, the other America. His political writing was sharp and provocative. His last written words before his death in Cuba set the tone for all future Latin American disaffection with the other America: "I have lived in the monster and I know its entrails."[32]

Martí was a great stylist, and his flair for provocative prose is most dramatically displayed in his later anti-imperialist, anti-American

30. Gonzales, *José Martí*, 27–29, 34, 54–55. The American essays are reprinted in José Martí, *The America of José Martí: Selected Writings*, trans. Juan de Onis (New York, 1953); Corbitt, "This Colossal Theater," 29. See John M. Kirk, "José Martí and the United States: A Further Interpretation," *Journal of Latin American Studies*, IX (1977), 275–90.

31. See Philip S. Foner, "Introduction," in Martí, *On Art and Literature*, 30. For a detailed analysis of the Emerson-Martí connection see Esther Elise Shuler, "José Martí: Su crítica de algunoes autores norteamericanos," *Archivo José Martí*, XVI (1950), 175–77. For Whitman's influence see John E. Englekirk, "Notes on Whitman in Spanish America," *Hispanic Review*, VI (1938), 133–38; Lewis, *Main Currents in Caribbean Thought*, 300.

32. See esp. Martí, "Washington Pan-American Conference," 339–67; Martí, *Our America*, 440; John M. Kirk, *José Martí*, 58; Lewis, *Main Currents in Caribbean Thought*, 301–303.

phase and especially in his best essay, "The Washington Pan-American Congress," which he wrote in November, 1889. Raising polemical hyperbole to an art, Martí compared the "condor and the lamb" and warned his Latin American readers of the dangers of dependency: "The nation eager to die sells to a single nation, the nation eager to live sells to many." Convinced that the United States' sole interest was to rid itself of "unsalable merchandise" through Latin America, Martí told his readers, "the nation that buys, commands, the nation that sells, serves." He bravely tried to imbue Latin America with both cultural and political independence, envisioning "Spanish-America [as] the world's balance of power." Blaine's Pan-American policies as well as Cuba's worsening political relationship with Spain contributed to Martí's bitter last phase. Martí foresaw that Latin America's static society of rich landowners and poor peasants would be dominated by the growing strength of the United States' democratic capitalism. He also predicted the North American shift from competitive to finance capitalism with its new pressures for economic expansion. He saw that Latin America could not hope to be an equal partner, not only failing economically and politically but culturally as well.[33]

Martí was dramatically successful in establishing a strong tradition of Pan-Hispanicism to counter Blaine's Pan-Americanism of the early 1890s, which Martí regarded as an attempt to manipulate Latin America to suit the United States' new industrial capacity and surplus. He was equally successful in changing the direction of Latin literature from European romanticism to *modernismo*. This change was as much a "general change in sensibility" as a new style or subject matter. Poets were changing independently of one another in scattered parts of Latin America. Martí's enormous gifts as well as his wide dissemination helped unify the scattered aesthetic revolution into a well-defined movement that had already begun in Buenos Aires and Mexico City.[34]

Literary *modernismo* was less radical than its cultural implications. The *modernismo* writers rejected Spain as their chief influence, instead adopting France. *Modernismo* was almost as derivative as what it replaced. France was the symbol of cosmopolitan and international cul-

33. Martí, "Washington Pan-American Conference," 371, 373, 340, 372, 367; Lewis, *Main Currents in Caribbean Thought*, 298–301.
34. Paz, "Prologue," 8–9; Gerald Martin, "The Literature, Music, and Art of Latin America, 1870–1930," in *CHLA*, IV, 456–69; Isaac Goldberg, *Studies in Spanish-American Literature* (New York, 1920), 1–16. For a bibliography on Spanish modernism see Anderson, *Spanish American Modernism*, 1–19.

ture. Parisian culture had nurtured the great nineteenth-century Russian novelists, as well as such French novelists as Honoré de Balzac and Gustave Flaubert. Spanish romanticism, sterile to begin with, lacked the sense of divided self that distinguished European and English romanticism. It also had no sense of irony or the conviction—essential to the English romantics—that poetry had replaced religious revelation. The *modernismo* poets were not adopting a new French culture, they were rejecting the old Spanish bond. The example of Martí as a cosmopolitan artist-revolutionary was inspiring to a culture searching for a cosmopolitan language and a way of seeing the world that rejected both Madrid and local provincial culture. Not only France but the United States and England were sources of the new *modernismo*, which was intent on release from the old traditions and exploring its new-found creativity.[35]

Although primarily a literary movement, *modernismo* was intimately connected with Martí's new anti-imperialism and Pan-Hispanicism. Technology gave writers and publishers the means of wide communication; new wealth created an international cultural market. The new professionalism of international culture made writing for limited local markets less appealing. "Everything connects, everything rhymes," defines the spirit of both Martí's odyssey in the other America and his leadership of a new literary sensibility. His essay "Our America" in 1891 marked the intellectual separation of Latin America not only from the other America but from Europe as well. "Our America" is a cultural and political declaration of independence as striking and eventually as influential as Ralph Waldo Emerson's "American Scholar" of 1837.[36]

Many Latin American authors, inspired by Martí's example, were goaded by the increasing disparities of Latin American and North American wealth and power to write angrily about how to deal with Martí's monster. Venezuelan César Zumeta's *Sick Continent* published in 1899 is more violent than any of Martí's polemical prose. Zumeta viewed the events that followed Martí's death as catastrophic for Latin America. In seeing the Spanish defeat in the Philippines as the end

35. Paz, "Prologue," 8–9; Keith Ellis, *Critical Approaches to Rubén Darío* (Toronto, 1974), 49; Goldberg, *Studies in Spanish-American Literature*, 11–16; Franco, *The Modern Culture of Latin America*, 14–39.

36. Ellis, *Critical Approaches to Rúben Darío*, 53; see esp. Angel Rama, *Rúben Darío y el modernismo* (Caracas, 1970), 9; Paz, "Prologue," 9; Onis, *The United States as Seen by Spanish American Writers*, 197–99.

of the last remaining hope for Bolívarian nationalism, Zumeta was convinced that armed resistance was Latin America's only defense against an increasingly rapacious United States. His melodramatic strategy included arming all citizens, establishing shooting clubs in all local parishes as well as national military academies, and defending the coasts, streams, and rivers of a Latin America under the threat of imminent attack. Zumeta was a master of polemical hyperbole. He envisioned "defenders behind every bush" challenging "the apologists of force and mercantilism."[37]

Zumeta's impassioned broadside was not wholly impractical. Suggesting that elevated natural fortresses were the equal of the most modern navies, Zumeta correctly observed that Latin America was well suited to a guerrilla war of resistance. He was equally vehement in opposition to the three institutions he blamed for Latin American weakness: the banks, the church, and the military. Zumeta portrayed an ideal world in which Latin American values triumphed, "saved only by the handful of wise men, artists, and dreamers." Zumeta, who used historical analogy with the license of a poet, urged Latin America to follow Bolívar's advice of seventy-five years before to "fight a brilliant, very prolonged, very arduous, very important war."[38]

Like many of the new Latin American anti–North American essays, Zumeta's angry prose reflects not only fear of the United States but a crisis of confidence in Latin America's relation to the world. The sickness of the continent in Zumeta's title is the weakness of Latin America. The enemy is not only the United States but Latin America itself. With Europe effectively eliminated from Latin American influence, Latin American writers had the luxury of being able to unify against a new common enemy, stronger, closer, and less congenial than the old European oppressors. But Latin American shortcomings no longer could be excused by the newness of the New World nations. The success of the United States made the issue no longer one of Old World versus New World but of New World versus New World. Zumeta cited Martí's rationale that Latin America did not have the time to develop because it was preoccupied with "expelling from our blood the impurities we have inherited." The expulsion of Spain and the strik-

37. César Zumeta, *El Continente Enfermo* (1899; rpr. Mexico City, 1979), 12–13. These passages were translated by Dolores J. O'Connor, University of New Orleans. For other Latin American writers on the sick continent theme see Stabb, *In Quest of Identity*, 13–33. For Darío's reaction in 1898 see Balseiro, *The Americas Look at Each Other*, 61–62.

38. Zumeta, *El Continente Enfermo*, 12–14.

ing success of the United States made it necessary for Latin American intellectuals and writers to create a new sense of self-identity upon which a new national tradition could be built. Zumeta's *Sick Continent* is primarily an exhortation for Latin American nationalism and pride and only secondarily an attack on the United States. Until Latin American cultural independence was securely established, the United States and the real and imagined threats it projected could be used as a convenient rallying device. Hatred was much more creative than self-hatred. Like Martí's most polemical pieces, Zumeta's passionate essay came from "inside the monster"; it was written in New York City. Although the prose of enmity had become a tradition, the relationship of modern Latin and North America was increasingly one of symbiosis, aided by increasing efforts at self-definition, many remarkably acute.[39]

When José Enrique Rodó, a Uruguayan writer, critic, educator, and man of letters, published *Ariel* in 1900, he had produced one of the most influential works of all time. *Ariel* was comparable in its effect to works like Tom Paine's *Common Sense*, which in 1776 captured in clear, telling prose the complex causes of the American Revolution, unifying literature and politics in one work. *Ariel's* genius lies equally in its impeccable literary style and the timeliness of its message. Rodó was twenty-nine when he wrote his cultural declaration of Spanish-American independence. *Ariel*, which appeared five years after Martí's death in Cuba, brilliantly amplified Martí's distinction of two conflicting Americas. Rodó's most famous peroration, the fifth part of *Ariel*, compared the two Americas through the metaphor of Shakespeare's last play, *The Tempest*, in which the coarse Caliban is contrasted with the gentle and spiritual Ariel. The materialistic United States is portrayed as both Caliban and Sparta, while Latin America in its pure poetic gentleness is Ariel and Athens. Although Rodó's eloquent reiteration of Martí's original theme established in literary prose the dominant Latin American–United States antipathy of the twentieth century, the first parts of *Ariel* are equally important in explaining why Rodó's book became a cultural declaration of independence for the youth of Latin America.[40]

39. *Ibid.*, 11; see Lewis, *Main Currents in Caribbean Thought*, 299–303; Crow, *Epic of Latin America*, 699–703; Stabb, *In Quest of Identity*, 27–33.

40. José Enrique Rodó, *Ariel*, trans. F. J. Stimson (Boston, 1922); Clemente Pereda, *Rodó's Main Sources* (San Juan, 1941); Crawford, *A Century of Latin American Thought*, 79–94; Lewis, *Main Currents in Caribbean Thought*, 306–307; Goldberg, *Studies in Spanish American Literature*, 184–245. For a Rodó bibliography see Anderson, *Spanish American Modernism*, 134–43.

Latin America in 1900 was caught in a cruel historical context. *Modernismo*, though well under way, was yet to establish a new literature, though it had destroyed faith in the old. In literature as in politics, Latin America was at sea. Cuba had exchanged one colonial overseer for another, and when the United States displaced Spain as the main foreign power in Latin America, the new configuration was far less pleasing than the old. A weak but familiar culture had been replaced by a completely foreign and monumentally powerful overseer. Positivism, industrialization, and urbanism had not transformed Latin America, which obviously lagged behind the United States in culture, politics, and wealth. The images in Rodó's *Ariel*, however, served to transform Latin American weakness into potential strength. For Rodó the symbolic Ariel is synonymous with youth, promise, and Latin America. Latin American excellence was not to be measured in the ledgers of the West, but "Ariel triumphant signifies ideality and order in life, noble inspiration in thought, unselfishness in conduct, high taste in art, heroism of action, delicacy and refinement in manners and usages." Neither European positivism nor North American Calvinist capitalism was the solution for Latin America. By excluding from his hierarchy of values all the established virtues of the West, Rodó beckoned Latin America's restless young to a new order, clearly designed for an antimaterial sensibility as well as for those who wanted a nationalism uncorrupted by foreign success.[41]

Rodó and *Ariel* became instantly famous. *Ariel* achieved much of its success by stating briefly and clearly a sense of the crisis and a solution. Though Rodó's theme parallels the Fugitive American agrarian manifesto of 1930, *I'll Take My Stand*, it speaks for all Latin America and not, as John Crowe Ransom's Fugitives did, for a small segment of disaffected southern elitist writers and intellectuals arguing against northern industrial materialism. Like the Fugitives who spoke about the glory of the South from northern universities, many of Rodó's followers praised Ariel but coveted Caliban.[42]

Rodó was not as anti-American as part five of *Ariel* taken out of context or used as political symbolism appeared. Unlike most Latin Ameri-

41. Rodó, *Ariel*, 144. For a useful review of Latin American positivism and an anthology of its major writers see Woodward, *Positivism in Latin America*; also see Zea, *Latin American Mind*, 26–34, 121–289; Crawford, *A Century of Latin American Thought*, 95–103; and Stabb, *In Quest of Identity*, 5, 11–12.
42. Stabb, *In Quest of Identity*, 35–39; Twelve Southerners, *I'll Take My Stand* (New York, 1930); Louis Cowan, *The Fugitive Group: A Literary History* (Baton Rouge, 1959); Paul K. Conkin, *The Southern Agrarians* (Knoxville, Tenn., 1988); Pereda, *Rodó's Main Sources*, 64.

can writer-activists, Rodó remained rooted in his native Uruguay and rarely traveled from Montevideo. His knowledge of the United States was based on a skewed reading of Alexis de Tocqueville and a stereotyped conception of North American Protestant culture: "The ideal of beauty does not appeal to the descendants of the austere Puritan." Emerson and Edgar Allan Poe, both greatly admired by Rodó and most of the Latin American writers, were easily dismissed as "estrays of a fauna expelled from their true habitat by some geological catastrophe." Rodó was scathing and effective in his charge that wealth and materialism destroyed culture in the United States, "the levelling by the middle classes tends ever. . . . to plane down what remains of the *intelligentsia*; the flowers are mown by the machine when the weeds remain." He believed that Benjamin Franklin and the *Federalist Papers* were the most representative products of a civilization that openly boasted, "America can beat the world." The imperialism that Rodó feared was the palpable North American success and pride in achievement that made them not likable—they might "even revise the Book of Genesis, to put themselves upon the front page."[43]

Rodó's portrait of the United States was meant to deter Latin America's youth from trying to imitate North American values as a previous generation had admired and imitated Europe. *Ariel's* most important message was Spanish-American unity. Rodó did not hate the United States. "I do not love the United States, but I greatly admire it," he wrote. But he did not want others to share his admiration. *Ariel* is filled with admiring comparisons with European culture; by 1900 Europe was no longer a direct cultural or diplomatic threat to Latin America. Positivism had failed, the Spanish had been expelled, the United States had made it clear that other European activity would not be tolerated. Martí had already made the other America the only enemy. Intense Spanish efforts in the 1890s to win Latin American support for the coming encounter with the United States helped make the United States the only devil in the new Latin American nationalism.[44]

To Rubén Darío fell the task of solidifying the new union of anti-Americanism, Pan-Hispanicism, and the cosmopolitan Latin Ameri-

43. Rodó, *Ariel*, 111, 110, 113, 114–21, 122.

44. Pereda, *Rodó's Main Sources*, 113; J. Fred Rippy, "Literary Yankeephobia in Hispanic America," *Journal of International Relations*, XII (1922), 352. For Latin American criticism of Rodó's Arielism see Crawford, *A Century of Latin American Thought*, 88–90; Lewis, *Main Currents in Caribbean Thought*, 307; Charles A. Hale, "Politics and Social Ideas in Latin America," in *CHLA*, IV, 414–17.

can art and literature. Darío, born in 1867 in Metapa, a small Nicaraguan town now renamed Ciudad Darío, published his first poem in 1880 and remained a prolific poet until his death in 1916. In spite of Darío's identification with political protest, especially in his 1904 poem "To Roosevelt," he never wavered in his dedication to art and disinterest in politics. Darío's significance lies in the strength of his poetry, his place as the first modern professional writer in Latin America, and his international audience. Although he did not reject or forget his Nicaraguan roots, Darío returned to his homeland only rarely, generally for financial or personal reasons. Martí's rejection of the Spanish-American romantic literary style lacked a unifying focus until Darío's *Azul* (Blue), a volume of poems and short fiction published in 1888, formally launched the *modernismo* movement. Innovation in literature—poetry, fiction, and essays—and life as a world traveler established Darío's international literary reputation.[45]

Before he left Nicaragua, Darío's work was both precocious and provincial, a representative measure of the state of pre-*modernismo* Latin American literature in the hands of a gifted young poet. Darío worked within the conventions of standard Spanish-American romanticism, writing on lyric and civic themes that extolled love, democracy, Central American unity, and progress. Darío worked with Nicaraguan President Adán Cárdenas in 1884 on a serious plan for a Central American union. On Darío's first international venture, a modest trip to El Salvador in 1883, he met President Rafael Zaldívar. As Martí had widened Latin American contact with the world from New York, so Darío, moving freely and frequently through Latin America, widened the new Latin American literary context from local to national and regional and eventually to continental. When Darío read his poem "The Liberator Bolívar" at San Salvador's National Theater in July, 1883, he began his role as one of the founding fathers of modern Latin American cultural pride, which eventually became a source of Latin American self-identity and a counterpoint to North America's financial and political skill. Politics and literature were far more intimately connected in Latin America, and Latin American political leaders considered advancing the arts and the fortunes of gifted

45. Paz, "Prologue," 7–18; Ellis, *Critical Approaches to Rúben Darío;* Goldberg, *Studies in Spanish American Literature,* 122–83; Crow, *Epic of Latin America,* 698–703; Martin, "Literature, Music, and Art, 1870–1930," in *CHLA,* IV, 460–63; Balseiro, *The Americas Look at Each Other,* 59–80; for a bibliography see Anderson, *Spanish American Modernism,* 24–61.

artists as high government priorities. When General Juan Cañas urged Darío to go to Chile because of its advanced literary community, President Cárdenas offered financial support. Darío became an active force in the literary communities of Valparaiso and Santiago, contributed pieces to Nicaraguan and Chilean newspapers, and continued writing. His travels included stops in Lima, Peru, El Salvador, Guatemala, Costa Rica, and Cuba. Europe followed in 1892, when Darío represented Nicaragua in Madrid at the Spanish celebration of the founding of America. Rafael Núñez, Colombia's president, convinced Darío in 1893 to become Colombian consul to Argentina, thus permitting Darío access to the advanced literary community in Buenos Aires.[46]

After meeting Martí briefly in New York in 1893, Darío went on to Paris to meet with Stéphane Mallarmé and Paul Verlaine, leaders of the new French symbolist movement. Darío was more worldly than the provincial Parisian Verlaine. By 1898 Darío was an international literary figure, reporting the Spanish reaction to the War of 1898 for Buenos Aires' influential *La Nación*. In 1900 he covered the Paris Exposition for *La Nación*, toured Italy, met with Pope Leo XIII, and in 1902 was appointed Nicaragua's consul in Paris. Darío's consular appointments were reflections of cultural support and not the result of political affiliations. Throughout his life Darío's primary commitment to art and the international literary community made him intellectually and emotionally aloof from national politics. Darío's aestheticism ran counter to the Latin American tradition of political commitment, and he was often criticized for his independence. When José Rodó first encountered Darío's new poetry, he was unhappy with the absence of a formal commitment to Latin America and he equated Darío's new modernism with decadence. By 1900, Rodó praised Darío's new poetry as well as his independence, realizing that Darío's literary gifts transcended national subject matter.[47]

When Darío wrote his most famous poem, "To Roosevelt," in 1904, he was superficially reacting to the waves of anti-Americanism begun by Martí's anti-imperialism and exacerbated by the dispute over Theodore Roosevelt's Panama Canal policies. But Darío was not interested in politics. "To Roosevelt" is a much more complex poem than simple political polemics would suggest. Like Martí and Rodó, Darío

46. Paz, "Prologue," 12; Ellis, *Critical Approaches to Rúben Darío*, 12–13.
47. Paz, "Prologue," 12–13; Ellis, *Critical Approaches to Rúben Darío*, 13–14, 27–30. For Rodó's criticisms of Darío see *ibid.*, 30–34.

was ambivalent to the other America, attracted by many of its writers, repelled by its size and its appearance of aggressiveness. Darío never wavered in his admiration of Poe, Whitman, and Emerson, whom he considered strong influences on his writing.[48]

Nor did Darío underestimate Roosevelt's formidable cultural achievements. "You are cultured and able," Darío wrote of Roosevelt, a substantial concession for a Latin American writer. Darío used Roosevelt's distaste for Leo Tolstoy's writing to demonstrate his awareness of Roosevelt's literary taste. For many Latin American intellectuals fear and distaste for the other America was as much cultural as economic and diplomatic. Darío was indifferent to the political imperialism that troubled César Zumeta and at times Martí. The main point of "To Roosevelt" is Darío's refusal to accede to North American cultural superiority. "But our own America, which has had poets / since the ancient times of Nezahualcóyotl," is a reminder that culturally North America is *nouveau riche*.

> The United States is grand and powerful.
> Whenever it trembles, a profound shudder
> runs down the enormous backbone of the Andes
> If it shouts, the sound is like the roar of a lion.

Darío concedes the disparity in strength. Unlike Zumeta and the more narrow nationalists, he was not willing to wage a military war though he did threaten that

> Roosevelt, you must become, by God's own will,
> the deadly Rifleman and the dreadful Hunter
> before you can catch us in your iron claws.

Darío was more interested in affirmation than in conflict. The magnificent lyricism of Darío's second stanza builds to a crescendo as he lists the uniqueness of

> Catholic America
> Spanish America,
> the America where a noble Cuauhtémoc said:
> "I am not a bed of roses"—our America
> trembling with hurricanes, trembling with Love:

48. Rúben Darío, "To Roosevelt" (1904), in Darío, *Selected Poems*, 69–70. For an analysis of "To Roosevelt," see Ellis, *Critical Approaches to Rúben Darío*, 97–102; For the Emerson-Poe-Whitman connection see Paz, "Prologue," 16; and Balseiro, *The Americas Look at Each Other*, 59–60.

Mammon is contrasted with love, power with naïveté, progress with ancient culture.[49]

After his Roosevelt poem became famous, Darío denied any real antipathy toward the United States and Roosevelt. "I myself hurled a trumpet blow which was also inoffensive at Mr. Roosevelt." Darío remained fascinated with the ambiguous symbol Theodore Roosevelt represented for Latin Americans. In his preface to *Cantos de vida y esperanza* (1905), he argued that "the politics is universal" and warned, "Tomorrow we may well be Yankees; in fact we probably shall be." He praised Roosevelt's patronage of poets, "which goes to show this kerosene hunter is a sensible man." Two years after "To Roosevelt," Darío's "Greeting to the Eagle," written in 1906 on the occasion of the Pan-American Conference in Rio, was unabashedly pro-American. Darío, appointed Nicaraguan secretary to the conference, remained indifferent to politics: "I propagandized for Pan-Americanism with a vague fear and with very little faith." Writing of Roosevelt's 1910 visit to Paris in "Roosevelt en Paris" (1912), Darío described him as a "superman" and a "marvelous example of free, untamed humanity." Remarking that "this jovial Nimrod has had a good press," Darío even excused Roosevelt's "big stick," explaining that rather than threatening "a dubbing from Cousin Jonathan" it was a variation of the Roman phrase "*Suavitier in modo, fortiter in re*" (the more gentle in manner, the stronger in deed). Calling Roosevelt "a force of nature," Darío praised both the Monroe Doctrine and Roosevelt's naval building program.[50]

Darío's most important function was to build on Martí's foundation of a dynamic modern Latin American cultural establishment as part of an active professional literary community. Darío's status as a great poet helped create a sense of national pride for all Latin America in much the same way Walt Whitman had done as the bard of North America. Although Whitman did more to establish the identity of the United States than his contemporary political leaders, even as late as 1900 he was probably more influential outside the United States than within. Nonetheless, Whitman's poetry was identified with the United States; the influence of his writing may have tempered Latin Ameri-

49. Darío, *Selected Poems*, 69–70.
50. "I myself" and "I propagandized" are quoted in Ellis, *Critical Approaches to Rúben Darío*, 100, trans. Dolores J. O'Connor; *El canto errante* and "Roosevelt en Paris," originally in *Cabezas*, are quoted in Balseiro, *The Americas Look at Each Other*, 74–75. For Columbia's use of TR as a symbol for its rage and frustration in 1903–1904 see Joseph L. Arbena, "The Image of an American Imperialist: Colombian Views of Theodore Roosevelt," *West Georgia Studies in the Social Sciences*, VI (June, 1967), 3–20.

can distaste for North America. Unlike Whitman, Darío was honored by his nation and respected and revered throughout Latin America. Darío's vision of a miraculous if mystical future for Latin America prefigured the modern apocalyptic and ironic view of Latin American history in the unique work of Gabriel García Márquez and Latin American magic realism.[51]

Latin America's cultural rediscovery of its own identity and the unity fostered by fear of the aggressive superpower to the north made the relationships that began the new century much more complicated than simple opposition to North American aggrandizement. The expulsion of Europe from active participation in American diplomacy both north and south made it necessary to redefine all the relationships between the Old and New Worlds. The rise of a new American culture—again both north and south—displaced the European cultural hegemony that had troubled ambitious writers in the New World. When Ulíses Heureaux, the Dominican Republic's political leader and student of changes in world relations, declared in 1882, "I have always lived in distrust of Yankees," his words reflected most post-Sarmiento Latin American sentiment. But the two regions were contiguous, and they had to deal with each other regardless of cultural and political antipathies. In spite of the mythology of helplessness encouraged by Darío ("If it [the United States] shouts, the sound is like the roar of a lion") and later by Colombians over the loss of Panama, Latin Americans were as adept at dealing with the new superpower as they had been in dealing with the Europeans they successfully dislodged. Heureaux had reason not to trust anyone. He played complex games of manipulation with European and North American bankers, using one against the other with remarkable skill. In 1892 Heureaux tried to force the United States to accept the gift of Samaná Bay, one of the handsomest ports of the Caribbean, in return for underwriting Heureaux's debtor economy and profligate personal lifestyle. Such overt acts of apparent imperialism were frequently initiated by political leaders or business interests in Latin American and Caribbean nations. The United States frequently declined involvement, even when the offer was attractive, partly because of the antipathy it shared with the Latin American intellectuals on merging the two different cul-

---

51. Barrett Wendell, *Literary History of the United States* (Boston, 1901), the standard contemporary work, cites the French admiration of Whitman as the poet's chief virtue. For Whitman's influence see Englekirk, "Notes on Whitman in Spanish America," 133–38; Paz, "Prologue," 12; Martin, "Music, Literature, and Art, 1870–1930," in *CHLA*, IV, 461.

tures. North America was well aware of the gulf between the two Americas and for most of its history unwilling to encourage, let alone force, a union.[52]

Sugar brought the two Americas closer. Until the same Ten Years' War that began José Martí's role as a political activist and martyr, Cuba's sugar industry was locally controlled and run on a small scale. The Ten Years' War destroyed the Cuban economy and society as well as its sugar industry. When the war ended and sugar agriculture resumed, the world had changed. New technology, not the United States, caused the changes. Increased competition from both beet and cane sugar came from new sugar-producing centers in Argentina, Peru, Mexico, Austria, France, and Germany, as well as from Cuban exiles resettled in the Dominican Republic. Even as uncapitalistic a country as Spain joined in the worldwide competition for sugar sales. To regain any significant share of the world sugar market Cubans would have to reorganize their sugar industry. North American capital financed the changes, but world technology in sugar agriculture, refining, transportation, and marketing contributed to the social chaos of the sugar plantations. The major North American investments were not an organized government-industry initiative but largely haphazard, made by business interests working independently of government. The dislocation of the peasantry that occurred throughout Latin America because of the sugar industry involved three cooperating international regions, Europe, Latin America, and North America. The upheaval in the sugar industry was part of a series of international cultural and economic changes that affected many extractive agricultural economies. Developmental capitalism was not part of a rational plan to dispossess the poor. The severe social dislocations were accidental and largely unforeseen liabilities arising from experiments with new agricultural, industrial, and marketing techniques.[53]

In a sense Latin America was caught up in its usual historical misfortune. When the United States first established its agricultural economy, tobacco, not sugar, was the profitable cash crop. Pedro Bono,

52. Hoetink, *Dominican People*, 164; Sumner Welles, *Naboth's Vineyard: The Dominican Republic, 1844–1924* (2 vols.; New York, 1928), I, 486–94; Lewis, *Main Currents in Caribbean Thought*, 306–307; Martin, "Music, Literature, and Art, 1870–1930," in *CHLA* IV, 460–61.

53. For Cuba's relationship to sugar see Pérez, "Vagrants, Beggars, and Bandits," 1093–1100; also see Richard D. Weigle, "The Sugar Interests and American Diplomacy in Hawaii and Cuba, 1893–1903" (Ph.D. dissertation, Yale University, 1939), 187–353; and Migdal, "Capitalist Penetration in the Nineteenth Century," 72–74.

an acute Dominican observer, knew how critical the difference was: "Tobacco is democratic. It takes six months and little capital." Sugar was economically more profitable but socially catastrophic. Sugar demanded enormous capital, disrupted the rural agricultural society, and replaced landownership with wage labor. Attracting labor through high seasonal wages, sugar made migrant workers out of settled farmers, added to the unrest of a poor economy, and by involving the capitalist nations with the undeveloped ones precipitated the main struggle of the twentieth century between the old West and the newly defined Third World.[54]

Like culture, sugar had become international. Poverty had always ignored national boundaries. Latin America's problems with New World market economies were far from unique. What was unique was the new voice that Latin American poets had developed. Martí, Rodó, and Darío were able to articulate Latin American nationalism, a new internationalism, and to unite against the nearest symbol of the new modern discontent, the United States. But the two Americas remained united in rejecting European politics and eventually European cultural leadership. Both Americas had bardic poets who spoke for an international literature rising above the primitive reality, Emerson's New England of the 1830s and Martí's Cuba of the 1880s. Both Americas were confounded by modernism and the changes in transportation, finance, agriculture, and technology. In the twentieth century's first decade all the nations of the world had to face the new problems and attempt to work out new relationships.[55]

54. Manuel Moreno Fraginals, "Plantation Economics and Society in the Spanish Caribbean, 1860–1930," in *CHLA*, IV, 187–231; Bono quoted in Hoetink, *Dominican People*, 66. Also see Bono's comments on the noncapitalist origins of sugar agriculture, *ibid.*, 30–31.

55. For the United States' accommodation to the cultural and legal differences in its new Catholic possessions see Reuter, *Catholic Influence in American Colonial Policies*. For the changes in world diplomacy see Calvin DeArmond Davis, *The United States and the Second Hague Peace Conference: American Diplomacy and International Organization, 1899–1914* (Durham, N.C., 1975), 3–60. For useful summaries of European change see Jan Romein, *The Watershed of Two Eras: Europe in 1900*, trans. Arnold Pomerans (Middletown, Conn., 1978); and Eric Hobsbawm, *The Age of Empire, 1875–1914* (New York, 1987). For Colombia's crisis see Charles W. Bergquist, "The Political Economy of the Colombian Presidential Election of 1897," *HAHR*, LVI (1976), 1–30. For the Generation of 1898 movement in Spain see Raymond Carr, *Spain, 1898–1939* (Oxford, 1966), 528–32. For a summary of the changes confronting Great Britain see R. G. Neale, *Great Britain and United States Expansion, 1898–1900* (East Lansing, Mich., 1966), esp. xiii–xxii. For examples of the problems and changes in the United States see William Reynolds Braisted, *The United States Navy in the Pacific, 1897–1909* (Austin, Tex., 1958); Stephen Skowronek, *Building a New American State: Expansion of National Administrative Capacities, 1877–1920* (Cambridge, Mass., 1982); and Cecilia Tichi, *Shifting Gears: Technology, Literature, Culture in Modernist America* (Chapel Hill, 1987), are especially useful.

2   The North American Context

North America, barren, colder, less hospitable, and clearly the second choice to South America, remained unsettled for over a century while Latin America, preferred for its temperate climate, its existent Indian civilization, its palpable and removable wealth and resources, became a victim of its own abundance. The Portuguese first settled Brazil in 1500, England established a colony at Jamestown, Virginia, in 1607, and Samuel de Champlain began New France at Quebec in 1608. Timing was a decisive influence on the character of the settlements. The century that separated Brazil from Jamestown saw the rise of Western capitalism, the spread of Renaissance culture, the decline of Iberian supremacy, the destabilization of the European economy caused by the influx of new Spanish precious metals, and England's Elizabethan efflorescence. With no gold to export and no northwest passage to exploit, North America became a process, not the path to riches South America offered. As the struggle to wrest a living from the inhospitable land continued, so did the defining struggles within England itself. England experimented with the bloodbath of religious civil wars, the dramatic elimination of royalty, and, wearily and futilely, the restoration of an inappropriate Catholic king. Finally, in 1688 the Glorious Revolution not only gave England its Protestant royal succession but guaranteed life, liberty, and property, no matter who governed.[1]

North America, mostly uninvolved with the worst excesses of the English conflict, benefited handsomely from its resolution. Locke's redefinitions of man's political obligations to the state became a part of

---

1. For the settlements see John H. Parry, *Europe in a Wider World, 1415–1715* (London, 1949); Parry, *The Age of Reconnaisance* (Cleveland, 1963); Hubert Herring, *A History of Latin America from the Beginnings to the Present* (New York, 1955), 58–239, esp. 150–53; and James Lang, *Conquest and Commerce: Spain and England in the Americas* (New York, 1975).

North American custom, law, and tradition. North America became an Enlightenment utopia, unique and exceptional. Not only were the forests and the rivers undeveloped, so was the society. There was no established church, no established government, no established old wealth, no established ways of doing things. There was, in fact, blessedly, no establishment except the land; there was no history because life was wholly in the present; and there was little of Europe, which in colonial eyes remained distant and increasingly irrelevant. Although the Americans of the 1680s still thought of themselves as Englishmen, they were in fact a world apart.[2]

The gulf that the American Revolution revealed in 1776 was organic. The new Americans were vastly different from their English antecedents. England worried about continental Europe, America about the continental West. England relied on the outside world, colonies, and trading partners for sustenance. America needed the outside world, not for sustenance but for profit. With the American Revolution the Americans more carefully defined their uniqueness by establishing a government without a king and raising the idea of democracy to an ideology of exceptionalism.[3]

The North American belief in the contradictory axioms of democracy and exceptionalism remained consistent, proclaimed in the Declaration of Independence and the Constitution, affirmed in the Monroe Doctrine of 1823, trumpeted by American writers from Emerson through Whitman, and used in slogans such as Manifest Destiny to justify absorbing adjacent territory and murdering Indians. The Civil War confirmed both the democracy and the exceptionalism. Americans confronted a dreadful and serious division and fought four years over whether an indissoluble Union had really been consummated in 1789. In the end the Union won, the slaves were grudgingly freed,

2. For Locke and the Enlightenment see Chapter 1, note 2. For the significance of Protestant supremacy in the Glorious Revolution see Henry May, *The Enlightenment in America* (New York, 1976), 3; for American exceptionalism see Henry Bamford Parkes, *The American Experience* (New York, 1959), 1–137; C. Vann Woodward, "The Comparability of American History," in Woodward (ed.), *The Comparative Approach to American History* (New York, 1968), 4–9; Merrill Jensen, "The Colonial Phase," *ibid.*, 18–33; and Louis Hartz, "United States History in a New Perspective," in Hartz (ed.), *The Founders of New Societies: Studies in the History of the United States, Latin America, South Africa, Canada, and Australia* (New York, 1964).

3. Parkes, *American Experience*, 34–41; Bernard Bailyn, *The Ideological Origins of the American Revolution* (Cambridge, Mass., 1967); Joyce Appleby (ed.), "Republicanism in the History and Historiography of the United States" (special issue), *AQ*, XXXVII (1985), 461–598.

and the now politically unified nation launched a social, economic, and cultural development that in two generations after 1865 made the United States a real (if only partially recognized) major world power, still led by ordinary commoners, not kings or emperors, and only on rare occasions (and by accident, not design), gentlemen.[4]

Freed from the political and economic constraints of the sectional struggles centering on slavery, post–Civil War America grew, unified, and became a prodigious nation. Using the advantage of geographic isolation, the Americans nurtured their abundant sense of exceptionalism. The beckoning western hinterland absorbed not only Europe's expendable excess population and its excess capital but the industrial production of the new urban East and Midwest as well and freed the United States from the urgency of Europe's advanced industrial states to seek new imperial markets. America's size and its natural wealth gave it an enormous geographical advantage. Developing an industrial aesthetic, a vernacular architecture, a language based on English but markedly different, the Americans could choose their degree of involvement with the civilized worlds of both Europe and Asia. In 1837 Ralph Waldo Emerson appealed for a distinctive American national culture, a difficult task for a provincial, materialistic people on the verge of a long moral preoccupation with the slavery issue. In 1855 America had its first national poetic voice when Walt Whitman published his *Leaves of Grass*. "I was simmering, simmering, simmering," Whitman proclaimed. "Emerson brought me to a boil." After the Civil War, however, a less exuberant Whitman complained in *Democratic Vistas* (1871) about the materialism of the newly unified nation and warned that "our New World democracy" was "an almost complete failure."[5]

Spanish efforts in the Dominican Republic, the French occupation of Mexico, and European diplomacy during the Civil War transformed

4. The classic texts about American exceptionalism are Michel Guillaume St. Jean (J. Hector St. John) de Crevècoeur, *Letters from an American Farmer* (London, 1782); and Alexis C. H. M. C. de Tocqueville, *Democracy in America* (1835), trans. Henry Reeve, ed. Phillips Bradley (2 vols., rev. ed.; New York, 1945). For a recent treatment see Stephen Skowronek, *Building the New American State: The Expansion of National Administrative Capacities, 1877–1920* (New York, 1982), 5–10. For the view that the native Indian was central to American culture see Richard Slotkin, *Regeneration Through Violence: The Mythology of the American Frontier, 1600–1860* (Middletown, Conn., 1973).

5. Allan Nevins, *Ordeal of the Union* (2 vols.; New York, 1947); David M. Potter, *The Impending Crisis, 1848–1861* (New York, 1976); John Hope Franklin, *Reconstruction After the Civil War* (New York, 1961); Kenneth M. Stampp, *The Era of Reconstruction* (New York, 1954). For the American language see Robert Spiller *et al.* (eds.), *Literary History of*

the vague Monroe Doctrine into a "national dogma" opposed to the old as well as any new European presence in the New World. Lincoln's secretary of state, William H. Seward, effectively courted Latin American nations threatened by overt European expansion and expansionists from the American South with ambitions in the Caribbean. After the Civil War President Ulysses S. Grant's secretary of state, Hamilton Fish, made the emancipation of Latin America from European dependence the main agenda for American foreign policy well into the twentieth century. Fish explicitly opposed transfers of New World dependencies between European powers, formally encouraged European withdrawal from the Caribbean and South America, and initiated active American participation to mediate European–Latin American disputes. Grant himself used ill-defined European threats to promote further American expansion, which he favored. But the Senate, more concerned with domestic issues, not only rejected territorial expansion but maintained high tariffs and strict budgets. In 1874, when a congressman complained, "The whole of South America is without a consular clerk," the West reeled from the effects of the severe depression that began in 1873 and encouraged farmers to seek new export markets.[6]

A disastrous wet and cold European spring wiped out Europe's 1879 grain crop at the same time that American farmers harvested their largest wheat and corn crops. Europe desperately needed food; the United States not only had grain in abundance, it had an efficient railroad system that could dispatch the harvest to the coastal ports to

the United States (3rd ed.; New York, 1963), 663–93; for the vernacular tradition in nineteenth-century American industrial art see John A. Kouwenhoven, Made in America (Garden City, N.Y., 1948); and H. Wayne Morgan, Unity and Culture (London, 1971), 22–33. Whitman quoted in William Sloane Kennedy, Reminiscences of Walt Whitman (London, 1896), 76; Whitman, Leaves of Grass and Selected Prose, ed. Scully Bradley (New York, 1949), 497.

6. Dexter Perkins, The Monroe Doctrine, 1867–1907 (Baltimore, 1937), 1–32; Nathan L. Ferris, "The Relations of the United States with South America During the American Civil War," HAHR, XXI (1941), 51–78; Tennant S. McWilliams, "The Lure of Empire: Southern Interest in the Caribbean, 1877–1900," Mississippi Quarterly, XXIX (1975), 44; Lester D. Langley, Struggle for the American Mediterranean: United States-European Rivalry in the Gulf-Caribbean, 1776–1904 (Athens, Ga., 1976), 107–93; Tom E. Terrill, The Tariff, Politics, and American Foreign Policy, 1874–1901 (Westport, Conn., 1973), 3–67; consular clerk quoted in Paul S. Holbo, "Economics, Emotion, and Expansion: An Emerging Foreign Policy," in H. Wayne Morgan (ed.), The Gilded Age (Rev. ed.; Syracuse, N.Y., 1970), 202; John A. S. Grenville and George Berkeley Young, Politics, Strategy, and Diplomacy: Studies in American Foreign Policy, 1873–1917 (New Haven, 1966), 77–78; William Appleman Williams, The Roots of American Empire (New York, 1969), 176–202.

be shipped to Europe's eager markets. Thus a European famine combined with domestic railroad technology unexpectedly propelled the United States into a world market. By 1880 American wheat exports had quadrupled. The wheat bonanza created great American prosperity. When Europe exchanged scarce gold for American grain, Americans used the money to invest in increased industrial capacity for export, especially of iron. Americans were not universally pleased with their good fortune. Many critics warned that the shift from reliance on agricultural exports to the production and marketing of manufactured goods was dangerous. The new prosperity forced many American businessmen to ponder the problems of world market industrialism for the first time.[7]

Events of the 1880s gave many thoughtful Americans pause. Although the European grain disaster gave the United States a temporary advantage, Europe still controlled the major world export markets. In 1881 Britain outsold American cotton, a traditionally strong American commodity, thirteen to one, and iron, even in a banner American sales year, by a hundred to one. British predominance in Latin America and Far Eastern markets rankled some ambitious Americans, mainly because it threatened the Americans with total exclusion. Changes in traditional international relations, not the continuation of the status quo, worried America. Benjamin Disraeli's expansionist foreign policy and Germany's new power following the Franco-Prussian War of 1870–1871 made Europe appear more powerful and more threatening during the 1870s. Ferdinand de Lesseps' campaign for the French Panama canal was in fact an innocent and inept French aesthetic conceit rather than an imperial expansion, but Americans well remembered French opportunism in Mexico during the Civil War and recoiled from the memory of previous recent European intrusions.[8]

7. David M. Pletcher, *The Awkward Years: American Foreign Relations Under Garfield and Arthur* (Columbia, Mo., 1961), 4–6; John F. Stover, *American Railroads* (Chicago, 1961), 97–103; see also Howard B. Schonberger, *Transportation to the Seaboard: The "Communication Revolution" and American Foreign Policy* (Westport, Conn., 1971). For European reaction to increased American agricultural exports see John L. Gignilliat, "Pigs, Politics, and Protection: The European Boycott of American Pork, 1879–1891," *Agricultural History*, XXXV (1961), 3–12

8. Pletcher, *Awkward Years*, 7–8; Milton Plesur, *America's Outward Thrust: Approaches to Foreign Affairs, 1865–1890* (DeKalb, Ill., 1971), 128–39; Gerstle Mack, *The Land Divided: A History of the Panama Canal and Other Isthmian Canal Projects* (New York, 1944), 281–316; David McCullough, *The Path Between the Seas: The Creation of the Panama Canal, 1870–1914* (New York, 1977), 45–152.

Latin America suddenly seemed volatile. The War of the Pacific (1879–1883), a conflict in which Chile defeated Peru and Bolivia, involved the United States directly and actively in Latin American affairs. Although Britain had financed and built Chile's navy and had invested extensively in the border nitrate fields, thereby contributing to the conflict, both the causes and the conduct of the war remained purely Latin American. The decisive Chilean victory consolidated Chile's role as a dominant Latin American power and eased the unfounded American fear that the British would exploit the Latin American conflict to establish a Chilean protectorate. The confluence of separate European actions in Latin America appeared to some concerned Americans as unified European action.[9]

The primitive American diplomatic apparatus of 1880 existed more as a function of domestic spoils politics than as a functioning foreign office. "Our foreign policy is a domestic policy," exulted the New York *Herald* in 1881. Secure in its geographic isolation and supported by the twin ideologies of democracy and exceptionalism, the United States had no foreign policy. What matter that, because of their lower relative diplomatic rank, America's foreign diplomats always marched toward the rear in diplomatic receptions? Almost no one in Washington spoke or read foreign languages well enough to assess world conditions intelligently; "Lemonade Lucy" Hayes's refusal to serve wine at official diplomatic functions added to the provincial flavor of American diplomacy. Until 1880 the indifferent image accurately reflected the studied absence of any unified American policy. What changed the American attitude in 1880 was not ambition but fear.[10]

James G. Blaine was one of the most popular and gifted political figures of his time. A bright, well-read, and cosmopolitan American,

9. For the War of the Pacific see Russell H. Bastert, "A New Approach to the Origins of Blaine's Foreign Policy," *HAHR*, XXXIX (1959), 375–412; Pletcher, *Awkward Years*, 9; V. G. Kiernan, "Foreign Interests in the War of the Pacific, *HAHR*, XXXV (1955), 14–36; Frederick Pike, *Chile and the United States, 1880–1962* (South Bend, Ind., 1963), 47–59; Robert Greenhill, "The Nitrate and Iodine Trades, 1880–1914," in D. C. M. Platt (ed.), *Business Imperialism, 1880–1914* (London, 1977), 231–83; and William F. Sater, *Chile and the War of the Pacific* (Lincoln, Neb., 1986).

10. New York *Herald*, December 19, 1881, p. 6; for the State Department's shortcomings see Pletcher, *Awkward Years*, 17–21. For Lucy Hayes see H. Wayne Morgan, *From Hayes to McKinley: National Party Politics, 1877–1896* (Syracuse, N.Y., 1969), 16–18. See also Morton Keller, *Affairs of State: Public Life in Late Nineteenth Century America* (Cambridge, Mass., 1977), esp. 97–98; Grenville and Young, *Politics, Strategy, and Diplomacy*, 77–78; Lester D. Langley, "James Gillespie Blaine: The Ideologue as Diplomat," in Frank J. Merli and Theodore A. Wilson (eds.), *Makers of American Democracy from Benjamin Franklin to Henry Kissinger* (New York, 1974), 257.

Blaine was equally gifted in domestic and foreign policy. After he came within a few hundred votes of being elected president in 1884, he declined almost certain election in 1888 to avoid the divisions his candidacy inevitably excited. He has often been unjustifiably dismissed as a simple American jingo and insensitive expansionist in his two separate terms as secretary of state. Actually, Blaine was one of the most innovative and sophisticated of American diplomats. His diplomacy failed because of domestic political opposition, the reluctance of many Americans to support any foreign policy, the inept and unprofessional practice of American diplomats, including Blaine himself, and the suspicion Latin Americans directed toward any active North American diplomatic initiative.[11]

As President James Garfield's secretary of state, Blaine tried to deal with a sea of Latin American troubles that stretched from Chile to Mexico. The most important subject in Blaine's new Pan-American policy was to redress not British economic superiority but the "existence and menace" of the little wars of Latin America. United States mediation helped settle the Argentine-Chilean dispute over control of Patagonia in 1881. Unable to convince Mexico to mediate its border dispute with weaker Guatemala, Blaine initiated an ambitious Pan-American policy in which the United States in concert with Latin America would attempt to resolve hemispheric issues short of war and without the threat of European coercion. Blaine's foreign policy was designed both to expel Europe and to court Latin America. Although Blaine's foreign activism harmonized with the growing American need for export markets and recognized the new competition from agricultural exporters such as Argentina, Blaine was genuinely interested in closer relations between North and South Americans and fearful of the dangers of unchecked European influence and expansion.[12]

The context of fear in which Blaine's diplomacy developed is the

11. See Charles S. Campbell, *The Transformation of American Foreign Relations, 1865–1900* (New York, 1976), 161–76, for a persuasive view of "Unjingo Jim"; see also Langley, "James Gillespie Blaine," 253–78; Plesur, *America's Outward Thrust*, 234–35; Pletcher, *Awkward Years*, esp. xiv–xv, 12–16, 40–86. For a more critical view see Justis D. Doenecke, *The Presidencies of James A. Garfield and Chester A. Arthur* (Lawrence, Kan., 1981), 13–14, 56, 60–74. For a favorable assessment of Blaine's political significance see Lewis L. Gould, "The Republican Search for a National Majority," in Morgan (ed.), *Gilded Age*, 178–81; see also Morgan, *From Hayes to McKinley*, 65–71; and Joseph B. Lockey, *Essays in Pan-Americanism* (Berkeley, 1939), 51–84.

12. Bastert, "New Approach to the Origins of Blaine's Foreign Policy," 375–412; Langley, "James Gillespie Blaine," 259–72; Campbell, *Transformation of American Foreign Relations*, 162–63.

most important aspect to consider in assessing it. Neither Blaine nor Garfield was an overt or passive expansionist in 1881. Garfield, as much of an activist as Blaine in supporting improved relations with Latin America, fought Britain's unchallenged trade supremacy "on general principles," while also trying to improve a trade deficit that in 1880 showed U.S. imports from Latin America of $176 million and exports of only $58 million. Both reacted to a series of events that may have appeared more threatening than they actually were. But an unsophisticated America, newly unified economically and politically, surprised by its own wealth and its frequent economic depressions, thrust into the world sooner than expected by the new transportation technology and the changes in European leadership, was forced to consider almost for the first time its place in international politics. American art collectors were out in the world learning the art market and competing with European museums. American businessmen were testing the economic waters in Latin America and Asia. Under Blaine, American diplomacy, though stumbling and frequently inept, supplanted the smug fortress America mentality that attempted to ignore a rapidly changing world. The world gradually began to impinge upon the once isolated Americans. Britain and Europe remained matters of concern, but nothing impressed reluctant American congressmen of the need to modernize the wooden American navy more than the substantial increase in the number of Latin American naval vessels. In the congressional debates of 1881, the superiority of any single new Chilean vessel to any of the United States' older ships was as compelling as William Cullen Bryant's observation that even a third-rate European power like Spain could afford museums. Once American tranquillity and smugness had been breached, national enthusiasm spread quickly.[13]

Economic development on a national scale accelerated in the 1880s. Two new transcontinental railroads, the Southern Pacific and the Atchison, Topeka, and Santa Fe, completed in 1883, linked the South and Southwest with the West. In 1883 Congress reluctantly recog-

13. Pletcher, *Awkward Years,* xiii. For Garfield's role see Allan Peskin, "Blaine, Garfield, and Latin America: A New Look," *Americas,* XXXVI (1979), 79–89; Garfield quoted *ibid.,* 87. The trade deficit is discussed in Robert Freeman Smith, "Latin America, the United States, and the European Powers, 1830–1930," in *CHLA,* IV, 88–89. W. G. Constable, *Art Collecting in the United States of America: An Outline of a History* (London, 1962); Nathaniel Burt, *Palaces for the People: A Social History of the American Art Museum* (Boston, 1977), 91; Harold Sprout and Margaret Sprout, *The Rise of American Naval Power, 1776–1918* (Princeton, 1939), 184.

nized the end of the age of wooden sailing vessels by funding the navy's first new steel ships. The naval appropriation was a compromise. The new *Chicago, Atlanta,* and *Boston* were unarmored vessels with full rigging and sails. The navy's highest-ranking officer, Admiral David D. Porter, boasted that these ships could go around the world exclusively on sail power. The new steel ships were as inept as the sailing ships the navy continued to rely on. Americans had neither experience in the new naval architecture of steel and coal nor the materials to make new ships, armor, or weaponry. No one thought of it as a turning point at the time, but the establishment of the Naval War College at Newport, Rhode Island, in 1884 gave the sailing navy a professional foundation for the future. In 1886 Congress passed a domestic manufacture law requiring that the new modern steel navy be built with American materials, thus establishing a domestic naval material industry that not only freed Americans from dependence on European shipbuilders but assured a vigorous naval building lobby in the 1890s.[14]

With Benjamin Harrison's election as president in 1888, a new activism entered American diplomacy, led by James Blaine, once again secretary of state, and Secretary of the Navy Benjamin Franklin Tracy, a vigorous former Civil War general. Blaine revived the Pan-Americanism he had introduced in 1881, and Tracy, an able administrator and financier, initiated a brilliant new naval program. Both domestic and foreign critics attacked Blaine's proposed Pan-American Congress meeting in Washington in 1889. Cuban writer José Martí warned Latin Americans of the perceived dangers; "Never in [Latin] America, from its independence to the present, has there been a matter requiring more good judgment or more vigilance, or demanding a clearer and more thorough examination, than the invitation which the powerful United States (glutted with unsalable merchandise and determined to extend its dominions in America) is sending to the less powerful American nations (bound by free and useful commerce to the European nations) for purposes of arranging an alliance against Europe and cutting off transactions with the rest of the world."

14. Stover, *American Railroads,* 82–88; Sprout and Sprout, *Rise of American Naval Power,* 182–95; George T. Davis, *A Navy Second to None: The Development of Modern American Naval Policy* (New York, 1940), 37–55; Ronald Spector, *Professors of War: The Naval War College and the Development of the Naval Profession* (Newport, R.I., 1977), 1–37; Robert Seager II, "Ten Years Before Mahan: The Unofficial Case for the New Navy, 1880–1890," *MVHR,* XL (1953), 491–512.

Martí's warning defined the criticism of the United States by contemporaries and many later historians, who saw a powerful acquisitive nation with an urge for conquest, economic domination, and empire.[15]

Benjamin Tracy was well aware that his new policies would be viewed with concern. "Not conquest, but defense," he declared, was the sole purpose of his new navy. The United States in 1889 was "absolutely at the mercy of states having less than one-tenth of its population, one-thirtieth of its wealth, and one hundredth of its area." Its "coast line of 13,000 miles" with twenty major cities was "wholly unprotected against modern weapons." Any power could, Tracy claimed, "secure in a single raid upon our coast, an amount of money sufficient to meet the expenses of a naval war." Tracy tried to reassure not only critics like Martí but American congressmen as well that the new navy was wholly defensive. "The policy of military aggrandizement is totally repugnant to American institutions." Perhaps Tracy's most compelling argument was the statistics that dramatically demonstrated the relative weakness of the American navy. Even Austria-Hungary, with twelve armored ships and a total of fifty-six vessels, exceeded the United States' eleven armored vessels and forty-two total vessels.[16]

15. Grenville and Young, *Politics, Strategy, and American Diplomacy*, 88–93; Campbell, *Transformation of American Foreign Relations*, 162–64; J. Lloyd Mecham, *The United States and Inter-American Security, 1889–1960* (Austin, Tex., 1961), 48–58; Langley, "James Gillespie Blaine," 270–72; Homer E. Socolofsky and Allan B. Spetter, *The Presidency of Benjamin Harrison* (Lawrence, Kan., 1987), 95–156; José Martí, "The Washington Pan American Congress," *La Nación* (Buenos Aires), December 19–20, 1889, rpr. in José Martí, *Inside the Monster: Writings on the United States and American Imperialism*, ed. Philip Foner, trans. Elinor Randall (New York, 1975), 340; Thomas Karnes, "Pan-Americanism," in Alexander De Conde (ed.), *Encyclopedia of American Foreign Policy* (3 vols.; New York, 1978), II, 735; Thomas F. McGann, "Argentina at the First Pan-American Conference," *Inter-American Economic Affairs*, I (1947), 21–53. For the conference proceedings see James Brown Scott (ed.), *The International Conferences of American States, 1889–1928* (New York, 1931), vii–47. For the American political background see Russell H. Bastert, "Diplomatic Reversal: Frelinghuysen's Opposition to Blaine's Pan-American Policy in 1882," *MVHR*, LXII (1956), 153–71.

16. See Benjamin Franklin Cooling, *Benjamin Franklin Tracy: Father of the Modern American Fighting Navy* (Hamden, Conn., 1973), 62–78; Walter R. Herrick, "Benjamin F. Tracy, 6 March 1889–6 March 1893," in Paolo E. Coletta (ed.), *American Secretaries of the Navy* (2 vols.; Annapolis, 1980), 415–24; Spector, *Professors of War*, 1–74; John D. Hayes and John B. Hattendorf, *The Writings of Stephen B. Luce* (Newport, R.I., 1975), 14–18, 203–204; Samuel P. Huntington, *The Soldier and the State: The Theory and Politics of Civil-Military Relations* (New York, 1964), 274–79; W. D. Puleston, *Mahan* (New Haven, 1939), 66–105; and Robert Seager II, *Alfred Thayer Mahan: The Man and His Letters* (Annapolis, 1977). Tracy's report is in *House Executive Documents*, 51st Cong., 1st Sess., No. 1, Pt. 3, Serial 2721, pp. 3–4.

Although the new American diplomacy was dramatic, it had no underlying unity or design. Tracy's appointment as head of the navy was a fortuitous consequence of American domestic politics, which still dominated American governance. Tracy, an able New York local politician, won the navy appointment when Harrison refused to make New York Republican Boss Thomas Platt his secretary of the treasury. When the incensed Platt threatened to break with Harrison, Tracy's appointment as navy secretary appeased both Platt and New York's badly split Republican party factions. Blaine's appointment, though richly deserved, owed as much to domestic politics as to foreign affairs. In spite of the rare Republican control of both the presidency and Congress, the deep and varied congressional opposition to virtually all of Blaine's diplomatic initiatives demonstrated a continuing diversity in America foreign policy, reflecting domestic priorities and increasing individualism, not unity or design. Rear Admiral Stephen B. Luce, the first head of the Naval War College, recognized Captain Alfred Thayer Mahan's gifts as a teacher and writer, brought him to Newport as his successor in 1885, and in 1889 helped him find a publisher for his Naval War College lectures, which as *The Influence of Sea Power upon History* (1890) established the idea of sea power as a popular public concept. Tracy the political organizer, Luce the naval intellectual, and Mahan, an imaginative and appealing historian of naval warfare, complemented each other's considerable gifts and made a compelling case for a new American naval activism. It was Tracy who began the practice of naming battleships for states and cruisers for cities, one way of marshaling local support for his ambitious programs.[17]

In spite of the enormous interest generated by Alfred T. Mahan's expansionist naval theories, strong congressional opposition to the Navy Policy Board's recommendation for two hundred new warships, branded as "naval fanaticism" by the New York *Herald*, limited but did not end naval expansion. Efforts to attain a new Caribbean coaling station were unsuccessful. Negotiations for Haiti's Môle St. Nicholas, the Dominican Republic's Samaná Bay, and Peru's Chimbote all failed but for different reasons, including continuing American ambivalence. An extended confrontation with Chile in 1891 threatened ac-

17. Walter R. Herrick, Jr., *The American Naval Revolution* (Baton Rouge, 1966), 42; Campbell, *Transformation of American Foreign Relations*, 165; Cooling, *Benjamin Franklin Tracy*, 43–45; Ernest May, *Imperial Democracy: The Emergence of America as a Great Power* (New York, 1961), 11.

tual war. Chile was the aggressor, British involvement a complication, and Harrison's willingness to go to war over a naval incident involving the cruiser *Baltimore* indicated both an increased national sensitivity to and frustration over continuing foreign slights during America's transition from inactive to major power. Europe recognized the new American consciousness when in 1892 all the major European nations (except Austria-Hungary) raised their American legations to embassies. The United States followed suit in 1893, thereby allowing American ministers to march nearer the front of diplomatic receptions.[18]

Theodore Roosevelt was an American political anomaly. An aristocrat and a graduate of Harvard's class of 1880, Roosevelt rejected the customary gentleman's career of corporation law or writing and became a politician in 1881. Unlike other gentlemen in politics, he remained a Republican in 1884 though his party nominated Blaine, whom Roosevelt detested. After a promising career as a New York State legislator and a disastrous third-place finish in the 1886 New York City mayoralty election, Roosevelt was rewarded upon Harrison's election in 1888 with a minor federal appointment as civil service commissioner, a post he held until 1895. In Washington, Roosevelt emerged as one of the leaders of the activist and expansionist Republicans often engaged in vitriolic combat with the Democrats and the antiexpansionists.[19]

One must view with extreme caution the rhetoric of American politicians and journalists, especially in the 1890s. Their words must be

18. New York *Herald*, January 31, 1890, p. 6. For the efforts to obtain Môle St. Nicolas, see Rayford W. Logan, *Diplomatic Relations of the United States with Haiti* (Chapel Hill, 1941); Frederick Douglass, "Haiti and the United States: Inside History of the Negotiations for Môle St. Nicolas," *NAR*, CLIII (1891), 337–45, 450–59. For the frequent negotiations on Samaná Bay, see Sumner Welles, *Naboth's Vineyard: The Dominican Republic, 1844–1924* (2 vols.; New York, 1928); see also Alice Felt Tyler, *The Foreign Policy of James G. Blaine* (Minneapolis, 1927), 91–98. For Chimbote see A. T. Volwiller, "Harrison, Blaine, and American Foreign Policy, 1889–1893," *Proceedings of the American Philosophical Society*, LXXIX (1938), 644. For the changes in legation rank see May, *Imperial Democracy*, 13–24. For the *Baltimore* incident see Joyce Goldberg, *The Baltimore Affair* (Lincoln, Neb., 1986).

19. John Morton Blum, *The Republican Roosevelt* (Cambridge, Mass., 1954), 1–36; William H. Harbaugh, *The Life and Times of Theodore Roosevelt* (New York, 1975), 26–83; Carleton Putnam, *Theodore Roosevelt: The Formative Years* (New York, 1958); James C. Malin, "Roosevelt and the Elections of 1884 and 1888," *MVHR*, XIV (1927), 25–38; for Roosevelt's role in 1884 see John Garraty, *Henry Cabot Lodge: A Biography* (New York, 1953), 75–87; see also David Healy, *US Expansionism: The Imperialist Urge in the 1890s* (Madison, Wisc., 1970), 110–26.

read in the context of American accommodation politics and not as rigid ideology. Until Benjamin Harrison's election in 1888, no party since Reconstruction had controlled both the Congress and the presidency. Harrison's triumph was partial, however, because his opponent, Grover Cleveland, won the popular vote. For a politician like Roosevelt, a Republican victory meant a job in Washington. But even within the parties there was almost no unity. Republicans were bitterly divided between stalwarts and half-breeds and later between railroad conservatives and reformers such as Roosevelt and Robert La Follette of Wisconsin. Even close friends like Roosevelt and Henry Cabot Lodge disagreed on many issues. The genius of American politics was its ability to accommodate an atomistic individualism verging on eccentricity, especially in its members of Congress, and to accept one-vote victories or defeats with equanimity. Indeed, American politics was based on the narrow victory. With a two-thirds majority required for Senate ratification of foreign treaties, it was rare for any treaty to win by more than a handful of votes. Domestic consensus was exceedingly rare, and many issues won passage only because of the custom of vote-trading, which crossed regional, ideological, and party alliances. Even legislation that passed had to run the gauntlet of an often unpredictable Supreme Court, by its nature out of phase with the predominant political fashions of the moment and eternally fond of bitter five-to-four decisions that were as binding in law and custom as rarer unanimous nine-to-zero decisions. American accommodation politics encouraged independence. Consensus was achieved politically but almost never intellectually. Nor was ideological consistency considered a virtue. Regional political preferences, the shifting alliances of the moment, the context of other issues being debated, all counted for more than ideology.[20]

20. Perceptive overviews of Gilded Age America include Keller, *Affairs of State*, esp. 188–96; Robert Wiebe, *The Search for Order, 1877–1920* (New York, 1967); David Rothman, *Politics and Power: The United States Senate, 1869–1901* (Cambridge, Mass., 1971); Paul Holbo, "Trade and Commerce," in DeConde, *Encyclopedia of American Foreign Policy*, III, 950–53; and Morgan, *From Hayes to McKinley*. For the resolution of political divisions see Skowronek, *Building a New American State*; James Livingston, *Origins of the Federal Reserve System: Money, Class, and Corporate Capitalism, 1890–1913* (Ithaca, N.Y., 1986); and Martin J. Sklar, *The Corporate Reconstruction of American Capitalism, 1890–1916* (New York, 1988). For tariff, reciprocity, and historiographical issues see David M. Pletcher, "1861–1898: Economic Growth and Diplomatic Adjustment," in William H. Becker and Samuel F. Wells, Jr. (eds.), *Economics and World Power: An Assessment of American Diplomacy Since 1789* (New York, 1984), 119–72. For a summary of the diversity see Morgan, *Unity and Culture*, esp. 118–27.

The question of Hawaiian annexation, the first expansion issue, debated in the press and the Congress for five years, well demonstrated the way the system operated. American sugar planters living in Hawaii had urged annexation by the United States since as early as 1854. Domestic American politics made Hawaii an issue in 1890, when the McKinley Tariff put sugar on the free list, ending Hawaii's price advantage and depressing its sugar exports. In 1891 Queen Liliuokalani assumed the throne and took new autocratic powers favoring the natives over the American planters. In 1893 the planters, led by Sanford B. Dole, overthrew the queen and claimed Hawaii for America. Unexpectedly and suddenly, the nation was plunged into a debate on the merits of expansion. Americans were completely divided. Should business or conscience dictate American policy? San Francisco's businessmen were the first to back annexation, but on patriotic rather than economic grounds and because they were sure that increased Pacific Ocean trade would undermine the local Southern Pacific Railroad's monopoly. Carl Schurz, a leading Mugwump writer, argued against annexation on strategic grounds. The island would be "an Achilles heel," exposed to a sudden enemy attack and therefore practically indefensible. Theodore Roosevelt in 1897 thought that "if we don't take Hawaii it will pass into the hands of some strong nation, and the chance of taking it will be gone forever." Andrew Carnegie opposed taking the Philippines but favored Hawaii as a "strictly defensive" coaling station. Both the *Catholic World* and the Protestant *Independent* favored annexing Hawaii and bitterly opposed American activities in the Philippines. William McKinley resisted the pressure for annexation and a war with Spain over Cuba. When war seemed inevitable, McKinley moved to annex Hawaii, citing Manifest Destiny. American opinion on Hawaii was mixed. Although the war of words was violent, everyone involved knew that the intense rhetoric and the compromise consensus politics were part of the same system of dialogue and decision.[21]

21. For the divisions on the Hawaii question see May, *Imperial Democracy*, 5; Carl Schurz, "Manifest Destiny," *Harper's New Monthly Magazine*, LXXXVII (1893), 743–44, rpr. in Norman A. Graebner (ed.), *Ideas and Diplomacy: Readings in the Intellectual Tradition of American Foreign Policy* (New York, 1964), 347–49; TR to William Chanler, December 23, 1897, in *MRL*, I, 747; Andrew Carnegie, "Distant Possessions—The Parting of the Ways," *NAR*, CLXVII (1898), 239–48, rpr. in Graebner (ed.), *Ideas and Diplomacy*, 361–65; Richard D. Weigle, "The Sugar Interests and American Diplomacy in Hawaii and Cuba, 1893–1903" (Ph.D. dissertation, Yale University, 1939); George W. Baker, "Benjamin Harrison and Hawaiian Annexation: A Reinterpretation," *PHR*, XXXIII

Theodore Roosevelt was adept at both parts of the process. Before he became president, he played the role of partisan Republican expansionist advocate; as president his policies were much less radical than his earlier words, though the Democratic and Mugwump press acted as if there had been no change. Roosevelt played the role of *enfant terrible* well, using his image as an explosive and impulsive man of action to win numerous political compromises. Roosevelt played many roles in his life; as a well-bred gentleman he knew the rules of social context and adapted to them quickly. It is a mistake to blur the nonpresidential Roosevelt with the man who as president well understood the institutional requirements of the office. As president he consulted cabinet, Congress, opposition leaders in both parties, intellectuals, and journalists before making well-considered decisions, often disguising the process for maximum political effectiveness. Both before and after he became president, Roosevelt played the role of partisan advocate for various causes including the superiority of the Republican party, territorial and naval expansion, and the need to go to war. Although he remained a passionate partisan believer, as president he not only understood how to meliorate his independence, but he deeply enjoyed the challenge of working within the consensus requirements of the American political process—and at times pushing it to its outermost limits. Later he equally enjoyed the independence of being free from the responsibilities of presidential constraints when he could make shocking statements publicly.[22]

In spite of all the passionate and violent arguments of the 1890s and the enormous divisions within the American political system, America's political leaders understood the underlying unity of dialogue and consensus, a process exemplified by Roosevelt's early career in national government and demonstrated by Democratic President Grover

---

(1964), 295–304; William A. Russ, Jr., *The Hawaiian Revolution (1893–1894)* (Selinsgrove, Pa., 1959); Russ, *The Hawaiian Republic (1894–1898)* (Selinsgrove, Pa., 1961); Holbo, "Economics, Emotion, and Expansion," 218–19; and Socolofsky and Spetter, *Presidency of Benjamin Harrison*, 200–206.

22. A perceptive analysis of Roosevelt's combination of cultivation and political ability is Lewis Einstein, *Roosevelt: His Mind in Action* (New York, 1930), 28–29. For TR's self-conscious use of exaggerated speech styles see William A. Behe, "Theodore Roosevelt's Principles of Speech Preparation and Delivery," *Speech Monographs*, XII (1945), 112–22. For a good example of TR's ability to dramatize himself as a "cyclone assemblyman," see Edmund Morris, *The Rise of Theodore Roosevelt*, 158–82; see also Frederick W. Marks III, *Velvet on Iron: The Diplomacy of Theodore Roosevelt* (Lincoln, Neb., 1979), 58–60; and John Morton Blum, *The Progressive Presidents* (New York, 1980), 23–24.

Cleveland's reappointment of the Republican Roosevelt as civil service commissioner in 1893. In 1897 President William McKinley, a public advocate and a passionate believer in peace, brought Roosevelt, the most outspoken advocate of belligerence, into his administration in the key role of assistant secretary of the navy. The two men agreed that Roosevelt was free to speak his mind as long as he faithfully carried out the president's decisions. Neither had any difficulty in this agreement; it was the established custom in American national politics.[23]

Roosevelt had written about America's place in the world since his graduation from Harvard in 1880. His first book, *The Naval War of 1812* (1881), was a revisionist account of American naval accomplishments in the War of 1812. His *Winning of the West* (1889–1896) was favorably reviewed by Frederick Jackson Turner and led to an affectionate correspondence between the two historians of the West. In his periodical articles and especially in his letters Roosevelt in the 1890s revealed a concern for America's changing position in the world, a process ignored by many American politicians, who were still wholly absorbed in domestic political issues.[24]

In a remarkable article for the *Sewanee Review*, Roosevelt in 1894 assessed his time and the prospects for the future. He decried the "morose and dyspeptic temper" of railing at the present, which Roosevelt

23. Harbaugh, *Life and Times of Theodore Roosevelt*, 77–83; Morris, *Rise of Theodore Roosevelt*, 554–60; HCL to TR, December 2, 1896, in *Selections from the Correspondence of Theodore Roosevelt and Henry Cabot Lodge* (2 vols.; New York, 1925), I, 241–42. For Blaine's sensible rejection of Roosevelt as assistant secretary of state in 1889 see Harbaugh, *Life and Times of Theodore Roosevelt*, 77.

24. For the view that Roosevelt was the preeminent naval intellectual of the two see Peter Karsten, "The Nature of 'Influence': Roosevelt, Mahan, and the Concept of Sea Power," *AQ*, XXIII (1971), 585–600; see also Noel F. Busch, *TR: The Story of Theodore Roosevelt and His Influence on Our Times* (New York, 1963), 42, 115; and Holbo, "Economics, Emotion, and Expansion," 213–14; for disagreement with Karsten's view see Michael T. Gorgan, "Mahan and Theodore Roosevelt: The Assessment of Influence," *Naval War College Review*, XXXIII (1980), 88–97; and Richard W. Turk, *The Ambiguous Relationship: Theodore Roosevelt and Alfred Thayer Mahan* (Westport, Conn., 1987). For assessments of Roosevelt as a writer see Aloysius A. Norton, *Theodore Roosevelt* (Boston, 1980); John A. Gable, "Theodore Roosevelt as an Historian and Man of Letters," in TR, *Gouverneur Morris* (Oyster Bay, 1985), xi–xxiv; Russel B. Nye, "Theodore Roosevelt as Historian," *Nassau County Historical Journal*, III (1940), 3–7; Morris, *Rise of Theodore Roosevelt*, 154–56, 387–89, 462–66; and David H. Burton, *The Learned Presidency: Theodore Roosevelt, William Howard Taft, and Woodrow Wilson* (Cranbury, N.J., 1988), 47–55. For Roosevelt as a writer on the West see G. Edward White, *The Eastern Establishment and the Western Experience: The West of Frederic Remington, Theodore Roosevelt, and Owen Wister* (New Haven, 1968); and Frederick Jackson Turner, "Winning of the West," *Dial*, X (1889), 71–73.

exuberantly found "full of interest . . . excitement, and enjoyment." He admired the new technological advances, the achievements of Lincoln and Bismarck, who "have taken their places among the world's worthies," and the rise of new empires. But he opposed colonial rule. "The English rulers of India will some day in the future—for the good of mankind . . . themselves be absorbed and vanish." Roosevelt's key distinction, between ethnic and political conquest, defined his opposition to colonialism. Making any people subject to another was both ineffective and immoral. Britain's development of Australia with men of English stock was far more significant and useful than holding India in subjection and making "the usurer rather than the soldier the dominant type." When Roosevelt wrote of the superiority of the white race, he was usually referring to national development and not innate racial characteristics. In rejecting other writers' fears of eventual domination by prolific nonwhite races, Roosevelt dismissed the problem: "If any of the tropical races ever does reach a pitch of industrial and military prosperity which makes it a menace to European and American countries, it will almost necessarily mean that this nation has itself become civilized in the process; and we shall then simply be dealing with another civilized nation of non-aryan blood, precisely as we now deal with Magyar, Fin, and Basque, without any thought of their being ethnically distinct from Croat, Roman, or Basque."[25]

Civilization was the controlling idea of Theodore Roosevelt's world and life. A cosmopolitan American nationalist, an aristocrat, and an intellectual, he saw himself as a citizen of the world. His major purpose was to make his own country the leader of the civilized world, but by equating independence with civilization, Roosevelt rejected territorial, political, or economic domination as a means of achieving national progress. Such expansion by conquest was doomed to failure because arbitrary mixing of different peoples diminished the vigor of both.[26]

Educated Americans like Roosevelt began to lose their unquestioned faith in civilized European superiority in the 1890s. When

25. TR, "National Life and Character," *Sewanee Review* (1894), rpr. in *TRWN*, XIII, 200–222; Thomas G. Dyer, *Theodore Roosevelt and the Idea of Race* (Baton Rouge, 1980). For a corrective of the oversimplified characterizations of Roosevelt as a Social Darwinist, see Burton, *Learned Presidency*, 38–44.

26. See Frank Ninkovich, "Theodore Roosevelt: Civilization as Ideology," *DH*, X (1986), 221–45; also see John P. Mallan, "Roosevelt, Brooks Adams, and Lea: The Warrior Critique of the Business Civilization," *AQ*, VIII (1956), 216–30.

Spanish ineptitude in Cuba became painfully obvious as American export trade increased, the unrest threatened to disrupt Cuba's Caribbean sea lanes, now vital to the depressed American economy. European insensitivity was dramatically underscored in 1894, when none of the great powers, Britain, France, or Russia, intervened when the Ottoman Turks massacred ten thousand Armenians, an event that shocked many Americans. When Europe, more and more viewed as seriously flawed, began its most active phase of expansion in 1895 and after, American uneasiness increased. The Monroe Doctrine, a vaguely worded but passionate icon of American independence from European hegemony, was revived as Americans worried about European intentions and ability. European acquiescence in the Monroe Doctrine was vital to American foreign policy. Only after Europe accepted North American hegemony could the United States use the arbitration process to prevent European intervention in Caribbean or Latin disputes. Without clear European acceptance of the Monroe Doctrine, the Americans feared that the doctrine itself might become an arbitratable issue, a disaster that the State Department worked hard to avoid. When the Anglo-Venezuela border erupted in 1895, the Americans remained oblivious to and ignorant of the specific issues and transformed the minor border dispute into an eventually successful attempt to force British acceptance of both the Monroe Doctrine and arbitration.[27]

No one in American politics understood the mystique of the Monroe Doctrine better than Theodore Roosevelt. He summarily dismissed British legal objections or questions of historical precedent. In March, 1896, Roosevelt declared, "If the Monroe Doctrine did not already exist it would be necessary forthwith to create it." But Roosevelt rejected using the doctrine as a catechism. "It is not desirable to define

27. On the criticism of European civilization see T. J. Jackson Lears, *No Place of Grace: Antimodernism and the Transformation of American Culture, 1880–1920* (New York, 1981), 116–17; and John Patrick Diggins, "Republicanism and Progressivism," *AQ,* XXXVII (1985), 572–76. For Cuba's increasing importance see Campbell, *Transformation of American Foreign Policy,* 241; for the reaction to the Ottoman atrocities see May, *Imperial Diplomacy,* 27. European expansion is described in Robert Beisner, *From the Old Diplomacy to the New, 1865–1900* (Arlington Heights, Ill., 1975), 102. On the Monroe Doctrine see Alvey A. Adee to Richard Olney, July 10, 1895, quoted in May, *Imperial Democracy;* and TR, "The Monroe Doctrine," *Bachelor of Arts* (1896), rpr. in *TRWN,* XIII, 168–81; see also TR to *Harvard Crimson,* January 2, 1896, in *MRL,* I, 505–506. For American ignorance of Venezuelan issues see May, *Imperial Democracy,* 36–37; Perkins, *Monroe Doctrine, 1867–1907,* 224–52; Grenville and Young, *Politics, Strategy, and American Diplomacy,* 158–229; and Richard E. Welch, Jr.; *The Presidencies of Grover Cleveland* (Lawrence, Kan., 1988), 180–92.

it so rigidly as to prevent our taking into account the varying degrees of national interest in varying cases." The United States did not want a universal protectorate over any part of Latin America or to prevent normal Latin American-European disputes. Roosevelt consistently used historical perspective to shape foreign policy. To explain the Monroe Doctrine's purpose, he used the Louisiana Territory as an example. In 1803 Americans accepted Louisiana's possession by Spain, a weak European power, but fought its transfer to France, a strong power, an example of the Monroe Doctrine principle before it was enunciated in 1823. In 1896, Roosevelt wrote, the same principle would exist "if Germany sought to acquire Cuba from Spain, St. Thomas from the Danes." If such an unlikely event occurred, the United States must interfere "if necessary, by force of arms."[28]

Within the context of the Monroe Doctrine Roosevelt made significant distinctions of his own concerning international relations and obligations. Nations must be strong to serve the international community best: "No country will ever accomplish very much for the world at large unless it elevates itself." Roosevelt was unequivocal in his insistence that "the most useful member of the brotherhood of nations is that nation which is most thoroughly saturated with the national idea." Strong nationality precluded any idea of colonization: "As long as the Canadian remains a colonist, he remains in a position which is distinctly inferior to that of his cousins, both in England and the United States." Roosevelt was hopeful about the future of Latin America: "The history of most Latin American republics has been both mean and bloody; but there is at least a chance that they may develop, after infinite tribulation and suffering, into a civilization quite as high and stable as that of such a European power as Portugal. But there is no chance for any tropical American colony owned by a Northern European race. It is distinctly in the interest of civilization that the present States in the two Americas should develop along their own lines" and not under European control. Roosevelt used British Guiana as an example of colonial ineffectiveness. It is "a colony where a few hundred or few thousand white men hold superior positions, while the bulk of the population is composed of Indians, negroes, and Asiatics. Looked at through the vista of the centuries, such a colony contains less promise of true growth than does a State like Venezuela or

28. TR, "Monroe Doctrine," 168, 169, 171; for TR on expelling Europe from the New World see TR to William A. Chanler, December 23, 1897, in *MRL*, I, 746–47; for strategic alternatives to various European threats see TR to Francis C. Moore, February 5, 1898, *ibid.*, 768–69.

Ecuador." Roosevelt's preference for strong nationalism was consistent. He decried "milk and water cosmopolitanism" as a poor substitute for patriotism. "Love of country is an elemental virtue, like love of home, or like honesty and courage." Wealth and education can corrupt men, "who undervalue the great fighting qualities, without which no nation can ever rise to the first rank." Roosevelt's views were sufficiently specific and unique to resist being comfortably classified in any single category, though he frequently wrote in Darwinian or racist diction.[29]

Americans were still far more absorbed with domestic matters than with foreign relations. In July, 1896, Roosevelt wrote his sister, "Not since the Civil War has there been an election fraught with so much consequence to the country. The silver craze surpasses belief. The populists, populist-democrats, and silver- or populist-Republicans who are behind Bryan are impelled by a wave of genuine fanaticism." Roosevelt, who then and later could not abide Bryan, concluded, "Bryan's election would be a great calamity, though we should in the end recover from it." New concerns about foreign relations were inevitable as European stability wavered, but Americans, who much preferred arguing over silver and tariffs, were forced to confront the new issues at once as Spain's hold on Cuba disintegrated, a matter of grave significance in American eyes. Under Spain, regarded by Americans as Europe's weakest nation, Cuba was safe from Germany or any other stronger European power. Americans were free to enjoy Cuba's economic benefits with none of the racial problems or duties of colonial administration. With Cuba in question, the entire Caribbean was vulnerable. Grover Cleveland recognized the growing problem in his final address and warned in 1896 that American intervention would be necessary if Spain could not reassert sovereignty.[30]

It is a mistake to overemphasize the influence of the sensationalist American press, which exploited the Cuban conflict to win new readers. American leaders were horrified at the ramifications of the Cuban disintegration, which fed the atomistic disunity of American domestic politics already in turmoil over currency and tariff questions. Winning a war with Spain was not at issue. Roosevelt wrote Henry Cabot Lodge at the end of 1896, "I do not think a war with Spain would be serious enough to cause much strain on the country, or much inter-

29. TR, "Monroe Doctrine," 172–73.
30. TR to Anna R. Cowles, July 26, 1896, in *MRL*, I, 550; Campbell, *Transformation of American Foreign Policy*, 245; Grenville and Young, *Politics, Strategy, and American Diplomacy*, 180–200.

ruption in the revival of prosperity; but I certainly wish the matter could be settled this winter." For the future, Roosevelt wanted "the ultimate removal of all European powers from the colonies they hold in the Western hemisphere." American business resisted war though American exports to Cuba dropped by over two-thirds. President McKinley resisted pressure from the press and from belligerents like Roosevelt and sought a peaceful solution. McKinley understood, perhaps intuitively, that for the United States the best solution was a restoration of the status quo with weak Spain in control of a pacified Cuba. Americans who thought about the Cuban problem remained divided. Cleveland's secretary of state, Richard Olney, would have been satisfied by any restoration of Spanish authority; McKinley wanted a restoration satisfactory to the Cuban rebels. Europe's response to a possible American intervention remained a constant uncertainty. Kaiser Wilhelm II, furious at the prospect, asked, "Just to suffer this event, is Europe ready to do that?" The kaiser's anger remained a marginal note on a diplomatic record because Europe, even more disunited than the United States, would not fight for Spain. Germany troubled the United States more than Spain. What eventually moved the American business community to support a war over Cuba was German expansion in China at Kiaochow in November, 1897, and in Shantung Province in March, 1898.[31]

The Spanish-American War of 1898 was a "splendid little war" (John Hay's phrase) only in comparison to the dreadful conflicts that preceded and would follow it. For Americans it was only partly splendid. The United States demonstrated to itself and to Europe that it could fight and win a foreign war. With former Confederates fighting side by side with Union soldiers, military unification cemented the political and economic reunion that had already given the post–Civil

31. TR to HCL, December 4, 1896, in *MRL*, I, 567; TR to William S. Cowles, April 5, 1896, *ibid.*, 524; Campbell, *Transformation of American Foreign Policy*, 245–47. For the shift in business sentiment see Walter LaFeber, *The New Empire: An Interpretation of American Expansion, 1860–1898* (Ithaca, N.Y., 1963), 354–406; see also TR to William Wirt Kimball, December 17, 1897; TR to Cecil Spring Rice, August 13, 1897, both in *MRL*, I, 644–49, 743; the kaiser's marginal notes are quoted in May, *Imperial Democracy*, 196–97. Welch, *Presidencies of Grover Cleveland*, 194–98, assesses Cleveland's Cuba policy. For McKinley see Lewis L. Gould, *The Presidency of William McKinley* (Lawrence, Kan., 1980), 59–121. For a review of the historiography see Joseph A. Fry, "William McKinley and the Coming of the Spanish-American War: A Study of the Besmirching and Redemption of an Historical Image," *DH*, III (1979), 77–98; also see David F. Trask, *The War with Spain in 1898* (New York, 1981); Pletcher, "1861–1898," 165–69; and Paolo E. Coletta (ed.), *Threshold to American Internationalism: Essays on the Foreign Policies of William McKinley* (New York, 1971).

War United States its awesome economic and political unity. But the war brought Americans into the maelstrom of turn-of-the-century nationalism and threatened to undo America's cherished exceptionalism by transforming the unique and isolated continent into a pale copy of imperial Europe, imitating Europe's mistakes. Much of the conflict over the fate of the Philippines and Cuba was a debate about whether the United States was surrendering its uniqueness and some of its democratic beliefs. Except for an occasional extremist like Albert Beveridge, who saw American conquest as "the hand of God" and the United States as a "redeeming nation," American expansionists viewed their new involvement with misgivings.[32]

Both Cuba and the Philippines revealed to Americans what Europe already knew: there were no good solutions. America in its first century enjoyed almost complete freedom from the world's problems. Between 1815 and 1870, the peak period of American continental development, there were no world wars to distract domestic energies or deflect investors. Blessed with the fortuitous world situation through which expendable European emigrants and surplus European profits gave the growing United States an inexhaustible fund of labor and capital to complement its seemingly inexhaustible land, the nation flourished, secure in its exceptionalism and democracy, both of which survived its bloody Civil War. William McKinley's anguished war message to Congress on April 10, 1898, sums up the ambivalence over fighting for Cuba much better than Hay's "splendid little war." Often criticized for its failure to galvanize the public with the nationalistic fervor of later American war messages, McKinley's careful exposition of the complex diplomatic problems and his own uncertainties, even with a state of war inevitable, made his war message a neglected American classic. McKinley's reluctance, not William Randolph Hearst's jingoism, was at the heart of the American war in 1898. As McKinley expressed it, "The fire of insurrection may flame or may smolder with varying seasons, but it has not been and it is plain that it cannot be extinguished by present methods. The only hope of relief and repose from a condition which can no longer be endured is the enforced pacification of Cuba. In the name of humanity, in the name

---

32. Albert Beveridge, Senate speech, January 9, 1900, in *Congressional Record*, 56th Cong., 1st Sess., 704–12, rpr. in Graebner (ed.), *Ideas and Diplomacy*, 370–73; see Gerald F. Lindeman, *The Mirror of War: American Society and the Spanish American War* (Ann Arbor, Mich., 1974); and David F. Healy, *The United States in Cuba, 1898–1902: Generals, Politicians, and the Search for Policy* (Madison, Wisc., 1963).

of civilization, in behalf of endangered American interests which give us the right and the duty to speak and to act, the war in Cuba must stop."[33]

Business had resisted war until March, 1898, the president until April. Although the war of 1898 is often cited as a turning point in American history, it marked more of a transition than a decisive change. When Theodore Roosevelt became president in September, 1901, he had, like McKinley before him, to deal with the complications following the successful war. No solutions would entirely satisfy most Americans, who were as divided over foreign affairs as they had been over purely domestic matters. William Graham Sumner, the Yale sociologist, called the war "a conquest of the United States by Spain." Sumner complained that "we are paying twenty million dollars for the privilege of tutoring tagals for self-government." George Hoar, the oratorical Massachusetts senator, compared American "lust for empire" with Athens and Sparta. John Tyler Morgan, one of the most dedicated of American expansionists, opposed taking the Philippines for racial reasons. But Americans maintained the luxury they had enjoyed for the first 110 years of their nation, fiercely arguing, overstating, indulging in grand rhetorical flourishes, and refusing to become part of any rigidly defined movement or orthodoxy. Under Theodore Roosevelt the same argumentativeness flourished, encouraged by a president who, unlike his predecessor, publicly enjoyed the give and take of political battle. America had changed. It had major urban art museums, more recognized women painters than any other nation, a flourishing industrial economy, and world recognition. Europe had not meliorated its distaste for the American ideology of democracy nor its Eurocentricity, but when the United States entered a diplomatic discussion, the Americans were regarded as a major power.[34]

By making foreign relations a new and prominent part of American government, the war of 1898 radically changed American politics. The

33. For the authorship, response, and a thoughtful analysis of McKinley's war speech see Gould, *Presidency of William McKinley*, 84–90; the text is in Graebner (ed.), *Ideas and Diplomacy*, 350–56.

34. William Graham Sumner, "The Conquest of the United States by Spain," *Yale Law Journal*, VIII (1899), 168–93, rpr. in Graebner (ed.), *Ideas and Diplomacy*, 367. For Hoar's speech see *ibid.*, 358; for Morgan's views and other examples of American diversity on the Philippine protectorate, see May, *Imperial Democracy*, 249; for the growth of American culture see Morgan, *Unity and Culture*, 75–109; for women artists see Burt, *Palaces for the People*, 144; for the British accommodation see H. A. Tullock, "Changing Attitudes Towards the United States in the 1880s," *Historical Journal*, XX (1977), 825–40;

constitutional powers of the president in conducting foreign affairs, heretofore more a matter of theory than of practice, changed the relationship of Congress and the president and forced both to reconsider their recent historic roles. Domestic issues still dominated American politics, even into the epochal political contest between Theodore Roosevelt and Woodrow Wilson in the 1912 presidential election, but the sudden prominence of foreign relations, even before the impetus added by Roosevelt's style and temperament, changed the way the country was governed. Europe could not be expected to accept the new American power willingly. Great Britain, the friendlier power, resisted American desires for complete hegemony over an interoceanic canal; Spain longed for a concert of Europe in 1898; Britain and Germany moved against Venezuela in 1902; France had interests in Panama and throughout the Caribbean; Germany was unpredictable and volatile; smaller European powers such as Holland, Belgium, and Denmark held extensive Caribbean investments or territory; and Italy was closely involved in Venezuela and the Dominican Republic. Europe would not relinquish its interests casually. Latin America was wary of the new relationships. The American Senate that resisted William McKinley's assumption of war powers and superintendence of foreign affairs could not be expected to accede to Theodore Roosevelt's further expansion of the chief executive's role. When Theodore Roosevelt assumed the presidency in September, 1901, Europe was still the center of the world economy and of world affairs, affecting the United States and Latin America almost equally. Roosevelt's main concern as president was to secure and consolidate United States' freedom from European interference and to challenge Congress' dominance of American government. He had no desire to add to American holdings in Asia, Latin America, or the Caribbean, though he did hope to expand the American people's sense of global consciousness and to make the United States a world rather than a regional power.[35]

Langley, *Struggle for the American Mediterranean,* 175–76; Charles S. Campbell, Jr., *Anglo-American Understanding, 1898–1903* (Baltimore, 1957), 23–55; A. E. Campbell, *Great Britain and the United States, 1895–1903* (London, 1960), 42–55; Kenneth Bourne, *The Balance of Power in North America, 1815–1908* (Berkeley, 1967), 342–51; and R. G. Neale, *Great Britain and United States Expansion, 1898–1903* (East Lansing, Mich., 1966), 142–58.

35. Robert Osgood, *Ideals and Self-Interest in America's Foreign Relations* (Chicago, 1965), 29; Beisner, *From the Old Diplomacy to the New,* 115–39; Raymond Esthus, *Theodore Roosevelt and the International Rivalries* (Waltham, Mass., 1970), 3.

3　Europe, Debt, Caudillos, and Conflict

With the national unification of Germany and Italy, the opening of the Suez Canal to world commerce, and Germany's defeat of France in the Franco-Prussian War of 1870–1871, the modern world began to emerge in the 1870s. In the New World the eastern and western United States were linked by the first transcontinental railroad in 1869, and the North and South compromised their Reconstruction differences. In Latin America Antonio Guzmán Blanco, the first and most successful of the new national caudillos, became president of Venezuela. Great Britain began to consolidate its empire with the granting to Canada of dominion status in 1871. The changes that began in the 1870s would become most apparent in the 1890s as the New World became dramatically involved in an increasingly volatile international world order.[1]

By the end of the nineteenth century Great Britain was no longer the unchallenged world power, but it is a mistake to consider new American and German activity a signal of British decline. Indeed, the golden age of British foreign investment occurred after 1900. Both Germany and the United States had become important economic activists, but their entry into world finance was still dwarfed by Britain's overwhelming predominance. In 1877 Britain's foreign capital invest-

1. For the significance of the Franco-Prussian War see Paul Kennedy, *The Rise and Fall of the Great Powers: Economic Change and Military Conflict from 1500 to 2000* (New York, 1987), 182–249; Manfred Jonas, *The United States and Germany: A Diplomatic History* (Ithaca, N.Y., 1984), 26–30; Henry Blumenthal, *France and the United States: Their Diplomatic Relations, 1789–1914* (Chapel Hill, 1970), 121–27, 132; and Michael Howard, *The Franco-Prussian War* (London, 1961). For U.S. economic growth see Harold G. Vatter, *The Drive to Maturity: The U.S. Economy, 1860–1914* (Westport, Conn., 1975); David M. Pletcher, "1861–1898: Economic Growth and Diplomatic Adjustments," in William H. Becker and Samuel F. Wells (eds.), *Economics and World Power: An Assessment of American Diplomacy Since 1789* (New York, 1984), 119–72. For Europe see David S. Landes, *The Unbound Prometheus: Technological Change, 1750 to the Present* (Cambridge, Eng., 1969), 193–358. For Latin America see *CHLA*, IV (topical essays); V (individual nations).

ments totaled 1.7 million pounds; in 1911 it was 185 million pounds. British foreign investment multiplied 500 percent in the first four years of the twentieth century and 1000 percent in the first ten years, all of it from the profits of past foreign investments. Demand for manufactured goods grew so rapidly after 1890 that new markets accommodated both the United States and Germany without punishing Britain. Between 1893 and 1913, when America entered the world trade market, United States manufactured exports increased 563 percent, German exports by 239 percent. In the rapidly growing world market the British increased their exports 121 percent, which in view of Britain's already prodigious foreign trade is more remarkable than the rise in exports of the relative newcomers.[2]

With regional centers increasingly replaced by unified national governments in the United States, Italy, Germany, and Latin America, it is tempting to see the new nationalism as an overly cohesive ideology and to emphasize the cooperation of business and government. Some American historians are especially fond of linking markets in China and Latin America with diplomatic expansion. Germany more than any of its rivals combined commercial expansion with diplomatic ambitions, but only after Kaiser Wilhelm II became emperor in 1888. Until then there was almost no coordination between finance and foreign policy. British investment policies remained independent by custom and policy, and until 1907 the British government showed little interest in colonial investments. France did use commerce to help make political policy, but French foreign investment and nationalism after the defeat by Germany in 1871 were defensive. The United States followed the British precedent, with remarkably little coordination between international finance and government until after World War I. The gentlemen who directed William McKinley's and Theodore Roosevelt's State Department had as little liking for businessmen as did the aristocratic Roosevelt. Moreover, America's major export manufacturers regarded government help as a nuisance and wanted no part of it. International world trade at the turn of the century was remarkably self-sustaining. In the United States, Germany, and Britain a minority of peripheral businessmen, investment losers, and outsiders clamored for government assistance, but the majority of suc-

2. Herbert Feis, *Europe: The World's Banker, 1870–1914* (New Haven, 1930), ix, 5, 11; D. C. M. Platt, *Latin America and British Trade, 1806–1914* (London, 1972), 99; see also J. Fred Rippy, *British Investments in Latin America, 1822–1949: A Case Study in the Operations of Private Enterprise* (Minneapolis, 1949).

cessful private bankers and corporate businessmen were satisfied with as little government interference as possible.[3]

Latin America remained isolated until the 1850s and did not become an integral part of the world economy until 1875. Only the largest of the Latin American republics offered incentives to world traders. Selling was difficult and expensive, the market for European consumer goods almost nonexistent, and the cost of transport prohibitive. Europe's population in 1808 was nine times greater than that of all Latin America. A century later, Venezuela, with a land area greater than Germany, Italy, France, and Greece combined, imported only 10 percent as much as Norway did. The entire Mexican market in 1900 for British consumer goods consisted of about seven thousand upper-class families. The majority of Latin Americans lived in the interior in primitive economies; because of extreme poverty Latin America by necessity remained self-sustaining. Latin America never became a good market in the nineteenth century, but when railroads penetrated the interior it became an attractive secondary market. Railroads, financed and built by the British, transformed Argentina in the 1870s, allowing European immigrants to go beyond Buenos Aires. The immigrant settlers changed Argentina from an importer of wheat to one of the world's largest exporters. Immigrants also constituted a market for familiar European goods. Argentina, Brazil, and Chile were the most attractive potential Latin American markets, and the British developed and dominated them, leaving the less attractive areas to the Germans, French, Belgians, Italians, Dutch, and eventually the newly enterprising Americans.[4]

War, revolution, and poverty became a way of life in Latin America. One historian wrote that "war in Venezuela seemed to follow a natu-

3. See Hugh de Santis, "Imperialist Impulse and American Innocence," in Gerald K. Haines and J. Samuel Walker (eds.), *American Foreign Relations: A Historiographical Review* (Westport, Conn., 1981), 70–79; Feis, *Europe*, 85, 38–39; William H. Becker, *The Dynamics of Business-Government Relations: Industry and Exports, 1893–1921* (Chicago, 1982), viii, xiv; Mira Wilkins, *The Emergence of Multinational Enterprise: American Business Abroad from the Colonial Era to 1914* (Cambridge, Mass., 1970); and David M. Pletcher, "Rhetoric and Results: A Pragmatic View of American Economic Expansionism, 1865–98," *DH*, V (1981), 93–108. For the strict limitations on Foreign Office help for commercial ventures see D. C. M. Platt, *Finance, Trade, and Politics in British Foreign Policy, 1815–1914* (London, 1968), 126–40. For the second-class status of Britain's commercial consuls see Joseph Smith, *Anglo-American Diplomacy Toward Latin America, 1865–1896* (Pittsburgh, 1979), 6, 16–21. For Latin American trade see Platt, *Latin America and British Trade*, 3, 6, 67, 68, 117, 118.

4. Platt, *Latin America and British Trade*, 99, 306; Colin Lewis, "British Railway Companies and the Argentine Government," in D. C. M. Platt (ed.), *Business Imperialism,*

ral cycle like earthquakes and floods." Latin America, poor to start, had little economic margin for destructive civil wars that moved the debt problem from precarious to catastrophic. In spite of the compelling imagery of gunboat diplomacy, European creditors never intervened solely to collect defaulted debts, although local consuls frequently and effectively threatened intervention. The two major European interventions, in Mexico in 1861 and Venezuela in 1902, were more political than economic. When Mexico defaulted on its European debt following Benito Juárez's revolution, Britain, Spain, and France took Mexico City to force reparations for seized foreign assets. With the United States distracted by its own Civil War, France, tempted by a rare opportunity, occupied Mexico and unsuccessfully tried to reestablish its influence in the New World. Although the French failed, the precedent worried post–Civil War Americans and newly emerging Latin American nationalists.[5]

The French occupation of Mexico, though a result of the personal ambitions of Louis Napoleon and the political opportunism of the anti-Juárista Mexican Conservatives, who encouraged the alliance, underscored Europe's growing need to expand beyond its continent. By 1860 Europe could no longer feed its growing population or reproduce the raw materials consumed by industrialization. Latin America, an obvious source of raw materials, attracted increasing European investment and trade. Serious debt defaults by Spain in 1872, Portugal almost constantly from 1851, and Turkey in 1876 made British investors wary of traditional European debtors. The British turned to other markets, especially in Argentina, Africa, and India. At the same time Germany and later France had developed sufficiently to seek opportunities for foreign investment. Britain's withdrawal from Europe opened up an established if secondary market well suited to the lim-

---

1840–1930 (London, 1977), 395–427; Robert Greenhill, "Merchants and the Latin American Trade: An Introduction," *ibid.*, 159–97; Greenhill, "The Brazilian Coffee Trade," *ibid.*, 198–230; and William Glade, "Latin America and the International Economy, 1870–1914," in *CHLA*, IV, 1–56, 597–603. For the problems Germany faced in Latin America see Holger H. Herwig, *Germany's Vision of Empire in Venezuela* (Princeton, 1986); see also Charles Jones, "Business Imperialism and Argentina, 1875–1900: A Theoretical Note," *Journal of Latin American Studies*, XII (1980), 437–44.
   5. Guillermo Moron, *A History of Venezuela* ed. and trans. John Street (London, 1963), 184; William H. Wynne, "Introduction," in Edwin Borchard, *State Insolvency and Foreign Bondholders* (2 vols.; New Haven, 1951), I, xxv. For the Mexican problem see Dexter Perkins, *The Monroe Doctrine, 1826–1867* (Baltimore, 1933), 318–548; for Latin American sympathy see Nathan Ferris, "The Relations of the United States with South America During the American Civil War," *HAHR*, XXI (1941), 51–78.

ited investment ambitions of the continental Europeans. The British, pioneers in railroad development, found fertile ground in Argentina. But Latin America outside of the larger southern nations remained extremely difficult, "a thorn in the flesh of British investors for half a century." Eventually, Britain left most of Latin America to the newcomers, Germany and the United States, shifting its priorities to its own colonies. Sophisticated British traders regarded the "muck and truck" of Latin American investment as suitable for foreigners and declined the hard selling required in Latin America.[6]

Before the British retreated from their investments in Latin America the intricate and well-developed London banking community established the dubious practices that institutionalized Latin America's cycles of debt, fraud, and default. As yields from European investments declined, the lure of an extra percentage point or two of interest swayed small English investors into the riskier Latin American investments, which appeared to have the backing of some of Britain's most respected private banking houses. By the 1870s Britain's banking apparatus had become both highly specialized and increasingly volatile. One large and successful loan could change the fortunes of even a Baring or Rothschild bank. Many smaller banking houses, underwriting specialists, and promoting companies joined the parade of highly competitive retail investment bankers. Latin American caudillos eager for cash agreed to the most outrageous terms. The Hartmont Loan of 1869 to the Dominican Republic is a representative example. The face value of the 420,000-pound loan included a 100,000-pound commission for London's Hartmont Bank. Requiring the Dominican government to pay 1,472,500 pounds over twenty-five years in exchange for only a net 320,000 pounds advance was bad enough, but Hartmont gave the Dominicans only a partial advance totaling 38,095 pounds and sold the debt to a retail investment firm, which in turn sold 757,700 pounds of bonds to a public attracted by the 25 to 50 percent discount. The Dominican Senate disavowed the Hartmont loan in 1870, but the bonds had already been sold to unsuspecting small investors, and the credit failure was blamed on the victimized Dominicans.[7]

6. Platt, *Latin America and British Trade*, 66, 121; Feis, *Europe*, 19–21; Blumenthal, *France and the United States*, 74–116; Jan Bazant, "Mexico from Independence to 1867," in *CHLA*, III, 464–70; Lewis, "British Railway Companies and the Argentine Government," 395–427.

7. Feis, *Europe*, 8, 9; Jacob Hollander, "Debt of Santo Domingo," in *Confidential Executive Documents*, 59th Cong., 1st Sess., No. 1A, p. 4.

Latin American caudillos as well as unscrupulous European small bankers were attracted to the profitable new bond market. The caudillo received cash, the bank, frequently an enterprising small mercantile house, its commission; since the lender retained the first two years of interest from the cash advanced, default was not possible until the third year, when the retail market had been exploited. Many large banks routinely bought small quantities of bad bonds, but because their names were included in the retail promotional material greedy small investors were deceived into the unwarranted assumption that the bonds were respectably underwritten. Governments were only peripherally involved. European investments remained private and unregulated. Lenders encouraged excess borrowing in Latin America by temporary heads of state. In Britain a new breed of external debt speculator manipulated the retail bond markets in London to inflate the value of Latin American bonds sold to pensioners and lower-middle-class small investors looking for better returns on their retirement savings. After default, speculators would buy up greatly depreciated securities at a fraction of the face value and lobby with the governments to collect the securities at face value.[8]

As the practice was established, many conventions became routine. New caudillos tried to escape obligations of previous governments; guarantees or collateral were offered to different creditors at the same time. Latin American leaders became adept at renegotiation. Honduras, noting that its original defaulted bonds had been sold at 2 percent of their face value, proposed that this sum be established as its new external debt. An alliance between the Latin Americans seeking credit and the British loan brokers marketing bonds foisted mostly worthless paper on naive though greedy small investors. The system was an international loan-sharking scheme with little if any redeeming economic or social value. As foreign investment increased in the poorer countries, the influx of capital made the dream of profit more tempting to European bankers and Latin American caudillos alike. It also destroyed the system. Only in the last part of the nineteenth century did pressure for government coercion to collect debts increase. The Council of Foreign Bondholders, the most active private group, began its lobbying for British investors in 1873, was incorporated in 1898, and became prominent in early twentieth-century default and

8. Wynne, "Introduction," xx; D. C. M. Platt, "British Bondholders in Nineteenth Century Latin America—Injury and Remedy," *Inter-American Economic Affairs*, XIV (Winter, 1960), 9, 13.

intervention politics. None of the other European countries had as active a lobbying group. But even in Britain, the center of foreign bond investments, the government resolutely refused to coerce foreign nations to collect the debts of its nationals, even in cases of extreme distress. In the nineteenth-century balance, the debtor, not the creditor, held the advantage.[9]

Debtor nations were helped by the enormity of their debt. When only one foreign country dominated the external debt, simple financial pressure was sufficient to bring about a settlement on pain of discontinuing further credit. When more than one country was involved, there were alternate sources of credit, and because of the most-favored-nation status that went with increased financial activity, any single creditor nation using coercive pressure became a collector for its rival creditors. Revolution more than finance disrupted the system. As debts piled up and commercial activity increased, Latin American nations fell into a state of almost continuous civil war and anarchy. New caudillos canceled the debts of previous governments. At the same time the incessant civil wars produced a new series of claims—the British called them "outrages"—such as imprisonment of foreign nationals and destruction of foreign property.[10]

Unlike Britain, which already possessed strategic overseas naval ports through its extensive colonies, neither Germany nor the United States was prepared for the new demands of steamship technology. Coaling stations became the gold of world trade, and all mercantile nations except Britain scrambled to acquire isolated islands on the main sea route. Newly nationalized and industrialized Germany desperately needed coaling stations, not for expansion but for trade commensurate with its growing productivity. Since Britain controlled many of the better markets, the Germans needed access to more distant areas in Asia and Latin America. Unfortunately, the Germans and the Americans eventually contested for the same markets. After his stunning victory over France in 1871, Chancellor Otto von Bismarck was content to limit German diplomatic ambitions to continental Europe. Relations between Germany and the United States had been extremely cordial, but the strain of competing for markets and coaling stations made adversaries of the two nations even before Kaiser

9. Platt, "British Bondholders," 24–25; see Feis, *Europe,* 113–14; D. C. M. Platt, "The Allied Coercion of Venezuela, 1902–3—A Reassessment," *Inter-American Economic Affairs,* XV (Spring, 1962), 9.
10. Platt, "British Bondholders," 24, 25.

Wilhelm II's ambitious world diplomacy. The American navy not only had to deal with the Germans and other Europeans looking for new naval bases but with a Congress determined to resist steamship technology and coaling stations. Congress feared alliance with tropical peoples who might dilute American political or racial purity.[11]

The two nations clashed dangerously in Samoa, an island archipelago in the distant South Pacific that possessed a great natural harbor at Pago Pago. The rivalry began in 1884, was complicated by Britain's involvement on behalf of New Zealand, and climaxed, after an unsuccessful German attack on the American-backed Samoans, when a hurricane destroyed the American and German vessels in 1889. Nature's intervention inspired a diplomatic resolution, and the three contesting nations agreed in the Berlin Conference of 1889 to a tripartite protectorate over Samoa, which became America's first overseas possession.[12]

The clash over Samoa underscored the dangerous natural rivalry between America and Germany that eventually ripened to open diplomatic conflict in the 1890s and military combat in World War I. Each nation routinely made the other a part of its secret war contingency plans. In 1889, Otto von Bismarck, in his last year as German chancellor, and Carl Schurz, an American mugwump journalist and editor of the New York *Post*, engaged in a rare exchange of views. Schurz had fought in the German revolution of 1848 and then served as a Union general in the American Civil War. A German revolutionary in 1848, Schurz was also a founding member of Abraham Lincoln's Republican party in 1856. Schurz and Bismarck were completely frank in their assessments of national strengths and weaknesses. Bismarck in 1889 understood that American wealth made a war of attrition unattrac-

11. On congressional reluctance for coaling stations see Charles S. Campbell, *The Transformation of American Foreign Relations, 1865–1900* (New York, 1976), 50, 73–74. For the developing German-American rivalry see Jeanette L. Keim, *Forty Years of German-American Political Relations* (Philadelphia, 1919); Clara Eve Schieber, *The Transformation of American Sentiment Toward Germany* (Boston, 1923); Charles C. Tansill, *The Purchase of the Danish West Indies* (Baltimore, 1932); Alfred Vagts, *Deutschland und die Vereinigten Staaten in Der Weltpolitik* (2 vols.; New York, 1935); Herwig, *Germany's Vision of Empire in Venezuela*; and Wilfrid Hardy Calcott, *The Western Hemisphere: Its Influence on United States Policies to the End of World War II* (Austin, Tex., 1968), 96–98.

12. Campbell, *Transformation of American Foreign Relations*, 72–83; Jonas, *United States and Germany*, 41–49. For Bismarck's colonial policies see Paul Kennedy, *The Rise of the Anglo-German Antagonism, 1860–1914* (London, 1980), 167–83; Holger H. Herwig, *Politics of Frustration: The United States in German Naval Planning, 1889–1941* (Boston, 1976), 14–18.

tive, and the Atlantic Ocean made the threat of European invasion unlikely. But the Americans were vulnerable to a German war of privateering. Schurz also favored privateering as an effective war weapon. Bismarck, smarter than Wilhelm II, clearly saw the ultimate American advantage: "Even burning down New York, Philadelphia, and Boston would bring no decision, and the eventual winner in a German-American naval war would be Britain freed by attrition of two maritime and naval rivals." Germany and America had begun testing the waters of war even before Kaiser Wilhelm II took control of German diplomacy in 1890.[13]

Germany held no advantages in its competition with other industrial powers. Britain had its colonies and an enormous lead in banking, industry, and investment. France recovered from the 5 billion franc indemnity paid to Germany after the war in 1871 to become an adept small international investor. France attracted unaligned investment customers who enjoyed French art, food, and banking and the pleasures of conducting business in Paris. The United States held the advantage of proximity to Latin America, which along with Asia was one of only two remaining open world markets. Thus Britain had its colonies and an established world trade, France had Paris, and the United States had its enormous geographic advantages. Germany had no advantages. Voltaire had once predicted that Germany was condemned to eternal poverty. Even after its remarkable national consolidation and rapid industrialization, Germany's place in the world was perilously close to meeting Voltaire's prophecy. Desperate, Germany became aggressive, willing to take the scraps Britain and France declined but also inclined to combine commercial expansion with an ambitious foreign policy. "Two needs for every mark" became a tradition as Germany coordinated investment, strategy, and territorial expansion.[14]

13. Carl Schurz to Count Arco, February 3, 1889, and Arco to Otto von Bismarck, February 5, 1889, in Alfred Vagts, "Hopes and Fears of an American-German War, 1870–1915," *Political Science Quarterly*, LIV (1939), 517–20, which summarizes the correspondence. For Schurz see Chester Varne Easum, *The Americanization of Carl Schurz* (Chicago, 1929); Claude M. Feuss, *Carl Schurz, Reformer, 1829–1906* (Boston, 1932); and Robert Beisner, *Twelve Against Empire: The Anti-Imperialists, 1898–1900* (Chicago, 1985), 18–34. For TR's antipathy to Schurz see TR to Sherman S. Rogers, February 1, 1899, in *MRL*, II, 927–28; for Schurz as a "prattling foreigner" see TR to HCL, October 20, 1899, *ibid.*, II, 1086; for the causes of the antipathy see John A. Garraty, *Henry Cabot Lodge: A Biography* (New York, 1953), 81–84.

14. See Feis, *Europe*, 33–80. For the trade conflicts between Germany and the United States see David M. Pletcher, *The Awkward Years: American Foreign Relations Under Garfield and Arthur* (Columbia, Mo., 1962), 158–69.

German threats to Cuba and to Spain's Caroline Islands in the Pacific in 1884–1886 concerned Americans and made Germany the chief American worry as Cuban unrest spread. German foreign investment in Latin America reached its high point between 1887 and 1890, when Bismarck, disturbed by European defaults that cost German investors a billion marks—10 percent of total German foreign investment—turned to Argentina, Venezuela, and Mexico. German interest in the French Panama canal continually perturbed the Americans. Much of the bad feeling reflected growing American economic competition with Germany and increased controversy over the tariff. Germans feared American supremacy in the balance of trade and resented the effects of the protectionist McKinley and Dingley tariffs in the 1890s.[15]

When Wilhelm II ousted Bismarck as chancellor in 1890, Germany's aggressive investment tactics combined with a new policy of diplomatic competition on a worldwide scale. The mercurial kaiser was far more of a threat to America than the less ambitious Bismarck. Bismarck saw any war with America as a war of attrition, unwinnable through conventional military or naval means by either nation. Under Wilhelm II Germany contested in every part of the world, frequently irrationally, often as a whim, or even through habit. Such incursions might be excused by Germany's pressing need for strategic coaling stations. After the kaiser assumed power, German aggression continued, but often with no discernible purpose. In 1893 German warships prominently appeared in Rio de Janeiro to protect German nationals during the Brazilian civil war. In 1894 Germany attempted to take sole possession of Samoa, battled with the British over the Congo, Morocco, and Sudan, and frequently confused its continental allies. In 1896 the kaiser infuriated the British by clumsily and publicly interfering in the Boer conflict. German interest in Latin America and especially the Caribbean continued to harass the Americans, uncomfortable with their new involvement in foreign affairs. Two German vessels shelled Port-au-Prince, Haiti, on December 6, 1897, when a former Berlin officer was arrested. The kaiser refused to accept an arbitration board's verdict "when I can obtain my rights with cannon."[16]

15. Feis, *Europe*, 63, 70. For the tariff disputes see H. Wayne Morgan, *William McKinley and His America* (Syracuse, N.Y., 1963), 123–51; Tom E. Terrill, *The Tariff, Politics, and American Foreign Policy, 1874–1901* (Westport, Conn., 1973); and John L. Gignilliat, "Pigs, Politics, and Protection: The European Boycott of American Pork, 1879–1891," *Agricultural History*, XXXV (1961), 3–12.

16. Campbell, *Transformation of American Foreign Relations*, 240–41; Gordon A. Craig, *Germany, 1866–1945* (New York, 1978), 242–44; Herwig, *Politics of Frustration*, 67–69.

Wilhelm II's enmity toward the Americans was not only economic and strategic but ideological. He detested the idea of American democracy and began serious diplomatic initiatives in 1897 to unite Europe with Spain, to show "the rascals that Europe's kings really stand together." Such an intervention would also "be a very excellent device for futhering and establishing the continental union against America planned by myself and the Tsar." From 1897, the kaiser explored various plans for a war with America, including physical occupation of parts of the American mainland. In 1901 the kaiser's war plans called for occupation of either New York City or Cape Cod as a starting point for the occupation of the United States. In the final plan, and the most promising from the German point of view, attempts on the American mainland were abandoned and instead Puerto Rico would be captured as a staging area for raids on the main American naval bases at Hampton Roads and Newport News. The kaiser was fascinated with the East Coast. Although he abandoned the idea of invading America, he never got over the desire to feel the sands of Cape Cod beneath his feet, an improbable fantasy but one that in 1900 he enthusiastically approved in excited marginal comments on one of the more detailed German plans.[17]

The "grizzly terror" (Henry Adams' apt description), combined bellicose rhetoric with opportunistic diplomacy. No single German move inspired as much fear in both Europe and America as the seizure of Kiaochow, a key Chinese port, by German troops in November, 1897. Europe was stunned and pondered possible countermoves that America feared would result in a European partition of China. American fears were also more immediate. What little American export trade had developed in North China and Manchuria was threatened by lack of access to the port of Kiaochow. The German seizure so disturbed America's ambassador to China, Charles Denby, that he suggested armed American intervention to keep Kiaochow free. The Germans, fearing a possible attack by the Russians, quickly made

17. Kaiser quote in Ernest May, *Imperial Democracy: The Emergence of America as a World Power* (New York, 1961), 196–97; see Walter LaFeber, *The New Empire: An Interpretation of American Expansion, 1860–1898* (Ithaca, N.Y., 1963), 354–55; Herwig, *Politics of Frustration*, 18–21, 40–66; John A. S. Grenville and George Berkeley Young, *Politics, Strategy, and American Diplomacy: Studies in Foreign Policy, 1873–1917* (New Haven, 1966), 305–307; Holger Herwig and David F. Trask, "Naval Operations Between Germany and the USA, 1898–1913: A Study of Strategic Planning in the Age of Imperialism," in Paul M. Kennedy (ed.), *The War Plans of the Great Powers, 1880–1914* (Boston, 1985), 39–74; and Herwig, *Germany's Vision of Empire in Venezuela*, 15–16, 147, 157, 163, 195–96.

peace with America and allowed it access to the port. The American shock over the German move may have been as deep as the British outrage over the kaiser's clumsy intervention in the British dispute with the Boers in 1896. Kiaochow was one of the major influences in convincing America to maintain possession of the Philippines after the Spanish war the following year. Although Germany opened the port of Kiaochow the adjoining Shantung Province, an area where Americans traditionally traded, was dominated by German commerce secured by concessions wrested from the Chinese government. The American Open Door notes regarding China in 1899 and 1900 were heavily influenced by German success in limiting American trade expansion in China.[18]

If strategic necessity alone dictated the German moves, perhaps other nations would have been less anxious. But the kaiser, even when acting for strategic purposes, colored his actions with a terrifying messianic zeal and a display of personal ego. When the troops landed in Kiaochow, the kaiser issued a declaration explaining the surprise move. "I am firmly determined to give up our over cautious policy which is regarded as weak throughout eastern Asia, and demonstrate through the use of sternness and if necessary the most brutal ruthlessness toward the Chinese, that the German Emperor cannot be trifled with." Apparent German aggression at Kiaochow and Port-au-Prince, Haiti, just three weeks apart combined with Chancellor Count Bernhard von Bülow's December 6 speech supporting Germany's new naval building program—"We too demand our place in the sun"—convinced the United States that Germany was a dangerous rival.[19]

During the Spanish-American War, especially at Manila Bay, friction between Germany and America intensified. When naval forces from all the major powers converged on Manila, the victorious Commodore George Dewey was faced with complex diplomatic problems while preparing for a possible Spanish counterattack. The German naval contingent under Admiral Otto von Diederichs gave Dewey many anxious moments and provided a classic example of German aggression and clumsiness. Dispatched by the kaiser's brother Prince Henry and acting on an incredible thirdhand tip from a German wine merchant in Manila that Filipinos desired German protection, Die-

18. LaFeber, *New Empire*, 354–55; William L. Langer, *The Diplomacy of Imperialism* (New York, 1935), 451–52.
19. Langer, *Diplomacy of Imperialism*, 452; Jonas, *United States and Germany*, 50–51; kaiser quoted in Herwig, *Politics of Frustration*, 69.

derichs's large naval group headed by the new cruiser *Kaiserin Augusta* clashed continuously with Dewey's fleet still on war duty and engaged in conflict with Spanish shore batteries.[20]

When the Germans refused to yield to Dewey as wartime commander in the harbor, the American threatened, "If Germany wants war, all right, we are ready." Dewey and Diederichs worked out a compromise, but the bad feelings festered. Washington, mostly uninformed of the friction—Dewey was not a meticulous report writer—and optimistic that European intentions were honorable or that the British would help in an emergency, remained innocent and aloof until July 24, 1898, when Ambassador Andrew Dickson White expressed American "uneasiness" to the German Foreign Office. When the United States ended world uncertainty by accepting responsibility for the Philippine Islands, the crisis passed and the Germans withdrew. The scars remained, helped by vivid newspaper stories of German-Spanish fraternization at Manila, the British ability to publicize the American-German friction, and Dewey's own frequent and intemperate remarks.[21]

Although American sensitivity about the Monroe Doctrine was well known, the kaiser refused to recognize its existence unless he was specifically trying to allay American fears. German plans for a naval base in Baja California at Magdalena Bay were well known. When Ambassador Theodor von Holleben warned the kaiser that the Americans would go to war if sufficiently provoked, the kaiser responded, "We will do whatever is necessary for our navy, even if it displeases the Yankees. Never fear!" Although Holleben was told to burn the inflammatory message, the Americans were constantly aware of German contempt and ambition. Dewey never forgot the tensions at Manila Bay. His remark, "Our next war will be with Germany," made to a New York *Herald* reporter at Trieste on his return trip to Washington from Manila Bay, was widely publicized in Europe and America. German papers were violently anti-American, and American newspapers responded to the attacks and generated

20. Lester Shippee, "Germany and the Spanish-American War," *AHR*, XXX (1925), 754–77; J. Fred Rippy, "The European Powers and the Spanish-American War," *James Sprunt Historical Studies*, XIX (1927), 22–52; Thomas Bailey, "Dewey and the Germans at Manila Bay," *AHR*, XLV (1939), 59–81. For the view that the Germans were reasonable at Manila see Jonas, *United States and Germany*, 57–59.

21. Bailey, "Dewey and the Germans at Manila Bay," 62, 64, 66, 70, 77, n.68, 79; Ronald Spector, *Admiral of the New Empire: The Life and Career of George Dewey* (Baton Rouge, 1974), 24.

anti-German stories of their own, even before the Spanish-American War added to the friction.[22]

Not only provocative actions but well-formulated public plans exacerbated the tension. In 1901 Franz von Edelsheim's *Operations upon the Sea: A Study* discussed in detail the success of a German invasion of the United States. Edelsheim's proposals were even more frightening than the usual German plans for naval victory in the Caribbean; he suggested major land battles to secure the key American eastern cities. Edelsheim's war plans revealed substantial ignorance of twentieth-century American conditions (he envisaged a ten-thousand-man army in the West to neutralize the Indians); his basic strategy repeated the same tactics that caused the British defeat in the American Revolution. The book was seriously reviewed by German military journals, one of which praised the author for suggesting the idea of a war with America, which until 1900 German Foreign Office documents referred to as "the United States of North America." The kaiser told his uncle King Edward VII that the United States had replaced Britain as the main focus of new German naval construction; the king told Andrew Carnegie, who told Theodore Roosevelt.[23]

American plans for an isthmian canal were of genuine strategic concern for the Germans, who needed to be able to unite naval forces on two oceans as much as did the Americans. German naval planners, heavily influenced by Alfred Mahan's *Influence of Sea Power upon History* (1890), were unrealistic in their attempt to surpass British naval superiority or override America's obvious geographical advantage in the nearby Caribbean. Admiral Alfred von Tirpitz envisioned not simply a series of bases that would enable Germany to maintain a naval presence in the West, but eventually a union with Central and Latin America against the United States, with a Latin American navy yet to be built by Germany and German control of the Panama canal, also yet unbuilt. Economics and strategy were blended with fanatical romantic nationalism. "Behind every German [merchant] vessel must stand the German battleship," was the battle cry of Albert Ballin,

22. Herwig, *Politics of Frustration*, 67–70; Herwig, *Germany's Vision of Empire in Venezuela*, 108–109, 195–96, 240–41; Charles C. Tansill, *The Purchase of the Danish West Indies* (Baltimore, 1932), 378–80; Keim, *Forty Years of German-American Political Relations*, 210; Bailey, "Dewey and the Germans at Manila Bay," 79.

23. Herwig, *Politics of Frustration*, 67–70; see also British intelligence concern over a fictional invasion of England in Erskine Childers, *The Riddle of the Sands* (1903; rpr. New York, 1976), in Kennedy, *Rise of Anglo-German Antagonism*, 252; Herwig, *Germany's Vision of Empire in Venezuela*, 168–69.

operator of the Hamburg-American Line. Ballin tried privately to purchase land in the West Indies to be transferred to the German government for use as a naval base. The Americans, fearful and suspicious of the Germans, were not deceived. The Germans were even blamed when they were innocent. Although Danish domestic politics was responsible for the decision not to sell the Danish West Indies to America in 1902, it was widely believed in America that Germany was behind the Danish rejection, a view often repeated in later diplomatic histories.[24]

Before Theodore Roosevelt became president and during his first term, he regarded Germany as the greatest single European threat to American security: "Germany's attitude toward us makes her the only power with which there is any reasonable likelihood or possibility of clashing within the future." Roosevelt dismissed the real possibility of conflict with Britain once American Anglophobia had been eased by British friendship during the Spanish-American War and public suspicion of Germany increased.[25]

As vice-president, Roosevelt had little if any influence on official American policy, but he had already worked out some of the possibilities in the fast-changing world situation. He thought it unlikely that the United States would have to face a British-German alliance, but "the last two years have shown that British statesmen are capable of committing the wildest follies." Roosevelt thought a showdown with Germany on the Monroe Doctrine the most likely possibility, and though he favored renegotiating or abrogating the Clayton-Bulwer Treaty with Britain (successfully renegotiated as the Hay-Pauncefote Treaty II, in December, 1901) Roosevelt wanted to make sure of Brit-

24. Herwig, *Politics of Frustration*, 70–71; Tansill, *Purchase of the Danish West Indies*, 397–413. For Tirpitz's naval plans see Herwig, *Germany's Vision of Empire in Venezuela*, 149–58, 200–201; Jonathan Steinberg, *Yesterday's Deterrent: Tirpitz and the Birth of the German Battle Fleet* (London, 1965); and Ernest L. Woodward, *Great Britain and the German Navy* (London, 1935), 15–53; for German concern about an American Panama canal see Herwig, *Germany's Vision of Empire in Venezuela*, 141–74. For Ballin and the Hamburg-American Line see Lamar Cecil, *Albert Ballin: Business and Politics in Imperial Germany* (Princeton, 1967).

25. TR to George von Lengerke Meyer, April 12, 1901, in *MRL*, III, 52; for earlier assessments of the potential German threat see TR to Bowman H. McCalla, August 3, 1897, *ibid.*, I, 636; to Cecil A. Spring Rice, August 13, 1897, *ibid.*, 644–49; to John Davis Long, September 30, 1897, *ibid.*, 695–96; to William W. Kimball, December 17, 1897, *ibid.*, 743; to Francis C. Moore, February, 5, 9, 1898, *ibid.*, 768–69; to Kimball, January 9, 1900, *ibid.*, II, 1130–31. For an assessment of TR's relationship to the Anglo-German rivalry see Raymond A. Esthus, *Theodore Roosevelt and the International Rivalries* (1961; rpr. Claremont, Calif., 1985).

ish friendship before taking on Germany. He wrote to Henry Cabot Lodge: "The only power which may be a menace to us in anything like the immediate future is Germany." Roosevelt's letter to Lodge shows his ability to combine his colorful, intemperate prose with sound and extremely cautious diplomatic instincts. He managed to insult Lord Lansdowne ("mischievous and ridiculous"), the "Bryanite party," the "Godkin-Parkhurst-Atkinson type of mendacious mugwump," and "creatures like [William] Mason in our own party" (placed with the British statesman in the "utmost folly" school). Yet what emerged was a rational strategy: keep the British as allies, convince the Germans of American seriousness, and establish an army and navy capable of winning a showdown, if it came, with Germany.[26]

Venezuela was the logical site for the almost inevitable showdown between Germany and the United States, the two most ambitious new world powers. Born as Gran Colombia in a revolution against Spain in 1821, led by its first and most illustrious citizen, Simón Bolívar, the new country, beset by problems including a debt default in the 1820s, divided into three sparsely settled nations, Venezuela, New Granada (Colombia), and Ecuador. Venezuela was a product of a dual cultural heritage, New World republicanism wedded to traditional Spanish culture, economy, and society. Bolívar, the quintessential Spanish-American romantic figure, an aristocrat who wrote and led successful revolutions, became ingrained in the Venezuelan imagination, remaining at the center of the nation's intellectual and literary life. Bolivarian independence remained a constant dominant theme of Venezuelan literature and life.[27]

When Antonio Guzmán Blanco, almost as prodigious a historical personage as Bolívar, seized power in 1870, he began an eighteen-year reign that changed Venezuela from a loose confederation of rural regions into northern Latin America's first integrated national state. Guzmán Blanco transformed the classic regional caudillo, in temporary control of the state treasury, to a powerful constitutional leader of an integrated modern nation. In many ways as brilliant as Bolívar, whose imagery of independence Guzmán Blanco used, "the Illustrious American,"—his preferred self-image—radically transformed Venezuela's government and its place in the outside world. Cherish-

26. TR to Henry Cabot Lodge, March 27, 1901, in *MRL*, III, 31–32.

27. John V. Lombardi, *Venezuela: The Search for Order, the Dream of Progress* (New York, 1982), 255; John Lynch, *The Spanish American Revolutions, 1808–1826* (2nd ed.; New York, 1973), 191–227.

ing the role of Latin American and Caribbean nationalist, Guzmán Blanco made Venezuela an active diplomatic and nationalistic force when he encouraged Cuba to revolt from Spain in 1871. His aggressive "little stick" policies made Venezuela a constant antagonist of all foreign influence in the Caribbean.[28]

At the same time the Illustrious American fought against Europe, he borrowed heavily from European bankers to enrich himself and provide the power and the symbolism for his autocratic regime. Guzmán Blanco was an artist of nineteenth-century Latin American power, and Caracas became his masterpiece. When he assumed power, Caracas was an ordinary Latin American provincial city. When he left, it was a modern city with electricity, sewers, Parisian boulevards, massive public buildings, and excellent public transportation. Using the money borrowed from European bankers, Guzmán Blanco installed a modern telegraph system linking the entire nation with the impressive capital city. In the new Caracas foreign bankers felt comfortable in familiar surroundings, impressed with Venezuela's obvious progress. The city foreshadowed twentieth-century totalitarian architecture. Venezuela's new national army was equipped with modern weaponry, especially new repeating rifles that, when combined with the national telegraph system, made threats from regional caudillos difficult if not impossible.[29]

The regional caudillos, however, were made a part of Venezuela's new prosperity, supported by Caracas in return for their allegiance. Guzmán Blanco, who lacked the charisma of the classic caudillo, paid his regional leaders to maintain the tradition, using the modern bureaucracy he installed in Caracas to govern. As long as the local warlords maintained law and order they were free to control their regions as they wished. Guzmán Blanco eventually borrowed more than his country could repay, always taking a large share of the loans for himself. But unlike other failed Latin American caudillos, he left Venezuela richer than he found it. By modernizing the military he made revolution more costly because rival caudillos needed foreign funds to buy

28. See Julian Nava, "The Illustrious American: The Development of Nationalism in Venezuela Under Antonio Guzmán Blanco," *HAHR*, XLV (1965), 527–43; George S. Wise, *Caudillo: A Portrait of Antonio Guzmán Blanco* (New York, 1951); Lombardi, *Venezuela*, 190–96; Robert L. Gilmore, *Caudillism and Militarism in Venezuela* (Athens, Ohio, 1964); and Judith Ewell, *Venezuela: A Century of Change* (Stanford, 1984).

29. Nava, "Illustrious American," 537; Lombardi, *Venezuela*, 193–95; Wise, *Caudillo*, 151–59; Malcolm Deas, "Colombia, Ecuador, and Venezuela, 1880–1930," in *CHLA*, V, 670–74.

the weaponry necessary to challenge the established Caracas government. The excessive financing helped integrate Venezuela into a world market system. Venezuela's export economy of coffee and cacao worked well enough in times of high demand but suffered from the inevitable world market cycles. Guzmán Blanco managed to flourish in two different cultures, Venezuela's old archaic Spanish tradition and the new milieu of modern world trade. But he was unable to transcend the tradition of caudillo opportunism or to give Venezuela a developed diverse economy immune to the inevitable cycles of agricultural monoculture.[30]

Nor was Guzmán Blanco's genius transferable to later leaders. By bullying and bluster he was able to maintain a balance between Venezuelan nationalism and reasonable international relations. Battles with the British over neighboring Trinidad frequently threatened war, especially since the British usually protected antigovernment factions. Guzmán Blanco fiercely fought the established powers. When Britain failed to expel the antigovernment forces from Trinidad, Guzmán Blanco's radical 30 percent duty on all Trinidad trade economically crippled the British colony. In 1880 the United States mediated a debt dispute between Venezuela and France. Troubled by disputes with both Britain and Chile in 1883, Guzmán Blanco suggested that the United States establish a "moral protectorate" over Venezuela but Secretary of State Frederick T. Frelinghuysen was not prepared to make such a sweeping American commitment.[31]

Venezuelan history is still customarily and logically divided into two main periods, before Guzmán Blanco and after. The old tradition of independence fostered by Bolívar and the "standing up to foreigners" policies of the Illustrious American remained in post–Guzmán Blanco Venezuela along with the constantly growing strain of foreign indebtedness. A new series of civil wars after Guzmán Blanco's exile to Paris in 1888 added to that indebtedness but did not soften Venezuela's willingness to battle with foreign interests, a

30. Wise, *Caudillo*, 151–59; Lombardi, *Venezuela*, 196–97; Ewell, *Venezuela*, 29–30. For agriculture see William M. Sullivan, "The Rise of Despotism in Venezuela: Cipriano Castro, 1899–1908" (Ph.D. dissertation, University of New Mexico, 1974), 25–28; for the struggle with regional caudillos see Mary Bernice Floyd, "Antonio Guzmán Blanco: The Dynamics of Septenio Politics" (Ph.D. dissertation, Indiana University, 1982), 112–16.

31. Miriam Hood, *Gunboat Diplomacy, 1895–1905: Great Power Pressure in Venezuela* (2nd ed.; London, 1983), 71–72, 80; Pletcher, *Awkward Years*, 128–32; Blumenthal, *France and the United States*, 138–39.

custom that infuriated even the generally calm British as well as the quarrelsome Americans. In 1890 the United States was tempted to the point of war over Venezuelan intransigence concerning an unresolved 1871 dispute involving an American-owned Venzuelan steamship company. Venezuela settled the American dispute and used the Americans as allies when the British tried to gain control of the Orinoco River during the gold discovery border dispute of 1894–1896. The Anglo-Venezuela border disputes made the United States and Venezuela into allies in the developing struggle of North and Latin America to end European dominance in the hemisphere. There was no common culture or even a sympathetic understanding between the two American nations, both of which were quarrelsome and independent, united only in convenience against a temporary common enemy. Guzmán Blanco's ability to juggle his many loans by using proceeds of a new one to pay an old one, and when it suited him to heap abuse on foreigners as an excuse for not paying a debt, became part of a tradition of scorn for foreign indebtedness that eventually infuriated the debtors into wanting to teach the rascals a lesson.[32]

After Guzmán Blanco's regime collapsed in 1888, Venezuela began a ten-year search for a new leader using its traditional selection process of civil war. Cipriano Castro, the eventual winner, won his first victory on May 23, 1899, at the head of an army of only sixty soldiers. His army and his influence grew when he won control of western Venezuela. After defeating President Ignacio Andrade's six-thousand-man army at the Battle of El Tocuyito in September, 1899, Castro settled with the other generals, sent Andrade into exile in the Antilles, and on crutches triumphantly entered Caracas on October 22, 1899, as the new president of Venezuela.[33]

Although Cipriano Castro, an educated leader, was a gifted soldier and politician, the dreadful condition of Venezuela in 1899 might well have defeated the political genius of a Guzmán Blanco. Venezuela's income had declined precipitously from 40 million to a little over 27 million bolivares in the two years since 1897. Venezuela's acknowl-

32. Hood, *Gunboat Diplomacy*, 66; for the war threat see Sheldon Liss, *Diplomacy and Dependency: The United States, Venezuela, and the Americas* (New York, 1982), 19; Ewell, *Venezuela*, 27–28; Chester Lloyd Jones, "Development of the Caribbean," in Jones, Henry Kitteridge Norton, and Parker Thomas Moon, *American Policies Abroad: The United States and the Caribbean* (Chicago, 1929), 55; for details on Venezuela's debt default, see Sullivan, "Rise of Despotism in Venezuela," 30–32.

33. Moron, *History of Venezuela*, 184–85; Sullivan, "Rise of Despotism in Venezuela," 105–33; Ewell, *Venezuela*, 9.

edged foreign debt, even before the astronomical claims caused by civil war damages, was 190 million bolivares ($38 million). Castro did not consolidate his hold on power until 1903, simultaneously fighting his main rivals for control of the national government at Caracas and Europeans, who were suddenly disturbed both by the size of the Venezuelan debt and the diminished prospects for repayment.[34]

Castro was indebted to Guzmán Blanco not only for Venezuela's permanent debt but also for his cavalier attitude toward repayment. Guzmán Blanco made the juggling of payments and constant refinancing of loans into an art form, possible only as long as the mortgaged Venezuelan customs revenues could pay the interest on the debt. With the decline in Venezuelan exports in 1897 and the interruption of the economy through constant civil war, Venezuela was on the verge of default. Venezuela's tradition of revolutionary independence was useful in forging a new national consciousness, but it became self-serving and reckless during the crises of Castro's civil wars. Castro used Guzmán Blanco's tactic of nationalist rhetoric but did not know when to stop. Venezuela's folk culture encouraged a disrespect for wealthy and powerful adversaries. In battles between Uncle Rabbit (*Tio Conejo*) and Uncle Tiger (*Tio Tigre*) in the 1890s Venezuela countryside, the rabbit using a unique Venezuelan cleverness (*astucia* or *viveza*) defeated the rapacious and much stronger tiger. In Venezuelan folk conventions, cleverness and deceit were valued, absolute power was disliked, equality was more important than liberty, and the purpose of justice was to punish the powerful, not to remedy a wrong. Wealth and advantage, it was widely believed, came from fate, not work—it was a stroke of luck. Such widely held beliefs might partly explain why Castro's Venezuela not only refused to conciliate its foreign debtors but went out of its way to insult European diplomats, destroy foreign property, and humiliate foreign nationals as the debt increased and the domestic and foreign crises deepened.[35]

On December 11, 1901, German Ambassador Theodor von Holleben informed the United States "that further negotiations with Venezuela

34. Moron, *History of Venezuela*, 185–86; Sullivan, "Rise of Despotism in Venezuela," 150–62; Hood, *Gunboat Diplomacy*, 149.

35. Ewell, *Venezuela*, 32–33; Sullivan, "Rise of Despotism in Venezuela," 162–69; see Wayne Lee Guthrie, "The Anglo-German Intervention in Venezuela, 1902–03" (Ph.D. dissertation, University of California, San Diego, 1983), 10–11. For German naval officers' views of Castro see Holger Herwig and J. Leon Helguera, *Alemania y el bloqueo internacional de Venezuela, 1902/03* (Caracas, 1977), 19.

are hopeless" and it was necessary to consider "what measures of coercion should be used against it." He outlined the possibilities: blockade or "the temporary occupation . . . of different Venezuelan harbor places and the levying of duties in those places." Holleben assured the American secretary of state that "under no circumstances would Germany acquire or permanently occupy Venezuelan territory." Hay's reply of December 16 assured the Germans that the Monroe Doctrine prohibited territorial aggrandizment and was not intended to be "hostile to any nation in the Old World," to interfere with commercial relations, or to "guarantee any state against punishment if it misconducts itself." The United States was well acquainted with Venezuela's economic problems because American claims against the Venezuelan government eventually totaled over $15 million, well in excess of the German claims of $1,423,700. At the start, American sympathies were with the Europeans, not the Latin Americans.[36]

Most European nations had substantial claims against Venezuela, but international coercion was not a simple remedy. If Germany acted on its own, at best it would have to share the proceeds with its rivals, at worst it would find itself in an ugly confrontation with other European powers. The Germans looked for an alliance. The German Foreign Office had examined the options and reported to Chancellor Count Bernhard von Bülow that a peaceful blockade of Venezuela was the best tactic although it would entail substantial diplomatic difficulties. In a peaceful blockade all ships, including those of neutral na-

36. *FRUS*, 1902, pp. 192–94. The claims against Venezuela are in U.S. Senate Documents, 58th Cong., 3rd Sess., No. 119, Serial 4769 as follows: U.S., 260; Germany, 641–42. U.S. claims amounted to 81,410,952 bolivares, the German claim to 7,376,686 bolivares. The exchange rate for 1902–1904 was 19.3 bolivares to the dollar. For American awareness of Venezuela's problems see Calvin DeArmond Davis, *The United States and the Second Hague Peace Conference: American Diplomacy and International Organization, 1899–1914* (Durham, N.C., 1976), 74–75; see also J. Fred Rippy, "The Venezuelan Claims Settlements of 1903–05: A Case Study in the Cost of Disorder, Despotism, and Deficient Capital and Technology," *Inter-American Economic Affairs*, VIII (1954), 65–67. For American-German diplomacy on the Venezuelan coercion see Howard K. Beale, *Theodore Roosevelt and the Rise of America to World Power* (Baltimore, 1956), 396–430; Alfred L. P. Dennis, *Adventures in American Diplomacy, 1896–1906* (New York, 1928), 282–308; Herwig, *Politics of Frustration*, 76–78; Jonas, *United States and Germany*, 65–73; and Howard C. Hill, *Roosevelt and the Caribbean* (Chicago, 1927), 110–15. For the debate on who initiated the intervention see Warren G. Kneer, *Great Britain and the Caribbean, 1901–1913* (East Lansing, Mich., 1975), 3–15; George Monger, *The End of Isolation: British Foreign Policy, 1900–1907* (London, 1963), 21, 104–107; Dexter Perkins, *The Monroe Doctrine, 1867–1907* (Baltimore, 1937), 327–29; Charles S. Campbell, *Anglo-American Understanding, 1898–1903* (Baltimore, 1957), 274–76; and Platt, "Allied Coercion of Venezuela," 3–4.

tions, were denied access. In a war blockade, neutral ships were unaffected whereas ships of belligerents were not just barred but sunk or confiscated. In his note of January 20, 1902, Bülow informed the kaiser that the British and Italians were interested in a joint effort, that a peaceful blockade was permitted under international law, and that a declaration of war was not required. A war would require the Bundesrath's approval after a public debate. International law prohibited belligerent ships from using neutral ports for supplies or coal so a Venezuelan war would place the Germans in a precarious logistical situation because Germany had no naval base nearby. Seizing a port in Venezuela would solve the logistic problem but might cause a direct confrontation with the United States. President Theodore Roosevelt in his First Annual Message to Congress, December 3, 1901, warned Europe that the United States would not tolerate "territorial aggrandizement by any non-American power at the expense of any American power on American soil." Roosevelt defined America as the entire hemisphere, not just the United States.[37]

Both Britain and Germany were aware of the diplomatic difficulties in dealing with the sensitive Americans, but for different reasons both chose to ignore the problem. Britain's Foreign Office, generally sure and sensitive, was in a transitional state. When Julian Pauncefote, the longtime British ambassador in Washington, died, there was no one to deflect Lord Lansdowne's desire for possible reconciliation with Germany. The British were badly distracted by Lord Salisbury's retirement, the sudden illness of King Edward, which forced postponement of his coronation, and the end of the Boer war.[38]

Germany and Kaiser Wilhelm II were equally obtuse about the Americans. The kaiser's brother Admiral Prince Henry was dispatched

37. Count von Bülow to Wilhelm II, June 20, 1902, in E. T. S. Dugdale (ed.), *German Diplomatic Documents, 1817–1914* (4 vols.; London, 1930), III, 160–61; TR, Message to Congress, in *TRWN*, XV, 116; TR to HCL, June 19, 1901, in *MRL*, III, 97–98; Kneer, *Great Britain and the Caribbean*, 23–25; Campbell, *Anglo-American Understanding*, 270–73; Hill, *Roosevelt and the Caribbean*, 115; Herwig, *Politics of Frustration*, 76–79; Herwig, *Germany's Vision of Empire in Venezuela*, 93–101. For the German Admiralty's view that a pacific blockade was useless see *ibid.*, 222–23; for the debate over the type of blockade see Guthrie, "Anglo-German Intervention," 23–25, 62–69; for the complications over French claims see *ibid.*, 89–90; for an analysis by the State Department's solicitor see W. L. Penfield, "The Anglo-German Intervention in Venezuela," *NAR*, CLXXVII (1903), 86–96.

38. For a perceptive overview of Britain's diplomatic options see R. G. Neale, *Great Britain and the United States, 1898–1900* (East Lansing, Mich., 1966), xiii–xxii; for British ambivalence to German diplomacy see Kennedy, *Rise of Anglo-German Antagonism*, 239–61; Campbell, *Anglo-American Understanding*, 274.

in February, 1902, on a goodwill mission to the United States. On the surface Prince Henry's trip was a complete success. Alice Roosevelt, the president's eldest daughter, christened the kaiser's yacht *Hohenzollern* being built in America; the kaiser in turn renamed a torpedo boat *Alice Roosevelt*. But friction lurked below the surface. The American press attacked Alice's relationship with Prince Henry. The Germans were badly divided on the nature of the prince's mission. Possible scenarios called for Henry to demand outright a German sphere of influence in South America, candid (and presumably critical) discussions of the German friction with Dewey at Manila, and the "injustice of the Spanish-American War." Baron von Holstein of the German Foreign Office intervened and prevented such gaffes. Latin America was not discussed, and the prince's visit did little but assure the Germans—incorrectly—that all was well with the Americans.[39]

The Germans would have been less sanguine about the success of Prince Henry's mission had they known of Roosevelt's thoughts on Alice's speech when christening the *Hohenzollern*. "The only motto sufficiently epigrammatic that came to my mind," Roosevelt wrote, "was 'Damn the Dutch!'" Neither Roosevelt nor his wife, Edith, "could be dragged to meet Prince Henry if it were not our official duty." Roosevelt, practiced in the complexities of official entertaining, complained of the difficulties of entertaining the prince. "How in the name of Heaven will we avoid hurting various Teuton susceptibilities? . . . I am quite clear that I ought not to walk in with my wife on one arm and the Prince somewhere alongside—but further than this I will not go."[40]

The meager fruits of Henry's mission are revealed in two letters Roosevelt wrote to Speck von Sternburg, his closest German diplomatic friend. He mentioned his reservations about how friendly Germany wanted to be and said he enjoyed the prince's visit. But Roosevelt never mailed the letter, instead sending Sternburg a short note complaining of German reluctance to appoint him to the diplomatic corps in Washington. The German mission was ill conceived and

39. Herwig, *Politics of Frustration*, 73–74; *MRL*, III, 219n; Henry Pringle, *Theodore Roosevelt: A Biography* (New York, 1931), 281–82; Jonas, *United States and Germany*, 69–70. Prince Henry's instructions are in *GP*, XVI, 243; J. Fred Rippy, *Latin America in World Politics* (3rd ed.; New York, 1938), 184; Nelson Manfred Blake, "Ambassadors at the Court of Theodore Roosevelt," *MVHR*, XLII (1955), 184–85. Henry's visit and Alice's role are well covered in the TR Scrapbooks, Reels 461–62, 471, in RP.

40. TR to JH, January 18, 1902, in *MRL*, III, 219; TR to Douglas Robinson, February 3, 1902, to JH, February 3, 1902, both in RP.

served to deepen justified American suspicions of Germany's ambitions. The kaiser was not concerned with the American reaction directly but of the possibly perfidious British. "If we can make sure that the Britons will not use the opportunity to make the Americans suspicious of us and so weaken the effect of my brother's visit," Wilhelm wrote, a joint action with the British against Venezuela was possible, but only after Prince Henry's American mission. The kaiser also considered letting the prince formally negotiate with Roosevelt but abandoned the idea. On June 19, 1902, when Roosevelt was asked by the German consul-general in New York for his opinions on American-German relations, a message to be directly relayed to the kaiser, the American president was unequivocal: "No European nation, Germany or any other, should gain a foot of soil in any shape or way in South America, or establish a protectorate under any disguise over any South American country." Roosevelt supported an open door for Germany in Latin America and accepted the possibility that a predominantly German community there might secede and govern itself. He assured the kaiser's emissary of his fondest wishes "for the Germans both individually and as a nation." [41]

Britain and Germany, preoccupied with their European and colonial conflicts, alternated between being sensitive and obtuse about American concerns. Although Arthur James Balfour, the first lord of the treasury before he became prime minister in 1902, and Joseph Chamberlain, the colonial secretary, had no illusions that the Germany of Tirpitz and Wilhelm II was Britain's most serious threat, many political leaders still reflected the traditional view that France and Russia were Britain's primary continental enemies. When British newspapers countered the publicity from Prince Henry's American trip by emphasizing the growth of Anglo-American friendship, German papers answered with an embarrassing charge that in 1898 it was Germany, not Britain as was commonly believed, that had effectively ended the Austrian-Spanish initiative for a new Concert of Europe against America's proposed intervention in Cuba, and that British Ambassador Julian Pauncefote had been the chief drafter of the pro-

41. TR to Speck von Sternburg, March 6, 1902 (unmailed), to Sternburg, March 8, 1902, to HCL, June 19, 1901, in *MRL*, III, 239, 242, 97–98; Herwig, *Politics of Frustration*, 72–78; Hill, *Roosevelt and the Caribbean*, 113–15; Kneer, *Great Britain and the Caribbean*, 12–19; Scheiber, *Transformation of America Sentiment Toward Germany*, 143–46; Campbell, *Anglo-American Understanding*, 272–76; Lionel Gelber, *The Rise of Anglo-American Friendship: A Study in World Politics, 1898–1906* (London, 1938), 106–10. Kaiser quoted in Dennis, *Adventures in American Diplomacy*, 286.

posed European note. Although Pauncefote's role can be explained—
he wrote the note as the senior European diplomat, and there were
problems in the French translation—it was not entirely innocent. As
a traditional English gentleman, Pauncefote temperamentally sympathized more with Austrian-Spanish pleas on behalf of Old World
values than with the brash American diplomatic style he officially tolerated but personally disliked. During the 1895 Venezuelan boundary
dispute, Pauncefote wrote Salisbury to explain the "bad taste and
such bad form" of Secretary of State Richard Olney's note: "It was
probably written by the President sitting in his shirt sleeves between
two bottles of whisky under which conditions he is reported to have
penned his previous message about Venezuela." The dispute over
whether Germany or Britain was the better friend of the United States
remained rooted, as had the entire European diplomatic debate over
the war of 1898, in European affairs with the United States in the role
of a formidable but distant provincial power. In 1897, in response to a
Dominican offer to Germany of a naval base (not genuine but a domestic Dominican political tactic), Wilhelm II refused because he "did
not wish to be at logger-heads with the United States." In 1902 the
Germans remained divided. Tirpitz waited for the completion of his
thirty-eight-battleship navy, the Germans remained unrealistic about
American perceptions and ability, and the kaiser was eager, albeit intermittently, for conflict.[42]

A serious debt default in Guatemala offered the still tentative Europeans a chance to try out their new strategy of coercion. Guatemala's president Manuel Estrada Cabrera, an old hand at clumsy debt
evasions, had by 1901 infuriated both the Council of Foreign Bondholders and several European governments. Lord Lansdowne initiated the idea of a joint European response; Germany, Italy, France,
and Belgium joined Britain in issuing a formal warning to Guatemala on September 4, 1901. Guatemala made an attractive target. As
Francis Villiers, the British under secretary for America, noted, "We

42. Neale, *Great Britain and the United States*, xiii–xxii, 1–42; Julian Pauncefote to
Lord Salisbury, June 26, 1896, *ibid.*, 40–41; George Smalley, *Anglo-American Memories:
Second Series* (London, 1912), 179–82; H. C. Allen, *Great Britain and the United States: A
History of Anglo-American Relations, 1783–1952* (New York, 1955), 574–76. For the af-
finity between TR and Chamberlain, and Hay and Lansdowne, see *ibid.*, 568–69; Jonas,
United States and Germany, 56; Tansill, *Purchase of the Danish West Indies*, 396–97; Herwig,
Politics of Frustration, 75–76.

don't often get a chance" to put pressure "upon these C. American rogues."[43]

The "rogues" had learned that intervention, though often threatened, rarely occurred. The beleaguered Latin American nation would appeal to the United States for protection, not necessarily under the aegis of the Monroe Doctrine but through a practice that had become, if not a tradition, a routine procedure. Efforts at collection were thus delayed, often indefinitely. But because the tactic had worked so well in the past, Latin American debts had become substantial enough to cause concern in Europe and the United States. On February 26, 1902, at the request of the American chargé in Guatemala, Estrada Cabrera transmitted copies of the diplomatic correspondence to the United States. John Hay waited almost a month, but his response echoed the American reply to the German note on Venezuela. No comment was needed from the United States "as it is within the right of the creditor nations to require payment of debts due to their nationals." The German invitation to join in the pressure on Guatemala on April 3 enabled the United States to define its own new policy in Latin America: "The United States would not join any coercive action against Guatemala" but reserved the right to share in the benefits the Europeans won through coercion. The American policy was shrewd and self-serving, yet by not joining the diplomatic coercion, the United States remained partly neutral and partly (a very small part) in sympathy and possible alliance with Guatemala and Caribbean Latin America.[44]

Long frustrated by Latin America's ability to evade debt payments, the Europeans were eager to make an example of vulnerable Guatemala, though the small country had settled some of its claims. The British minister to Guatemala, Ralph S. Paget, used the visit of the British warship *Grafton* to coerce Estrada Cabrera without telling the Foreign Office. He threatened to seize the customs houses on April 16 if all British claims were not immediately settled. Since the German gunboat *Vineta* was scheduled to arrive within a few days, and the various European ministers in Guatemala made it appear as if overwhelming force would be used, Estrada Carbrera gave in. At least,

43. Kneer, *Great Britain and the Caribbean*, 1–3. For the details of the debt and the diplomatic correspondence between the European powers see *FRUS*, 1902, pp. 569–77.
44. Kneer, *Great Britain and the Caribbean*, 1–7; JH to W. Godfrey Hunter, March 22, April 10, 1902; Pro memoriâ, April 3, 1902; JH to Theodor von Holleben with enclosed Memorandum, April 5, 1902, all in *FRUS*, 1902, pp. 578, 426–27.

everyone agreed that he had. Guatemala's total external debt was estimated to be $7,778,640 (1,600,000 pounds sterling). The settlement
amounted to about $188,049. The Europeans had established the pre-
cedent that coercion worked better than persuasion in balky Latin
American countries.[45]

In response to the new European initiatives the Americans continued their passive policy of accepting limited European intervention
but refusing to participate in coercion. After careful consultation, Assistant Secretary Alvey Adee, the State Department scholar William F.
Penfield, and Secretary of State John Hay continued the calm, almost
indifferent posture in the face of obvious European intrusion into
Central America. Guatemala, impressed with the "friendly attitude"
of the United States, pledged not to discriminate against friendly and
lenient creditors when paying its debts, a gesture that was not reflected in any payments.[46]

Not one but two precedents had been set. Europe began its short-
lived policy of coercion to collect debts, and the United States refused
to participate in such action. Many historians and virtually all Latin
American intellectuals see the age of Roosevelt's diplomacy as the
foundation of later military coercion and dependency. Indeed, many
members of Roosevelt's administration became prominent policy
makers in William Howard Taft's administration, when dollar diplomacy began the American policy of almost continuous military and
economic intervention in the Caribbean and Central America. But
Roosevelt's and Taft's policies were radically different. By the time of
Taft's presidency the United States was the dominant Caribbean
power. In 1901, when America was still fighting for European respect
and recognition, it might have been logical for the United States to
join with Europe against Guatemala. Few Americans were concerned
with Latin America; the most interested group, the investors who suffered in the same manner as the European investors, would have welcomed American pressure. Instead, the United States, at considerable
cost to its own investors, chose to stand with the Latin American nations against a unified Europe. The new European strategy conflicted

45. Kneer, *Great Britain and the Caribbean*, 3–5. The claims totaled 304,591 Guatemalan
pesos, 523,534 French francs, and 56,872 German marks. Britain's minister to Guatemala
estimated the settlement at 40,000 to 45,000 pounds, which is slightly lower than the
total of $188,049 given in *FRUS*; see Dana Munro, *Intervention and Dollar Diplomacy in
the Caribbean, 1900–1921* (Princeton, 1943), 143.
46. Kneer, *Great Britain and the Caribbean*, 6.

with the Monroe Doctrine's prohibition against European intervention and increasing Latin American sensitivity toward forced collection of debts. On December 29, 1902, Argentine Foreign Minister Luis M. Drago invited the United States to support the Drago Doctrine formally to oppose any government's intervention to collect public debts in Latin America.[47]

Drago, who endorsed the Monroe Doctrine because he considered it not only compatible but complementary, understood that for a very brief moment the two Americas were united in their rejection of European intervention. Although the Roosevelt Corollary of 1905 offended Latin Americans by its diction and its unilateral assertion of the right of intervention, the two doctrines converged in rejecting the European practice of coercion. Drago was unable to win approval of his doctrine from the Argentine Congress, which divided between factions favoring Latin American solidarity and those fearful of offending Argentina's European trading partners. Nor could he win over John Hay, who may have viewed even an ideological alliance with Drago as entangling and therefore likely to upset the American Congress—which had never formally approved the Monroe Doctrine. Because of Latin America's diversity, the many economic and cultural differences between the Americas, and fear that Roosevelt's protective diplomacy would prove to be as imperial as European domination, the extremely short ideological union of the Drago and Monroe doctrines is often overlooked or unrecognized.[48]

47. Luis M. Drago to Martin Garcia Méron, December 29, 1902, in *FRUS*, 1903, pp. 1–5. For the earliest and most influential linkage see the chapter "Roosevelt Corollary and Dollar Diplomacy, 1899–1913," in Samuel Flagg Bemis, *The Latin American Policy of the United States: An Historical Interpretation* (New York, 1943), 142–67; for the context of the Drago (originally Calvo) Doctrine see Robert Freeman Smith, "Latin America, the United States, and the European Powers, 1830–1930," in *CHLA*, IV, 103–104; Donald Shea, *The Calvo Clause: A Problem of Inter-American and International Law and Diplomacy* (Minneapolis, 1955), 9–32; and Alejandro Alvarez, "Latin America and International Law," *American Journal of International Law*, III (1909), 269–353. For the differences between Roosevelt's and Taft's foreign policies see Eugene F. Trani, "Cautious Warrior: Theodore Roosevelt and the Diplomacy of Activism," in Frank J. Merli and Theodore A. Wilson (eds.), *Makers of American Diplomacy from Benjamin Franklin to Henry Kissinger* (New York, 1974), 324–26; and Trani, "Dollar Diplomacy," in Alexander DeConde (ed.), *Encyclopedia of American Foreign Policy* (3 vols.; New York, 1978), I, 268–74.

48. For the origins of Drago's letter see Thomas F. McGann, *Argentina, the United States, and the Inter-American System, 1880–1914* (Cambridge, Mass., 1957), 218–30; and Perkins, *Monroe Doctrine, 1867–1907*, 350–53. For the change of Bemis' phrase, "protective imperialism" to "protective diplomacy," see Harold Eugene Davis, John J. Finan, and F. Taylor Peck, *Latin American Diplomatic History: An Introduction* (Baton Rouge, 1977), 152–55; for European predominance in Latin American trade until well into the

Europe moved slowly. It was diplomatic friction between Britain and Venezuela, not the issue of Drago's debt default, that pushed the British to exasperated action. Britain felt that Venezuela had violated the long-standing Anglo-Venezuelan commerical treaty of 1825 by levying a 30 percent surtax on imports from Trinidad and the West Indies. This tax had disrupted normal Caribbean commerce, encouraged smuggling, and led to open warfare between Venezuelan naval vessels and British ships suspected of avoiding the tax. Each side was convinced that the other was the cause of the trouble, making a diplomatic resolution almost impossible. With the Venezuelan civil wars in full fury, Cipriano Castro was more concerned with controlling the supply of arms to the rebels than with the niceties of big power relations. Continued Venezuelan seizures of British-owned ships, some of which carried munitions, added to the sense of confrontation and crisis.[49]

France dramatically demonstrated that force was more effective than diplomacy in Venezuela. When French merchants were jailed in a customs dispute at Carúpano, the French cruiser *Suchet* obtained the release of the prisoners and a public apology by holding a Venezuelan naval vessel at gunpoint until the demands were met. The French minister at Caracas refused to accept the Venezuelan protest. Infuriated, the American minister Herbert Bowen called the French action "irregular and reprehensible." Washington, unperturbed by yet another European show of force, considered the incident "a closed matter." Alvey Adee blandly instructed Bowen to be discreet and helpful in adjusting differences rather than using force.[50]

---

twentieth century see Smith, "Latin America, the United States, and the European Powers," 88; and Platt, *Finance, Trade, and Politics in British Foreign Policy*, 136–40. For a view emphasizing the differences between Drago's and the United States' positions see Arthur P. Whitaker, *The Western Hemisphere Idea: Its Rise and Decline* (Ithaca, N.Y., 1954), 86–107. Although many accounts date the Roosevelt Corollary from the text of TR's fourth annual message to Congress, December 6, 1904 (in *TRWN*, XV, 256–58), its first application occurred with the Dominican Republic crisis of January, 1905. See Chapter 14.

49. Kneer, *Great Britain and the Caribbean*, 1–9; Sullivan, "Rise of Despotism in Venezuela," 316–21, 326–27; Hood, *Gunboat Diplomacy*, 174–77. For the Venezuelan seizure of the British merchant vessel the *Queen* in May, 1902, as a turning point see Guthrie, "Anglo-German Intervention," 37–38.

50. Kneer, *Great Britain and the Caribbean*, 15–16; Herbert Bowen to JH, August 10, 1902, Despatches from United States Ministers to Venezuela, M79, Roll 56, RG 59, NA; Alvey Adee to Bowen, August 16, 1902, Diplomatic Instructions of the Department of State, M77, Roll 175, RG 59, NA. Adee's handwritten draft of the instruction is on the second copy of Bowen to Hay, August 10, 1902, in Despatches, M79, Roll 56.

Castro's forces went beyond simple search and seizure. Passengers and crew members of British ships were taken prisoner to be released in remote areas, and some ships were destroyed on the spot. Normal British diplomatic protests were ignored. If the French were able to act decisively "in a case *comparatively* mild," the British could not endure such a relationship between a "great power" and a "petty statelet." Lord Lansdowne agreed that "we cannot let this pass," and a detailed memorandum on the troubles with Venezuela was drawn up. Britain complained that such "unwarrantable interference" was "an outrage that justifies and, with the other outrages, requires reprisal." Further attempts to negotiate with Venezuela broke down. The British minister complained that over a four-month period the Venzuelan government had ignored seventeen diplomatic notes. On July 23, 1902, just three days after the British reprisal memorandum, Germany suggested that "the Powers interested in Venezuela" exert pressure through a "pacific blockade."[51]

The United States Navy had been preparing for a possible showdown with Germany since William McKinley's presidency. In 1901–1902, Culebra, an island about five miles east of Puerto Rico, became the main American Caribbean naval base. The navy received regular reports from Commander Nathan Sargent aboard the *Scorpion*, a warship that observed the Venezuelans and reported regularly on German activities in Venezuela. From its inception in 1900 the navy's General Board regarded Germany as the major threat to American interests, and under Admiral Dewey, its presiding officer for seventeen years, no possible German threat was taken lightly.[52]

The United States prepared to coerce the coercion. The developing Venezuelan crisis was treated realistically and seriously. By July 9, 1902, Navy Secretary William Moody completed the plan to assemble an entire fleet at Culebra. Since Americans expected a confrontation with Castro as early as 1902, new naval appropriations had already

51. Kneer, *Great Britain and the Caribbean*, 15–16; William Haggard to Lord Lansdowne, June 30, 1902; "Memorandum by A. Larcom on Existing Causes of Complaint Against Venezuela," July 20, 1902; Lord Lansdowne to George Buchanan, July 23, 1902, all in FO 420/206 (Venezuela, Confidential), PRO; Sullivan, "Rise of Despotism in Venezuela," 327; Hood, *Gunboat Diplomacy*, 181–82.

52. Tansill, *Purchase of the Danish West Indies*, 400–401, 427–28; Herwig, *Politics of Frustration*, 78, 99–109; Richard Challener, *Admirals, Generals, and American Foreign Policy, 1898–1914* (Princeton, 1973), 16–17, 28–29; Grenville and Young, *Politics, Strategy, and American Diplomacy*, 297–307. For the history of the General Board see Daniel J. Costello, "Planning for War: A History of the General Board of the Navy, 1900–1914" (Ph.D. dissertation, Fletcher School of Law and Diplomacy, 1958).

been requested, and inquiries on Venezuela's principal roads and landing places had begun in February. By June the fleet was mobilized for battle, and Dewey, the first four-star admiral to command an American fighting naval force, took command at Culebra. German naval attachés were banned from viewing the American fleet's movements, an unusual action that made Germany aware of the extraordinary concentration of American warships in Caribbean and Central American waters. In July the American Caribbean commander was ordered to report on where the Germans might land and to prepare both offensive and defensive plans to deal with such an invasion.[53]

On August 19, 1902, Britain and Germany agreed to begin a blockade of "one or more Venezuelan ports" in November. Lord Lansdowne at first suggested inviting the Americans to join the "naval demonstration." The Germans at this point seemed more aware of the possible conflicts with American policy than the British. The United States had consistently followed its passive policy toward claims, resisting active enforcement, but had not objected to other nations pursuing an active policy. At the same time the Americans made certain that everyone understood that the Monroe Doctrine must not be violated. The Monroe Doctrine, however, was capable of enormous flexibility and modulation depending on the circumstances. Coercion appeared to be acceptable if no territory was taken. But the Monroe Doctrine was as much a state of mind as a legal or diplomatic policy. The planned Anglo-German coercion of Venezuela might not violate the American diplomatic guidelines, which had never been carefully formulated, but it would gravely disturb America's state of mind. Europeans understood the Monroe Doctrine's emotional dimension and were careful not to disturb the Americans. At times, however, the ingrained European distaste for the American doctrine triumphed over diplomatic wisdom and the Europeans seemed almost eager to test American resolve. Perhaps the old resentment against the Americans, their doctrine, and America's olympian tendency to remain aloof from European diplomatic concerns explains why Lansdowne inexplicably backed off from inviting the Americans to join or even keeping them informed. The Americans would be put on notice only "when the time drew nearer."[54]

53. Seward W. Livermore, "Theodore Roosevelt, the American Navy, and the Venezuelan Crisis of 1902–1903," AHR, LI (1946), 455; for British awareness of Culebra's significance as the major American Caribbean naval base see Kenneth Bourne, Britain and the Balance of Power in North America, 1815–1908 (Berkeley, 1967), 346.

54. Kneer, Great Britain and the Caribbean, 20, 26; Lord Lansdowne to Sir Frank Lascelles, August 19, 1902, in FO 420/206, PRO; Perkins, Monroe Doctrine, 1867–1907,

The Germans continued to overreact to small Caribbean grievances. During a Haitian civil war, insurrectionists took a government boat and stopped a German vessel and prevented it from unloading its cargo of arms. The German gunboat *Panther* destroyed the offending Haitian vessel, *Crête-à-Pierrot*, in September, 1902. "Bravo, *Panther*," the kaiser enthusiastically cabled to the captain. In reply to Assistant Secretary of State Alvey Adee's troubled inquiry, diplomatic scholar and consultant John Bassett Moore termed the German action illegal and excessive.[55]

In spite of serious ambivalence and confusion about their new alliance and joint naval operation, both Britain and Germany proceeded. Considerable criticism from the British press during the kaiser's twelve-day visit to Britain that began on November 8 further demonstrated the serious problems of the new alliance. On November 13, British Minister Michael Herbert obliquely informed the United States that if Britain's final ultimatum to Venezuela failed, the British would take further measures. In reply Hay regretted the need for coercion but reiterated that the Americans had no objections to such operations, providing no territory was acquired.[56]

For the first time the British and Germans classified their claims against Venezuela. British first-rank claims included shipping losses, personal injury, and wrongful imprisonment; those of Germany included losses in the Venezuelan civil wars of 1898–1900. National matters rather than financial default constituted the main—and the decisive—European complaint. Not until the naval operation plans were almost fully set did the Europeans consider including the enormous Venezuelan external debt or dealing with their bondholders' requests for government intervention. Germany suggested ranking the European claims against Venezuela. In the first rank the Germans proposed placing the $340,000 in losses German nationals sustained in the Venezuelan civil wars of 1898–1900. If coercion became necessary, the Germans wanted to add an additional $600,000 for property losses suffered in Venezuela's ongoing civil war as well as an interest

---

319–49; Campbell, *Anglo-American Understanding*, 274–75; Gelber, *Rise of Anglo-American Friendship*, 111. For the British reservations about the intervention see Lord Newton, *Lord Lansdowne: A Biography* (London, 1929), 256; Herwig, *Germany's Vision of Empire in Venezuela*, 99; for the confusion see Guthrie, "Anglo-German Intervention," esp. 70–94.

55. Herwig, *Politics of Frustration*, 71–72; JBM to Alvey Adee, September 15, 1902, in Hay Papers, LC.

56. Kneer, *Great Britain and the Caribbean*, 25–26; Gelber, *Rise of Anglo-American Friendship*, 111–12; Kennedy, *Rise of Anglo-German Antagonism*, 258–60.

guarantee on Venezuelan loans of $8.2 million held by German credi-
tors. Britain limited its first-line claims to about $27,500, including di-
rect losses of British shipping and related materials resulting from
Venezuelan aggression, or what the British called "outrages." Following the German suggestion that joint action include Venezuela's large
external debt, the British placed their share of Venezuela's defaulted
external debt in the third or lowest rank of claims. Nonetheless, the
diplomatic and economic claims were now unified and supported by
European governments planning to collect the debts through armed
naval and military coercion.[57]

The United States remained passive but wary of the Anglo-German
intervention. An American naval memorandum in November, 1902,
summarized the basis for American concern. In twelve terse points
the memo painted a vivid picture of the possible disasters in Venezuela arising not from any careful German plan but from the many possible misadventures. Since the navy was convinced that the Germans
had no long-range invasion plans, the main American concern centered on the possible accidents that might turn a small episode into
a protracted crisis. The United States Navy had considered almost
every possible contingency. It predicted President Castro's worst over-
reactions: "He is a perfectly irresponsible dictator and would violently oppose" German occupation of all customs houses, which
would be necessary because "occupying a port only . . . would divert trade to others." Once the Venezuelans opposed military occupation, war would result. Though not seeking war with Venezuela,
Germany, once started on this expedition, "would not go out of her
way to avoid it."[58]

The memo became more ominous. If war began, Germany must
win it and would then demand further indemnity for port expenses.
Venezuela, with no assets, would be forced to offer either land or a
mortgage on future revenue. Either solution would effectively make
Venezuela a German protectorate. Venezuela's political and economic

---

57. Kneer, *Great Britain and the Caribbean*, 21–22; Lord Lansdowne to George
Buchanan, November 11, 1902, in *GTBD*, II, 156. For the debt see Guthrie, "Anglo-
German Intervention," 50–58, 77–80; for early American concern on the questions
posed by the Venezuelan blockade see JBM to Alvey Adee, November 20, 1902, Box 9,
John Bassett Moore Papers, LC.

58. Dennis, *Adventures in Diplomacy*, 291–92. The undated memorandum with the
initials H.C.T. (Rear Admiral Henry C. Taylor, chief of the Bureau of Navigation and
chairman of the Executive Committee of the General Board) was filed under Venezuela
in the premicrofilm Roosevelt Papers, LC.

dependence on Germany would be disastrous for the United States. The navy was firm in its warning: "The United States . . . must not allow Germany, during its attempt on Venezuela, to occupy, fit up, or fortify any port so as to allow of its being used as a base against us." Further, the navy warned, no fortifications or materials for future fortifications could be tolerated. American naval forces equal to those of Germany should be maintained at nearby bases. Ground forces stationed at Puerto Rico should be maintained in sufficient force to defend against any German intervention or invasion in the Caribbean area. The navy's point that Roosevelt took most seriously may explain the thoroughness of his precautions: "Our aim must be at all times to be in a better state of preparation for war than Germany is, and her every move must be met by corresponding preparatory action on our part." The attitudes of German diplomats and naval officers in Venezuela justified the American circumspection. The commander of the German cruiser *Vineta* on Caribbean duty favored European occupation of the customs houses as the only effective tactic against this "rotten state," a view shared by the admiralty staff. In September, German chargé Giesbert von Pilgrim-Baltazzi suggested to British Minister William Haggard in Caracas a joint action that included "something of a permanent administrative nature . . . beyond the occupation of one or more customs houses." Although Haggard reminded him of the Monroe Doctrine, in October even the British minister favored "one or more of the foreign powers" administering the customs houses "for a prolonged period." [59]

Hay's diplomatic responses to Britain and Germany were calm and almost passive. American naval preparations were just the opposite. Nor did the Americans keep the naval buildup a secret. Dewey's appointment as active fleet commander was well publicized; his antipathy toward Germany was well known, especially to the Germans. Officially, the Americans were conducting extensive naval exercises in the Caribbean. Dewey was ordered to the Caribbean on November 18, a week before the State Department was formally told of the Anglo-German intervention plan. Dewey arrived at Culebra on De-

59. Dennis, *Adventures in Diplomacy*, 291–92; Baltazzi-Haggard conversation quoted in Kneer, *Great Britain and the Caribbean*, 9–10; "rotten state" quoted in Herwig, *Germany's Vision of Empire in Venezuela*, 93–94; for further discussion of possible German occupation see *ibid.*, 238–39. For an alarmist naval intelligence report showing substantial German naval superiority see Charles D. Sigsbee, memorandum, March 22, 1902, in Reel 25, RP.

cember 1 and assumed command on the flagship *Mayflower* December 8, 1902.[60]

Britain and Germany severed diplomatic relations with Venezuela and delivered their final formal diplomatic ultimatum on December 7, 1902. By prearrangement the United States took charge of both the British and German legations in Caracas. President Castro refused to placate the great powers. Instead, he ordered the arrest of all German and British nationals, who now fell under the protection of American Minister Herbert Bowen. The armed conflict began on December 9, 1902.[61]

60. Livermore, "Theodore Roosevelt," 460–61; TR to George Dewey, June 14, 1902, in *MRL*, III, 275 and 275 n; for the Culebra exercises see TR to Thomas C. Platt, June 28, 1902, *ibid.*, 283; Spector, *Admiral of the New Empire*, 146–53; and *Annual Report of the Secretary of the Navy, 1903*, Serial 4642, pp. 646–50.

61. The details are in Herbert Bowen to JH, December 13, 1902, Despatches, M79, Roll 56, RG 59, NA; *FRUS*, 1903, pp. 788–91.

4 Venezuela: Coercion and Confrontation, 1902–1903

Venezuela's size and the physical impossibility of winning any military conflict should have deterred the Europeans, but both intervening powers were aware of only a small fraction of the obstacles. December was chosen to avoid the hurricane season of late summer and early fall. That date seemed to satisfy the British wariness about Venezuela's "unhealthy" tropical ports. But yellow fever was a constant threat, as strong in winter as in summer. At least as important as their geographic ignorance was the cultural obtuseness of the British and Germans. Initially they were angered by Cipriano Castro's failure to observe minimal diplomatic amenities. That Castro was a provincial who did not know the amenities made him appear to the Europeans more vulnerable. In fact, it made Castro more dangerous and almost invulnerable. The various ultimatums that were delivered on December 7, 1902, went on interminably, and though the meaning of "immediately" might be clear to a European diplomat, the Venezuelans did not realize that this time the European threats were serious. Indeed, even the British on the scene did not know when the attempt at coercion would begin. The British commodore at Trinidad urgently cabled the Admiralty on December 9 for specific instructions, noting that the German commander "has direct orders from Kaiser, if no satisfactory reply to ultimatum received, to seize Venezuelan government ships at 3 P.M., 9th December."[1]

1. See Bowen to JH, December 13, 1902, Despatches from American Ministers to Venezuela, Microcopy M79, Roll 56, RG 59, NA; Admiralty to Foreign Office, Inclosure, December 9, 1902, in FO 420/206, PRO. For the confusions of the ultimatums see Wayne Lee Guthrie, "The Anglo-German Intervention in Venezuela, 1902–03" (Ph.D. dissertation, University of California, San Diego, 1983), 115–18; for the Venezuelan view see William M. Sullivan, "The Rise of Despotism in Venezuela: Cipriano Castro, 1899–1908" (Ph.D. dissertation, University of New Mexico, 1974), 316–73; and Miriam Hood, *Gunboat Diplomacy, 1895–1905: Great Power Pressure in Venezuela* (2nd ed.; London, 1983). For the German intervention see Holger H. Herwig and J. Leon Helguera, *Alemania y el*

Castro may well have appeared to the Europeans as a provincial who failed to understand big power diplomacy, but the Europeans were equally provincial in failing to understand the Venezuelan tradition, begun by Guzmán Blanco and followed by Castro, of alternately using and defying foreigners. By the time Castro took power, Venezuela's established tradition of independence made backing down before European gunboat pressure almost unthinkable. Venezuela's defiance, not its fiscal irresponsibility, goaded the powers into action. But Venezuela, like the United States, was too large and too wild to be controlled through the capture of the equivalent of a Berlin or a London. Castro could have defended Caracas with twenty thousand troops. How many casualties could the Germans and British accept—politically or militarily—to teach Latin America a lesson? To have any chance of success, the interveners had to win control of Venezuela at the beginning of hostilities. Failing a quick resolution, the attempted coercion could not succeed, and then the powers would demonstrate that the exceptionalism suggested by the Monroe Doctrine did in fact exist, not merely as myth or political propaganda but in the physical reality of unhealthy Venezuela.[2]

Almost as soon as the coercion began, the Venezuelans achieved a stalemate. One cannot know how many lessons the British and Ger-

---

bloquero internacional de Venezuela 1902/03 (Caracas, 1977); Herwig, *Germany's Vision of Empire in Venezuela, 1871–1914* (Princeton, 1986), 80–109; and Guthrie, "Anglo-German Intervention." For the United States see Seward W. Livermore, "Theodore Roosevelt, the American Navy, and the Venezuelan Crisis of 1902–03," *AHR*, LI (1946), 452–71; Howard K. Beale, *Theodore Roosevelt and the Rise of America to World Power* (Baltimore, 1956); Howard C. Hill, *Roosevelt and the Caribbean* (Chicago, 1927), 125–47; and Alfred L. P. Dennis, *Adventures in American Diplomacy, 1896–1906* (New York, 1928), 282–308. For Great Britain see Warren G. Kneer, *Great Britain and the Caribbean, 1901–1913* (East Lansing, Mich., 1975); Charles S. Campbell, *Anglo-American Understanding, 1898–1903* (Baltimore, 1957); Lionel Gelber, *The Rise of Anglo-American Friendship: A Study in World Politics, 1898–1906* (London, 1938); H. C. Allen, *Great Britain and the United States: A History of Anglo-American Relations, 1783–1952* (New York, 1955); and D. C. M. Platt, "The Allied Coercion of Venezuela, 1902–3—A Reassessment," *Inter-American Economic Affairs*, XV (Spring, 1962), 3–28; also see Holger H. Herwig, *Politics of Frustration: The United States in German Naval Planning, 1889–1941* (Boston, 1976); Richard Challener, *Admirals, Generals, and American Foreign Policy, 1898–1914* (Princeton, 1973); Manfred Jonas, *The United States and Germany: A Diplomatic History* (Ithaca, N.Y., 1984); and Alfred Vagts, *Deutschland und die Vereinigten Staaten in Der Weltpolitik* (2 vols.; New York, 1935).

2. Hood, *Gunboat Diplomacy*, 66–72; Judith Ewell, *Venezuela: A Century of Change* (Stanford, 1984), 27–29, 36–46; John V. Lombardi, *Venezuela: The Search for Order, the Dream of Progress* (New York, 1982), 201–205; Guthrie, "Anglo-German Intervention," 124–29. For German motives see Herwig, *Germany's Vision of Empire in Venezuela*, 99; and Herwig, *Politics of Frustration*, 79; J. Fred Rippy, *Latin America in World Politics* (3rd ed.; New York, 1938), 182–99. For the twenty thousand men see Frederick W. Marks III, *Velvet on Iron: The Diplomacy of Theodore Roosevelt* (Lincoln, Neb., 1979), 74, n. 18.

mans might have been willing to teach Castro had the American fleet not been in place and ready to intervene. German and British violence in the early encounters suggests a mixture of hostility and ineptitude. Outraged public opinion might have prevented further excess, but only after additional conflict. But with the American fleet in position and an American president dedicated to educating Europe that the newly self-conscious United States must be treated with proper respect, Venezuela had a powerful diplomatic ally. The Germans and British were already divided and preoccupied with problems from their own confused alliance.[3]

Italy's use of imperial African affairs to join the coercion further demonstrated European insularity and insensitivity to both Americas. Italian Foreign Minister Giulio Prinetti, Lansdowne wrote, "impressed upon me the connection between the Venezuelan and Somaliland questions, and the importance of our acting together in both cases." In recommending that Italy be permitted to join the intervention, Lansdowne remarked that "it was . . . better that all the teeth should be pulled out at once" and that Italy should not have to wait and intervene later separately. Germany objected that the Italian claims were not as weighty as its own but permitted the Italians to join the intervention after the opening actions. On December 11 Lansdowne still failed to perceive or comprehend the worldwide revulsion against the use of force. He joked with Count Metternich that the Germans avoided the difficulties of prize courts for captured ships by sinking them, a reference to the two Venezuelan ships sunk by the *Panther* on December 9. This "might, I suppose, be regarded as a form of 'sequestration,'" the British foreign minister humorously suggested. Afterward, Lansdowne would work hard to separate Britain from the clumsy German actions, but both powers were almost equally insensitive at the start.[4]

The Venezuelan conflict was fought in three theaters. Cipriano Castro and American Minister Herbert Bowen were the principals in Venezuela, where the war began; Lord Lansdowne, Count Metternich, and American diplomat Henry White played decisive roles in

3. Sullivan, "Rise of Despotism in Venezuela," 334–36; Challener, *Admirals, Generals, and American Foreign Policy*, 116–18. For TR's early awareness of possible naval intervention see Beale, *Theodore Roosevelt*, 416; for Castro's control of the crisis see Guthrie, "Anglo-German Intervention," 127–28.

4. Lord Lansdowne to Sir R. Rodd, December 5, 1902; Lansdowne to George Buchanan, December 7, 11, 1902, all in FO 420/206, PRO; Guthrie, "Anglo-German Intervention," 95–97. For the Italian claims see Maurizio Vernassa, *Emigrazione, diplomazia e cannoniero: L'inteventi italiano in Venezuela, 1902–1903* (Leghorn, 1980).

the battle in London. Between these two contests the most controversial battle took place in Washington when Theodore Roosevelt summoned German Ambassador Theodor von Holleben for an interview that produced one of the most controversial episodes in modern diplomatic history. Even the exact date remains uncertain. Theodore Roosevelt later asserted that between December 6, before the shooting began, and December 10, well before it ended, he delivered a verbal ultimatum to von Holleben that armed intervention in Venezuela was forbidden by the United States government, which insisted that the dispute be settled by international arbitration and not by force of arms. Historians have disagreed since 1916, when Roosevelt's revelations were first made public, over whether such an ultimatum was ever given. There is substantial evidence to support Roosevelt's contention that it was but no definitive physical evidence in the diplomatic archives to prove it. Some historians have questioned whether Roosevelt, confused over dates, erred years later in recalling both the timing and the nature of the episode. The latest historical research shows persuasively—though not definitively—that an exchange between the president and the kaiser did take place through the German ambassador and that Roosevelt's account is substantially correct.[5]

One of the chief arguments against Roosevelt's contention that he delivered a direct ultimatum raised by historians familiar with German diplomatic archives is the strong evidence that Germany had no clear-cut plan for a major intervention in Venezuela. German archives show a healthy respect for American sensitivity on the Monroe Doctrine, and beyond the opportunistic desire to create some havoc, blaming the British and causing minor dissension and chaos, the Germans were not ready or willing to risk a major confrontation with the United States over occupation of any part of Venezuela or the Caribbean. Mischief, not conquest, was the German goal. Roosevelt was convinced that its goals were weightier: "Germany intended to seize some Venezuelan harbor and turn it into a strongly fortified place of

5. TR to William R. Thayer, August 21, 1916, in *MRL*, VIII, 1101–1105; TR to Henry White, August 14, 1906, in *MRL*, V, 357–59. For comprehensive treatments of the dispute see Beale, *Theodore Roosevelt*, 399–431; Marks, *Velvet on Iron*, 38–54, 70–73. For a summary of how the historiographical debate developed see Edward D. Parsons, "The German-American Crisis of 1902–1903," *Historian*, XXXIII (1971), 436–52; see also Paul S. Holbo, "Perilous Obscurity: Public Diplomacy and the Press in the Venezuela Crisis, 1902–1903," *Historian*, XXXII (1970), 428–48. A detailed reconstruction of the chronology of Roosevelt's ultimatum and a defense of Roosevelt's accuracy are in Edmund Morris, "'A Few Pregnant Days': Theodore Roosevelt and the Venzuelan Crisis of 1902," *TRAJ*, XV (Winter, 1989), 2–13.

arms, on the model of Kiauchau, with a view to exercising some degree of control over the future isthmian canal and over South American affairs generally."[6]

Although Roosevelt possibly exaggerated German motives, Germany's actual intentions were only a part of the problem. The navy's November, 1902, memorandum was more concerned with accidental German encroachments than with possible occupation plans. Roosevelt overstated German intentions, but he was justifiably fearful of a German occupation of Venezuelan territory by misadventure, sudden opportunity, or anger. The crisis caused by the presence of the large German-British fleet at Venezuela was eased, not by Roosevelt's diplomatic ultimatums but because America's diplomatic and naval contingency planning gave the United States complete control in Venezuelan waters. The tough diplomatic rhetoric Roosevelt directed at Germany reflected American naval superiority in the Caribbean and confidence that Britain, though temporarily allied with Germany, remained friendly to America. By being prepared for the worst, Theodore Roosevelt was able to limit the diplomatic confrontation. As soon as the Anglo-German ultimatum had been delivered to Venezuela, Lieutenant Marbury Johnston, the official United States naval liaison officer in Caracas, took over direction of American intelligence, accurately reporting on all Venezuelan troop detachments, armaments, and ammunition supplies. Roosevelt had this information, including the precise deployment of all American, British, and German vessels, before confronting the German ambassador. Because the navy was well prepared, diplomacy could limit the problem by concentrating on immediate relief from invasion and blockade without raising potentially more inflammatory matters such as grandiose German ambitions in Central America.[7]

Arbitration was the preferred American diplomatic strategy to prevent Europe from establishing a new precedent for naval intervention

6. TR to William R. Thayer, August 21, 1916, in *MRL*, VIII, 1102; for German ambivalence on the Monroe Doctrine see Herwig, *Germany's Vision of Empire in Venezuela*, 175–235; Beale, *Theodore Roosevelt*, 403–407; Dexter Perkins, *The Monroe Doctrine, 1867–1907* (Baltimore, 1937), 311–18.

7. Livermore, "Theodore Roosevelt," 460; for German opinion favoring European customs control see Kneer, *Great Britain and the Caribbean*, 9–10; Herwig, *Germany's Vision of Empire in Venezuela*, 93–98; for the view that Roosevelt exaggerated the German naval threat see Hill, *Roosevelt and the Caribbean*, 129–32; for the actual German war plans see Holger H. Herwig and David F. Trask, "Naval Operations Plans Between Germany and the USA, 1898–1913: A Study of Strategic Planning in the Age of Imperialism," in Paul M. Kennedy (ed.), *The War Plans of the Great Powers, 1880–1914* (Lon-

in Latin America. Since 1858, when Argentine lawyer Carlos Calvo formalized Latin objections to the practice of collecting private commercial debts through military or naval coercion, the Calvo Clause became a part of most Latin American contracts though it was either rejected or ignored by non–Latin American businessmen. The resolution of British and American Civil War maritime claims through international arbitration in 1871 marked the beginning of a substantial legal movement toward peaceful mediation. In 1895 President Cleveland demanded arbitration to end the Anglo-Venezuelan border dispute. When Tsar Nicholas II convened the First Hague Peace Conference on May 18, 1899, he was seeking a way to prevent costly wars over resolvable disputes. The Hague conference proved disappointing, but it did establish a Permanent Court of Arbitration, which its backers hoped would encourage greater use of formal mediation. Theodore Roosevelt, an early advocate of arbitration, gave the new Hague Court its first case, the Pious Fund of the Californias dispute with Mexico that had festered since 1848. The impressive formal proceedings began on September 15, 1902, with the United States represented by English and Russian attorneys and the Mexicans by two Dutch jurists. When the court ruled for the United States a month later, Roosevelt was encouraged by the efficiency of a precedent that offered an expeditious means of peacefully settling Latin American economic disputes.[8]

Germany led the opposition to arbitration at the Hague confer-

---

don, 1979), 39–74; see also Alfred Vagts, "Hopes and Fears of an American-German War, 1870–1915," *Political Science Quarterly*, LIV (1939), 514–35, LV (1940), 53–76; John A. S. Grenville and George Berkeley Young, *Politics, Strategy, and American Diplomacy: Studies in Foreign Policy, 1873–1917* (New Haven, 1966), 305–307; and Ronald Spector, *Admiral of the New Empire: The Life and Career of George Dewey* (Baton Rouge, 1974), 146–53; for the view that the American navy feared a German confrontation see Spector, "Roosevelt, the Navy, and the Venezuelan Controversy, 1902–1903," *American Neptune*, XXXII (1972), 257–63.

8. Calvin de Armond Davis, *The United States and the First Hague Peace Conference* (Ithaca, N.Y., 1962), 2–3, 210–12; for the Pious Fund case see *FRUS*, 1902, Appendix II, pp. 9–15, 17–18; see Peter Martin Di Meglio, "The United States and the Second Hague Peace Conference: The Extension of the Use of Arbitration" (Ph.D. dissertation, St. John's University, 1968); Helen May Cory, *Compulsory Arbitration of International Disputes* (New York, 1932); and Montague Hughes Crackanthorpe, "Arbitration, International," in *Encyclopaedia Britannica* (26 vols.; New York, 1910), II, 327–33. For Roosevelt's use of arbitration see Marks, *Velvet on Iron*, 136–38. See also David S. Patterson, *Toward a Warless World: The Travail of the American Peace Movement, 1887–1914* (Bloomington, Ind., 1976), 109–10. George Crichfield, *American Supremacy* (2 vols.; New York, 1908), 159–369, provides an extensive history of Latin American concession and arbitration disputes.

ence in 1899 and continued to oppose arbitration proceedings, which generally favored debtor nations by neutralizing superior European navies. The Germans, who knew the Americans were sensitive to the prospect of protracted hostilities in Venezuela, might be clumsy, but they were not foolhardy and reckless. American wariness verging on hysteria was well publicized in American and British newspapers; German diplomats were gravely concerned with their worsening image. Roosevelt's very presence, one historian has suggested, would have been sufficient ultimatum, with the navy ready, the British uneasy, and the Venezuelans far from defeated.[9]

Roosevelt was certain that "Germany was the leader and the really formidable party in the transaction." Arbitration gave the Americans a policy that would accomplish their primary goals: removal of European armies and navies from Caribbean waters, extrication of Britain from the misbegotten alliance with Germany with a minimum of damage to the Anglo-American détente, and a ringing reaffirmation of the Monroe Doctrine. When Roosevelt told Holleben that the German presence made Americans uneasy, the German diplomat offered the usual reassurances that Germany had pledged not to seize any territory permanently. Holleben's defense gave the president a chance to make his ultimatum as clear and forceful as possible. Roosevelt told Holleben: "Kiachau was not a 'permanent' possession of Germany— that I understood was merely held by a 99-year lease; and that I did not intend to have another Kiachau, held by similar tenure, on the approach to the Isthmian canal."[10]

Holleben repeated his government's refusal to arbitrate, whereupon Roosevelt responded that unless the Germans agreed to arbitration an American fleet under Admiral Dewey would "see that the German forces did not take possession of any territory." To underline the point, as well as the careful advance preparation, Roosevelt pointed out on a map the relative strength of Dewey's and the Germans' forces and America's enormous advantages fighting a na-

9. For Roosevelt's presence see Calvin de Armond Davis, *The United States and the Second Hague Peace Conference* (Durham, N.C., 1975), 82; for the politics of the arbitration movement see Donald Shea, *The Calvo Clause: A Problem of Inter-American and International Law and Diplomacy* (Minneapolis, 1955); and Margaret Robinson, *Arbitration and the Hague Peace Conferences, 1899 and 1907* (Philadelphia, 1936). For the reassuring style of both powers' diplomatic messages to the United States see Wilfred Hardy Calcott, *The Caribbean Policy of the United States* (Baltimore, 1942), 129.

10. TR to William R. Thayer, August 21, 1916, in *MRL*, VIII, 1101–1105; for the conversation see Joseph B. Bishop, *Theodore Roosevelt and His Times* (2 vols.; New York, 1920), I, 224–25.

val battle near its own coast. "A glance" at the map, Roosevelt told his startled listener, "would show him that there was no spot in the world where Germany in the event of a conflict with the United States would be at a greater disadvantage than in the Caribbean Sea."[11]

Too much of the Venezuelan historical controversy focuses on peripheral details that are mostly irrelevant. Holleben is a bit player in a larger historical confrontation between the new America and the new Germany, each using Britain as a foil, an ally, or a red herring depending on the circumstances. The contest between the countries was also a contest between two young and determined leaders, Theodore Roosevelt and Kaiser Wilhelm II, neither of whom, despite brilliance or determination, could change the geography of the world, which favored the Americans. Germany still had to play the aggressive imperialist to have any chance of overtaking Britain's enormous lead in colonial possessions and naval power. America remained protected by Britain's power and the enormous advantages of relying on a defensive naval strategy three thousand miles from Germany's nearest home base. Theodore Roosevelt did not have to be a genius to grasp a fundamental advantage which only ignorance or surprise could eliminate. The kaiser's entire Latin American strategy was based on an assumption of American innocence or ignorance.[12]

Roosevelt's personal diplomacy was dramatic, colorful, and interesting but in the Venezuelan episode not decisive. Arguments over Roosevelt's precise words to Holleben, who was a simple-minded figurehead and a dolt, are mostly irrelevant. As long as the American navy was on war alert in the Caribbean and the president was willing to use the navy, the Germans had no choice but to give up their coercive plan. The diplomats would work out the details of how and when Germany would concede. Once the kaiser received Holleben's message indicating American opposition, he appointed Speck von Sternburg, Roosevelt's close personal friend, to salvage what he could from Germany's Venezuelan diplomatic debacle.[13]

11. TR to William R. Thayer, August 21, 1916, in *MRL*, VIII, 1101–1105.

12. See Herwig, *Germany's Vision of Empire in Venezuela*, esp. 236–45; Herwig, *Politics of Frustration*, 77; Livermore, "Theodore Roosevelt," 455–65; Donald E. Shepardson, "Theodore Roosevelt and William II: The New Struggle for Atlantic Supremacy," in Harold T. Parker, *Problems in European History* (Durham, N.C., 1979), 165–76; and Paul Kennedy, "British and German Reactions to the Rise of American Power," in R. J. Bullen, H. Pogge von Strandmann, and A. B. Polonsky (eds.), *Ideas into History: Aspects of European History* (London, 1984), 15–24.

13. For Hay's negative assessment of Holleben see Beale, *Theodore Roosevelt*, 422, b; see also Henry Pringle, *Theodore Roosevelt: A Biography* (New York, 1931), 288; and Per-

Sternburg's appointment marked a major reversal of Roosevelt's influence on German diplomacy. Roosevelt had been unsuccessful earlier in 1902, when he appealed to both the kaiser and Prince Henry to appoint his young friend and regular correspondent as Berlin's American ambassador. On December 10, 1902, Sternburg was summoned to a personal meeting with the kaiser at which he stated "rather roughly" that the Americans were wary and shared with the German leader Roosevelt's views on Germany and Latin America that Holleben had failed to communicate clearly. Although he lacked the age, the rank, or the ability for a major diplomatic post, Sternburg was sent to the United States as emergency ambassador to replace Holleben, who was "ill." American Ambassador Charlemagne Tower in Berlin shortly confirmed that the kaiser wanted Roosevelt to know that though a formal appointment as ambassador had not been made, "the Emperor has decided to make Baron Sternburg his Ambassador to Washington." Sternburg's appointment meant that Germany was willing to conciliate but not necessarily to concede.[14]

Herbert Bowen, the American minister in Caracas, was not well liked even before he became a central figure in the Venezuelan dispute. Alvey Adee, the usually imperturbable assistant secretary of state, thought little of Bowen, who was dismissed from the service in 1905 after a bitter press scandal. On December 2, 1902, Bowen first suggested arbitration as a means of settling the Venezuelan dispute. Bowen won the confidence of all the principals when he successfully interceded with President Castro, who had imprisoned as many British and German civilians as his police could find. Castro, furious over what he considered an unprovoked attack on his navy, argued that the Anglo-German ultimatum on December 7 was not a declaration of

kins, *Monroe Doctrine, 1867–1907*, 368–69. For the French surprise at Holleben's sudden removal see Chargé de Margerie to MAE, January 12, 1903, in MAE, *Documents diplomatiques français, 1871–1914* (2nd ser., 14 vols.; Paris, 1930–55), III, 23–27.

14. TR to Speck von Sternburg, March 6, 1902 (unmailed); to Sternburg, March 8, 1902, in *MRL*, III, 239, 242; Sternburg to TR, December 15, 1902, in RP; Beale, *Theodore Roosevelt*, 429; Charlemagne Tower to JH, January 9, 15, 1902, in Despatches from United States Ministers to Germany, Microcopy M44, Roll 79, RG 59, NA; for Sternburg's relationship with TR see Nelson Manfred Blake, "Ambassadors at the Court of Theodore Roosevelt," *MVHR*, XLII (1955), 180–89; for German criticism of Sternburg's appointment see Herwig, *Germany's Vision of Empire in Venezuela*, 202–203; for Sternburg's inadequacy as a diplomat see Raymond A. Esthus, *Theodore Roosevelt and the International Rivalries* (1970; rpr. Claremont, Calif., 1985), 18–19; for Sternburg's birth in England, his English mother, his diplomatic career, and his American wife, see Guthrie, "Anglo-German Intervention," 218–220.

war. Bowen calmed the angry Castro, who declared that he would not accept humiliation or "try to placate with phrases." Instead, Castro "assured me [Bowen] several times that he would like to have the matter settled by arbitration." On December 11 John Hay approved Bowen as arbitrator and on December 12 the American minister framed Venezuela's formal request for arbitration. Bowen was in a unique position. He was acting as the representative of the British and German governments, as the American minister, and as Venezuela's representative in the proposed arbitration proceedings.[15]

Arbitration, though not an ideal solution, satisfied the immediate goals of both the Americans and the Venezuelans by removing armed European navies from New World waters. For the Europeans arbitration presented serious problems. It was much slower than an immediate settlement won through armed force, and because it was proposed by Venezuela and supported by the Americans, it would shift the diplomatic initiative from the Old to the New World. If the Americans were at one pole in favoring arbitration, the Germans were at the other, opposing arbitration at the Hague peace conferences in 1899 and 1907. At issue as well in 1902 was whether the Venezuelan dispute could be arbitrated. The Europeans had undertaken their coercive action because they were angry at Venezuela's aggressive behavior, rather than its failure to pay its debts. Only after the proceedings were under way did Venezuela's fiscal sins seem important. National honor, exacerbated by Venezuela's refusal to "placate with phrases" or deal in accepted diplomatic form with serious complaints, made the coercion more emotional and nationalistic than a demand for payment on defaulted loans. Economic issues were arbitrable, national or political issues were not. The Europeans had sound reasons for resisting the arbitration proposal.[16]

15. Platt, "Allied Coercion of Venezuela," 4–5; Lord Newton, *Lord Lansdowne: A Biography* (London, 1929), 259–60; Kneer, *Great Britain and the Caribbean*, 42–50. For the scandal in 1905 involving Bowen and Assistant Secretary of State Francis B. Loomis, see Dennis, *Adventures in American Diplomacy*, 298–99; Herbert Bowen, *Recollections Diplomatic and Undiplomatic* (New York, 1926), 287–313; and Guthrie, "Anglo-German Intervention," 328–29; a summary is in *MRL*, IV, 1164 n. Bowen to JH, December 2, 8, 9, 10, 1902; JH to Bowen, December 9, 11, 1902, all in *FRUS*, 1903, pp. 788–90; Bowen to JH, December 13, 1902, in Despatches, Venezuela, M79, Roll 56, NA.

16. Kneer, *Great Britain and the Caribbean*, 16–17, 35–39; Beale, *Theodore Roosevelt*, 413–16; Rippy, *Latin America in World Politics*, 197; Hood, *Gunboat Diplomacy*, 181–83; Platt, "Allied Coercion of Venezuela," 11–15. For German opposition to arbitration see Robinson, *Arbitration and the Hague Peace Conferences*, 132–36; Herwig, *Germany's Vision of Empire in Venezuela*, 98–101.

When Secretary Hay transmitted the Venezuelan request to the Germans and British, the Americans and Venezuelans became united in a common cause, the removal of European armed intervention from the New World. Neither of the American allies liked the other, but they liked the intervening European powers even less. Their co-operation deprived the Europeans of their only advantage, the ability to overwhelm a powerless adversary. Venezuela enjoyed some substantial additional advantages. The Europeans were fearful of the unhealthiness of the terrain and feared the casualties that would result from armed conflict. La Guaira, a key customs port, could be defended from nearby hills. By resisting at La Guaira, Castro could have inflicted substantial casualties on an invading force. Infuriated by the attacks, more than one hundred thousand Venezuelans enlisted to battle the invaders. The British had realized from the start that they would be at a disadvantage in any land contest. By refusing to surrender when its navy was sunk and then enlisting the Americans as diplomatic allies, Venezuela survived the critical first blows.[17]

The scene of battle shifted from Caracas and Washington to London, where public shock over the violence seriously undermined the Anglo-German alliance. Not only was "acting with Germans unpopular in this country, sinking of ships certainly is," Henry White informed John Hay. White, the acting American ambassador, who had many friends in the British government, including Prime Minister Arthur Balfour, began his diplomatic campaign to divide the British and Germans and to convince the British that continuing the coercion would strain American friendship. White was immediately assured that the British did not intend to land troops in Venezuela or to participate in the German plan for a "pacific blockade." In an extraordinary interview with Balfour, White spoke frankly and warned the British against being led by Germany, alienating American public opinion, or extending the conflict. Balfour told White to assure Secretary Hay privately that landing of troops in Venezuela would be a "positive calamity." Debates in Parliament were sharply critical of the German alliance, and to placate American feelings, several members of Parliament spoke glowingly of the Monroe Doctrine.[18]

17. Lord Lansdowne to Count Metternich, December 2, 1902, in *GTBD*, II, 160; Sullivan, "Rise of Despotism in Venezuela," 333–34; Hood, *Gunboat Diplomacy*, 166–70, 184; Gelber, *Rise of Anglo-American Friendship*, 112–17; Platt, "Allied Coercion of Venezuela," 8–9.

18. Henry White to JH, December 15, 16, 17, 1902, in Despatches from United States Ministers to Great Britain, Microcopy, M30, Roll 193, NA; see also Lord Lansdowne to

On December 15 Lord Lansdowne, yielding to American pressure, refused German Ambassador Count Metternich's plea for a joint German-British seizure of the Venezuelan ports. The American initiative for arbitration was well conceived and well executed. On December 12 the Americans simply transmitted Venezuela's request. On December 15 Hay wrote of the "great desirability" of arbitration, which impressed Lansdowne, who gradually softened his initial opposition. By December 18 Lansdowne had capitulated; White's wire to Hay was jubilant: "You will receive shortly important and very satisfactory cipher cablegram from me. Principle of arbitration accepted." [19]

Theodore Roosevelt thrived as the American-European diplomatic confrontation dominated the news. In a well-publicized December 16 cabinet meeting the president ordered four American battleships and two cruisers to Trinidad and Curaçao, thereby giving the United States absolute naval superiority over the combined German and British forces in the blockade area. When Roosevelt released maps of the war zone to the press, major newspapers in Chicago, New York, and Washington carried news of the dramatic new naval plans. To underscore the possible gravity of the situation, Secretary of the Navy William Moody personally took over supervision of the Caribbean fleet. Dewey remained the fleet commander, but it was clear that Washington was orchestrating the moves. Detailed analyses of the meaning of the new naval moves appeared in the major newspapers. Rarely has a cabinet meeting been as effectively publicized. [20]

By now the combined American diplomatic and naval offensive was irresistible; as the Germans and the British became more suspicious of each other's motives, the temporary alliance disintegrated. As late as December 15, 1902, both Britain and Germany were proceeding with invasion and against arbitration. By December 18, when Count Metternich advised the kaiser to accept arbitration, both nations were grateful to accept that face-saving solution. The avalanche of reports of further American naval or diplomatic action had made Britain fear-

---

Michael Herbert, December 15, 1902, British Blue Book, Venezuela, No. 1, 1903, rpr. in *Senate Documents*, 58th Cong., 3rd Sess., No. 119, Serial 4769, p. 675, hereinafter cited as British Blue Book, Ser. 4769; Allan Nevins, *Henry White: Thirty Years of American Diplomacy* (New York, 1930), 210; Campbell, *Anglo-American Understanding*, 278–81.

19. Henry White to JH, December 18, 1902, in Despatches, Great Britain, M30, Roll 193.

20. Holbo, "Perilous Obscurity," 433–35; Livermore, "Theodore Roosevelt," 463–64. For an analysis of the press reaction see Guthrie, "Anglo-German Intervention," 138–47.

ful, and an isolated Germany could no longer resist the American pressure. Even in retrospect it is astonishing that the United States could deliver a formal ultimatum to the two most powerful European powers on December 17, 1902, and achieve total acceptance the following day. So great was the diplomatic reversal that Lord Lansdowne requested that the United States not use the word *urgently* when it published the diplomatic correspondence. Lansdowne did not want to appear to have submitted to pressure.[21]

The intense American sense of victory over the Europeans' backing down from their coercive action and accepting the principle of arbitration in the Venezuelan dispute was short-lived. Summarizing the conflict to former President Grover Cleveland on December 26, Roosevelt cited "getting England and Germany explicitly to recognize the Monroe Doctrine . . . and in getting all of the parties . . . to accept arbitration by the Hague Court" as his main accomplishments. Roosevelt was tempted to honor European requests that he rather than the Hague Court act as arbitrator, but the United States still feared placing the Monroe Doctrine principle even indirectly before the whims of an international court, a skepticism justified by the Hague Court's ultimate decision in favor of the coercing powers. Had Europe insisted, Roosevelt, despite his support for the Hague Court principle, might have accepted the role of arbitrator, though by so doing he would have sacrificed any hope of settling the large American private claims against Venezuela.[22]

Although Roosevelt publicly insisted that acceptance of the Hague arbitration principle was "a great triumph," he knew that the United States had won not a victory but a stalemate. "We are not out of the woods by any means," he confided to his friend the editor Albert Shaw. The dangers were painfully obvious: "the chances of complication from a long and irritating little war between the European powers and Venezuela" were considerable. A diplomatic resolution of the dispute was neither routine nor certain. There was "a chance of complications in connection with the terms of the arbitration." Europe, the United States, and Venezuela all shared the sense of urgency for a speedy resolution of the stalemate, the main reason everyone wanted

21. For a detailed description of other British and German suppressed diplomatic documents, see Marks, *Velvet on Iron*, 43–47.

22. TR to Grover Cleveland, December 26, 1902; to Albert Shaw, December 26, 1902, both in *MRL*, III, 398, 396–97; Davis, *United States and the Second Hague Peace Conference*, 82–83.

Roosevelt himself to arbitrate. There would be no "red tape or pedantry," Lord Lansdowne declared, if the president decided the issues.[23]

Although the original coercion had ended, the situation remained menacing. British Prime Minister Arthur Balfour publicly dismissed the German contention that blockades could be peaceful. "A blockade does involve a state of war," Balfour told the House of Commons. The formal declaration of blockade of December 20, 1902, dealt leniently with neutral ships but harshly with Venezuela. The combined European naval force of fourteen vessels, including British (28,750 tons), Italian (14,800 tons), and German (11,147 tons) squadrons, was dwarfed by the American fleet of fifty-four vessels (129,822 tons). The Americans used their overwhelming naval superiority to exert pressure on the German diplomatic corps in Washington, thoroughly demoralized by the intensity of American public antipathy toward Germany. Chargé Albert von Quadt, concerned about press reports of the continued American naval buildup, was hardly calmed when John Hay threatened to unleash Congress as well as the navy on a recalcitrant Germany, while reiterating America's peaceful intentions. Putting naval pressure on Germany and diplomatic pressure on Great Britain remained effective American tactics throughout the entire Venezuelan crisis.[24]

The German warship *Panther*, which had complicated the initial coercion by sinking rather than capturing two Venezuelan ships, compounded the situation when it leveled a Venezuelan fort on January 21. The actions of the *Panther*'s Commodore Georg Scheder accurately reflected his government's unyielding attitude, which remained the main obstacle to an easy settlement. While Britain's first-line claims—a modest $27,500 (£5,500) to satisfy national honor for direct outrages—remained constant throughout the dispute, German demands (high to begin with) fluctuated sharply. By including Venezuela's external debt as part of its first-line claims Germany demanded

23. TR to Albert Shaw, December 26, 1902; to Carl Schurz, December 26, 1902, both in *MRL*, III, 396–97; Lord Lansdowne to Michael Herbert, in British Blue Book, Ser. 4769, p. 686.

24. Henry White to JH, December 18, 1902, in *FRUS*, 1903, p. 455; Herwig, *Politics of Frustration*, 81; Parsons, "German-American Crisis of 1902–1903," 444–45; Albert von Quadt to German Foreign Office, December 18, 1902, in *GP*, XVII, 269. For British and German naval inadequacy see Guthrie, "Anglo-German Intervention," 24, 61–62, 91–94. For the French confusion over whether a blockade was in effect, what it covered, and the official British notice from Vice-Admiral Sir Archibald Lucius Douglass, December 12, 20, 1903, see the loose correspondence in Mission du *Troude* (1901–1906) in BB⁴, 1623, Archives de la Marine, Château de Vincennes.

an immediate Venezuelan payment of $325,000. The Germans insisted throughout the negotiations that their $325,000 was equal to Britain's $27,500 and must be paid in cash before any other claims could be arbitrated. Even after the negotiations had reached a critical stage, complicated by the disparity of the Anglo-German claims, the Germans wanted to add the cost of the blockade to their demands.[25]

If Germany created constant friction in the negotiations, so did Herbert Bowen, the American minister to Venezuela. Bowen had made himself indispensable in the Venezuelan crisis, mainly by winning the confidence of President Cipriano Castro. But Bowen was a mean opportunist, disliked in the State Department and despised by the British. British Ambassador Michael Herbert thought Bowen "a blustering, insolent, untrustworthy cad"; A. L. P. Dennis, an American diplomat and historian, thought Bowen "an injudicious and officious person." The authenticity of Bowen's pose as champion of Venezuela was questionable. A year before he had confided to the British minister William Haggard that Caracas should be occupied by foreign troops when the Castro government collapsed. Later, in 1905, when Bowen's indiscretions resulted in a public scandal, Roosevelt had an "iridescent dream" in which "Castro would execute Bowen and thereby give us good reason for smashing Castro." Although they despised him, the British preferred dealing with Bowen to lengthy Hague Court proceedings or to dealing directly with a Venezuelan. When the United States assured the Europeans that Bowen would be independent of any American instructions or guidance, they accepted him as the negotiator.[26]

All of the disputants dreaded the prospect of a Hague Court proceeding. The Europeans insisted that national claims, as opposed to monetary or commerical matters, were not subject to arbitration, much as Theodore Roosevelt refused to arbitrate anything remotely connected with the Monroe Doctrine. Venezuela objected to the cost and the time involved in a judicial proceeding. The blockade hurt

25. The original discussion is in Lord Lansdowne to George Buchanan, November 11, 1902, in *GTBD*, II, 156–57; Germany's first-line claims are in Charlemagne Tower to JH, December 24, 1902, in *FRUS*, 1903, pp. 426–27; Kneer, *Great Britain and the Caribbean*, 46–47; Lansdowne to Sir Frank Lascelles, January 22, 1903, in *GTBD*, II, 164–65; Platt, "Allied Coercion of Venezuela," 16–27.

26. Kneer, *Great Britain and the Caribbean*, 58; Dennis, *Adventures in American Diplomacy*, 295; Platt, "Allied Coercion of Venezuela," 4–5. For a survey of the diplomatic corps in Caracas see Guthrie, "Anglo-German Intervention," 109–13; TR to William Howard Taft, April 20, 1905, in *MRL*, IV, 1163.

Venezuelan civilians; the loss of its small navy interfered with Venezuela's civil war, always Castro's first priority. There were so many revolutionists, Bowen reported, that if they obtained supplies and arms, disorder could become permanent. Venezuela preferred settling as many claims as possible for cash, getting the blockade lifted and its warships returned, and resuming its civil war.[27]

Castro was an impatient Latin American caudillo, indifferent to big power diplomacy and scornful of foreign intrusions. Whatever the immediate cost, Castro wanted to end the blockade and the negotiations, which were distracting him from his main and pressing concern, consolidating his power as Venezuela's president. Citing Venezuelan helplessness, he agreed quickly and shrewdly to all of Bowen's proposals. He first agreed to accept Roosevelt as arbitrator, then to Hague arbitration, and finally to every European claim. Castro insisted that all the claims against Venezuela would already have been settled if the civil wars had not distracted the government. Castro was unrepentant. "The time has arrived" not to pay debts but "to yield to force." Castro probably still believed on January 7, 1903, as he told Bowen, "that the claims against him are purely commercial." If the powers wanted to take the case to the Hague, at least they should raise the blockade and let Venezuela continue its civil wars. Castro's belief that the controversy "could be settled at Washington, easily, quickly, and at little expense," was echoed by Lord Lansdowne, who thought the whole matter could have been settled in twenty-four hours. But there was no quick resolution. Even after Castro recognized the European claims in principle on January 1, 1903, and then pledged Venezuelan customs receipts as a guarantee for them, the blockade and the proceedings continued. No one trusted Castro, Bowen enjoyed the limelight as the chief negotiator, and Germany refused to be reasonable.[28]

Germany nullified many of its apparent agreements by adding onerous conditions. Germany's January 5 acceptance of Bowen as Venezuela's representative was dependent on Venezuela's "unconditional acceptance of the three preliminary conditions" listed in Germany's December 22, 1902, memorandum and an acceptable method of pay-

<hr/>

27. *FRUS*, 1903, pp. 461–62, 427–28; Herbert Bowen to JH, December 20, 1902, *ibid.*, 800; Bowen to JH, December 13, 1902, Despatches, Venezuela, M79, Roll 56.
28. See *FRUS*, 1903, pp. 802–803; Herbert Bowen to JH, January 6, 1903, in Despatches, Venezuela, M79, Roll 56; Kneer, *Great Britain and the Caribbean*, 40–41. For Castro's ambitions to conquer Columbia and British encouragement of a Colombia-Trinidad alliance against Castro see Hood, *Gunboat Diplomacy*, 76–81.

ment. The impatient Castro agreed to all German demands by return cable. When on January 8 Castro agreed to pay all outstanding claims and guaranteed the payment from future receipts of Venezuela's two customs houses, the Anglo-German blockade should have been lifted. When the Germans delayed, Venezuela fought back. Castro circumvented some of the effects of the blockade by opening the Colombian-Venezuelan border. When the *Panther* tried to tighten the blockade by closing the narrow channel at Maracaibo, Castro ordered Fort San Carlos not to permit the German ship to pass. The *Panther*, undamaged from the attack on January 17, returned with the *Falke* on January 21 and destroyed the Venezuelan fort. The Germans were justified in firing on the fort but not in intentionally "punishing" it with a barrage of 110 shots. The *Panther*'s shots reverberated through a world shocked at such a gross overreaction while negotiations were proceeding so well.[29]

When the news of the incident reached Washington, Roosevelt roared at Quadt, "Are people in Berlin crazy? Don't they know that they are inflaming public opinion more and more here? Don't they know they will be left alone without England?" Prime Minister Balfour was anxious and annoyed at the Germans; the public unhappiness led Henry White on January 24 to suggest that if it "became known that Germany is the obstacle to or even delaying settlement public opinion here would compel the abandonment" of the alliance. Two days later White reported that the British were losing patience with their German allies and were considering a separate settlement.[30]

British Ambassador Sir Michael Herbert had noted American anger in December: "The outburst in this country against the Germans has been truly remarkable, and suspicion of the German Emperor's designs in the Caribbean Sea is shared by the Administration, the press, and the public alike." At the time British participation was welcomed as a reassuring check on further German aggression. American suspicions of Germany were not eased by a report in early January that Germany planned to acquire the unfinished Panama Canal. The report was taken seriously by the Americans, who discussed two ver-

29. William Russell to JH, January 28, 1903, Despatches, M79, Roll 56, NA; Beale, *Theodore Roosevelt*, 423; Kneer, *Great Britain and the Caribbean*, 44; Herwig, *Politics of Frustration*, 79; Guthrie, "Anglo-German Intervention," 205–209; Herwig and Helguera, *Alemania y el bloquero internacional de Venezuela*, 34–38.

30. TR's conversation with Quadt is in Vagts, *Deutschland und die Vereinigten Staaten in Der Weltpolitik*, II, 1595; Henry White to JH, January 24, 26, 1903, in Despatches, Great Britain, M30, Roll 193.

sions of the rumored sale, one for $40 million to "German interests" and one as an exchange with Colombia for liquidation of German claims. Baron Oswald von Richthofen denied the report as "a pure invention." Herbert said that after the Fort San Carlos incident "there is a feeling of intense irritation in the United States against Germany" and advised that political pressure on Roosevelt would result if it appeared Germany was delaying settlement.[31]

Meanwhile, Herbert Bowen's first settlement proposal called for all claims against Venezuela to be paid from 30 percent of customs receipts collected at La Guaira and Puerto Cabello, Venezuela's two major ports. By not specifying special payments to the blockading nations Bowen tried to avoid the question of preferential treatment, an issue that threatened to break down the negotiations and eventually had to be settled by the Hague Court. Thirty percent of Venezuela's customs receipts would not pay all of Venezuela's creditors, though it might pay Britain, Germany, and Italy. The blockading nations demanded preferential payment, not out of greed but because Venezuela's instability made long-term payment plans impractical. The blockading powers' claims of $4.5 million and the nonblockading nations' claims of nearly $6 million were to be paid in Bowen's proposal from dedicated customs revenues of about $1 million annually. Venezuela's total annual income (all from customs revenues) was only $6 million. The 30 percent would be levied on the $3.6 million annual revenue from the two ports. Therefore, for Britain preferential treatment was not a principle but a practical matter. Lansdowne feared lumping all claims together with everyone waiting an equal time for payment.[32]

The British, trying to work out a practical arrangement, were eager to compromise, at first by accepting a five-year settlement, later by suggesting several alternatives. Bowen resolutely refused to favor the blockading powers, insisting, mistakenly it turned out, that the Hague Court would not support preferential payments. Bowen was at his intemperate best in apparently genuine revulsion at the idea: "I can not accept even in principle that preferential treatment can be rightly obtained by blockades and bombardments. It would be absolutely offensive to modern civilization to recognize that principle."

31. Michael Herbert to Lord Lansdowne, December 29, 1902, in *GTBD*, 163–64; Charlemagne Tower to JH, January 9, 13, 1903, in Despatches, Germany, M44, Roll 97; Herbert to Lansdowne, January 26, 1903, in *GTBD*, II, 166.

32. Bowen Correspondence in *Senate Documents*, 58th Cong., 2nd Sess., No. 316, Serial 4620, p. 1039.

Herbert countered with an intelligent compromise that proposed dividing the 30 percent in thirds, with two-thirds going to the blockading nations and one-third to the "peace powers." But Bowen and the British remained equally unconvinced as the ideological stalemate complemented the naval stalemate and tempers grew short in London and Washington. Bowen's proposal that Belgium administer the two Venezuelan ports and both customs and payments caused no objections in Washington, though the idea clearly violated the Monroe Doctrine. A year later, when Castro refused to pay other debts, Roosevelt suggested to Hay that "we had better take possession of the custom house and put in Belgium or other representatives of the Hague Court."[33]

German aggressiveness, Bowen's frequent obtuseness, and the issue of preferential treatment all threatened the negotiations. Bowen was on respectable ground with his objections to preferential treatment, which he hoped could be satisfied "simply as a point of honor." When Bowen boasted to the Italian minister that his main aim was to divide the German and British representatives, and when he gave the press confidential information on the negotiations with Britain, these indiscretions goaded the usually calm Herbert into a rage.[34]

Roosevelt became pessimistic. When Speck von Sternburg arrived on February 1 as the new German ambassador, Roosevelt confided to his son, "I do not believe he can do anything on the Venezuela matter." American naval maneuvers remained prominently in the news. New battleships joined Rear Admiral Francis J. Higginson's squadron at Culebra and other warships remained close by at different Caribbean stations. As part of the continuing naval publicity, all naval yards and stations were ordered to a state of full mobilization on January 29, and the press was given details of a cabinet discussion concerning naval and military appropriations and the strengthening of American coastal defenses. In conversations with "nice little Baron Speck," Roosevelt informed the new German ambassador that Admiral Dewey, always useful as a red flag to wave at the Germans, had "secret orders" from 1902, which were still in effect. As Roosevelt in-

33. For Venezuela's income see Michael Herbert to Lord Lansdowne, January 24, 1903; for Lansdowne's reasons for preferential treatment and the difficulties with Bowen's projections, see Lansdowne to Herbert, January 26, 1903, both in British Blue Book, Ser. 4769, pp. 733–35; Bowen Correspondence, 1036; TR to JH, August 30, 1904, in MRL, IV, 914; Lord Lansdowne to Frank Lascelles, January 27, 1903, in GTBD, II, 167.

34. Kneer, Great Britain and the Caribbean, 50; Lord Lansdowne to Frank Lascelles, February 6, 1903, in GTBD, II, 171; Beale, Theodore Roosevelt, 426.

tended, Sternburg warned his Foreign Office of Roosevelt's continued strong feeling. Roosevelt was genuinely concerned. He asked for specific information on German Caribbean naval strength on February 5. Britain warned that the Germans were buying two Chilean battleships; though they were unsuited to the American navy, the British urged the Americans to buy them to keep them from Germany. The report proved unfounded but caused concern. Henry Adams compared the kaiser and the president: "Our Emperor . . . more irrepressible than ever . . . sits in the midst of a score of politicians and reporters describing his preparations for a war with Germany."[35]

Britain, under extreme political pressure from the United States and from its Germanophobic press and public opinion, wanted the Venezuelan matter finished. The alliance with Germany was fraying badly. Metternich and Bülow defended the Fort San Carlos incident and continued to press Bowen for a larger cash settlement than Britain. The British considered appealing to Roosevelt once again to arbitrate even though Count Metternich was sure that the president would rule against preferential treatment. On February 4, Metternich became concerned that the continuing Venezuelan problems might bring down the British government.[36]

The British were caught in a desperate political situation. The reasonableness of their proposals was lost in being tied in with the German and Italian demands, which were at best questionable and at worst greedy. Already under pressure because of the increasingly burdensome German alliance, the British were also frustrated by Bowen's alternating idealism and opportunism. Who could the British turn to? They had chosen Bowen over the Hague because that choice had seemed faster. Now the Hague seemed preferable. The Americans and British had grown closer during the dispute because of their common purpose. Both desperately wanted to be done with the situation and to be rid of the fear of further dangerous incidents. The Germans did not share this sense of urgency. Germany wanted its settle-

35. Livermore, "Theodore Roosevelt," 466–69; TR to TRJR, February 9, 1903, in *MRL*, III, 423; Beale, *Theodore Roosevelt*, 425; Adams quoted *ibid.*, 424; Sternburg warning is in *GP*, XVII, 286.

36. Count Metternich to Count von Bülow, February 4, 1903, in E. T. S. Dugdale, *German Diplomatic Documents, 1817–1914* (4 vols.; London, 1930), III, 164–65; Lord Lansdowne to Frank Lascelles, January 27, 28, 1903, in *GTBD*, II, 167, 168; Beale, *Theodore Roosevelt*, 426.

ment. The Germans appeared to be willing to take risks to get what they wanted, but actually they were unaware that any risks were involved. For Germany the debt existed, it must be paid, and no one could question something so obvious. Nor were the Germans greedy. They remained single-minded and insensitive, at odds with their increasingly reluctant British allies as the Venezuelan blockade continued into February.[37]

On February 6, the British pleaded for help from Theodore Roosevelt. They proposed accepting all the settlements already made and having the president "decide the single point"—preferential treatment—that blocked a complete agreement. Roosevelt demurred. Although there is no evidence that he even considered undertaking such a role, Roosevelt and Hay (like Bowen) were probably confident that the Hague Court would not reward acts of war such as blockades and therefore were willing to have that court suffer the onus of an unpopular decision. If ever there was a golden opportunity to use a big stick, this was it. Roosevelt could have dramatically rejected preferential treatment as vociferously as Herbert Bowen had but much more effectively. But the Americans were not thinking of big sticks or looking for opportunities to win confrontations even against the troublesome Germans. In December, when Roosevelt had originally moved the dispute to the Hague, he was hailed as a peacemaker and a statesman. In turning down the British plea of February 6, although he may have missed a rare opportunity to impose an American settlement on Europe, he genuinely preferred an impartial judicial settlement to direct American intervention.[38]

When it became clear that the preferential treatment issue would be decided at the Hague, the resolution of the first-rank claims became the last obstacle to lifting the blockade. Britain agreed to a cash payment of $27,500, Germany demanded $330,000 in cash at once, and Italy $560,000 in cash. Germany rejected Bowen's offer that each power receive $27,500 and refused to lift the blockade while negotiations continued. German attempts to compromise centered on con-

37. Gelber, *Rise of Anglo-American Friendship*, 120–25; Allen, *Great Britain and the United States*, 605–607; Dennis, *Adventures in American Diplomacy*, 294–95; Beale, *Theodore Roosevelt*, 425–29.

38. Michael Herbert to JH, February 6, 1903; JH to Herbert, February 6, 1903, both in *FRUS*, 1903, pp. 473–75. For examples of praise for TR's original Hague decision see Davis, *United States and the Second Hague Peace Conference*, 83; Tyler Dennett, *John Hay* (New York, 1933), 389.

vincing the Italians to postpone their questionable first-rank claims. Collecting the large sum of money was "a point of honour" and one the Germans pursued with extreme pressure on Bowen.[39]

Britain seriously considered ending the alliance. On February 7, Ambassador Herbert called the German demands "unfair" and argued that the British, who had managed to balance friendship with the United States and an alliance with Germany, must make a formal choice. "A great change has taken place" in American feeling. Continued alliance with Germany, Herbert warned, would damage Anglo-American relations: "The time has almost come, in American opinion, for us to make the choice between the friendship of the United States and that of Germany." Britain's alliance with Germany had never been popular with the public or the press. Kipling's anti-German poem "The Rowers," which concluded with the phrase "the shameless Hun," was published in the London *Times* in December; its popularity summarized British feelings about the alliance. Lansdowne's words to Metternich were the diplomatic equivalent of Kipling's verse. "Utmost frankness," "gravity," and "almost intolerable" well described the Anglo-German alliance; although Lansdowne added that "we had no intention of deserting Germany," his assurance was followed by a "but." Theodore Roosevelt did not address Count Metternich, but he shared Britain's exasperation: "My chief difficulty at the moment is the Venezuela matter in which Germany takes an impossible stand."[40]

Germany became both more impossible and totally and unexpectedly victorious. Bowen and Sternburg agreed to a complicated compromise whereby all the intervening powers would be paid $27,500 at once. Italy waived its immediate demands, and Germany was to re-

---

39. For a summary of the British claims and Venezuela's external debt see the long letter and memorandum, Lord Lansdowne to Michael Herbert, British Blue Book, Ser. 4769, pp. 719–27; for the German claims see *FRUS*, 1902, pp. 429–31; for the Italian claims see Vernassa, *Emigrazione, diplomazia e cannoniero;* see also J. Fred Rippy, "The Venezuelan Claims Settlements of 1903–05: A Case Study in the Cost of Disorder, Despotism, and Deficient Capital and Technology," *Inter-American Economic Affairs,* VII (1954), 65–77; Lord Lansdowne to Frank Lascelles, February 10, 1903, in FO 420/213, PRO.

40. Michael Herbert to Lord Lansdowne, February 7, 1903; Lansdowne to Herbert, February 7, 1903, both in *GTBD*, II, 172–73; TR to TRJR, February 9, 1901, in *MRL*, III, 423; see also Henry White to JH, February 10, 1903, in Despatches, Great Britain, M30, Roll 193; Kipling's "The Rowers" is in London *Times*, December 22, 1902; for the poem's significance as a watershed for European history see Herwig, *Germany's Vision of Empire in Venezuela,* 240; and Guthrie, "Anglo-German Intervention," viii–ix.

ceive half of its first-class claims in three months. Metternich rejected the compromise, reiterating the German demand for full cash payment even though the British were furious that the Germans would be paid $180,000 compared to their own $27,500. When the Germans insisted on full payment, Lansdowne was fully prepared to withdraw from the alliance, an action that might have convinced the Germans to yield. But Bowen, not the Germans, finally gave up as the German tactic of unrelenting pressure paid off. Bowen agreed to all the German demands, paying the entire first-rank claim of $343,763 with $27,500 in cash and five monthly payments of $63,305. The protocols were signed on February 14, and the blockade was lifted.[41]

The protocols of February 14, 1903, signed by Germany, Britain, Italy, and Venezuela, specified lifting the blockade, returning Venezuela's captured naval vessels, and the terms of payment reached in the Bowen agreement. Mixed claims commissions, a customary means of settling international commercial disputes, decided how much Venezuela had to pay each nation. Both Venezuela and the claiming nation chose one representative, and President Roosevelt appointed a neutral who would decide the case if the two nationals could not agree. The queen of the Netherlands was named the umpire for the substantial American claims against Venezuela. To pay the claims and awards, 30 percent of the customs receipts from the Venezuelan ports at La Guaira and Puerto Cabello were remitted monthly and secured in a Bank of England account until the Hague Court determined what proportions should be paid to each claiming power.[42]

There were no winners in the Venezuelan coercion crisis. Venezuela lost very little because it had the least to lose. True, Castro had to settle the enormous debt as well as pay the substantial war claims of the blockading powers. But for Castro winning the civil war in Venezuela was all that mattered. He used the world powers as adjuncts to his own limited—parochial—goal of winning his civil war. He sought to be free both from the distraction of big power diplomacy and from British aid to the threatening anti-government forces. Castro won his civil war, consolidated his power, and changed the nature of Venezuelan politics. Although Castro was driven from power in 1908,

41. Kneer, *Great Britain and the Caribbean*, 54–55, has the clearest summary. For the rejected compromise see "A Concession to Germany," Bowen Correspondence, 1040.
42. Protocols are in Bowen Correspondence, 1041–57; the Venezuela–United States Mixed Claims Commission decision awarding $7,691,716 is in *FRUS*, 1904, p. 871.

his successor and former ally, Juan Vicente Gómez, followed the structure Castro had created and ruled until 1935—an unprecedented period of stability for revolutionary Venezuela. Gómez' long reign may not have benefited the people of Venezuela, but that is another question. Castro had won, and his tactics of hectoring foreigners and playing one nation off against the other proved remarkably successful in maintaining power in a country whose leaders and constitutions changed almost with the seasons.[43]

Germany neither won nor lost. German honor was upheld, and the Venezuelans had to pay dearly, but German diplomatic and naval excesses did not win it any new markets or friends. Bowen had rebelled at the German demands and warned Sternburg that the money Venezuela had to pay under duress would cost the Germans much more in loss of goodwill and trade in Latin America. There is no evidence that the Germans lost any more Latin American goodwill than the Americans did. The Germans had little to lose except possible expansion in the Caribbean, which was unlikely anyway. Extremely wary of German expansion, the American Congress and public were willing to support building a larger navy as assurance that the Germans could be checked. Alfred Vagts, a distinguished German historian, dismissed the Venezuelan episode as a gambit for both sides to win domestic support for larger navies. Vagts is correct about the effect but not the cause. American and German naval expansion, in full flower before Venezuela, demonstrated the continued overwhelming superiority of the British navy. Only the informal alliance with Britain gave the Americans the appearance of naval superiority. Long-range German losses were inconsequential, but the short-term German gain was equally small. Even the German loss in Europe was minor. Any permanent alliance with Britain was impossible, but it had been before Venezuela.[44]

43. Ewell, *Venezuela*, 46–59; Hood, *Gunboat Diplomacy*, 192–94. For Castro's victory see Sullivan, "Rise of Despotism in Venezuela," 349–50; for the German "Pyrrhic victory" see Guthrie, "Anglo-German Intervention," 316–25; Holbo, "Perilous Obscurity," 447; Parsons, "German-American Crisis of 1902–03," 450–51.

44. Bowen's threat is in JH to Henry White, February 16, 1903, in Hay Papers, LC; Vagts, *Deutschland*, II, 1525–1635; Guthrie, "Anglo-German Intervention," 297; for the end of German ambitions in Venezuela see Herwig, *Germany's Vision of Empire in Venezuela*, esp. 67–68, 207–208, 240; for the Anglo-German naval rivalry see Gelber, *Rise of Anglo-American Friendship*, 128–29; and Ernest L. Woodward, *Great Britain and the German Navy* (Oxford, 1935), 3–86. For increased naval cooperation between the United States and Britain see Arthur J. Marder, *The Anatomy of British Naval Policy in the Pre-Dreadnought Era, 1880–1905* (New York, 1940), 442–50. For the American navy's fears of German naval superiority see Spector, "Roosevelt, the Navy, and the Venezuela Con-

Some historians find striking similarities—and some equally sharp dissimilarities—between Wilhelm II and Theodore Roosevelt. Perhaps the more useful comparison among the principals in the Anglo-German intervention is between Cipriano Castro and Wilhelm II. Both were single-minded, used other nations to achieve their own ends, acted belligerently, swaggered when they walked, and when pressed retaliated with an excess of violence. Although both leaders were superficially successful, Castro in resuming and winning his civil war, the kaiser in winning a large cash settlement, both leaders' triumphs eventually damaged their own countries as well as future world peace. The kaiser's diplomacy ended in the trenches of Europe and a ghastly world war; Castro's repeated acts of irresponsibility helped make intervention and dependency legacies of an increasingly authoritarian Latin America.[45]

Theodore Roosevelt did not win the Venezuelan episode. By following a policy of mediation he acquitted himself well in the confrontation. By preparing the navy for any contingency he assured that the Germans would not be tempted by New World opportunities while enforcing their point of honor on Venezuela. Roosevelt did not so much overstate his role in the Venezuelan crisis as wrench it out of its proper historical context. He undoubtedly gave ultimatums to a weak German ambassador, and Berlin took his warnings about the Monroe Doctrine seriously. In 1916 Roosevelt used his 1902 diplomacy—effective then because it was confidential and not public—to try to influence President Woodrow Wilson's foreign policy, ignoring the huge differences between 1916 and 1902, when preventive diplomacy was still possible and Germany was not involved in a European war. By making history serve a political purpose Roosevelt undermined both his own credibility and the necessary confidentiality of personal diplomacy. Historians, annoyed by the spectacle of the

---

troversy," 257–63. For Britain's urging of American assumption of Caribbean responsibility see Perkins, *Monroe Doctrine, 1867–1907*, 362–63; and Kneer, *Great Britain in the Caribbean*, 61–62. For the German diplomatic and naval retreat see George T. Davis, *A Navy Second to None: The Development of Modern American Naval Policy* (New York, 1940), 123–27. See also Herwig and Helguera, *Alemania y el bloquero internacional de Venezuela*, 41–47.

45. For comparisons of TR and Wilhelm II see Beale, *Theodore Roosevelt*, 441–42; Jonas, *United States and Germany*, 67–68; Marks, *Velvet on Iron*, 174; For the "Teddy-Willy" correspondence see Herwig, *Germany's Vision of Empire in Venezuela*, 206–207. For a perceptive analysis of Roosevelt's relationship with Wilhelm II see Esthus, *Theodore Roosevelt and the International Rivalries*, 38, 55–56, 59–63, 80, 126–31. For the kaiser's objections to Castro's swaggering see Herwig, *Politics of Frustration*, 79.

principal actor in a diplomatic drama also playing a role as its first historian (with his own newly created sources), demanded further documentary evidence. Roosevelt, who used nuance masterfully in diplomacy but seldom in the history he wrote, may have overstated the severity of his personal ultimatum to Holleben. Roosevelt's several ultimatums—naval, diplomatic, and personal in 1902—did not prevent the Germans from coercing Venezuela but effectively limited the nature of the coercion and the likelihood of further German adventures. Roosevelt chose his targets and tactics to make specific points. In 1916 Woodrow Wilson as much as Germany was the target. In 1903, when it suited President Roosevelt to be gracious and generous, he reprimanded Admirals Taylor and Dewey for their intemperate remarks against the Germans after the crisis, though privately he sympathized with Dewey's attitude. In 1916 he had no choice but to play the polemicist since Wilson was America's duly elected president.[46]

Although the eventual Hague Court ruling turned out to be disastrous for the American strategy of international arbitration, in moving the dispute out of the seas and into the courts Roosevelt practiced just the opposite of big stick diplomacy. By bellowing at two different German diplomats and revealing his diplomatic conversations fourteen years after the events, Roosevelt was not speaking softly. Nevertheless, Roosevelt's intemperance was measured. Even while president Roosevelt peppered his letters with abusive, humorous, and acerbic remarks. Although his informal conversations tended to be even more colorful, President Roosevelt's official actions were calm, well reasoned, and carefully modulated. Both before and after his presidency Roosevelt was an effective polemicist who enjoyed playing the role of a partisan advocate. But as president Roosevelt measured his words carefully, often using specific events such as the Venezuelan crisis to promote a long-range policy. In his April 2, 1903, speech at Chicago, Roosevelt exploited the Monroe Doctrine's new visibility to

46. Beale, *Theodore Roosevelt*, 430, suggests that historians in their "false assumptions" may share the blame for the controversy over Roosevelt's ultimatum. For Sternburg's public assurance of the kaiser's acceptance of the Monroe Doctrine see Jonas, *United States and Germany*, 72–73; for the kaiser's later rejection of the doctrine see Herwig, *Germany's Vision of Empire in Venezuela*, 205; TR to Rear Admiral Henry C. Taylor, March 28, 1903, to George Dewey, March 20, 1903, both in Bishop, *Theodore Roosevelt and His Times*, I, 239; for Roosevelt's private support of Dewey see Spector, *Admiral of the New Empire*, 145–46; see John Gary Clifford, "Admiral Dewey and the Germans, 1903: A New Perspective," *Mid-America*, XLIX (1967), 214–20. For the Roosevelt-Wilson relationship see John Milton Cooper, *The Warrior and the Priest: Theodore Roosevelt and Woodrow Wilson* (Cambridge, Mass., 1983), 266–87, 303–37.

dramatize the need for a stronger navy: "If the American nation will speak softly and yet build, and keep at a pitch of the highest training, a thoroughly efficient navy, the Monroe Doctrine will go far."[47]

Roosevelt won substantial advantages from his Venezuelan diplomacy. The friendship with Britain was stronger after Venezuela than before and possibly aided the Americans in the Alaskan boundary dispute issue in 1903. By dramatizing the European threat to Latin America, Roosevelt set the stage for a more realistic American naval and diplomatic policy. By aligning with the Venezuelans Roosevelt began the first stage of a promising Pan-American policy that eventually failed because of Latin American instability and narrower U.S. interpretations of America's best interests after Roosevelt's presidency. In conversations with German Ambassador Sternburg on February 19, 1903, Roosevelt encouraged both German commercial expansion and the possible establishment of a separate German state in Brazil, ideas the kaiser endorsed with the comment "right" in the margin. Roosevelt's approval—indeed encouragement—of a separate German state in the heart of Latin America suggests that he was unconcerned with either expanding American trade in Latin America or limiting German ambitions south of the Caribbean. Roosevelt's suggestions to Germany were at worst innocent, perhaps naïve in giving up so much, at best shrewd, in consenting to what was already a strong German enclave. His secretary of state, John Hay, might have shuddered at such an abrogation of the Open Door and Monroe Doctrine in one breath. But Roosevelt was a determined internationalist who most of all wanted order and stability. Since he did not feel that German influence in Brazil threatened American security, he believed that German settlement might benefit Latin America by increasing prosperity while lessening American responsibility for continuing Latin American disorder. Prime Minister Arthur Balfour in a widely publicized speech in the House of Commons as well as in a private letter to Andrew

47. The Chicago address is in TR, *Presidential Addresses and State Papers* (8 vols.; New York, 1910), I, 265; for the effectiveness of TR's diplomatic diction, esp. Baron Holstein's use of the "big stick phrase" in German diplomatic correspondence, see Marks, *Velvet on Iron*, 173; for an analysis of Roosevelt's unique diction and the new words he introduced into the language see Edmund Morris, "Theodore Roosevelt as Writer," Paper presented at the Woodrow Wilson Colloquium, Washington, D.C., May 17, 1983; for the view that Roosevelt's original ultimatum to Holleben was friendlier in tone than historical accounts have made it appear see Beale, *Theodore Roosevelt*, 430. For a description and analysis of Roosevelt's effectiveness in political conversation see James E. Amos, *Theodore Roosevelt: Hero to His Valet* (New York, 1927), 62–63.

Carnegie in December, 1902, urged that the United States assume the role of hemispheric policeman, a view echoed by Argentina's Luis Drago but as late as 1904 still resisted by the kaiser. By 1904 Britain planned radical reductions in its Caribbean naval and military establishments, evidence not only of increasing demands on its resources elsewhere but of growing American diplomatic and naval capacities.[48]

In 1904, the Hague Court's ruling in favor of the intervening powers, Britain, Germany, and Italy, demolished Roosevelt's policy of compelling arbitration. But by then the combination of ambitious American naval manuevers during the Venezuelan confrontation and Roosevelt's forcefully stated diplomacy convinced Europe that conflict with the United States for any reason was costly and perilous. In 1902 for the first time, all the scattered warships of the American navy assembled at the Culebra naval base for operations as a single fleet. After the manuevers, the United States redeployed its naval forces, replacing the scattered battleship stations with cruisers and using the eleven battleships to form the first two unified American fleets—eight battleships in the Atlantic and three in Asian waters. The naval redeployment and the favorable press coverage created additional pressure on Congress not only for more battleships but for smaller warships and improvements to naval bases as well. The new naval deployment helped reinforce Roosevelt's diplomacy by lessening the major fear of naval planners, that Germany might acquire an effective naval base in the Caribbean.[49]

48. For the Alaskan boundary issue see Campbell, *Anglo-American Understanding,* 301–47; John A. Garraty, *Henry Cabot Lodge: A Biography* (New York, 1953), 242–56; Thomas A. Bailey, "Theodore Roosevelt and the Alaska Boundary Settlement," *Canadian Historical Review,* XVIII (1937), 123–30; and Charles C. Tansill, *Canadian-American Relations, 1875–1911* (New Haven, 1943). Sternburg's report is in *GP,* XVII, 291–92, translated with the kaiser's marginal remarks in Howard C. Hill, *Roosevelt and the Caribbean* (Chicago, 1927), 145–46. For TR's non-dollar-diplomacy view of trade in Latin America see TR, "The United States and the South American Republics," Address at Progressive Party Farewell Dinner, New York, October 3, 1913, in *TRWN,* 294–95; Rippy, *Latin America and World Politics,* 199; Hill, *Roosevelt and the Caribbean,* 143–46. For British military and naval reductions following the Venezuelan dispute see Gelber, *Rise of Anglo-American Friendship,* 132–33; and Samuel F. Wells, Jr., "British Strategic Withdrawal from the Western Hemisphere, 1904–1906," *Canadian Historical Review,* XLIX (1968), 335–56. For strengthening of American-British ties see Campbell, *Anglo-American Understanding,* 288–90, 299–300.

49. For the Hague Court decision see George Grafton Wilson (ed.), *The Hague Arbitration Cases* (Boston, 1915), 34–39; Davis, *United States and the Second Hague Peace Conference,* 82–90. For Roosevelt's personal planning of the Culebra manuevers see TR to Thomas C. Platt, June 28, 1902, in *MRL,* III, 283; see also Davis, *A Navy Second to None,* 114–27; Gordon Carpenter O'Gara, *Theodore Roosevelt and the Rise of the Modern Navy*

Perhaps as important, Europe felt more comfortable dealing with an American leader who was not only conversant with the style of European diplomacy—Weltpolitik and Realpolitik—but effectively practiced a personal diplomacy many European diplomatic leaders favored, including Wilhelm II, King Edward VII, French Foreign Minister Théophile Delcassé, Bülow, and Tsar Nicholas II. European actions affecting the Caribbean or Latin America could no longer be undertaken casually or without clearly defined and delimited objectives. During the Christmas holiday in 1902 more than eight thousand American sailors and their ships traveled from Culebra to many Caribbean ports for Christmas liberty, a peaceful but dramatic demonstration of the new and active American presence in the Caribbean and American determination to replace and supplant European influence and power. Europe, caught up in its continental and colonial problems, had little choice but to accept Roosevelt's newly dramatized Monroe Doctrine.[50]

(Princeton, 1943), 74–75. For American fears of German acquisition of a Caribbean naval base see Charles Sigsbee, "Germany Versus the United States—West Indies," May 21, 1900, File 425, in General Board War Portfolios, RG 80, NA. For the establishment of the Culebra base and its early operations see TR to John D. Long, General Order No. 75, December 18, 1901, File 10602, Box 477, General Records of the Navy, RG 80, NA. For Roosevelt's use of Venezuela to win congressional approval for a larger navy see Albert C. Stillson, "Military Policy Without Political Guidance: Theodore Roosevelt's Navy," *Military Affairs*, XXV (Spring, 1961), 22. For the Culebra naval maneuvers see Spector, *Admiral of the New Empire*, 143–46; George Dewey, "Journal of the Commander in Chief, 1 Dec., 1902 to Jan. 1903," in Box 2, George Dewey Papers, LC; for the Culebra naval manuevers and the subsequent fleet redeployment see *Annual Report of the Secretary of the Navy, 1903*, Serial 4642, pp. 646–50; Nathan Sargent, "General Rules for Fleet Evaluations," *ca.* January, 1903; "Tactical Evolutions off Culebra," memorandum for Chief of Staff, January 12, 1903, both in 1902–1903 folder, Box 3, Nathan Sargent Papers, LC. For Culebra's significance as a strategic Caribbean naval base see Kenneth Bourne, *Britain and the Balance of Power in North America, 1815–1908* (Berkeley, 1967), 346–47.

50. For the new popularity of the Monroe Doctrine see J. Michael Hogan, *The Panama Canal in American Politics: Domestic Advocacy and the Evolution of Policy* (Carbondale, Ill., 1956), 36; for the assessment of the Christmas liberty see *Annual Report of the Secretary of the Navy, 1903*, 648; for the personal diplomacy comparison see Eugene Trani, "Cautious Warrior: Theodore Roosevelt and the Diplomacy of Activism," in Frank J. Merli and Theodore A. Wilson (eds.), *Makers of American Diplomacy from Benjamin Franklin to Henry Kissinger* (New York, 1974), 312.

Part II

Panama

5   Prelude, 1513–1899

Dreams of building a canal at Panama began almost as soon as the narrow isthmus was first discovered. Invariably the dream ended in disaster or tragedy. Spanish explorer Vasco Núñez de Balboa glimpsed the possibilities of the future when he climbed a mountain on the Isthmus of Panama on September 25, 1513, and became the first recorded human to view the Pacific Ocean and the Caribbean Sea from a single vantage point. Balboa was sure he had found the elusive Northwest Passage that could link Europe and the Orient by sea, the potential pathway that motivated the European discoveries and the eventual settlement of the New World. Balboa, like Ferdinand de Lesseps and Theodore Roosevelt later, found that Panama was not the place to establish a historical reputation. Balboa spent the last six years of his life vainly trying to convince the colonial authorities that his discovery was worth far more than the gold the Spanish were carrying out of Latin America. Panama, as Balboa found it, an open savanna, was a more accessible site for a canal than the mixture of wild jungle and mountains that it had become by the nineteenth century. Instead of being hailed as a genius, Balboa was beheaded for political crimes. The first plan for a canal at Panama, designed in 1529, was not implemented because Spain, already the dominant power in Central America, remained content to use the forty-seven-mile land route across the isthmus rather than risk building a canal that would challenge British sea power.[1]

1. The most useful overall histories of Panama and the canal are Miles P. DuVal, Jr., *Cadiz to Cathay: The Story of the Long Diplomatic Struggle for the Panama Canal* (Stanford, 1940); Duval, *And the Mountains Will Move: The Story of the Building of the Panama Canal* (Stanford, 1947); Gerstle Mack, *The Land Divided: A History of the Panama Canal and Other Isthmian Canal Projects* (New York, 1944); Dwight Carroll Miner, *The Fight for the Panama Route: The Story of the Spooner Act and the Hay-Herrán Treaty* (New York, 1940); E. Taylor Parks, *Colombia and the United States, 1765–1934* (Durham, N.C., 1935); Philippe Bunau-Varilla, *Panama: The Creation, Destruction, and Resurrection* (London, 1913), cited as *BVC;*

In 1815 Simón Bolívar, in his prophetic "Letter to an English gentle-man," envisioned the isthmus of Panama "as the capital of the world" and offered Britain the chance to control canals in Nicaragua and Panama in exchange for help in his revolution against Spain. Hoping for a Western Hemispheric balance of power with British help against continental Europe, or "under the auspices of a liberal nation which lends us its protection," an early vision of the Pan-Americanism he began, Bolívar struggled with the question of how the Latin American peoples might govern themselves. He rejected the idea of monarchy and dismissed the possibility that the freed Latin American peoples might create a single great nation like the United States. Bolívar shared with the United States a commitment to republican idealism, a distrust of European intentions, and a continuing interest in building an isthmian canal.[2]

Inspired by the writings of the German naturalist and canal enthusiast Alexander von Humboldt, the German poet Johann Goethe in 1827 made a remarkable prediction of how intimately interwoven were the destinies of Panama, the United States, and a future canal:

This much is certain: If by a crosscut of this kind it could be accomplished that vessels with all sorts of cargoes and of every size could go through such a canal from the Gulf of Mexico to the Pacific Ocean, quite incalculable results would follow for the entire civilized and uncivilized human race.

I, however, would be surprised if the United States would miss the chance to get such a work into her hands. It is to be foreseen that this young State, with its decided tendency toward the West, will in thirty to forty years have also taken possession, and will have populated, the large areas of land on the

---

David McCullough, *The Path Between the Seas: The Creation of the Panama Canal, 1870–1914* (New York, 1977); Gustave Anguizola, *Philippe Bunau-Varilla: The Man Behind the Panama Canal* (Chicago, 1980); Ira E. Bennett, *History of the Panama Canal: Its Construction and Builders* (Washington, D.C., 1915); and Jesús María Henao and Gerardo Arrubla, *History of Columbia*, trans. and ed. J. Fred Rippy (Chapel Hill, 1938). On the dramatic change in topography see Mary W. Helms, *Panama: Chiefs in Search of Power* (Austin, Tex., 1979), 7; for Panama's climate and geography see Louis E. Guzmán, *Farming and Farmlands in Panama* (Chicago, 1956), 32–44.

2. Joseph Lockey, *Essays in Pan-Americanism* (Berkeley, 1939), 138–39; for a translation of Bolívar's letter see John A. Crow, *The Epic of Latin America* (3rd ed.; Berkeley, 1980), 441–44; John Lynch, *The Spanish American Revolutions, 1808–1826* (2nd ed.; New York, 1975); for the interactions between Bolivarian America and the United States see especially José de Onís, *The United States as Seen by Spanish American Writers, 1776–1890* (New York, 1952), 1–88; John T. Reid, *Spanish American Images of the United States, 1790–1960* (Gainesville, 1977); Hubert Herring, *A History of Latin America* (New York, 1955), 260–69.

other side of the Rocky Mountains. It is furthermore to be foreseen that in this entire coast of the Pacific Ocean, where nature had already created the most roomy and safest harbors, in course of time very important commercial towns will carry on a large traffic between China and the East Indies with the United States. In such a case it would not only be desirable, but almost necessary, that merchant as well as war vessels should be able to have quicker connection with the western and eastern coast of America. I therefore repeat that it is entirely indispensable for the United States to make a passage from the Gulf of Mexico to the Pacific Ocean, and I am certain that she will accomplish it.[3]

History by its very nature is not a study of the inevitable. In 1827 Goethe thought a future union of the United States and the isthmus perfectly logical. But until 1914 the canal remained an extravagant hope expressed in different ways—for the French, a metaphor of water and engineering; for Panamanians, a deliverance from poverty; for North Americans, the realization of a national destiny; and for many others in the world, a combination of man-made engineering and natural wonder. From Balboa, the first visionary, through the French—the engineers, the promoter de Lesseps, and nationalist poet Victor Hugo—the building of a canal was regarded as a symbol of mankind's peaceful progress. But the poetry of the canal fell victim to the dense isthmian jungles, the fierce political struggles within the Colombian and American Senates, and the conflicting national visions of four diverse peoples, American, Colombian, French, and Panamanian.[4]

The diplomacy of the Monroe Doctrine, the defining act of North American, Latin American, and European relations, addressed the ideological clash between American republicanism and Holy Alliance monarchism, and whether revolutionary Latin America could possibly be ruled by Bourbon princes installed by the French navy, or—with the United States' support—exist as independent nations. Monroe's doc-

3. Quoted in Frankfurt *Zeitung*, February 26, 1904, trans. and rpr. in *House Documents*, 58th Cong., 2nd Sess., No. 53, Serial 4679, p. 613; for another version see DuVal, *Cadiz to Cathay*, 27; for the background on Goethe's remarks see Mack, *Land Divided*, 111–19.

4. See William Whatley Pierson, "The Political Influences of an Interoceanic Canal, 1826–1926," *HAHR*, VI (1926), 205–31. Colombia is known by many names: the Vice-Royalty of New Granada (1717–24, 1740–1819), Gran Colombia (1819–30), New Granada (1830–58), Granadine Confederation (1858–61), United States of Colombia (1861–86), and the Republic of Colombia (since 1886). For a useful brief history see Bernard Moses, "Antecedents of the Constitution of the Republic of Colombia," in *Senate Documents*, 57th Cong., 2nd Sess., No. 75, Serial 4472, pp. 9–16.

trine, the result of complex domestic political and intense diplomatic negotiations, was made public as part of President Monroe's annual message to Congress in 1823. Britain, involved with its own decision on whether to unify with continental Europe, remain aloof, or align with the United States, was disappointed that Monroe went beyond Foreign Secretary George Canning's proposed joint recognition of the new Latin American nations to reaffirm American exceptionalism. Austrian Chancellor Prince Richard von Metternich was furious, declaring that the United States now opposed Europe "altar against altar" by threatening that "this flood of evil doctrines and pernicious examples should extend over the whole of America." But Monroe and Secretary of State John Quincy Adams' new doctrine of American exceptionalism was intended to exclude Europe, not embrace Latin America. Europeans were not welcome as allies, but neither were "our Southern Brethren," the new Latin American republics. Although the Monroe Doctrine affirmed a new Pan-Americanism, it envisioned the United States as the senior (and only voting) partner. Monroe's exclusionary doctrine—no Europe in the New World— stated a principle implicit in American foreign policy until Theodore Roosevelt's Corollary in 1905 made it formal. Because the United States' early Pan-Americanism was rooted in ideological republicanism, it offered incalculable support to the new Latin American nations in their political seed time. But the United States, firmly committed to George Washington's rejection of any foreign alliances, refused to go beyond this limited ideological affinity in its early relations with the new Latin American republics.[5]

When Simón Bolívar won the battle of Ayachucho on December 9, 1824, Spain lost its last vestige of Latin American military power. Bolívar, who at times compared himself to Napoleon and at other times to George Washington, sought diplomatic support from Great Britain and the United States to prevent a Holy Alliance war of resto-

5. Dexter Perkins, *A History of the Monroe Doctrine* (Boston, 1963), 69–72; Metternich quoted *ibid.*, 27; Perkins, *The Monroe Doctrine, 1823–1826* (Cambridge, Mass., 1927), 185–92; text of the Monroe Doctrine *ibid.*, 83–85; for reaction to the Monroe Doctrine see *ibid.*, 144–84; for the European and American political contexts see Ernest May, *The Making of the Monroe Doctrine* (Cambridge, Mass., 1975); Samuel Flagg Bemis, *John Quincy Adams and the Foundations of American Foreign Policy* (New York, 1949); Harry Ammon, "The Monroe Doctrine: Domestic Politics or National Decision?" *DH*, V (1981), 53–70; Ernest May, "Response to Harry Ammon," *ibid.*, 71–72; "our Southern Brethren" (capitalized) quoted from Monroe Doctrine original Senate file text in Bemis, *John Quincy Adams*, 393 (text, 391–93); see also Timothy E. Anna, *Spain and the Loss of America* (Lincoln, Neb., 1983), 256–87.

ration. Cuba, the strategic key to the Caribbean, became the main diplomatic focus as the United States and Britain manuevered to replace
Spain as the dominant Central American commercial power. As part
of its intense diplomatic effort to encourage the continuation of Spanish control of Cuba, the United States enlisted Russia to urge Spain to
make peace and not risk losing Cuba and Puerto Rico. The United
States also warned Mexico and Colombia that it regarded their further
designs on Cuba as wars of conquest, not of liberation.[6]

Even as Bolívar planned his "Amphictyonic Assembly" to promote
the interests of the new American states to convene at Panama in
1826, Colombia's Foreign Minister Pedro Guál was playing off Britain
and the United States to assure that neither would be able to dominate the newly independent region, a strategy realized when both nations agreed to participate in the Panama Congress of 1826. Secretary
of State Henry Clay's glowing eighteen-thousand-word letter of instructions to the United States delegates, perhaps the nation's most
idealistic statement of its commitment to Pan-Americanism, is striking evidence of how domestic politics could impinge even on a foreign policy of goodwill. Clay's letter was not published until the
1889–1890 Washington Pan-American Congress because the American Congress, which did not share Clay's vision, only reluctantly and
after intense debate approved funds for United States participation
and then refused to publish the documents for fear of making the
Adams administration look good. Because of the congressional delay—and also because one American delegate refused to go to Panama during the "unhealthy" tropical season—the American delegates arrived too late to participate fully. Yet the very presence of the
United States and Britain was dramatic support of Latin American independence and a guarantee against the lingering threat of Spanish
reconquest aided by the French navy and France's own Caribbean
ambitions.[7]

Bolívar's dream of a united Latin America failed first in the Panama
Congress, then in his ill-fated Federation of the Andes, and he died in

6. Bemis, *John Quincy Adams*, 537–65; Víctor Andrés Belaúnde, *Bolívar and the Political Thought of the Spanish American Revolution* (Baltimore, 1938), esp. for the Washington
and Napolean comparisons, x, xi, 127, 173; for Símon Bolívar, "Views on the Congress
of Panama," see David Bushnell (ed.), *The Liberator, Simón Bolívar: Man and Image* (New
York, 1970), 79–81; Perkins, *Monroe Doctrine, 1823–1826*, 205–22.

7. For Bolívar's "I wanted to make a noise . . . to discourage Spain" letter see
William R. Shephard, "Bolívar and the United States," *HAHR*, I (1918), 293–94; see also
ibid., 270–98; and Bemis, *John Quincy Adams*, 544–49. For the early history of the Pan-

1830 an exile from the New Granada he liberated and governed. In spite of United States support, the Central American Federation, a promising union of the five small Central American states, was beset by British opposition and internal disagreements and dissolved in 1839, to be replaced by the five separate republics of Costa Rica, Niacaragua, Honduras, El Salvador, and Guatemala. This separation, a diplomatic victory for Britain and a defeat for the United States, was a permanent catastrophe for Central American political stability.[8]

Renewed interest in a possible Panama canal coincided with Central American political unrest. During the New Granadan civil war of 1839–1841, Panama, exercising its constitutional right, seceded for the second time (1830 was the first). New Granada before the secession, Panama as an independent nation, and New Granada and Panama reunited in 1842 negotiated with Britain, France, Spain, Holland, and the United States for a guarantee of sovereignty in the isthmus in exchange for the right to build a canal. Britain, concerned about continued American westward expansion that threatened to spread toward Central America as well as California and Oregon and encouraged by its own aggressive diplomats in Central America, used the issue of protecting the Mosquito Indians to establish a political foothold in Central America. Since an American transcontinental railroad in the 1840s was not possible, attention focused on control of a Central American route, which each nation feared would give the other total dominance in the region. Britain's aggressive diplomacy back-

American movement see Joseph Lockey, *Pan-Americanism: The Beginnings* (New York, 1920); and J. Lloyd Meecham, *The United States and Inter-American Security, 1889–1960* (Austin, Tex., 1961), 28–29; Frances L. Reinhold, "New Research on the First Pan-American Congress Held at Panama in 1826," *HAHR*, XVIII (1938), 342–63. For Spanish refusal to concede the loss of Central America see Anna, *Spain and the Loss of America*, 267–75, 294. For a summary of and the documents relating to the Congress of Panama see James Brown Scott (ed.), *The International Conferences of American States, 1889–1928* (London, 1931), vii–xxix.

8. For assessments of Bolívar see Belaúnde, *Bolívar and the Political Thought of the Spanish-American Revolution;* John Lynch, "Bolívar and the Caudillos," *HAHR*, LXIII (1983), 3–35; Simon Collier, "Nationality, Nationalism, and Supranationalism in the Writings of Simón Bolívar," *HAHR*, LXIII (1983), 37–64; David Bushnell, "The Last Dictatorship: Betrayal or Consummation?" *HAHR*, LXIII (1983), 65–105; Joseph B. Lockey, "Bolívar After a Century," in Lockey, *Essays in Pan-Americanism*, 135–42; Gerhard Masur, *Simón Bolívar* (Albuquerque, N.M., 1969). For a useful selection of Bolívar's political texts and a summary of older historical assessments see Bushnell (ed.), *The Liberator;* for the Central American Federation, see Thomas L. Karnes, *The Failure of Union: Central America, 1824–1860* (Chapel Hill, 1961), 3–125; for Central America see Ralph Lee Woodward, Jr., *Central America: A Nation Divided* (2nd ed.; New York, 1985).

fired. By supporting Mexico and Texas, the British encouraged the United States to intensify its already popular Manifest Destiny ideology and to annex Texas more quickly. Resentment against the British may have contributed to President James K. Polk's strong reaffirmation of the Monroe Doctrine in his December, 1845, message to Congress.[9]

Shaken by the British refusal to consider a treaty guaranteeing New Granadan sovereignty over the isthmus and concerned by the serious threat of Ecuador's former president General Juan José Flores, who was assembling an expedition with apparent British support to reestablish Spanish political institutions in Ecuador and Central America, New Granada turned to the United States for help. Although Britain and Spain finally ended the threat that a Flores expedition would land on the isthmus, General Tomás Cipriano de Mosquera, elected president of New Granada on April 1, 1845, became wary of British ambitions, especially persistent rumors of British intentions to seize the isthmus.[10]

Secretary of State James Buchanan was also concerned. In his instructions to Benjamin A. Bidlack, appointed as chargé to New Granada on May 14, 1845, Buchanan noted the talk of a proposed rail line across the isthmus and warned that "no other nation should obtain either an exclusive privilege or an advantage." Bidlack was instructed to prevent New Granada "from granting privileges to any other nation which might prove injurious to the United States." Britain was so dominant in Central American affairs that Bidlack's ostensible mission,

9. For the 1830 separation see Arnold M. Freedman, "The Independence of Panama and Its Incorporation in Gran Colombia, 1820–1830" (Ph.D. dissertation, University of Florida, 1978), 321–27; for the 1840 separation see J. Ignacio Méndez, "*Azul y Rojo*, Panama's Independence in 1840," *HAHR*, LX (1980), 269–93. For British-American diplomacy see Robert Naylor, "The British Role in Central America Prior to the Clayton-Bulwer Treaty of 1850," *HAHR*, XL (1960), 361, 375–82; see also Parks, *Colombia and the United States*, 137–47, 199–200; DuVal, *Cadiz to Cathay*, 46–65; J. Fred Rippy, *Rivalry of the United States and Great Britain* (Baltimore, 1929), 217–46; Mary W. Williams, *Anglo-Isthmian Diplomacy, 1815–1915* (Washington, D.C., 1916), 40–52; David Pletcher, *The Diplomacy of Annexation: Texas, Oregon, and the Mexican War* (Columbia, Mo., 1973), 9–30, 236–41; Mack, *Land Divided*, 181–87; Richard W. Van Alstyne, "The Central American Policy of Lord Palmerston, 1846–1848," *HAHR*, XVI (1936), 339–59; Perkins, *History of the Monroe Doctrine*, 86–89, 298–99; and Joseph B. Lockey, "A Neglected Aspect of Isthmian Diplomacy," *AHR*, XLI (1936), 295–305.

10. Lockey, "Neglected Aspect of Isthmian Diplomacy," 296–305; Parks, *Colombia and the United States*, 202–203; Joseph L. Helguera, "The First Mosquera Administration in New Granada" (Ph.D. dissertation, University of North Carolina, 1958), 377–85, 432–61.

to negotiate a revised commercial agreement with New Granada, was all that could reasonably have been expected. When Mosquera boldly decided to reverse New Granada's dependence on Britain as the major power, he turned the tables on the British and made the United States the new dominant power in isthmian and Central American affairs. Bidlack was the innocent middleman in the negotiations, but Secretary Buchanan, aware of the momentous changes inherent in Mosquera's proposed treaty, was a willing and effective accomplice in replacing British with American influence in the isthmus.[11]

Mosquera and his two most influential advisers, Manuel Ancízar and Pedro Fernández Madrid, were fully aware of the radical nature of the treaty they proposed to the willing Bidlack. Mosquera agreed to abolish all differential duties on American trade, a sticking point for many years, in exchange for including Article 35, written by Mosquera himself, which would give the United States "the right of way or transit across the Isthmus" in exchange for guarantees of "perfect neutrality" and New Granadan sovereignty over Panama. Manuel María Mallarino, who became foreign minister in May, knew that the proposed guarantee came perilously close to an entangling alliance, which the American Senate abhorred. His plea to the United States to ratify the proposed Bidlack-Mallarino Treaty emphasized British dominance and arrogance and suggested that British ambitions would soon extend from Argentina to California. The New Granadans kept the treaty, especially Article 35, secret until it was signed on December 12, 1846, to prevent British Chargé Daniel Florencio O'Leary from influencing the negotiations. O'Leary understood that New Granada had made the United States its isthmian protector. Certain that the American Senate would reject so sweeping a treaty, O'Leary underestimated Mosquera's—and Buchanan's—determination. Bidlack justified negotiating the treaty without instructions on the grounds that the British menace was a "threatened emergency" and assured Buchanan that Mosquera did not regard the treaty as a general alliance but rather a limited guarantee.[12]

11. James Buchanan to Benjamin Bidlack, June 23, 1845, in William R. Manning (ed.), *Diplomatic Correspondence of the United States: Inter-American Affairs* (12 vols.; Washington, D.C., 1935), V, 357; Helguera, "First Mosquera Administration," 443–56; Lockey, "Neglected Aspect of Isthmian Diplomacy," 305; Parks, *Colombia and the United States,* 202–10.

12. Helguera, "First Mosquera Administration," 443–56; Manuel María Mallarino, "Report upon the reasons that make the stipulations of the Treaty proposed, useful and acceptable to the United States of America," December 10, 1846, in Manning (ed.), *Dip-*

Mosquera appointed former president Pedro Alcántara Herrán as minister to Washington to lobby the Bidlack-Mallarino Treaty through an American Senate that remained unenthusiastic about Bidlack's "golden opportunity." With great patience and skill, the English-speaking Herrán courted influential senators and eventually over-came French and British efforts against the treaty. When the Senate finally approved the treaty before its ten-day recess on June 3, but failed to include an additional article on maritime registry, Buchanan gathered enough senators to ratify the omitted article in a secret ses-sion, dated the exchange of signatures June 10 (not the actual procla-mation date of June 12), and allowed a Granadan clerk to translate the treaty into Spanish as the official copy he endorsed. Mosquera, who was further enraged when the British replaced the Nicaraguan flag with that of the Mosquito Kingdom at San Juan (which they renamed Greytown) in January, 1848, won his battle to check British domina-tion and reversed Bolívar's original policy of using Britain as a balance against the potentially more powerful Americans. The ratification of the Bidlack-Mallarino Treaty effectively ended British ambitions in Central America at the critical moment when the discovery of gold in California made a railroad line across the isthmus irresistible.[13]

Panamanian diplomat Justo Arosemena complained that none of the powers wanted a canal: Britain preferred a railroad, the French interest was mainly scientific, and the United States was not yet ca-pable of undertaking so large a project. What Britain and the United States most wanted was to deny the other a canal that would make either power dominant in the region. British Foreign Secretary Lord Palmerston's dubious strategy, based on an alliance with the Mosquito Indians, was a shambles. American diplomatic agents Elijah Hise and George Squier were as aggressive—and as effective—as Palmerston's Frederick Chatfield. After the Bidlack-Mallarino Treaty and the Ameri-can victory in the Mexican War of 1846–1848, Britain had little choice but to give up its hopes of Central American domination. In the

lomatic Correspondence, V, 630–33. Bidlack's diplomatic correspondence is in Manning (ed.), Diplomatic Correspondence, V, 628–50; treaty is in Senate Documents, 61st Cong., 2nd Sess., No. 357 (William M. Malloy, Treaties, Conventions, International Acts, Protocols, and Agreements Between the United States of America and Other Powers, 1776–1909), I, 302–14; Howard C. Hill, Roosevelt and the Caribbean (Chicago, 1927), 38–46.

13. Helguera, "First Mosquera Administration," 451–61; for the Senate debate see Parks, Colombia and the United States, 206–15; Lockey, "Neglected Aspect of Isthmian Diplomacy," 305.

Clayton-Bulwer Treaty of 1850 both Britain and the United States agreed not to build or fortify an isthmian canal unilaterally. Britain ended its abrasive alliance with the Mosquito Indians, acknowledged the United States as a diplomatic equal in Central America, and, in return for the easing of immediate tensions, won a temporary delaying action against further informal American expansion in Central America. By 1856 the British, who expected the United States to occupy both Mexico and Central America, hoped gracefully to abrogate a treaty the United States might not honor and Britain was unable to enforce. The Clayton-Bulwer Treaty ultimately served the British well, however, by inhibiting American canal ambitions until both sides agreed to end the agreement in 1901.[14]

With the entrance of Oregon and California to the Union in 1848, followed quickly by the discovery of gold in California, the isthmus became the first effective link between the American East and West coasts. Even before the Gold Rush began in earnest, when President James K. Polk's December 5, 1848, message to Congress confirmed the early rumors from California, New Granada's President Mosquera and Minister Herrán awarded a transit concession to a French syndicate headed by Mateo Klien on June 8, 1847. When Klien could not raise the initial surety fee of 600,000 francs, William Aspinwall, a New York businessman, took over the concession. In 1848 Aspinwall's Pacific Mail Steamship Company also won the federal mail contract between San Francisco and Panama. New Granadan Minister Herrán preferred American businessmen to European speculators (they asked fewer concessions), and Aspinwall better suited Ancízar's and Mosquera's new "eminently American" policy. When Congress refused to subsidize Aspinwall's railroad, he raised private capital and in five years (1850–1855) built the Panama Railroad, thereby firmly establishing American interests in the isthmus. Meanwhile, bitter competition between Charles Morgan and Cornelius Vanderbilt and William

14. Van Alstyne, "Central American Policy of Lord Palmerston," 339–59; Richard W. Van Alstyne, "British Diplomacy and the Clayton-Bulwer Treaty, 1850–1860," *Journal of Modern History*, XI (1939), 149–83; Mark Van Aken, "British Policy Considerations in Central America Before 1850," *HAHR*, XLII (1962), 54–59; Kenneth Bourne, "The Clayton-Bulwer Treaty and the Decline of British Opposition to the Territorial Expansion of the United States, 1857–1860," *Journal of Modern History*, XXXIII (1961), 287–91; Bourne, *Britain and the Balance of Power in North America, 1815–1908* (Berkeley, 1967), 170–205; Pletcher, *Diplomacy of Annexation*, 18–19; Parks, *Colombia and the United States*, 326–32. For the later effectiveness of the Clayton-Bulwer Treaty see Jackson Crowell, "The United States and a Central American Canal, 1869–1877, *HAHR*, XLIX (1969), 27–52.

Walker's filibustering activities—which included invasions, civil wars, and gunboat diplomacy—devastated Nicaragua and its alternate interoceanic transit route. A Honduran firing squad finally ended Walker's reign of destruction in 1860, but the Central American distrust stemming from Walker's activities lingered long after his death. In spite of Aspinwall's overwhelming success, the rivalry between Nicaragua and Panama continued unabated into the twentieth century.[15]

Although the American Civil War (1861–1865) and New Granada's War of the Hundred Fights (1857–1863) occurred at about the same time, they had little else in common. New Granada's tradition of civil conflict was rooted in its geography and history. The three large Andean mountain chains that divided the already sparse Colombian population into regional rivalries made any effective national transportation system impossible until the twentieth century. Even as Spain's waning authority over the Viceroyalty of New Granada gave way to Bolívar's Gran Colombia, the persistent contradictions of Colombia's history became a part of the mountainous and divided country. Beset by recurring disputes centered on the issues of centralism versus federalism, clericalism versus secularism, a strong executive versus a weak legislature, and institutionalism versus caudilloism, Colombia remained an extremely poor country even by Latin America standards. Throughout the nineteenth century Colombia struggled with export agriculture—tobacco until the 1870s, salt, and finally coffee—to stave off the continuous threat of bankruptcy. Colombia's promising industrial and railroad development initiatives, difficult because of the geographic barriers, were hindered by chronic poverty and by frequent changes in political leadership and ideology. As one writer observed, "Economic anarchy produces political anarchy which in turn makes economic anarchy worse," a succinct summary of Colombia's nineteenth-century political and economic history.[16]

15. Helguera, "First Mosquera Administration," 501–11; Mack, Land Divided, 136–60; Alex Perez-Venero, Before the Five Frontiers: Panama from 1821–1903 (New York, 1978), 51–78; Anguizola, Philippe Bunau-Varilla, 14–23; DuVal, Cadiz to Cathay, 36–38. For the Panama route see John Haskell Kemble, The Panama Route, 1848–1869 (Berkeley, 1943); for the Nicaraguan route and Walker's filibusters see David I. Folkman, Jr., The Nicaragua Route (Salt Lake City, 1972); see also Bennett, History of the Panama Canal, 86–95. For Aspinwall's ambitions and accomplishments see DuVal, And the Mountains Will Move, 3–30.

16. See Frank Safford, "Foreign and National Enterprise in Nineteenth-Century Colombia," Business History Review, XXXIX (1965), 503–26; Safford, The Ideal of the Practical: Colombia's Struggle to Form a Technical Elite (Austin, Tex., 1976); J. Leon Helguera, "The Problem of Liberalism Versus Conservatism in Colombia, 1849–85," in Frederick B.

Liberal General Tomás de Mosquera won the struggle for power and in 1863 instituted the Liberal Rionegro constitution that changed New Granada into a federation renamed the United States of Colombia. The victorious Liberals banished the Society of Jesus, exiled its members, and seized the church's property. By giving the nine separate states effective sovereignty, by excluding the Conservatives from both the constitution-framing process and any participation in government, and by outlawing the Catholic church, the Rionegro constitution assured that Colombia would remain in a state of almost constant civil war (there were more than forty) as Conservatives fought for their religion and their political freedom. Rafael Núñez's Regeneration of 1885 reversed the radical Liberal rule, restored the church, ended federalism, and banished the Liberals from power.[17]

Odd new taxes, the possibility of foreign canal concessions, constant bickering over the meaning of the Bidlack-Mallarino Treaty, frequent changes in government, and finally overt American naval intervention plagued American–New Granadan relations. In 1850 American Chargé Thomas M. Foote worried that New Granada planned to redeem the Aspinwall railway concession and sell it to the British in 1859, the first of three possible redemption dates. New Granada disputed the American right to transport troops across the isthmus without making an advance reservation. In 1854 New Granada imposed a one-dollar passenger tax on "certain" persons crossing the isthmus. Since Britons and New Granadans were exempt, "certain" and American became synonymous. New Chargé James S. Green was especially frustrated when he could not deliver his protest during Holy Week,

---

Pike (ed.), *Latin American History: Select Problems, Identity, Integration, and Nationhood* (New York, 1969), 224–58; Marco Palacios, *Coffee in Colombia, 1850–1970* (Cambridge, Eng., 1980); Malcolm Deas, "The Fiscal Problems of Nineteenth-Century Colombia," *Journal of Latin American Studies,* XIV (1982), 287–328; William Paul McGreevey, *An Economic History of Colombia, 1845–1930* (Cambridge, Eng., 1971); Hernán Horna, "Transportation, Modernization, and Entrepreneurship in Nineteenth-Century Colombia," *Journal of Latin American Studies,* XIV (1982), 33–54; David Bushnell, "Two Stages in Colombian Tariff Policy: The Radical Era and the Return to Protection (1865–1885)," *Inter-American Economic Affairs* IX (1956), 3–23; and J. Fred Rippy, "Dawn of the Railway Era in Colombia," *HAHR,* XXXIII (1943), 650–63.

17. Henao and Arrubla, *History of Colombia,* 483–91; Helguera, "Problem of Liberalism Versus Conservatism in Colombia," 224–32; Deas, "Colombia, Ecuador, and Venezuela," 644–46; see also Carey Shaw, Jr., "Church and State in Colombia as Observed by American Diplomats, 1834–1906," *HAHR,* XXI (1941), 577–613. For the historiography of Colombian Liberalism see Helen Delpar, "The Liberal Record and Colombian Historiography," *Revista Americana de Bibliografía,* XXXI (1981), 524–37.

"when no public business is transacted," or on Monday, when "the Government was subverted and I could do nothing." Green suggested that a warship and the use of force might soon be required. The new government, the fully independent State of Panama (1855), was still subject to "constant agitation and revolutions," which United States Minister James B. Bowlin in Bogotá was sure resulted from "causes inherent in the State," namely the preponderance of non-whites in Panama's population. Bowlin thought it "a fixed fact that a Ship Canal will follow the Rail Road." He found the threatened boundary war between Colombia and Venezuela incomprehensible because the Andes made invasion by either side impossible and neither nation had a navy. The "annual annoyances and petty schemes to plunder" included a ship tax to replace the withdrawn passenger tax. The assessment of forty cents a ton for sailing vessels and twenty cents for steamers took effect on November 1, 1855, for American vessels and two months later for "the rest of the world," except British vessels, which were exempt. After New Granada annulled the passenger tax with appropriate apologies, on May 14, 1856, Panama's new tax of $3.25 per pound for crossing the isthmus (again the British were exempt) generated a new series of American protests.[18]

The growing bad feelings between Americans and Panamanians erupted in a serious riot on April 15, 1856. The "Watermelon War," a racial melee over a ten-cent piece of watermelon, resulted in the deaths of fifteen Americans and two Panamanians and the wounding of twenty-nine persons. On September 19 two American sailing warships, *Independence* and *St. Mary's*, landed 160 men to occupy the railroad station. Although the riot did not directly involve or interrupt transit across the isthmus, the United States justified its intervention by citing the Bidlack-Mallarino Treaty's provision to protect the tran-

18. Thomas J. Foote to John M. Clayton, March 29, 1850; Victoriano de Diego Paredes to William L. Marcy, June 6, July 19, 1853, April 8, 1854; James S. Green to C. Pinzon, April 15, 22; Green to Marcy, April 22, 1854; James B. Bowlin to Marcy, May 10, 17, August 18, 1855; Bowlin to Lino de Pombo, October 10, 1855; Pombo to Bowlin, October 12, 1855; Pedro Alcántra Herrán to Marcy, January 24, 28, 1856; Bowlin to Marcy, May 14, 1856, all in Manning (ed.), *Diplomatic Correspondence*, V, 656–725. For Justo Arosemena's argument that a tonnage tax was Panama's only chance to benefit from a railroad, see Perez-Venero, *Before the Five Frontiers*, 96. For Arosemena's 1845 proposal that New Granada build its own macadam road across the isthmus rather than negotiate with foreign powers for a canal or railroad, see Parks, *Colombia and the United States*, 202. For the new Panama government and the Granadine Confederation era see Henao and Arrubla, *History of Colombia*, 475–77.

sit. Eleven such interventions occurred between 1856 and 1903, some at the request of Colombia, others by American initiative. In the 1865 intervention, Secretary of State William H. Seward rejected Colombia's request for a longer intervention. Both the Bidlack-Mallarino Treaty and the Colombian federal system were ambiguous about responsibility for the frequent Panamanian squabbles, which caused friction, intervention, and constant arguments over indemnities for damage and injury. Isaac E. Morse expressed the American frustration:

Relying upon their poverty, their want of an army or a navy, they do not hesitate to treat the most powerful nations, with perfect indifference, if not contempt, as they are now doing us and Great Britain; and it would seem they are perfectly persuaded that their insignificance is their strongest protection, and that if any one nation should dare to seize upon any thing of theirs, that the rest of the world would instantly rush to their rescue.

Their self conceit is perfectly sublime. Stuck up here nine thousand feet in the Andes they look upon the rest of the world with supreme contempt, and when Peru, Chile, and some other South American States are held up to them, as models for honesty and punctuality in the payment of their obligations they affect to consider them as only half civilized when compared with New Grenada [sic].

Yet Morse was as self-righteous as the Colombians he criticized. Although foreign witnesses absolved the local police and identified Americans as the aggressors in the riot, the United States made outrageous demands for control of the railroad and the use of naval bases before settling for a cash award of $412,394. In 1866, after Mosquera appeared ready to buy out Aspinwall and sell the railroad to English interests, the Colombian Congress gave him a new ninety-nine-year contract.[19]

When the Senate on March 19, 1866, requested the navy to report on possible isthmian canal sites, Rear Admiral Charles H. Davis responded on July 11 with nineteen possible sites in Tehuantepec, Mexico, Honduras, Nicaragua (eight routes), Panama (six routes), and Darién (three routes). Davis also listed seven land crossings, including

19. For summaries of the American naval interventions of 1856, 1860, 1865, 1868, May and September, 1873, January and March, 1885, 1901, 1902, and 1903, see Milton Offutt, *The Protection of Citizens Abroad by Armed Forces of the United States* (Baltimore, 1928), 37, 48, 52, 60–61, 66–67, 89, 94, and 96; Isaac E. Morse to Marcy, February 20, 1857, in Manning (ed.), *Diplomatic Correspondence*, V, 848–49. For the "Watermelon War," see Mack, *Land Divided*, 161–68; and Perez-Venero, *Before the Five Frontiers*, 98–103.

Aspinwall's Panama Railroad. On May 4, 1866, Colombia initiated negotiations for a canal concession, preferably with the United States. Although President Andrew Johnson sent the Sullivan-Semper-Cuenca Ship-Canal Convention to the United States Senate on February 15, 1869, the Colombian Senate, acting first, rejected the clumsy treaty, an act that provoked secession sentiment in Panama. President Ulysses S. Grant, an ardent expansionist with memories of a harrowing 1852 isthmus crossing with the army, supported an American canal (not under international auspices like the Suez Canal of 1869), an exclusively American policy begun by Secretary of State Seward in 1857. Under Grant and Commodore Daniel Ammen, chief of the Bureau of Navigation, the navy undertook surveys of the major sites in Davis' report, which were then consolidated by the Interoceanic Canal Commission the Senate initiated on March 15, 1872. As a result of the navy's investigations, Tehuantepec (144 miles and 142 locks) and Darién (five rejected sites) were eliminated. Although the surveys were detailed, the results were often unscientific, colored by favorable personal impressions and underestimates of technical difficulties. Because Panama was saved for last, Aniceto G. Menocal, the gifted Cuban chief engineer of the Nicaragua survey, and Commander Edward Lill, a Darién veteran, had probably already made Nicaragua their preferred choice. Both failed to realize that building a dam would solve the Chagres River problems, and they perfunctorily dismissed Panama as impractical and too expensive. The canal commission report of February 7, 1876, unanimously favored Nicaragua, a diplomatic complication for the United States because the Clayton-Bulwer Treaty barred the kind of exclusive control in Central America that President Grant and the Senate preferred.[20]

On November 17, 1869, French promoter Ferdinand de Lesseps' company finished the Suez Canal, a major French aesthetic, engineering, and economic achievement. De Lesseps became a folk hero because he refused to pay Baron Rothschild a 5-percent commission for financing the canal and instead raised the money through a public subscription from French citizens, mainly shopkeepers of modest means. The French were already justifiably proud of their engineer-

20. DuVal, *Cadiz to Cathay*, 73–79; Parks, *Colombia and the United States*, 338–50; Mack, *Land Divided*, 166–70; *Senate Documents*, 56th Cong., 1st Sess., No. 237, Serial 3853, pp. 45–61; Crowell, "The United States and a Central American Canal," 26–52; Williams, *Anglo-Isthmian Diplomacy*, 271–74; and Kenneth J. Hagan, *American Gunboat Diplomacy and the Old Navy, 1877–1889* (Westport, Conn., 1973), 143–59.

ing genius, and building the Suez Canal fulfilled their belief in social philosopher Henri de Saint-Simon's idea that canals were a service to humanity and helped promote peace. The French made the Suez Canal opening a major international cultural event celebrated by Italian Giuseppe Verdi's opera *Aida*, which had been commissioned to open Cairo's new opera house.[21]

When the American transcontinental railroad was completed in 1869, it replaced the Panama Railroad as the primary link between the East and West. In 1867 Colombia renegotiated its Panama Railroad contract, extending it for ninety-nine years and giving up the right to buy it back for $5 million in 1869, the twentieth anniversary of the concession. The railroad, still valuable though much less so than when it held a monopoly on transcontinental transit, paid Colombia $1 million and an annual rental of $250,000 for the extension of the contract and gave up the right of veto over the route of a new Panama canal. The new contract restricted the railroad's share in a Panama canal to a site west of Darién along a line from Cape Tiburón to Point Garachiné and required that the railroad receive "reasonable" compensation to be divided equally with Colombia.[22]

Success at Suez and defeat in the Franco-Prussian War in 1871 combined to push the French into an attempt to duplicate their Suez triumph in the isthmus. Poet Victor Hugo publicly asked de Lesseps to "astonish the world by great deeds that could be done without a war." De Lesseps, an aristocrat and a promoter but not an engineer, was rebuffed in his first attempt to win a concession for a lock canal in Nicaragua in 1872, just after President Grant's expeditions made Americans popular in Nicaragua. When Anthoine de Gogorza—an American of French parents—failed to interest the United States in his Darién canal plans, he turned to Paris' Société de Géographie, which in 1875 appointed a "Committee of Initiative" to investigate all feasible canal routes. Almost simultaneously, the Türr Syndicate (La Société Civile International du Canal Interocéaniqe du Darién), a new French private company, headed by General Istvan Türr (a Hungarian friend of de Lesseps), Baron Jacques de Reinach, and French navy Lieutenant Lucien Napoléon-Bonaparte Wyse, agreed to finance the expeditions. On May 28, 1876, de Gogorza won a provisional eighteen-month concession from Colombia. Wyse and a party of fifteen techni-

21. McCullough, *Path Between the Seas*, 45–55; André Siegfried, *Suez and Panama*, trans. H. H. Heming and Doris Heming (New York, 1940), 61–76, 239.
22. Mack, *Land Divided*, 156–60.

cians found De Gogorza's proposed Darién route unworkable as a sea-level canal. Following de Lesseps' preference for a sea-level canal on the railroad line, Wyse returned to Panama, perfunctorily examined the favored route, and immediately negotiated with Colombian Minister of Foreign Affairs Eustorgio Salgar a concession to build a Panama canal. The Wyse-Salgar concession, approved by the Colombian Congress on May 18, 1878, gave the French company twelve years (or eighteen at Colombia's option) to build its canal and directed it to make an "amicable" arrangement with the Panama Railroad Company. The contract could be sold to a private company but not to a government. On October 20, 1878, the Compagnie Universelle du Canal Interocéanique de Panamá with de Lesseps as president bought the Wyse concession and the contract of the Société Civile. Although de Lesseps' International Congress for Consideration of an Interoceanic Canal made a pretense of examining the five best routes, on May 29, 1879, the conference chose the Gulf of Limón–Bay of Panama route. At seventy-four, de Lesseps, one of the most famous and celebrated men in the world—and in France—prepared to repeat the miracle of Suez at Panama.[23]

De Lesseps' son Charles did not share his father's confidence, nor did French bankers and newspapers. De Lesseps' publicity campaign failed to attract investors. When only 60,000 of the 800,000 shares (at 500 francs) of the initial organizing issue were sold, de Lesseps had to turn to the financiers he had spurned at Suez for help. Undercapitalized from the start, authorized by the French legislature to raise only 300 million francs by public subscription (half of what was needed), and hampered by unusually large promotional costs, de Lesseps launched his new Panama canal project with the first shovelful of earth on January 1, 1880. Backed by 104,315 subscribers (mostly French middle-class investors), who, influenced by heavy press support and memories of the success at Suez, oversubscribed the issue, de Lesseps tried to assuage American feelings by offering the presidency of the canal company to former President Ulysses S. Grant. On March 5, 1880, de Lesseps conferred with Secretary of State William M. Evarts and President Rutherford B. Hayes, and on March 8 he pleaded for support before the House Interoceanic Canal Committee. But on that same day, Hayes, in a strong special message to Congress, de-

23. DuVal, *Cadiz to Cathay*, 102–107; DuVal, *And the Mountains Will Move*, 31–45; Mack, *Land Divided*, 283–99; McCullough, *Path Between the Seas*, 43–69; Siegfried, *Suez and Panama*.

clared that any isthmian canal was "virtually a part of the coast line of the United States" and that "the policy of this country is a canal under American control." Also on March 8 the House Select Committee on Interoceanic Canals urged Congress to bar any form of European protectorate in the New World and to assert American control over any "artificial" means of communication across the isthmus and urged the president to take steps to abrogate "any treaty in conflict with this declaration," a direct reference to the Clayton-Bulwer Treaty with Britain. Grant not only refused the presidency of de Lesseps' canal but publicly rebuffed the French project. "I commend an American canal, on American soil to the American people" and warned that rival powers, "whether friendly or hostile," should be watched carefully. De Lesseps' efforts revived interest in the Monroe Doctrine and in a Nicaraguan canal under American control and began the American association of a Panama canal with French or foreign interests.[24]

Upset by the French canal initiative, a group of influential private American investors, including Grant, General George B. McClellan, Admiral Ammen, Menocal, and Levi Morton, organized the Provisional Interoceanic Canal Society in 1880 to seek an American-controlled canal franchise. On April 24, 1880, this group formed the Maritime Canal Company of Nicaragua and was awarded a ninety-nine-year concession for a canal with the provision that it be built and operating within twelve years. When Secretary of State Frederick T. Frelinghuysen negotiated a canal convention with Nicaragua's special commissioner Joaquín Zavala on December 1, 1884, he ignored the Clayton-Bulwer Treaty, which prohibited a unilateral American canal. On December 15, Secretary of the Navy William E. Chandler ordered another survey of Nicaragua. Menocal's revised report called for a route from Greytown to Brito, seven locks instead of twenty-one, and a proposed length of 169 miles. The Frelinghuysen-Zavala convention, which proposed that a canal be "built by the United States . . . and owned by them," attracted wide debate in the press and in January, 1885, failed by only five votes to win the required two-thirds for ratification in the Senate. When Cleveland, who opposed public ownership of a canal, became president in March, 1885, he withdrew

24. For the financial details see Mack, *Land Divided*, 300–316. Hayes's message is in *Senate Executive Documents*, 46th Cong., 1st Sess., No. 112, Serial 1885, pp. 1–2; the House report is in *House Reports*, 46th Cong., 3rd Sess., No. 390, Serial 1983, pp. 8–9; DuVal, *Cadiz to Cathay*, 95–96; DuVal, *And the Mountains Will Move*, 45–66; Perkins, *Monroe Doctrine, 1867–1907*, 69–87; McCullough, *Path Between the Seas*, 118–23. Grant's statement is in *NAR*, CXXXXII (1881), 115–16.

the convention and opened the way for a new private canal company. On December 3, 1886, Ammen and Menocal formed the Provisional Canal Association, negotiated a new concession, approved by the Nicaraguan Senate on April 23, 1887, which called for a payment of at least $4 million to Nicaragua (or 6 percent of the proposed canal's value). The company also agreed to pay Costa Rica $1.5 millon (or 1.5 percent of the proposed canal's value), although a legal decision rendered by President Cleveland, acting as arbitrator, ruled that Costa Rica was not entitled to compensation. By February 20, 1889, Congress passed and Cleveland approved bills to incorporate the Maritime Canal Company of Nicaragua as a private company. Hiram Hitchcock became president and Menocal chief engineer of the new company, which took over the Provisional Canal Association's concession, and formed the Nicaraguan Canal Construction Company to begin work.[25]

Because Panama was so different from Suez, de Lesseps' experience proved to be a disadvantage in dealing with a situation so new that every phase became an experiment. Panama's rock formations were radically different from Europe's; the rare European engineers who were willing to improvise faced massive opposition from the traditionalists. Oppressive humid heat, devastating fevers, racially complicated labor problems, and de Lesseps' insistence on a sea-level canal all contributed to making the enterprise a disaster. Real estate speculators along the canal route made everything more expensive, especially the Panama Railroad, which de Lesseps finally had to spend nearly $20 million to acquire, more than five times its real value. As yellow fever and malaria took a dreadful toll, French subscribers were repeatedly asked for more money. In 1885, Lieutenant William W. Kimball, an American naval intelligence officer sent to inspect and report on the Panama situation to a House committee, admired "the

25. Mack, *Land Divided*, 215–18; DuVal, *Cadiz to Cathay*, 82–87; Miner, *Fight for the Panama Route*, 25–30; Roscoe R. Hill, "The Nicaraguan Canal Idea to 1913," *HAHR*, XXVII (1948), 197–211; Paul J. Scheips, "United States Commercial Pressures for a Nicaraguan Canal in the 1890's," *Americas*, XX (1964), 333–58; Lawrence A. Clayton, "The Nicaraguan Canal in the Nineteenth Century: Prelude to American Empire in the Caribbean," *Journal of Latin American Studies*, XIX (1987), 333–52. For the public debate on the Frelinghuysen convention see David M. Pletcher, *The Awkward Years: American Foreign Relations Under Garfield and Arthur* (Columbia, Mo., 1962), 278–83; for the Menocal report see *Senate Executive Documents*, 49th Cong., 1st Sess., No. 99, Serial 2337; Hagan, *American Gunboat Diplomacy and the Old Navy*, 155–59. See also Joseph Smith, *Illusions of Conflict: Anglo-American Diplomacy Toward Latin America, 1865–1896* (Pittsburgh, 1979), 104–13.

courage of the French and the determination to finish the canal" but noted that for the "500,000,000 francs already spent and not one-tenth of the work accomplished," only de Lesseps' prestige had prevented the company's bankruptcy. Kimball advised Congress "that with a sufficient expenditure of money, time, brains, energy, and human life, the canal can be finished is self-evident." French brains might do the job but not French money. French money and de Lesseps' magic were both exhausted.[26]

Jean Philippe Bunau-Varilla, born in 1859, was educated at the Ecole Polytechnique, the great Paris engineering school that imbued its students with the spirit of its motto—for country, science, and glory." When de Lesseps addressed a convocation at the Ecole on his return from America in 1880, he inspired the young Bunau-Varilla to make the Panama canal his life's work. When Bunau-Varilla fretted that he had missed the great opportunity at Suez, his mother reassured him: "You still have the Panama Canal left." Trained as a civil engineer, Bunau-Varilla began his required five years of state service by building roads in colonial North Africa. Yellow fever so decimated the French ranks in Panama that when Bunau-Varilla volunteered for Panama duty in 1884, he was quickly accepted. He spent the three-week sea journey immersed in the Panama project. He was appointed head of the Pacific slope excavation and began to solve the canal's most vexing engineering problem, the creation of an artifical lake as a reliable source of water for the canal. As head of the Colón excavation, Bunau-Varilla solved the demolition problem involving Panama's especially hard rock, a procedure that éventually transformed de Lesseps' original sea-level canal into a more sophisticated, cheaper lock canal originally thought possible only in Nicaragua. When yellow fever claimed General Manager Charles Dingler and his replacement, Maurice Hutin, Bunau-Varilla at age twenty-six became the canal's general manager and chief engineer.[27]

Bunau-Varilla's ascension to the head of the Panama canal company coincided with the rise of Colombia's President Rafael Núñez, whose victory in the war of 1884–1885 and his Regeneration program replaced the Liberal federalism of the Rionegro constitution of 1863.

26. Anguizola, *Philippe Bunau-Varilla*, 47–50; Mack, *Land Divided*, 315–17; DuVal, *And the Mountains Will Move*, 67–96. Kimball's report is in *House Miscellaneous Reports*, 59th Cong., 1st Sess., No. 395, Serial 2422, pp. 30–32.

27. *BVC*, esp. 35–49, 82–83; Anguizola, *Philippe Bunau-Varilla*, 53–58. For the role of the Ecole Polytechnique as a military school specializing in scientific education for future engineers see *BVC*, 35 n.

The conflict between the Liberals and Conservatives, clearly defined since the 1850s and exacerbated by the deeply rooted regionalism of Colombia's history and geography, resulted in almost constant ideological warfare in nineteenth-century Colombia. Núñez, an intellectual, poet, writer, cosmopolitan world traveler, and noted philanderer, first ran for the presidency as a Liberal in 1875. When the ruling Liberals divided between Radicals, who supported the Rionegro ideology, and Independents, who wanted reforms, Colombia's tendency toward virtual anarchy in its nine regional states put Liberal governing power in jeopardy, especially after Conservatives won control of two of the nine states. When Núñez won the presidency in 1880, he put through a protective tariff, a national bank, and new public works, all of which signaled a radical break with ideological Liberalism and its devotion to laissez-faire economic programs. Plagued by the collapse of its tobacco and quinine agriculture and a decline in world coffee prices, Colombia faced increasing deficits, a gold drain, and a growing trade imbalance. Núñez pledged the annual $250,000 Panama Railroad lease income (until 1908) to secure a $3 million loan from a New York bank to fund Colombia's first national bank. When Núñez won his second term as president in 1884 and formed a coalition of Independent Liberals and Conservatives, the Radicals went to war to resist the modernizing nationalism of the Regeneration. After the war, Núñez instituted the Regeneration constitution of 1886, which gave Colombia a highly centralized government, restored and protected the Catholic church, restored the death penalty, extended the president's term to six years, limited the freedom of the press, barred the private sale, possession, or manufacture of arms and ammunition, and gave presidential decrees the force of law. The nine sovereign states of the Rionegro era became departments headed by presidentially appointed governors and elected assemblies.[28]

Nowhere was the "enervating particularism" that Núñez fought to eradicate more pronounced than in Panama, the final battleground of the war of 1884–1885. Panama's position as a center of commerce be-

28. James William Park, *Rafael Núñez and the Politics of Colombian Regionalism, 1863–1886* (Baton Rouge, 1985); Thomas R. Favell, "The Antecendents of Panama's Separation from Colombia" (Ph.D. dissertation, Fletcher School of Law and Diplomacy, 1951), 71–101; Helen Delpar, *Red Against Blue: The Liberal Party in Colombian Politics, 1863–1899* (University, Ala., 1981); Charles W. Bergquist, *Coffee and Conflict in Colombia, 1886–1910* (Durham, N.C., 1978); Helguera, "Problem of Liberalism Versus Conservatism in Colombia"; Bushnell, "Two Stages in Colombia Tariff Policy," 3–23; Jane Meyer Loy, "Primary Education During the Colombian Federation: The School Reform of 1870,"

gan in the seventeenth century, when the trading fair at the Caribbean port of Portobello attracted merchants from all over South America, who came to make their annual purchases. When Spain closed the Portobello fair in 1739, Panama endured a depression that lasted until the wars of independence allowed a renewed trade in contraband. After winning its independence from Spain in a bloodless coup, Panama reluctantly allied with Bolívar's Gran Colombia, hoping to exploit its potential as a trade crossroads. Bogotá then, as Bogotá later, resisted Panama's ambitions. In a statement to the Colombian Congress in 1823, Panama complained that Colombia did not understand Panama's unique geography or encourage its commercial potential. When Panama separated from Colombia in 1830 and 1840, it cited Colombian insensitivity to Panama's uniqueness, a belief that became the controlling myth of the isthmus. Calmed by the wealth the Panama Railroad produced, content with the regionalism of Rionegro, its extensive international contacts, and a remoteness from Bogotá virtually all Colombia shared, Panama was effectively an independent state between 1861 and 1885, ill prepared for the unifying ideology of the Núñez Regeneration, which it fiercely resisted.[29]

Although Núñez, anticipating Panamanian resistance to the Regeneration, put Panama under a military governor, two serious insurrections destroyed Colón and partially destroyed Panama City. Because Panama, Colombia, and the United States were all in a transitional period between governments, their confused initial reactions to the crisis made it worse. On January 18, 1885, twelve marines from the American warship *Alliance* landed overnight to guard the Panama

HAHR, LI (1971), 275–94; Helen Delpar, "Aspects of Liberal Factionalism in Colombia, 1875–1885," *HAHR*, LI (1971), 250–74. For the collapse of tobacco and quinine exports see Charles W. Bergquist, "The Political Economy of the Colombia Presidential Election of 1897," *HAHR*, LVI (1976), 4; also see Delpar, "The Liberal Record and Colombian Historiography," 524–37; Herring, *History of Latin America*, 482–84; text of the constitution of 1886 is in "Constitution of Republic of Colombia," trans. Bernard Moses, in *Senate Documents*, 57th Cong., 2nd Sess., No. 75, Serial 4422.

29. For the Portobello fairs see Murdo J. Macleod, "Aspects of the Internal Economy of Colonial Latin America," in *CHLA*, I, 352–54, 385, 410–11; Donald Lee DeWitt, "Social and Educational Thought in the Development of the Republic of Panama, 1903–1946" (Ph.D. dissertation, University of Arizona, 1972), 2–24; and Freedman, "The Independence of Panama and Its Incorporation in Gran Colombia," 4–7. "Myth of the Isthmus" is Ricuarte Soler's phrase quoted *ibid.*, 18. For a political denunciation of Núñez and Colombia and a history of Panamanian separatism see Ramon Valdes, "The Independence of the Isthmus of Panama—Its History, Causes, and Justification," trans. U.S. State Department, in *FRUS*, 1903, pp. 319–33; for a sympathetic history of Panama see Perez-Venero, *Before the Five Frontiers.*

Railroad Company offices. On March 16, Rafael Aizpuru, a former president of Panama, led a Liberal revolt in Panama City. When General Carlos A. Gonima moved against Aizpuru, Pedro Prestán took advantage of the army's absence to take control of Colón, where he took hostage the Americans, who refused to release a shipment of arms to him, and threatened reprisals against the other Americans in the city. When the captain of the American warship *Galena* refused to yield the arms, Prestán took his captives to the front lines. In the battle that followed between Gonima's and Prestán's forces, a fire broke out that destroyed Colón. Meanwhile, Aizpuru regained control of Panama City. The Americans, confused by the changing of administrations from the more activist Republican Chester A. Arthur to the Democrat Cleveland and because the Panama crisis was far more complicated than previous incidents such as the Watermelon War of 1856, did not arrive in strength until the isthmus was out of control at both ends. Aizpuru, a serious political revolutionary, may have tried to win United States protection for an independent Panama. When the massive American force of seven warships and 740 marines assembled between March 31 and April 15 finally intervened, the fighting quickly ended.[30]

The American commander, Rear Admiral James E. Jouett, wary of the possibility of having to fight two Colombian forces and fearful of any American political involvement in the isthmus, at first refused to permit General Rafael Reyes's national forces to land on the isthmus. Unaware that Reyes, in his dirty uniform from his long journey from Colombia, was not one of the revolutionary rabble they usually encountered, the Americans made disparaging remarks, certain that Reyes could not understand them. Before Bunau-Varilla, whom Jouett asked to act as interpreter, could begin, Reyes, speaking in his Oxford accent, astonished the Americans by citing the treaty of 1846 as his authority to restore Colombian order in the isthmus. Jouett congratulated him, and the Americans gave the Colombians full military honors as they embarked. Jouett, Reyes, and Bunau-Varilla, working well

---

30. Anguizola, *Philippe Bunau-Varilla*, 60–61; Mack, *Land Divided*, 350–52; Offutt, *Protection of Citizens Abroad by the United States*, 66–70. For an account emphasizing American economic motives see Hagan, *American Gunboat Diplomacy and the Old Navy*, 160–87; Perez-Venero, *Before the Five Frontiers*, 113–15. See also Daniel H. Wicks, "Dress Rehearsal: United States Intervention on the Isthmus of Panama, 1885," *PHR*, XLIX (1980), 581–605; and Jack Shulimson, "U.S. Marines in Panama, 1885," in Merrill L. Bartlett (ed.), *Assault from the Sea: Essays on the History of Amphibious Warfare* (Annapolis, 1983), 107–20.

together, restored order in the isthmus. Aizpuru was tried in Bogotá and sentenced to ten years in exile; Prestán, ostracized by both sides, who blamed him for the Colón fire, was captured at Cartagena, returned to Colón, and hanged on August 18, 1885. Impressed with how quickly the American troops restored order, Bunau-Varilla and José Arango both remembered the event and made it the cornerstone of their strategy in Panama's successful revolution of 1903.[31]

Bunau-Varilla survived yellow fever in 1886 and, after recuperating in Paris, returned to Panama as an independent contractor. He convinced the company to give up de Lesseps' dream of a sea-level canal and to accept his lock canal solution for the Culebra Cut. After de Lesseps' desperation lottery bond issue failed, on December 15, 1888, however, the Compagnie Universelle was declared bankrupt. Although a French engineering committee estimated that a completed canal would cost 3 billion francs ($600 million) and would take twenty years, Wyse negotiated the Wyse-Roldán agreement, an extension of the original Salgar-Wyse concession, due to expire on March 3, 1893. On December 26, 1890, Colombia granted a ten-year concession in return for 10 million francs in cash and 5 million francs in stock, provided a new canal company resumed work by February 28, 1893. In the criminal trials that followed the scandals over the Panama canal fiasco in 1892, many company officials, including de Lesseps and his son, were convicted of fraud. Because of his age and distinction, de Lesseps escaped jail, though Charles and other convicted company officials were briefly imprisoned for their roles in the French debacle at Panama.[32]

When Bunau-Varilla left the isthmus in 1889, he carried with him the obsession that Panama was still the "great idea which would give France one more glorious page in the history of Humanity." After narrowly failing to win a seat in the Chamber of Deputies in 1889, Bunau-Varilla followed the suggestion of John Bigelow, the American minister to France during the Civil War, to write his first book on the

31. Anguizola, *Philippe Bunau-Varilla*, 61–64; Mack, *Land Divided*, 353–54; Perez-Venero, *Before the Five Frontiers*, 113–15; Miner, *Fight for the Panama Route*, 47–52; BVC, 41. For the naval intervention see *Senate Documents*, 58th Cong., 2nd Sess., No. 143, Serial 4589 (*The Use of Military Force in Colombia*), 103–58; Offutt, *Protection of Citizens Abroad by the United States*, 66–70; and Hagan, *American Gunboat Diplomacy and the Old Navy*, 172–87. For American concern about French influence in Panama see Wicks, "Dress Rehearsal," 587.

32. Anguizola, *Philippe Bunau-Varilla*, 111–56; Mack, *Land Divided*, 374–404; McCullough, *Path Between the Seas*, 204–41; Siegfried, *Suez and Panama*, 271–83.

canal, *Panama: Past, Present, and Future*. Bunau-Varilla had met Bigelow in 1886 when de Lesseps, trying to win American interest, invited distinguished persons to visit and write about the canal. Bigelow, representing the New York Chamber of Commerce, became friends with Bunau-Varilla and remained his close confidant and the main American supporter of a Panama canal. Although Francis Loomis, in 1903 the American diplomat most directly involved in the Panama canal, wrote (in January, 1904) to President Roosevelt that he had known Bunau-Varilla casually and only since 1901, Bunau-Varilla's biographer places the beginning of their relationship in 1890, when Loomis became the American consul at St. Etienne. Loomis, who worked for American minister to France Whitelaw Reid when Reid was editor of the New York *Tribune*, delivered a message from Bigelow to Bunau-Varilla, and they then became lifelong friends. Looking for a means of defending and supporting the Panama canal, the brothers Philippe and Maurice Bunau-Varilla bought an interest in the French newspaper *Le Matin* after their attempts to buy *Le Temps* and *Figaro* failed.[33]

Bunau-Varilla tried unsuccessfully to get Russia, which in 1892 began its Trans-Siberian railroad and its new alliance with France, to finish the canal. After Colombia agreed to extend the deadline for the canal company's reorganization to October 31, 1894 (over United States objections), the Compagnie Nouvelle du Canal de Panama was ingeniously organized by raising its capital of 60 million francs (plus 5 million francs in stock to Colombia) from forced investments imposed on the Compagnie Universelle's contractors, banks, and directors under threat of criminal prosecution for fraud claims. Bunau-Varilla and his brother were assessed 22,000 one-hundred-franc shares because Maurice, appointed as general manager of Bunau-Varilla's Paris contracting office, had set aside a regular salary for Phillipe as a way of evading the law that prohibited government engineers from receiving any private income during their five years of required service. Bunau-Varilla, like the other "penalty stockholders," was barred from participation in the new company's management. Bunau-Varilla's sudden wealth remains unexplained. He had been a scholar-

33. "Humanity" quoted in *BVC*, 429; Margaret Clapp, *Forgotten First Citizen: John Bigelow* (Boston, 1947), 306–307; *BVC*, 139–44; Anguizola, *Philippe Bunau-Varilla*, 157–59. For the dating of their active collaboration in Caracas in 1898, when Loomis was appointed minister to Venezuela, see *ibid.*, 175–77; Francis Loomis to TR, January 5, 1904, Panama Folder 19, Reel 5, in Francis B. Loomis Papers, Stanford University, Palo Alto, California.

ship student at the Ecole Polytechnique, and his wife was an eccentric, unmonied semirecluse. Although speculation often connects him with the Isaac Seligman family banking interests in New York, through mutual concerns with both Alfred Dreyfus and Panama, there is no evidence that he received financial support from the Seligmans. French hopes of salvaging anything from the de Lesseps debacle were negligible, especially since the public scandals of the de Lesseps trials reinforced America's predisposition for a Nicaraguan route. Bunau-Varilla, who defended his classmate Alfred Dreyfus in 1894 and later lost a leg as a volunteer at Verdun, remained determined to fight for Panama though he was now branded as a *panimiste* (thief). The *Nation* wrote in 1893: "The word Panama now suggests so universally huge a scandal that its association with an actual canal across an actual isthmus seems only a figure of speech."[34]

Senator John Tyler Morgan, the chairman of the Senate Committee on Interoceanic Canals, was a complex southern nationalist. He was a Selma, Alabama, lawyer, born in 1824, who became a brigadier general after leading a cavalry charge at Chickamauga. Elected to the United States Senate in 1876, Morgan became a member of the Foreign Relations Committee in 1878. In 1890 Morgan, already a strong advocate of a Nicaraguan canal, supported John T. Sherman's bill to convert the Maritime Canal Company from a private to a publicly funded enterprise. Sherman's proposal to guarantee $100 million of canal bonds was opposed by senators wary of violating the Clayton-Bulwer Treaty or of using public funds to benefit a private company. The Maritime Canal Company began work in Nicaragua on October 9, 1889, and in the following year bought dredges and other idle equipment from the Panama canal's construction company. But its original capitalization of $3 million was not enough to build a canal. Just before Britain's Baring Bank failed in 1890, it rejected a proposed loan to the Maritime Canal Company. Morgan argued that public funding would prevent private foreign capitalists from controlling an American canal. Although Morgan failed to sway the Senate, by 1893 he was

34. The Russian overture is described in *BVC*, 145–51; for the United States objection see *SP*, 209; Anguizola, *Philippe Bunau-Varilla*, 161–63; for the Dreyfus connection see *ibid.*, 163–64; Mack, *Land Divided*, 406–409; for *panimiste* and the *Nation* see *ibid.*, 377; *Nation*, LVI, March 30, 1893, p. 229; for the reasons why Bunau-Varilla was made a penalty stockholder, his connection with the Seligmans, and the mystery of his wealth see McCullough, *Path Between the Seas*, 288–94; for the figure of 11,000 shares instead of 22,000, and speculation about the Seligman connection see Earl Harding, *The Untold Story of Panama* (New York, 1959), 15, 58–60.

the leading champion of an American-owned and controlled isthmian canal. Like other southerners, Morgan feared that the transcontinental railroad interests were opposed to any interoceanic canal that could compete with existing American railroads. In support of a Nicaraguan canal, Morgan cited duty, profit, the natural hand of Providence, and the need to break the railroad industry's monopoly in transcontinental and long-distance transportation. Morgan argued that canals should receive government subsidies as the railroads had.[35]

Morgan, who could play demogogue or realistic politician as the occasion demanded, was regarded by his colleagues—until he became a single-minded fanatic—as almost an intellectual. Morgan's best arguments were inspired by his southern interests. A Nicaraguan canal near the Gulf of Mexico would give the ports of Mobile and New Orleans advantages over Atlantic ports, especially in shipments to the Pacific and Latin America. Morgan envisioned a new south transformed into a manufacturing and export center with cheap and effective access to Latin American as well as world markets through an isthmian canal. Since a trip from the Atlantic to the Pacific was six hundred miles shorter, Morgan's early preference for a Nicaraguan canal route was sound. The major problem was that these arguments applied almost equally to Panama. Panama might be farther from the Gulf ports than Nicaragua, but the advantages of any Central American canal were similar and of almost equal benefit to the South. When Congress refused to fund the Maritime Canal Company, and the company's own bond issue of $5 million failed as the depression of 1893 began, the company was declared bankrupt on August 30, 1893.[36]

35. August C. Radke, "Senator Morgan and the Nicaragua Canal," *Alabama Review*, XII (1959), 5–34; Radke, "John Tyler Morgan: An Expansionist Senator, 1877–1907" (Ph.D. dissertation, University of Washington, 1953); A. L. Venable, "John T. Morgan, Father of the Inter-Oceanic Canal," *Southwestern Social Science Quarterly*, XIX (1939), 376–87; O. Lawrence Burnette, Jr., "John Tyler Morgan and Expansionist Sentiment in the New South," *Alabama Review*, XVIII (1965), 163–82; Scheips, "United States Commercial Pressures for a Nicaraguan Canal in the 1890's," 333–58; Hill, "The Nicaraguan Canal Idea to 1913," 207–208; Miner, *Fight for the Panama Route*, 24–32; Mack, *Land Divided*, 219–22; Clayton, "The Nicaraguan Canal in the Nineteenth Century," 323–32; John T. Morgan, "Government Aid to Nicaragua," *NAR*, CLXVI (1983), 195–203.

36. "Statement of John T. Morgan on the Nicaraguan Canal, December 14, 1892, Before the Committee on Interstate and Foreign Commerce," in Box 26, John Tyler Morgan Papers, LC; Tennant S. McWilliams, "The Lure of Empire: Southern Interest in the Caribbean, 1877–1900," *Mississippi Quarterly*, XXIX (1975–76), 43–63; Joseph A. Fry, "John Tyler Morgan's Southern Expansionism," *DH*, 9 (1985), 336; Morgan, "The Choice of Isthmian Canal Routes," *NAR*, CLXXIV (1902), 672–86.

At first there was no opposition to Morgan's Nicaragua canal, though there were questions about its funding, precise location, and other technical details. Some of these were addressed by the Ludlow Commission on March 2, 1895, which estimated the cost of a canal at $133,472,893. For Americans a canal and Nicaragua were synonymous. After de Lesseps' bankruptcy in 1889, Bunau-Varilla assumed the leadership of the French Panama canal initiative. In 1896 the Compagnie Nouvelle hired American railroad attorney and political lobbyist William Nelson Cromwell to represent its American interests. Cromwell was an ideal choice, a specialist in railroads, mergers, and corporate troubleshooting, experienced in Panama as attorney for the Panama Railroad since 1894, and an influential contributor to the Republican party. Cromwell's connections were important but no more so than his ability to understand corporate balance sheets and to work hard and effectively for his clients. Cromwell, the self-made American manipulator, and Bunau-Varilla, the polished French gentleman, disliked each other but worked efficiently and separately (they did not meet until 1902) as one of history's most effective lobbying teams. In 1896 no one disputed that Nicaragua would be the site of America's future canal. For Cromwell the task of persuading Americans that Panama was preferable was bleak even without the dedicated opposition of Senator Morgan. Cromwell summed up the situation in 1896:

Public opinion demanded the Nicaragua Canal. The only canal known, the only (canal) wanted, the only (canal) spoken of was looked upon as a vanished dream. The desire for a canal meant only the desire for the Nicaragua Canal. The constant activity of the Maritime Co. and its friends throughout the country had aroused interest and created a demand for its construction. Boards of trade, State legislatures, party conventions all over the country had passed resolutions in which action in favor of the Nicaragua Canal was demanded. . . . It was evident that in one form or another the United States was about to adopt the Nicaragua Canal.[37]

Theodore Roosevelt's assessment of Colombian society before the chaos of civil war is both patronizing and fairly accurate: "There is among them a circle of high-bred men and women which would reflect honor on the social life of any country; and there has been an

37. DuVal, *Cadiz to Cathay*, 84–87; *Report of the Nicaragua Canal Board*, October 31, 1895, in *House Documents*, 54th Cong., 1st Sess., No. 279, Serial 5172; for Cromwell's role see Miner, *Fight for the Panama Route*, 75–77; Cromwell's own account is in "Cromwell's Brief," *SP*, 197–298; Cromwell quote in *SP*, 209.

intellectual and literary development within this small circle which partially atones for the stagnation and illiteracy of the mass of the people." In the three decades following 1850, Colombia had developed a wealthy upper class with a taste for European luxuries that contrasted sharply with the primitive poverty of both Bogotá and the countryside. In the early 1890s the coffee boom made Bogotá's upper classes active consumers of European culture. Clothes from Paris and London tailors, opera performances, and a social calendar of parties and dances gave Bogotá the air, if not the substance, of cosmopolitan culture. Opera companies stayed for seven months in opulent Bogotá; the Teatro Colón, an elegant theater, had the most expensive actors and singers from Europe. After attending the evening's cultural event, Bogotá society enjoyed a round of lavish suppers and parties. The money was new, the culture imported, and the wealth temporary, but the golden age of coffee gave wealthy Colombians a false sense of security and the Liberals who were Bogotá's social leaders a conviction that the new Colombia reflected the worldly Liberal political philosophy. Colombia's extreme good fortune ended abruptly in 1896, when Brazil came to dominate the coffee market. When world coffee prices plummeted, coffee growers, coffee merchants, and Bogotá's lavish lifestyle were equally devastated, precipitating a crisis that soon destroyed Colombia's fragile political peace.[38]

Colombia's politicians were not only well educated, they tended to be scholars or intellectuals. It was customary for Bogotá politicians to own and edit their own newspapers. Miguel Antonio Caro, the most important of the political leaders and philosophers, was a central figure in all three of Colombia's political crises between 1886 and 1903. Caro's ideology dominated the Regeneration era, the civil wars, and the ultimate Colombian rejection of the Panama Canal treaty. Born and raised as a member of the gentry, educated as a Jesuit, Caro translated Virgil, was a distinguished philologist and literary critic, and remained a determined—perhaps even an ideological—provincial. Caro's intellect was impressive though narrowly focused on Colombia's Spanish Catholic heritage. He was the paradigm of the well-to-

38. TR, *Autobiography* (1913), rpr. in *TRWN*, XX, 515; Parks, *Colombia and the United States*, 111, 115–16; Bergquist, *Coffee and Conflict in Colombia*, 35–36; Jonathan C. Brown, "The Genteel Tradition of Nineteenth Century Colombian Culture," *Americas*, XXXVI (1980), 445–64; see also Jane Meyer Loy, "Modernization and Educational Reform in Colombia" (Ph.D. dissertation, University of Wisconsin, 1969); Loy, "Primary Education During the Colombia Federation," 275–94.

do gentleman who had servants do his shopping and never left the intellectual confines of Bogotá Catholicism. An intelligent and articulate true believer, Caro lacked the temperament for practical politics; his attempts to impose the "right" system on intellectual opponents polarized an already divided society.[39]

President Rafael Núñez was both a scholar and an effective practicing politician. When Núñez won his first presidential term in 1880, he campaigned as a Radical Liberal against the Catholic church. As president he made peace with the church, centralized political power in Bogotá, and promulgated Vice-President Caro's constitution of 1886. But Núñez, unlike Caro, had traveled in Europe and the United States and served as Colombian consul in Liverpool. A liberal who became a conservative, a rational skeptic who attacked the church and then negotiated a concordat with the pope and made an ally of the church to stabilize Colombian society, Núñez was a consummate and worldly politician—an intellectual eclectic and a political opportunist. Núñez thought the Regeneration was politically necessary to restore Colombian stability; Caro regarded it as an absolute good. When Núñez died in 1894, the leadership of the Regeneration passed to the rigid absolutism of Caro, who had become president in 1892.[40]

Under Caro's leadership, and with the fall in world coffee prices, a serious crisis was made worse by Colombia's increasingly factionalized politicians. In January, 1896, twenty-one Conservatives who had supported the Regeneration of 1886 and had become members of Núñez's new Nationalist party, left that party and formed a new group called Historical Conservatives. "Motives of Dissidence," a manifesto written by Carlos Martínez Silva, attacked the increasing authoritarianism of the regime and its narrow economic policies, which failed to encourage export trade, retire the foreign debt, or discourage corruption. Instead of trying to placate an important dissident constituency, Caro rejected the valid grievances of the Historical Conservatives and in his insensitive response widened the breach. Colombian politics became a battleground characterized by frequent declarations of principles. Conservatives, Historicals, Liberals—the

39. Bergquist, *Coffee and Conflict in Colombia*, 42–43; Favell, "Antecedents," 152; Park, *Rafael Núñez and the Politics of Colombian Regionalism*, 275–77. For Caro's role in the philological movement as a leader in the rejection of French influence and a return to Spanish roots see Brown, "Genteel Tradition of Nineteenth Century Colombian Culture," 460.

40. Crow, *Epic of Latin America*, 620–21; Bergquist, *Coffee and Conflict in Colombia*, 43; Palacios, *Coffee in Colombia*, 126–27.

latter soon to break into two disparate groups—and the ruling Nationalists all became increasingly doctrinaire. Núñez might have worked out a compromise to avert a confrontation; Caro and the nationalists relished the ideological war and increased repressive measures against the clamoring minority groups.[41]

The Nationalists enjoyed two advantages: the power of the government and an ideology that, though inflexible, was more appealing than the doctrinal schisms of their opponents. Even the dissenting Historical Conservatives approved the fundamental Nationalist reforms of a more highly centralized government and a closer relationship with the Catholic church. Catholic fundamentalism, opposition to wealthy export agricultural capitalists, and repression of dissent were as appealing in Colombia as the rhetoric of the common man was in America. Rafael Reyes, the most likely politician to put aside ideology for compromise and to unite Liberals and Conservatives under a modernist program to bring technology to Colombia, was rejected because he was too flexible. A cosmopolitan who had served as Colombia's minister to France, a Conservative popular with both factions, a businessman and agricultural developer, Reyes was out of step with Colombia's increasingly doctrinal politics. Any figure with connections in another party was suspect. The very possibility that a candidate might compromise was unappealing in Colombia's presidential election of 1897.[42]

Colombian presidential elections were curious mixtures of ideology, opportunism, and fraud. Each of the parties and schisms presented elaborate programs; the Nationalists offered an odd ticket of two elderly men designed to appeal to specific constituencies, even though as the government in power the Nationalists controlled the ballot boxes, especially in the provinces. The victorious Nationalists offered a ticket headed by Manuel Antonio Sanclemente, who, at eighty-three, was expected to be a figurehead. Sanclemente was both old and ill and made it clear that he would not live in Bogotá because of his failing health. The new president's only political experience

41. Bergquist, *Coffee and Conflict in Colombia*, 57–59; Crow, *Epic of Latin America*, 621; "Motives of Dissidence" is in Luis Martínez Delgado, *A proposito de Carlos Martínez Silva* (Bogotá, 1926), 157–78; Delpar, *Red Against Blue*, 160–63; Favell, "Antecedents," 118–27.

42. Bergquist, *Coffee and Conflict in Colombia*, 59, 220–22. For the primacy of the religious issue in the Colombian conflict see Delpar, "Aspects of Liberal Factionalism in Colombia," 251; Favell, "Antecedents," 128; Delpar, *Red Against Blue*, 164–69; Bergquist, "Political Economy of the Colombian Presidential Election of 1897," 21–24.

consisted of a term as senator from the large western province of Cauca and a brief role as minister of state under Caro that he had resigned for medical reasons.[43]

Vice-President José Manuel Marroquín at seventy-one was a lifelong Conservative and even less of a politician than Sanclemente. Marroquín, a writer and educator, had taught Caro, and the two had become friends associated with many educational projects. If there was a strategy in Caro's odd choice of presidential tickets, it was the reasonable expectation that Sanclemente would not govern effectively because of his age and poor health and Marroquín would serve as a figurehead for his friend and pupil Caro because of his distaste for public life.[44]

The plan backfired badly. Economic conditions were so bad by 1897 that any elected government would be faced with an immediate crisis. A government headed by two gentlemen who had no taste for politics and even less experience was impractical enough. When neither Sanclemente nor Marroquín played his expected role, the result would have been comic had Colombia's desperate situation not made it tragic. Colombian law specified that the president must govern from Bogotá. When Sanclemente refused to leave his home province of Cauca, Vice-President Marroquín was sworn in as acting president. Neither of the new leaders was an experienced politician, and neither was inclined to learn a new profession or stand aside and allow Caro to govern. Marroquín surprised everyone with his authority and initiative, but his policies appealed to the Historical Conservatives and even some Liberals more than to his own party.[45]

Caro's initial strategy had failed badly. As an alternative plan, he brought the reluctant Sanclemente to Bogotá to take over the symbolic governing authority while presumably allowing Caro to run the government. The president was miserable in Bogotá and pleaded to be allowed to resign and return to the healthier air of Cauca. Instead, he

43. Bergquist, *Coffee and Conflict in Colombia*, 61; Miner, *Fight for the Panama Route*, 52–53; Vincent Baillie Dunlap, "Tragedy of a Colombian Martyr: Rafael Uribe Uribe and the Liberal Party, 1896–1914" (Ph.D. dissertation, University of North Carolina, 1979), 120–23; Favell, "Antecedents," 143; Luis Martínez Delgado, *Historia de un cambio de gobierno* (Bogotá, 1958), is a basic history of Sanclemente's presidency.
44. Bergquist, *Coffee and Conflict in Colombia*, 61; Miner, *Fight for the Panama Route*, 53–54.
45. Bergquist, *Coffee and Conflict in Colombia*, 76–78; Miner, *Fight for the Panama Route*, 53–54; McGreevey, *Economic History of Colombia*, 180–81; Dunlap, "Tragedy of a Colombian Martyr," 141.

was kept outside of Bogotá close enough to maintain the legal fiction of power and prevent Marroquín from assuming the presidency. The Colombian Congress seethed with political activity. The Nationalists only marginally controlled the Congress, and the various parties, sensing weakness in the executive branch, attempted to undo the Regeneration. The result was deepening political chaos. No one was in command, the schisms widened, the struggle for control of the government became ominous, and increasingly the Nationalist control of the army became more important than its hold on the electorate.[46]

Colombia, one of the rare Latin American nations with a tradition of orderly government, ruled by scholars and gentlemen rather than caudillos, was on the brink of chaos. The economy had disintegrated. When he assumed office in August, 1898, Marroquín found a treasury with no money, an external debt of 7 million pesos, no prospect of further loans, and an 85 percent decline in the exchange rate of the peso from its 1887 rate of one dollar for one peso. Military expenditures had increased, the government payroll could not be met, and Colombia's economy was paralyzed. Coffee exports had almost completely halted; what little customs revenue there was had already been spent.[47]

The ideological battles of the Regeneration had sapped Colombia's capability for political accommodation. Colombia had not mastered political compromise, but its occasional successes put it far above the caudillo rule of most of its neighbors. Colombia drifted dangerously toward war. The church and the economy were not only divisive issues, they were potentially explosive. The leader of the Liberals, Rafael Uribe Uribe, understood the dangers and the absurdity of a "religious war at the end of the nineteenth century." He believed "only a Turk could conceive of such a thing!" Colombia's politics was so civilized that at first the real threat of civil war was disregarded.[48]

But the Liberals, frustrated by the repressive Nationalist government, unable to win any ideological or political accommodation, split into two groups, Peace Liberals and War Liberals, a schism that proved deadly to the party and the nation. War seemed a way out of the stale-

46. Miner, *Fight for the Panama Route*, 54–55; Bergquist, *Coffee and Conflict in Colombia*, 76–79; Favell, "Antecedents," 143–50.
47. Miner, *Fight for the Panama Route*, 55; Bergquist, *Coffee and Conflict in Colombia*, 76; Favell, "Antecedents," 150.
48. Rafael Uribe Uribe, in *El Autonomista*, July 6, 1899, trans. in Bergquist, *Coffee and Conflict in Colombia*, 129; Delpar, "Aspects of Factional Liberalism in Colombia," 251.

mate—but not a real war. Colombia's nineteenth-century conflicts were gentlemen's wars in which paid armies under chivalric generals fought limited battles on the order of pre-Napoleonic Europe. They were wars of words, rarely of blood. No one dreamed that the gentlemen's war would turn into a cataclysmic civil war that would last nearly three years. Yet the politics of ideas can be dangerous when there is no leader capable of finding a compromise. Obviously, the erratic Sanclemente, a hostage to his political mentors as well as to his infirmities, could not prevent a war. Nor was José Marroquín any more able to understand the dangers. The gentlemanly politics of Colombia had long demonstrated a penchant for ideological cul de sacs, celebrated by a popular poem:

> In Colombia, which is a land
> Of the most singular things,
> The soldiers bring peace
> And the civilians cause wars.[49]

The Compagnie Nouvelle was demoralized and unrealistic, its directors passive. The French had picked a bad time to be ambivalent. The Americans were at last ready for seriously planning a canal. The war with Spain in 1898 had publicized the need for a canal, especially when the flagship of the American fleet, the *Oregon*, nearly missed the war after a monumental twelve-thousand-mile voyage from San Francisco to Cuban waters. With the Spanish-American War, Americans suddenly realized that their extensive interests in Europe, Asia, and Latin America had made them a naval power. An interoceanic canal had become a necessity. In 1898, when new Secretary of State John Sherman, a strong supporter of a Nicaraguan canal as a senator, began to push for a treaty to enable the United States to build a canal in Nicaragua, Cromwell turned to Colombia's diplomatic representative in Washington and in a joint formal presentation to the United States government proposed Panama as an alternate site. In Paris, Bunau-Varilla first attempted to persuade the Compagnie Nouvelle to build a small barge canal as a dramatic demonstration of the Panama canal's potential. When this failed, he enlisted his old friend John Bigelow, Lincoln's ambassador to France, to write Secretary of State

49. Bergquist, *Coffee and Conflict in Colombia*, 81–90, 153; for the war and peace divisions in the Liberal party see Dunlap, "Tragedy of a Colombian Martyr," 128–43; Delpar, *Red Against Blue*, 174–81; poem quoted in Crow, *Epic of Latin America*, 618.

John Hay in November, 1898, "not to commit himself" publicly on a choice of canal routes until a thorough study of the Panama route could be done.[50]

Although Nicaragua had tired of the repeated efforts of the Maritime Canal Company and canceled its contract, President José Santos Zelaya was persuaded to negotiate a new concession in October, 1899, for an American canal through Nicaragua. To gain time and prevent an immediate Senate vote for Nicaragua, Cromwell used his political connections to persuade the McKinley administration to reconsider all possibilities, including Panama. When President William McKinley appointed the Isthmian Canal Commission in 1899, Cromwell actively lobbied for members likely to favor Panama. He was only partly successful, winning three friendly appointees against four advocates of Nicaragua among the nine commissioners. By persuading Rear Admiral John G. Walker, the chairman, to begin the commission's work in Paris with the Compagnie Nouvelle, Cromwell achieved a substantial victory.[51]

Yet the French continued to deal in abstractions, delaying realistic negotiation. Maurice Hutin, president of the Compagnie Nouvelle, proposed several unwieldy plans for reorganizing the company with only partial American participation, an unrealistic policy given the American insistence on absolute control. When McKinley's canal commission approached the Compagnie Nouvelle directly, Hutin de-

50. See Alfred Charles Richard, "The Panama Canal in American National Consciousness, 1870–1922" (Ph.D. dissertation, Boston University, 1969), 93; McCullough, *Path Between the Seas*, 254–57; John Bigelow to Philippe Bunau-Varilla, December 1, 1898, in *BVC*, 160.

51. *SP*, 214; Miner, *Fight for the Panama Route*, 30. For the conflict between the Grace interests and the original Maritime Canal Company see Clayton, "The Nicaraguan Canal in the Nineteenth Century," 323–32; Mack, *Land Divided*, 423–27. For Rear Admiral Walker's two canal commissions, the Nicaragua Canal Commission of 1897 (called the first Walker Commission) and the Isthmian Canal Commission of March 3, 1899 (called the second Walker Commission), which issued three reports: November 30, 1900 (preliminary), November 16, 1901 (final), and January 18, 1902 (supplementary), see Mack, *Land Divided*, 423–25. For Walker's comments on the significance of his work and the men he appointed to the second Walker Commission see Walker to Editorial Department, *Review of Reviews*, March 10, 1902, in John Grimes Walker Papers, LC. For Walker's naval career see Daniel H. Wicks, "New Navy and New Empire: The Life and Times of John Grimes Walker" (Ph.D. dissertation, University of California, Berkeley, 1979). See also George Abbott Morison, *George Shattuck Morison, 1842–1903: A Memoir* (Peterborough, N.H., 1940), 12–13. For a summary of continuing American diplomatic and naval interest in Nicaragua see William Roger Adams, "Strategy, Diplomacy, and Isthmian Canal Security, 1880–1917" (Ph.D. dissertation, Florida State University, 1974), esp. 89–109.

layed and refused to negotiate meaningfully with a willing Admiral Walker. The Walker Commission took its charge seriously, personally visiting the successful Kiel and Manchester canals and examining the French records for the Panama canal in Paris. On-site inspections of proposed canal sites in Panama and Nicaragua concluded the commission's research, but, without active French cooperation, there seemed no possibility of an American canal at Panama.[52]

The political crisis of Panama's future had begun, but none of the principal nations seemed to be aware that their relationships had changed. Colombia, on the verge of a disastrous civil war, relied on American protection under the Bidlack-Mallarino Treaty of 1846 to prevent Panama from seceding. Both Colombia and Panama were concerned over Nicaragua. The United States and Britain had to settle the fate of the Clayton-Bulwer Treaty. Panama chafed at the restraints imposed by the constitution of 1886. There was never any question in 1885, 1895, or later that should Colombia's and Panama's interests diverge, Panama would secede—but only with United States acquiescence. For Panama, the canal was the only hope for the future. For Colombia, it remained secondary to the bitter struggle for political control about to engage all its energies.[53]

52. For the original and supplementary Isthmian Canal Commission reports see *Senate Documents*, 58th Cong., 2nd Sess., No. 222, Serial 4609; for the correspondence between the Compagnie Nouvelle and the United States see *Senate Documents*, 57th Cong., 2nd Sess., No. 34, Serial 4417, pp. 1–47; Anguizola, *Philippe Bunau-Varilla*, 178–79.

53. Favell, "Antecedents," 146–47, 150–51; Richard, "Panama Canal in American National Consciousness," 93–101.

6 War, 1899–1901

The War of the Thousand Days began in October, 1899, in the same way Colombian civil wars frequently began. The armies were composed of lower-class conscripts, dupes, or volunteers attracted by romance, plunder, or simply an escape from drudgery. The government army was better-trained and more capable than the War Liberals anticipated and in the first skirmishes in October the Liberals failed to win control of the important ports at Barranquilla and Cartagena, Colombia's link with the outside world and an essential source of customs house revenue needed to finance the war. The first major battle, on December 15–16 at the Peralonso River near Cúcata, should have been decisive. Led by Rafael Uribe Uribe, a gentleman scholar, now a general, a small group of Liberals turned likely defeat into a major victory against a larger government force. When the overly cautious General Gabriel Vargos Santos failed to follow up the Liberal victory with a quick strike at Bogotá, however, the Liberals lost their chance to win the war.[1]

1. The most useful sources for this period are Thomas R. Favell, "The Antecedents of Panama's Separation from Colombia" (Ph.D. dissertation, Fletcher School of Law and Diplomacy, 1951), esp. 132, 144; Charles W. Bergquist, *Coffee and Conflict in Colombia, 1886–1910* (Durham, N.C., 1978), esp. 142–64; Miles DuVal, *Cadiz to Cathay: The Story of the Long Diplomatic Struggle for the Panama Canal* (Stanford, 1940); Dwight Carroll Miner, *The Fight for the Panama Route: The Story of the Spooner Act and the Hay-Herrán Treaty* (New York, 1940); Philippe Bunau-Varilla, *Panama: The Creation, Destruction, and Resurrection* (London, 1913), cited as *BVC*; Gerstle Mack, *The Land Divided: A History of the Panama Canal and Other Isthmian Canal Projects* (New York, 1944); David McCullough, *The Path Between the Seas: The Creation of the Panama Canal, 1870–1914* (New York, 1977); *SP*; Helen Delpar, *Red Against Blue: The Liberal Party in Colombian Politics, 1863–1899* (University, Ala., 1981); Vincent Baillie Dunlap, "Tragedy of a Colombian Martyr: Rafael Uribe Uribe and the Liberal Party, 1896–1914" (Ph.D. dissertation, University of North Carolina, 1979); E. Taylor Parks, *Colombia and the United States* (Durham, N.C., 1935); and Luis Martínez Delgado, *Historia de un cambio de gobierno* (Bogotá, 1958). For the effect of Cipriano Castro's revolution in Venezuela and its encouragement of Colombian Liberals see Helen V. Delpar, "The Liberal Party of Colombia, 1863–1903" (Ph.D. dissertation, Columbia University, 1967), 360.

The Liberals, who were more successful in their political efforts than in their military battles, controlled Cúcata and all of Panama except the cities of Colón and Panama. For the first six months the conflict followed the usual Colombian pattern of war between two opposing ideological elites. Liberals, though divided between war and peace advocates, were united in resistance to the oppressive government. Conservatives, who had also divided into two major groups— the ruling Nationalist party (the renamed regular Conservatives) and Historical Conservatives—were so ideologically divided that when the government army marched to battle, it was led by thirty-nine generals, each representing a different Conservative faction. Ideological division had already paralyzed the political process. Colombia faced two dreadful alternatives—a settlement won by power, not ideas, or a stalemate that would plunge the country into an endless and bloody civil war.[2]

Colombia's already precarious economy could not afford a war. In 1892 the Colombian peso and the American dollar were even—one hundred pesos equaled one hundred cents or one dollar. At the beginning of 1899 the peso cost 235 cents. By January, 1900, wartime inflation had devalued the peso to 714 cents. The desperate state of Colombia's economy, with the peso exchange rising to 18,900, eventually led to frantic attempts to raise money by selling the right to build a canal. For a proud nation that valued its role in the "concert of world civilization" and abhorred the caudillo society of its less fortunate Latin American neighbors, the continuing financial catastrophe was unimaginable. Since paper money was the government's only recourse to finance the war, the money printers were the only government employees paid regularly. Money was printed so quickly that no one bothered to change the peso's serial numbers. The rebel forces, unable to print money, seized property and conscripted civilians. In early 1900, a quick victory by either side and the end to a ruinous war was the best of the terrible alternatives. Military and political paralysis reflected the nation's ideological stalemate. Colombia was too divided to wage a decisive civil war.[3]

2. Favell, "Antecedents," 165; Bergquist, *Coffee and Conflict in Colombia,* 142–43; Dunlap, "Tragedy of a Colombian Martyr," 136–59.

3. Colombian exchange rate and inflation tables in Bergquist, *Coffee and Conflict in Colombia,* 33, 109, 145; William Paul McGreevey, *An Economic History of Colombia, 1845–1930* (Cambridge, Eng., 1971), 180. For Colombia's shortage of paper for printing currency and its use of candy wrapper paper for printing pesos see Malcolm Deas, "The Fiscal Problems of Nineteenth-Century Colombia," *Journal of Latin American Studies,* XIV (1982), 324–25.

Manuel Sanclemente was not a war leader. Most of the time the president was not even in the capital but conducted his government by rubber stamp and through temporary deals with whatever faction was momentarily willing to yield its doctrinal purity for a share of the ruling power. Foreign loans were not possible so the problem of financing the war remained paramount. Expropriating personal property and selling Panama offered the only possibilities for immediate cash. Sanclemente sold the Compagnie Nouvelle a six-year extension of its concession (from 1904 to 1910) for a cash payment of 5 million francs, perhaps one-quarter the amount a stable government could have negotiated. The Liberals, who did not share in the proceeds, charged that the extension was illegal, a claim that continued to cloud the American-French-Colombian negotiations for a Panama canal.[4]

The war became ugly at the dreadful battle of Palonegro on May 11, 1900, when fourteen thousand Conservatives faced seven thousand Liberals. The bitter fighting lasted two weeks, decimated both sides, and led to a stalemate that ended the Liberals' formal military effort. When the Liberals divided into smaller guerrilla units, the War of the Thousand Days, already one of the worst in Colombia's history, entered its bloodiest phase.[5]

In a bloodless coup on July 31, 1900, Vice-President José Manuel Marroquín replaced President Manuel Sanclemente. Even the coup was indecisive, reflecting Colombia's growing political incoherence rather than one group's determined drive to power. When the Historical Conservatives aligned with the Peace Liberals to seek a political settlement to the civil wars, their hope coalesced around Conservative Vice-President Marroquín. Sanclemente, who detested Bogotá, had moved with his war minister to a village about fifty miles west of the capital. The originator of the coup, Historical Conservative Jorge Moya Vásquez, marched on Bogotá and, finding no support for his position and his officers divided, followed the gentlemanly style of Colombian war by offering to surrender his sword to Minister of War Manuel Casabianca. When Casabianca refused to act, Director of Police Aristides Fernández, the next in command, kept both sides in doubt while massing his troops in the center of the capital. When

4. Bergquist, *Coffee and Conflict in Colombia*, 110, 112. A picture of the rubber stamp is in Martínez Delgado, *Historia de un cambio de gobierno*, 56–57. The most detailed history of the concession negotiations is in Miner, *Fight for the Panama Route*, 57–60; Bergquist, *Coffee and Conflict in Colombia*, 148.

5. Bergquist, *Coffee and Conflict in Colombia*, 149–51; Dunlap, "Tragedy of a Colombian Martyr," 161.

Fernández reluctantly sided with the opposition, the coup took place by default and Marroquín assumed power.[6]

What appeared to the outside world and to Theodore Roosevelt as a typical Latin American seizure of power was just the opposite. Marroquín's indecisive accession to power reflected the Byzantine complexity of Colombia's cerebral politics and the general dissatisfaction with the leadership of the always absent Sanclemente. The Historical Conservatives and Liberals, who had undertaken the coup in the hope that their new leader would negotiate a peace settlement, were quickly disappointed. Although Marroquín appointed many Historical Conservatives to cabinet positions, the center of power in the new government was occupied by Aristides Fernández, an opportunist and a gifted administrator, one of the few Colombian leaders who was not a member of the educated elite. Fernández became military governor of the important southern department of Cundinamarca. His alliance with Marroquín conferred on Fernández the social credentials he lacked, and Fernández' control of Cudinamarca widened the authority of the Marroquín government.[7]

The most effective political alliance of the Colombian wars was also an ideological disaster that served to prolong rather than shorten the civil war. Despite their different backgrounds, Fernández and Marroquín shared fundamentalist views that made political accommodation impossible. Both men were implacable Spanish Catholics, provincial in their outlook and experience. They were convinced that Liberals, influenced by Enlightenment political and social philosophy, were part of an international conspiracy to undermine established conservative Catholicism and end Colombia's cultural and economic isolation from the modern world. Fernández' administrative ability helped make the Marroquín government effective, but his extremism and opportunism made him a symbol of Liberal hatred. Fernández, an unprincipled and deadly opponent, became the main obstacle to a negotiated political settlement of the war.[8]

The learned Historical Conservatives, who had elevated Marroquín to the presidency, had mistaken his scholarly achievements and his gentlemanly class for intellectual flexibility. Marroquín, a well-educated, frequently articulate gentleman, was an ideologue rather

6. Bergquist, *Coffee and Conflict in Colombia,* 152; Delpar, "Liberal Party of Colombia," 368–71.

7. Bergquist, *Coffee and Conflict in Colombia,* 153, 178; Favell, "Antecedents," 178. For a brief biography of Marroquín see Martínez Delgado, *Historia de un cambio de gobierno.*

8. Bergquist, *Coffee and Conflict in Colombia,* 178.

than an intellectual and a provincial, who remained incurious and un-exposed to the intellectual and geographic world beyond the confines of Bogotá and its narrow Spanish Catholic heritage. Before entering his political career, Marroquín had dedicated himself to preserving the union between Catholicism and Colombia. He worked to estab-lish a Catholic university and served as its first rector in 1883. He was in constant opposition to Liberalism and its intellectual rivalry with Spanish Catholicism. Marroquín directed the Regeneration's policy to replace secular ideas with a return to Catholic principles at all levels of Colombian education. Upon his retirement in 1892, José Marroquín became the paradigm of a gentleman farmer, a well-dressed hacienda owner tending to his rich family lands, who wrote four social novels celebrating the golden age of Colombian Catholicism uncorrupted by outside forces. Marroquín was a determined fundamentalist, much more extreme in his views than the Regeneration that inspired the civil wars.[9]

Marroquín's seemingly unyielding diplomacy confounded Theo-dore Roosevelt and other Americans, who were unfamiliar with Co-lombia's conservative Catholic ideology or with twentieth-century re-ligious wars. Marroquín's ideology made what amounted to the selling of a part of Colombia to an outside power, especially a Protestant one, abhorrent. Marroquín had as little understanding of the commercial aspects of Panama canal diplomacy as Theodore Roosevelt had for Colombia's religious politics. Marroquín rejected any political process that did not allow him to impose his beliefs on everyone. In his novel *Blas Gil* (1896) he portrayed an opportunist who used a political career to make money while avoiding having to work for a living. In the end, the corrupt politician was saved from moral disaster through his love of a good woman and the miraculous rediscovery of his Catholic faith. Marroquín's second novel, *Entre primos* (1897), suggested Colombia's later metaphorical insistence on questions of sovereignty, the leitmotiv of the Panama negotiations. He used a cultural confrontation between an effete English outsider and an idealized, hardworking Colombian to show the silliness of the outside world and the superiority of the insular Colombian culture. Marroquín detested the Protestant world of Theodore Roosevelt's Americans and the much closer world of Co-lombian Liberals and Historical Conservatives with equal vehemence. He fought both, resisted any compromise, and turned the War of the Thousand Days into a religious war. In much the same way, he trans-

9. *Ibid.*, 155.

formed the routine negotiations for a canal at Panama into another religious war. Marroquín never pretended to play the politician's role. The Liberals and the bookish Historical Conservatives who elevated him to power were as confounded by his implacable ideology as Theodore Roosevelt and came to hate him with equal vigor.[10]

Marroquín's refusal to negotiate with the Liberal revolutionaries made a political settlement of the war impossible. When the superior forces of the government were balanced by the guerrilla tactics of the Liberal revolutionaries—many of whom were intelligent upper-class merchants and farmers—the conflict became a bloody military stalemate. Dissidents controlled the countryside, the repressive government the urban areas. The Liberals were so politically divided that they were unable to wage any unified military action. Forced to fight a defensive and reactive guerrilla war, the Liberals helped destroy the heart of Colombia's ruling classes, regardless of political belief. Both the ethos of Marroquín's Spanish gentleman and the world of the cultivated cosmopolitan Liberals were devasted by a war that killed the upper classes while destroying their property and Colombia's future.[11]

United States interest in a possible Panama canal involved the Americans in the War of the Thousand Days, resulting in a confluence of Colombian and American destinies that could not have occurred at a worse time. In 1900 the United States was successful, ambitious, prosperous, and optimistic. As the frontier period closed, Americans embraced and mastered the new ethos of technology and modernity, adding a major new chasm to the already immense cultural gulf between the new nations. When José Concha wrote in the most grandiloquent prose to John Hay of Colombia's eagerness to participate in an international Panama canal project, his message sincerely reflected the nation's idealistic and enlightened view of its place in the world. Unfortunately, these high national aspirations remained unrealizable as the agony of the thousand-day war destroyed Colombia's elite society.[12]

10. *Ibid.*, 155–56. For Marroquín's view of revolutionaries as "evildoers" and his re-institution of the death penalty to deal with them see Favell, "Antecedents," 182–83.

11. For Marroquín's rejection of Uribe Uribe's "Manifesto of Peace," April 12, 1901, see Dunlap, "Tragedy of a Colombian Martyr," 170–72; for the effect of the war on a coffee plantation see Malcolm Deas, "A Colombian Coffee Estate: Santa Bárbara, Cundinamarca, 1870–1912," in Kenneth Duncan and Ian Rutledge (eds.), *Land and Labour in Latin America* (Cambridge, Eng., 1977), 285–98.

12. José Concha to John Hay, March 31, 1902, *House Documents*, 57th Cong., 1st Sess., No. 611, pp. 2–3; Favell, "Antecedents," 180–81.

Although Rear Admiral John G. Walker's Isthmian Canal Commission recommended a route through Nicaragua in its preliminary report of November 30, 1900, and its "final" report of November 16, 1901, the commission clearly preferred Panama. Nicaragua was a second choice dictated by French unwillingness to sell its equipment, completed excavation, and engineering plans in Panama for a reasonable price. Both the original Walker report and the supplementary report of January 18, 1902, favored Panama as the ideal site: "The Panama route would be 134–57 [miles] shorter from sea to sea than the Nicaragua route. It would have less summit elevation, fewer locks, 1568 degrees and 26.44 miles less curvative." In addition, maintenance of a canal at Panama would cost $300,000 a year less; it was estimated that a ship could pass through the canal in twelve hours at Panama and thirty-three at Nicaragua. The estimated cost of building was $189,864,062 for Nicaragua and $144,233,358 for Panama. Why, then, was Nicaragua chosen? The commission blamed the Colombian concessions that gave control to the French Compagnie Nouvelle. "If the Panama route is selected these concessions must be removed in order that the two Republics may enter into treaty to enable the United States to acquire the control upon the Isthmus that will be necessary to fix the consideration." After many delays the Compagnie Nouvelle set a price of $109,141,500 for assets the American commission valued at $40 million. When the $69 million overvaluation was added to the construction estimates, the Panama route would cost over $25 million more than the Nicaraguan alternative though construction costs in Panama were cheaper. The French price "is so unreasonable that its acceptance cannot be recommended by this Commission." Therefore, "the most practicable and feasible route" for an isthmian canal "under the control, management and ownership of the United States" [quoting the congressional charge to the commission] "is that known as the Nicaragua route."[13]

American insistence on ownership and control of any isthmian canal became apparent during the diplomatic negotiations with Britain to remove the Clayton-Bulwer Treaty's stipulation of joint British and American jurisdiction over a Central American canal. Britain, which had never wanted an isthmian canal, conceded primary interest in the Caribbean to the United States as part of its new policy of informal

13. Both the original and the supplementary Isthmian Canal Commission reports are in *Senate Documents*, 58th Cong., 2nd Sess., No. 222, Serial 4609. The Panama recommendation is on pp. 173–75.

détente. In graciously acknowledging the power of Britain's navy to control any canal, Secretary of State Hay, a longtime Anglophile, failed to specify American control and fortification in his new treaty with Britain. Both the United States Senate and governor of New York Theodore Roosevelt were horrified. Hay was shocked at the Senate's violent response and considered resigning. But Roosevelt and the Senate reflected the consistent American feeling forcefully articulated by Presidents Grant and Hayes that any new canal must be wholly American. Getting the United States out of the restrictive Clayton-Bulwer Treaty and any vestige of British participation out of the revised Hay-Pauncefote Treaty I took two years. When the British finally relented and ceded in words what already existed in reality, the United States became the dominant Caribbean power. Colombia, which relied on the continued British presence to limit America's growing power, was deeply disappointed with the Hay-Pauncefote Treaty II, President Theodore Roosevelt's first signed treaty. Although the Colombians thought they had lost their buffer against American domination, the United States was more concerned with eliminating all formal European influence from the Caribbean—even the friendly British—than with taking over Latin America. It is doubtful that the United States was fully aware of its new inter-American power. The Americans did not suddenly change their diplomatic practices in Spanish America, but Colombia, confused by its civil war and the loss of possible British leverage, became deeply divided over its policy alternatives.[14]

The American government's shift in preference from Nicaragua to Panama was gradual. William Nelson Cromwell, the Compagnie Nouvelle's counsel and public relations representative, convinced the Republicans to substitute the phrase "isthmian canal" for Nicaragua in the 1900 platform. Senator John Tyler Morgan, the Alabama Democrat who headed the Nicaragua advocates, told President McKinley in

14. For the British linkage of the Clayton-Bulwer renegotiation with the ongoing American-Canadian boundary dispute in Alaska see Tyler Dennett, *John Hay: From Poetry to Politics* (New York, 1934), 248–63; and Allan Nevins, *Henry White: Thirty Years of American Diplomacy* (New York, 1930), 143–60. For the British considerations in renegotiating the Clayton-Bulwer Treaty see J. A. S. Grenville, "Great Britain and the Isthmian Canal, 1898–1901," *AHR*, LXI (1955), 48–69; for Britain's strategic considerations see Kenneth Bourne, *Britain and the Balance of Power in North America, 1815–1908* (Berkeley, 1967), 340–51; for the British diplomatic context see R. G. Neale, *Great Britain and United States Expansion, 1898–1900* (East Lansing, Mich., 1966), esp. xii–xxii, 163–67; for the negotiations see Charles S. Campbell, *Anglo-American Understanding, 1898–1903* (Baltimore, 1957), 186–239; see also Board of Trade to Foreign Office, February 2, 1899;

September, 1900, that "French politics and other entanglements" would make a Colombian canal impossible for Americans "at any cost," for there "is no diplomatic effort that seems to be more difficult than such a tripartite arrangement" between the United States, Colombia, and France. At this point, when the prospect of a Panama route looked hopeless, Philippe Bunau-Varilla interceded. Bunau-Varilla, a prolific writer and a gifted speaker, chose his audiences carefully, working independently of Cromwell, the Compagnie Nouvelle's official paid lobbyist.[15]

During his Ohio speaking tour Bunau-Varilla convinced Senator Mark Hanna in January, 1901, and shortly afterward converted the New York Chamber of Commerce. In his pamphlet *Nicaragua or Panama* and in his conversations with influential Americans, Bunau-Varilla emphasized the dangers of earthquakes in Nicaragua, even though the Walker Commission report considered earthquakes equally dangerous at either site. A master of adversarial writing, Bunau-Varilla made Nicaraguan earthquakes appear terrifying but ignored Panama's considerable medical dangers even though as a yellow fever victim in 1885 he knew firsthand of Panama's perils. Not only yellow fever and malaria but exotic illnesses such as beriberi, insect and snake bites, encephalitis, and a variety of tropical fevers made Panama a deadly construction site. While Bunau-Varilla inundated the politicians with his persuasive pamphlets, conversation, and propaganda, William Nelson Cromwell convinced the Colombian government, which had no permanent American diplomatic representative, to push actively for the canal. Cromwell urged Arturo de Brigard, Colombia's New York commercial counsel, to convince the Colombian

---

Memorandum respecting the Clayton-Bulwer Treaty, January 3, 1899; Memorandum on the Amendments . . . to the Hay-Pauncefote Convention, January 16, 1901; Cabinet Memorandum, July 6, 1901, all rpr. *ibid*, 348–68; J. A. S. Grenville, *Lord Salisbury and Foreign Policy: The Close of the Nineteenth Century* (London, 1964), 378–89; H. C. Allen, *Great Britain and the United States: A History of Anglo-American Relations, 1783–1952* (New York, 1955), 601–603; Lionel Gelber, *The Rise of Anglo-American Friendship: A Study in World Politics, 1898–1906* (1938; rpr. Hamden, Conn., 1966), 47–58, 97–102; and Bradford Perkins, *The Great Rapprochement: England and the United States, 1895–1914* (London, 1969), 174–84. For Roosevelt's views see TR to JH, February 18, 1900, in *MRL*, II, 1192; to Arthur Lee, April 24, 1901, *ibid.*, III, 64–65; text of Hay-Pauncefote II is in *FRUS*, 1902, pp. 513–17.

15. Cromwell's Brief, in *SP*, 234; John T. Morgan to William McKinley, September 22, 1900, in Hay Papers, L.C.; *BVC*, 178–87; Charles D. Ameringer, "The Panama Canal Lobby of Philippe Bunau-Varilla and William Nelson Cromwell," *AHR*, XLIII (1963), 346–63.

government that it would lose any hope of a canal at Panama if it did not establish a senior diplomatic mission able to negotiate directly with the United States.[16]

Secretary of State Hay understood the potential difficulties of any three-way arrangements, especially one involving France and Colombia. Hay played his diplomatic role shrewdly, patiently, and well. As soon as the Walker Commission report favoring Nicaragua was released on November 30, 1900, Hay signed agreements with Costa Rica and Nicaragua for rights to an American canal, a major prerequisite for final congressional approval. Until Congress formally decided on the route, the question of the canal's location remained open. Hay, who shared a common predilection with many others of his generation toward transcontinental railroads, did not care which route was chosen and would have preferred no isthmian canal at all. When Cromwell was able to convince Colombia to negotiate, Hay was willing to listen.[17]

Like John Hay, Colombia's Acting President José Manuel Marroquín would have preferred no isthmian canal. If the approaching United States congressional consideration of a canal route had not made further delay impossible, Marroquín would have ignored the canal issue while his attention was focused on the Colombian civil war. But with the disruption of the already depressed Colombian economy, possible revenue from an American canal at Panama offered an apparent solution. Colombia sent its foreign minister, the distinguished Carlos Martínez Silva, to Washington as envoy extraordinary and minister plenipotentiary to negotiate a Panama canal concession with the United States. Martínez Silva, the prototypical Latin American scholar-gentleman-diplomat, had not only written constitutions but, unlike most of his compatriots, had traveled widely and had attended the First Pan-American Congress at Washington in 1890. He played a central role in the coup that elevated Marroquín to the presidency.[18]

16. *BVC*, 178–87; *Senate Documents*, 58th Cong., 2nd Sess., No. 222, Serial 4609, p. 113. For a detailed description of Panama's diseases, see Gustave Anguizola, *Philippe Bunau-Varilla: The Man Behind the Panama Canal* (Chicago, 1980), 91–100; Cromwell's Brief, in *SP*, 238–39.

17. The text of the Nicaragua and Costa Rica agreements is in *House Documents*, 57th Cong., 1st Sess., No. 611, Serial 4377, pp. 23, 24. For Hay's indifference to any canal see N. T. Bacon to John Hay, October 6, 1904, in Dennett, *John Hay*, 378–79.

18. For Martínez Silva's life and his mission see Miner, *Fight for the Panama Route*, 63–64n; Martínez Delgado, *Historia de un cambio de gobierno*, 254–64; DuVal, *Cadiz to Cathay*, 173–74; Antonio José Uribe to Carlos Martínez Silva, January 12, 1901, in *LA*, 3–4; Favell, "Antecedents," 180–81.

Marroquín's instructions to Martínez Silva called the Panama canal "the most grave, delicate, and transcendental question, which today affects Colombia in relation with other governments." Only the outcome of its civil war was more important for Colombia. Martínez Silva was instructed to "procure . . . the definite adoption of the Isthmus of Panama for the location of the interoceanic Canal." Martínez Silva, certain that Panama's technical advantages diminished any threat from Nicaragua, was shocked when Cromwell convinced him that the United States overwhelmingly preferred Nicaragua. As long as British involvement remained a possibility, an American canal through Nicaragua was out of the question and Martínez Silva remained confident. When he perceived the strength of the new American nationalism, however, he knew that even Britain would eventually yield and consent to a wholly American canal project. Martínez Silva's reaction was revealing: "If England . . . submits to the United States, we are out of the fight, and the Panama enterprise will be dead." [19]

After a week of actively courting influential congressmen and promoting Panama over Nicaragua, Martínez Silva met with Secretary Hay on March 13, 1901, and formally proposed that the United States acquire the Panama canal properties from France. At the same time the Colombian minister asked Bogotá for additional money to finance his active campaign in the American Congress. Following this promising start, tripartite negotiations between Admiral Walker of the Isthmian Canal Commission, Cromwell, representing the Compagnie Nouvelle, and Martínez Silva, representing Colombia, produced a partial preliminary agreement on May 16, 1901. Colombia agreed to the sale of the French canal properties to the United States and also to America building the canal. The Compagnie Nouvelle agreed to sell its holdings to the United States. When the company refused to set a price and insisted on arbitration rather than negotiation to fix the American payment, Admiral Walker balked, insisting on a fixed price. Walker agreed to withhold his preliminary report favoring Nicaragua until July 20 to allow Cromwell time to communicate the terms to the Compagnie Nouvelle. [20]

Martínez Silva represented Colombia well. Had the French company taken its golden opportunity, the Panama route might have

19. For the evolution of Martínez Silva's appraisal see Miner, *Fight for the Panama Route*, 110–11; his views on Britain are in DuVal, *Cadiz to Cathay*, 173.
20. *SP*, 161; Cromwell's Brief, in *SP*, 238–40; Memorandum of June 25, 1901, in *LA*, 37–59.

been secured by the end of 1901. But the French remained dilatory and refused to comply with Admiral Walker's request and Cromwell's urgent pleas for a set price. Martínez Silva understood the part of the problem that frequently eluded Bogotá's domestically oriented politicians: "For [the Panamanians] the canal is a matter of life and death . . . I am sure there is not a single Panamanian who would not consider it a supreme misfortune, a thousand times worse than an earthquake, should hope be lost for a canal via that route. What could Colombia be able to do then for the benefit of the isthmus, and what right would we have to prevent this section of our country from taking care of its own interests even to seeking annexation to the United States?" Martínez Silva also understood the fatal flaw in Marroquín's thinking. Certain that the passage of time favored Colombia and extremely ambivalent about a canal settlement, the increasingly beleaguered Colombian leader turned away from what he had first called Colombia's "transcendental problem," concentrating his political energy on revolutionary domestic politics. Although Martínez Silva understood the problem, he was unable to direct Bogotá's attention back to the Panama question. Martínez Silva compared Colombia's self-defeating attitude with Spain's attitude in its recent conflict with the United States. "False pride and an exaggerated sense of national honor" were doomed to failure. Colombia's best policy, Martínez Silva advised, was to take the threat of Nicaragua seriously and to cooperate with the United States in negotiating a settlement.[21]

But direct negotiations between Martínez Silva and Maurice Hutin, president of the Compagnie Nouvelle, moved slowly. Cable communications with Bogotá, always a problem, seriously hampered the Colombian diplomat's ability to negotiate. When Cromwell pushed for a specific price, Hutin dismissed him, and the Compagnie Nouvelle remained without an American representative. Only when the Walker Commission submitted a draft treaty for Martínez Silva's comments was any progress made. The Colombian raised four major points. He objected to a perpetual lease and the inclusion of the cities of Panama and Colón in the American canal zone; he preferred a percentage of tolls over a fixed indemnity; and he insisted that the question of Colombian sovereignty be explicitly addressed. These remained unresolved issues throughout the negotiations as both sides became less flexible and more attached to their original proposals or objections.

21. Favell, "Antecedents," 187.

Continued negotiation was out of the question without meaningful communication with an increasingly indifferent Bogotá and Cromwell's active presence to prod the French company. The promising negotiations had faltered badly.[22]

When Theodore Roosevelt assumed the presidency on September 14, 1901, the canal question was still confused. The French were inert, the Colombians distracted by civil war, the Hay-Pauncefote renegotiations incomplete. In reality there was no canal issue. Unless the champions of Panama—Colombia, the French Compagnie Nouvelle, and a handful of other advocates—could somehow unify and work out an attractive proposal, Nicaragua would remain the American choice. The consequences probably would have been disastrous since earthquakes in 1911, 1931, and 1972 all occurred near the center of the proposed canal.[23]

Since the negotiations with the Compagnie Nouvelle and Colombia failed to resolve even the preliminary difficulties involved in considering a Panama route, on November 16, 1901, the Walker Commission formally recommended Nicaragua as the site for the canal. Events moved quickly. On December 10, the United States signed a canal convention with Nicaragua. A week later the Senate approved the Hay-Pauncefote Treaty II, eliminating British participation in a Nicaraguan canal. On December 19, the Hepburn Bill, the enabling legislation for a Nicaraguan canal, was placed on the House agenda for January 7, 1902. In Paris, Philippe Bunau-Varilla began his last-minute efforts to reverse the Walker Commission's recommendation.[24]

Bunau-Varilla began to use his newspaper connection with increasing frequency. On November 29, 1901, a day before the preliminary Walker report was released, Bunau-Varilla, who already knew its recommendations, demanded in Le Matin that the Compagnie Nouvelle's management resign and that negotiation of a fixed price continue. During December Bunau-Varilla's intensive campaign convinced the

22. Memorandum of June 25, 1901, in LA, 37–50, 53–54; Favell, "Antecedents," 188; Ameringer, "Panama Canal Lobby," 348; SP, 162; Miner, Fight for the Panama Route, 112; Carlos Martínez Silva to John G. Walker, July 5, 1901 (printed as June 5, 1901), in LA, 59–61.

23. Gustave Anguizola, review of David McCullough, Path Between the Seas, JAH, 65 (1978), 201–202; Anguizola, Philippe Bunau-Varilla, 6.

24. SP, 244; Mack, Land Divided, 424–27. The report was dated November 16, 1901, leaked to the New York Tribune, which published it on November 21–22 with George S. Morison's Minority Report, and formally released on November 30, 1901. See DuVal, Cadiz to Cathay, 154.

Compagnie Nouvelle's shareholders to replace the lethargic leadership with a new negotiator and a new policy. Le Matin's pages crackled with Bunau-Varilla's imprecations: "What is needed is not to negotiate; it is to fix a price; yesterday you might have negotiated and got perhaps, sixty, perhaps seventy million dollars; today the battle is lost. You can make an offensive attack again only if you accept the figure of forty million dollars at which the Commission has valued that part of the company's property which she can still use in her project." Bunau-Varilla warned Marius Bo, the company's new president, that new arrangements would have to be concluded quickly because the American congressional debate to confirm the Nicaraguan route was to begin on January 7, 1902.[25]

Bunau-Varilla used Le Matin effectively, not only for editorials but as a source of news on canal issues. The French newspaper reprinted a cable from Senator Mark Hanna on December 25, 1901, promising that Hanna's Senate Canal Committee would reconsider the Nicaraguan decision "should the owners of the French works be disposed to sell their enterprise for forty million dollars." Until Bunau-Varilla's campaign, the French assumed there was ample time to deal with both the difficult Colombians and the American government agencies—canal commissions, congressmen, committees, and lobbyists—that merited comparison with the legendary French bureaucracy. Until Bunau-Varilla's articles in Le Matin, Bo had been unaware that once the Senate met the American decision-making process would move quickly and decisively. One of Bunau-Varilla's most important functions in the Panama conflict was his intimate knowledge of the different cultures and bureaucracies. No one knew more about French and Colombian customs than Bunau-Varilla, who served more as a cultural intermediary than a conniving conspirator. By knowing when to intervene and how, the Frenchman was able to exercise an uncanny control over the complex issues and often appeared able to manipulate the French, American, and Colombian bureaucracies at will.[26]

Bunau-Varilla's concentrated campaign in Le Matin, which attacked the company's patriotism as well as criticizing specific policies, embarrassed the company sufficiently to force its agreement to the American terms. On January 4, 1902, Bo wired Admiral John Walker his

25. Anguizola, Philippe Bunau-Varilla, 153; DuVal, Cadiz to Cathay, 154; BVC, 209–10.
26. BVC, 209–10; for Bunau-Varilla's 1898 trip to Venezuela to meet with Loomis and his first overtures to the Colombians on the possibility of an American-controlled canal see Anguizola, Philippe Bunau-Varilla, 175–78.

acceptance of the Isthmian Canal Commission's $40 million offer. The agreement was formally confirmed after the company agreed to Walker's demand for "all maps and archives in Paris," the official French liquidator in bankruptcy agreed to the price, and the American consul general certified the Compagnie Nouvelle's legal power to sell. After years of fruitless delay, the French had finally agreed to the American commission's evaluation of the French holdings in Panama. With that agreement in hand, Panama became the official first choice of the Walker Commission. Until the Compagnie Nouvelle's agreement to sell at the American price, George S. Morison was the only member of the Isthmian Canal Commission who consistently favored the Panama route. After the sale, Lewis Haupt became the sole dissenting member in the commission's consistent eight-to-one votes, as the majority shifted from Nicaragua to Panama.[27]

Congress had not waited for the French. On January 9, 1902, the House approved the original arrangement for a canal through Nicaragua by an overwhelming vote of 308 to 2, a misleading margin that reflected common knowledge of the changing developments in Paris and agreement that the Senate rather than the House would ultimately decide the route. Once the French offer and the Walker Commission's acceptance were made public, no one doubted that the debate between the Morgan Democrats favoring Nicaragua and the Hanna Republicans favoring Panama would be bitter, close, and dramatic.[28]

Until now, Theodore Roosevelt had remained neutral. His message to Congress the month before had strongly recommended a Central American canal but had refrained from backing either site. Roosevelt was thoroughly conversant not only with the Walker Commission's formal reports but with its deliberations. George S. Morison, a brilliant engineer and an influential member of the commission, kept Roosevelt fully informed, especially about the rapid changes in canal technology, a phenomenon comparable to computer technology in the 1980s. On December 10, 1901, Morison in a detailed letter informed Roosevelt that new technology not only made Panama the su-

27. *Senate Documents*, 57th Cong., 2nd Sess., No. 34, Serial 4417, p. 47. See the Minutes for the Committee Sessions, November 14, 15, 16, 1901, January 10, 17, 1902, in Box 4, Lewis Haupt Papers, LC; for Haupt's reasons for making the vote unanimous see Haupt to John Tyler Morgan, September 14, 1903, in John Tyler Morgan Papers, LC.

28. For the view that the House vote for Hepburn was sentiment not for Nicaragua but for "a canal, any canal," see Alfred Charles Richard, Jr., "The Panama Canal in American National Consciousness, 1870–1922" (Ph.D. dissertation, Boston University, 1969), 127–30; see also "Panama or Nicaragua," *LD*, January 4, 1902, p. 1.

perior engineering choice but eliminated Nicaragua as anything but an emergency alternative. It was Morison, not Cromwell or Hanna, who moved Roosevelt from observer to active participant and advocate of a Panama route. On January 16, 1902, when Roosevelt, at a White House meeting with the Isthmian Canal Commission, requested a revised supplementary report unequivocally and unanimously supporting the Panama route, the members agreed. Although four commission members voiced some reservations, subsequent examination by skeptical congressmen revealed no serious objections except for Lewis Haupt, who continued to support Nicaragua. Technological advances and French acceptance of the American terms—not politics or pressure—persuaded the commission to reverse its original recommendation. Cromwell, often cited as a direct influence on Roosevelt, was not a factor because he was not reinstated as the Compagnie Nouvelle's representative until the week following the president's intervention, and then only after Bunau-Varilla's and Hanna's intercession. On January 18, 1902, Roosevelt publicly submitted the revised Walker report recommending the Panama route to both Houses of Congress.[29]

29. For TR's neutrality on the canal route see Miner, *Fight for the Panama Route*, 120; for TR's preference for Nicaragua in 1894 see TR to Anna Roosevelt, May 20, 1894, in *MRL*, I, 379; Walter McCaleb, *Theodore Roosevelt* (New York, 1931), 155. For the widespread professional support of the Panama route for its technological advantages see Richard, "Panama Canal in American Consciousness," 116–40. For contemporary scientific support see George A. Burt, "A Comparison of the Isthmian Canal Projects," *Engineering Magazine*, XIX (1900), 19–27; "The New Panama Canal," *Scientific American*, LXXXIII (February 4, 1899), 66; "Panama and Nicaragua Canals—A Comparison," *ibid.*, LXXIII (February 18, 1899), 98; "Nicaragua or Panama," *ibid.*, LXXXV (December 21, 1901), p. 406; *SP*, 166; *Senate Documents*, 58th Cong., 2nd Sess., No. 222, Serial 4609, contains Isthmian Canal Commission reports, the correspondence between the commission and the Compagnie Nouvelle, and TR's message transmitting the report to Congress. For evidence that the technological evidence weighed most heavily on TR's Panama decision see McCullough, *Path Between the Seas*, 326, who cites a detailed letter of George S. Morison to TR, December 10, 1901, which gives in detail the technological advantages of Panama over Nicaragua; see also the important note in *MRL*, III, 567 n. For Morison's life, career, and summary of his letter to TR, see George Abbott Morison, *George Shattuck Morison, 1842–1903: A Memoir* (Peterborough, N.H., 1940), 13–14. For Morison's detailed analysis of the Panama route's superiority see George S. Morison, Draft of Address, American Geographical Society, *ca.* December 23, 1902, in 1902 Letterbook, pp. 648–75, in George S. Morison Papers, Smithsonian Museum of American History, Washington, D.C. For Morison's views of technological changes and their effect on modern society see Morison, *The New Epoch: As Developed by the Manufacture of Power* (Boston, 1903). For the views of an Isthmian Canal Commission member see Emory R. Johnson, "Reasons for the Panama Route," *Independent*, LIV (1902), 313–15.

Roosevelt was not the only one to change his mind. After the Compagnie Nouvelle agreed to the Walker Commission evaluation, many newspapers began to reexamine the issue. The Chicago *Evening Post* called the notion that most people favored Nicaragua "sheer nonsense." Panama had picked up a number of new journalistic supporters, and some previously committed newspapers believed the question would still be open in the upcoming congressional debate.[30]

The two leading canal protagonists in the Senate, Mark Hanna and John T. Morgan, agreed on few matters. But on the difficulty of dealing with Colombia they were in complete harmony. Hanna knew that no case could (or should) be made for a Panama canal without Colombia's formal consent. Hanna was determined to resolve the diplomatic problems with Colombia before the critical Senate debate. But the increasingly chaotic condition of Colombian politics made serious negotiations difficult. Martínez Silva had been unable to communicate effectively with his government for nearly a year. He was generally told to await new instructions which never arrived. Fearing the loss of Panama by default, the unhappy Colombian diplomat drew up his own treaty draft. It was never formally presented to John Hay, but he probably knew the substance of it from William Cromwell, who helped write it. It called for a renewable one-hundred-year lease, a six-mile-wide canal zone, American guarantees of the canal zone's perpetual neutrality, and Colombian sovereignty over the zone and the cities of Colón and Panama. Colombia would be responsible for defending the zone but could call for assistance from the United States, which could intervene in an emergency without prior Colombian permission. The Compagnie Nouvelle would transfer its property and concessions to the United States, which would pay Colombia a yearly annuity of $600,000 to be increased by 3 percent on subsequent lease renewals.[31]

Martínez Silva's economic arrangements were remarkably close to the final figures of the Hay-Herrán Treaty. But Marroquín, critical of Martínez Silva's uninstructed diplomacy, reluctant to agree to any canal on Colombian soil, and distracted by Colombia's civil wars, refused to send new instructions or to negotiate as meaningfully and realistically as Martínez Silva. The related questions of sovereignty

30. Miner, *Fight for the Panama Route*, 120n; Richard, "Panama Canal in American Consciousness," 123–25.
31. Martínez Silva's draft is in *LA*, 90–102; Miner, *Fight for the Panama Route*, 129–30.

and control resisted easy diplomatic resolution for both symbolic and substantive reasons. Colombia had long relied on the United States to maintain its claim to sovereignty over Panama. Many observers, including a prominent Panama historian as well as State Department advisers, felt that Colombia had compromised its claim to sovereignty in Panama in the Bidlack-Mallarino Treaty of 1846 and later compounded its difficulties through the many concessions to France and an increasing reliance on the American navy to control Panama.[32]

Instead of sending new instructions and allowing Martínez Silva to complete the promising negotiations, Marroquín replaced him. Martínez Silva bitterly remonstrated with Marroquín, describing "the last six months [as] . . . a real torture." In an eloquent and prophetic communiqué, Martínez Silva told Marroquín that Panama would not tolerate losing the canal and would join with the United States against Colombia if need be. Comparing himself to Cordelia in *King Lear*, Martínez Silva complained that the "other daughters of the unfortunate king offered him everything" for personal gain, while Cordelia remained faithful and a true friend. Martínez Silva returned to Bogotá a broken man. Imprisoned as part of Marroquín's purge of his old Historical Conservative allies, he died on March 3, 1903, of pneumonia.[33]

Eventually Panama became the decisive war zone that brought the revolution to an end. The Americans and the other Western powers represented by naval forces in the Caribbean maintained a strict neutrality during the revolution. Most observers considered both sides equally unkempt and disorderly. As the war progressed, ideological differences were blurred by the brutality of battle. Panama, which had experienced only sporadic fighting, became a major war zone late in 1901. Eventually the American, British, and French naval forces at Panama intervened to prevent the same destruction and loss of life that had already occurred in mainland Colombia. Two warships, the battleship *Iowa* at Panama and the cruiser *Machias* at Colón, repre-

32. Ernesto J. Castellero Reyes, *La causa immediata de la emancipa de Panama* (Panama City, 1933), 104–105. For a critical discussion of the financial terms see the British counsel Spencer S. Dickson's Memorandum rpr. in *FRUS*, 1903, pp. 169–71; *BVC*, 221; and Parks, *Colombia and the United States*, 411–12. For Marroquín's criticism see Miner, *Fight for the Panama Route*, 130, n. 38; for the additional influence of geographical regionalism see Joseph L. Arbena, "Colombian Reactions to the Independence of Panama, 1903–04," *Americas*, XXXIII (1976), 137.

33. Miner, *Fight for the Panama Route*, 131–34; Concha's instructions are in Felipe Paúl to José Concha, March 24, 1902, in *LA*, 102–17; Carlos Martínez Silva to José Marroquín, March 11, 1902, in DuVal, *Cadiz to Cathay*, 176–77.

sented American interests. Although life for the Americans at Colón was mainly one of unrelieved monotony, Lieutenant Commander Henry McCrea of the *Machias* reported on October 8, 1901, that "the Liberals are becoming more impatient and aggressive."[34]

The American monotony was abruptly broken when "about 150 Liberals boarded the regular train," paid their fares to Gatun, and then cut the telegraph wires between Panama and Colón. The Liberals, who had previously tried to bring Venezuela into the civil war, were now attempting to involve the United States. Captain Thomas Perry of the *Iowa*, refusing to take the bait, informed Hezekiah A. Gudger, the American consul at Panama, about the difficulties and requested Colombian police protection for the transit line. On November 19, 1901, when Colón was taken by the Liberals, Perry informed Washington that he would "land force if there should be further interference." As Perry had anticipated, Colombia formally pleaded its inability to "protect transit," anticipating that its requested American intervention would neutralize the Liberal offensive and give the government forces a powerful ally. Perry, who refused to be drawn into the war on either side, declined to provide the police force Colombia demanded, saying the "transit is open and normal." Because the area was already dominated by the Liberal revolutionaries, the rail line was no longer a target. "Liberals along line inclined to protect rather than interfere," Perry cabled Washington.[35]

When the government forces dispatched the gunboat *Pinzon* with six hundred troops, threatening total war on the isthmus, the United

34. Henry McCrea to John D. Long, October 12, 1901, in *Senate Documents*, 58th Cong., 2nd Sess., No. 143, Serial 4589, pp. 200–201. For the report that "there is no more evidence of war or insurrection . . . on the isthmus . . . than there is in Dupont Circle, Washington, D.C. on a midsummer afternoon," see Thomas Perry to Secretary of the Navy, September 16, 1901, in Subject File VI, Correspondence Relating to Panama, RG 45, Box 667, NA. A summary of the intervention is in Milton Offutt, *The Protection of Citizens Abroad by the Armed Forces of the United States* (Baltimore, 1928), 88–92. For Liberal negotiations with Venezuela see Dunlap, "Tragedy of a Colombian Martyr," 166–68. For prior Venezuelan encouragement of the Liberals see Delpar, *Red Against Blue*, 181–82. For the evolution of the State Department's concurrence in the naval intervention see Alvey Adee to Secretary of the Navy, August 7, 1901, "Interference with Transit in Isthmus of Panama," in Panama Affair Subject File, Box 134, John Bassett Moore Papers, LC. For earlier fighting in Panama see Alex Perez-Venero, *Before the Five Frontiers: Panama from 1821–1903* (New York, 1978), 129–37.

35. Thomas Perry to U.S. Consul General, Panama, November 21, 1901; Perry to John D. Long, November 21, 22, 1901 (two letters). The best description of the encounter is in Perry to Long, November 25, 1901. All sources in *Senate Documents*, 58th Cong., 2nd Sess., No. 143, Serial 4589, pp. 202–13.

States landed troops at both ends of the railroad. The Panama railway station was occupied by 250 sailors from the *Iowa*, and a shore party from the *Machias* landed at Colón. Secretary of the Navy John D. Long's orders reflected the American interest: "Our duty is to protect free transit. You will exercise your discretion in determining whether landing . . . will endanger that." Captain McCrea quickly intervened. He ordered the *Pinzon* not to open fire and convinced the Liberals to hold their fire as long as a landing was not attempted. Although the immediate crisis passed when the Colombian gunboat sailed to the east, a major test of Liberal and Nationalist strength as well as growing American involvement in the Colombian war was imminent.[36]

Commander Francis H. Delano, the chief American naval officer in the Panama area, and Consul Gudger tried to prevent the impending battle. Liberals controlled the Panama Railroad line, subjecting trains to frequent searches and harassment, while a force of six hundred men under Panama's Governor General Carlos Alban planned to attack the Liberals holding Colón. When it became clear that the American forces could decide the struggle, both Colombian sides tried to move the Americans to active involvement. When government forces took the advantage, Liberals blatantly interrupted train service to force American intervention. The nationalists were equally resourceful. At Colón the Colombian gunboat *Pinzon* at anchor and ostensibly neutralized by the American ship *Machias* at its side opened fire on the Liberals after dark and turned off its lights so the American ship absorbed the return fire of the Liberals. At one point the Nationalists, threatened by a possible Liberal attack on Panama, openly contrived to involve the Americans to prevent the attack. Captain Perry resented the tactic: "In their weakness and incapacity they want the United States to protect them from their enemies, while they sit hopelessly incompetent." The Americans were joined by French and British ships in attempting to prevent a battle for Colón that would place the city's mostly foreign population at risk. Liberal and Nationalist commanders met on the British cruiser *Tribune* and after hard negotiations for more than four hours reached an agreement to wage the battle for Colón outside the city.[37]

36. John Long to Thomas Perry, to Henry McCrea, November 23, 1901; Perry to Long, Long to McCrea, McCrea to Long, November 24, 1901, all *ibid.*, 203–13.

37. Francis A. Delano to John D. Long, November 25, 1901; Henry McCrea to Long, November 26, 1901; Thomas Perry to Long, November 25, 1901, all in *ibid.*, pp. 204–209; "Interference with Transit on the Isthmus of Panama."

But the warring forces continued to try to involve the Americans. A substantial battle occurred along the rail line on November 25; when the Nationalists won, Governor General Alban wanted to transport his troops on the railroad in search of more Liberals to fight. At this point Captain Perry took control of the railroad. An armored car with "an American flag, part of a company and two Colt guns" preceded the train, which was heavily guarded by an armed United States Navy force. In a bizarre confrontation between Captain Perry and Governor Alban, Perry insisted that Alban could not transport any troops on the trains. Arguing that Alban's request to use the trains in war went against the "demand made upon me by his government," Perry told Alban he must cooperate with the American forces carrying out American obligations to Colombia's government. Colombia, he said, had been told "that if it called upon the United States to protect . . . he no longer enjoyed the privilege of having his troops transported." Perry reported that "it was completely understood from one end of the line to the other that in the future, and while this disturbance continues, the trains would be guarded by United States forces under the United States flag." The American commander was satisifed with his effective demonstration of American efficiency. "In just one day perfect order has been secured out of a condition that was unendurable yesterday." Perry was adamant: "The same order will continue indefinitely"; every passenger train would be guarded by forty American marines. Perry's intervention pointed the way to the eventual end of the grim and bloody war as both sides increasingly hoped the neutral United States would help negotiate a settlement.[38]

On November 28, 1901, General Domingo S. de la Rosa, the Liberal leader whose troops held Colón, and General Alban, representing the Nationalist government, met aboard the American warship *Marietta* to arrange a peace that would avoid a battle for Colón. The American naval officers Perry, McCrea, and Delano were joined by the commanders of the French warship *Suchet* and the British cruiser *Tribune*. Both Colombian sides welcomed the international mediation, which avoided another bloody and destructive battle. The war had become a habit, the continued destruction increasingly senseless, and in Pan-

---

38. Thomas Perry to John D. Long, November 25, 1901, in *Senate Documents*, 58th Cong., 2nd Sess., No. 143, Serial 4589, p. 211; Offutt, *Protection of Citizens Abroad by the Armed Forces of the United States*, 90–91.

ama, distant from Bogotá's interests and ethos, a bloodbath between Liberals and Nationalists seemed almost absurd. The American and European presence allowed a peaceful face-saving solution for both sides. The government guaranteed "life and liberty and a passport out of the country" to Liberals who would lay down their arms. The plan called for the Liberals to surrender Colón to the American, French, and British forces on November 29, 1901, at 11 A.M. After a three-hour interval General Alban, who waited with his troops seven miles away at Gatun, would take control of the city.[39]

In an emotional surrender ceremony witnessed by British, French, and American consuls and naval officers, three hundred American marines and bluejackets, and small British and French contingents, one hundred Liberal troops laid down their arms as the revolutionary flag was taken down. Captain Perry reported: "Much feeling was shown at the time by the whole Liberal command, a large majority of them being in tears." At 2 P.M. the same ceremony took place in reverse. Three hundred occupying Colombian troops lined the streets as the foreign contingents witnessed the raising of the government flag over Colón. By the end of the next day all American sentries were replaced by Colombians, and the four-day restriction of Colombian troop movements on the Panama Railroad was ended. Ten days later Perry could report that "the condition of affairs at the Isthmus for the week . . . is peaceful, tranquil, and orderly."[40]

Captain Perry was not content with a simple armistice. He reported on December 9, 1901, that "permanent peace was near." Perry was understandably optimistic, having dealt with Panama's General Alban and not Bogotá's President Marroquín. When Perry reported that "the force of the insurrection was broken and the spirit of the revolution disappearing," he was impressed with General Alban's "generous terms" and the eagerness with which both sides in Panama sought an end to the war. Perry, a sincere neutral, hated the mindless war, wrote of "the blessings of peace," and worked hard to negotiate a prisoner exchange because the condition of the prisoners on both

39. Thomas A. Perry to John D. Long, December 2, 1901, in *Senate Documents*, 58th Cong., 2nd Sess., No. 143, Serial 4589, pp. 216–17.

40. Thomas Perry, A. Galloway, Francis H. Delano, P. Le Bris, and Henry McCrea to John D. Long, November 28, 1901; Perry to Long, December 2, 1901, all in *Senate Documents*, 58th Cong., 2nd Sess., No. 143; Serial 4589, pp. 214–19. On the United States landing forces see Perry to Long, December 9, 1901, *ibid.*, 221.

sides was "most pitiable . . . and it would appear to be only humane" to help arrange an exchange. Perry's efforts were significant, though making peace in Panama was easier than settling the war in Bogotá. When President Marroquín refused to offer similar guarantees of fair treatment and safety to the minority Liberals in the rest of Colombia, the war continued. In Panama, American control of communications and transportation and willingness to mediate fairly persuaded both sides to seek peace. The Colón peace initiative, though not as lasting as Captain Perry hoped, established the precedent for the peace treaty of *Wisconsin* that a year later finally brought the War of the Thousand Days to an end.[41]

41. Thomas Perry to John D. Long, December 9, 1901, *ibid.*, 218, 220; "Interference with Transit on the Isthmus of Panama."

7 Diplomacy, 1902

José Vincente Concha, Colombia's new minister, a thirty-five-year-old journalist and founder of the Bogotá newspaper *El Día*, was an intellectual, Colombia's war minister, and a Conservative revolutionary who helped Marroquín take power. He arrived in the United States on January 26, 1902, with fresh instructions from Bogotá. Concha became Colombia's president in 1914, but in 1902 he was a provincial who spoke no English and had never traveled outside of Colombia. He did not have the training, experience, or temperament to be an effective diplomat. Concha's instructions were broad, vague, and unrealistic. There was no way Colombia could retain its sovereignty while giving the United States absolute control over a canal. Neither side could find a compromise for what had become as much a battle over symbolism as substance. Symbolism was equally important for each side. The Americans had fought bitterly with their new allies, the British, to eliminate even the diction of compromise in the original Hay-Pauncefote Treaty. In the second Hay-Pauncefote Treaty the British were persuaded to relinquish any vestige of participation, even though, as Theodore Roosevelt pointed out to his English friends, the Americans were acutely aware that without British support they could not control or defend a canal. For Colombia the passion for diction was equally strong. *Soberanía* meant history, struggle, and aspiration to Colombians. But Colombia's traditional regionalism, rooted in its geography as well as its political history, had encouraged the United States to act as police force, peacekeeper, and the most effective authority in Panama. The weaker its claim to sovereignty became, the more Colombia struggled to regain it through legal means; the more Colombia struggled to hold on to Panama, the more the United States feared that any concession would make governing or defending Panama a jurisdictional nightmare. The conflict between Colombian love of legal abstraction and American passion for efficiency and order created a cultural stalemate.[1]

What followed was a series of shadow negotiations. Martínez Silva had begun the process; José Concha continued it. Colombia, disorganized by the civil war and by changes within its government, remained out of touch with its new envoy in Washington. Instructions to Concha were sent by boat mail or in garbled cable transmissions. Temporary Foreign Minister Miguel Abadía Méndez instructed Concha to demand $20 million from the United States, far more than the $2 million Martínez Silva proposed. Although Marroquín's advisory canal commission appointed on February 2, 1902, confirmed the higher figure, some Colombians dissented. Constantino Arosemena, José Obdalia, Federico Boyd (all from Panama), and Colombian Oscar Terán opposed any transfer payment whereas Colombian economist Francisco Groot favored full cooperation with the United States as an alternative to European imperialism. Luis M. Isaza, a member of the Colombian canal commission, warned that cooperation with the United States to build the canal was the only way to maintain Panama's allegiance. Abadía Méndez based his demands on possible profits from a canal, Colombia's loss of revenue from the Panama Railroad, and the value of the veto power Colombia held over a Panama route. But what Colombia held was worthless without the expensive investment and development that only the United States could furnish. Although Colombia's diplomats brought to Washington the un-

1. For Concha's career see Gustave Anguizola, *Philippe Bunau-Varilla: The Man Behind the Panama Canal* (Chicago, 1980), 195; for questions about Concha's bad health, inexperience, and sanity see David McCullough, *Path Between the Seas: The Creation of the Panama Canal, 1870–1914* (New York, 1977), 329–31; for Concha and the issue of sovereignty see Dwight Carroll Miner, *The Fight for the Panama Route: The Story of the Spooner Act and the Hay-Herrán Treaty* (New York, 1940), 130–32; for Concha's initial "repugnance" for talking with Americans, see Cromwell's Brief, *SP*, 256; a brief biography is in Luis Martínez Delgado, *Historia de un cambio gobierno* (Bogotá, 1958), 265–74. For Colombia's unrealistic view of the sovereignty issue see Thomas R. Favell, "The Antecedents of Panama's Separation from Colombia" (Ph.D. dissertation, Fletcher School of Law and Diplomacy, 1951), 200–201; see also Joseph L. Arbena, "Colombian Reactions to the Independence of Panama, 1903–1904," *Americas*, XXXIII (1976), 137. For Concha's inept war ministry and his failed invasion of Venezuela in July, 1901, see Charles W. Bergquist, *Coffee and Conflict in Colombia, 1886–1910* (Durham, N.C., 1978), 174–75. For the Hay-Pauncefote Treaty negotiations with Britain and Roosevelt's role see Chapter 6, note 14. For Roosevelt's canal correspondence with his English friends see David H. Burton, *Theodore Roosevelt and His English Correspondents: A Special Relationship of Friends* (Philadelphia, 1973), 40–42.

realistic expectations of almost all Bogotá patriots and intellectuals, they soon understood the very real alternative that the Nicaraguan route offered to the Americans. None was able to convince Bogotá that Panama was a substantial if limited asset, not an infinite dream or a *deus ex machina* that would suddenly make Colombia wealthy and solve its political divisions.[2]

Although Bunau-Varilla and Cromwell, who had been restored as the Compagnie Nouvelle's agent at Mark Hanna's and Bunau-Varilla's urging, gave Concha a crash course in canal diplomacy, he remained uneasy in his unfamiliar diplomatic role. Everything had to be translated, generally by the legation secretary Tómas Herrán; Cromwell was too American, Bunau-Varilla too French, Bogotá too unreasonable in its expectations, and events moved far too quickly. When Felipe Paúl became foreign minister in February, like most of Marroquín's canal commissioners he believed that "the Nicaragua route is not practical and the inter-oceanic canal will be constructed across Panama." On March 20 Concha warned Paúl of strong separatist sentiment in Panama and that the United States was about to choose a Nicaraguan route. Concha went ahead on his own because Paúl's elaborate instructions sent by boat did not arrive until late April.[3]

One of Philippe Bunau-Varilla's most impressive gifts was his ability to reduce complex matters to simpler and more easily understandable terms. The Frenchman was particularly acute in his ability to translate different economic terms into a usable formula. Bunau-Varilla calculated that $14 million was the maximum amount Colombia could expect to receive from the United States for the right to a Panama route. A cash indemnity of $9.8 million capitalized at 3 percent annually plus a yearly annuity of $250,000 equaled $14 million, which he proposed to

2. For the garbled cables and other communication difficulties see Gerstle Mack, *The Land Divided: A History of the Panama Canal and Other Isthmian Canal Projects* (New York, 1944), 437; for the administrative breakdown in Colombia see Charles B. Hart to JH, February 3, 1902, Despatches from United States Ministers to Colombia, Microcopy T33, Roll 58, RG 59, NA; for Marroquín's canal commission see Favell, "Antecedents," 200–204; the commission report and Groot's and Rivas' comments are in *LA*, Appendix, 3–9, 18, 34–35; Abadía Mendéz' proposal is in Miner, *Fight for the Panama Route*, 134–38.

3. For Cromwell's reinstatement see Charles D. Ameringer, "The Panama Canal Lobby of Philippe Bunau-Varilla and William Nelson Cromwell," *AHR*, XLIII (1963), 350; see also Philippe Bunau-Varilla, *Les 19 documents du drame de Panama* (Paris, 1939), copy in Tomás Herrán Papers, Special Collections Division, Georgetown University Library, Washington, D.C. *SP*, 164–69; Miles P. DuVal, Jr., *Cadiz to Cathay: The Story of the Long Diplomatic Struggle for the Panama Canal* (Stanford, 1940), 178; Concha-Paúl correspondence quoted in Favell, "Antecedents," 203–204; Mack, *Land Divided*, 436–37.

Concha as a realistic demand upon the United States. At first Concha refused to budge. Whereas Martínez Silva had asked for a $600,000 annual payment, Concha demanded an immediate indemnity of $7 million plus an annual payment of $600,000, or in Bunau-Varilla's formula, the equivalent of $27 million. Since Nicaragua would settle for one-quarter of this or a little under $7 million, Concha's demands could not realistically be the basis for any meaningful negotiations.[4]

Bunau-Varilla's intercession was shrewd, flamboyant, and effective. He sent a grandiloquent threatening cable to the publisher of the Panama *Star and Herald*. Bunau-Varilla explained to Cromwell, who was shocked by the tone of the cable, that derogatory telegrams were not printed in Panama but were sent on to Bogotá and served the ingenious purpose of indirectly advising Colombia the best way to proceed. Bunau-Varilla also wrote directly to Concha telling him that to demand any amount over $12.5 million—in Bunau-Varilla's formula—from the United States would jeopardize any chance of a canal at Panama. Concha bristled at Bunau-Varilla's implied charge of Colombian greed, arguing that money was only a small part of the issue. But Bunau-Varilla's intercession worked, for on March 31, 1902, in his first formal communication to John Hay, Concha demanded an indemnity of $7 million (a reduction of nearly $3 million) and an annuity to be set by arbitration.[5]

Although the figures were still high compared to the cost in Nicaragua and the Americans had no taste for the uncertainties of arbitration, Concha's proposals offered at least a basis for continued negotiation. Concha's letter to Hay cited the international importance of a canal at the shortest and best route: "Colombia widely and generously opens her doors so that the grand work may be achieved within the shortest possible time." Not only would Colombia "not place any obstacle whatever" but she would enlarge the concessions, grant a larger zone than France enjoyed, and forgo many other demands in the interest of cooperation. In a final burst of generous prose Concha, with a good heart but a poor sense of prophecy, assured Hay that "a final convention on this subject will not be hampered by pecuniary

4. *BVC*, 220–21; Anguizola, *Philippe Bunau-Varilla*, 196–97; for British Chargé Claude Coventry Mallet's view that the American offer of $7 million in gold was attractive, especially in view of Colombia's desperate financial condition, see C. Mallet to Lord Lansdowne, August 7, 1902, in FO 55/408, PRO.
5. Philippe Bunau-Varilla to Panama *Star and Herald*, March 26, 1902; Bunau-Varilla to José Concha, March 27, 1902 (two letters), all in *BVC*, 221–25. For the reduction from $20 million to $9.8 million to $7 million see DuVal, *Cadiz to Cathay*, 178–80.

considerations." Concha's letter is important in establishing that he, like Martínez Silva before him, actively courted the Americans and tried to reverse their initial preference for Nicaragua. Although Bogotá tried to keep all its options open by not communicating in a timely way with its own representatives and both Cromwell and Bunau-Varilla were successful in influencing Concha, Concha's March 31, 1902, letter to John Hay does not have the tone of a coerced or manipulated response. At this stage of the canal negotiations, the interests of Cromwell, Bunau-Varilla, and Concha were similar if not identical. The United States with its alternative routes at Panama or Nicaragua held an imposing advantage; the other negotiators did not have the luxury of options. In his March 31 letter, Concha's eagerness, friendliness, and repeated assurances of Colombia's refusal to profit from what nature had placed within her boundaries led the Americans to believe that negotiations with Colombia were serious and finite. On the basis of Concha's willingness to negotiate, and as a result of his subsequent negotiations with John Hay, Senator Mark Hanna prepared to fight in the Senate for a Panama route, which would benefit all of the principals in the negotiations, the Compagnie Nouvelle, the United States, Colombia, and Panama.[6]

The negotiations with Colombia, however, proved to be even more difficult than Senator John T. Morgan had predicted. In a clumsy attempt to counter the threat of the Nicaraguan option, Colombia asserted its frequent claim of sovereignty over Nicaragua as well as Panama. Colombia, which owned fifty thousand shares of Compagnie Nouvelle stock, made it clear through its Paris consul that its representative on the company's board would veto any sale to the United States that preceded an American treaty with Colombia. Although Concha in his initial letter to Hay had denied Colombia's monetary motives, it was clear, as Cromwell observed, that Colombia was interested in money as well as reassurances about sovereignty.[7]

6. José Concha to JH, March 31, 1902, House Documents, 57th Cong., 1st Sess., No. 611, Serial 4337, pp. 2–3. This essential letter is not included in the standard collections of the Concha-Hay correspondence (see note 7, Serial 6582) but is reprinted in this different collection ("Letters from the Colombian Minister"); SP, 174–75.

7. José Concha to JH, April 8, 1902, Senate Documents, 63rd Cong., 2nd Sess., No. 474, Serial 6582 (Diplomatic History of the Panama Canal), 250–52; SP, 173–74; Miner, Fight for the Panama Route, 133. Cromwell's Brief, in SP, 246–47, has a good summary of the situation. For the Nicaraguan claim see José Concha to JH, April 8, 1902, Notes from the Colombian Legation to the United States, RG 59, Microcopy M51, Roll 11; for the historic basis of the Colombian claim on a Spanish decree of 1803 which transferred Mosquito to the captaincy-general of New Granada for military purposes and was origi-

The problems with the Panama route continued to multiply. Concha and Colombia remained equivocal, and the Compagnie Nouvelle's offer to the United States required the stockholders' approval, which could not be obtained until Colombia made its arrangements with the United States. Meanwhile, the Senate had begun to consider the alternative routes in hearings before Senator Morgan's Interoceanic Canal Committee. Concha well understood that by delaying an agreement with the United States, Colombia risked the secession of Panama, either spontaneously or with encouragement from the United States, which would produce "incalculable evils" for Colombia. Concha warned Bogotá that many American newspapers had urged, even in 1902, that the United States denounce the treaty of 1846 and occupy Panama. The Colombians were ready to denounce the 1846 treaty if Europe could be persuaded to replace the United States as Colombia's protector. Bogotá's hope of such a possibility was highly unrealistic. Even before Theodore Roosevelt became president, the revived Monroe Doctrine defined a new American sensitivity to any foreign involvement in Central America. When Concha dutifully asked the French ambassador in Washington to initiate a European intervention to offset the threat of the United States, the French quickly declined and the negotiations continued.[8]

Since Concha spoke no English and Hay no Spanish, William Cromwell became the intermediary. Both Hay and Hanna refused to consider the original $10 to $20 million indemnity specified in Concha's original instructions. Cromwell worked out many of the other differences and helped write and edit Concha's draft agreement, which was based on Concha's original proposal of March 31 plus Hay's and Concha's many amendments and changes. Concha formally submitted the final draft—the Hay-Concha Protocol—to Secretary Hay on April 18, 1902. In this memorandum the United States agreed to

---

nally inspired by the prospect of a Nicaraguan canal, see Richard Van Alstyne, "The Central American Policy of Lord Palmerston, 1846–1848," *HAHR* (1936), 344–45; for similar Colombian claims in 1825, 1838, 1892, and 1894, see E. Taylor Parks, *Colombia and the United States, 1765–1934* (Durham, N.C., 1935), 389.

8. DuVal, *Cadiz to Cathay* 181; Miner, *Fight for the Panama Route*, 134; José Concha to Felipe Paúl, April 1, 10, 1902, both in *SP*, 177. For American sentiment for dealing with Panama separately see Frederick Penfield, "Why Not Own the Panama Isthmus?" *NAR*, CLXXIV (1902), 269–72; "Our Relations to the Isthmus," "Importance of the Isthmus," and "Advantages of Annexation," all in *Review of Reviews*, XXIV (1901), 276, 524; Alfred Charles Richard, Jr., "The Panama Canal in American Consciousness, 1870–1922" (Ph.D. dissertation, Boston University, 1969), 121–22.

pay $7 million indemnity and an annual annuity of $250,000 to cover Colombia's loss of income from the Panama Railroad. To avoid a complete breakdown of negotiations Cromwell postponed the question of an additional "fair and reasonable" canal annuity that Concha's draft specified would be set by additional negotiations or arbitration.[9]

Throughout the Colombian-American negotiations, the difficulties of communications between the cities of Bogotá and Washington constituted an additional complication. Not only were the cable transmissions hampered by technical difficulties, but Bogotá's foreign ministry remained ambivalent, indecisive, or willfully confusing in its dealings with Washington and its own diplomatic representatives. Martínez Silva waited a year for instructions that never arrived. Concha was told on March 19, 1902, that new instructions were on the way. Bogotá ignored the urgency imposed by the United States congressional debate as well as the real threat of Nicaragua. When Foreign Minister Felipe Paúl gave American minister Charles B. Hart a copy of Concha's new instruction, Hart immediately wired them to Washington on March 6, 1902. Hay received them on March 17 and rejected them on March 18, an astonishing three weeks before Concha received a copy of his own—after he had drafted and submitted his treaty proposal. Once again the new Colombian instructions ignored the previous negotiations and reiterated demands that had been summarily rejected. Had Concha received them early in March and followed Colombia's demands, even the efforts of the intrepid Cromwell and Bunau-Varilla could not have saved the Panama option. In its delayed instructions Colombia asked for complete sovereignty, an international guarantee of the canal's neutrality, Colombian police powers paid for by American funds, a reversion of all property and improvements after ninety-nine years, and a stipulation that Colombian congressional approval was required. Even worse, further negotiations were to await a financial settlement between the French company and Colombia.[10]

Concha immediately cabled Bogotá objecting to the obvious bad faith of his own government. Following the instructions, Concha argued, would precipitate an immediate American commitment to Nicaragua. Withdrawing a proposal already submitted would be dip-

9. *SP*, 176–77; DuVal, *Cadiz to Cathay*, 182.

10. Miner, *Fight for the Panama Route*, 137–42; text of the Hay-Concha Protocol, *ibid.*, 397–407; Charles B. Hart to JH, March 6, 1902, Despatches, T33, Roll 58; JH to Hart, Diplomatic Instructions of the State Department, Microcopy M77, Roll 48, RG 59, NA.

lomatically offensive to the United States, which "would consider me *persona non grata* . . . I believe I ought to retire." In a later communication Concha reiterated that Martínez Silva had authorized direct negotiations between the United States and the Compagnie Nouvelle, and Colombia could not now revoke them. Bogotá ignored Concha's protests, ordered him not to leave, and dispatched no new instructions. When on April 21, 1902, John Hay accepted the Hay-Concha Protocol, Concha's draft served as the Senate's basis for consideration of Panama as a serious alternative to Nicaragua. Colombia and the United States agreed that an American canal at Panama was not only desirable but in the best interests of both countries and the world. Nonetheless, Bogotá felt the threat of Nicaragua was a Yanqui trick to make the best bargain possible, even after the 308 to 2 vote in January, 1902, for a canal in Nicaragua.[11]

Although the Americans were not sanguine about any part of the Colombian negotiations, their aims have been frequently misunderstood. With remarkable patience those Americans who believed that the French canal route at Panama was the best choice tried to satisfy as many of Colombia's wishes as possible, though many of these demands were irrational, self-defeating, and diplomatically irresponsible. As its more worldly diplomats warned, the Colombian misperception of American options was suicidal. But the Americans tried, by dealing with one problem at a time, to prevent the Colombians from foreclosing by inadvertence what the Americans were convinced was in everyone's best interests. Diplomatically Nicaragua offered the United States a much less painful political alternative. But the search for an acceptable arrangement with Colombia was evidence, not of American pressure or bullying, but of sympathy with a confused but proud smaller nation, as well as a determination to build the canal at the optimal site.[12]

Colombia remained determinedly uncooperative. While its Washington diplomats continued to work with the United States, Bogotá played the role of constant adversary. The Hay-Concha Protocol satisfied one of Senator Hanna's two prerequisites for Senate consideration of Panama as an alternate to Nicaragua. Hanna's second requirement, that the Compagnie Nouvelle's shareholders agree to transfer

11. Miner, *Fight for the Panama Route,* 142–43.
12. Tyler Dennett, *John Hay: From Poetry to Politics* (New York, 1934), 370–71; for Concha's fear that the United States could "embrace whatever tendency there may be toward separation" in Panama, see Concha to Paúl, April 1, 1902, in *SP,* 177.

its ownership to the United States, presented problems. Once before the Colombian representative in Paris had prevented the transfer. Instead of calling another general meeting that would involve a public vote of the stockholders, the Compagnie Nouvelle's directors obtained formal written consent from a majority of the stockholders authorizing the sale. This device satisfied Hanna and prevented Colombia from attempting to extract further concessions in Paris. Had the Colombians succeeded they would have prevented any further consideration of Panama in the American Senate.[13]

It has been frequently misunderstood that the French did not sell Colombia's Panama canal concession to the United States—the concession was not France's to sell but Colombia's. The United States had to make two separate purchases, first a new concession from Colombia, and second the physical material owned by the original de Lesseps company in Panama and Paris. Concessions were never any part of the American-French negotiations or arrangements. All of the Colombian concessions, land rights, rentals, and related matters were specifically and expressly reserved for separate arrangements and negotiation between the United States and Colombia and never constituted any part of the $40 million to be paid to the Compagnie Nouvelle's stockholders.[14]

What the Americans bought for $40 million included 56 parcels of land totaling 30,000 acres, 2,431 buildings including two hospitals and general office buildings, "an immense amount of machinery" which the Walker Isthmian Canal Commission regarded as virtually useless, and, most important, 39,586,332 cubic yards of excavation that could be used to complete the canal. The final evaluation amounted to $27,474,033 for excavation completed, $6,886,300 for Panama Railroad Company stock, $2,000,000 for maps, drawings, and records, and 10 percent for possible omissions. Thus the $40 million was paid for tangible property, not sovereign rights. Subsequent investigations confirmed the accuracy of the original conservative American evaluation that provided a fair payment to the French company for usable equipment, property, and the immense amount of work already completed, mainly in planning and excavation. The Walker Commission, even when recommending Nicaragua, had consistently pointed out the engineering advantages in the Panama route. The shorter estimated time needed to build a canal at Panama, eight years instead of

13. *SP*, 260–61.
14. *SP*, 174; Cromwell's Brief, *SP*, 256–58.

ten at Nicaragua, was the most telling comparison of the Walker Commission's revised supplementary report that reversed its Nicaraguan recommendation in favor of Panama. The total estimated cost of a Panama canal was $5 million less than at Nicaragua.[15]

With an apparent agreement between the United States and Colombia, an actual agreement between the United States and France, and Colombia's written consent to the principle of the arrangement, Senator Hanna prepared to argue in favor of a Panama route in the United States Senate. Hanna, now satisfied that the Colombians and French fully understood that the American offer was final, especially the $40 million purchase from the Compagnie Nouvelle, had William Nelson Cromwell write the draft of Hanna's Senate subcommittee report in favor of the Panama route, which became the basis for his arguments during the Senate debate.[16]

For those who argue that all America needed was patience or the willingness to settle for Nicaragua, John Hay's plaintive letter to Senator John T. Morgan, on the eve of the debate on the route, is evidence that there was no simple solution for a Central American canal. "I regret to say," Hay wrote Morgan on April 22, 1902, "that I have not yet been able to get a firm offer from the Government of Nicaragua." Hay, who had no preference, insisted that the American agreements with both Colombia and Nicaragua be submitted to Congress simultaneously. Hay wrote Morgan, "The principal difficulty [is] that both in Colombia and Nicaragua great ignorance exists as to the attitude of the United States. In both countries it is believed that their route is the only one possible or practicable, and that the . . . . United States in the last resort, will accept any terms they choose to demand. The Ministers here of both powers know perfectly well that it is untrue and they are doing all they can to convince their people at home that no unreasonable proposition will be considered by the Government of the United States; but it is slow work convincing them."[17]

The American negotiations with both Nicaragua and Costa Rica were not reassuring. Hay had rejected a draft submitted by William

15. A detailed inventory is in *House Documents*, 58th Cong., 3rd Sess., No. 226, Serial 4853, pp. 54–60; a summary is in *Senate Documents*, 57th Cong., 1st Sess., No. 123, Serial 4609–1, pp. 677–80; an analysis of the value is in Mack, *Land Divided*, 485–86.
16. *SP*, 174.
17. JH to John T. Morgan, April 22, 1902, in Hay Papers, LC; for Hay's lack of preference see Kenton J. Clymer, *John Hay: Gentleman as Diplomat* (Ann Arbor, 1975), 203–205. For problems with Nicaragua see Dana G. Munro, *Intervention and Dollar Diplomacy in the Caribbean, 1900–1921* (Princeton, 1964), 59–60.

Merry, the American minister at Managua, and renegotiation was slow. Costa Rica's president worried about whether he had the constitutional power to make a canal treaty. For a brief time it appeared that Panama might be the Senate's only possible choice by default. On May 13, Hay threatened Nicaragua that he would send forward only the Hay-Concha Protocol for Senate consideration. Only on May 14, 1902, did Nicaragua submit to Hay an incomplete draft, still subject to possible changes. On May 15, 1902, President Roosevelt submitted the Hay-Concha Protocol and Foreign Minister Luis Corea's Nicaraguan proposal to Congress.[18]

On the eve of the Senate debate, President Theodore Roosevelt was not considered a public advocate of Panama, though he remained in contact with the Panama interests through Senator Mark Hanna and Republican lobbyist William Cromwell. Bunau-Varilla thought Roosevelt favored Nicaragua, and the New York *Sun* regarded him as uncommitted. John Hay remained indifferent, preferring no canal at all, or possibly leaning toward Nicaragua. He was having as many "exasperating difficulties" negotiating with the Nicaraguans as with the Colombians. When President Roosevelt called a special session of Congress for June 4, 1902, to decide the canal route, Democratic Senator John T. Morgan led the Nicaragua advocates and Republican Mark Hanna led the Panama group, which was still in the minority. The Hepburn bill, passed by the house, specified the Nicaraguan route. On March 29 John Spooner introduced a substitute amendment, which called for a Panama route. Spooner's bill was introduced after consultation with Roosevelt, not to advocate Panama but to assure that if the Nicaraguan route was defeated, Panama could be designated without the procedural delay involved in calling another special session. Although the original House vote for Nicaragua of 308 to 2 reflected the strength of the sentiment for Nicaragua, by the time the Senate debate opened in June a shift had occurred, not in favor of Panama but away from absolute certainty about Nicaragua. More senators and newspapers now viewed the canal route as an open question and the Senate debate as a genuine forum for deciding the proper American option.[19]

18. Miner, *Fight for the Panama Route,* 144–45; for the Nicaragua and Costa Rica protocols see *House Documents,* 57th Cong., 1st Sess., No. 611, pp. 16–25.

19. For TR's public neutrality see *BVC,* 229. Dorothy Fowler, *John Coit Spooner: Defender of Presidents* (New York, 1961), 275–76, establishes Spooner's authorship of the Spooner Act claimed by Cromwell; Dennett, *John Hay,* 367–69; for the shift in con-

On June 4, 1902, Senator John Tyler Morgan began the nineteen-day debate by summarily dismissing the charge that Nicaragua was frequently beset by serious earthquakes. He dramatically presented a letter from Nicaragua's Foreign Minister Luis Corea, stating that "Nicaragua had not had any volcanic eruption since 1835," an obvious falsehood since Momotombo, an old volcano one hundred miles from the proposed canal route, had erupted on May 13. On June 5, Senator Hanna, ill and looking old, took the Senate floor for two days to argue for the Panama route. Hanna's final significant Senate debate was a rare performance, a speech that changed men's minds as well as Senate votes.[20]

On the eve of the vote, Bunau-Varilla may also have helped change some minds. He supplied each senator with an official Nicaraguan stamp, showing a beautiful engraving of Mont Momotombo erupting. Bunau-Varilla's dramatic gesture was made even more effective by the actual eruption of Mont Pelée in Martinique on May 7, 1902, which destroyed the city of St.-Pierre killing its twenty-five thousand inhabitants, a tragedy the New York *Sun* compared with Pompeii. Bunau-Varilla's stamp was an irrefutable rebuttal of Senator Morgan's main arguments that Nicaragua offered a safer canal route. The Senate now had a clear choice—dangerous volcanic eruptions in Nicaragua or difficult politics in Colombia. The key vote came on June 19, when Senator Spooner proposed to substitute his Panama amendment for the Nicaragua bill. After Panama won 42 to 34, the final bill, now renamed the Spooner Act, passed by a 67 to 6 margin with even John T. Morgan voting in favor. The Spooner Act was a statesmanslike compromise that provided for the president to purchase the French rights and property for $40 million, negotiate a satisfactory arrangement with Colombia, and build a Panama canal. If he failed to accomplish any of these in a reasonable time (unspecified), the Senate directed that the Nicaragua route be taken. The Spooner Act limited payment

---

gressional sentiment from Nicaragua to Panama see Miner, *Fight for the Panama Route*, 120; an opposite view is in *BVC*, 241. For Hepburn's political struggle for an American-controlled canal in Nicaragua and his acquiescence to the Spooner compromise see John Ely Briggs, *William Peters Hepburn* (Iowa City, 1919), 200–222.

20. Morgan's argument is in *Congressional Record*, 57th Cong., 1st Sess., p. 6269. On Hanna's effectiveness see Shelby Cullom, *Fifty Years of Public Service* (Chicago, 1911), 281; for Morgan's role see August C. Radke, Jr., "John Tyler Morgan: An Expansionist Senator, 1877–1907" (Ph.D. dissertation, University of Washington, 1953), 419–30; for the opinion shift see Richard, "Panama Canal in American Consciousness," 117–30; Ameringer, "Panama Canal Lobby," 356–59.

to $10 million for either route and also limited the cost for either route to the estimates given in the two Walker Commission reports. The House concurred by a 252 to 8 vote.[21]

Senator Morgan had not given up. Still convinced that dealing with Colombia was impossible, he was certain that eventually the United States would have to turn to Nicaragua as an alternative, and he was equally determined that reasonable time would be interpreted as strictly as possible. The Senate, not the president, still maintained the original initiative in directing American canal policy. It was the Senate that first had persuaded President McKinley to appoint the decisive Walker Isthmian Canal commission, and it was the Senate that had made a shambles of John Hay's first English treaty, not only rejecting but rewriting it. Although he strongly favored the Panama route for technological reasons, like McKinley Roosevelt remained committed to an American canal at a site chosen by the Senate. In mid-1902, Roosevelt, in his first year as an elevated vice-president, would have been hard-pressed to fight either the Republican leadership or the Senate if either body had chosen Nicaragua.[22]

The Spooner Act was signed by President Roosevelt on June 28, 1902. To satisfy congressional skepticism concerning the company's title, an exhaustive two-month legal examination of the soundness of the Compagnie Nouvelle's title and whether it could legally sell its holdings to the Americans was conducted. Attorney-General Philander C. Knox went to Paris to complete the legal work. On September 29, 1902, Roosevelt wrote to Hanna that "the Panama title is all right." To satisfy Senate objections to parts of the Hay-Concha Protocol, Hay and Cromwell worked out amendments which Concha sent on to Bogotá for approval.[23]

Roosevelt, like Morgan and other congressional leaders, remained wary of the diplomatic problems that still remained to be resolved. Morgan suggested buying Panama, "the entire State," from Colom-

21. New York *Sun* article in *BVC*, 241–42, 178, 228. For the debate and text of the Spooner Act see Miner, *Fight for the Panama Route*, 147–55, 408–12; *BVC*, facing 247, has a picture of the volcano stamp; Anguizola, *Philippe Bunau-Varilla*, 213–15. For a balanced assessment of the Spooner Act see John G. Walker to Lewis Haupt, February 1, 1902, Box 2, John G. Walker Papers, LC; Ameringer, "Panama Canal Lobby," 356–61. For the 252–8 vote (not the 259 or 260 in many accounts) see New York *Times*, June 27, 1902, p. 9.

22. Miner, *Fight for the Panama Route*, 154–56; Radke, "John Tyler Morgan," 434–37.

23. TR to Mark Hanna, September 29, 1903, in *MRL*, III, 333; Cromwell's Brief, in *SP*, 265–67; Miner, *Fight for the Panama Route*, 156.

bia. Hay promised Morgan to consult "some of the leading members of the senate." One of these, chairman of the Foreign Relations Committee Shelby Cullom, disturbed by the delays in dealing with Colombia, publicly suggested the unilateral appropriation of the canal zone as a "universal public utility," with compensation to be arranged after the fact. "Why cannot we buy the Panama Isthmus outright instead of leasing it from Colombia? I think they would change their Constitution if we offered enough," Theodore Roosevelt wrote Secretary of state John Hay on August 21, 1902. "It seems to me a good thing." Such proposals mirrored American frustration at the delays, not serious imperial policies. Roosevelt and the Senate in 1902 wanted control with as little colonial responsibility as possible.[24]

When the Senate approved Spooner's amendment to the original Hepburn bill, a Senate-House conference committee had to decide which of the two diametrically opposed bills to adopt. The House's concurrence with the Senate by a 252 to 8 vote did not necessarily mean that the Panama advocates had convinced the House to change its views. Lewis Haupt, a member of the Isthmian Canal Commission and a fervent public advocate of the Nicaraguan route, suggested to Senator Morgan the tactic of supporting Panama to get the enabling legislation for a canal, then restoring Nicaragua in the House-Senate conference. Morgan supported the Spooner Act, however, because it was a shrewd political compromise. So sure were the Nicaraguan canal advocates that Colombia would not agree or that the French title was defective that they regarded the Senate's adoption of the Panama route as a prelude to eventual retreat to the politically more manageable Nicaraguan route. Ironically, the senators who favored Nicaragua had no better ally than the Colombian government at Bogotá.[25]

The War of the Thousand Days entered its last painful stages as both sides turned more and more to foreign help to end the fighting. Although Colombians remained ambivalent about any foreign presence, both sides cooperated when neutral powers intervened to negotiate

24. TR to JH, August 21, 1902, in MRL, III, 318; JH to John Spooner, July 15, 1902, in William R. Thayer, The Life and Letters of John Hay (1915; 2 vols., rpr. Boston, 1929), II, 303; Tomás Herrán to Felipe Paúl, December 19, 1902, in DuVal, Cadiz to Cathay, 196. See also Penfield, "Why Not Own the Panama Isthmus," 269–72; and "Advantages of Annexation," 524.

25. Lewis Haupt to John Tyler Morgan, January 19, 1902, on page 2 of minutes of final commission meeting, Box 3, Lewis Haupt Papers, LC.

local armistices. In 1902, when Panama became a war zone and American naval reinforcements were dispatched, both Liberals and Nationalists openly prepared to contest control of the isthmus, knowing that such a conflict would bring the United States directly into the war. How clearly the opponents understood that extending the war to Panama was the best means of ending it through American intercession is impossible to estimate, but both were aware of the likelihood. The Panama canal problem had already indirectly influenced the Colombian civil war. When War minister José Concha replaced Carlos Martínez Silva in the Washington negotiations, the Spooner Act debate was just beginning. In Colombia, Aristides Fernández, the most extreme of the Nationalists, replaced Concha as minister of war. Fernández' partisan measures brought the already bitter war to its most draconian phase at a time when Liberal war fortunes appeared momentarily promising. As Liberal guerrilla strength grew in the south, Rafael Uribe Uribe's Liberal army, in its march from the Venezuelan border, threatened both Bogotá and a union with the guerrillas.[26]

But Fernández, who combined administrative brilliance with authoritarian brutality, rallied the Nationalists, who decisively defeated Uribe Uribe's army and implemented Fernández' new policy of "inexorable repression" of the revolutionary spirit. The Liberals, once again defeated by strength of arms, were forced to continue their resistance while the efficient and insensitive Fernández insisted on fighting his religious-ideological war to the bitter end. On June 12, 1902, Marroquín wavered, offering the Liberals a general amnesty coupled with a vague promise of future representation. Fernández' monetary inducements to Liberal guerrilla groups to surrender were more successful. But Fernández remained an opportunistic ideologue, not a politician in search of peace. Prominent political adversaries were summarily executed; when Carlos Martínez Silva and eleven other Historical Conservatives signed a declaration opposing execution for political activities, Martínez Silva was among the group arrested and imprisoned. Some were executed, others were jailed and then exiled to isolated areas away from the capital.[27]

26. W. W. Mead to General Benjamín Herrera, January 20, 1902; J. A. Ramíerez to Mead, January 20, 1902, both in *Senate Documents*, 58th Cong., 2nd Sess., No. 143, Serial 4589, pp. 229–31; Bergquist, *Coffee and Conflict in Colombia*, 178–80.

27. Bergquist, *Coffee and Conflict in Colombia*, 184–85; Delpar, "The Liberal Party of Colombia, 1863–1903" (Ph.D. dissertation, Columbia University, 1967), 373–74. For Marroquín's use of fake truce talks to trap Liberal soldiers see C. Mallet to Lord Lansdowne, August 7, September 15, 1902, in FO 55/408; on Marroquín's shaky hold on power see Charles B. Hart to JH, August 29, 1902, in Despatches, T33, Roll 58.

Panama became the key to end the war and the hope of creating a workable peace. Panama also stood as the only remnant of Colombian wealth that could produce revenue for an economy that had virtually ceased to function. When inflation reached 25,000 percent, large numbers of troops were not paid or fed regularly, thus leading to increased looting and expropriation. Liberal Benjamín Herrera suddenly emerged as the war's most successful military leader. By winning a series of decisive victories in Panama, Herrera made it impossible for the impoverished Bogotá government to dislodge his forces. The Nationalists had won the mainland; the Liberals under Herrera controlled Panama. A negotiated peace was now more appealing because both sides controlled territory and armies and neither was strong enough to dislodge the other.[28]

Colombia's desperate economic conditions were vividly described by Henry Eder, an American sugar planter living in the large western province of Cauca, who wrote to John Hay on March 1, 1902, asking for American diplomatic help. Eder complained that Bogotá was only interested in Cauca's potential for supplying money to the war effort. Because communication between Cauca and Bogotá was sporadic, the local government maintained almost autonomous authority, and foreigners—especially Americans—fared badly since local officials knew that the United States had refused to intervene in domestic matters of Latin American nations to protect its citizens' business interests. Colombians "have long ago become accustomed to regard Panama as an entirely different nation and of an exceptional and particular interest to the American government," Eder wrote. Although both sides reinforced their claims to Panama, the government's financial problems worried Captain W. W. Reisinger, commander of the cruiser *Philadelphia*, more than the threat of a rebel attack. Reisinger reported on March 31, 1902, an "audacious" Liberal attack on the railroad line. When Colombian troops proved unable to protect the rail line, the American naval officer asked how much discretion he was permitted.[29]

28. Bergquist, *Coffee and Conflict in Colombia*, 200, 185; Favell, "Antecedents," 205–208; for the gravity of Colombia's economic situation see George Welby to Lord Lansdowne, March 17, 1902; and Spenser Dickson to Lansdowne, June 5, December 10, 1902, all in FO 55/409.

29. Henry J. Eder to JH, March 1, 1902, Naval Records Collection of the Naval Records and Library, Subject File VI, International Relations and Politics, Colombia, in RG 45, NA; W. W. Reisinger to William Moody, April 7, 1902, in *Senate Documents*, 58th Cong., 2nd Sess., No. 143, Serial 4589, pp. 248–49. For internal problems of expropriation during the war see Malcolm Deas, "A Colombian Coffee Estate: Santa Bárbara, Cundinamarca, 1870–1912," in Kenneth Duncan and Ian Rutledge (eds.), *Land and Labour in Latin America* (Cambridge, Eng., 1977), 285–90.

Bogotá was too preoccupied with the ebb and flow of the revolution to celebrate the news of the passage of the Spooner Act in the American Congress on June 26, 1902. Few Colombians viewed the decision for a canal at Panama as a substantial Colombian victory. Colombia, historically more attracted to abstract ideas than to practical diplomacy, refused to enjoy its victory and instead continued to raise questions of sovereignty and national honor, especially ironic at a time when the revolutionists were about to take control of Panama. One Liberal leader publicly supported the idea of an American canal—but only after the civil war, Colombia's first priority, was resolved. Many Colombians viewed a canal as a way to pay for the civil war damages, an idea that became more attractive as the costs of the war grew. The idea of a canal as an economic panacea was unfortunate because the expense of the war and the cost of the foreign war claims arising from it far exceeded what the United States could conceivably pay.[30]

When on July 26, 1902, President Marroquín postponed his decision on the canal, he feared that he would be held responsible either for losing the canal or for allowing Americans to control Panama. Marroquín planned "to free myself of the responsibility for this matter if I could transfer it to the Congress and only God knows when Congress can be convened." José Concha, negotiating the amendments to the Hay-Concha Protocol in Washington, was not instructed until August to inform the United States of the tentative nature of Marroquín's commitment. Concha chided the president for his lack of will.[31]

The last phase of the war took several dramatic turns. After the Liberals won a decisive naval battle in Parita Bay on July 31, when the *Padilla* captured two government vessels, took control of the sea near Panama, and captured Aguadulce, Rafael Uribe Uribe returned to lead a new Liberal army on the mainland. In September the Liberals made another peace overture to Marroquín, demanding the removal of Fernández as a prerequisite to peace negotiations. On October 5, 1902, Marroquín yielded to the Liberals' only remaining condition and announced Fernández' retirement. Uribe Uribe controlled an important area on the Magdalena River, denying the government full commercial control of Colombia's most important waterway. Just as the Liberals, with strength in Panama and in mainland Colombia, appeared to be in a position to win the war, Uribe Uribe

30. Favell, "Antecedents," 211; John Crow, *The Epic of Latin America* (3rd ed.; Berkeley, 1980), 619; Anguizola, *Philippe Bunau-Varilla*, 196.
31. José Marroquín to General Pompillio Gutiérrez, July 26, 1902; Felipe Paúl to José Concha, August 13, 1902, both in Favell, "Antecedents," 212–13.

lost a key battle and surrendered. The defeated Liberals were allowed safe-conduct and guaranteed retention of their property but did not receive any further political concessions. But Marroquín's concessions and Uribe Uribe's surrender helped end the habit of war in a nation that was understandably war weary.[32]

On September 11, 1902, Colombia formally asked the United States to mediate a settlement of its civil war. The Americans, who were asked to intervene both for humanitarian reasons and to facilitate the submission of the canal question to the Colombian Congress, had independently begun a naval intervention to restore uninterrupted transit on the embattled railroad line. When Acting Secretary of State Alvey Adee advised President Roosevelt to place the negotiations in the hands of the naval forces at Colón rather than with the minister at Bogotá, the American naval intervention and the Colombian initiative for mediation merged under Commander Thomas C. McLean, captain of the cruiser *Cincinnati*, who became the chief American negotiator. McLean's first priority was to restore order. Secretary of the Navy William Moody reaffirmed the neutrality of the isthmus but suggested that the use of the railroad line by government troops, "which will not endanger transit or provoke hostilities, may not be objectionable." Because the American decision to intervene to restore the transit under the Bidlack-Mallarino Treaty's provisions and Marroquín's request for mediation were but a day apart and became effectively merged under McLean's direction, Colombia, never aware of the independent American decision to intervene, remained convinced that the Americans had overstepped the purpose of its request. McLean, given wide latitude to deal with the problem, treated both sides as belligerents. The navy understood the dangers of such interventions. On October 4, 1902, when the navy's permanent Caribbean squadron was established to deal with trouble spots in Central America, American naval officers were instructed to be friendly to Latin American natives, learn their language, and, of utmost importance, avoid "any assumption of superiority." Because communications were so irregular and the military and political events complex and pressing, neither the Americans nor the Colombians were aware of their mutual misunderstanding about the dual nature of the American intervention.[33]

32. Bergquist, *Coffee and Conflict in Colombia*, 186–88; Rafael Santos V. to General Benjamín Herrera, July 31, 1902, in *Senate Documents*, 58th Cong., 2nd Sess., No. 143, Serial 4589, pp. 280–81.

33. Charles Hart to JH, September 11, 1902; Alvey Adee to William Moody, September 16, 1902; Moody to Thomas McLean, September 20, 1902, all in *Senate Documents*,

On September 19, 1902, the United States took control of the Panama Railroad. In identical letters to General Tomás Quintero, commander of the government forces, and General Benjamín Herrera of the revolutionary forces, McLean declared that "no armed men except forces of the United States will be allowed to come on or use the line." Marines were dispatched to occupy the Panama railway station and guard all trains. In addition, the United States extended the neutrality zone to include Panama Bay, prohibiting any naval activity by either side. Colombia had barred "persons suspected of Liberal tendencies" from being "in the streets" of Colón. When Rear Admiral Silas Casey arrived on September 30 with the battleship *Wisconsin*, he continued McLean's policy of neutralizing the railroad to separate it from the conflict. Casey quickly ended the government's practice of stopping trains to search for and remove Liberals. At first the Americans refused to permit armed troops to ride on the trains but allowed "limited numbers" of troops to ride as long as their arms were checked in the baggage car. Casey, who was not optimistic, wrote that "the conflict will last indefinitely, and it will be necessary to guard the trains until the revolution is at an end." Keeping either side from controlling the trains was central to the continuing American policy of strict neutrality while restoring peace to the isthmus.[34]

On October 3, Casey stopped permitting Colombian troops to ride on the trains even with their arms carried separately. All trains were heavily guarded by thirty-five to forty American marines or bluejackets. The only potentially dangerous incident occurred when a group of Liberals tried to remove a Colombian army officer from a train. The American guards pointed their machine gun at the insurgents, who then retreated. By October 13, Admiral Casey had no doubt that the American presence was helping the government by preventing insurgents from controlling both the railroad and the isthmus.[35]

58th Cong., 2nd Sess., No. 143, Serial 4589, pp. 284–85; Richard Challener, *Admirals, Generals, and American Foreign Policy* (Princeton, 1973), 152–53. For Adee's decision see Adee to Moody, September 12, 1902, memorandum, "Interference with Transit on Isthmus of Panama," in Henry B. Armes to JBM, Panama Affair Subject Folder, Box 134, John Bassett Moore Papers, LC.

34. Thomas C. McLean to Generals Tomás Quintero and Benjamín Herrera, September 22, 1902; McLean to Lieutenant Colonel B. R. Russell, September 23, 1902; Rear Admiral Silas W. Casey to William H. Moody, October 6, 1902, all in *Senate Documents*, 58th Cong., 2nd Sess., No. 143, Serial 4589, pp. 287–92.

35. N. E. Mason to Silas Casey, October 5, 1902; Casey to William Moody, October 13, 1902, both *ibid.*, 295–97, 300.

But the Marroquín government was not satisfied with the even-handed aid of the Americans. Even though the government had originally asked the United States to mediate the revolution, after the American presence on the isthmus prevented the Liberals from taking complete control Colombia insisted that the Americans become co-belligerents rather than peacekeepers. Colombia objected to the American policy of treating both sides as belligerents, particularly Commander McLean's practice of sending identical letters to insurgent and government leaders. The Marroquín government also objected to the use of American troops on shore, which it insisted was unnecessary and might provoke confrontations with government troops. Invoking the treaty of 1846 to protect the transit was interpreted by Marroquín as protection against insurgents, not as a means of maintaining neutrality or keeping the rail line open.[36]

Marroquín's ambivalence about the American insistence that good offices must be neutral is hardly surprising. The War of the Thousand Days was waged as ferociously and lasted as long as it did because Marroquín was unwilling at some times and unable at others to seek a political remedy. Calling for American help was dictated by the immediate necessity of preventing a Liberal takeover of Panama. But Marroquín was no more interested in a negotiated peace in late 1902 than he had been earlier. What he wanted was not to lose Panama—either to the Liberals or ultimately to the United States. The president was candid about his motives even when defending his actions the following year. "Triumphant at Aguadulce, the revolutionary army overran the whole Isthmus, invaded the line of the railroad and threatened Colón and Panama in a most serious manner. . . . My government was obliged to take an extreme resolution . . . for American forces to reestablish the freedom of transit of the Panama Railroad." Good offices meant different things to Marroquín and the Americans. When the United States refused to become a co-belligerent, the Marroquín government talked about Colombian honor and patriotism, as if the Liberals were neither Colombians nor patriots. The Americans continued to regard both sides as Colombian.[37]

Marroquín's deception was more than simple opportunism. Not only did he use American intervention to neutralize growing Liberal

36. A summary of the Marroquín government's protests is in Miner, *Fight for the Panama Route*, 177–78.
37. Marroquín's message to Colombian Congress, July, 1904, quoted in Miner, *Fight for the Panama Route*, 174.

strength in Panama, but he misled his own minister in Washington into thinking that the Americans had intervened on their own rather than at Colombia's request. José Concha, already troubled by the negotiations, was outraged by the new American intervention because he assumed they had acted on their own, which was shocking for a nation engaged in diplomatic negotiations concerning the area it was occupying. Foreign Minister Felipe Paúl understood the appearance of duplicity but, instead of explaining to Concha that the Americans had been invited by the government, he ordered Concha not to interfere or comment in Washington. The instructions to "abstain from treating the American intervention in Panama; the Minister of Foreign Relations will handle it here" were seriously misleading because Concha was not told that the problem was of Colombia's own initiative. Concha resigned in anger, but Marroquín rejected the action as "unpatriotic and inadmissible." Concha, however, well understood the most troubling part of the Colombian attempt to manipulate the United States, Panama, and the entire question of sovereignty: "Between a Power which thus imposes its force, and a Government which cannot or will not defend the national sovereignty, treaties cannot be made."[38]

Concha's anger made it difficult to continue negotiations on Panama. To ease the diplomatic tension, Hay ordered Admiral Casey to meliorate his absolute neutrality and allow government troops access to the Panama Railroad. The Marroquín government continued its increasingly successful manipulation of the Americans. Once the United States had been persuaded to allow Colombia to use the American presence as a partial alliance, the government was able to assemble a large army in Panama to challenge Liberal control. By the end of October, General Nicolás Perdomo moved a Nationalist army of six thousand men to Colón under American cover. The Colombian strategy was not accidental. Although the Marroquín government had anticipated less difficulty in getting American cooperation and had intimated that cooperation would expedite the canal negotiations, after American neutrality was reversed through diplomatic pressure the plan proceeded as intended. On September 20, Marroquín told Concha that Perdomo's army was about to land on the isthmus and the time had come to demand that the United States honor its obligation for free transit of a government army across the isthmus. Only after

38. *Ibid.*, 176; José Concha to Felipe Paúl, October 3, 1902; José Marroquín and Felipe Paúl to Concha, October 7, 1902, both in *LA*, 254–57.

the army had neutralized Liberal strength on the isthmus did the Marroquín government act to neutralize its Washington minister, who had been as badly used during the proceedings as the Americans. Concha's own government purposely undermined him by giving him "consolation" instructions while telling the Americans not to take his protests seriously. Felipe Paúl told American Minister Charles Hart that Concha's "nervous excitement" accounted for his difficulties and also gave Hart different instructions from those given to Concha for critical points in the canal negotiations. Thus the Americans, who had yielded Liberal control of Panama to the Marroquín government, were now negotiating directly with Marroquín on the canal, still unaware that Marroquín did not intend to fulfill either his implied or his actual promises.[39]

Admiral Casey remained pessimistic about the prospects of peace. "Panama and Colón are practically besieged; troops at neither place dare to go beyond their intrenchments . . . if our men were removed from shore the insurgents would be in Panama in forty-eight hours." Casey viewed Colombia's continued objections to land-based American troops as face-saving and not meant "to be taken seriously." Casey was only partly right. As long as the Liberals had the advantage, the Nationalists did not mind the American troops, but when the advantage changed, Colombia insisted on less American control.[40]

General Herrera's acceptance of the American offer to mediate the war reached Admiral Casey on October 26 after being held up by government troops at Colón. Herrera's note, though mostly an amalgam of revolutionary rhetoric and political polemic, was also touching and eloquent: "The war with us is only an act of instinctive and vehement despair." The revolutionists were ready to lay down their arms as soon "as they can secure something republican." The government's previous peace terms were "simply the replacing of the white for the red terror." Herrera and the Nationalists shared a common fear of

39. Miner, *Fight for the Panama Route*, 236, 185–86; Concha to Paúl, October 23, 1902, in *LA*, 259–67; Concha's distress is expressed in Concha to Marroquín, October 2, 1902, and Concha to Paúl, October 30, 1902, both in *SP*, 188. Casey's melioration order is in Charles P. Darling to Silas B. Casey, October 29, 1902, in *Senate Documents*, 58th Cong., 2nd Sess., No. 143, Serial 4589, p. 333; see also the commendation of Casey's actions in Darling to Casey, December 10, 1902, in Box 1, Silas B. Casey Papers, LC. Concha to JH, JH to Concha, October 26, 28, 1902, in *Senate Documents*, 63rd Cong., 2nd Sess., No. 474, pp. 255–56; Charles B. Hart to JH, November 3, 14, 1902, in Despatches, T33, Roll 58; JH to Hart, October 16, 1902, in Instructions, M77, Roll 48.

40. Silas Casey to William Moody, October 20, 1902, in *Senate Documents*, 58th Cong., 2nd Sess., No. 143, Serial 4589, p. 305.

the American presence on the isthmus. For Herrera, Marroquín's "obstinacy" was responsible for that "officious guardianship which—why should I hide it—hurts the feelings of those who know our rights, our duties, and our responsibilities as a sovereign and independent nation." Nevertheless, Herrera wrote glowingly of a future American-built Panama canal, which was an integral part of the proposed peace talks: "The conference could fix the basis which might insure the construction of the canal by the United States, which is the universal desire of Colombians, a wish that is condensed into a national interest." How Colombians, Liberal or Conservative, could accommodate their distaste for the American presence in the isthmus with their almost equally strong desire for the Americans to build and operate a canal on the isthmus was not addressed. But in almost every way the Americans were reassured that all Colombians wanted a Panama canal—at least in theory.[41]

Herrera's acceptance of Casey's mediation effectively ended the Liberal war effort. When Nationalist reinforcements arrived at Colón on October 31, the Liberals as well as the Americans regarded the war as ended. Casey, swayed by Secretary of State Hay's requests to meliorate his ban on troop movements by train and by the increasing dominance of Nationalist forces, permitted the Colombians to use the Panama Railroad to move their army, though Casey still insisted that the troops use special trains. In a report published in the Colón *Starlet*, Nationalist General Perdomo was effusive and agreeable: "I am a great friend of the United States and I admire that country. I and all Colombians favor the construction of a canal by the Americans, and my principal object in pacifying the Isthmus is to make possible a meeting of the Colombian Congress to consider the canal bill." At the same time Perdomo made it clear that he expected to have a ten-thousand-man army on the isthmus that would "then be able to relieve the American forces doing shore duty on the Isthmus."[42]

When both sides agreed to meet on the American battleship *Wisconsin* on November 19, 1902, to settle their long war, the final arrangements seemed almost anticlimactic. The Liberals, represented by Benjamín Herrera, General Lucas Caballero (the Liberal secretary of war), and Eusebio Morales (secretary of the treasury for the departments of Panama and Cauca), discussed the peace terms offered by

41. Benjamín Herrera to Silas Casey, October 18, 1902, *ibid.*, 307–309.

42. Silas Casey to William Moody, November 3, 1902; Casey to Felix Ehrman, October 31, 1902; Colón *Starlet*, October 30, 1902, enclosed in Casey to Moody, November 3, 1902, all *ibid.*, 310–11, 313, 315–16.

Governor Victor M. Salazar and General Alfredo Vásquez Cobo, representing the government. When the Liberals agreed to the terms and General Perdomo confirmed the government's acquiescence, the War of the Thousand Days was over; the Nationalist forces prepared to withdraw, leaving only a small police force on the isthmus.[43]

The Treaty of *Wisconsin* gave the Liberals a general amnesty, the release of all political prisoners from jail, and a promise to restore normal and peaceful government functions in the embattled nation. The Liberal demand of April 14, 1902, for congressional elections was accepted as the occasion to decide three specific issues: the Panama canal negotiations, the Marroquín reform program of 1898, and a reformation of the monetary system to ensure that revenues from the canal would not be compromised by the paper money problems that had plagued Colombia during the revolution. Similar terms were included in two previous peace treaties, the Treaty of Nerlandia signed after Rafael Uribe Uribe surrendered on October 24, 1902, and the Treaty of Chinácota signed on November 21. The three treaties confirmed the formal end of the War of the Thousand Days.[44]

Colombia lay devastated by the long civil war. Probably close to one hundred thousand men were killed, Colombia currency had lost 99 percent of its prewar value, and the deficit of over 16 million pesos a month was compounded by printing over half a million pesos in new paper money each day. So great was the need for currency that at one point paper bought to wrap candy was used for printing currency. Few government employees could be paid. The Marroquín government was politically bankrupt as well. Both the United States and Panama had been promised prompt action on a canal. But Marroquín, who had relied on force rather than persuasion to maintain power, had almost no political allies nor a functioning party structure in postwar Colombia. Although he had raised expectations in both the United States and Panama, Marroquín now needed vast sums of money simply to restore the day-to-day operations of a government

43. Silas Casey to William Moody, November 22, 1902, *ibid.*, 318–19. See the accounts of the war and the peace negotiations by Herrera's chief of staff Lucas Caballero, *Memorias de la guerra de los mil días* (Bogotá, 1939); and Nationalist Governor Victor M. Salazar, *Memorias de la guerra (1899–1902)* (Bogotá, 1943).

44. Text of the Treaty of *Wisconsin, Senate Documents*, 58th Cong., 2nd Sess., No. 143, Serial 4589, pp. 319–21; for the advantages Herrera won and the secret payment of 16,000 pounds see Bergquist, *Coffee and Conflict in Colombia*, 187. For the Treaty of Nerlandia and Uribe Uribe's advice to Herrera to seek greater concessions in Panama see Vincent Baillie Dunlap, "Tragedy of a Colombian Martyr: Rafael Uribe Uribe and the Liberal Party, 1896–1914" (Ph.D. dissertation, University of North Carolina, 1979), 184–85. For the treaty of Chinácota see Miner, *Fight for the Panama Route*, 237.

long disrupted by revolution. Colombia's economy was at a standstill. Agriculture and exports remained crippled, the huge army remained mostly unpaid, and immense international claims for damages incurred in the revolution added to Colombia's external debt, already in default. Although the hope of a Panama canal had finally ended the war, any reasonable settlement for Panama could not possibly produce enough money to pay even a fraction of Colombia's war losses, let alone provide for the prospect of future mainland prosperity. Once the war had ended, Panama and its possible canal became the focus of Colombian hopes, not for its future development but as an easy means of rescuing the nation from its desperate economic situation.[45]

Negotiations between John Hay and José Concha had disintegrated. Concha, still upset by the American intervention, though it had ultimately brought peace, and with the continuing duplicity of his own government, became frustrated, quarrelsome, and abstract. Colombia, concerned that Concha might so exasperate the United States that it would abandon the Panama route, ordered the tired diplomat to sign the proposed treaty to maintain Colombia's stake in a canal. Hay rejected most of Concha's new amendments, compromised the diction in some of his suggestions to satisfy a minor point, and returned the amended treaty for Concha's signature with a firm but respectful note. Both diplomats were aware that Concha was regarded as an embarrassment by his government. Concha complained to Hay on October 26 that because of his instructions from Bogotá "I am not now at liberty to express my opinion." Foreign Minister Felipe Paúl assured American Minister Charles Hart in Bogotá that "Colombia wants the canal." Paúl also gave Hart a copy of Concha's instructions that gave him the option either to sign the agreement or to turn the legation over to secretary Tomás Herrán, who in turn was instructed to sign the agreement only if he received a written ultimatum from the United States. The Colombians planned to convene a congress in April. Paúl told Hart that "the ratification of the treaty would be more probable if price increased, but notwithstanding Government will exert itself to secure ratification."[46]

45. Bergquist, *Coffee and Conflict in Colombia*, 133 and n., 201; Favell, "Antecedents," 216–17.

46. José Concha to JH, October 26, 1902; JH to Concha, November 18, 1902, both in *Senate Documents*, 63rd Cong., 2nd Sess., No. 474, Serial 6582, pp. 254–55, 260–61; text, *ibid.*, 261–63; Charles Hart to JH, November 25, 1902, in Despatches, Microcopy T33, Roll 57. For Liberal concern that the war endangered the Panama canal see Dunlap, "Tragedy of a Colombian Martyr," 184–85.

An embittered Concha refused to sign the draft and left Washington without formally visiting Hay. His successor, Tomás Herrán, described Concha's failures as a diplomat. Instead of evading obstacles, Concha tried to overcome them: "Not only in diplomacy but in private life it is well to be a little pliable when vital principles are not at stake." But Concha was part of a milieu in which doctrinal battles had become a way of life. As a Historical Conservative, already a part of one Colombian ideological schism, he played a central role in the coup that brought Marroquín to office, and he managed to negotiate with John Hay a workable arrangement building on Martínez Silva's promising foundation. But Concha could not stand to acquiesce in the failure of Colombia's dream of being able both to sell and hold the canal simultaneously. Simón Bolívar had observed that "Venezuela is an armed camp, Colombia a university, and Ecuador a convent." With the War of the Thousand Days and the encroachment of modernism, Colombia had to adapt its love of abstraction and learn to compromise. Concha was too much a nineteenth-century Colombian gentleman-scholar to accommodate to the change, though he probably understood more of what was required of Colombia in a difficult period than most of his compatriots.[47]

The problem was probably insoluble. The man who replaced Concha, Tomás Herrán, the son of the Colombia minister who had negotiated the original Bidlack-Mallarino Treaty in 1846 and a graduate of Georgetown University, had served as secretary of the Colombian legation under Carlos Martínez Silva and José Concha. He knew more about the Colombian-American negotiations than any other person. Yet all of Herrán's intelligence, knowledge, and diplomatic ability could not change Colombia's situation or its leaders' view of the world. The provinciality of Bogotá, reflected equally by its geography and its political leaders, insulated the most learned Colombians from a world that was changing far more rapidly than they wished or understood. The War of the Thousand Days pitted Marroquín's provincial and protective Catholicism against the European modernism that influenced the Liberals. If Colombia's dominant political party could not accommodate the relatively mild modernism of its own scholar-gentlemen, how could it possibly deal with the United States? One of the finest intellectual gentlemen of the age, the learned and

47. Miner, *Fight for the Panama Route*, 188. For Herrán's remarks on Concha see Du-Val, *Cadiz to Cathay*, 190; Bolívar quoted in Crow, *Epic of Latin America*, 619.

passionate Carlos Martínez Silva, languished in a Nationalist jail as the revolutionary war ended. Herrán would argue eloquently that the United States and Colombia were not adversaries, that the canal at Panama was, as José Concha had written in his first letter to John Hay, an international undertaking: "Colombia widely and generously opens her doors so that the grand work may be achieved in the shortest possible time." But in Bogotá that wider vision of a world community became increasingly repugnant as the government's energies were freed from surviving a civil war.[48]

Although the religious elements in the Colombian civil war and in the conflict with the United States have been overshadowed by the diplomatic disputes, they should not be ignored. Both Caro and Marroquín were Conservative Catholic ideologues who despised Liberalism and Protestantism. Rafael Reyes was rejected for the presidency that Sanclemente and Marroquín won in 1897 because of his Liberal views. Reyes linked religion and modernism in his speech before the Second Pan-American Conference in Mexico City in February, 1902: "In times past it was the Cross or the Koran, the sword or the book that accomplished the conquests of civilization; today it is the powerful locomotive." The speech was criticized in the Bogotá press though Reyes was commended in a conference resolution for his pioneering work in developing steam navigation on South American rivers. Rafael Uribe Uribe wrote that "among modern men only a Turk could conceive [of] religious wars at the end of the nineteenth century." He wrote that tyranny in Colombia was "equaled only in the European Middle Ages." With their new colonial responsibilities in Catholic Cuba, Puerto Rico, and the Philippines, Americans were increasingly aware of the sharp cultural difference between Protestant and Catholic cultures. In 1821 John Quincy Adams described to Henry Clay his view of how Latin American nations differed from the United States: "They have not the first elements of good or free government. Arbitrary power, military and ecclesiastical is stamped upon their education, upon their hearts, and upon all their institutions." The church and Colombia's deep tradition of Catholicism played a major role in the war; the cultural differences between Protestant American society and Catholic Colombia played a significant if indirect role in the Colombian-American discord.[49]

48. José Concha to JH, March 31, 1902, in *House Documents*, 57th Cong., 1st Sess., No. 611, Serial 4377, p. 3.
49. For Catholicism as the main Colombian ideological conflict see Helen Delpar, "Aspects of Liberal Factionalism in Colombia, 1875–1885," *HAHR*, LI (1974), 251; for

Although the Americans efficiently helped to settle the war, there remains a substantial question of who was the more adept manipulator. Bogotá promised America a quick resolution of the canal question, a pledge it had no means or intention of carrying out. Liberals, barred from taking either of the key cities in Panama, Colón or Panama, could not exercise full control. Although the American use of the Bidlack-Mallarino Treaty of 1846 to further their own interests has received more historical attention, both Colombia's Nationalist government and the revolutionary Liberals were much more adept at maneuvering the United States than they were each other. The Americans had provided an effective and neutral police force in the isthmus since 1900. When both sides in the revolution decided that the war had gone far enough, they used the Americans to end it.[50]

British Chargé Claude Mallet understood the flaw in Marroquín's tactic of negotiating a canal treaty with Colombian congressional approval as an escape hatch. A postwar Colombian congress convened in the usual way would inevitably be anti-Marroquín, anticanal, concerned almost wholly with Colombian domestic politics, and unrepresentative—with few Panamanians and no Liberals. Mallet's solution was a special congress with one member from each department and the Panama canal the only matter for consideration. Neither side of the Colombian revolution was concerned over how seriously the Americans took the assurances of an expedited canal settlement, the *quid pro quid* both sides repeatedly offered for help in settling the war.

Caro's fundamental Catholic ideology see Charles Bergquist, "Political Economy of the Colombian Presidential Election of 1897," *HAHR*, LVI (1976), 11. For Latin American intellectuals' rejection of "the English Protestant Reformation and its bastard children—empirical rationalism and the Industrial Revolution," see Mary Patricia Chapman, "Yankeephobia: An Analysis of the Anti-United States Bias of Certain Spanish South American Intellectuals, 1898–1928" (Ph.D. dissertation, Stanford University, 1950), esp. 20–22. See also John Lynch, "The Catholic Church in Latin America, 1830–1930," *CHLA*, IV, esp. 557–84. Reyes is quoted in Bergquist, *Coffee and Conflict in Colombia*, 221; Rafael Uribe Uribe quoted, *ibid.*, 129; for Reyes's commendation see James Brown Scott (ed.), *The International Conferences of American States, 1889–1928* (New York, 1928), 107. For the basic Protestantism of the formative American Enlightenment see Henry May, *The Enlightenment in America* (New York, 1976), 3. For the Catholic colonial problems see Frank Reuter, *Catholic Influence on American Colonial Policies, 1898–1904* (Austin, Tex., 1967); Adams quoted in Samuel Shapiro, "A Common History of the Americas?" in Shapiro (ed.), *Cultural Factors in Inter-American Relations* (South Bend, Ind., 1966), 62. See also Glen Caudill Dealy, *The Public Man: An Interpretation of Latin American and Other Catholic Countries* (Amherst, Mass., 1977).

50. Favell, "Antecedents," 212; Bergquist, *Coffee and Conflict in Colombia*, 188; for the view that the United States was the manipulator, see Challener, *Admirals, Generals, and American Foreign Policy*, 153.

Once the war was settled, the Colombians were content to go back to their war of words and let the Americans wait. Neither the Nationalists, the Liberals, nor the Americans comprehended the immense cultural gulf or its seriousness. But the Colombians were in no hurry, and the Americans could not wait. If Marroquín was an appropriate representative of Colombia's divided but patient politics, then Theodore Roosevelt was an appropriate representative of the United States' preference for decisive resolution. Neither Roosevelt nor Marroquín realized that their Panama diplomacy reflected unresolvable cultural, political, and temperamental differences between their two nations.[51]

51. Favell, "Antecedents," 212–13; C. Mallet to Lord Lansdowne, August 7, 1902, in FO 55/408. For the French chargé's certainty that the American intervention was an American-Liberal alliance and a prelude to a protectorate see Emile Guy to Gabriel Hanotaux, September 18, October 17, 1902, N.S., Colombre 5, AMAE. For Liberal consideration of a possible American alliance see Belisara Parras, Public Declaration, August 19, 1902, translated by Naval Cadet Percy W. Foote in Office of Naval Intelligence, Subject File VI, Panama Correspondence, Box 667, RG 45, NA.

8 Debate, 1903

With the civil war finally at an end in Colombia, the American press and the Congress were impatient to resolve the canal question. Pressure intensified on President Roosevelt to drop the idea of Panama and settle on Nicaragua. Senator Morgan, many newspapers, and the Nicaraguan diplomatic corps were eager to sign a canal treaty. Colombia's refusal to believe the United States might choose Nicaragua was compounded by its chaotic diplomatic representation in Washington. Only Tomás Herrán's presence made continued negotiations possible. As Cromwell agonized over Colombia's unpromising course, the Roosevelt administration continued to negotiate, hopeful that the differences could be resolved diplomatically.[1]

Roosevelt, concerned about Senate resistance to any further economic concessions to Colombia, suggested that Senator John Spooner join Secretary of State Hay and new Colombian minister Herrán in a discussion. Hay wrote Spooner that he expected Colombia to make its "last stand on something like half a million a year rental, claiming that Colombia loses $400,000 a year port dues and customs and $250,000 a year revenue from the railroad, and they think we ought to make this good to them. The President wants me to ask you what concession to them in that respect could be made without rewriting the treaty in the Senate." Roosevelt respected the Senate's power to approve treaties, but he feared the politicization of the Senate amendment process that permitted a small minority to reject a treaty without openly opposing it. Amendments also might create the need for endless negotiations with other nations and their senates. Senator Morgan used the amend-

---

1. The most useful histories include Thomas R. Favell, "Antecedents of Panama's Separation from Colombia" (Ph.D. dissertation, Fletcher School of Law and Diplomacy, 1951); Dwight Carroll Miner, *The Fight for the Panama Route: The Story of the Spooner Act and the Hay-Herrán Treaty* (New York, 1940); Miles DuVal, *Cadiz to Cathay: The Story of the Long Diplomatic Struggle for the Panama Canal* (Stanford, 1940); and *SP*, esp. 190.

ment as a tactic at every opportunity, and even senators friendly to the administration used it to demonstrate their support for both sides, a process the exasperated Roosevelt tried desperately to avoid.[2]

Hay and Roosevelt still assumed that Colombia was driving a hard bargain and not simply using delaying tactics. Hay resisted Colombia's demand for $600,000, wildly at odds with the American offer of $10,000. Marroquín instructed Herrán to demand $600,000 but, if the United States issued its anticipated formal Nicaragua ultimatum, to sign the treaty. Roosevelt and Hay, after assessing the Senate's willingness to approve more money, substantially raised both parts of the American offer. The proposed initial payment was increased from $7 to $10 million, and the annual rental from $10,000 to $100,000. Hay argued that 5 percent interest on $10 million amounted to $500,000, which when added to $100,000 met the Colombians' demand for $600,000. Herrán, a good negotiator, argued that Nicaragua's unimproved land was not comparable to Panama's already well-developed land, working facilities, and established railroad. But the Americans regarded the Panama facilities as products of French development for which the French were being adequately compensated. Knowing that Congress would not go any higher, Hay tried to put Herrán off by agreeing to discuss increasing the payment only after the canal opened.[3]

When Marroquín refused to budge, even the usually optimistic Cromwell despaired of finding a way to end the stalemate. Herrán, aware of congressional impatience with the continued haggling, warned Marroquín that Roosevelt "is determined to terminate negotiations" before the congressional session ended on March 4, 1903. "He is a decided partisan of the Panama route, but he does not reject that of Nicaragua, and probably will adopt the latter in case he does not arrive at a satisfactory arrangement with Colombia." Senator Shelby Cullom had suggested expropriation of the canal zone on the grounds that it was "a universal public utility." Herrán thought adoption of Cullom's proposal was "very improbable" but not "absolutely impossible."[4]

Colombia, which had agreed to separate its diplomatic negotiations

2. JH to John Spooner, December 8, 1902, Box 58, John C. Spooner Papers, LC. TR to Shelby Cullom, February 10, 1905, in *MRL*, IV, 1118–19, gives TR's view of the Senate's abuse of its treaty-amending powers.
3. Favell, "Antecedents," 220; *SP*, 270; Miner, *Fight for the Panama Route*, 191.
4. Tomás Herrán to José Marroquín, January 8, 1903, in *SP*, 319.

for a Panama canal concession from the sale of French property to the United States—part of Senator Hanna's prerequisite for Senate consideration of a Panama route—now reopened an issue the United States had regarded as settled. Colombia not only asked for a share of the Compagnie Nouvelle's proposed sale to the United States, it reintroduced the Concha amendments that Foreign Minister Felipe Paúl had advised the United States to ignore. An exasperated Hay warned Colombia on January 16 that if it "persists in its present attitude it will make impossible further negotiations." With the United States ready to end the Panama negotiations, Cromwell worked desperately to salvage the situation. Herrán, troubled by the frequently conflicting instructions he received from Bogotá as well as the delay in receiving new instructions, found himself in the same situation as his predecessors, dealing with a critical situation in Washington while Bogotá's attention wandered.[5]

Cromwell convinced Herrán to dismiss the Concha amendments that the United States had resolutely refused to consider. The gap between Colombia's demand of $600,000 annually and the United States' offer of $100,000 made a financial settlement unlikely. Herrán, putting the best light on the disparity, wrote Paúl on January 18 that though the American offer fell short of Colombia's expectations, it was far in excess of the $35,000 Nicaragua was asking for its canal concession, a figure that Herrán explained realistically defined "the value which the American government places upon the privilege and the use of the desired zone." Since the United States did not consider the Panama canal a money-making commercial enterprise but an international improvement that would benefit everyone, especially Colombia, Hay resented Colombia's demands for more money.[6]

On January 22, 1903, the United States dramatically raised its annual payment offer from $100,000 to $250,000 and simultaneously issued its long postponed ultimatum. Hay warned, "I am not authorized to consider or discuss any other change." Herrán, unaware that new instructions ordering him not to sign any treaty were on the way and convinced that the American offer was fair, signed the Hay-Herrán Treaty at Secretary Hay's home that evening with William Cromwell in attendance. Though Herrán defended his acceptance of the treaty, which he noted gained concessions totaling $7,250,000, he knew his

5. *SP*, 319; JH to Tomás Herrán, January 16, 1903, in *SP*, 320.
6. DuVal, *Cathay to Cadiz*, 203; *SP*, 271.

efforts would remain unappreciated in Colombia. Marroquín's new instructions reiterated the familiar demands for more money and better sovereignty terms, matters that had been discussed and rejected several times. Marroquín argued that Colombia had regained its stability and was in a better bargaining position, ignoring that the Treaty of *Wisconsin* that brought peace to Colombia had been arranged by the same Americans Marroquín wanted more money from.[7]

Roosevelt quickly submitted the Hay-Herrán Treaty to the Senate, where it faced a determined attack led by Senator John Tyler Morgan. Morgan first added sixty amendments in committee and ended the regular session with a filibuster. Roosevelt, forced to call a special session, wrote on March 12, "I am now sweating blood" to get the Panama treaty confirmed. Roosevelt was impatient with his floor leader, John Spooner. "He is an admirable man of great intellect, but I wish that every Tomcat in his path did not strike him as an unusually large and ferocious lion."[8]

Morgan's proposals, including thirty-one deletions, thirty-five additions, and two amendments, amounted to a rewriting of the treaty. Roosevelt, well aware that a small minority of senators could defeat a treaty through amendments, was fortunate that Morgan continued to overplay his hand. Although Morgan opened the Hay-Herrán Treaty debate with a speech supporting a Panama route, by proposing wholesale changes and amendments and verbally abusing Colombia he made the treaty not only unacceptable but offensive to Colombia. Particularly egregious among Morgan's xenophobic attacks on Colombia was his proposed anti-Catholic "additional amendment number 2," specifically exempting Americans in Colombia from adherence to the "Spanish Inquisition" and Pope Leo XIII's concordat of 1888. Morgan publicly compared Nicaragua's "orderly, industrious, thrifty, peaceable, and easy to control" people with Panama's large element of "degraded, dissatisfied, turbulent, mixed, and filthy" population.[9]

7. DuVal, *Cathay to Cadiz*, 204–207; *SP*, 322–23; JH to Tomás Herrán, January 22, 1903, in *SP*, 322. For Herrán's calculations see Herrán to Felipe Paúl, January 29, 1903; for Marroquín's promise of new instructions see José Marroquín to Herrán, January 24, 1903, both in Tomás Herrán Papers, Special Collections Division, Georgetown University Library, Washington, D.C. Instructions to Herrán are in Favell, "Antecedents," 222. Herrán's assessment of the U.S. reluctance is in Tomás Herrán to José Marroquín, n.d., *ibid.*, 223.

8. TR to JH, March 12, 1903; in *MRL*, III, 445; see August Carl Radke, "John Tyler Morgan: An Expansionist Senator, 1877–1907" (Ph.D. dissertation, University of Washington, 1953), 454–66.

9. TR to John C. Spooner, July 7, 1905, in *MRL*, IV, 1264; *Congressional Record*, 58th Cong., Spec. Sess., March 9, 1903, pp. 15–16.

It is impossible to separate Morgan's love of hyperbolic rhetoric from his real sentiments, but many of his arguments against ratification were based on charges that the United States had conceded too much to Colombia, thereby submitting "to the humiliation of a galley slave of Colombia." Much of the Senate took a far more extreme view than the administration. Several senators asserted that the United States should go to war with Colombia if necessary, that Colombia's sovereignty over Panama was only theoretical, and that the United States was giving up far too much in the negotiations. Historians have paid little attention to the Senate debates that pitted ultra-nationalists like Morgan against an administration that tried to satisfy some of Colombia's more unrealistic demands. Morgan insisted on American rights to land troops, build fortifications, and take control of the terminal ports at Panama and Colón. The draconian treaty suggested by Morgan's amendments and changes provides a classic example of a truly imperial arrangement. Many of Morgan's proposed changes, which were later incorporated in the Hay–Bunau-Varilla Treaty to neutralize his continued opposition, made that later treaty with Panama much harsher. Morgan's attacks on the Hay-Herrán Treaty are a defense of its comparative reasonableness. All of Morgan's proposed changes were eventually defeated, and on March 17, 1903, by a surprisingly large margin of 73 to 5, the Senate ratified the Hay-Herrán Treaty unchanged.[10]

The victory was a hollow one. The treaty was doomed from its inception. The length of the negotiations, the increasing gulf between each nation's perceptions of its own best interests, and the loss of the first impulse of benign internationalism shared by both sides gave way to petty and frequently irrelevant bickering over points of national honor and too narrowly conceived national self-interest. Both chief executives, Roosevelt in America and Marroquín in Colombia, had to deal with demanding senates, sensitive to any extension of executive power, even in foreign relations. Marroquín, the head of a nation divided by civil war, and Roosevelt, an elevated vice-president battling for an unprecedented renomination and reelection, were on equally precarious political ground; both were dealing with sensitive senators jealous of yielding political power to vulnerable chief executives. Marroquín faced a newly elected Senate unified only by its opposition to the Marroquín government, its policies, and its responsibility for Colombia's devastating civil war. The Colombian Congress

10. *Congressional Record*, 58th Cong., Spec. Sess., March 9, 1903, pp. 21–22.

that was elected to debate the Hay-Herrán Treaty gathered instead to debate Marroquín himself.[11]

Colombia's new Congress was elected on March 8, 1903, while the American Senate was meeting in special session on the Hay-Herrán Treaty. The first Colombian election since the beginning of the War of the Thousand Days reflected Colombia's continuing and severe political divisions. A repressive central government had granted amnesty but not political equality to the Liberals; the failure to institute needed structural political reforms limited the election to the ruling National party. Criticism of the Catholic church, civil authorities, currency, or the military remained illegal. Since politically controlled newspapers played a critical role in Colombian political debate, legal sanctions against newspapers that attacked government policy muzzled political dialogue. As a result, only two Liberals were elected to Colombia's first postwar Congress. The Marroquín government once again moved to consolidate its power rather than conciliate Colombia's political minorities, almost as if the War of the Thousand Days had not occurred. Authoritarian conservatives, more interested in repression than reform, ideology than mediation, abstraction than solving practical problems, controlled the government and its policies, creating an oppressive atmosphere that discouraged any calm attempt to deal with the Panama canal, a matter that demanded all of Colombia's political energies and intellectual ability.[12]

Bogotá did not share Tomás Herrán's joy at the American Senate's approval of his treaty. For Herrán the treaty offered "the prospect for Colombia of a period of peace and prosperity such as she has never yet known, of her development and aggrandizement to an extent as yet hardly imagined." William Gordon, the British vice-consul at Medellín, surprised at how Colombians reacted to the treaty, wrote that "Mr. Morgan has no better friends than public opinion in Colombia. . . . Whether the Colombians are acting 'the dog in the manger' policy—or with extreme selfish aims—or whether real patriotism or personal ambition is moving them against the canal treaty I cannot understand . . . opposition is read in every paper and it is accepted,

11. See W. Stull Holt, *Treaties Defeated by the Senate: A Study of the Struggle Between President and Senate over the Conduct of Foreign Affairs* (Baltimore, 1933); Charles W. Bergquist, *Coffee and Conflict in Colombia, 1886–1910* (Durham, N.C., 1978), 218–19.

12. For Colombian political conditions see Bergquist, *Coffee and Conflict in Colombia*, 197–209; for the elections see *ibid.*, 199; for the limited press freedom see Favell, "Antecedents," 225–26.

without any doubt that the canal scheme will be thrown over by the Colombian Congress." The Colombians, encouraged by the Marroquín government's confusion and ambivalence, never considered their actual choice, a Panama canal with the Hay-Herrán Treaty or no Colombian canal at all. By ignoring both the American Nicaraguan option and intense Panamanian separatist sentiment, Colombians transformed a diplomatic problem into an abstraction. Herrán's view—"the treaty made is not perfect but it was the best possible to make of a very difficult question"—never became a part of the increasingly abstract and self-defeating Colombian debate.[13]

The Hay-Herrán Treaty's main provisions gave the United States the right to build a canal zone three and a half to fifteen miles wide around the canal; excluded the cities of Colón and Panama from the American zone; set the grant's term at one hundred years, renewable at the sole option of the United States; established three judicial systems, Colombian, American, and mixed, depending on the nature of the dispute; reserved sovereignty to Colombia and defense to the United States; and called for an immediate payment of $10 million in cash on exchange of ratification and a $250,000 annual rental, the surrender by Colombia of its right to bargain separately with the Compagnie Nouvelle, and the transfer to the United States of Colombia's economic interests in the Panama Railroad.[14]

Colombia's main objections to the treaty included the inadequate amount of money, the prohibition against additional bargaining with the Compagnie Nouvelle, and sovereignty. The United States considered an ultimate cost that included not only the payments to Colombia and the Compagnie Nouvelle but the prodigious investment of building the canal, which eventually totaled $302 million in congressional appropriations, an unprecedented sum in pre–World War I America. Colombia looked only at the final revenues the United States would receive, not at the investment required to produce them. The Americans regarded the canal zone as undeveloped land which was economically worthless until the canal transformed it. The two sides could not even agree on the ground rules. The United States held that Colombia's agreement to the transfer of the French assets to the

13. Tomás Herrán to Foreign Ministry, March 20, 1903 (submitting the Hay-Herrán Treaty); William Gordon to Tomás Herrán, April 16, 1903; Herrán to Germán Villa, April 3, 1903, all in Herrán Papers.

14. The treaty is in *Senate Documents*, 63rd Cong., 2nd Sess., No. 474, Serial 6582, 277–88, and in DuVal, *Cadiz to Cathay*, 462–75.

Americans, concluded before the Spooner Act debate, constituted a moral and legal bar to any further negotiations by Colombia about French property or French rights. In the American view, Colombia's agreement had eliminated the French from the negotiations. For the Colombians the French constituted a continuing irritation and an opportunity to wring more money from the increasingly outraged Americans. The disparity over the two nations' conceptions of what the treaty actually meant increased as the time approached for the Colombian Senate's consideration.[15]

For the sensitive position of American minister at Bogotá, Theodore Roosevelt chose Arthur M. Beaupré, an Illinois politician who had first been appointed to a Latin American diplomatic post by William Mc-Kinley. Though Beaupré has often been blamed for the deterioration of American-Colombian relations, he was an able diplomat in a difficult situation. He not only reported the status of the Hay-Herrán debate in Colombia but became involved in the Colombian Senate debate, a reflection not of his own ineptitude but of the American-Colombian stalemate. Experienced in Latin American affairs as American consul in Guatemala and as secretary and consul in Bogotá from 1899 to 1901, Beaupré was a rare nonprofessional diplomat who was equally at home in American local domestic politics and foreign affairs.[16]

The discrepancy between the $40 million to be paid to the French company and the $10 million to be paid to Colombia was the biggest continuing source of friction. The Americans were convinced that a contractual arrangement already existed and any exchange of property between French interests and the American government must remain independent of the diplomacy for a canal zone concession. Although the Americans were legally correct, the discrepancy between the $10 million and $40 million payments was a continuing aggrava-

15. For the cost figures see David McCullough, *The Path Between the Seas: The Creation of the Panama Canal, 1870–1914* (New York, 1977), 310. For a good summary of the Colombian view see Howard C. Hill, *Roosevelt and the Caribbean* (Chicago, 1927), 30–68. For a defense of the American view see Frederick W. Marks III, *Velvet on Iron: The Diplomacy of Theodore Roosevelt* (Lincoln, Neb., 1979), 99–100; for the overall debate see Favell, "Antecedents," 220–62.

16. Except for H. W. Howard Knott (in the *Dictionary of American Biography*), Miles DuVal (*Cadiz to Cathay*, 216–17), the State Department, and Theodore Roosevelt, almost no one has a good word for Beaupré. Dwight Miner found him "lacking in penetration and unfriendly in tone" (*Fight for the Panama Route*, 389–90). After Colombia, Beaupré served as minister to Argentina (four years), the Netherlands, Luxembourg, and Cuba; see Calvin James Billman, "Backgrounds and Policies of Selected United States Diplomats to Latin America, 1898–1938" (Ph.D. dissertation, Tulane University, 1954), 24–29.

tion. William Cromwell, the French company's shrewd and capable American legal representative, probably erred in not conceding a small part, $5 million, of the $40 million to the Colombians as a goodwill gesture. The Roosevelt administration refused to bargain with what it regarded as French money and refused to yield to what it also regarded as Colombian blackmail, asserting that a deal is a deal. The Colombians might not have been moved by $5 million, but the gesture might have eased the tension, swayed some sentiment, and made Colombia's sale of its own land for needed money more palatable. But William Cromwell, a corporation lawyer steeped in American adversary property law, would probably have been judged guilty of legal malpractice had he offered and Colombia accepted a goodwill gift of $5 million. When the Colombians tried to renege on Sanclemente's sale in 1900 of a six-year extension of the French concession three years after receiving and spending the money, it reinforced the American view of Colombia as shifty and dishonorable.[17]

Marroquín's continuing ambivalence about the Panama canal, reflected by his frequent contradictory diplomatic instructions, enraged the Americans when he failed forcefully to advocate the passage of a treaty his own government had negotiated. On January 1, 1903, Marroquín remained publicly uncommitted. When he used the Colombian Congress to try to force the United States to make additional concessions, he infuriated the now thoroughly frustrated Americans, who became increasingly shrill and intemperate. Beaupré's messages to Marroquín reflected the American view of Marroquín's lack of support for his treaty as a diplomatic breach of faith verging on belligerence.[18]

17. See DuVal, *Cadiz to Cathay*, 213; Favell, "Antecedents," 223–24. A conservative Colombian historian argues that the failure to resolve the transfer issue was the main reason for the failure of the treaty; see Luis Martínez Delgado, *A propósito del Dr. Carlos Martínez Silva, capítulos de historia política de Colombia* (Bogotá, 1926), 294. For the argument that Colombia should have insisted from the start on a payment from the French Compagnie Nouvelle see Favell, "Antecedents," 223–24. Had the Colombians been sufficiently sophisticated financially and as unambivalant as this tactic suggests, there would have been fewer diplomatic problems in the settlement negotiations; see Miner, *Fight for the Panama Route*, 213–16, 273–75; and Antonio José Uribe, *Colombia y los Estado Unidos* (Bogotá, 1931), 81.

18. For the argument against making the Colombian congressional debate comparable to that of the United States Senate, see Marks, *Velvet on Iron*, 99. Marroquín's New Year message is in *Diario oficial* (Bogotá, 1836–1904), No. 11784, January 2, 1903; Favell, "Antecedents," 220. For a criticism of the United States' warlike messages, see Henry F. Pringle, *Theodore Roosevelt: A Biography* (New York, 1931), 311.

Marroquín was not loath to use his considerable executive power when it suited him. He had broken with Aristides Fernández, his most militant Nationalist ally, during the later stages of the War of the Thousand Days. Fernández, who had been at the center of power, was suddenly reduced to political obscurity. Marroquín, who had remained a Nationalist in a nation divided between Conservatives and Liberals, was not a weak politician, but his peacetime power was hampered by the lack of a national political organization. As an authoritarian war leader he had not needed a normal political party. The Americans were firmly convinced that Marroquín did not need to convene the Colombian Congress to ratify the Hay-Herrán Treaty. When the Panama problem refused to go away, and the United States as well as Colombia's Washington diplomats remained insistent, Marroquín may have used Colombian congressional approval as a means of keeping his options open. Only after the United States Senate adopted the Spooner Act in June, 1902, did the Marroquín government begin to emphasize the need for approval by a Congress that had not met since the beginning of the civil war in 1899. Before and after the treaty of *Wisconsin* Marroquín had assured the Americans that congressional approval was a formality. When Herrán could not extract the monumental sum of money from the United States that would make the loss of Panama seem politically palatable, Marroquín fell back on a congressional option not as a constitutional requirement—hardly one of Marroquín's primary concerns—but as a political delaying tactic. Although Conservatives, elected on local issues and probably even less concerned with Panama and foreign relations than Marroquín, won majorities in the congressional elections, Marroquín remained a powerful executive. Two of his supporters were elected as president and vice-president of the newly convened Colombian Senate. He easily defeated opponents on a peripheral treaty issue by a 38 to 5 vote, and he demonstrated sufficient political power on issues the government found important. The passage of the Hay-Herrán Treaty was not one of them.[19]

Marroquín unexpectedly relaxed the government's control of the press to permit open discussion of the upcoming Hay-Herrán debate. The anti-Marroquín journals that were the ones most affected by government control responded to their new freedom by attacking the Hay-Herrán Treaty, mainly because it appeared at first to be the Marroquín

19. Marks, *Velvet on Iron*, 101; for the origins of the congressional delaying tactic see José Marroquín to General Pompillio Gutiérrez, July 26, 1902, in Favell, "Antecedents," 212–15.

government's chief policy. Bogotá's newspapers, inexperienced in both foreign affairs and open debate, were not only bastions of partisan political opposition, they were extraordinarily misinformed. "Without question," Beaupré observed, "public opinion is strongly against its ratification, but, of course, public opinion in Colombia is not necessarily a potent factor in controlling legislation." Because the Congress was dominated by Conservatives and Nationalists opposed to Marroquín for various reasons, approval of any government measure was politically difficult. Without a "thoroughly in earnest" government effort, Minister Beaupré gave the possibility of approval almost no chance of success at the end of March.[20]

By April 15, Beaupré described how the Marroquín government had manipulated public opinion. In March most Colombians had been indifferent about the disposition of Panama or a canal. The prospect of receiving the $10 million from the Americans was welcomed by some overly sanguine Bogotáns as a panacea that would end Colombia's financial crisis. Beaupré cited Colombia's sudden drop in inflation of 37 percent to support his view that Colombia's first reaction to the passage of the Hay-Herrán Treaty was favorable, especially since a rumor of its rejection caused a rise of 37 percent. Apathy changed to concern and eventually to opposition after Finance Minister Fernández "issued a circular to the Bogotá press (which had suddenly sprung into existence), inviting discussion on the canal convention. The circular was to the effect that the government had no preconceived wishes for or against the measure; that it was for Congress to decide, and Congress would largely be guided by public opinion. At the same time, what purported to be a translation of the text of the convention was published."[21]

The press printed the wildest rumors. It was hinted that Herrán had sold out, that the United States had already derived a profit of $180 million, that the deal was a demonstration of Yankee imperialism, robbing Colombia of her birthright and paying only a paltry sum for the theft, and that the United States was more interested in keeping out other Europeans than in developing the canal. Many Colombians still believed that a European country might build a canal, and rumors of new British or German initiatives clouded the debate and offered solutions to American dominance that were unrealistic.

20. Favell, "Antecedents," 226–28; AMB to JH, March 30, 1903, in FRUS, 1903, pp. 133–34.
21. AMB to JH, April 15, 1903, in FRUS, 1903, pp. 134–35. The exchange remained catastrophic, fluctuating between 10,000 and 6,750 percent.

After the American Senate debate finished, Senator Morgan's intemperate remarks were reprinted in the Colombian press, causing wide and justifiable resentment. The developing Colombian turmoil was a case of politics turned inside out. The main forces against the government's treaty included the government, the anti-government press, and one of the most implacable of Colombia's foes, Senator John Tyler Morgan, who wanted nothing more than the rejection of the route the Colombians had first suggested. Much of the public debate focused on irrelevancies and rumors.[22]

America's Nicaragua option and Panama's separatist sentiments were conspicuously absent from the newspaper debate. One writer who submitted an article favorable to the treaty was advised to stay out of the debate for his own good; his article was declined. Beaupré reported to Hay on May 4, 1903, "It is entirely impossible to convince these people that the Nicaragua route was ever seriously considered by the United States; that the negotiations concerning it had any other motive than the squeezing of an advantageous bargain out of Colombia; nor that any other than the Panama route ever will be selected." Colombians were convinced that they could prolong the negotiations indefinitely and without risk to their interests, confident that the American offer—perceived as ridiculously low—would eventually be raised and that somehow Colombia could both give up Panama and retain it through an unspecified but more favorable arrangement. In the press and in private conversation Colombian honor and sovereignty were the main topics. Colombians remained convinced that they could negotiate a great deal more money. The debate ignored specific issues that might have produced additional American concessions such as protection of the canal or specific guarantes of Colombian sovereignty over Panama's two ports at Colón and Panama City. On the money issue, the United States remained adamant; the senators favoring Nicaragua could block any further payment even if the Roosevelt administration was willing to buy Colombian approval.[23]

22. AMB to JH, April 15, 1903, in *FRUS*, 1903, pp. 134–35; Favell, "Antecedents," 225–30. For German ambitions for a Panama canal see Holger H. Herwig, *Germany's Vision of Empire in Venezuela, 1871–1914* (Princeton, 1986), 156–61, 168–69; and Gustave Anguizola, *Philippe Bunau-Varilla: The Man Behind the Panama Canal* (Chicago, 1980), 233.
23. Tomás Herrán to Germán Villa, April 3, 1903, Herrán Papers; AMB to JH, May 4, 1903, in *FRUS*, 1903, pp. 142–43. Miner, *Fight for the Panama Route*, 256–66, disputes Beaupré's report of the totality of censorship and the effect of its lifting. See Joseph L. Arbena, "The Panama Problem in Colombian History" (Ph.D. dissertation, University of Virginia, 1970).

By May, the unleashing of public opinion, originally undertaken by the Marroquín government to pressure the Americans into a higher payment, had backfired badly and the often postponed call for Congress to convene was moved back again to June 20. A confidant told Beaupré that the government viewed the press attacks more as opposition to the Marroquín government than to the canal treaty. He was assured that though the government expected an initial adverse vote, it remained confident of eventual passage. One option, Beaupré's confidant casually mentioned, was "forcing confirmation through Congress," a tactic that Theodore Roosevelt might have envied. One of the three Panamanian senators had already acrimoniously predicted the unanimous defeat of the treaty: "The Herrán treaty will be rejected, and rejected by a unanimous vote in both chambers. . . . The insult, however, which Herrán has cast upon the Colombian name will never be wiped out. The gallows would be a small punishment for a criminal of this class." There was heat but little light in the limited Colombian discussion of the canal and of Colombia's possible new relationship with the United States.[24]

By June the situation in Colombia had deteriorated further. Hay instructed Beaupré to "discreetly and properly . . . exert your influence in favor of ratification." Searching for inside information, Hay asked about "the intricacies of Colombian politics," and, reflecting the American fear of European intervention, Hay inquired about possible "opposition . . . from European sources." Colombia was equally paranoid, transforming the arrival of three American engineers in Panama to a corps of 150 troops. Hay instructed Beaupré to "deny it [the "absolutely false" rumor] promptly and emphatically." The unbridled press caused a serious Colombian domestic crisis. Militant Conservatives Fernández and José Joaquin Casas, outraged by "the licentious and insolent press," quit after Marroquín, assured of support from the more moderate Conservatives, accepted their proffered resignations rather than approve the draconian and repressive measures they demanded. On June 1, 1903, Marroquín officially proclaimed the end of the war. Concerned Americans, trying to explain Colombia's obvious inattention to the Panama question, blamed Byzantine domestic politics, greed, shrewd economic bargaining, or even a European plot. The Americans were worried, the Colombians

24. AMB to JH, May 7, 1903; excerpt of article by Juan B. Pérez y Soto in *El Correo Nacional*, trans. and rpr. in Beaupré to JH, May 12, 1903; JH to AMB, June 2, 1903, all in *FRUS*, 1903, pp. 143–46.

incomprehensible, and the congressional session about to convene almost completely unpredictable. Colombian politics and Marroquín's policies, puzzling to the Americans, were equally unpredictable for the Colombians themselves.[25]

In a long message to Foreign Minister Luis Rico on June 10, 1903, Beaupré once again resisted Colombia's attempt to wrest a share of the French sale of the Panama properties. John Hay's peremptory and severe note to Colombia on June 9, 1903, reflected the American sense that Colombia was misusing the treaty negotiation process: "The Colombian Government apparently does not appreciate the gravity of the situation. The canal negotiations were initiated by Colombia, and were energetically pressed upon this government for several years. The propositions presented to us by Colombia, with slight modifications, were finally accepted by us. In virtue of this agreement our Congress reversed its previous judgment and decided upon the Panama route." Although Hay's statement is oversimplified and self-serving— Colombia was pushed at various stages by William Cromwell—José Concha's first formal communication opening the treaty negotiations with the United States had assured the Americans that "a final convention on this subject will not be hampered by pecuniary considerations." Thus, when the Americans refused to budge on money, the Colombians refused to believe them.[26]

Marroquín's opening address to the Colombian Congress on June 20, 1903, argued that the canal was "an immensely beneficial enterprise for our country, and also that once the canal is opened by the United States our relations will become more intimate and more extensive, while our industries, commerce, and wealth will gain incalculably." But at the same time Marroquín raised the question of loss of sovereignty and loss of "pecuniary advantages," presumably income from the railroad. Marroquín sealed the fate of the treaty by telling the Congress, "I leave the full responsibility the decision of this matter brings with Congress. I do not pretend to make my opinion weigh." In an authoritarian state such a policy is tantamount to disapproval. "There is," Beaupré reported, "a full and ample majority of the friends of the Government in both houses of Congress, and such legislation

25. AMB to JH, May 28, 1903 (two letters), JH to AMB, May 28, 1903, all in *FRUS*, 1903, pp. 145–46. An account of Marroquín's struggle with the Conservatives is in Bergquist, *Coffee and Conflict in Colombia*, 204–11.

26. AMB to Luis Rico, June 10, 1903; JH to AMB, June 9, 1903, both in *FRUS*, 1903, pp. 147–50, 146; José Concha to JH, March 31, 1902, in *House Documents*, 57th Cong., 1st Sess., No. 611, Serial 4377, p. 3.

as the Government may seriously desire will be enacted." The Colombian Senate confirmed Beaupré's view of Marroquín's control by defeating an antigovernment, anticanal parliamentary maneuver by a 38 to 5 vote. One cannot assess the relative strength or weakness of Marroquín's power in the extremely fluid and volatile state of Colombian politics because it varied enormously, changing from issue to issue, a common enough phenomenon even in stable political cultures. But the combination of Marroquín's ambivalence and vulnerability made the treaty debate a shambles.[27]

Panama was represented in the Colombian Congress by three members, but José Agustín Arango, one of the eventual leaders of the Panamanian revolution, refused to attend, feeling the meetings were useless and the treaty doomed. Another senator, Juan Pérez y Soto, though elected as a Panamanian, was a successful Cartagena merchant, whose opposition to the treaty may have reflected his fears about the possible decline of the port of Cartagena once a canal was built. Discussions on the canal began July 2, but the Congress became embroiled in a trivial dispute over whether Marroquín had actually signed the treaty that took two weeks and was ended by a narrow vote allowing substantive discussions to continue. The Congress worked at a dilatory pace. A meeting with Marroquín at the San Carlos Palace failed to produce any support for the treaty. When the procedural squabble ended, the Senate sent the treaty to a committee headed by Senator Pérez y Soto, one of its most determined foes. Beaupré could find no cause for optimism in his report to Washington.[28]

Except for the Panamanians, no one wanted the treaty; few Colombians thought of its implications; an extraordinarily ambivalent chief executive not only did not support his own treaty but failed to sign it. Nor did the majority of the Senate feel any urgency in dealing with the matter. Pérez y Soto declared, "There is no urgency in this matter, ten or twenty years are nothing in the lives of nations." The return of Rafael Reyes, one of the few Colombian political leaders who remained untainted by the War of the Thousand Days, in May, 1903, from a five-year exile in Mexico and Paris, gave new hope to treaty advocates.[29]

Reyes tended toward the American belief that the proposed canal

27. Translation of Marroquín's address is in *FRUS*, 1903, pp. 154–55; AMB to JH, June 23, 25, 1903, *ibid.*, 155.
28. Favell, "Antecedents," 238, AMB to JH, July 2, 1903, in *FRUS*, 1903, p. 157.
29. Favell, "Antecedents," 248, 250–51.

was an international improvement that would help Colombia by encouraging regional development. In describing his discussions with Roosevelt and an American congressman in December, 1901, shortly after Roosevelt had become president, Reyes suggested that "we can make a favorable deal that would permit us to valorize our paper money while at the same time placing us in a position to master the frightening fiscal and economic crisis which grips the nation." Reyes apprised Marroquín of his views and urged him to "make sure the canal is constructed through Panama." Reyes, like Marroquín, insisted on getting as much money as possible, but unlike either Marroquín or most Colombians, Reyes was not troubled by the question of sovereignty. For him development and economic regeneration were the significant issues; he regarded sovereignty as a nineteenth-century, premodern concern. Reyes, neither an ideological Conservative nor a Liberal intellectual, remained a firm believer in the need for Colombia to accommodate to modern developmental capitalism. In his 1897 presidential effort he had been called a materialist, who would substitute material progress for Christian morality in Colombia.[30]

Reyes was firmly committed to a canal treaty with the United States and became the government liaison spokesman, attempting to salvage the unpopular treaty through amendments. Reyes and Marroquín forged a political alliance, making it likely that Reyes would succeed Marroquín in the 1904 Colombian presidential election. What Reyes said and did, though not official government policy, reflected more than one man's views, a familiar Colombian tactic that tended to confuse everyone. Nonetheless, Reyes's offer to Beaupré on July 9, 1903, reflected Colombia's new—perhaps negotiable—demand for an additional $5 million from the United States and $10 of the $40 million from the proposed Compagnie Nouvelle payment. Hay turned down the now familiar overture with an equally familiar rejection: neither of Reyes's proposals "would stand any chance of acceptance by the Senate of the United States." Both the Americans and the Colombians were using their senates as reasons (or excuses) for not reopening negotiations to arrive at an acceptable compromise for a canal that was in both nations' best interests. Caught in a cultural stalemate, both nations persisted in their now habitual intransigence. They could no

30. Bergquist, *Coffee and Conflict in Colombia*, 215, 221–22; Rafael Reyes to M. J. Ortiz and D. A. de Castro, December 13, 1901; to José Marroquín, July 6, 1902, both *ibid.*, 215.

longer communicate, let alone negotiate. Neither José Marroquín nor Theodore Roosevelt was particularly willful; the actions of both chief executives reflected the beliefs and political cultures of their respective countries.[31]

Reyes tried hard to convince both the Americans and the Colombian Senate to compromise. But there was far too much ill feeling on both sides and too great a disparity in what each thought possible. Without a gesture from the United States that included an additional and substantial sum of money, the Colombians remained obdurate. Roosevelt and Hay feared what Morgan might do to a renegotiated treaty in the American Senate and refused to negotiate further. The cutting of the main cable link between Bogotá and Washington for three weeks during the Colombia Senate debate shut off communications. In the Alaskan boundary dispute with Britain in September, 1903, at almost the same time of the Colombian debate, Roosevelt retreated; after compromising a number of substantial points, he won a satisfactory settlement through flexible negotiation. But over the canal issue, with two third parties involved—Cromwell representing a French company and Morgan the Nicaraguan option—direct negotiations between the chief executives were almost impossible. Had Reyes already assumed control of Colombia, it might have been possible to negotiate an arrangement between him and Roosevelt. But the timing was bad. The anti-American rhetoric of Marroquín's political rivals offended the Americans as deeply as Senator Morgan's outbursts in the American Senate wounded Colombian sensitivities.[32]

In seeking to gain an advantage, both sides further damaged the possibility of compromise. The Colombians, preying on American fears of European intervention, attempted to interest both Britain and Germany in constructing a canal. At the same time, the Americans used a press leak to pressure Colombia. Roger Farnham, Cromwell's

31. Favell, "Antecedents," 231; Bergquist, *Coffee and Conflict in Colombia*, 215; AMB to JH, July 9, 1903; JH to AMB, July 13, 1903, both in *FRUS*, 1903, pp. 162, 164.
32. For the view that the cable disruption resulted from a contractual dispute between the Panama *Star and Herald* and the Central and South American Cable Company, see Favell, "Antecedents," 249. For the argument that the break was intentional, a part of Colombian duplicity, see Marks, *Velvet on Iron*, 101–102. For the Alaskan boundary dispute see *ibid.*, 105–11; A. E. Campbell, *Great Britain and the United States, 1895–1903* (London, 1960), 89–126; Charles C. Tansill, *Canadian-American Relations, 1875–1911* (New Haven, 1943); and Lewis Green, *The Boundary Hunters: Surveying the 141st Meridian and the Alaskan Panhandle* (Vancouver, 1982).

press agent, told the New York *World,* that in a White House meeting between Roosevelt and Cromwell, Roosevelt had said he would not give up the Panama route for Nicaragua because the United States had already invested millions of dollars in choosing the most efficient route. Assigning greed and factionalized politics as the main reasons for Colombian resistance, the *World* presented a scenario for revolution in Panama, American support of such a revolution, and a legal interpretation of the Bidlack-Mallarino Treaty of 1846 arguing the American right to recognize Panamanian sovereignty. The article ended with the hopeful conclusion that Cromwell "still expects ratification." Threats were ineffective because they reinforced the stubbornness of the deadlocked nations and drove them even further from an accommodation, an atmosphere reflected in the sarcastic tone that replaced the customary amenities even in routine diplomatic notes.[33]

On August 5, a week before the final vote, Beaupré estimated that an unamended Hay-Herrán Treaty would win only eight votes in the twenty-seven-member Colombian Senate. Even the prospect of an amended treaty diminished after a severely critical committee report offering nine substantial amendments won the support of the majority of the senators. By the day of the final debate, the only question that remained was by how many votes the treaty would be rejected. Before the debate began, the president's son, Lorenzo Marroquín, joining the tide against ratification, asked that the full diplomatic correspondence be read publicly. Poor Beaupré's stern messages, sounding even more aggressive in translation, moved an already disapproving legislative body to anger.[34]

In the tumultuous final debate, Marroquín, the United States, and the Hay-Herrán Treaty were equally excoriated. Leading the attack was Colombia's most gifted orator, Miguel Antonio Caro, one of the most doctrinaire leaders of the Regeneration movement, president of Colombia from 1894 to 1898, and a supporter of Marroquín's vice-presidency. Caro broke with his friend after Marroquín joined with

---

33. AMB to JH, July 13, 1902, in *FRUS,* 1903, p. 166; *SP,* 344; New York *World,* June 14, 1903, rpr. in Miner, *Fight for the Panama Route,* 293–95. Both Rico and Beaupré refer to the other's communications as "polite" (*FRUS,* 1903, p. 167). The text of the article is in McCullough, *Path Between the Seas,* 334–35.

34. AMB to JH, August 5, 1902, in *FRUS,* 1903, pp. 172–73; Favell, "Antecedents," 252.

the Historical Conservatives in an alliance that eventually deposed Caro's friend President Sanclemente. Caro never forgot or forgave Marroquín. On August 12, 1903, he used the Hay-Herrán Treaty debate to punish his former political ally. Caro introduced his bill to reject the Hay-Herrán Treaty and then launched his vicious attack on the bill and especially on President Marroquín. Caro decried the constitutionality of the arrangement, doubted that Panamanian separatism or American retaliation was likely, and urged Colombia to take a strong position. But the primary target of Caro's enmity was not the canal, to which he was mostly indifferent, but Marroquín. He meticulously and unmercifully took Marroquín to task for all his political errors, beginning with his assumption of the presidency in July, 1900. Some of the spectators cheered Caro's performance, but others found it ineffective because of the obvious personal bias.[35]

Much if not all of the public debate was prearranged. No one expected the treaty to pass in its original form; many Colombians seriously expected the Americans to renegotiate a more acceptable arrangement shortly after the rejection, and most of the participants dedicated the day to an attack on the president. The treaty remained a secondary issue, and neither of its two most fervent opponents spoke. When Luis Rico presented the government's position, he followed the consistent Marroquín policy of presenting both sides and making no recommendations. Not a single voice defended the treaty, and when the final vote was taken, the Colombian Senate rejected the Hay-Herrán Treaty by a 24 to 0 vote with three abstentions. The president's son Lorenzo voted with the majority.[36]

In spite of the predictions, the stunningly unanimous rejection of the Hay-Herrán Treaty shocked the United States. In his surrealistic explanation of the event, Reyes claimed that it was part of a planned strategy by canal supporters to get a treaty adopted without amendments. Reyes told Beaupré he expected intense Colombian public protest to the rejection, which was improbable in mostly indifferent Bogotá and already fatalistic Panama. The main concern in Bogotá's press was the election of a new pope, not the Panama canal. A flurry

35. Miner, *Fight for the Panama Route*, 52–54, 302, 323–25; Favell, "Antecedents," 252–53.

36. Miner, *Fight for the Panama Route*, 322–27; Favell, "Antecedents," 254–55; AMB to JH, August 12, 1903, in *FRUS*, 1903, p. 179.

of excitement occurred when it was erroneously reported that American troops had invaded the isthmus. Senator (and General) Pedro Nel Ospina, who had argued that the treaty was unconstitutional, proposed a casual reconvening of the Congress both to amend the constitution and to pass the treaty, a process the general suggested would mysteriously allow the Senate to pass the treaty without "publicly speaking in favor of it." Since twenty Colombian senators publicly supported amendments the State Department had labeled "fatal to treaty," there was little hope for a reversal although Reyes continued to try.[37]

Beaupré's analysis of the treaty's failure was detailed and perceptive. Ratification was not possible

without the active influence of the government, and this it has never used. The nationalists, under the lead of Senator Caro, have been too deeply concerned in their efforts to belittle the government to consider the merits of the treaty at all. The Liberals, while not represented in congress, are the most active factors in creating public opinion, and have taken an almost identical position. The coffee planters and exporters, who think their business would be ruined by low foreign exchange, have been unpatriotic enough to place personal interests above national good and have been against the treaty because the $10,000,000 once paid Colombia would send exchange so low that coffee could not be exported from the interior. Even the Panama representatives have lately become so thoroughly imbued with the idea of an independent Republic that they have been more or less indifferent to the fate of the treaty . . . the treaty, as such, has had no active friends or supporters.[38]

One Bogotá newspaper argued that the Colombian Senate missed its best opportunity by not passing a heavily amended treaty instead of indulging in its empty show of political oratory. Although an amended treaty would have deeply disappointed the Americans, it would not have outraged as many influential leaders—including Roosevelt, Hay, the American Senate, and the press—as the unanimous rejection did. An amended treaty might have forced the Americans to negotiate on Colombia's terms while giving Colombia the appearance of flexibility and slowing Panama's ardor for separation. A

37. AMB to JH, August 12, 1903 (two letters), August 15, 1903, all in *FRUS*, 1903, pp. 179–84; Miner, *Fight for the Panama Route*, 326–27; Favell, "Antecedents," 255.
38. AMB to JH, August 15, 1903, in *FRUS*, 1903, pp. 185–87; for Colombian coffee exports see Marco Palacios, *Coffee in Colombia, 1850–1970* (Cambridge, Eng., 1980), 136–47; Bergquist, *Coffee and Conflict in Colombia*, 229–31.

counterproposal might have inspired either the American Senate or the Compagnie Nouvelle to concede more money. Colombia's few conciliatory gestures were ineffectual. Even the news at the end of August that Reyes would succeed Marroquín and that, as president, he would support the treaty came too late to do any good.[39]

Any dim hope that the Reyes government would change the fate of the canal treaty ended on September 2, 1903, when the final Colombian congressional committee report endorsed the already unacceptable amendments of the Colombian Senate committee of July and added further onerous stipulations that doubled the initial payment to $20 million, increased the rental from $250,000 to $400,000, and required an addtional payment of $10 million from the Compagnie Nouvelle. Following Colombia's frequently Byzantine political logic, Marroquín, perhaps hoping to appease disappointed Panamanians, appointed José Obaldía, a well-known Panamanian separatist, governor of Panama. Obaldía had publicly proclaimed Panama's desire to secede and negotiate a new treaty with the Americans, and he informed Marroquín that if Panama seceded his loyalties would be with Panama and separation.[40]

The Colombian Senate was already disbanding; all hope was lost. Beaupré reported in retrospect that an additional $15 million at the height of the Senate debate might have won enough support for ratification. The press had turned violently against ratification, provoking "rivalry among the newspapers as to which could produce the most violent and bitter attacks." Only two supporters of the treaty appeared in the press, and they were subjected to personal abuse. On September 12, Foreign Minister Luis Rico formally asked the Senate to reconsider its rejection of the treaty, an empty gesture that marked the Marroquín government's only formal act of support for the treaty. Beaupré offered little future hope. He discounted Reyes's continued optimism, noting that whenever the issue was reopened "they will insist upon more money and other modifications."[41]

Marroquín's politics often appeared inept, but they may have served

---

39. AMB to JH, August 15, 30, 1903, in *FRUS, 1903*, pp. 185–87. For the possible complications the Americans considered see Alvey Adee to JH, August 19, 20, 21, 1903, Hay Papers, LC. On the question of whether the president is obligated to present amendments to the Senate see Adee to JH, August 21, 1903, *ibid.*

40. Favell, "Antecedents," 257–58; Miner, *Fight for the Panama Route*, 330; AMB to JH, September 5, 1903, in *FRUS, 1903*, p. 191.

41. AMB to JH, September 5, 1903, in *FRUS, 1903*, p. 191.

his country well. By burning his diplomatic bridges in leading Colombia to the debacle that eventually lost Panama, Marroquín may have gained more for Colombia than even the millions of dollars he had sought from the United States. In losing Panama, Colombia was forced to confront modernism and its hated symbol in Catholic Latin America—the United States. In the end Colombia received the $25 million it originally wanted, but it also received a far greater gift—a new sense of national unity that even the bloodiest of revolutionary wars had failed to provide.[42]

42. See Arbena, "Panama Problem in Colombian History"; Arbena, "Colombian Reactions to the Independence of Panama, 1903–1904," *Americas*, XXXIII (July, 1976), 133, 135, 147; for Reyes's *concordia nacional* program see Bergquist, *Coffee and Conflict in Colombia*, 228–29. For explicit statements by Marroquín of his policy to "leave the project to the Yankees only as a last resort, then only if our sovereignty doesn't suffer," see his speeches, January 1, June 20, 22, 1903, in *Diario oficial*, No. 11, 784, 11, 861, *ibid.*, 215–16. See also Mary Patricia Chapman, "Yankeephobia: An Analysis of the Anti-United States Bias of Certain Latin American Intellectuals, 1898–1928" (Ph.D. dissertation, Stanford University, 1950), esp. 20–21.

9   Revolution, 1903

Panama's revolution in 1903, the most predicted revolution of modern times, was a bitter American diplomatic defeat that marked the end of President Theodore Roosevelt's attempt to reach a peaceful accommodation with Colombia for building a canal. Panama's revolution against Colombia was first predicted in 1886, nearly seventeen years before it actually happened. All three of Colombia's ministers to the United States in the twentieth century warned their government of impending revolution—Martínez Silva in 1901, José Concha in 1902, and Tomás Herrán in 1903—if Colombia continued to treat Panama badly. Ironically, the United States was the main impediment to Panama's secession from Colombia. According to an American State Department memorandum, dated August 18, 1903, Panama's widespread sentiment for separation was inhibited by the "fear, that in some way, the United States will crush their efforts," not surprising since the Americans had intervened thirteen times after the Bidlack-Mallarino Treaty of 1846 to thwart previous Panamanian secession attempts. In 1903 the most dedicated political activists in Panama perceived the United States, not Colombia, as the biggest obstacle to revolution. Panamanian revolutionary energy was directed mainly at the United States, not to promote American participation but to assure American neutrality before the revolution and diplomatic support and recognition afterward. Fully aware of Panama's feelings and American frustration, Herrán on September 11 discussed the possibilities of both revolution and American intervention.[1]

Since the Americans were prepared for Colombian rejection of the Hay-Herrán Treaty (it was the unanimity that surprised and shocked

1. For press predictions see Thomas R. Favell, "Antecedents of Panama's Separation from Colombia" (Ph.D. dissertation, Fletcher School of Law and Diplomacy, 1951), 274; and Alfred Charles Richard, Jr., "The Panama Canal in American National Consciousness, 1870–1922" (Ph.D. dissertation, Boston University, 1969), 159–70. "The Proposed

the United States, not the rejection), there was no sense of crisis in American relations with Colombia. In his calm report to Roosevelt, Hay explained, "I would come at once to Oyster Bay to get your orders, but I am sure there is nothing to be done for the moment. You will, before our Congress meets [in December] make up your mind which of the two courses you will take, the simple and easy Nicaragua solution, or the far more difficult and multifurcate scheme, of building the Panama Canal *malgré* Bogotá." Colombia's rejection was a disappointment but not a catastrophe for Roosevelt, though for all the other principals—Philippe Bunau-Varilla, Cromwell, and the Panamanians—it was a serious crisis and possibly a disaster. Hay and Roosevelt knew the United States had many options, which they planned to examine without publicity. Hay suggested discussions with "some of the leading Senators, Hanna, Spooner, Aldrich, etc." (but not Morgan) and a talk with Secretary of War Elihu Root, who was about to leave for Europe as a member of the Alaskan Boundary Arbitration Commission. Hay further suggested a reexamination of the Bidlack-Mallarino Treaty of 1846 to clarify the obligations imposed upon both Colombia and the United States. Since Nicaraguan Minister Luis Corea was in Europe, no further negotiations with Nicaragua were possible until his return. Hay proposed doing nothing until Congress convened and then allowing the Senate to make the ultimate decision on how, where, and when to proceed.[2]

On August 18, 1903, Assistant Secretary of State Alvey Adee acknowledged the possibility that Panama would revolt and make an "offer of annexation to the United States," then refused to consider such a proposal. "Our policy before the world should stand, like Mr. Caesar, without suspicion. Neither could we undertake to recognize and protect Panama as an independent state, 'like a second Texas.'" In discussing the Colombian rejection Adee wryly observed, "It is human nature to do the idiotic thing sometimes." State Department specialists considering the diplomatic ramifications of a separate Panamanian state speculated on whether neighboring Costa Rica might

---

Panama Secession," *LD*, September, 1903, pp. 343–44, summarizes widespread American press sentiment for Roosevelt to exercise the right of "international eminent domain." John Crawford to Alvey Adee, August 18, 1903, John Hay Papers, LC; Tomás Herrán to Luis Rico, September 11, 1903, *LA*, 363–64. For the history of U.S. naval intervention in Panama see *Senate Documents*, 58th Cong., 2nd Sess., No. 143, Serial 4589 (*The Use of Military Force in Colombia*).

2. JH to TR, August 16, 1903, in RP; for press predictions of Colombia's reaction see Richard, "Panama Canal in American National Consciousness," 160–63.

recognize Panama or even merge with it to enjoy the benefits of a canal.[3]

Although Theodore Roosevelt's rhetoric was heated, his demeanor remained calm and his policies patient. "What we do now will be of consequence, not merely decades, but centuries hence, and we must be sure we are taking the right step before we act." Roosevelt was furious over Colombia's actions because he felt the United States had been badly used, but his view of Panama as an international project remained as consistent as his insensitive rhetoric: "I do not think the Bogota lot of jack rabbits should be allowed permanently to bar one of the future highways of civilization," he wrote Hay. But Roosevelt kept his anger and disappointment to himself. He assured Mark Hanna that "I shall say nothing publicly about what to do with Panama, and I shall not come to any conclusion, even tentatively and in private, before the fullest discussion with you."[4]

In 1903 Assistant Secretary of State Francis Loomis, a close adviser of Adee and Hay, was the link between President Roosevelt and Philippe Bunau-Varilla. Loomis, formerly the New York *Tribune's* Washington correspondent, entered the diplomatic service in 1890 as American consul in France. American minister to France Whitelaw Reid, also a former journalist, introduced him to Bunau-Varilla's social circles. Loomis claimed that the two men did not meet until 1901, when they became close friends while Bunau-Varilla was attempting to transfer French canal interests to the United States. John Bassett Moore, another central figure in the evolving American post–Hay–Herrán Panama policy, trained as a State Department diplomatic clerk under Alvey Adee in 1885 to 1886, then became a distinguished scholar and teacher, the first Hamilton Fish Professor of Law and Diplomacy at Columbia University and a frequent and important State Department adviser in the McKinley and Roosevelt administrations. Moore had been influential in dealing with legal questions relating to the end

3. John Crawford to Alvey Adee, August 18, 1903; Adee to JH, August 18, 1903, both in Hay Papers. For the origins of the revolution see Miles DuVal, *Cadiz to Cathay: The Story of the Long Diplomatic Struggle for the Panama Canal* (Stanford, 1940), 273–83; Favell, "Antecedents," 263–80; G. A. Mellander, *The United States in Panamanian Politics: The Intriguing Formative Years* (Danville, Ill., 1971), 10–22.

4. TR to JH, August 19, 1903; to Mark Hanna, August 22, 1903; to Jacob Schurman, September 10, 1903; to William H. Taft, September 15, 1903, all in *MRL*, III, 566–67, 569, 595–96, 598; for the contrast between TR's heated prose and his reasoned actions see John A. S. Grenville and George Berkeley Young, *Politics, Strategy, and American Diplomacy: Studies in Foreign Policy, 1873–1917* (New Haven, 1966), 310n.; see also Alfred L. P. Dennis, *Adventures in American Diplomacy, 1896–1906* (New York, 1928), 317–20.

of the Spanish-American War and was an international authority on the world arbitration movement and the State Department's adviser on Caribbean and Latin American affairs.[5]

On August 8, 1903, four days before the Colombian Senate rejected the Hay-Herrán Treaty, Francis Loomis initiated the process that ultimately led to active American confrontation with Colombia. Loomis asked Moore whether he thought the Bidlack-Mallarino Treaty of 1846 could be applied to the Colombian canal negotiations of 1903. When Moore wrote that the right of transit in Article 35 of the Bidlack-Mallarino Treaty gave the United States the right to finish the French work on the Panama canal without Colombia's consent, an excited Loomis wrote immediately to Roosevelt. After Roosevelt asked for further details, Loomis wrote Moore, "I had an interesting talk with the President on the canal question . . . and told him something of your views with reference to the possibility of proceeding under a license to dig without a formal treaty. Your suggestion interested him very much, and he said he would like to have you prepare a memorandum on the subject." Moore wrote his memorandum quickly and sent it to Loomis, who dispatched it to Roosevelt on August 15 with a note: "I think you will find some strong and well supported suggestions in this memorandum, which, in the event of the failure of the treaty at Bogotá which now seems probable, may be of the very greatest importance."[6]

Moore's memorandum is an ingenious legal justification for American intervention in Panama to build a canal. Moore's argument is based on the premise—almost universally challenged—that the canal project would benefit international civilization more than it would gratify the United States' strategic or commercial self-interest. Moore, who may have tailored his legal opinion to the needs of his client— the State Department—argued against accepting a second-best route

5. For Loomis' claim that his first meeting with Bunau-Varilla occurred in 1901 see Francis Loomis to TR, January 4, 1904, Francis Butler Loomis Papers, Stanford University; *BVC*, 304–305; for the 1890 relationship between Loomis and Bunau-Varilla and the 1898 meetings in Caracas, when Loomis as American minister to Venezuela and Bunau-Varilla met and "first plotted the [Panama] revolution," see Gustave Anguizola, *Philippe Bunau-Varilla: The Man Behind the Canal* (Chicago, 1980), 158–59, 175–77. A brief summary of Loomis' career, his role in Panama, and his papers is in Stanford University Library, *Francis Butler Loomis and the Panama Crisis* (Stanford, 1965). For John Bassett Moore's career see Richard Megaree, "The Diplomacy of John Bassett Moore: Realism in American Foreign Policy" (Ph.D. dissertation, Northwestern University, 1963).

6. Francis B. Loomis to John Bassett Moore, August 12, 1903; to TR, August 15, 1903, both in Loomis Papers.

through Nicaragua just because it was diplomatically expedient since "the United States, in undertaking to build the canal, does a work not only for itself but for the world. . . . The United States now holds out to the world for the first time a certain prospect of a canal. May Colombia be permitted to stand in the way?" Moore's answer, based on Secretary of State Lewis Cass's opinion on a Central American canal in 1858, was an unqualified no. As if speaking to order for the Roosevelt administration, Cass's words defined the new American policy and attitude toward Colombia: "Sovereignty has its duties as well as its rights, and none of these local governments . . . would be permitted . . . to close these gates of intercourse on the great highways of the world, and justify the act by the pretension that these avenues of trade and travel belong to them." So much for Colombia's ideas of sovereignty—or Panama's, which Colombia and the United States ignored with almost equal disdain.[7]

Moore used President James K. Polk's message in support of the Bidlack-Mallarino Treaty of 1846 to establish the concept of joint American-Colombian sovereignty over the canal zone. "The treaty does not propose to guarantee a territory in a foreign nation in which the United States will have no common interest with that nation. On the contrary, we are more deeply and directly interested in the subject of the guarantee than New Granada itself, or any other country." Polk's message is essential to understanding the American view of the Bidlack-Mallarino Treaty and America's long-standing proprietary view of an interoceanic canal in Central America. Moore as a lawyer was impressed with precedents, but his citations establish not only the American legal claim to the "right of transit" but the historical American sense of sovereignty over the isthmus as compelling—and as abstract and passionate—as Colombia's.[8]

Moore used the American interventions on behalf of Colombia under the Bidlack-Mallarino Treaty to dispute Colombia's claim to sovereignty over Panama. By demanding intervention in domestic disputes, Colombia "has in reality approached the point of making us the responsible sovereign on the Isthmus." Because the United States had fulfilled its treaty obligations in keeping the transit open for fifty years, "the United States is in a position to demand that it shall be

7. Text of Moore's memorandum is in Dwight Carroll Miner, *The Fight for the Panama Route: The Story of the Spooner Act and the Hay-Herrán Treaty* (New York, 1940), Appendix D, pp. 427–32; Lewis Cass to Mirabeau B. Lamar, July 25, 1858, *ibid.*, 427–28.
8. *Ibid.*, 429.

allowed to construct the great means of transit which the treaty was chiefly designed to assure." Thus, breathtakingly, because the unfinished canal was built under American protection, "the United States would be justified in maintaining and asserting a right to finish it." Moore insisted that the unbuilt Panama canal was the real subject of the 1846 treaty. That treaty "looked to the future as well as the present, and above all to the construction of a canal." Further, the benefits of the treaty had already been enjoyed by Colombia, which had been granted sovereignty over Panama in exchange for its guarantee to the United States of a place to build a canal. Thus Colombia could not in 1903 deny the United States its part of the diplomatic contract, which "would be realized only when the ships of the United States and its citizens should be able to pass from ocean to ocean by way of the Isthmus." Moore concluded his remarkable memorandum by comparing a private contract, which requires prior arrangements in satisfying local jurisdictions, to dealings between governments in which the negotiations over details can be handled as the work itself proceeds.[9]

Moore's memorandum was the decisive influence on Roosevelt's canal policy. Writing to Hay on August 19, 1903, Roosevelt enclosed the "important" paper from John Bassett Moore. Roosevelt was not fully convinced by Moore's self-serving arguments, but he grasped that Moore had given a mantle of respectability to the American urge to take the canal zone. "If under the treaty of 1846 we have a color of right to start in and build the canal, my offhand judgment would favor such proceeding." Virtually all historical studies of Roosevelt's canal policies focus almost exclusively on the diplomatic aspects, making Roosevelt's preference for Panama a matter of presidential impatience and classic big stick diplomacy. But in August, 1903, Roosevelt was acutely aware of the superiority of the Panama route. "It seems that the great bulk of the best engineers are agreed that the route is the best," Roosevelt wrote to Hay in the same letter in which he discussed Moore's memorandum and exploded in anger at the "Bogota lot of jack rabbits." Because of the radical changes in naval architecture and the technological advances in canal engineering, by 1903 the Nicaragua route had become not only inferior but of questionable utility. Larger ships would have difficulty passing through Nicaragua's rivers. In the 1870s damming the Chagres River on the Panama

9. *Ibid.*, 430–32.

route was not possible, but in 1903 it was not only possible but desirable. Roosevelt fully understood the engineering preference for Panama from his conversations with George S. Morison, the chief professional engineer on the Second Walker [Canal] Commission. The combination of Panama's enormous engineering advantage, the annoyance with apparent Colombian bad faith, greed, and flouting of American pride, and the hopeful arguments of the Moore memorandum all combined to move Roosevelt to a preference for Panama. He still kept the Nicaragua option open, but after August 15 the energies of the Roosevelt administration were directed toward finding an acceptable Panama strategy.[10]

The Senate was more aggressive than the president. When Shelby Cullom, the chairman of the Senate Foreign Relations Committee, an early advocate of the idea of seizing the canal zone by "international eminent domain," conferred with Roosevelt at Oyster Bay, he talked candidly with the press afterward. "I do not think we are ready to abandon Panama yet, not by any means," Cullom told the reporters after talking with Roosevelt. When pressed, the senator declared, "We might make another treaty, not with Colombia, but with Panama." Cullom summed up the consistent American attitude from the start of the canal negotiations: "This country wants to build that canal and build it now. It needs it for its own defense, and it is needed by the whole world." Self-interest and international good works gave the Americans the same righteous self-confidence that arguments of sovereignty violation gave the Colombians.[11]

Moore's memorandum supplied Roosevelt with an alternative that was more satisfying than reopening negotiations with Colombia or convening Congress to admit defeat and accept Nicaragua as a second choice. "I fear we may have to give a lesson to those jack rabbits," Roosevelt had written to Hay on August 17. Moore's memorandum pointed the way for Roosevelt to rebuke Colombia, win the best canal route, and still remain on the right side of international morality. Moore's initiative gave him the cover of legality while allowing him to do both things he most wanted to do—build a canal on the best route

10. TR to JH, August 19, 1903, in *MRL*, III, 566–67. On the engineering question see David McCullough, *The Path Between the Seas: The Creation of the Panama Canal, 1870–1914* (New York, 1977), 326–27; and *MRL*, III, 567n.; see also Alfred D. Chandler, "Theodore Roosevelt and the Panama Canal: A Study in Administration," in *MRL*, VI, 1547–57.

11. New York *Herald*, August 15, 1903, p. 3, rpr. in DuVal, *Cadiz to Cathay*, 264; see also Richard, "Panama Canal in American National Consciousness," 162–67.

and teach Colombia a lesson. What made Moore's memorandum most attractive was its statement of moral and legal principles, a necessity for the aristocratic and moralistic Roosevelt. In his later defense of his Panama policies Roosevelt reported, "I had done everything possible . . . to persuade the Colombian government to keep faith." In Roosevelt's view, Herrán's signature meant that Colombia's authoritarian government had agreed to the Hay-Herrán Treaty. The convening of the Colombian Congress was a sham for the purpose of seizing the French assets and selling them to the United States for $40 million. Roosevelt's righteousness in listing the moral obloquy of Marroquín crackles in his retelling. Colombia was "wicked and foolish," the government was "anti-social," and treating Colombia as a serious sovereign of Panama was "a travesty of justice." Roosevelt regarded the Colombian Senate's action on the Hay-Herrán Treaty not as a rejection but as a repudiation of its January agreement.[12]

By the end of August, the Roosevelt administration had virtually given up hope of coming to an agreement with Colombia. Minister Beaupré's cables from Bogotá confirmed this view. Colombia continued to believe that eventually it would be able to dictate its own terms to the United States and that Nicaragua was not a serious option, a correct assessment in September, 1903, but based more on faith than on Roosevelt's actual reason—the engineering factor. Reyes admitted to Beaupré that he had gravely mismanaged his pro-canal tactics. Rumors, new plans, promises of the anticanal faction that would add even more anti-American amendments to the treaty, and threats to any public proponents of a treaty with the United States made relations between the two countries almost actively hostile. In Bogotá, confidence that the United States would eventually be forced to come to terms gave the Colombian Senate and press a bumptious euphoria hardly justified by the longtime Panamanian separatist sentiment. The Colombians, in spite of their deep suspicions of American imperialism, remained confident in the face of dire warnings from their own diplomats, Panama's leaders, and the world press that the vulnerable isthmus would not secede—with or without American encouragement—and make its own canal deal. Herrán understood what Bogotá did not. "The least grave thing that can possibly happen to us would be the definite choice by the United States of the Nicaragua

12. TR to JH, August 17, 1903, RP; TR, *Autobiography* (1913), rpr. in *TRWN*, XX, 509–16. See Frederick W. Marks III, "Morality as a Drive Wheel in the Diplomacy of Theodore Roosevelt," *DH*, II (1978), 43–62.

route, but in this event the Panamanian enterprise will be value-less, because [the United States] will not permit a rival canal to be constructed."[13]

Panama's revolution was first conceived in April, 1903, when Sena-tor José Arango, Panama's elected representative to the Colombian Congress, certain that ratification would fail, made his decision not to attend the Colombian Senate debate in June. Arango held a series of discreet discussions in April, and by May a small revolutionary group was active. In June, Dr. Manuel Amador Guerrero, the Panama Railroad's company physician, joined the junta and became its chief spokesman. By the time the Colombian Senate debate was under way in June and well before its rejection ended the formal diplomatic phase of the Panama canal episode, Amador had put together a small but potent revolutionary group in Panama, including Carlos C. Arose-mena and Nicanor A. de Obarrio, an active separatist writer. Amador, the revolution's acknowledged leader, was chosen by common con-sent to be the first president-to-be of the new republic of Panama.[14]

Philippe Bunau-Varilla was the catalyst who brought the innocent Panamanians and the aloof Americans together; Assistant Secretary of State Francis Loomis became the active link between the American government and Bunau-Varilla. Loomis had asked Moore to write his memorandum for President Roosevelt, and, as acting secretary of state in Hay's summer absence, he had skillfully presented Moore's memo-randum to Roosevelt at a time when the government was examining alternatives. Bunau-Varilla was willing to play the role of activist to allow the Americans the appearance on noninvolvement. Roosevelt summed up the situation afterward: "Bunau-Varilla, I believe, (though of course I cannot prove it) did actually start the revolution that went off; but there were a dozen different trains of powder laid, and some of them were certain to go off." Although Roosevelt and the Americans were hardly innocent, Panama was the most active agent of its own revolution. When Panama needed help in organization and assurance

13. AMB to JH, September 24, 25, 1903, in FRUS, 1903, pp. 201–204; Tomás Herrán to José Concha, June 12, 1903, Herrán Papers, Special Collections Division, George-town University Library, Washington, D.C. For Herrán's view that the United States would abandon Nicaragua if and when Panama separated from Colombia, see Herrán to Julio Uribe, May 22, 1903, ibid. For Colombian proposals to sell Panama to the United States for $100 million or to seize the Compagnie Nouvelle's property because Sancle-mente's concession extension was illegal see Anguizola, Philippe Bunau-Varilla, 224–25.

14. José Arango, Datos, para la historia de la independencia del istmo (Panama, 1922), 11–17; Mellander, United States in Panamanian Politics, 10–11; Miner, Fight for the Pan-ama Route, 336–39; DuVal, Cadiz to Cathay, 273–79.

of an American alliance, Bunau-Varilla organized Panama's revolutionary nucleus and convinced America—opportunistic enough to be swayed by its own self-interest—to break its prior allegiance with Colombia and support a revolution that promised an immediate canal treaty. Without Colombia's unique diplomacy of brinksmanship with the very United States it depended on for military—and therefore political—control of Panama, however, neither the United States nor Panama would have seriously considered revolutionary separation.[15]

Panama had been willing to endure its alliance with Colombia only as long as the canal through the isthmus was assured. Once the Colombian Senate rejected the Hay-Herrán Treaty on August 12, a small revolutionary nucleus became a public and popular movement. On the floor of the Colombian Congress, in communiqués from Tomás Herrán in Washington, in letters from prominent Panamanians, Panama's desire for separation from Colombia became a passionate and effective popular movement that needed no encouragement from Bunau-Varilla or the United States. An alliance of Panamanian separatists and discontented liberals forged a network of revolutionary committees directed from Panama City that covered all of Panama. Panama wanted its canal; it had never accepted its dependent status as a department of Colombia, what Elihu Root later termed "unlawful subjection." Had the United States' alliance with Colombia not prevented separation, Panama would have revolted earlier.[16]

The Americans knew not only that Panama wanted to separate from Colombia but that planning for secession was under way. James R. Beers, the American freight agent of the Panama Railroad, who was friendly with Cromwell, the general counsel of both the railroad and the Compagnie Nouvelle, had joined the revolutionary junta in May. After Beers returned from a visit with Cromwell in New York in June, he assured the revolutionaries of Cromwell's support. The purpose of Beers's trip was known not only to the Americans but to Colombia, which suspected that the United States had made diplomatic

15. The main and best source for Bunau-Varilla's participation is *BVC*; see also Anguizola, *Philippe Bunau-Varilla*; TR to William R. Thayer, July 2, 1915, in *MRL*, VIII, 944–45; Mellander, *United States in Panamanian Politics*, 10–35.

16. Favell, "Antecedents," 270–71; Root is quoted in Frederick W. Marks III, *Velvet on Iron: The Diplomacy of Theodore Roosevelt* (Lincoln, Neb., 1979), 98; *SP*, 347–50; Luis Velez to José Marroquín, July 6, 1903, in *SP*, 347. For British Chargé Claude Chauncey Mallet's estimate in September, 1902, that 75 percent of Panama's citizens were Liberals who would actively support independence or United States annexation see C. Mallet to Lord Lansdowne, September 15, 1902, in FO 55/408, PRO.

inquiries about Europe's response to possible Panamanian independence. When a Colombian governor visiting the United States confronted Cromwell, the lawyer assured him that the United States "never followed a crooked path." Though not officially encouraging a Panamanian revolution, the United States was unofficially and informally involved. The American consul general from Panama City was one of the principal speakers at a Savannah, Georgia, meeting at which more than twenty Americans and Panamanians discussed a possible revolution.[17]

By the beginning of September, American newspapers were openly predicting the events that would occur in November. The *Outlook* indicated that Panamanian secession and prompt American recognition were likely. The Indianapolis *Sentinel* mildly protested the possible inciting of a revolution, which though "hypocritical . . . in this case . . . would almost be justifiable." The Boston *Advertiser*, in an anti-imperialist editorial, ironically suggested, "Why not annex all Central America while we are about it?" The most important newspaper column was published in Paris. In his article in *Le Matin* on September 2, 1903, Philippe Bunau-Varilla predicted that a Panamanian revolution would take place on November 3, 1903. Bunau-Varilla, who had purchased *Le Matin* in 1892 specifically to influence Panama canal issues, intended to influence President Roosevelt openly through a public newspaper article. Bunau-Varilla made sure that Roosevelt and influential members in the State Department received copies of *Le Matin* with his revolutionary scenario.[18]

One of Bunau-Varilla's most useful gifts was his ability to understand foreign cultures well enough to know what course of action would be most appealing. His September 2 *Le Matin* proposal embraced the same principles presented in Moore's memorandum, hardly an accident because an unidentified source had informed him about Moore's memorandum. "A telegram from New York, though somewhat obscure, convinced me that the idea which had occurred to me of using the text of the Treaty of 1846 to coerce Colombia had simul-

17. *SP*, 347–50. For the convenient connections of the Panama Railroad Company with the revolutionary junta see Walter LaFeber, *The Panama Canal: The Crisis in Historical Perspective* (Rev. ed.; New York, 1979), 31–32; Gerstle Mack, *The Land Divided: A History of the Panama Canal and Other Isthmian Canal Projects* (New York, 1944), 456–58; Earl Harding, *Untold Story of Panama* (New York, 1959), 23–26; and Charles D. Ameringer, "Philippe Bunau-Varilla: New Light on the Panama Canal Treaty," *AHR*, XLVI (1966), 30.
18. Quoted in *LD*, August 29, 1903, p. 246; *BVC*, 288.

taneously been entertained in America." In his article Bunau-Varilla suggested that President Roosevelt "can wait . . . until the Revolution, which is smoldering in the State of Panama bursts out, and until that province declares itself independent as it has already done twice during the last century—in 1840 and 1856. In that case the President would merely have to make a Treaty with the new State of Panama," and "nobody could blame President Roosevelt even for employing force." Closely following Moore, Bunau-Varilla wrote that private property could be limited by the principle of international eminent domain, a "superior law" legally justified by the language of the treaty of 1846 that could support or mandate American intervention.[19]

The first attempt at discourse between Panama's revolutionaries and the United States occurred on September 1, when Amador, armed with a complex codebook, arrived in New York hoping to receive assurances from the United States that American forces would not be used to prevent Panamanian secession. Amador's mission became a comedy of errors. His first mistake was traveling with J. Gabriel Duque, a Cuban who had become an American citizen and published the Panama *Star and Herald*. Although Duque knew about the planned revolution, he was not a member of the junta. Duque had better connections than Amador, and when he landed, one of Cromwell's agents met him. When Duque talked with William Cromwell in New York on September 1 and with John Hay in Washington on September 3, the air was already thick with rumors of unrest. On September 3, Hay came perilously close to officially sanctioning if not encouraging the revolutionary movement when he told Duque that "the United States would build the Panama Canal and that it did not propose to permit Colombia's standing in the way." Although Hay refused to pledge direct support for a revolution, he indicated that the Americans would support a new government after a successful revolution. If the revolutionaries took the cities of Panama and Colón, Hay told Duque, the United States would no longer support Colombia but would honor its obligation to maintain the right of transit by barring the landing of Colombian troops, in effect supporting the Panamanian revolutionaries. This assurance of American neutrality was precisely the message Amador had hoped to hear. Cromwell and Hay told Duque, a peripheral figure, of the significant American policy change but assiduously ignored Amador.[20]

19. Telegram in *BVC*, 286; text of article, *ibid.*, 286–88.
20. *SP*, 359–60, 365; codebook is in McCullough, *Path Between the Seas*, 343–44; see Mack, *Land Divided*, 457–59; Miner, *Fight for the Panama Route*, 336–39.

The fiasco was compounded when Duque immediately reported his conversation to Herrán, one of his many friends from Colombia, in the mistaken hope that Colombia might yield in the face of a revolutionary threat. Herrán needed no prodding to warn his government of possible trouble. "Revolutionary agents here," Herrán dramatically warned. "If treaty is not approved by September 22 [the deadline mandated by the American Senate in ratifying the Hay-Herrán Treaty], it is probable there will be a revolution with American support." Herrán took the offensive in America, hiring private detectives to follow Amador and forcing a frightened Cromwell to cease any further instigations by threatening to terminate the Compagnie Nouvelle's concession. Amador, now pointedly ignored by Cromwell as well as by the American diplomats, lost all of his contacts and became disheartened.[21]

Bogotá was discreetly interested in the American response to the treaty rejection. Herrán had heard about some of Roosevelt's private pronouncements on Panama, which convinced him that the president was "hostile" toward Colombia. Roosevelt's private warnings, Herrán reported, indicated that the United States would promptly recognize an independent Panamanian state: "President Roosevelt is a decided partisan of the Panama route, and hopes to begin excavation of a canal during his administration. Your excellency already knows the vehement character of the President, and you are aware of the persistence and decision with which he pursues anything to which he may be committed." Roosevelt and Hay were pursuing a tactic that had worked effectively in other recent American diplomatic confrontations. In December, 1902, the Roosevelt administration had used private threats, the press, and official pressure to force Germany to back down in the Venezuelan coercion crisis. Roosevelt and Hay together were using similar methods against the British and Canadians in the Alaskan boundary dispute taking place at the same time the Panama crisis was unfolding. Although the strategy worked well against the Western powers, Colombia was unmoved by American cajoling, informal diplomacy, last-minute concessions, and varying degrees of pressure. Bogotá and Washington remained worlds apart, interested in but essentially untouched by the other's words or actions in a way that resembled the diplomacy that preceded the Spanish-American War of 1898. Like the Spanish, the Colombians refused to yield, compromise, or even believe that the worst could happen. In 1898 Spain hoped that

21. *SP*, 361–62; Mellander, *United States in Panamanian Politics*, 12–15.

the concert of Europe might save it from defeat in a war with the United States. In 1903 Colombia refused to budge from its collision course with the determined and powerful colossus.[22]

Contrary to popular legend, Theodore Roosevelt was not an impulsive leader. Few presidents consulted with as many persons in as many different capacities as Roosevelt did. He spoke with senators, newspapermen, novelists, local politicians. He had an enormous number of correspondents, including English historian Sir George Treveleyan, public figures such as Lord James Bryce, and many Americans with a wide spectrum of opinions. He read newspapers actively, frequently complaining to friends and political allies about articles or editorials he liked or that displeased him. On September 10, 1903, Roosevelt wrote, "I should of course infinitely prefer to get title to the Canal outright, and I do not consent for a moment to the view that Colombia has the right permanently to block one of the world's great highways." But Roosevelt knew that "to announce my feelings would undoubtedly be taken as equivalent to an effort to incite an insurrection in Panama." Waiting "a few months, or even a year or two, is nothing compared with having the thing done rightly." Although Roosevelt was an active chief executive who extended the constitutional powers of the presidency to their limits, he did not openly flaunt congressional constitutional prerogatives. "If Congress will give me a certain amount of freedom and a certain amount of time, I believe I can do much better than by any action taken out of hand. But of course what Congress will do I don't know."[23]

In early September the administration remained unsure of its future plans. Secretary Hay's September 13 memorandum of options, written after consultation with Roosevelt, is an accurate reflection of American uncertainty. The United States could issue a peremptory rejection of any Colombian amendments, or, Hay advised, "say nothing and let them go on making fools of themselves until you are ready to act on some other basis." Hay was convinced that "we cannot now—

22. For the Alaskan boundary confrontation see Chapter 8, note 32; for the Spanish-American War see Chapter 2, note 31; for the Spanish delays see David F. Trask, *The War with Spain in 1898* (New York, 1981), 36–51; for Roosevelt's Venezuelan diplomacy see Chapter 4; *SP*, 361–62.

23. For a persuasive refutation of TR's legendary impatience, see Marks, *Velvet on Iron*, 129–70; TR to Jacob Schurman, September 10, 1903, in *MRL*, III, 595–96. For examples of historical condemnations of TR see Robert A. Friedlander, "A Reassessment of Roosevelt's Role in the Panamanian Revolution of 1903," *Western Political Quarterly*, XIV (1961), 535. For the most striking example see George E. Mowry, *The Era of Theodore Roosevelt and the Birth of Modern America, 1900–1912* (New York, 1958), 155.

nor for some time to come—make a satisfactory treaty with Colombia." Hay succinctly outlined Roosevelt's options: "It is altogether likely that there will be an insurrection on the Isthmus against the régime of folly and graft that now rules at Bogotá. It is for you to decide whether you will (1) await the result of that movement, or (2) take a hand in rescuing the Isthmus from anarchy, or (3) treat with Nicaragua." Hay advised that in the event of an insurrection the United States would need "to keep the transit clear. Our intervention should not be haphazard, nor this time should it be to the profit, as heretofore, of Bogotá." Clearly, the Americans had three options: to wait, to pursue the Nicaraguan route, or to support Panamanian separatism and renounce the previous alliance with Colombia. A fourth option which Roosevelt considered was unilaterally to seize the canal zone and allow an international tribunal to settle accounts with Colombia later.[24]

Sensitive to American failure to arrive at an agreement with Colombia, Roosevelt complained that "treaties are not made by one party *in vacuo* but with other contracting parties. As yet no one has pointed out one step we have taken in the matter which could have been better taken." The urge to punish the Colombians, the convenience of the Panamanian separatist movement, and further discouragement from Colombia encouraged a Panama-first policy. Henry Cabot Lodge, who was in Paris before beginning his Alaskan Boundary Commission duties in London, urged Roosevelt on September 5 "that either under the treaty of '46 or by the secession of the Province of Panama we can get control of what is undoubtedly the best route." American newspapers echoed Lodge's sentiments. "Up to the present moment the United States has conducted its side of the negotiations in open and honorable fashion," the Pittsburgh *Gazette* declared, but the United States now has the right to proceed against an "unreasonable and unfaithful" Colombia. The Moore memorandum and the possibility of Panamanian separation became familiar American newpaper subjects.[25]

24. JH to TR, September 13, 1903, RP, rpr. in Tyler Dennett, *John Hay: From Poetry to Politics* (New York, 1933), 377. Dennett's attempt to make Hay's memorandum a plea for Nicaragua is unconvincing.
25. TR to Albert Shaw, October 7, 1903, in *MRL*, III, 625–26; AMB to JH, September 30, 1903, in *FRUS*, 1903, p. 205; HCL to TR, September 5, 1903, in *Selections from the Correspondence of Theodore Roosevelt and Henry Cabot Lodge, 1884–1918* (2 vols.; New York, 1925), II, 54; for the Pittsburgh *Gazette* and other American press reports see "Proposed Panama Secession," *LD*, September 19, 1903, p. 343; Richard, "Panama Canal in American National Consciousness," 163–69; Dennett, *John Hay*, 376.

After meeting with John Bassett Moore in September, Roosevelt decided to address a special session of Congress in November to urge unilateral American seizure of the canal zone. Such a policy, legally supported by Moore's memorandum, would probably have won overwhelming support. The American view of Colombia's political dilemma was not entirely unsympathetic. Alvey Adee's analysis on September 21 recognized that the Marroquín government had lost control of the canal issue to an unrestrained Colombian Senate. Adee thought that the Colombian political stalemate could be solved either by the Congress giving Marroquín the right to reopen negotiations without going through additional congressional ratification or if "Reyes gets up a revolution." The Colombian policy—in reality, a nonpolicy—was to ask the United States to wait until the new Congress of August, 1904, convened to reconsider a canal treaty. Adee summed up the American view of the stalemate: "It seems to me that the Colombian cow, having kicked over the pail, says 'see here; if I kick over this pail, would you give me an extension of time to see what I can do with another pailful tomorrow?'" The initiative had shifted not only from Marroquín to his Congress but from Colombia altogether. Another American assistant secretary observed, "They appear to be waiting in Colombia for us to do something, but it seems to me they will have to pull themselves out of the hole into which they have fallen." [26]

In Panama the revolutionary movement flourished. Panama's Liberals and Conservatives worked well together in planning the revolution. Although there were more Liberals, the original Conservative nucleus controlled the work of the junta from Panama City. The Americans in the canal zone were aware of the revolutionary movement, but they were excluded from planning or active participation. Bogotá, though aware of the unrest, did little to discourage it, maintaining only a small garrison of troops, hardly enough to offer resistance to a determined uprising. Many of the soldiers garrisoned in Panama were related to Panamanians and increasingly sympathetic to local rather than national interests. Bogotá ignored the Colombian governor's frequent requests for additional troops. When Colombia failed to pay its small Panama garrison regularly, many of these

26. Moore's meeting with TR is described in Moore's unpublished manuscript memoir, Box 211, John Bassett Moore Papers, LC; TR, *Autobiography*, in *TRWN*, XX, 510; text of rough draft of congressional message, *ibid.*, 549–50; TR's defense of the choice of Panama over Colombia, *ibid.*, 514; Alvey Adee to JH, September 21, 1903, in Hay Papers; Francis Loomis to William N. Cromwell, August 29, 1903, in Loomis Papers. For some of the Colombian proposals see Anguizola, *Philippe Bunau-Varilla*, 224–25.

troops became as embittered toward the Bogotá government as the Panamanians and the Americans already were.[27]

Marroquín's appointment of José Obaldía as Panama's new governor in September was part of a complex political maneuver that raised as many questions as it answered. Obaldía, a Conservative who appointed many Liberals to department offices, was part of the new Reyes-Marroquín coalition and a Panamanian who openly supported separatism. Panamanians, pleased with their new governor, excluded him from the revolutionary activity, a remarkable feat since Obaldía stayed with Arango for over a month before moving to his governor's quarters. As one Panamanian explained, "The high esteem in which we hold Obaldía makes it our duty to leave him in ignorance of everything . . . his position is a difficult one; but his ideas are the same as before in what touches our separation from the step-mother."[28]

In New York, meanwhile, a disheartened Amador, isolated by Herrán and unable to make any further American contacts, prepared to return to Panama. With his knack for fortuitous timing, Philippe Bunau-Varilla arrived on the scene and dramatically took charge. The Frenchman claimed that he had decided at the last minute to accompany his wife, who was taking their thirteen-year-old son to Maine for hay fever treatments. A discouraged Amador told Bunau-Varilla in New York on September 23, 1903, that "a revolution would today meet with no obstacle." Not only was Colombia's garrison weak but the Colombian commander, General Esteban Huertas, sympathized with Panama. But Amador could not envision a successful insurrection without control of the sea. "The Colombians have the command of the sea, their ships crews are loyal," Amador told Bunau-Varilla. Amador knew that soldiers could be easily bribed, but Colombia's sailors could not be neutralized, and Amador assumed that Panama needed its own fleet to control the seas. Even the imperturbable Bunau-Varilla blanched at Amador's request for $6 million to buy a navy.[29]

Sensing a rare opportunity to manipulate the incipient revolution, Bunau-Varilla told Amador, "Don't speak to anyone. If you want

27. Favell, "Antecedents," 273. For the absence of Americans see Oscar Teran, *Del Tratado Herrán-Hay al Tratado Hay–Bunau-Varilla* (2 vols.; Panama, 1934), I, 392–93.

28. On Obaldía's appointment see Favell, "Antecedents," 272; M. Carlos Arsomena to Dr. Manuel Amador, September 20, 1903, translation of extract in Box 207, Folder C, Moore Papers; *BVC*, 309–10.

29. *BVC*, 293–97; for Huertas see Mellander, *United States in Panamanian Politics*, 21–22.

to speak to me over the phone take the name of Smith. I shall take that of Jones. The extremely articulate Bunau-Varilla conversed more than he plotted. His main weapon was publicity; his schemes were flamboyant, public, and terrifyingly simple. Instead of asking for help, he openly told everyone what was going to happen, as well as where and when, thereby setting in motion the forces that fulfilled his predictions.[30]

Through his old friend Columbia University engineering professor William H. Burr, an isthmian canal commissioner who supported the Panama route and who may have been the mysterious source who first told Bunau-Varilla of Moore's views, Bunau-Varilla arranged to meet John Bassett Moore, Burr's colleague at Columbia. Besides wanting to make friends with an important American, Bunau-Varilla hoped to learn Roosevelt's preferences regarding the Panama route. Even as late as September 29, Bunau-Varilla thought Theodore Roosevelt was neutral on the route but leaning slightly toward Nicaragua. Moore, fully aware of how dangerous any association with the Frenchman might be (or appear to be), was uncomfortable talking with Bunau-Varilla. Although nothing was said directly about Roosevelt's views, Bunau-Varilla's conversation with Moore convinced him that Roosevelt preferred the Panama route and might be sympathetic to a Panamanian revolution.[31]

Bunau-Varilla used his meeting with Moore as a conduit to President Roosevelt. He knew that his letters to Moore would reach the president's eyes. This arrangement suited the Americans as well. In his October 3, 1903, letter Bunau-Varilla urged support of the Moore memorandum and advised that "sentiment in all classes of the population of the Isthmus is for a secession from Colombia, and for a direct treaty of the independent State of Panama, with the United States, strictly on the basis of the Hay-Herran Treaty." Bunau-Varilla suggested that, though an advance sign of American support would encourage the impending revolution, he understood that "Machiavelli's principles" were not in harmony with American custom. Citing a letter from a Panamanian to Amador, which he enclosed, Bunau-Varilla argued that Reyes would have difficulty obtaining a more malleable Congress than Marroquín's. His perceptive analysis of Colombian motives appealed to an administration that often found Colombia's

30. *BVC*, 293.
31. *BVC*, 296–98.

diplomacy incomprehensible: "Spaniards and Spanish-Americans . . . have admirable moral qualities, but when the Don Quixote side of their character gets stronger than the Sancho Panza side, nothing will stop them, and the strong arm of the windmill is the only thing that can bring them to reason."[32]

The Frenchman equated Colombian actions with feudal South African savages extorting money from passing caravans. He concluded by asking the United States to protect the world—presumably from both Colombian extortion and South African banditry. The letter is a classic demonstration of Bunau-Varilla's manipulative techniques, planting ideas while observing the moral amenities, and persuasive in spite of its breathless polemic. The idea that because the United States had assumed the role of protector of Colombia it now had to protect the world against Colombian rapacity—"the right of protecting involves the duty of policing"—was a brilliant extension of Moore's principles and suggested the direction Roosevelt eventually took in the Roosevelt Corollary to the Monroe Doctrine.[33]

Bunau-Varilla could "advise" the Americans without conspiring by offering "useful suggestions in the garb of information without giving them the slightest ground for suspecting my participation in the revolutionary movement." His old friend Francis Loomis became the major conduit for Bunau-Varilla's suggestions. The conversations between Bunau-Varilla and the Roosevelt administration were exercises in gentlemanly diplomacy, resembling nothing so much as characters in a Henry James novel talking around a subject with perfect comprehension of what was unsaid as well as what was between the lines of what was unsaid. It was a gentlemen's game, and the principals enjoyed themselves immensely. Roosevelt, Hay, Loomis, and Moore cooperated without moral compunctions, convinced that Colombia was immoral, that Panama was entitled to its independence, and that the world—and the United States—was entitled to a canal. Roosevelt and his administration activists never doubted that they were acting morally and in America's best interests. Their actions were no more ethically skewed than the opposing Colombian tactic of continually raising its price for a canal at Panama.[34]

32. Philippe Bunau-Varilla to JBM, September 3, 1903, in *BVC*, 307–309.
33. *BVC*, 308–309.
34. *BVC*, 310. For TR's preoccupation with his renomination and an example of a Jamesian conversation between Bunau-Varilla and Hay see Anguizola, *Philippe Bunau-Varilla*, 233–35.

Roosevelt's canal policy was determined by two dramatic Sunday visits at the White House in October. On October 9, the president and Bunau-Varilla met for the first time. Loomis, who had arranged the meeting, stood as still as a statue as the two men maneuvered toward the unspoken question of revolution. Roosevelt asked what Bunau-Varilla thought might be the outcome of the Panama question. Without hesitation Bunau-Varilla replied: "A revolution." The president appeared surprised. Turning to Loomis, who was standing "impassible," according to Bunau-Varilla's written account, Roosevelt said in a low tone as if speaking to himself, "A revolution." Roosevelt was pleased that Bunau-Varilla had corroborated the rumors, but he was not as surprised as he pretended to be. Roosevelt already had his own remarkable source of information on the imminence of a Panamanian revolution. Shortly before the Senate had ratified the Hay-Herrán Treaty in March, 1903, a concerned Roosevelt, determined to investigate persistent rumors of continued European interest in Panama, asked Secretary of War Elihu Root "for two or three first class men" to gather information on the Gulf, Caribbean, Venezuela, Colombia, and the Guianas—virtually any area that might be involved in a future canal. "The probability of our beginning work on the canal would justify such action," Roosevelt added. "Can this not be done at once?" the president asked his secretary of war.[35]

A clandestine operation in an area shattered by civil war and suspicious of foreigners was extremely difficult to arrange through conventional means. General Leonard Wood, Roosevelt's old army friend from Cuba, volunteered to lead a group of army officers disguised in civilian dress using a commandeered private boat. Wood even found a yachtsman willing to take them. The way the mission was ultimately implemented was only slightly less unorthodox. The army ordered Captain Chauncey B. Humphrey and Lieutenant Grayson Mallet-Prevost Murphy, a new West Point graduate, to conduct a routine military survey in Venezuela. The original orders, limiting the assignment to Venezuela—with President Cipriano Castro's official assent—gave no hint of the grandiose scheme the president had in mind.[36]

35. Meeting and conversation in *BVC*, 311–12; TR to ER, March 14, 1903, in RP; see also TR to ER, March 15, 1903, in *MRL*, III, 447.

36. One of the best accounts of the mission is in Henry F. Pringle, *Theodore Roosevelt: A Biography* (New York, 1931), 320–21; see also typescript of an interview with Grayson M. P. Murphy, April 3, 1930, Henry Pringle Notes, TR Collection, Harvard College Library, Harvard University, Cambridge, Mass. The original War College Division files for this period were destroyed as part of a general housecleaning program in the 1920s

It is not entirely clear why the mission changed. Humphrey said he received a letter from a friend in Washington who unofficially suggested a trip to Panama. Both Humphrey and Murphy, excited by the prospect of the new mission but fearful that it was too unconventional for standard army procedures, followed their instincts and, after wiring the War Department of their destination, left without waiting for permission. Once in Panama, Humphrey and Murphy more than fulfilled Roosevelt's original plan. They talked with many native Panamanians, took copious notes, and gathered so much firsthand information that on hearing their oral report to the General Staff, Army Chief of Staff Lieutenant General Samuel B. M. Young called the president and arranged for them to meet with him.[37]

Humphrey and Murphy were able to confirm Bunau-Varilla's certainty of a revolution to the president on October 16. This second critical White House meeting marked a turning point for Theodore Roosevelt's plans for Panama. Murphy and Humphrey not only confirmed the accuracy of Bunau-Varilla's prediction of revolution, they gave the president the names of prominent Panamanians who were involved as well as other specific details. The young soldiers were impressed with how much Roosevelt already knew about conditions in Panama. Their own plans to take advantage of the coming revolution, however, took the president's breath away. The enterprising soldiers planned to ask J. P. Morgan, whom they had never met, for a $10 million loan to finance a joint enterprise—the Humphrey-Murphy-Morgan Panama Canal in post-revolutionary Panama. Roosevelt ordered the two men to the Philippines to keep them out of mischief. Before going, they dictated all of their notes to the General Staff,

(see Judith Koucky, *National Archives Microfilm Publications Pamphlet Describing M1023* [Washington, D.C., 1979], pp. 7–8). Much of the correspondence can be traced in summary form through record cards to the Correspondence of the War College Division in Microcopy 1023, RG 165, NA. For Humphrey's appointment as military attaché in Caracas, June 10, 1903, and Murphy's orders as assistant attaché, June 16, 1903, see record card 646, Military Information Division (MID), M1023, roll 1; for the mission's limits to Venezuela see June 10, 1903, *ibid.*

37. Pringle, Murphy interview. The fullest account of the oral Humphrey-Murphy report is in Lieutenant General S. B. M. Young to Elihu Root, December 24, 1903, in vol. 177, pt. 1, pp. 427–28, in Elihu Root Papers, LC; see Miner, *Fight for the Panama Route*, 354. Root's request for the report is Root to Chief of Staff, December 24, 1903, vol. 183, pt. 1, p. 25, Root Papers. For Humphrey's "unclear" cable to MID and MID's response, August 28, 29, 1903, see record card 646d, M1023, roll 1; for a summary of the two-volume Venezuelan report see record card 1400 in M1023, roll 2; for Murphy see record card 715, in M1023, roll 1; see also record cards 716, 1190, and 1301, *ibid.*

which compiled and published in November, 1903, one of the most
bizarre of American government documents, a book on Panama "for
the sole use of the officer to whom issued." The manual gathered the
scattered material from government documents and offered survival
tips for American military men in the Panama theater of war.[38]

Assured that a revolution in Panama was imminent, Roosevelt
moved the navy to a state of readiness. Although he was certain a
revolution would take place, he could not know exactly when. On
October 17 he ordered three ships into the area and alerted the Army
General Staff to prepare for possible action in the isthmus. After consulting with his cabinet and with John Hay, Roosevelt issued further
naval orders on October 19. On October 20 the *Boston* was dispatched
to Nicaragua to arrive November 1 with sufficient fuel to return to Aca-
pulco—or proceed to Panama. The *Dixie* with four hundred marines
and the *Kearsrage* were ordered to ports close to Panama. Roosevelt
still continued with his original plan to put the question of Panama
before Congress. If Panama remained "quiet . . . I was prepared to
recommend to Congress that we should at once occupy the Isthmus
anyhow, and proceed to dig the canal; and I had drawn out a draft of
my message to this effect." On October 20 Roosevelt called a special
session of Congress for November 9, 1903, to consider the Cuban reciprocity treaty. Had the reports of an imminent Panamanian revolution proved premature, Roosevelt planned to make his recommendations to Congress to allow the seizure of the canal zone under the
legal justifications of the Moore memorandum.[39]

Bunau-Varilla, convinced that the Americans would deal with the
revolution as they had in previous interventions, deduced that their
first objective would be to seize the Panama Railroad to prevent its
military use by either side. This suited Bunau-Varilla, who reasoned
that once the railroad was secure the Americans, though they acted in
good faith in maintaining neutrality, would be sympathetic toward

38. *SP*, 369–70; Captain H. C. Hale, *Notes on Panama*, War Department Military Information Division, Chief of Staff Document, 217. *SP*, 369–70, describes Humphrey's
contribution to *Notes on Panama*. For the order requesting "all information possible respecting military forces in isthmus of Panama and of defensive works at Colon and
Panama," see MID to Humphrey, September 15, 1903, summary in record card 812,
M1023, roll 2. TR to William R. Thayer, July 2, 1915, in *MRL*, VIII, 944.

39. Naval orders are in TR, Message to Congress, January 4, 1904, in *FRUS*, 1903,
pp. 260–78; *SP*, 368–70; TR, *Autobiography*, in *TRWN*, XX, 510. For a summary of the
naval orders see Richard W. Turk, "The United States Navy and the 'Taking' of Panama,
1901–1903," *Military Affairs*, XXXVIII (1974), 92–96.

the Panamanians. Colombia's Panama garrisons had not been paid for two months; without access to the railroad—impossible without active American support—Colombia would be helpless to resist Panama's revolution. Bunau-Varilla suggested to Amador that bribery was the key to ensure a bloodless revolution. He was sure that a fund of $100,000—$40 for each Colombian soldier in Panama—would be sufficient. On October 14, Amador, giving up his dream of a million-dollar working navy, reluctantly agreed. When Bunau-Varilla went to Washington on October 17, he learned from Secretary Hay that American naval preparations were being made. From his other extensive Navy Department contacts, Bunau-Varilla, the master of discreet conversation, probably learned enough specific details to be sure that enough American ships would be near Panama to convince onlookers of active American participation. He knew that both sides would assume the United States had an ulterior motive, not realizing that the show of naval strength was actually a demonstration of neutrality.[40]

Returning to New York, Bunau-Varilla now greeted "President" Amador with the news of a *fait accompli*. Bunau-Varilla declared Room 1162 of the Waldorf-Astoria Hotel "the cradle of Panamanian independence" and lied to Amador about his trip to Washington by assuring him that American naval support had been arranged, leaving Amador with the mistaken notion that the Americans not only knew of the revolution but were voluntarily taking part in it. Amador was easily convinced. How could he resist the French whirlwind at the height of his most spectacular performance? Already Bunau-Varilla "had prepared the proclamation of independence, a methodical plan of the military operations, as well as the arrangements for the defense of the isthmus to be effected within the first three days, and finally a cipher code allowing Amador and myself to correspond secretly." Bunau-Varilla based Panama's new government on the constitution of Cuba, which he observed had recently been devised by the best legal talent in America, the reigning expert on republics and their constitutions. "It only remained to design the flag of the new republic," which task Bunau-Varilla delegated to his wife. But although

40. *SP*, 315–19. Captain John Hubbard's report to William Moody, October 17, 1903, which confirmed that 75 percent of Panamanians supported a canal on virtually any terms but lacked a leader to follow, may have contributed to TR's and Hay's willingness to give Bunau-Varilla a free hand in organizing the leadership (quoted in Richard D. Challener, *Admirals, Generals, and American Foreign Policy, 1898–1914* [Princeton, 1973], 154).

Panama, like the United States, was willing to use Bunau-Varilla to further its own interests, it resented his patronizing attitude. Panamanians rejected not only Madame Bunau-Varilla's flag but the Frenchman's declaration of independence and constitution, adopting instead a document written by Panamanians in Panama.[41]

Amador returned by boat from New York on October 20, arriving in Panama on October 27. With American ships setting sail for the war zone on October 20, Bunau-Varilla could plan on their arrival early in November. The Frenchman decided to stage the revolution on November 3, 1903, the American election day, which would dominate the news reports and make the Panamanian coup less prominent in the American press. Amador described the revolutionary plan to his son on October 18: "The plan seems to me good. A portion of the Isthmus declares itself independent, and that portion the United States will not allow any Colombian forces to attack . . . the new Republic remains under the protection of the United States." The main problem with Bunau-Varilla's plan was his requirement that he, not a Panamanian, be named to negotiate a canal treaty with the United States. The Panamanians had rejected Bunau-Varilla's proclamation, his constitution, and his flag, and they would have rejected his services as foreign minister. But the Frenchman's genius for manipulation enabled him to maintain control by winning the post of foreign minister, and in the process he corrupted the genuine and passionate revolution he had helped plan.[42]

When Amador landed in Panama on October 27, the revolution's initial phase—the bribing of Colombian officials—began. Armed with Bunau-Varilla's loan of $100,000 as a war chest, the Panamanians discovered that money was a far more effective tool than navies or rifles. Bogotá's financial difficulties had made its troops especially vulnerable. Colombia's government, committed to the raw exercise of power since the election of 1897, could offer the troops no national sense of purpose or ideological commitment to fight for. Panama's eagerness for independence was the only compelling ideology, and Colombian officers and soldiers eagerly took Panama's terms and its money. Gen-

---

41. *SP*, 320–23; DuVal, *Cadiz to Cathay*, 307; Mellander, *United States in Panamanian Politics*, 20.
42. Manuel Amador to Raul Amador, October 18, 1903, in *SP*, 71–72; *BVC*, 324. For Panama's attempted rejection of Bunau-Varilla, see DuVal, *Cadiz to Cathay*, 310–11; Anguizola, *Philippe Bunau-Varilla*, 240–41.

eral Ruben Varón accepted $35,000 in silver to neutralize most of the remaining officers in the Colombian navy. General Esteban Huertas, already sympathetic to Panama and as much a political figure as an army officer, also agreed to join the revolutionaries by not using his troops in opposition.[43]

When Governor José Obaldía ordered potentially uncooperative Colombian troops into the interior, an alarmed Bogotá sent two hundred new men as reinforcements to Panama, frightening Obaldía, who shared his concern with Amador. Amador's cable to Bunau-Varilla telling of the new danger set in motion an important meeting with Acting Secretary of State Loomis in Washington on October 27. When Bunau-Varilla referred to American actions in Panama's 1885 uprising, Loomis realized that it was essential for an American warship to be at Colón on November 3. After Loomis indicated that a warship was indeed on its way to Colón, Bunau-Varilla could easily deduce the rest of the American naval orders by using regular newspaper reports of ship movements. He knew the *Nashville* at Kingston, five hundred miles away, was the closest warship to Colón. Calculating the speed of the American vessel, Bunau-Varilla estimated its arrival at two and a half days.[44]

Certain that American vessels would be off the Panama coast when the revolution began, Bunau-Varilla falsely reassured Amador of support, though he knew the American presence was only symbolic, largely accidental, and not an indication of cooperation with the revolution. By talking to Loomis, Bunau-Varilla also made sure the Americans would react (overreact?) to the chain of events begun by Obaldía's initial order and assured a flurry of American naval activity in addition to the dispatch of the *Nashville*. Loomis ordered several ships to the scene. They arrived too late for the actual revolution but assured a measure of stability once the coup had achieved its initial success. Bunau-Varilla's information was hardly top secret because sailings of American warships were routinely printed in the New York *Times*. It is, of course, possible that Loomis or another American official told Bunau-Varilla directly of American ship movements and

43. *SP*, 382; for reproductions of the documents relating to Bunau-Varilla's bank loan of 500,000 francs from Credít Lyonnais see Philippe Bunau-Varilla, *Les 19 documents cles du drame de Panama* (Paris, 1939?), 42–54 (copy in Herrán Papers).
44. A summary of the orders is in DuVal, *Cadiz to Cathay*, 313–14; see also Turk, "United States Navy and the 'Taking' of Panama," 92–96.

together they fabricated elaborate fictions as a cover. Bunau-Varilla enjoyed the double game as well as his ability to manipulate every-one—America, Panama, and Colombia.[45]

Although the *Nashville* arrived on November 2 at 5:30 P.M.—only slightly behind Bunau-Varilla's predicted schedule—its commander, following the usual policy of strict American neutrality, completely misunderstood the purpose of his mission, which was to keep the Panama Railroad neutral and prevent troops of either side from taking control of it. At daybreak on November 3, Commander John Hubbard boarded the Colombian vessel *Cartagena*, apparently unaware that the 474 troops it carried made it a potential disaster for the impending revolution. Although Commander Hubbard was told that the troops were bound for Panama, he made no effort to stop them. The Pana-manians had taken the precaution of moving most of the available railroad cars from Colón to Panama to prevent any Colombian troops from crossing the isthmus. Only after the Colombian troops had al-ready landed did the State Department order the *Nashville* to "prevent Government troops [from] departing for Panama [city] or taking any action which would lead to bloodshed." Once General Juan Tobar's troops were ashore, the Americans had become bystanders in the en-folding revolutionary drama. Panama's revolutionaries were now badly outnumbered and in a precarious situation.[46]

45. For the controlled cooperation between Bunau-Varilla and Loomis, see *BVC*, 327–32; *SP*, 380–81. For evidence that Loomis' help was more direct see Philippe Bunau-Varilla to Francis B. Loomis, November 3, 1914, Loomis Papers; Stanford University Li-brary, *Francis Butler Loomis*, 3. For the New York *Times* prediction of November 1 see "*Nashville*, Sailed for Colombia?" cited in *BVC*, 333.

46. *SP*, 386–89. The best account is John Hubbard to William Moody, November 8, 1903, in TR to Congress, January 4, 1904, in *FRUS*, 1903, pp. 269–71; Challener, *Ad-mirals, Generals, and American Foreign Policy*, 154–56. Two contemporary personal jour-nal accounts appear to show that Roosevelt was more fully informed of the details of Bunau-Varilla's involvement than either claimed. See John Bigelow's Journal entry of his conversation with Bunau-Varilla, which describes a full discussion of the impend-ing Panama revolution between Roosevelt, Loomis, and Bunau-Varilla, in Margaret Clapp, *Forgotten First Citizen: John Bigelow* (Boston, 1947), 313. Also see "Memorandum of a Conversation Between Archibald C. Coolidge and Theodore Roosevelt in presence of Max Farrand, January 23, 1913, Harvard Club, N.Y., abstracted by F. J. Turner," in Thomas D. Schoonover, "Max Farrand's Memorandum on the U.S. Role in the Panama-nian Revolution of 1903," *DH*, XII (1988), 501–506. Clapp clearly sees the "wholly natu-ral mistake of failing to see any signal distinction either of a practical or moral nature between privately exchanged words and private, nonverbalized understandings" (*For-gotten First Citizen*, 313). Roosevelt, like the press, knew a great deal and may have speculated about the possibilities of revolution on the isthmus. How much of what was said or thought was speculative, conjectural, or lacking a modifying nuance in the rec-ollection or retelling is impossible to know.

The Panamanians reacted with shrewdness and zeal. The first of the many heroes of the day was seventy-seven-year-old Colonel James Shaler, the head of the Panama Railroad, who improvised an inspired maneuver to save the revolution. Knowing the new army could easily control any military situation, Shaler used a ruse to separate the commander from his troops. He escorted General Tobar and fifteen of his officers into a special railroad car, promising additional equipment for the troops. Tobar and the officers were whisked to Panama City while the now leaderless troops were left stranded in Colón. Only after Shaler's brilliant maneuver did the *Nashville*'s commander, John Hubbard, receive the message that might have prevented the crisis: "Prevent landing of any hostile force" read the overdue orders from Washington.[47]

The crisis forced Amador's hand. There were too many unexpected troops on the isthmus to put off the revolution any longer. Amador had to choose between postponement or a premature announcement that might end the opportunity. Although American support was in question and the reinforced Colombian garrison was formidable, Amador chose 5 P.M. on November 3 as the time officially to proclaim and begin the revolution. Coolly he proceeded with the grand reception at Panama City for General Tobar, who wondered why his troops had been delayed, not realizing that they had never left Colón. The general's hosts at the Panama City luncheon, Governor Obaldía and United States Vice-Consul General Felix Ehrman were aware that a coup was imminent but not of when it would happen or of the unforeseen crisis. The total American confusion led to a series of telegrams that have caused some historians to argue that the Americans were orchestrating the revolution. The nervous consul at Colón, who wired Washington at 2:35 P.M. to say revolution was "imminent," based his information on the sudden increase of American and Colombian naval activity, not specific local information. His cable was a plea to Washington for news. Assistant Secretary Loomis, anxiously awaiting word in Washington, cabled Ehrman at 4 P.M.: "Uprising on Isthmus reported. Keep department promptly and fully informed." Ehrman replied: "No uprising yet. Reported will be in the night. Situation is critical."[48]

47. *SP*, 388–90; *FRUS*, 1903, p. 248.
48. *SP*, 388–97, 439–59; Felix Ehrman to JH, Francis Loomis to Ehrman, November 3, 1903, both in *SP*, 393; Anguizola, *Philippe Bunau-Varilla*, 251–53; Oscar Malmros to JH, November 4, 5, 1903, in *FRUS*, 1903, pp. 237–38.

The only information the Americans had was Bunau-Varilla's frequently repeated prediction that there would be a revolution on November 3, a date he had chosen to make certain that American ships would appear on the scene to give the appearance of naval support and to ensure—in theory—that Colombian troops would not be landed to quell the revolution. While the Americans were exchanging confused cable messages Amador decided to begin his revolution. By this time the risks, the decisions, and the execution were wholly Panama's. The Americans remained substantially ignorant of what was happening and when. Amador's revolution changed from a comic opera to a serious historical event at 5 P.M. on November 3, 1903. The little doctor presented himself at the headquarters of the Colombian garrison and asked General Esteban Huertas for his surrender: "If you will aid us, you shall reach immortality in the history of the new republic. An American ship has arrived, more were coming. You and your battalion can accomplish nothing against the superior force of the cruisers, which have their orders. Choose here, glory and riches; in Bogatá, misery and ingratitude." The revolution hung in the balance. It was a dramatic moment when a civilian revolutionary using a wild bluff confronted a general with enough troops to quell the revolution, execute the leader, and change the course of isthmian history.[49]

Huertas knew it was his decision, his historic moment in the sun. He paused and then agreed to Amador's offer, beginning Panama's revolution of 1903. Huertas and Amador worked out the expensive details of their accommodation. Huertas was to receive about $50,000, each of his men, $50. Once Huertas had accepted, General Tobar could be dealt with firmly. At 5 P.M., while Tobar and his aides were wondering why their troops remained in Colón, Huertas and his aides arrested Tobar as a crowd began to gather outside the Government house in Panama City. The crowd began shouting, "Viva Amador," and the revolution spread from neutralization of the Colombian army to the people in the streets. Only now with the revolution officially proclaimed and under way did Amador notify the Americans. When Amador told Vice-Consul Ehrman that the revolution was a fact, Ehrman cabled Washington: "Uprising occurred tonight, 6. No

49. Amador quoted in McCullough, *Path Between the Seas*, 368. The most detailed account of the revolution is *ibid.*, 361–77; see *SP*, 456–57; DuVal, *Cadiz to Cathay*, 361–77. For the initial negotiations with Huertas see Mellander, *United States in Panamanian Politics*, 21–22; Joseph L. Arbena, "The Panama Problem in Colombian History" (Ph.D. dissertation, University of Virginia, 1970), 270–71; see also Eduardo Lemaitre, *Panama y su separción de Colombia* (Bogotá, 1971).

bloodshed. Army and Navy officials taken prisoner. Government will be organized tonight."[50]

The success of the revolution was not assured for several days. Even the usually optimistic Bunau-Varilla had moments of doubt while waiting for news from Panama. Panama City had been won, but Colón was controlled by Colonel Eliseo Torres' large force left behind when Tobar went to Panama City. Without control of Colón the insurrection was stalemated: revolutionaries controlled Panama, Colombia controlled Colón, and the United States held the railroad between the two cities. Tense moments occurred when the fifty-man United States landing party from the *Nashville* faced the nearly five hundred Colombian soldiers with rifles drawn. Commander Hubbard, the chief American naval officer at Colón, was careful to maintain his neutrality, even while "advising" and observing the revolutionaries' negotiations with the Colombians. He assured Colonel Torres that although he had relanded American troops, "I had no interest in the affairs of either party; that my attitude was strictly neutral." Hubbard went on to quote what had become the catechism of American isthmian diplomacy: "to maintain the free and uninterrupted transit of the Isthmus . . . by force if necessary."[51]

Finally, James Shaler and Colón Police Chief Porfirio Melindez used bribery, the Panama revolution's most effective weapon, to resolve the stalemate. Torres' price of $8,000 with $20 for each of his men was counted out on the spot in $20 American gold pieces. Tobar should have accepted the junta's offer to confer with Torres in Colón. When he refused, the junta bribed Torres, thereby removing the last vestige of Colombian sovereignty in Panama. The Panamanians, overjoyed at winning without bloodshed, felt no resentment toward the corrupted Colombians. Shaler, ostensibly an American but in spirit and tempera-

50. *SP*, 382, 446–47, 459; McCullough, *Path Between the Seas*, 368–71; Mellander, *United States in Panamanian Politics*, 26–31. There is wide disagreement on the amount of the bribes. The sum for Huertas is $25,000 (E. Taylor Parks, *Colombia and the United States* [Durham, N.C., 1935], 401); $25,000 to $35,000 (Mellander, *United States in Panamanian Politics*, 31); $30,000 (William H. Harbaugh, *The Life and Times of Theodore Roosevelt* [New York, 1975], 203); $50,000 (*SP*, 459); $65,000 (McCullough, *Path Between the Seas*, 369); $80,000 (Pringle, *Theodore Roosevelt*, 328); and $30,000 silver plus $50,000 American gold (Parks, *Colombia and the United States*, 401 n.).

51. John Hubbard to William Moody, November 5, 8, 1903, in *FRUS*, 1903, pp. 268–71. A full account of the *Nashville*'s arrival and the landing of Colombian troops is in DuVal, *Cadiz to Cathay*, 322–24; for the significance of Tobar's refusal see Mack, *Land Divided*, 462. For a detailed account of the crisis at Colón see French Vice-Consul P. Bonhenry to MAE, November 7, 1903, in N.S., Colombia, 5, AMAE.

ment a Panamanian, expressed the ebullience of the revolution when in bidding farewell to Torres and his men he delivered two cases of champagne as an additional gift. The Panamanians kept their word on all the monetary deals. General Huertas received $80,000—more than was originally agreed upon—General Ruben Varón, $35,000, Huertas' aide, Captain Marco A. Salazar, and several other officers, $10,000 each.[52]

The only casualty of the revolution occurred when the government gunboat *Bogatá*, confused by the absence of all its officers, fired wildly on the city, killing a Chinese shopkeeper and a donkey. Not until the garrison of Colombian troops left Colón on the *Orinoco* were the tension and uncertainty dispelled. On November 6 at 10 A.M. the official proclamation of revolution was completed. The Panamanian flag—designed by the revolutionaries and not Madame Bunau-Varilla—was raised and a Declaration of Independence patterned after the original American model was solemnly read. Vice-Consul Ehrman cabled John Hay at 10:40 A.M. of the revolution's success and the appointment of Phillipe Bunau-Varilla as "confidential agent of the Republic of Panama at Washington." At 1 P.M. on November 6, Secretary Hay cabled Ehrman formal American recognition of the new nation. In Panama the bloodless revolution was a happy one. Even the Colombians who had not been bribed wanted no part of the contest. In the midst of the revolution, General Pompillio Guitérrez arrived on a special mission from Bogotá. Informed by another Colombian officer that the revolution was a *fait accompli*, he immediately left with his troops. General Huertas, a rich man and the hero of the moment when Amador proclaimed the revolution, stayed in the Central Hotel with the revolutionaries, "nearly drowned in champagne, the contents of dozens of bottles poured over him."[53]

The usual question—what part did the American naval presence play in making the revolution possible?—must be paired with its historical twin—did the American naval presence prevent previous revolutions in Panama? Obviously, the answer to both questions is the

---

52. *SP*, 394, 446, 456–57, 462; McCullough, *Path Between the Seas*, 374–76; Parks, *Colombia and the United States*, 401.

53. TR, Message to Congress, January 4, 1904, in *FRUS*, 1903, pp. 271–72; Log of *Nashville* in *SP*, 430; log of *Dixie* in *SP*, 435; *BVC*, 344–46; DuVal, *Cadiz to Cathay*, 336–37. A useful guide is Appendix J, "Movements of United States Naval Vessels," in DuVal, *Cadiz to Cathay*, 510–11; Oscar Malmros to JH, November 4, 5, 1903, in *FRUS*, 1903, pp. 237–38; *SP*, 457–58. Naval orders are in *SP*, 382–83; Miner, *Fight for the Panama Route*, 368; *SP*, 453.

same: whoever the Americans backed controlled the isthmus. What was significant in 1903 was not the existence of an American naval force but the twofold shift in American policy, first from alliance with Colombia to neutrality, then from neutrality to alliance with Panama. The change from unquestioned support of Colombia to neutrality causes much of the historical misunderstanding of American involvement in the revolution. After 1855, American naval vessels were always on duty near or at Panama, and at times of insurrection these forces were routinely increased. The American naval presence was not a foreign intrusion but the center of Colombian policy and diplomacy, traditionally serving—at Colombia's behest—as the legal and practical guarantor of Colombian sovereignty over a consistently ambivalent Panama. Aside from a common language, the American naval force constituted the only consistent link between Colombia and Panama. Although Theodore Roosevelt was sympathetic to Panamanian independence, he refused to allow any American intervention before the expected revolution. Roosevelt accurately recalled American policy: "No one connected with the American Government had any part in preparing, inciting, or encouraging the revolution, and except for reports of our military and naval officers . . . no one connected with the government had any previous knowledge concerning the proposed revolution, except such as was accessible to anyone who read the newspapers and kept abreast of current questions and current affairs."[54]

The United States refused to support or recognize the revolution until after it had succeeded. In the Colón confrontations with Colonel Torres' troops, the American forces reacted only to threats against civilians and not in support of the revolutionaries. In defending American neutrality in his January 4, 1904, message to Congress, President Roosevelt noted that there had been only forty-two soldiers on hand when the insurrection occurred, and "at Panama [City], when the revolution broke out, there was no American man-of-war and no American troops or sailors." That the Americans sympathized with the Panamanians was no secret. Nevertheless, the Americans firmly withheld open support of the revolution until the Panamanians had emerged victorious. Panamanian determination, shrewdness, and Amador's own revolutionary eloquence—and the appearance of American help—convinced the Colombian officers not to resist. Once

54. TR, *Autobiography,* in *TRWN,* XX, 511–12.

the revolution was accomplished, Washington gave its complete blessing, providing naval support and instant diplomatic recognition. The cruiser *Boston* sailed from Nicaragua the day before the revolution with specific orders to "prevent landing of any armed force." The *Boston* was ordered to control the city, railroad depot, and harbor by landing artillery and controlling the key access points as recommended by Murphy and Humphrey in their Panama report. The *Dixie* arrived on November 5 and the *Boston* on November 7, the latter's function to bring the news of American recognition to the excited new nation.[55]

The American ships were useful in the long run. They served as a reminder that the revolution did have support, as a warning to Colombia not to reopen hostilities, and as a guarantee of stability to a troubled and unstable region. In 1903, as in the past, the Americans had prevailed with a show of force, not force itself. What changed was not fundamental American policy on the isthmus but the beneficiary of that policy. The United States and its navy remained the guarantor of isthmian sovereignty, but Panama, not Colombia, was the new sovereign in November, 1903.[56]

55. TR to Congress, January 4, 1904, in *FRUS*, 1903, p. 271; Miner, *Fight for the Panama Route*, 368; *SP*, 382–83. The policy of American neutrality in Colombian civil wars was established by Secretary of State William H. Seward in 1865, when he instructed that the Bidlack-Mallarino Treaty guaranteed "the Isthmus against seizure or invasion by a foreign power only. It could not have been contemplated that we were to become a party to any civil war in that country by defending the Isthmus against another party" (Seward to Allan A. Burton, November 9, 1865, cited in AMB to JH, November 9, 1903, in *FRUS*, 1903, p. 227). A dramatic account of the siege of the foreign consuls, civilians, and the Compagnie Nouvelle's employees is in P. Bonhenry to MAE, November 7, 1903, in N.S., Colombie, 5, AMAE.

56. Ameringer, "Philippe Bunau-Varilla," 34. See Arbena, "Panama Problem in Colombian History"; Lester D. Langley, *The Banana Wars: An Inner History of American Empire, 1900–1934* (Lexington, Ky., 1983), 22–26.

10   Resolution, 1903–1904

Philippe Bunau-Varilla's master plan succeeded handsomely. Panama declared its independence from Colombia; the United States recognized and supported the new nation; American newspapers, concentrating on local elections, relegated the news of the revolution to a corner of the front page; and Bunau-Varilla was named Panama's new emissary to negotiate a canal treaty with the United States. Yet its very success carried seeds that would cloud the apparent triumph. Neither Theodore Roosevelt nor John Hay ever understood the bad feeling the Panamanian revolution caused. "How can anyone criticize our action in Panama on the grounds upon which it is ordinarily attacked?" Hay complained in December. Theodore Roosevelt remained moral and resolute: "I did not lift my finger to incite the revolutionists. . . . I simply ceased to stamp out the different revolutionary fuses that were already burning."[1]

Part of the outcry that greeted the news of the convenient revolution originated in the highly partisan Democratic press, which like the New York *Times* castigated "the path of scandal, disgrace, and dishonor." The vocal anti-imperialist minority added to the furor. Within two weeks of the revolution, however, the partisan ranks were broken as some Democratic and even some anti-imperialist papers supported the Roosevelt administration's handling of the volatile situation. As the *Literary Digest* reported, "Journals like the Hartford *Times*, the Buffalo *Express*, and the Philadelphia *North American*, which disapprove of our Philippine policy, regard the Panama policy with favor; and such leading Democratic papers as the Atlanta *Constitution* and the New Orleans *Times-Democrat*, which would rather see Mr. Roosevelt President of Liberia than of this country, support his action in this

1. JH to James Ford Rhodes, December 8, 1903, Hay Papers, LC; TR, *Autobiography* (1913), in *TRWN*, XX, 514.

matter." Both the support and the criticism of the American Panama policy frequently assumed direct American involvement in the revolution and either favored or derided the intervention. Although Roosevelt and Hay continued to insist a narrower moral or legal justification, many Republican papers were wildly jingoistic in their approval of the quick recognition of the new Panama republic.[2]

The major error in Theodore Roosevelt's Panama policy was his ingenious but ultimately unsuccessful use of Bunau-Varilla to orchestrate the revolution without American involvement. By permitting Bunau-Varilla to take the initiative, Roosevelt gave up American control. Bunau-Varilla's intervention clouded the issues, did not absolve the Americans from the appearance of collusion, and—most important—interposed a third party between the Americans and the Panamanians. Roosevelt's expediency reversed a consistent American policy of total opposition to any European participation in an American-controlled canal in Central America. Well before foreign policy was a central concern in American government, the purity of any proposed canal was a paramount foreign policy principle. The first arrangements with Nicaragua in the Arthur administration, the complex negotiations with Britain over ending Clayton-Bulwer's stipulation of joint participation, the Senate's insistence on both the substance and the diction of total American control in refusing to accept Hay-Pauncefote I, and its insistence on isolating the French from the Colombian interests before considering the Panama route, as well as the revival of the Monroe Doctrine, all underlined consistent American nationalism under very different administrations.[3]

The American instincts were sound. First Britain, then France complicated diplomacy between America and Colombia and contributed to Colombia's failure to assess American determination. The Panamanians, who had rejected Bunau-Varilla's constitution and flag, would have rejected his presence as canal treaty negotiator if they could. But Bunau-Varilla had made himself so central to the revolution that Panama could not extricate itself from its unwelcome alliance with him.

2. *LD*, November 14, 1903, pp. 649–51. For detailed summaries of the American press response see *LD*, November 21, 1903, pp. 689–91; Hay's response is in *LD*, November 14, 1903, pp. 649–50. See Alfred Charles Richard, Jr., "The Panama Canal in American National Consciousness, 1870–1922" (Ph.D. dissertation, Boston University, 1969), 171–213.

3. For the evolution from international sponsorship to American insistence on exclusive control see Richard, "Panama Canal in American National Consciousness," 7–105.

The Roosevelt administration, frustrated by the complications of dealing with Colombia and wary of further prolonging the controversial Panama negotiations, decided to use Bunau-Varilla's involvement to facilitate a favorable canal treaty with two major objectives: sure passage in the United States Senate and absolute control in the isthmus. But though the Hay–Bunau-Varilla Treaty was superficially favorable to the United States, it caused more bad feeling and misunderstanding in Latin America than any other part of the Colombian difficulties. The concessions the Americans gained were unnecessary and politically motivated. Hay and Bunau-Varilla's motives were understandable. They wanted a treaty so overwhelmingly favorable to the United States that the Senate would find it irresistible. Although the treaty met this immediate political purpose, its long-range cost in bad feeling, resentment, misunderstanding, and ill will was immense. The Hay–Bunau-Varilla Treaty was a bad bargain both for the United States and Panama.[4]

The normally sophisticated Roosevelt erred in failing to perceive that even a benign European influence was dangerous and should have been avoided at all costs. Philippe Bunau-Varilla made the Panama revolution possible, kept the Americans out of the action, and facilitated the negotiation of a canal treaty, all without bloodshed, but he openly betrayed the Panamanians he ostensibly represented, corrupting their revolution, the previously honorable American canal diplomacy, and Roosevelt's entire Panama policy. Had Roosevelt followed his original inclination, to address a joint session of Congress and give the Senate the choice of unilateral American intervention in Panama or a canal through Nicaragua, he and the Americans would have fared better. Had the Senate followed Roosevelt's strong recommendation to proceed with building the canal "without any further parlay with Colombia," the matter of compensation would have been decided by negotiation, arbitration, or some other inter-

4. Panamanian resistance to Bunau-Varilla's full plenipotentiary powers is discussed in Dwight Carroll Miner, *The Fight for the Panama Route: The Story of the Spooner Act and the Hay-Herrán Treaty* (New York, 1940), 374–75; Gustave Anguizola, *Philippe Bunau-Varilla: The Man Behind the Panama Canal* (Chicago, 1980), 260–61; *BVC*, 353–54, 358–61. For Hay's ambivalance see William D. McCain, *The United States and the Republic of Panama* (Durham, N.C., 1937), 77; *BVC*, 374–75. For a detailed account of Panama's unhappiness with the treaty see McCain, *United States and the Republic of Panama*, 23–45; Miles DuVal, *Cadiz to Cathay: The Story of the Long Diplomatic Struggle for the Panama Canal* (Stanford, 1940), 384–90; *BVC*, 379–86. For the genesis of the treaty and a dramatic revision of Bunau-Varilla's account, see John Major, "Who Wrote the Hay–Bunau-Varilla Convention?" *DH*, VIII (1984), 115–23.

national legal device. Sovereignty would not have been a major issue because Roosevelt's international waterway would not have involved a painful change in existing sovereignty, as did American recognition of Panamanian independence. No doubt the outcry of imperialism would have been just as strong and the partisan press on both sides equally vituperative. But there would have been no third party acting independently of the vital interests of either Colombia, Panama, or the United States. Although bold and unique, Roosevelt's action would not have had the appearance of subterfuge that clouded Bunau-Varilla's convenient Panamanian revolution. Eventually a more balanced treaty arrangement would have resulted with whichever Latin American state held sovereignty over the canal zone. The abdication by the Americans and Panamanians of their own best interests to a Frenchmen, who acted for his own perceived national, practical, and moral interests, helped make Roosevelt's canal policy superficially successful but historically unpalatable.[5]

The revolution in Panama profoundly shocked Colombia, and its loss eventually helped unify the nation in a common sense of tragedy and made possible the emergence of a nationalism that nineteenth-century Colombia did not want and could not achieve. At the first news Colombians acted in anger and fear, not against Panama or the Americans but against President Marroquín. Minister Beaupré reported shortly after the news of the Panama revolution reached Bogotá, "Very great excitement here. Large crowds paraded streets yesterday [November 8], crying 'down with Marroquín.' Mass meeting denounced him; called for a change in government. Hundreds gathered at the palace, and their orator, a prominent national general, addressed the President, calling for his resignation. Troops dispersed gathering, wounding several. Martial law is declared here, and the city is being guarded by soldiers." There were additional demonstra-

5. Roosevelt's original policy is described in TR, "Colombia: The Proposed Message to Congress," in *Autobiography*, in *TRWN*, XX, Appendix B, 549–50; see "The Suppressed Panama Message," *LD*, November 28, 1903, p. 727. For Colombian views of Bunau-Varilla see Joseph Luther Arbena, "The Panama Problem in Colombian History" (Ph.D. dissertation, University of Virginia, 1970), 272–73; Charles D. Ameringer, "Philippe Bunau-Varilla: New Light on the Panama Canal Treaty," *AHR*, XLVI (1966), 28–52. For the Panamanian description of the "Bunau-Varilla sellout," see Frank Otto Gatell, "The Canal in Retrospect—Some Panamanian and Colombian Views," *Americas*, XV (July, 1958), 25. For the lingering distaste for the "Frenchman's treaty," see Walter LaFeber, *The Panama Canal: The Crisis in Historical Perspective* (Rev. ed.; New York, 1979), 38–39. For the guarded French diplomatic response to Bunau-Varilla's participation see Jean Jules Jusserand to MAE, November 8, 1903, N.S., Colombie, 5, AMAE.

tions against Lorenzo Marroquín's residence, which was stoned, but none against the heavily guarded American legation.[6]

General Rafael Reyes's official response to the news was dramatic and equally shocking. On November 6, Reyes offered either to approve the Hay-Herrán Treaty as signed "by decree," or, if the United States preferred, to "call extra session of Congress with new and friendly members next May to approve the treaty." The Americans had heard similar offers before, especially with the customary Colombian hedge that "this is the personal opinion of Reyes, and he will advise this government to act accordingly." At this stage the Colombians were grasping at straws. Reyes's proposal that the United States restore the status quo and allow Colombia to regain sovereignty in Panama with the aid of American troops was absurd. Beaupré's dispatch that "there is great reaction of public opinion in favor of the treaty, and it is considered certain that the treaty was not legally rejected by Congress" confirmed the American view of Colombia's ability to reverse its policies at will and further horrified the Americans.[7]

Theodore Roosevelt was seriously scarred by the acrimonious diplomacy with Colombia, which frustrated his main objective of extricating the United States from European influence by eliminating any pretext for European intervention in the Caribbean area. Constricted by the megalomaniacal dedication of Senator John Tyler Morgan to a Nicaraguan canal route and by his desire to make the United States a major power in image as well as substance, Roosevelt was further restricted by his understanding of the immense technological superiority of the Panama route. The best solution in the long negotiations with Colombia, France, and the Senate lay in a negotiated settlement with Colombia for Panama. Roosevelt made many more concessions to get Colombia's consent than he is commonly given credit for. When all the concessions led to naught, a frustrated Roosevelt determined that Colombia had to be punished for its apparent greed, frivolity, and dishonesty in its dealings with the Americans.[8]

6. AMB to JH, November 9, 1903, in *FRUS*, 1903, p. 227; see Arbena, "Panama Problem in Colombian History," 65–83.

7. AMB to JH, November 6, 1903, in *FRUS*, 1903, p. 225; for the next day's modification of Reyes's offer see AMB to JH, November 7, 1903, *ibid.*, 226; E. Taylor Parks, *Colombia and the United States, 1765–1934* (Durham, N.C., 1935), 403.

8. For Morgan's single-mindedness see Richard, "Panama Canal in American National Consciousness," 120–21, 156–59; for the Republican choice of "killing the treaty or killing Morgan," see *Nation*, LXXVI (1903), 219. See TR, "How the United States Acquired the Right to Dig the Panama Canal," *Outlook*, XCIX, October 7, 1911, pp. 315–

Roosevelt's new policy of acting like a great power precluded turning the other cheek when U.S. honor was challenged or its Senate openly rebuffed. When Colombia's Senate unanimously rejected the Hay-Herrán Treaty, it threw down the gauntlet to both the U.S. Senate and President. Roosevelt had invested too much of his own prestige in the Panama route and a Colombian settlement to withstand the Colombian Senate's unanimous rejection of the treaty. That Colombia was acting against its own best interests or stupidly was scant comfort for a governing president seeking reelection or a nation sensitive to any questions about its New World status.[9]

Colombia's extreme reaction influenced Roosevelt's solution. One cannot predict whether a mild modification of Colombia's policy might have influenced Roosevelt, but certainly the Colombian Senate's best course in the face of its genuine opposition to the Hay-Herrán Treaty was to adopt an amended treaty, even one grossly unacceptable to the Americans. The Colombians were clearly more interested in embarrassing their own leader, José Marroquín, by their rejection of the treaty, but they embarrassed Theodore Roosevelt at least as much and made some manner of retribution almost inevitable, not as a matter of personal pique but of practical national policy. Sovereign nations may squabble or disagree violently, but once a treaty is negotiated and the proceedings become matters of public record, normal diplomatic conventions of common courtesy must be followed, and under any circumstances, 24-to-0 rebuffs must be avoided. Such overwhelming disapproval leaves nothing to negotiate, and diplomacy can do little to repair the political breach. Even Senator Caro, Marroquín's and the United States' strongest opponent, admitted in the closing moments

16; TR to Cecil Spring Rice, November 9, 1903, in *MRL*, III, 651. Support for Roosevelt's contention is in Colombian historian Eduardo Lemaitre, *Reyes* (Bogotá, 1952), 202, who describes Colombia's rejection of the Hay-Herrán Treaty as "brutal," "unrealistic," based on a "disastrous misunderstanding of the international reality" and an "exacerbated juridical romanticism" (quoted in Arbena, "Panama Problem in Colombian History," 236).

9. For differing conclusions about the effect of the 1904 presidential election on Roosevelt's Panama policies see Anguizola, *Philippe Bunau-Varilla*, 235; and William H. Harbaugh, *The Life and Times of Theodore Roosevelt* (New York, 1975), 205. See William H. Becker, "1899–1920: America Adjusts to World Power," in Becker and Samuel F. Wells (eds.), *Economics and World Power: An Assessment of American Diplomacy Since 1789* (New York, 1984), 188–95. For U.S. fears of European temptation from Colombia's weakness see Richard L. Lael, *Arrogant Diplomacy: U.S. Foreign Policy Toward Colombia, 1903–1922* (Wilmington, Del., 1987), xii.

of the Colombian Senate session on October 27, 1903, that the insulting conduct of that body was damaging to Colombia.[10]

On October 10, Roosevelt clearly understood his options: "The alternatives were to go to Nicaragua, against the advice of the great majority of competent engineers—some of the most competent saying that we had better have no canal at this time than go there—or else take the territory by force without any attempt at getting a treaty. I cast aside the proposition made at this time to foment the secession of Panama. Whatever other governments can do, the United States cannot go into the securing by such underhand means, the secession. Privately, I freely say to you that I should be delighted if Panama were an independent state, or if it made it so at this moment; but for me to say so publicly would amount to an instigation of a revolt, and therefore I cannot say it." Roosevelt mistakenly thought that fulfilling the American wish for Panamanian independence through Bunau-Varilla shielded the United States and the Roosevelt administration from responsibility. He would spend a great deal of his future energy defending that misjudgment.[11]

When the news of the successful Panama revolution reached the White House on November 4, 1903, Roosevelt wrote one of his "posterity letters"—a statement clearly made for the historical record—on his position. "For half a century we have policed that Isthmus in the interest of the little wildcat republic of Colombia. Colombia has behaved infamously about the treaty for the building of the Panama Canal; and I do not intend in the police work that I will have to do in connection with the new insurrection any longer to do for her work which is not merely profitless but brings no gratitude. Any interference I undertake now will be in the interest of the United States and of the people of the Panama Isthmus themselves." Roosevelt knew that his Panama policies would produce "some lively times" and some "checks," but he was confident of putting "it through all right."[12]

10. For the political popularity of Roosevelt's Panama policy see cartoons such as "Held Up the Wrong Man," *Harper's Weekly*, November 21, 1903 (full page), and "To Spite His Own Face," New York *World*, part of the overwhelming press support cited in Richard, "Panama Canal in American National Consciousness," 171–78; AMB to JH, November 2, 1903, *FRUS*, 1903, pp. 219–20.

11. TR to Albert Shaw, October 10, 1903, in *MRL*, III, 628.

12. TR to Kermit Roosevelt, November 4, 1903, in *MRL*, III, 644.

The nucleus of Roosevelt's policy was already in place by November 5, when the Baltimore *Evening Sun*'s correspondent described the administration's views through an interview with an authoritative "source of the highest responsibility . . . who is never quoted in newspaper interviews." Significant in the American list of grievances was the disappointment of expectations arising from the U.S. intercession that produced the Treaty of *Wisconsin*, ending the long Colombian civil war in November, 1902. Washington rarely referred to the *Wisconsin* treaty in formal statements, possibly to deemphasize the large role naval diplomacy had begun to play in American foreign policy. The United States clearly believed that the peace settlement that ended the War of the Thousand Days removed the last obstacle to a satisfactory canal treaty. On November 5, the administration source in outlining the American choices unveiled the tentative diction of the new policy. The legal support of the right of transit, central to the Bidlack-Mallarino Treaty of 1846, was essential to any American legitimacy in the isthmus, but the alliance with Colombia had become an increasingly troublesome liability. Ingeniously the source suggested that the United States could continue to honor the Bidlack-Mallarino Treaty guaranteeing the safe transit of the isthmus—but without "construing it with reference to the interests of Colombia alone." Because the constant "throat-cutting" on the isthmus raised the question of whether U.S. authority should continue to be used against Panama, "which was at one time independent and has always desired to be so," the United States could come out of its critical shift of alliance supporting all good things—treaties, peace, self-determination of a previously subject people—while simultaneously punishing errant Colombia.[13]

John Bassett Moore's original arguments favoring unilateral isthmian intervention were adapted to the new context of recognizing an independent Panama. When diplomat and lawyer Oscar Straus suggested to Roosevelt at lunch on November 6 the idea of a legal "covenant running with the land," and Roosevelt asked Straus to explain the idea to Secretary Hay, it became one of the key arguments in the American policy statement Hay gave to the press the next day. Straus's covenant idea reinforced Moore's legal opinions and made the Ameri-

13. Baltimore *Evening Sun*, November 6, 1903, in John Bassett Moore Scrapbooks (JBMS), Box 250, John Bassett Moore Papers, LC. French Vice-Consul Emile Gey cited the peace Treaty of *Wisconsin* in his assessment of the growth of Panama's separatist sentiment, Gey to MAE November 8, 1903, in N.S., Colombie, 5, AMAE.

can policy of shifting its alliance from Colombia to Panama appear to be a matter of principle as well as convenience. Hay's statement argued that the guarantee of transit in the isthmus was independent of sovereignty and that the 1846 treaty gave the United States an implied right to build a canal. In the gospel according to Hay, Panama's despair over continuing its "connection with the Colombian Government, which had never proved entirely satisfactory," led to the quick revolution. The suddenness of the separation was not attributable to help from the United States but to the nature of Spanish America: "They went to work with their talent for prompt and secret organization to which there is no parallel among people of Northern blood; they prepared the machinery of revolution in advance, and suddenly, in a single day, without the firing of a shot . . . they accomplished their independence." The United States thus was intervening for "the imperative demands of the interests of civilization," to end "the incessant civil contests and bickerings which have been for so many years the curse of Panama," and in the interests of peace, commerce, Colombia, and Panama, and to preserve free transit in the isthmus.[14]

Although the arguments that Hay advanced had already been discussed many times in the nation's press, the knowledgeable *Evening Sun* was surprised at the speed of Roosevelt's policy decision. Roosevelt, confident in his own integrity, had already made Colombia the transgressor. He exulted in Albert Shaw's metaphor of "cutting off the dog's tail by inches" in reference to the separation of Panama from mainland Colombia. "Colombia's grip on Panama is gone forever," Roosevelt declared privately. Colombia "signed its own death warrant when they acted in such infamous bad faith about the signing of the treaty." Hay's official statement complained that Colombia not only rejected the Hay-Herrán Treaty unanimously but did so "without consideration." The Americans were aggrieved by Colombian rudeness, apparent Colombian greed, and the incessant delay and uncertainty. American self-righteousness, however, was inappropriate. The Americans were publicly admitting to having maintained Panama's unwilling subjection as long as Colombia cooperated in the proposed canal project. So many volatile issues were raised by the Panamanian revolution that the gratuitous slur about South America's gift

14. TR to JH, November 6, 1903, with Straus memorandum, November 6, 1903; TR to JBM, November 7, 1903, both in *MRL*, III, 648–50. See David S. Patterson, *Toward a Warless World: The Travail of the American Peace Movement, 1887–1914* (Bloomington, Ind., 1976), 123–25.

for quick revolutions and the long-standing American policy of sub-
verting what had suddenly become Panama's historical tradition of independence were mostly ignored.[15]

Colombia's reaction to the American shift of alliance was both threatening and ineffectual. Although expeditions of a thousand troops
each were prepared for dispatch to Colón and Panama City, once the
United States publicly supported Panama Colombia had no realistic
military or naval options. The United States could control any possible confrontation. Colombia's combination of military pressure and
diplomatic demands for restoration of the status quo reflected a mixture of fear, bluster, and ignorance. In truth, Colombia, shocked and
disbelieving at the loss of Panama without any compensation, had no
idea what to do. Its alternating rhythms of threats and offers of compromise represented dismay and doubt more than any rational strategy. In early November, Reyes still hoped that Panama's revolution
could be reversed and negotiations reopened with the Americans.
Not until the new year did Colombia give up its hopes of reconciliation and turn to the strategy of legal redress and political martyrdom
that seventeen years later proved successful.[16]

Roosevelt keenly felt the turbulence that threatened a war with Colombia and hampered negotiation of a new canal treaty with Panama.
"The entire fool mugwump crowd have fairly suffered from hysterics;
and a goodly number of the Senators even of my own party have
shown as much backbone as so many angle worms," Roosevelt complained in a letter to his son Ted on November 15. Roosevelt compared his "interesting time with Panama and Colombia" with Lincoln's
Civil War crises. "When I see how panic-struck Senators, businessmen and everybody else become from any little flourish of trouble,
and the wild clamor they all raise for foolish or cowardly action," he
could sympathize with Lincoln after Bull Run and other setbacks,
Roosevelt confided to his son. Roosevelt resisted some of the pressures but not all of them. His attitude toward Colombia was both violent and ambivalent. Colombia was "not merely corrupt. They are
governmentally utterly incompetent." The main trouble, Roosevelt
felt, was not Colombia's greed but its indecision—"they would not or

15. Baltimore *Evening Sun*, November 7, 1903, in JBMS; TR to Albert Shaw, November 6, 1903, in *MRL*, III, 649.
16. Joseph L. Arbena, "Colombian Reactions to the Independence of Panama, 1903–
1904," *Americas*, XXXIII (July, 1976); Arbena, "Panama Problem in Colombian History,"
109–11.

could not act on any terms." On reflection, Roosevelt was more disappointed and puzzled than angry: "The treaty we offered them went further in their interests than we by rights ought to have gone, and it would have given them a stability and power such as no other Spanish-American republic possessed between Mexico and Chile. But in spite of the plainest warnings they persisted in slitting their own throats from ear to ear." [17]

Bunau-Varilla had successfully manipulated Roosevelt and Amador, but he could not budge Senator John Tyler Morgan. Hoping to defuse a bitter partisan political battle over a new canal treaty, Bunau-Varilla pleaded with Morgan to transcend the old enmity over rival canal routes and join in an alliance. Bunau-Varilla flattered the senator's "indomitable will," surely a felicitous euphemism for dogged stubbornness, and explained the two men's substantial differences as purely generational:

I entered the field of active life about one-third of a century after you. . . . The solution which was a better one fifty years ago, when there was scarcely any ship drawing more than 17ft. of water, has gradually seen its superiority vanish and transformed into a marked inferiority owing to the steady increase of the draft and length of ships. . . . These gradual and scarcely noticeable changes in the technical necessities of the waterway are accountable for the differences between you, the champion of the solution of the middle of the nineteenth century [Nicaragua], and the champions of the solution of the beginning of the twentieth [Panama].

Bunau-Varilla's charm and tact were unavailing. Morgan, whom Bunau-Varilla called the "Father of the Isthmian Canal" and offered "the laurels of the victory that is yours," not only rejected Bunau-Varilla's overtures but used the letter to accuse Bunau-Varilla of acting as a foreign agent and interfering with American domestic politics. [18]

Without Morgan's cooperation any easy resolution of the canal issue was doomed. Partisan politics, not quiet statesmanship, dictated the new treaty with Panama. Democrats eagerly launched their presidential ambitions with the mistaken notion that Roosevelt was politically vulnerable on the Panama issue; General Reyes made common cause with American antiadministration forces while continuing

17. TR to TRJR, November 15, 1903; to Cecil Spring Rice, November 9, 1903, both in *MRL*, III, 651–52.
18. Philippe Bunau-Varilla to John Tyler Morgan, November 9, 1903, in *BVC*, 356; see also *BVC*, 356–68.

to escalate Colombia's military buildup; and Panama sought to take control of its own destinies from its French foreign minister. In response, Philippe Bunau-Varilla, seeking to complete his work before either the Reyes Commission arrived or Panama could negotiate its own canal treaty, approved a quick and thoroughly expedient treaty designed to mollify the extremists in the American Senate.[19]

John Hay, who was not in good health or good spirits, complained in a letter to his daughter on November 19, "As for your poor old dad, they are working him nights and Sundays. I have never, I think, been so constantly and actively employed as during the last fortnight." Drafting a new treaty with Panama began almost as soon as the revolution ended. Hay and Bunau-Varilla met for lunch on November 9; the first extant American draft was completed by November 10 and dispatched by Hay to Secretary of War Elihu Root and Senator John Spooner. Hay, Attorney General Philander C. Knox, and Spooner all revised the project before Bunau-Varilla received his first draft. Although Bunau-Varilla in recounting his own influence in writing the Hay–Bunau-Varilla Treaty claimed that the draft he received from John Hay on November 15 was "the Hay-Herrán Treaty with insignificant modifications" and with the indemnity figure blank, the American draft differed substantially from the failed Colombian treaty. Only ten of the original twenty-eight Hay-Herrán articles remained unchanged, three were deleted, and fifteen were modified in varying degrees. The original ten-kilometer canal zone was increased to ten miles, the previously shared judicial jurisdiction was made entirely American, and a number of islands that had been excluded from the American canal zone were included.[20]

That the treaty with Panama was far different from the Hay-Herrán Treaty with Colombia is hardly surprising. Panama, which owed its

19. August C. Radke, Jr., "John Tyler Morgan: An Expansionist Senator, 1877–1907" (Ph.D. dissertation, University of Washington, 1953), 471–73; DuVal, *Cadiz to Cathay*, 345–58; Lael, *Arrogant Diplomacy*, 14–15.

20. JH to Helen Hay Whitney, November 19, 1903, in William R. Thayer, *The Life and Letters of John Hay* (2 vols.; Boston, 1915), II, 318. The first draft of the treaty is in JH to ER, November 10, 1903, Elihu Root Papers, LC; other drafts are in *Drafts of Treaties*, IV (Isthmus Countries to Italy), pp. 54–55, RG 59, NA; Bunau-Varilla's account is in *BVC*, 368; Major, "Who Wrote the Hay–Bunau-Varilla Convention?" 115–23, is essential. Philip Jessup, *Elihu Root* (2 vols.; New York, 1938), 406, describes Hay's letter to Root of November 10, 1903, asking for Root's "emendations." See also Tyler Dennett, *John Hay: From Poetry to Politics* (New York, 1933), 381–83; Kenton J. Clymer, *John Hay: The Gentleman as Diplomat* (Ann Arbor, 1975), 205–209; DuVal, *Cadiz to Cathay*, 379–84; Miner, *Fight for the Panama Route*, 375–78; and *BVC*, 358–60.

independence to an American alliance, was in the weakest possible bargaining position. More important was the menacing presence of Senator John Tyler Morgan, who was expected to fight his last battle against a Panama canal with all the resources of an old and experienced Senate orator. The State Department's first text was an annotated draft of Morgan's once rejected amendments to the Hay-Herrán Treaty, which now served as the basis for the revision of that treaty and the new agreement with Panama. Roosevelt, under severe attack over the suspected American involvement in the Panamanian revolution and with Bunau-Varilla, had to ensure that Morgan did not gain enough senatorial allies to block the new treaty and postpone or cancel the prospect of a Panama canal. The new treaty had to be overwhelmingly favorable to the United States to assure Senate approval. John Hay, searching for a middle ground, suggested to Bunau-Varilla that the $10 million to be paid to Panama be divided between Colombia and Panama, a gesture that for all its good intentions might have inflamed both nations equally. Hay's halfhearted attempt to compromise may have reflected the political influence of some senators rather than his own preference.[21]

Bunau-Varilla substantially changed Hay's draft but not nearly as radically as he suggested in his account. Bunau-Varilla's modifications were written in two days with the help of New York attorney Frank Pavey, whose indiscreet boasts to the press about his work irritated John Hay. Not all of these modifications were favorable to the United States. Bunau-Varilla restored Colón and Panama City to Panama, reinstituted the eventual reversion of land to Panama, and limited the American right to develop the canal commercially. He did, however, accept twenty-three of Hay's twenty-seven articles and made minor changes favoring the United States in the four remaining articles. These substantive changes were bad enough, but the diction was worse—especially the most heavily revised third article. Given the enormous sensitivity of Colombians and Panamanians to the question of sovereignty, a stipulation that the United States had rights "as if it were the sovereign . . . to the entire exclusion of the exercise by the Republic of Panama of any such sovereign rights, power or authority," was inflammatory, unnecessary, and offensive.[22]

21. The Morgan draft is in *Drafts of Treaties*, IV; *BVC*, 368; see Major, "Who Wrote the Hay–Bunau-Varilla Convention?" 119, for a summary of the American changes.
22. *Drafts of Treaties*, IV; Major, "Who Wrote the Hay–Bunau-Varilla Convention?" 120–21; Philippe Bunau-Varilla to JH, November 16, 1903, in *BVC*, 370; *BVC*, 368–70.

Bunau-Varilla made no pretense of representing Panama's wishes. He openly regarded the Panamanians as rivals and worked feverishly to complete the treaty before Panama's Canal Commission, headed by Amador and Federico Boyd, a prominent Panamanian revolutionary, arrived in Washington. Both Hay and Bunau-Varilla feared that long, drawn-out negotiations with the Panamanians might make the Senate debate even more volatile. Piqued that the Panamanian delegation had stopped in New York to see Cromwell first, Bunau-Varilla was as vengeful toward the Panamanians as he was wary of Senator Morgan. He adamantly opposed Hay's suggestion that Panama and Colombia share the $10 million American indemnity (what the French had called a concession payment), a proposal that compounded American insensitivity to the new Panama republic and was probably intended to soften Senate sympathy for Colombia. Bunau-Varilla insisted that any payment to Colombia would constitute "blackmail" or conscience money for a "concealed crime." Latin America, Bunau-Varilla insisted, would look upon a payment to Colombia as an "insulting offer of a little money compensation for a patriotic wrong," and it would be construed as an admission of guilt, a view that was both patronizing and inaccurate. On November 16, Assistant Secretary of State Francis Loomis indicated to the British that the Americans were willing to divide the money, but Bunau-Varilla's arguments ended any such plan.[23]

Hay discussed Bunau-Varilla's amendments with Root, Knox, and Secretary of the Treasury Leslie Shaw and accepted all but one change. Following the American preference for control, Hay substituted a grant in perpetuity and occupation for Bunau-Varilla's proposed lease and landlord relationship. On November 18, after keeping Bunau-Varilla in doubt about whether his latest changes would be accepted, Hay signed the last revised draft with ceremony. Although Bunau-Varilla later claimed that his draft was preferable because it was cleansed of the circuitous Colombian diction of José Concha, "who never wished to accede to anything in one article without withdrawing it in the next one," both Hay's and Bunau-Varilla's final drafts owed more to a possible Senate revolt against Roosevelt, Panama, and the president's activist foreign policy than to Colombia. Bunau-Varilla observed that without Colombia's many qualifying particulars, the new treaty "offers less probability of eventual discussion

23. *BVC*, 370–76; Major, "Who Wrote the Hay–Bunau-Varilla Convention?" 122–23; Loomis' remarks are in Arthur S. Raikes to Lord Lansdowne, November 16, 1903, FO 420/210, p. 64, PRO.

between the two countries." The simplicity of Bunau-Varilla's draft, however, owed as much to the granting of every American Senate wish as to its style or format. In his only known communication at the time, Bunau-Varilla correctly identified his own work in the new treaty as the first seven articles. In truth, the drafting process was a close collaboration between Hay, his advisers, and Bunau-Varilla, all working under the threat of John Tyler Morgan's determined Senate opposition.[24]

When Amador and Federico Boyd, members of Panama's mission to help negotiate the new canal treaty, arrived in Washington, they were aghast when Bunau-Varilla, furious that the Panamanians had stopped first in New York to see Cromwell, told them he had already signed the treaty. Bunau-Varilla convinced the disappointed Panamanians that if they tried to renegotiate a treaty already on its way to the Senate, the United States would withdraw its legal and naval protection. Ironically, Colombia's continuing threats against Panama gave Bunau-Varilla's lame threat a momentary plausibility.[25]

Colombia's counterattacks were immediately frightening but ultimately self-defeating. A clumsy attempt to involve Europe in the dispute proved as futile as the well-publicized military preparations. On November 9, Colombia's consul in New York announced a plan to offer Germany land concessions on both the Pacific and Atlantic oceans in return for a German protectorate over Panama. But Colombia's history of cavalier diplomacy had left it without friends or allies. Italy remembered Colombia's refusal to recognize President Grover Cleveland's "ill-advised" decision in Italy's favor though both nations had chosen Cleveland as an impartial arbitrator. The Mexican government journal *Imparcial* blamed Colombia for its shortsightedness and lack of respect for the isthmians' interests, declaring, "Colombia has reaped what she sowed." Fears of growing American influence in both Europe and Latin America tempered the favorable response to Panamanian independence, but for Colombia there was no support or sympathy. Herrán knew Colombia's weak position well. Not only would the new Panama be recognized, but "this recognition . . . will

24. *BVC*, 370–77; Major, "Who Wrote the Hay–Bunau-Varilla Convention?" 123; English and Spanish texts in *Senate Documents*, 63rd Cong., 2nd Sess., No. 474, Serial 6582, pp. 295–313. A useful guide to the two treaties is Ricardo J. Alfaro, "Comparative Table," listing the principal differences in the two canal treaties, in DuVal, *Cadiz to Cathay*, Appendix L, 513–14.

25. *BVC*, 379–86.

come with the good wishes of the European powers; since the scandals which we persist in giving deprive us of the sympathy of the civilized world." Even in Latin America, Colombia had "alienated the sympathy of our sister American republics, and we remain alone, absolutely alone."[26]

Colombia's mission to win back the allegiance of Panamanians, headed by Rafael Reyes, was equally unsuccessful. Reyes, Colombia's most gifted leader, remained remarkably unrealistic about Colombia's ability to win friends, most glaringly in Panama itself. Reyes proposed visiting Panama to dissuade the revolutionaries from separation, an incredibly naive undertaking, though even as late as July, 1903, Panama had been sharply divided over a canal. Spenser Dickson, the British vice-consul in Bogotá, an articulate independent observer, described Panama's prerevolution divisions. The

enlightened party, consisting of the more educated classes, engaged in commerce on a large scale, and comprising nearly all the foreign element in the Department . . . is represented by Senator Obaldía, and is for the construction of the Canal at all costs, including secession and the assumption of an independent sovereignty. There is also a large body of . . . lower middle and poorer classes, who . . . have no sympathy with the larger issues, on which they prefer to adopt a *laissez faire* attitude. They have all the chauvinism and hatred of the foreigner so prevalent in other departments of Colombia, and are for the union at all costs.

After the revolution, Panama was solidly united and neither the Americans nor the Panamanians feared Reyes's visit, realizing that his presence would publicly confirm the solidarity of the Panamanian decision for separation. Reyes, who was barred from going ashore, met with a delegation of Panama's new government on board the neutral French ship *Canada* on November 19. The United States not only allowed the visit but encouraged Reyes, offering the American warship *Mayflower* as the site of the meeting and urging "a courteous reception and a considerate hearing" for the Colombian leader.[27]

26. For Germany see Baltimore *Evening Sun*, November 9, 1903; for Italy see New York *Times*, November 9, 1903, both in JBMS; for Mexico see the Panama *Star and Herald*, November 11, 1903; Tomás Herrán to Vicente Hurtado, November 11, 1903, Herrán to Autoro Brigard, November 22, 1903, both in Tómas Herrán Papers, Special Collections Division, Georgetown University Library, Washington, D.C.

27. For Reyes's mission see DuVal, *Cadiz to Cathay*, 358–61; Dickson memorandum, September 15, 1903, in FO 420/210, pp. 35–37, PRO. For the relatively small opposition to independence see G. F. Rothwinger to Lord Lansdowne, November 11, 1903, FO

When the Reyes Commission reached the United States, it became clear that even the most enlightened of Bogotá's political leaders had only a murky understanding of the Colombian-American conflict or Colombia's realistic options. Herrán observed that the Reyes party had "very erroneous ideas regarding the situation here. . . . 'What might have been' is now the burthen of their song." Reyes began to evolve Colombia's most promising strategy, international martyrdom and demands for legal redress of grievances, while Colombia continued to threaten both Panama and the United States with military action. A confused Reyes added to the tension by boasting to newsmen on his arrival by boat in New Orleans that Panama's army of 200 men was no match for Colombia's 250,000. Only after seeing President Roosevelt, Reyes told the newsmen, would his commission learn whether they "are peace or war commissioners." Some American papers used the visit of the Reyes mission for sensationalist stories; others like the Baltimore *Evening Sun* observed that the Reyes party "seemed well supplied with newly minted Colombian gold."[28]

As the ominous naval and military buildup continued, both sides became increasingly nervous. Roosevelt was concerned with the distinct possibility of full-scale war with Colombia. When Reyes—citing Colombia's right under the Bidlack-Mallarino Treaty of 1846—asked permission to land troops in Panama, Rear Admiral Joseph B. Coghlan, the American commander there, refused the request on November 21. Although Reyes agreed to suspend hostilities, minor naval incidents kept tension high. On December 3, the United States Army caught the war fever and, using disguised officers supplied with code names, established a secret observation mission near the border at Yavisa to guard against surprise attack. The War Department warned Admirals Henry Glass (at Panama) and Joseph Coghlan (at Colón) of "fears lest Colombia forces may advance on the Isthmus by land." On December 8, 1903, Admiral Walker reassured a nervous War Department that the Americans had "a sufficient number of troops here. No

420/210, p. 72. For the American meeting with the Reyes Commission see Rear Admiral Joseph B. Coghlan to Navy Department, November 17, 23, 1903, in Letters Sent to the Navy Department, Records of Naval Operating Forces, Caribbean Squadron, RG 313, entry 61, NA; and Albert C. Gleaves, Diary, 1902–04, Box 3; and chap. XI, Gleaves's autobiography draft, Box 12, both in Albert C. Gleaves Papers, LC.

28. Tomás Herrán to L. H. Andrews, December 9, 1903, Herrán Papers; DuVal, *Cadiz to Cathay*, 398–400; Baltimore *Evening Sun*, November 27, 1903. Reyes's troop figures varied wildly. He told the New York *World* reporter that Colombia would match 500,000 troops against Panama's 2,000.

probability of force advancing on Panama until after dry season has set in next month."[29]

On November 13, 1903, the United States formally recognized the new Republic of Panama. Roosevelt's message of recognition defended the new American policy toward Panama and argued for wide international recognition of the new state. In affirming "the act of the ancient territory of Panama in reasserting the right of self-control," Roosevelt cited the "opposed expression of the will of the people," a key consideration for international recognition. In response, Colombia asked all Latin American nations to refuse recognition and to join in a concert against American imperialism. American imperialism has always been a popular issue in Latin America, and Colombia's plea should have achieved a substantial measure of success solely on its political appeal. Its failure revealed a deep Latin American division on the Panama issue. Several Latin American governments went out of their way to reassure the United States of their support. On November 20, Brazil not only approved the American recognition of Panama, it formally rejected Colombia's plea for a Latin American boycott. Chile, a frequent American diplomatic adversary, resisted Colombian entreaties and supported the canal though without enthusiasm. The major Latin American nations, the ABC powers of Argentina, Brazil, and Chile, recognized Panama's new government by March, 1904. Many of the smaller Latin American countries indicated unofficial support of the United States and rejection of Colombia but wanted to wait for the ABC powers' reaction before proceeding officially. The Latin American press was equally supportive and temperate in its reaction to Panama's revolution. The *Literary Digest* on December 26, 1903, reported that "opponents of President Roosevelt's Panama policy who may have been counting upon an explosion of indignation throughout South America will, perhaps, be disappointed." Colombia's appeal "to take arms against 'the aggressor' from the north has been to a considerable extent ignored."[30]

---

29. Rear Admiral Joseph B. Coghlan to Rafael Reyes, November 21, 1903, in *SP*, 487; Rear Admiral John G. Walker to William Moody, December 8, 1903, in *SP*, 488; *SP*, 487–92.

30. John Patterson, "Latin American Reaction to the Panama Revolution of 1903," *HAHR*, XXIV (1944), 342–51; "South American Press on the Isthmus Coup," *LD*, December 26, 1903, p. 909; Louis E. Van Norman, "Latin-American Views of Panama and the Canal," *American Review of Reviews*, March, 1904, p. 335; E. Bradford Burns, "The Recognition of Panama by the Major Latin American States," *Americas*, XXVI (1969), 3–14.

Colombia also failed to convince Europe of its legitimate claim to sovereignty over Panama. The French recognized the new Republic of Panama on November 16. When Colombia's New York consul suggested a German protectorate for Panama on November 9, the German Foreign Office declared that such a proposal "would not be entertained for one moment," adding, "we hope to see our trade prosper better after the United States builds the canal." Britain was more concerned about Panama's share of Colombia's indebtedness and its Council of Foreign Bondholders' claims against Colombia than about the question of recognition. Lansdowne avoided offending the bondholders by ignoring their request. "Considering how averse the United States government are to act with any European government in American affairs," he asked Ambassador Sir Mortimer Durand to raise the matter unofficially with Hay. Colombia's diplomatic offensive fizzled completely because governments worried more about offending the United States than supporting Colombia. Even Latin American nations frequently at odds with the United States refused to support Colombia. After ascertaining that Britain would recognize Panama, Chile formally objected to Colombia's assertion that Chile opposed ratification of the Hay-Herrán Treaty. The Chilean minister in Bogotá informed the British that Chile favored a Panama canal: "This work of civilization . . . was impossible to obstruct, and Chile, like other countries, must endeavor to see how she could derive the greatest benefit from the new water-way." [31]

Later in November, China, Austria-Hungary, and Germany recognized Panama. In early December, Denmark, Russia, Sweden, Norway, and Belgium followed. On December 15, Nicaragua became the first Latin American nation to grant recognition, followed shortly by Peru and Cuba. By the end of the year Great Britain, Italy, Switzerland, Japan, and Costa Rica had joined the procession. [32]

The military tension increased when the Americans reinforced their

31. TR to Philippe Bunau-Varilla, November 13, 1903, in *FRUS*, 1903, p. 246; Francis Villers to Mortimer Durand, December 11, 1903, FO 420/210, pp. 79–80. For the bond-holder question see Arthur S. Raikes to Lord Lansdowne, November 16, 1903, FO 420/210, p. 64. The debt issue is in Council of Foreign Bondholders to TR, November 27, 1903, FO 420/210, pp. 67–69. The British memorandum discussing recognition is in A. H. Oakes memorandum, December 8, 1903, FO 420/210, pp. 74–76; Gerard Lowther to Lord Lansdowne, November 17, 1903, FO 420/210, p. 92, all in PRO. For early French approval of U.S. Panama policies see Jean Jules Jusserand to MAE, November 9, 1903, N.S., Colombie, 5, AMAE.

32. A list of recognitions is in DuVal, *Cadiz to Cathay*, 354.

garrison at Yavisa, a swampy outpost of questionable value in Darién, near the Colombia border. Idle press conjecture fanned the war fever. From Paris, where many papers speculated on the possibility of war, a detailed scenario of a Colombian war plan was reprinted in the United States. American newspapers reported that one hundred thousand Colombian troops were ready to fight and continued to print new Colombian threats of war. Reports that Colombian troops were massing near Yavisa continued to be received by American naval forces; the Americans responded by sending reinforcements.[33]

The tension accelerated until December 21, 1903, when Roosevelt, fearing an accidental war, finally stopped the buildup that he had helped institute. On December 10, Secretary of the Navy William Moody wrote a cable ordering Rear Admirals Henry Glass and Joseph B. Coghlan to "establish camps, seaman, and marine battalions fully equipped" to "forcibly prevent" a possible Colombian land invasion of Panama. Rear Admiral Henry C. Taylor, head of the Bureau of Navigation and the main force behind the General Board, wrote on the Navy Department file copy, "The above submitted by Secretary Moody to the President, who directed it not be sent now but withheld till further considered." On December 21 Roosevelt wrote to Moody formally countermanding the buildup order: "Would it not be well to issue instructions down at and around Panama that under no circumstances must they fire unless fired upon. If there should come a brush with Colombia I want to be dead sure that Colombia fires first." When Admiral Glass ordered most of the American force out of Yavisa, the crisis passed. The men who remained to gather information were ordered to withdraw to the safety of Darién in case of attack. Roosevelt's decision to ease the war crisis was one of the few times he overruled Secretary of War Elihu Root, one of his most influential advisers. Root and Navy Secretary Moody had urged the occupation of Yavisa, but Roosevelt, agreeing with them "from the

33. Rear Admiral Joseph B. Coghlan to Rafael Reyes, November 21, 1903, in *SP*, 487; Rear Admiral John G. Walker to William Moody, December 8, 1903, in *SP*, 488; *SP*, 487–92. For General Daniel Ortiz, General Order, November 23, 1903, that declared, "it is preferable to see the Colombian race completely extinguished than to submit to the infamous policy of President Roosevelt," see Box 6, Gleaves Papers. For the U.S. naval maneuvers see Panama Correspondence, RG 45, entry 304, NA. For the secret mission of Sydney A. Cloman and William Haan and the American mobilization see file 7113a, b, box 173, in RG 165, NA. Copies of many of the detailed army and navy dispatches were routinely sent to the White House and can be seen in RP, rolls 39–41. See also Richard Challener, *Admirals, Generals, and American Foreign Policy, 1898–1914* (Princeton, 1973), 156–60; and DuVal, *Cadiz to Cathay*, 362–78.

purely military standpoint," thought "the political reasons against seeming to court a clash with Colombia outweigh the military advantages of allowing them to seize unopposed a valuable base of possible operations against us. Accordingly, I have overridden for the present the views of the two departments in this matter."[34]

On December 6 Roosevelt met with Reyes at the White House in a spartan diplomatic meeting unmarked by the usual ceremonies. The two leaders had met once before at the White House to discuss the same subject, the Panama canal, in 1901, during the first months of Roosevelt's presidency. Although locked in a bitter struggle, Roosevelt and Reyes liked each other and remained on congenial terms. Roosevelt, abandoning the diplomatic protocol of a formal standing exchange of messages, engaged the Colombian in an earnest seated conversation in which Roosevelt told Reyes that had he been president instead of Marroquín the two men could have resolved the canal dispute amicably. Roosevelt, however, refused to deal personally with the Colombian leader and insisted that he conduct any further negotiations with John Hay. He asked Hay to "see Reyes and we could find out whether he has any practical proposal." The ensuing meetings were discouraging. After the two author-statesmen exchanged their most recent books, a disarmingly candid Reyes told Hay he was embarrassed by his mission in Washington because he was expected "to accomplish more than is possible under the circumstances." Fearing an "inevitable period of anarchy and general civil war in Colombia," Reyes seriously considered not taking the presidency and instead resuming his exile abroad.[35]

Senator John Tyler Morgan's dogged inflexibility and demagogic opposition more than anything else sealed Panama's fate. Few treaties have been signed by both principals with less enthusiasm. Panama

34. William Moody to Rear Admirals Henry Glass and Joseph B. Coghlan, December 10, 1903, annotation by Rear Admiral Henry C. Taylor, Translations of Cipher Messages Sent, entry 19, Naval Records Collection of the Office of Naval Records and Library, RG 45, NA; TR to William Moody, December 21, 1903, in *MRL*, III, 674; TR to Leslie Shaw, December 23, 1903, in *MRL*, III, 678; New York *Times*, November 22, 1903, in JBMS. For details of the Yavisa buildup see the correspondence in Vol. 177, Pt. 1, pp. 365–70, 382–84, 390–92, in Root Papers. For Taylor's influence see Daniel J. Costello, "Planning for War: A History of the General Board of the Navy" (Ph.D. dissertation, Fletcher School of Law and Diplomacy, 1969), 11–64.

35. The Reyes-Roosevelt meeting is described in Baltimore *Evening Sun*, December 6, 1903, JBMS; TR to JH, December 22, 1903, in *MRL*, III, 674; JH to Rafael Reyes, December 14, 1903; to TR, December 24, 1903, both in Hay Papers; TR to Reyes, February 20, 1905, in *MRL*, IV, 1124; Hay memo of meeting with Reyes, January 11, 1904, in RP.

officials signed reluctantly and under duress, and John Hay signed in a joyless ceremony on December 2. Writing with weariness to Republican Senate leader John Spooner a month later, Hay described the treaty as "very satisfactory, vastly advantageous to the United States, and we must confess, with what face we can muster, not so advantageous to Panama." The concessions made because of Morgan failed to mollify the irascible and inconsistent Alabama senator. Hay said, "If you should answer everything he said categorically, contradicting him with his own public utterances, it would have no effect on him. . . . He is as much the author of the present Canal Treaty as I am. Not only did I embody in it all his amendments to the Herran Treaty, but I went further than he has ever done in getting the proper guarantees for jurisdiction over the Canal." A year before, Morgan had insisted "that it was our bounden duty to aid them [the Liberals of Panama] in attaining their liberty." Now he accused the administration of having fomented the revolution he had demanded. An exasperated Hay complained, "How can you argue with a man whose prejudices are so violent and variable as this?" Unfortunately, Panama's sensitivity and interests ultimately were sacrificed to satisfy the unyielding Senator Morgan.[36]

Congress convened on December 7, 1903, to debate Roosevelt's canal policy. Roosevelt made his case in two substantial statements, the first his Annual Message, December 7, 1903, and the second a much longer message on January 4, 1904, delivered when Congress reconvened. In his first message, Roosevelt insisted that the United States had proceeded not from whim or impulse but from reason; he vigorously defended the American actions as both realistic and moral, demonstrating America's "consistent good faith" to the "peoples of the Isthmus" as well as the "civilized world." Regarding the diplomatic failure with Colombia, Roosevelt argued that "in drawing up this treaty every concession was made to the people and to the government of Colombia." He defended the American concessions: "In our scrupulous desire to pay all possible heed, not merely to the real but even to the fancied rights of our weaker neighbor, who already owed so much to our protection and forbearance, we yielded in all possible ways to her desires in drawing up the treaty." Roosevelt then described in detail the disturbances on the isthmus reported by American diplomats, "fifty-three in fifty-seven years," beginning with an

36. JH to John Spooner, January 20, 1903, in Hay Papers; JH to H. S. Pritchett, December 28, 1903, in Thayer, *Life and Letters of John Hay,* II, 326–27.

outbreak on May 22, 1850, that resulted in the death of two Americans to the July, 1902, revolution.[37]

Roosevelt documented the Colombian reliance on American naval forces. "In 1856, in 1860, in 1873, in 1885, in 1901, and again in 1902, sailors and marines from United States war-ships were forced to land. . . . In 1861, in 1862, in 1885, and in 1900, the Colombian Government asked that the United States Government would land troops to protect its interests and maintain order on the Isthmus." Roosevelt complained that though "only the active interference of the United States has enabled [Colombia] to preserve so much as a semblance of sovereignty," after fifty-seven years of American services that nation "peremptorily and offensively refused to do its part, even though to do so would have been to its advantage." Roosevelt declared that "every effort has been made by . . . the United States to persuade Colombia to follow a course which was essentially not only to our interests and to the interests of the world, but to the interests of Colombia itself." He closed with a plea for approval of the new treaty with Panama enumerating its advantages.[38]

Roosevelt's message marked the opening salvo of a bitter political battle over his Panama policy. It infuriated the partisan press. The New York *Times*, a wildly partisan Democratic paper unlike the later twentieth-century august journal of record, exploded with the "wish that part of President Roosevelt's message in which he explains and defends his course upon the Isthmus of Panama might be expunged from the National records." The *Times* thought Roosevelt's elaborate defense was evidence of a moral lapse, and it made the clarion call for "the Senate of the United States to check the President in the path of madness and danger which he is following." The *Literary Digest* looked forward to the struggle: "We have had the President and Panama; now we shall have Congress and Panama."[39]

Senator George Frisbee Hoar, a Massachusetts Republican and a vocal anti-imperialist, opened the Senate debate by demanding full disclosure of all government documents concerning Panama. Demo-

37. TR, Annual Message to Congress, December 7, 1903, in *TRWN*, XV, 202–14, 205, 207–209.

38. *Ibid.*; for summaries of all the American interventions except 1900 see Milton Offutt, *The Protection of Citizens Abroad by the Armed Forces of the United States* (Baltimore, 1928); for detailed accounts of the interventions, including the one in 1900, see *Senate Documents*, 58th Cong., 2nd Sess., No. 143, Serial 4589 (*The Use of Military Force in Colombia*).

39. New York *Times*, December 7, 1903, JBMS; *LD*, December 5, 1903, p. 765.

cratic leaders picked up on the implication of a conspiracy when Senator Arthur Pue Gorman, a Maryland Democrat, who was an early favorite for the Democratic presidential nomination, charged that the administration had suppressed evidence about its part in the Panamanian revolution. Roosevelt had sent the diplomatic correspondence to the House of Representatives on November 16 and sent the Senate the papers Hoar demanded on December 18. He could not believe the continuing suspicion of the government's cupidity in Panama: "How extraordinary it is that men can be taken in by arguments like those advanced. . . . by Senators Hoar, Morgan, and Gorman!" The Panama debate began with attacks on Roosevelt's aggressive executive leadership, an irony because letting Bunau-Varilla stage the revolution was less active than Roosevelt's original plan to seize the isthmus route directly. Despite accusations of conspiracy and imperialism, Roosevelt remained confident through most of the debate, mobilizing the administration's forces for the joint attack led by Democrats, who joined forces with Rafael Reyes to discredit Roosevelt.[40]

Reyes probably did his cause more harm than good. L. H. Andrews, Colombia's New York consul, shrewdly observed that sympathy for Colombia "will secure some consideration for Colombia if she does not do anything rash." Reyes, however, kept shifting his priorities, at first demanding Panama's return to Colombian sovereignty, several times threatening war, and only intermittently promoting Colombia's best option—an inclusive settlement with a large cash indemnity. Caught up in the American Senate debate, Reyes joined with the Democrats to defeat the treaty and discredit Roosevelt. In the process he made a compromise almost impossible and failed to take advantage of the considerable sympathy for Colombia. After a meeting with Roosevelt at the White House on the Hay–Bunau-Varilla Treaty, one Republican, convinced of the arguments for ratification but sympathetic to Colombia, told Hay, "Do it, but be as gentle as you can with Colombia." Hay, recounting the episode, compared it to a piece of American western folklore, "Kill him, but kill him easy."[41]

Because of the wording of the original Spooner Act, Secretary Hay ruled that the House did not have to reconsider its approval of the

40. TR to John Bigelow, January 6, 1904, in *MRL*, III, 689; "Gorman's Fight on Panama," Baltimore *Evening Sun*, December 19, 1903, JBMS. See Richard E. Welch, Jr., *George Frisbee Hoar and the Half-Breed Republicans* (Cambridge, Mass., 1971), 297–300.

41. L. H. Andrews to Tomás Herrán, November 10, 1903, in Herrán Papers; Hay conversation in Joseph B. Bishop, *Theodore Roosevelt and His Times* (2 vols.; New York, 1920), I, 305.

canal. The Senate would decide the entire issue in its debate on the Hay–Bunau-Varilla Treaty. The Republicans controlled the Senate and were confident that the treaty would eventually be approved. On December 15 Secretary of War Elihu Root assured a correspondent, "I think there is little doubt of the treaty with Panama being confirmed by the Senate." Root, sometimes erroneously regarded as unsympathetic to Roosevelt's policy because he was out of Washington when the Panama revolution occurred, was as forceful as Roosevelt and Hay in condemning Colombia's actions. Referring contemptuously to the "Bogotá patriots'" idea of holding up construction of the canal with the "very attractive idea of bilking the French people" by taking over the property and the $40 million payment, Root observed, "They are now in the position of a girl who keeps refusing a fellow, with the idea that she will marry him sometime or other when she gets ready, and who wakes up one fine morning to find that he has married another girl." [42]

How the French would have reacted had Colombia seized the Compagnie Nouvelle's canal property became a popular administration defense of its diplomacy. Assistant Secretary Francis Loomis made the French connection public in a speech before the Quill Club in New York on December 15. Had the negotiations with Colombia been delayed, and had Colombia, as it indicated it might do, reversed the extension of the Compagnie Nouvelle and seized its property, "the Government of France would not have stood serenely by. . . . A French squadron from Martinique would have borne down upon the Isthmus and perhaps landed marines at Colón and sent them across the Isthmus to Panama. . . . There would, in all probability, have been an armed conflict between France and Colombia, or France would have felt compelled to hold the Isthmus for a long period." Loomis even envisioned a world war over Panama: "The French warships might easily have been followed by those of England and Holland; and Panama, like the Balkan States, might well have been expected to furnish the spark to set half the world in flames." Senator Gorman protested that Loomis' speech was "a violation of sacred secrecy," but it is doubtful that he was referring to Loomis' eerie prophecy of how World War I would begin. [43]

42. ER to General Horace Porter, December 15, 1903, in DuVal, *Cadiz to Cathay*, 404.

43. Loomis' speech is in New York *Times*, December 16, 1903, JBMS; Gorman's criticism is in New York *Evening Post*, December 17, 1903, *ibid.* For TR's awareness of the possibility of French intervention see TR, *Autobiography*, in *TRWN*, XX, 513. Ambas-

The administration could do little for Colombia or Reyes without hurting Panama or appearing to back down. Reyes understood with startling acuity Colombia's tragic situation: "Sad indeed is the fate of my country, condemned at times to suffer calamities from its own revolutions and at others to witness unexpected attacks of a powerful but friendly state. . . . to deliver us pitilessly to the unhappy hazards of fortune." On December 29 Elihu Root assumed responsibility for further diplomatic negotiations with Colombia because John Hay was ill. Root painstakingly discussed Colombia's grievances in the longest cabinet meeting of Roosevelt's presidency in an unsuccessful search for a politically acceptable compromise. Since the United States feared that submitting any part of the Panama dispute to arbitration might appear as a concession of guilt, the cabinet remained unified against all of Colombia's demands. Nor could Panama be asked to assume its proportionate share of Colombia's external debt because that would raise questions about legal sovereignty and a storm of protest in Panama. Although the formal denials to Colombia awaited careful legal and diplomatic drafting, details on the cabinet's decisions to reject Colombia's redress of grievances were leaked to the press. The Colombians, by casting their net too widely and making accusations that were inflammatory and easily refuted, made the American response easier than it might have been and discouraged any chance for a compromise.[44]

The diplomatic exchange, already an exercise in futility, deteriorated into bitter polemics. Reyes announced that Colombia intended forcibly "subduing the rebellion," accused the United States of threatening war if Colombia intervened in Panama, and concluded with a proposal to present Colombia's case directly before the United States Senate during the Hay–Bunau-Varilla Treaty debate. The Americans took Reyes's war threats seriously. On December 30, 1903, Admiral Coghlan warned the president that a young and well-disciplined army of five thousand men armed with new weapons from Europe,

---

sador Jean Jules Jusserand and French Consul P. Bonhenry at Colón credited the United States with having prevented a bloodbath on the isthmus. Though Jusserand was concerned about further American ambitions, he remained sympathetic to the American intervention. See Jusserand to MAE, November 9, 1903; Bonhenry to MAE, November 7, 12, 1903; and Emile Gey to MAE, November 8, 1903, all in N.S., Colombie, 5, AMAE.

44. Rafael Reyes to JH, December 23, 1903, in FRUS, 1903, p. 291; New York Tribune, December 30, 1903; Baltimore Evening Sun, December 30, 1903, JBMS; JH to Rafael Reyes, January 5, 1904, in FRUS, 1903, pp. 294–306; Reyes's formal statement of grievances, ibid., 284–94; Lael, Arrogant Diplomacy, 26–27.

possibly headed by "General Castro, the best guerrilla in Colombia," was assembling in time for the advent of Colombia's dry season with "new roads improving daily."[45]

On January 8, while drafting yet another reply to Colombia, Hay asked Bunau-Varilla whether it would be safer to accede to Colombia's demands to divide the $10 million than to fight a war over it. Bunau-Varilla well understood that Colombia could not reconquer Panama: an "invasion of the Isthmus by land forces coming on foot from Colombia is a mere bugaboo. It can only frighten birds, or men with birds' brains. It is impracticable, it will never take place," the Frenchman reassured Hay. Bunau-Varilla then attacked the proposal to pay Colombia any sum of money as blackmail and declared that an invasion, even if it were possible, was preferable to such a payment. Bunau-Varilla threatened to resign as Panama's minister if Hay agreed to pay Colombia. Hay had not expected Bunau-Varilla to agree to Reyes's terms but needed some concession to "conclude with General Reyes," to make a gesture that might ease the dangerous war of words, and to conciliate senators sympathetic to Colombia. Hay incorporated Bunau-Varilla's suggestion of a plebescite and arbitration in the American reply of January 13 under which Panamanians could choose reaffiliation with Colombia or continued independence. The arbitration proposal, which did not mention the independence of Panama, appeared to conciliate Colombia while offering a plebescite only after Colombia recognized the new government of Panama. Marroquín rejected this transparent American gambit and continued his quixotic preparations for war, cabling Reyes to "gain time while we effect troop movements."[46]

Senator Gorman's political strategy was as wildly off the mark as Reyes's. Sensing the overwhelming public support for a canal, the Democratic leader focused his opposition on Panama and the revolution, insisting that the Spooner Act required Roosevelt to choose the Nicaraguan route. Unlike Senator Morgan, Gorman was not an ideologue but a politician in search of a path to the presidency who had no good alternatives—the tariff and post office fraud were less attractive campaign issues than the canal. Though Gorman was doubt-

45. Reyes to JH, January 6, 1904, in *FRUS*, 1903, pp. 306–309; Rear Admiral Joseph Coghlan to William Moody, December 30, 1903, in RP.

46. *BVC*, 417–20; JH to Rafael Reyes, January 13, 1903, in *FRUS*, 1903, pp. 313–14; José Marroquín to Rafael Reyes, January 25, 1904, in DuVal, *Cadiz to Cathay*, 401. For the consideration by Roosevelt, Hay, and Lodge of Reyes's proposal for an outright $5 million payment or a $10 million railroad grant see Lael, *Arrogant Diplomacy*, 30–32.

ful of defeating the president on the Panama question, he put on his best public face and tried to marshal the thirty-three Democratic Senate votes to block the treaty, which required sixty Senate votes for ratification, while at the same time hoping to block Roosevelt's renomination and reelection.[47]

By the time Congress reconvened in January, 1904, it was clear that Gorman had no chance of defeating the president. Too many Democrats liked both the treaty and Roosevelt's policy, and the Democratic press enthusiastically approved. The Atlanta *Constitution*, a staunchly anti-Roosevelt, southern Democratic paper, whose editor, Clark Howell, was a member of the Democratic National Committee, summed up the consensus: "The simplest observer of popular tempers in this country can not mistake how the American people feel about this matter. They approve what has been done to date, they want and mean to have that canal, and they will visit their wrath upon whatever man or party may defeat their treaty." The *Literary Digest* compared Gorman with the Spanish leader who, on urging his troops to annihilate the heretics, "discovered that most of his men were heretics themselves and refused to do the annihilating."[48]

Not only did dozens of newspapers cross party lines, but much of the southern Democracy rebelled and joined the Republican majority. Louisiana's wholly Democratic legislature unanimously urged its senators to approve the treaty. One southern senator predicted that southern state legislatures would pass resolutions favoring the treaty. The Brooklyn *Eagle* compared Gorman's opposition to that of the "obstructionists at Bogotá" and warned that "the country will have little patience" with Washington obstructionists. The turn of the political tide against the hopes of a unified Democratic opposition made the political debate even more bitter as Roosevelt's opponents engaged in a desperate search for a smoking gun, some evidence that would unmistakably link the president with Panama's revolution.[49]

Colombia's active alliance with the Democratic opposition contrib-

47. Gorman's program is in New York *Evening Post*, December 17, 1903, JBMS. For Gorman's reservations see John R. Lambert, *Arthur Pue Gorman* (Baton Rouge, 1953), 302–303; for an analysis of Gorman's political prospects and leadership, see *ibid.*, 301–308.

48. *LD*, January 2, 1904, p. 1. For anti-imperialist opposition to Roosevelt's Panama policies see Patterson, *Toward a Warless World*, 123–24; and E. Berkeley Tompkins, *Anti-Imperialism in the United States: The Great Debate, 1890–1920* (Philadelphia, 1970), 257–68.

49. *LD*, January 2, 1904, p. 2

uted to Roosevelt's polemical and defensive tone in his long message to Congress. His bitter personal feelings were revealed in a letter to Charles Lummis, a writer and explorer friend, who had urged patience with Colombia. Roosevelt, who thought within a histori- cal framework, compared Colombia to seventeenth-century Spain and contemporary Turkey, then in serious turmoil. "No more cruel despotism outside of Turkey exists than that of the so-called Colom- bia Republic, under its present political and ecclesiastical manage- ment. . . . Turkey is worse, but I know of no other power that is as bad. To the worst characteristics of 17th Century Spain, and of Spain at its worst under Phillip II, Colombia has added a squalid savagery of its own, and it has combined with exquisite nicety the worst forms of despotism, and of anarchy, of violence and of fatuous weakness, of dismal ignorance, cruelty, treachery, greed, and utter vanity. I cannot feel much respect for such a country."[50]

Yet Roosevelt remained conciliatory: "If I can do anything to make it better I shall try to, and try to in good faith." Roosevelt still preferred the original solution of a Colombian Panama canal: "If without detri- ment to the interests of the people of Panama, Panama can again be- come a state under Colombia, and desires to do so—why well and good." He believed that Colombian intransigence, not American am- bition, caused the problem: "They shall no longer tyrannize over Pan- ama nor longer block the pathway of the canal, if I can help it." His letter to Lummis reveals Roosevelt's thinking more clearly than his le- galistic and political message to Congress, written by several hands, including those of John Bassett Moore and Francis Loomis. In spite of his self-righteous anger against Colombia's unwillingness (inability?) to take the best deal possible, Roosevelt understood some of the dif- ferences between Latin and North American societies. He also knew that Panama would have remained content as a department of Colom- bia had Bogotá obtained the canal, which the Panamanians wanted even more than sovereignty.[51]

Roosevelt's second message to Congress on the canal on January 4,

50. Charles Lummis to TR, December 30, 1902, in RP; TR to Lummis, January 4, 1904, in *MRL*, III, 688–89. For TR's comparison of Panama's revolution to that of Greece from Turkey, see TR to David Thompson, December 22, 1903, in *MRL*, III, 675.

51. TR to Charles Lummis, January 4, 1904, in *MRL*, III, 688–89. The authorship of the congressional message is in TR to JBM, January 6, 1904, *ibid.*, 690–91. For a detailed description of the dictation of the message and Moore's legal emendations, see "Pan- ama Affair," Folder C, Box 211, pp. 9–18, Moore Papers. Loomis' memorandum is in "Suggestions (Canal)," Roll VII, Folder 34, Loomis Papers, Stanford University.

1904, addressed the main issue that was emerging in the debate—the president's new role as an active chief executive. Not until Roosevelt's presidency did foreign affairs become a major political issue rivaling domestic matters. William McKinley had struggled with Congress over presidential diplomacy on the timing of the war with Spain. Although McKinley preferred to placate rather than confront Congress, the increase of diplomatic problems as well as uncontrolled corporate growth would have caused congressional-presidential friction even without Roosevelt's openly activist style. The pressures of modernism were equally intense in North America as in Latin America, and they created challenges to Congress' late nineteenth-century dominance over the executive. When Congress, which shared domestic control with the corporate and railroad interests, remained unwilling to relinquish its preponderant political power, Roosevelt used the immense dormant powers of the presidency in foreign affairs to enlarge the chief executive's authority, while at the same time challenging Congress' absolute control over domestic politics.[52]

The Panama canal debate was the first major battleground between the president and Congress over the executive activism exemplified and symbolized by Theodore Roosevelt's Panama diplomacy. Honest disagreements over Panama caused only part of the bitterness of the debate. It also reflected reservations by Congress, not only about Panama and presidential activism but about the encroachment of world affairs on American politics. Roosevelt, the modern presidency, and modernism were the main texts of the Panama debate in which Panama itself was often relegated to the status of a subtext. There was far more consensus on Panama than on Roosevelt's new style of executive leadership. Because 1904 was a presidential election year, campaign politics further complicated the debate.[53]

52. For Roosevelt's battles with Congress see John M. Blum, *The Republican Roosevelt* (Cambridge, Mass., 1954); Willard B. Gatewood, Jr., *Theodore Roosevelt and the Art of Controversy* (Baton Rouge, 1970); Gordon Carpenter O'Gara, *Theodore Roosevelt and the Rise of the Modern Navy* (Princeton, 1943); Stephen Skowronek, *Building a New American State: The Expansion of National Administrative Capacities, 1877–1920* (Cambridge, Eng., 1982); George H. Mayer, *The Republican Party, 1854–1964* (New York, 1967), 272–99; G. Wallace Chessman, *Theodore Roosevelt and the Politics of Power* (Boston, 1969). See also Richard W. Leopold, "The Emergence of America as a World Power: Some Second Thoughts," and John Braeman, "The Square Deal in Action: A Case Study in the Growth of the 'National Police Power,'" both in John Braeman, Robert H. Brenner, and Everett Walters (eds.), *Change and Continuity in Twentieth-Century America* (New York, 1966), 3–34, 35–80. For McKinley's role as the "first modern president" see Lewis L. Gould, *The Presidency of William McKinley* (Lawrence, Kan., 1980), 231–53.

53. For the friction between president and Congress see W. Stull Holt, *Treaties Defeated by the Senate: A Study of the Struggle Between President and Senate over the Conduct of*

Roosevelt attacked Colombia for "violating the spirit and substantially repudiating the obligations of a treaty the full benefits she had enjoyed for over 50 years. My intention was to consult the Congress and either. . . . announce that the canal was to be dug forthwith; that we would give the terms that we offered and no others; and if such terms were not agreed to we would enter into an arrangement with Panama direct, or take whatever steps were needful in order to begin the enterprise." Roosevelt defended the administration's innocence in the Panamanian revolution. He cited newspaper accounts that "could be indefinitely multiplied," and though granting that "the administration had special means of knowledge," he insisted that the threat of secession "was a matter of common notoriety" that anyone could discover. The message included a vast array of documentary evidence, including naval orders, the Humphrey-Murphy mission and conference, and naval reports from Panama. Roosevelt argued that the American presence was "too long delayed" and that when they did intervene it was to prevent fighting between Panamanians and Colombians. "We, in effect, policed the Isthmus in the interest of its inhabitants, and of our own national needs, and for the good of the entire civilized world." Roosevelt vehemently denied any American participation in the revolution: "No one connected with this government had any part in preparing, inciting, or encouraging the late revolution in the Isthmus of Panama. . . . [or] any previous knowledge of the revolution except such as was accessible to any person of ordinary intelligence who read the newspapers and kept up a current acquaintance with public affairs."[54]

In addressing his failure to delay action until the dispute could be diplomatically resolved, the most common objection raised by historians, Roosevelt cited possible French complications. Suggesting a scenario in which Colombia demanded American protection when France attempted to take back French property in Panama, Roosevelt argued that the Colombian plan exhibited "wanton disregard of our own highest interests" and would have caused "further injury to the citizens of a friendly nation." In defending his decision to negotiate with Colombia, Roosevelt cited the resolution of the Second Pan-

---

Foreign Affairs (Baltimore, 1933), 178–248. For Roosevelt's role see Eugene P. Trani, "Cautious Warrior: Theodore Roosevelt and the Diplomacy of Activism," in Frank W. Merli and Theodore A. Wilson (eds.), *Makers of American Diplomacy* (New York, 1974), 305–31; William C. Widenor, *Henry Cabot Lodge and the Search for an American Foreign Policy* (Berkeley, 1980), 121–70; and Raymond A. Esthus, *Theodore Roosevelt and the International Rivalries* (1970; rpr. Claremont, Calif., 1982).
54. TR, Message to Congress, in *SP*, 579–94, 582.

American Conference at Mexico City on January 22, 1902, signed by Rafael Reyes: "The Republics assembled at the International Conference of Mexico applaud the purpose of the United States Government to construct an interoceanic canal and acknowledge that its work will not only be worthy of the greatness of the American people, but also in the highest sense a work of civilization and to the greatest degree beneficial to the development of commerce between the American States and the other countries of the world." Roosevelt argued: "Little could it have been foreseen that two years later the Colombian Government, led astray by false allurements of selfish advantage, and forgetful alike of its international obligations and responsibilities of sovereignty, would thwart the efforts of the United States to enter upon and complete a work which the nations of America, reechoing the sentiment of the nations of Europe, had pronounced to be . . . 'in the highest sense a work of civilization.'"[55]

Although even the opposition New York *Times* conceded on January 9, 1904, that the passage of the Panama treaty was sure and "the anti-treaty vote . . . is dwindling daily," Roosevelt learned that determined Senate opposition would charge that "Bunau-Varilla knew or had assurances from Hay or myself as to what our action would be, and advised the revolutionists." Francis Loomis, the most direct State Department link to Bunau-Varilla, responded to Roosevelt's request for complete disclosure with a detailed account of his relationship with Bunau-Varilla. Loomis wrote the president that though he had known Bunau-Varilla since 1901, his State Department visit around October 10, 1903, ostensibly to talk about the health of his children and a mining property in California, was their first meeting in eighteen months. When Bunau-Varilla asked Loomis' opinion on Panama, the assistant secretary wrote that he evaded answering by saying he had been on vacation for over a month.[56]

55. *SP*, 582, 589–90. The most detailed form of the delay argument is in Miner, *Fight for the Panama Route*, 388–92. In its various forms, relying on the stereotype of the impatient and impulsive TR, it has become a textbook commonplace, suggesting either that TR should have taken the Nicaragua option (Dennett, *John Hay*, 382–83) or waited until Reyes's presidency made the Colombian Senate more malleable. See *SP*, 592; TR, *Autobiography*, in *TRWN*, 512–13. For French intervention in Central America, see Warren G. Kneer, *Great Britain and the Caribbean, 1901–1913: A Study in Anglo-American Relations* (East Lansing, Mich., 1975), 15–16. A well-stated but anonymous contemporary argument against the efficacy of delay is in "Extract from a letter (translation), dated Panama 28th Sept. 1903," in Box 207, Folder C, Moore Papers.

56. TR to John Bigelow, January 6, 1904, in *MRL*, III, 689; Francis Loomis to TR, January 4, 1904, in Loomis Papers. For evidence that the Loomis–Bunau-Varilla relationship began in 1890 and involved active planning of a Panama canal in 1898, see Anguizola, *Philippe Bunau-Varilla*, 157–59, 175–77.

Loomis admitted that he told Bunau-Varilla that he had no hope that the Colombian Senate would reconsider its rejection of the treaty. At this point Bunau-Varilla, according to Loomis, gave him a copy of his September 2, 1903, *Le Matin* article and asked if he might see the president. Loomis and Roosevelt were already aware of the article, which Bunau-Varilla had mailed to virtually everyone of influence. Loomis described the meeting with Roosevelt in general terms but unequivocally declared that "nothing was said that could be construed as advising, instigating, suggesting, or encouraging a revolutionary movement." Bunau-Varilla visited Loomis' offices "once or twice later in the same month." When he asked what the United States would do "in the case of a serious outbreak at this juncture on the Isthmus," Loomis replied, "I did not know and could only venture the guess that this government would do as it had done in the past under like circumstances." When Bunau-Varilla suggested that the United States might consider doing more, Loomis insisted that he was an observer and "did not feel called upon either to confirm or combat what appeared to be his very settled opinion." [57]

Bunau-Varilla, who was not nearly as innocent as Roosevelt claimed but far less culpable than the Democrats and their newspapers argued, was saved on several occasions by American sensitivity. Offering John Bassett Moore an official post as counsel to the new Republic of Panama in November was a dreadful idea. Moore, obviously shocked by such gross impropriety, quickly declined the position. Roosevelt found Bunau-Varilla "a very able fellow, and it was his business to find out what he thought our government would do. . . . in finding out, as it was easy to find out, the movements of our ships; and in forecasting, not merely from the remote past but from the immediate past, what our action was likely to be." So cleverly did Bunau-Varilla use his *Le Matin* article of September 2, 1903, that Reyes's American attorney, Wayne MacVeagh, and Senator Morgan were continually confounded by their inability to connect Bunau-Varilla directly with the administration. Roosevelt, writing to Lodge on January 6, was pleased that Senator Morgan "quoted Bunau-Varilla's article to *Le Matin* September 2d and stated that it so foreshadowed the course I actually took that undoubtedly Hay or I must have inspired it. Now, I am very much pleased that he should have done this. MacVeagh and others have been threatening for some time to produce telegrams from Bunau-Varilla which would show an exact knowledge of our

57. Francis Loomis to TR, January 4, 1904, in Loomis Papers.

movements and even our intentions. . . . They have proved too much. They have proved that Bunau-Varilla knew what we were going to do six weeks before he ever saw any of us and some little time before I had even begun myself to make up my mind what I should do."[58]

Roosevelt intuitively understood Bunau-Varilla's role when he asked John Bassett Moore, "Do you ever remember meeting Bunau-Varilla? I wonder if he, being evidently a very clever man, could have formed his ideas on what he had heard were yours?" Roosevelt and the opposition were equally fascinated with Bunau-Varilla's achievement, Roosevelt because he knew how much Bunau-Varilla had done on his own, the opposition because they were sure there was a connection. Roosevelt in a paranoid moment even expected that an incriminating Bunau-Varilla telegram—presumably forged or ambiguous—might suddenly appear. He warned Lodge to be wary "if they spring any telegrams of Bunau-Varilla upon us in the Senate." When Roosevelt asked Bunau-Varilla at the diplomatic dinner on January 14, 1904, how he had managed to know so much, the delighted Frenchman replied, "Mr. President, it is purely a matter of logic. The same facts are bound to lead logical minds to the same conclusion, however far away from each other they may be." Roosevelt complimented Bunau-Varilla: "If that is so, you are the greatest logician I have ever known." The coincidence was too great, and Roosevelt as well as the opposition knew it. Columbia University engineering professor William H. Burr, a member of the Walker Isthmian Canal Commission and a friend and colleague of John Bassett Moore, was the most likely connection. Burr had brought Bunau-Varilla and Moore together for the first time in October, 1903, and probably sent Bunau-Varilla the mysterious "telegram from New York" that "convinced me [Bunau-Varilla] that the idea which occurred to me of using the text of Treaty of 1846 to coerce Colombia had simultaneously been entertained in America."[59]

"They are making an ugly fight in the Panama business," Roosevelt wrote Mark Hanna on January 14, "and I think it very desirable that you should be here." The most serious threat was a resolution jointly

58. The offer to Moore is in Box 211, Folder C, p. 9, Moore Papers. For Moore's account of his relationship with TR see JBM to TR, January 6, 1904, RP; TR to HCL, January 6, 1904, in MRL, III, 690.

59. TR to JBM, January 6, 1904; to HCL, January 6, 1904, both in MRL, III, 688, 690; conversation with TR is in BVC, 417; the Burr-Moore connection is in BVC, 294–95; the mysterious cable is in BVC, 286.

sponsored by Republican Senator Eugene Hale of Maine and Democrat Augustus O. Bacon of Georgia calling for the president to mediate differences between Panama and Colombia and indemnify Colombia for its loss of territory. Hale, a member of the Foreign Relations Committee, successfully delayed the reporting of the treaty from committee while Senator William Stone of Missouri opened an official Senate inquiry on Bunau-Varilla's connection with the administration. On January 17, the New York *World* charged that Bunau-Varilla and the Panamanian revolutionaries would make millions in speculation on the Compagnie Nouvelle's stock, which had risen on the Paris bourse after the revolution. Bunau-Varilla partially deflected the attack by offering to pay Colombia a million dollars based on a one-sixteenth share of Colombia's external debt. When the *World* failed to substantiate its sensational allegations, the possibility of the sudden appearance of yet another smoking gun failed.[60]

Once it became clear in the first week of January that the treaty had enough support to pass, the amendment process, which could subject the treaty to endless negotiation, became the most serious threat Roosevelt faced. Senator Morgan, a master at adding amendments to treaties, was more interested in rhetorical effect than practical politics. Roosevelt was more concerned with members of his own party, who in good conscience could register a serious reservation through an amendment while appearing to maintain their open support and party loyalty. Roosevelt's floor leader, John C. Spooner, who the president observed a year later "invariably uses his ingenious mind to put in meticulous and usually slightly improper amendments to every treaty," agreed not to amend this one only after Roosevelt and Hay exerted extraordinary personal and political pressure.[61]

Spooner's proposed amendments dealt with peripheral administrative jurisdictional matters in Panama's cities that were satisfactorily resolved through diplomatic memoranda and executive orders. In cajoling Spooner to give up his amendments, Hay warned that "the holiday spirit in which they [Panama] ratified the treaty in twenty-four hours no longer exists. . . . They are very suspicious." In a letter

60. TR to Mark Hanna, January 14, 1904, in *MRL*, III, 695; New York *Evening Post*, January 13, 1904; New York *Sun*, January 13, 1904; New York *World*, January 17, 1904, all in JBMS; *LD*, January 9, 1904, pp. 36–37.

61. For TR on Spooner and his thoughts on the Senate's amending powers see TR to Joseph B. Bucklin, March 23, 1905, in *MRL*, IV, 1144; see also TR to Shelby Cullom, February 10, 1905, *ibid.*, 1118–19.

the following day, Hay confided, "You and I know too well how many points there are in this treaty to which a Panama patriot could object. If it is again submitted to their consideration, they will attempt to amend it in many places, no man can say with what result." Hay flattered the senator effusively, accepting responsibility because he "had not been sufficiently lucid" and assuring him that the matter could be easily resolved outside of the amendment process.[62]

Roosevelt paid court to Spooner's expertise and pleaded with him not to insist on perfection but to pass "this treaty which in its present shape gives everything to the United States which we can possibly desire." The administration's arguments convinced Spooner and Cullom to report the treaty out of committee, accompanied by both the amendments and the chairman's recommendation that they be defeated. On January 18, Roosevelt wrote to Cecil Spring Rice: "I believe I shall put through the Panama treaty (my worst foes being those in the Senate and not those outside the border of the United States) and begin to dig the canal." It was the "weary length" of the debate that troubled Roosevelt. Hay reflected Roosevelt's impatience. Quick Senate passage, he told Spooner, would "leave us free to begin work at once."[63]

Once Cullom reported the treaty out of committee, its passage was assured. Roosevelt thought the treaty would win by a "three to one majority; but they are filibustering and talking every which way in vain hope that something will turn up to help them." Democrats in the Senate continued to demand documents from the administration. Roosevelt formally asked the War and Navy departments to "send me every dispatch or document of any kind, sort or description." These were gathered, screened for security, and added to the huge volume of diplomatic documents already printed on Panama. By February 10, Roosevelt confided to his son, "I think the opposition to Panama is pretty well over and I shall be surprised if within a week or so we do not have a treaty ratified." Senator Morgan alone refused to allow the treaty to come to the floor, insisting on making more speeches against

62. JH to John Spooner, January 19, 20, 1904, both in Hay Papers.
63. A description of the amendments and tactics for dealing with them is in JH to William I. Buchanan, January 11, 1904; to John Spooner, January 19, 20, 1904, all in Hay Papers; TR to John Spooner, January 20, 1904; to Cecil Spring Rice, January 18, 1904; to TRJR, January 18, 1904, all in MRL, III, 700, 701, 699. For Spooner's canal expertise, see Dorothy G. Fowler, John Coit Spooner: Defender of Presidents (New York, 1961), 283.

it, and was "absent from the Senate for several days, preparing further broadsides."[64]

Since the real Senate debate on the treaty was in executive session with no record kept, the public debate was mostly designed to allow senators to make a case for the press and the record with customary oratorical flourishes. Roosevelt's style and his activism rankled some senators as much as the Panama issue. Hernando Money, a Democrat from Mississippi, who favored the Nicaraguan route, vehemently objected to the increase of presidential power and the corresponding erosion of congressional power. On February 20, 1904, Money told the Senate, "It is dangerous for the Chief Executive to begin to think. The thinking belongs to Congress. It is the great political department of the country." After the Panama canal issue was resolved, the Senate and the president continued to struggle with the question of whether the president or the Congress was the "great political department of the country."[65]

On February 23, 1904, the Senate ratified the Hay–Bunau-Varilla Treaty without amendments by a vote of 66 to 14. On February 25, John Hay and Philippe Bunau-Varilla exchanged ratifications and Bunau-Varilla resigned as Panama's minister to the United States. The title to the canal property was transferred from the French company to the United States on April 22, and on May 9, 1904, the United States through the J. P. Morgan Bank paid $40 million to the Bank of France, which then distributed the 206 million francs to the legally designated creditors of the old and new French canal companies.[66]

64. TR to TRJR, January 29, 1904; to ER, January 26, 1904, both in *MRL*, III, 712, 711; TR to William Moody, January 26, 1904, in RP; TR to TRJR, February 10, 1904, in *MRL*, IV, 724; Baltimore *Evening Post*, February 10, 1904, in JBMS.

65. *Congressional Record*, 58th Cong., 2nd Sess., February 23, 1904, p. 2244; Radke, "John Tyler Morgan," 474–83.

66. For the Morgan payment and the French distribution of it see Anguizola, *Philippe Bunau-Varilla*, 290–92; Mack, *Land Divided*, 472, 480–82.

11   Aftermath, 1904–

Theodore Roosevelt had no doubts about the rightness of his Panama canal policies. He was acutely aware of the "great uneasiness caused among my friends by my action." Politically, Roosevelt had won a decisive victory. Senate Democratic leader Arthur Pue Gorman, defeated and discouraged, witnessed the dramatic collapse of his presidential hopes. The Democrats' compromise presidential nominee, lackluster conservative Judge Alton B. Parker, was no match for Roosevelt, who knew how much he owed to his activist Panama policies. During the presidential campaign Roosevelt advised a political aide to "tell our speakers to dwell more on the Panama Canal. . . . We have not a stronger card."[1]

Roosevelt, however, was increasingly frustrated over the lingering acrimony, ostensibly directed toward his Panama policies but fundamentally more concerned with his continuing struggle with Congress over the reapportionment of political power between the executive and the legislative branches. Indeed, Roosevelt's activist Panama policy marked the beginning of the modern American presidency, when attention to foreign affairs modified the previous total dominance of domestic affairs. The Constitution itself, as well as the new technologies that constitute what we call modernism—not an aggressive president—mandated the changes in American government that in turn were complicated by the inopportune timing of the Panama crisis. Roosevelt was one of the few men of his age who not only understood the immensity of the engineering problems involved in building any isthmian canal but who also grasped the greatest diplomatic danger—that the existence of an unfinished canal at Panama might poison Caribbean affairs for many years to come. If others—an ambitious

1. TR to John Spooner, January 20, 1904, in *MRL*, III, 701. For Gorman's political decline and the effect of his Panama policies, see John R. Lambert, *Arthur Pue Gorman* (Baton Rouge, 1953), 301–16; TR to Nathan Scott, October 9, 1904, in *MRL*, IV, 928.

European power or a European syndicate—were tempted to follow in
de Lesseps' footsteps, the combination of Colombia's chaotic political
situation and American resistance to any European threat could seriously unsettle the region and lead to even greater strife than the limited Anglo-German blockade of Venezuela or Panama's bloodless
revolution of 1903.[2]

Most members of the American Senate, the press, and indeed, the
historians who have written later viewed the Panama canal as a much
narrower issue than Roosevelt did. Much of what has been written
on the canal assumes—aggressively but with total inaccuracy—that
Nicaragua was a genuine and even a preferable option. But once the
French ended their work on a canal at Panama, it became essential, if
Europe were to continue to be excluded from the Caribbean, for the
United States to secure a monopoly on a hemispheric canal by controlling Panama. An American canal at Nicaragua, even had it been
possible to build and maintain, would have been vulnerable to the
threat of another canal through Panama. Eventually the Americans
would have been forced to come to terms with the better route through
Panama by the use of naval force, diplomatic accommodation, purchase, or a combination of these alternatives. During the Senate de-

2. For the congressional struggle see W. Stull Holt, *Treaties Defeated by the Senate: A
Study of the Struggle Between the President and Senate over the Conduct of Foreign Relations*
(Baltimore, 1933), 178–248; and E. Taylor Parks, *Colombia and the United States, 1765–1934*
(Durham, N.C., 1935), 427–28. For anti-imperialist opposition to Roosevelt's Panama
policies see E. Bradley Tompkins, *Anti-Imperialism in the United States: The Great Debate,
1890–1920* (Philadelphia, 1970), 257–68; Moorfield Storey, *The Recognition of Panama*
(Boston, 1904); and Alfred Charles Richard, Jr., "The Panama Canal in American
National Consciousness, 1870–1922" (Ph.D. dissertation, Boston University, 1969),
183–85. A useful summary of the opposition to Panama is in George L. Fox, *President
Roosevelt's Coup d'Etat: The Panama Affair in a Nutshell* (New Haven, 1904), copy in Pan-
ama Affair Folder, Box 134, John Bassett Moore Papers, LC. For the engineering prob-
lems and Roosevelt's awareness of them see George Abbott Morison, *George Shattuck
Morison, 1842–1903* (Peterborough, N.H., 1940), 12–14. For American concerns over
German ambitions in Panama see Captain Charles D. Sigsbee, "Report to the General
Board: Germany versus the United States—West Indies," in General Board File 425,
War Portfolios, RG 80, NA; Office of Naval Intelligence, Memorandum Comparing German and American naval strength, March 23, 1902, reel 23, RP; Richard D. Challener,
Admirals, Generals, and American Foreign Policy, 1898–1914 (Princeton, 1973), 16–17,
26–30; Holger H. Herwig, *Politics of Frustration: The United States in German War Plan-
ning, 1889–1914* (Boston, 1976), 67–109. For American naval orders to guard against
possible German or Chilean intervention at the time of the Panama revolution, see
William Reynolds Braisted, *The United States Navy in the Pacific, 1897–1909* (Austin,
Tex., 1958), 148. For concern over possible French intervention see "President Roosevelt's Fear of France," *LD*, January 16, 1904, p. 89. For Lucien Napoleon-Bonaparte
Wyse's urging of French and European intervention see *Le Rapt de Panama* (Toulon,
1904), esp. 4–14.

bate, Senator Morgan questioned whether the Panama canal could effectively compete with Suez, which in 1904 held a world shipping monopoly. The existence of two canals on the isthmus would have created serious economic and diplomatic rivalries, while the provocation—diplomatic, nationalistic, and economic—provided by the presence of a permanently unfinished Panama canal would have been immense. The Naval War College had already considered a possible German-American naval and military war in Panama in its summer, 1901, exercise.[3]

Eliminating Europe from the New World was the cornerstone of Roosevelt's foreign policy, more for strategic than for economic reasons. Securing Panama helped assure the success of Roosevelt's policy by eliminating the largest remaining New World temptation for European development. Roosevelt saw Panama in global terms. Many senators, both pro-Panama and anti-Roosevelt, saw the Panama issue as a domestic transportation problem as much as a diplomatic or strategic concern. Roosevelt was sincere when he spoke of acting on behalf of international civilization. He envisioned an American-controlled canal at Panama in a stable Caribbean and a peaceful world that would permit the development of Latin America as a prosperous region independent of both Europe and the United States. Roosevelt would not tolerate any proposal to take money from the French, which he felt not only violated international honor, a necessity for discourse between civilized nations, but, by infuriating the French, might endanger his practical policy of eliminating European gunboat diplomacy in Latin American waters.[4]

3. TR's account of the technology of canals is in TR, *Autobiography* (1913), in *TRWN*, XX, 516–17. For the most detailed accounts of the technological superiority of the Panama route, see George H. Morison to TR, December 10, 1901, cited in David McCullough, *The Path Between the Seas: The Creation of the Panama Canal, 1870–1914* (New York, 1977), 326–27; and Morison, *George Shattuck Morrison*, 12–14. For possible competition in building a canal see Senator John Tyler Morgan's remarks, February 8, 1904, in *Congressional Record*, 58th Cong., 2nd Sess., 1709–10. For the assumption of Nicaraguan superiority see Gerstle Mack, *The Land Divided: A History of the Panama Canal and Other Isthmian Canal Projects* (New York, 1944), 436; Tyler Dennett, *John Hay: From Poetry to Politics* (New York, 1933), 379. For plans for a Nicaraguan canal after Panama see Thomas A. Bailey, "Interest in a Nicaragua Canal, 1903–1931," *HAHR*, XVI (1936), 2–28. The navy war plan is in Problem of 1901, in RG 12, Naval War College Archives, Newport R.I.; see Richard W. Turk, "The United States Navy and the 'Taking' of Panama, 1901–1903," *Military Affairs*, XXXVIII (1974), 92–96. For the failed attempt to use the Naval War College's plan in Panama see Charles Darling to Rear Admiral Joseph Coghlan, April 5, 1904, Confidential Letters Sent, RG 45, entry 20, NA.
4. For the railroad competition issue see Richard, "Panama Canal in American National Consciousness," 126; Joseph Fry, "John Tyler Morgan's Southern Expansionism,"

Realizing that Panama had become a symbol for his active leadership style, Roosevelt defended his Panama policies by arguing that "our opponents can criticize what we did at Panama only on condition of misstating what was done. The administration behaved throughout not only with good faith but with extraordinary patience and with large generosity toward those with whom it dealt. It was also mindful of American interests. . . . Had not Panama been promptly recognized . . . there would have ensued endless guerrilla warfare and possible foreign complications; while all chance of building a canal would have been deferred, certainly for years, perhaps a generation or more." But when Roosevelt acquiesced to and benefited from Philippe Bunau-Varilla's organization of Panama's revolution, he committed the most serious foreign policy error of his presidency. By allowing the Frenchman to serve as a front man for American interests—even indirectly—Roosevelt put his administration's credibility in doubt. Bunau-Varilla's presence made Roosevelt's already controversial activist policies vulnerable to question as well as criticism. The Frenchman's actions required too much defending. In the process of defending the minutiae of the revolution itself—whether the United States actively helped, quietly encouraged, or engaged in quiet subversion—Roosevelt's larger policies remained offstage, and when debated were seen as peripheral. All the Panama debates—Senate, public, and historical—emphasized the question of direct American involvement in the Panama revolution of 1903 and rarely touched upon the global implications of Roosevelt's foreign policy.[5]

DH, IX (1985), 333–34. For Roosevelt's concern with the French see TR, "How the United States Acquired the Right to Dig the Panama Canal," *Outlook*, XCIX (October 7, 1911), 314–15; and "President Roosevelt's Fear of France," 89. For TR's careful diplomacy with French interests in the Caribbean during a Venezuelan crisis in 1905 see Philip Jessup, *Elihu Root* (2 vols.; New York, 1938), I, 495–97; see also Peter Larsen, "Theodore Roosevelt and the Moroccan Crisis, 1904–1906" (Ph.D. dissertation, Princeton University, 1984). TR, "The United States and the South American Republics, "Address, New York, October 3, 1913, rpr. in *TRWN*, XVI, 292–304. For a rejection of the thesis that an overt or informal alliance existed between American business and government, see William H. Becker, *The Dynamics of Business-Government Relations: Industry and Exports, 1893–1921* (Chicago, 1982), esp. vii–xiv; see also David M. Pletcher, "Rhetoric and Results: A Pragmatic View of American Economic Expansionism, 1865–98," *DH*, V (1981), 93–108. For German apprehension over an American canal in Panama see Holger H. Herwig, *Germany's Vision of Empire in Venezuela, 1871–1914* (Princeton, 1986), 156, 171; for Roosevelt's global context see Frederick Marks III, *Velvet on Iron: The Diplomacy of Theodore Roosevelt* (Lincoln, Neb., 1979), esp. 171–211; and John A. S. Grenville and George Berkeley Young, *Politics, Strategy and American Diplomacy: Studies in Foreign Policy, 1873–1917* (New Haven, 1966), esp. 309–13.

5. TR to Joseph Cannon, September 12, 1904, in *MRL*, III, 922 (the formal acceptance of the Republican presidential nomination in 1904). John Major, "Who Wrote the Hay–

Bunau-Varilla further corrupted Roosevelt's policies when he dealt dishonorably with his Panamanian associates by negotiating the one-sided Hay–Bunau-Varilla Treaty. The United States government, which had been honorable in its dealings with Colombia and had maintained a defensible balance between realism and innocence in the Panamanian revolution, had no defense other than expediency when it negotiated and ratified the treaty that became known in Panama as "the Bunau-Varilla sellout." Once Bunau-Varilla had been allowed to orchestrate the revolution and then as a consequence to substitute Panama for Colombia in the canal treaty, Roosevelt's policies became examples not of impeccable morality, as he claimed, but of political expedience. Bunau-Varilla, one of the cleverest men Roosevelt knew and a private individual, could act without the moral restraints placed on a head of government. Once Roosevelt permitted Bunau-Varilla to execute American policy, even indirectly, the president lost control of the Panama dispute as well as of his claim to absolute morality. When John Hay, in pleading with Senator John Spooner for quick passage of the Hay–Bunau-Varilla Treaty, concluded, "it is only a question of expediency and opportuneness," he summarized not only the irony of Roosevelt's dilemma but the tragedy of the inappropriate intercession of Bunau-Varilla in American foreign policy.[6]

Although Roosevelt erred, he did not err as grievously as many historians have argued. Historical accounts that blame Roosevelt unequivocally for America's Panama diplomacy give insufficient weight to the roles played by the other major principals in the drama; José Marroquín and Senator John Tyler Morgan are both relegated to minor

Bunau-Varilla Convention?" *DH*, VIII (1984), 115–23, raises serious new questions about Bunau-Varilla's credibility. Gustave Anguizola, *Philippe Bunau-Varilla: The Man Behind the Panama Canal* (Chicago, 1980), esp. 158–59, 175–77, 230, raises equally serious questions about Loomis and his relationship with Bunau-Varilla. See also Charles Ameringer, "Philippe Bunau-Varilla: New Light on the Panama Canal Treaty," *AHR*, XLVI (1966), 28–52; Richard, "Panama Canal in American National Consciousness," 179–85; August Carl Radke, Jr., "John Tyler Morgan: An Expansionist Senator, 1877–1907" (Ph.D. dissertation, University of Washington, 1953), 473–88; Richard E. Welch, Jr., *George Frisbee Hoar and the Half-Breed Republicans* (Cambridge, Mass., 1971), 298–99; and Lambert, *Arthur Pue Gorman,* 297–300.

6. Frank Otto Gatell, "The Canal in Retrospect—Some Panamanian and Colombian Views," *Americas*, XV (July, 1958), 27, discusses the phrase. For a history of Panama's dissatisfaction with the American canal relationship see Walter LaFeber, *The Panama Canal: The Crisis in Historical Perspective* (Rev. ed.; New York, 1979); Joseph L. Arbena, "The Image of an American Imperialist: Colombian Views of Theodore Roosevelt," *West Georgia Studies in the Social Sciences*, VI (June, 1967), 3–20. JH to John Spooner, January 20, 1904, Hay Papers, LC.

roles as gadflies in most histories of America's Panama diplomacy. Although Morgan was not Roosevelt's intellectual or political equal, his key position in the Senate enabled him to frustrate Roosevelt's maneuverability. Morgan's implacable opposition in the Senate, combined with José Marroquín's ambivalent diplomacy, effectively blocked Roosevelt's plan to build an American canal at Panama with Colombia's acquiescence and cooperation. Against two determined foes, Roosevelt ultimately prevailed, but his shift of American allegiance from Colombia to Panama required greater use of executive power in foreign policy than Congress was accustomed to. Because Senator Morgan could block further Senate concessions to Colombia, Roosevelt could not consider raising the additional funds to satisfy Colombia's politicians. Roosevelt reluctantly supported Panama's revolution because he felt it was the best remaining choice.[7]

Moreover, making the Panama canal primarily an episode of American imperial or big stick diplomacy relegates Colombia's acting president José Manuel Marroquín's role to an undeserved secondary status. When Marroquín stood up to Theodore Roosevelt and the Americans, he not only won as much as it was possible for Colombia to win, he may have achieved almost all he wanted. Roosevelt's view of Marroquín as a dictator whose *"coup d' état . . .* took away from Colombia herself the power of government, and vested it in an irresponsible dictator" only partly captured the spirit and purpose of Marroquín's convoluted diplomacy. Roosevelt's often quoted complaint—"you could no more make an agreement with them [Colombia] than you could nail currant jelly to a wall is not due to a nail; it is due to the currant jelly"—indirectly acknowledged Marroquín's undervalued ability to manipulate Roosevelt and the Americans for three years. Marroquín's credentials as an authoritarian dictator are not in question, but Roosevelt's charge of dishonesty is only partly correct. Americans considered Marroquín dishonest because they measured the Colombian leader by Roosevelt's moral calculus of the civilized, gentlemanly leader playing by the rules of international diplomacy. But the customs of diplomacy favored the big powers and

7. Marks, *Velvet on Iron,* 96–105; Robert A. Friedlander, "A Reassessment of Roosevelt's Role in the Panamanian Revolution of 1903," *Western Political Quarterly,* XIV (1961), 535–43; for Morgan's decisive influence see Major, "Who Wrote the Hay–Bunau-Varilla Convention?" 117. For the complaint that Panama historiography is often exaggerated see Waldo Heinrichs, "The Panama Canal in History, Policy, and Caricature," *Latin American Research Review,* XVII (1982), 247–61.

precluded Colombia from simply and irrationally refusing to deal with the United States while continuing to hold an unwilling Panama. What Marroquín really wanted—American money and technology for the Panama canal with Colombian ownership and control—was not diplomatically possible, but Marroquín did not believe in running the world by diplomacy. Marroquín never wavered. Although he wrote scholarly books and social novels, served as an educational administrator, and entered politics, Marroquín remained an authoritarian ideologue. He played the game of politics and diplomacy as an expert technician, but only as a means of manipulating his enemies, never as a form of compromise.[8]

From the beginning of Colombia's canal negotiations with the United States, Marroquín's unequivocal policy was to "leave the project to the Yankees only as a last resort, and then only if our sovereignty does not suffer." For Colombia, sovereignty was both a sacred word and an indefinable metaphor that did not meet any American legal definition. The American insistence on absolute control matched Colombia's obsession with sovereignty. The two nations would have needed more goodwill and mutual cultural comprehension than either could manage in 1902 to reach an accommodation that was even partly satisfactory to either. For Marroquín, yielding was out of the question. No price was too high to maintain a hierarchy of beliefs that he feared would be endangered by foreign influence, be it from Americans, from modernism, or from Colombia's own Liberals. A civil war that cost one hundred thousand Colombian lives and destroyed most of the nation's wealth was a price Marroquín was willing to pay to maintain the narrow, provincial, premodern authoritarian Catholicism of the Bogotán world he cherished in words—in his four novels—and in his deeds as acting president.[9]

Roosevelt was sure that Marroquín could have won ratification of the Hay–Herrán Treaty, and he knew that Marroquín's government

8. TR, *Autobiography*, in *TRWN*, XX, 508; TR to William R. Thayer, July 2, 1915, in *MRL*, VIII, 945. For Marroquín's life and politics see Charles Bergquist, *Coffee and Conflict in Colombia, 1886–1910* (Durham, N.C., 1980); Eduardo Lemaitre, *Panama y su separación de Colombia* (Bogotá, 1980); Joseph Arbena, "The Panama Problem in Colombian History" (Ph.D. dissertation, University of Virginia, 1970). One of the few American historians to consider Marroquín seriously is Marks, *Velvet on Iron*, 14–15, 96–105.

9. José Marroquín to Manuel Naría Astro V., August 21, 1901, quoted in Bergquist, *Coffee and Conflict in Colombia*, 216; Colombia's absorption with the question of sovereignty is discussed in Dwight Carroll Miner, *The Fight for the Panama Route: The Story of the Spooner Act and the Hay-Herrán Treaty* (New York, 1940), 132.

had broken its promises to the United States many times. Roosevelt was infuriated by the obvious inconsistency of an authoritarian leader who appeared to be defeated by the opposition of a weak Congress. At times, Roosevelt felt that Colombia's actions were dictated by a design that he could not explain or comprehend as much as by the commonly attributed motives of greed or ineptitude. Without knowing why, Roosevelt sensed that further diplomacy was futile, dismissing the arguments of those who thought that more negotiation would eventually convince Colombia. But Marroquín did not want a Panama canal, nor did he care about Panama. For Marroquín and the Conservative Colombians, no compensation would have been sufficient to permit a foreign canal in the isthmus. Had Marroquín been less determined to maintain the *status quo* of premodern Colombia, he would not have have risked losing Panama, especially since both Panama and the United States frequently threatened either separation or seizure.[10]

By 1900, Bogotá's almost complete isolation reflected Colombia's purposeful rejection of a changing world. Bogotá, at times impossible to reach even after a seven-week journey from the nearest Colombian coastal port, often interrupted its telegraphic link with the outside world. Telegraphic communications were the bane of Colombian-American diplomacy, and the frequent interruptions in service kept diplomats of both nations in Washington equally confused. The mysteries of Colombian telegraphy were generally blamed on classic Latin American technological ineptitude, though when the cable service broke down for three weeks during the Colombian Senate's Panama debate, precluding any possible last-minute compromise negotiations, some Americans grew suspicious.[11]

Colombia's ability to defeat the paraphernalia of modern technology has been consistently underestimated. The question over whether to build railroads was at the heart of the Colombian Liberal-Conservative struggle. Liberals wanted modernism with its new ideas, the railroads Conservatives hated, foreign capital, and foreign influence, all per-

10. See TR, "Colombia: The Proposed Message to Congress," November, 1903, in *TRWN*, XX, 550. Marks, *Velvet on Iron*, 99–102; for warnings to Marroquín and Colombia's unpreparedness see Arbena, "Panama Problem in Colombian History," 97; and Favell, "Antecedents of Panama's Separation from Colombia" (Ph.D. dissertation, Fletcher School of Law and Diplomacy, 1951), 235–36, 241, 262.

11. For the cable interruptions see Marks, *Velvet on Iron*, 101–102; and Favell, "Antecedents," 249. For Colombia's isolation see Richard L. Lael, *Arrogant Diplomacy: U.S. Policy Toward Colombia, 1903–1922* (Wilmington, Del., 1987), 40–45; and Miner, *Fight for the Panama Route*, 39–40.

ceived as serious threats to traditional Iberian Catholicism. The Panama canal was widely portrayed as a superefficient transcontinental
railroad. Many Latin Americans were more antimodern than anti-
American. Railroads and Americans were often related and could be
hated with equal passion. By focusing on the virulent anti-Americanism in Colombia following the Panamanian revolution, it is easy to
overlook the even fiercer hatred Conservatives reserved for Liberals
well before the Panama canal became an issue. Americans were a distant plague which Marroquín's conservatives wanted to keep that
way. Closer to home, Liberals appeared more dangerous—before the
Panama Canal united Liberals, Americans, and modernism.[12]

Sovereignty became a handy stalking-horse for defending Colombia against both modernism and Americanism. Colombia's—Marroquín's—idea of sovereignty might have shocked Theodore Roosevelt
even more than Marroquín's apparent perfidy and his overt authoritarianism. For Marroquín, ideal sovereignty was nothing less than
Bogotá permanently ensconced in a time warp centered in the coffee
prosperity of the early 1890s and the doctrinaire Catholicism of the
1850s, before Liberalism began its attack on the church and well before the threat of Protestantism and transcontinental railroads. What
so angered Theodore Roosevelt in retrospect was Bogotá's apparent
hypocrisy in arguing questions of sovereignty with the United States
while practicing the worst kind of oppression upon Panama. For
Marroquín, anything that was not orthodox Catholicism or part of the
intentionally narrow Bogotán view of the world was foreign and
worthless. Bogotá cared little about Panama. It had allowed the United
States to run Panama's affairs for half a century. The Americans ran
the railroad and policed the canal zone, all at Colombia's behest. The
French, too, were allowed to do what they wanted in Panama as long
as they continued to pay their tribute to the Bogotá treasury. Roosevelt complained, "As for Colombia's attitude, it is incomprehensible

12. Charles Bergquist, "Political Economy of the Colombian Presidential Election
of 1897," *HAHR*, LVI (1976), 1–30; Malcolm Deas, "Fiscal Problems of Nineteenth-
Century Colombia," *Journal of Latin American Studies*, XIV (1982), 287–328; Helen Delpar, *Red Against Blue: The Liberal Party in Colombian Politics, 1863–1899* (University, Ala.,
1981). For the argument (made by Morgan and others) that railroad interests opposed a
canal see Richard, "Panama Canal in American National Consciousness," 125–26; and
Fry, "John Tyler Morgan's Southern Expansionism," 345. See also Mary Patricia Chapman, "Yankeephobia: An Analysis of the Anti-United States Bias of Certain Spanish
South American Intellectuals" (Ph.D. dissertation, Stanford University, 1950), esp.
20–21.

upon any theory of desire to see the canal built upon the basis of mutual advantage alike to those building it and to Colombia itself." The Colombia that had just ended a religious war in 1902 did not understand North American niceties such as mutual advantage. "Obviously it is Colombia's duty to help toward such completion [of the canal]," well expressed the North American view of duty; Bogotá's view was far different. One revolutionary Panamanian complained in 1903, in much the same aggrieved tone as Theodore Roosevelt, that Colombia "did not bridge for us a single river, nor make a single roadway, nor erect a single college where our children could be educated, nor do anything at all to advance our industries." For Panama, "the building of that canal [was] a matter of life or death to us. We wanted that because it meant, with the United States in control of it, peace and prosperity for us."[13]

Marroquín and Colombia wanted nothing to do with United States control and as little to do with Panamanians as possible. When the combination of French and American pressure in 1901 convinced Marroquín that he had to negotiate at least the appearance of a canal settlement, his policies remained consistent throughout the diplomatic struggle. He would make impossible demands, then delay, and after his own exasperated diplomat told him that the tactic was no longer possible, he would outsmart the diplomat as well as the United States by shrewdly replacing him with a new representative who had to begin the negotiations anew. His appointment of José Concha in 1902 was the most effective example of this strategy because Concha did not even speak English. Marroquín's main objective was limited and defensive—to prevent Nicaragua from becoming the American choice. The ensuing stalemate—with no isthmian canal—maintained the *status quo* and defined Marroquín's ideal outcome.[14]

13. Sovereignty is discussed in Favell, "Antecedents," 229; and Miner, *Fight for the Panama Route,* 132. For the view that disputes over Catholicism were the main ideological issues in Colombian politics see Helen Delpar, "Aspects of Liberal Factionalism in Colombia," *HAHR,* LI (1974), 251; see Carey Shaw, "Church and State in Colombia as Observed by American Diplomats, 1834–1906," *HAHR,* XXI (1941), 577–613; and Jonathan C. Brown, "The Genteel Tradition of Nineteenth Century Colombian Culture," *Americas,* XXXVI (1980), esp. 451; Delpar, *Red Against Blue,* 27, 65, 78–80, 118–19. See also John Lynch, "The Catholic Church in Latin America, 1830–1930," *CHLA,* IV, 527–95; and Glen Caudill Dealy, *The Public Man: An Interpretation of Latin American and Other Catholic Countries* (Amherst, Mass., 1977). TR, "Colombia: The Proposed Message to Congress," November, 1903, in *TRWN,* XX, 550; New York *Evening Post,* December 8, 1903, quoted by TR, Message to Congress, January 4, 1904, in *SP,* 589.

14. Favell, "Antecedents," 180–202; for the delays during the Concha-Hay negotiations see Miner, *Fight for the Panama Route,* 136–47.

If one views Marroquín as a political leader of a national state, his performance was abysmal. As a religious leader who used politics to further his nineteenth-century views of the dominance of church over state, however, the educator turned national leader was a striking success. Before entering politics, Marroquín was a scholarly philologist specializing in Castillian spelling and grammar. He entered politics as a religious educator dedicated to maintaining Catholic ideals in an increasingly secular—Liberal—society. As a political religious leader, Marroquín was remarkably successful. He helped found an organization whose efforts to reestablish orthodox Catholicism in 1865 eventually led to the Regeneration movement that culminated in two major civil wars. Learned as well as pious, Marroquín helped establish a national Catholic university and served as its first rector. When he became the leader of a badly divided nation, chosen because he was old, apparently malleable, and nonpolitical, Marroquín turned an already divisive situation into an unrelenting civil war, personally rejecting every possible compromise while at the same time manipulating the various political factions and maintaining his own authoritarian power. Marroquín reached the summit of his career as the catalyst and leader of the War of the Thousand Days, in many ways a religious war.[15]

Not only Theodore Roosevelt but the Colombian Liberals and many of the Conservative faction, including old allies and friends of Marroquín such as Senator Miguel Antonio Caro, found that he could be dealt with effectively only on a field of battle. Marroquín's peculiar political genius required Roosevelt to fight for his canal. Roosevelt was shrewd enough to avoid doing the fighting himself or with American forces, but he was not shrewd enough to avoid being blamed for using force. Marroquín lived up to his ideal of an effective and deadly twentieth-century reactionary religious revolutionary. Roosevelt, like the Colombian Liberals before him, discovered firsthand the capabilities of the fanatic Colombian leader, who pretended to play politics only repeatedly to crush hopes of compromise he had encouraged during the War of the Thousand Days. He used the same tactic in the battle against an American canal at Panama. Marroquín remained obdurate though many Colombians could see no point in threatening to retake Panama or go to war with the United States. By appointing

15. For Marroquín's life and political career see Bergquist, *Coffee and Conflict in Colombia*, 154–56; Favell, "Antecedents," 178; Luis Martínez Delgado, *Historia de un cambio de gobierno* (Bogotá, 1958), 56–57; and Lemaitre, *Panamá y su separación de Colombia*, 258–62.

Reyes "Generalisimo of the Armies in operations along the Atlantic and Pacific coasts and in the Department of Panama," and falsely reporting that troops were on the way to the isthmus simply to keep up morale, Marroquín effectively ended any hope of early reconciliation and added a needless military complication to the crisis.[16]

Protestant American tenacity eventually defeated Marroquín. Roosevelt, who was as far from the stereotypical image of impatience as one could be, and the long-suffering John Hay put up with every one of Colombia's delaying tactics until the resourceful Marroquín ran out of ways to continue putting off a decision. Marroquín, however, came closer to complete victory than is generally recognized. Only Theodore Roosevelt's willingness to undertake an unprecedented and politically risky policy—independent of orthodox diplomacy—defeated Marroquín's masterful strategy. As one German newspaper observed: "The Americans got tired of being led around by the nose by the Colombians." The London *Times* accused Colombia of "wanton procrastination" and "blackmail" of the United States and the Compagnie Nouvelle.[17]

Those Colombians who left the narrow atmosphere of provincial Bogotá, even temporarily, knew that the energy of the North Americans was more powerful than the inertia of the Conservative Colombians. Carlos Martinéz Silva, then José Concha, and finally Tomás Herrán all predicted the eventual triumph of the United States. Each

16. For Caro's indictment of Marroquín see Favell, "Antecedents," 252–53; for Marroquín's obduracy see Decree No. 997, November 7, 1903, quoted in Arbena, "Panama Problem in Colombian History," 109. For the U.S. overreaction to Marroquín's war threat and its planned mobilization of ten thousand troops see General Staff memoranda, December 22–26, War College Division, file 7113b, Box 173, RG 165, NA.

17. Berlin *Vossische Zeitung*, quoted in "Europe on the Isthmian Situation," in *LD*, November 28, 1903, p. 748; London *Times*, November 5, 1903, quoted in Marks, *Velvet on Iron*, 124, n. 33. Examples of Marroquín's manipulations include his claim, "Colombia wants a canal," coupled with an ambivalent requirement to submit the treaty to a congress in Charles B. Hart to JH, November 25, 1902, in Despatches from American Ministers to Colombia, T33, Roll 58, RG 59, NA. Claude Chauncey Mallet's description of how Marroquín used the pretext of peace talks to trap Liberal soldiers leaving after the staged negotiations failed is in Mallet to Lord Lansdowne, August 7, September 15, 1902, in FO 55/408, PRO. For Marroquín's wangling the gunboat *Bogotá* to win control of the seas from the Liberals in Panama see DuVal, *Cadiz to Cathay*, 186; and JH to Hart, October 7, 1902, in Diplomatic Instructions, M77, Roll 48, RG 59, NA. For Marroquín's negative position in his opening address on the Colombian Senate's debate of the Hay-Herran Treaty as a means of remaining blameless see Favell, "Antecedents," 241. For Caro's charge that Marroquín manipulated the Senate by reading Beaupré's confidential correspondence, see George Welby to Lord Lansdowne, August 15, 1903, in FO 115/1276, PRO. For Marroquín's blaming the Colombian Senate for the loss of Panama see Arbena, "Panama Problem in Colombian History," 239.

of them told Marroquín that if he persisted, he would eventually lose both the proffered money and Panama. Marroquín may have realized instinctively that Panama was already all but legally lost and that a diplomatic and financial settlement with the United States that would breach Bogotá's premodern seclusion was a bargain with the devil for no useful purpose. What both the United States and Panama wanted was the antithesis of what the Marroquín Colombians wanted. Rafael Reyes may have understood the confrontation better than Roosevelt or Marroquín because Reyes was a part of both worlds, the new modernism of North America and the old orthodoxy of South America. In 1901, while in exile from the Colombian revolution, Reyes declared in a speech in Mexico City that "in times past it was the Cross or the Koran, the sword or the book that accomplished the conquests of civilization; today it is the powerful locomotive, flying over the shining rail, breathing like a volcano, that awakens people to progress, well-being and liberty . . . and those who do not conform to that progress it crushes beneath its wheels." There is no better prediction or description of the tragic American-Colombian confrontation that culminated in the Panama revolution of 1903 and the American-Panamanian alliance that followed.[18]

After the Marroquín-Roosevelt confrontation ended with Colombia's loss of Panama, Marroquín and the Liberal-Conservative center of Colombian politics gave way to a new bipartisan political order. Although the bitter 1904 election between Rafael Reyes and Conservative Joaquín Vélez was close, many Colombians blamed the old system of government that allowed Marroquín to set his own policies unchecked by an effective opposition party or advice from a cross section of his own party. Reyes's Quinquenio (as his presidency is called) restored Colombia's foreign credit, built new railroads, and increased support for export agriculture. Reyes reformed the military, appointed Liberals to his cabinet (over Marroquín's protests), and insisted that

18. Warnings to Marroquín about the loss of Panama include Tomás Herrán to José Marroquín, April 3, May 22, and June 26, 1903, in DuVal, *Cadiz to Cathay*, 218, 221, 231; Favell, "Antecedents," 235–36; José Pablo Uribe B. to Marroquín, September 8, 1903; and Juan B. Pérez y Soto to Marroquín, September 2, 1903, cited in Arbena, "Panama Problem in Colombian History," 97; Philippe Bunau-Varilla to Marroquín, June 13, 1903, in *BVC*, 267–68; Anguizola, *Philippe Bunau-Varilla*, 223–24. See also the charge by Alvaro Restrop E., December 3, 1903, that "this national catastrophe [was] predicted and announced since the year 1896," quoted in Arbena, "Colombian Interpretations of the Role of the United States in the Independence of Panama," *North Dakota Quarterly*, XLI (1973), 31. Reyes's statement is in *La Opinion*, February 10, 1902, quoted in Bergquist, *Coffee and Conflict in Colombia*, 221.

Liberals be fully represented in Congress. Reyes's reconciliation included making General Benjamín Herrera, the best of the Liberal generals, commander of Colombian forces on the Venezuela border and Rafael Uribe Uribe minister to Argentina, Brazil, and Chile. Although Reyes's presidency ultimately failed, by the time he left for exile in Europe in 1909, Colombia's economy, if not its pride, had recovered from the loss of Panama. Reyes encouraged the United Fruit Company to develop banana agriculture, and by the 1920s Colombia was the world's largest banana exporter. In 1914 the new union of Liberals and Historical Conservatives elected José Concha president and Rafael Uribe Uribe vice-president.[19]

The new Republic of Panama, freed from its ambivalent ties to Colombia, also developed a bipartisan Liberal-Conservative coalition which ruled until 1912. Panama's 1903 revolution closely resembled its original independence coup of 1821. In both revolutions, a small oligarchy subverted the troops garrisoned on the isthmus. Although Panama was dominated by Liberals, Conservatives initiated the 1903 revolution. Most Panamanians supported independence though influential Liberals Belisario Porras and Pablo Arosemena opposed it. Panama's constitution, influenced by the United States, formally separated church and state and restored the basic Latin American Liberalism that Panama historically favored, especially free trade, protection of property, and freedom from control by a distant capital. Panama fared less well economically than its leaders hoped. The better jobs were taken by Americans, who also dominated the business opportunities generated by the canal.[20]

In 1904, Senator John Tyler Morgan's obsessive fight against an American canal at Panama had little effect in a Senate that had learned to discount Morgan, but it deeply influenced contemporary Latin Americans, who in accepting and repeating Morgan's wildest charges failed to realize that his posturing was not serious political discourse

19. Bergquist, *Coffee and Conflict in Colombia*, 225–47; Arbena, "Panama Problem in Colombian History," 103–104, 107; Lael, *Arrogant Diplomacy*, 45–47. For the Reyes-Velez election contest from an American perspective see Captain John Hubbard to Rear Admiral Joseph B. Coghlan, February 4, 1904, in reel 41, RP.

20. Donald Lee De Witt, "Social and Educational Thought in the Development of the Republic of Panama, 1903–1946: An Intellectual History" (Ph.D. dissertation, University of Arizona, 1972), 27–33; William B. McCain, *The United States and the Republic of Panama* (Durham, N.C., 1937), 23–47; Ralph Eldin Minger, "Panama, the Canal Zone, and Titular Sovereignty," *Western Political Quarterly*, XIV (1961), 544–54; and G. A. Mellander, *The United States in Panamanian Politics: The Intriguing Formative Years* (Danville, Ill., 1971), esp. 192–94.

but a classic example of American senatorial oratory. Morgan was responsible not only for the skewed Hay–Bunau-Varilla Treaty but for the intense anti-Americanism that followed in the wake of the Senate's Panama canal debate. As a contemporary report observed, "The earliest comments on the independence of Panama and the canal treaty were mild, but later there has appeared a spirit of animosity, aroused, no doubt, by the reports of opposition to the President in this country and the utterances of senators and other public men on the 'unjustifiable interference' of the United States." John Tyler Morgan's politics of opposition cast a wide net. It was Morgan's bitter and mostly irresponsible harangues against the hated Panama route and President Theodore Roosevelt, explicable only in the exotic tradition of American congressional oratory with its conventions of hyperbole and exaggeration, more than Roosevelt's Panama policy that intensified the nascent tradition of Latin American opposition to the United States.[21]

Morgan and Marroquín were equally anachronistic twentieth-century religious warriors. Shelby Cullom, the pragmatic Republican chairman of the Senate Foreign Relations Committee, described Senator Morgan as "an extraordinary man in many respects. He had a wonderful fund of information on every subject, but was not a man of sound judgment, and I would not say that he was a man on whose advice one could rely in solving a difficult problem. . . . He did not have the faculty of seeing both sides of a question, and once he made up his mind, it was impossible to change him, or by argument or reason to move him from a position deliberately taken." Morgan refused to be called the father of the Panama Canal, declaring that he would not be "the father of such a bastard." Morgan, who led the Senate fight for Nicaragua in two long treaty debates, imposed his will so thoroughly upon the issue that many of his amendments, rejected by the Senate in the Hay-Herrán debate, were written into the Hay–Bunau-Varilla Treaty in a vain attempt to escape some of the Alabama senator's oratorical wrath. Cullom observed, "He was so intense on any subject in which he took an interest, particularly anything pertaining to an interoceanic canal, that he became almost vicious toward

21. "South American Press on the Isthmus Coup," *LD,* December 26, 1903, p. 909; Louis E. Van Norman, "Latin American Views of Panama and the Canal," *American Review of Reviews* (March, 1904), 335. See also Sydney A. Cloman to Military Information Division, December 23, 1903, in file 7113b, box 173, RG 165, NA; Chapman, "Yankeephobia," esp. 3–7.

anyone who opposed him." Cullom described Morgan's fierceness even in the final Hay–Bunau-Varilla debates, when all that remained was the final tallying of the vote. "He addressed the Senate about five hours every day on the subject, desisting only when we consented to publish his speeches and papers on the subject, notwithstanding they had been made and presented in executive session." [22]

Morgan was a master of isthmian canal history, as well as of obfuscation, pedantry, patriotism, and racism. In dealing with the subject of the new government of Panama, Morgan touched many bases in his Senate speech of February 1, 1904: "If the warmed viper, just hatched from the egg, so soon begins to warn us of its power to sting, we may well consider what will occur when swarms of them will be gathered in Panama from the lowest classes of all the peoples of the earth." Had Morgan's efforts been confined to oratory, his long-term effect would have been less significant. But Morgan embroidered the truth, distorted, and misconstrued on a wide scale. Because he was an expert on canal matters, his fiction easily became confused with fact and led not only the press but many of his colleagues astray. On one occasion Senator George Hoar confronted Roosevelt about a conversation between Panamanian newspaperman J. Gabriel Duque and Secretary of State John Hay, which upon investigation turned out to have occurred not in fact but in one of Morgan's Senate speeches, duly reported in the press and then cited as a real event by an honest if misinformed senator. When Morgan's diatribes were widely publicized in the American press (Democratic, anti-Roosevelt, pro-Nicaragua, or all three), the stories were eventually reprinted in Colombian papers. In a bizarre irony, the people who Morgan had called "the filthiest people in the world that claim to be civilized" made Senator John Tyler Morgan their new hero. [23]

The working Senate debate on the Hay–Bunau-Varilla Treaty was conducted confidentially in executive session. The public debate, consisting mainly of Senator Morgan's half-truths, innuendos, and misrepresentation, filled the pages of the *Congressional Record* and distort the historical record. Because the Panama issue was inextricably tied to the ongoing political drama of the Republican Roosevelt arrayed

22. Shelby Cullom, *Fifty Years of Public Service* (Chicago, 1911), 348–49; Radke, "John Tyler Morgan," 449–90; *BVC*, 355–57.

23. *Congressional Record*, 58th Cong., 2nd Sess., February 1, 1904, p. 1460; JH to George Hoar, January 11, 1904, in John Hay Papers, LC; *Congressional Record*, 58th Cong., Spec. Sess., March 9, 1903, p. 25; Favell, "Antecedents," 289.

against the Democratic party, the press was attracted by Roosevelt's colorful personality as well as his exercise of unprecedented executive power, which remained a source of constant and frequently bitter congressional debate. Roosevelt's tolerance for inaccurate newspaper reporting was low to begin with, but as his presidency drew to a close, his political instincts were often defeated by his moral outrage. When the New York *World*, a constant journalistic adversary, repeatedly misrepresented Roosevelt's Panama policies and accused him and his relatives of making a financial profit from the $40 million paid by the United States to the Compagnie Nouvelle's liquidators, Roosevelt was infuriated. After other Republicans claimed that the *World* and papers picking up its original inaccurate story had hurt the party in the 1908 election, Roosevelt decided to punish the newspaper with an unprecedented government libel action.[24]

From the start of the Panama controversy, Roosevelt insisted that he and the United States had nothing to hide, and he cooperated with congressional and journalistic requests for documents. Newspaperman Oscar K. Davis, attracted to the controversy between Roosevelt and the *World*, asked Roosevelt's help in tracing the documents containing French distribution of the $40 million payment that would prove or belie the *World*'s accusations. Roosevelt put his authority behind the search that had stymied Davis; with active government help the elusive document on the financial transaction was located and proved to be as innocent as the mountains of other documents uncovered through the years. But Roosevelt's own belligerence, especially fierce after his release from official presidential constraints, kept the controversy alive. Roosevelt's federal legal action against the Hearst papers kept the canal episode prominently in the news until the United States Supreme Court dismissed the case on January 3, 1911.[25]

Although Theodore Roosevelt's address at the University of California on March 23, 1911, appears to be vintage belligerent Roosevelt,

24. For the chronology and correspondence see TR to William Dudley Foulke, October 24, 1908; to Henry L. Stimson, December 9, 1908, both in *MRL*, VI, 1315–18, 1415–17. Brief summaries of the libel suit are in Henry Pringle, *Theodore Roosevelt: A Biography* (New York, 1931), 335–38; *MRL*, VI, 1315–16n., 1415–16n. For fuller accounts see *The Roosevelt Panama Libel Case Against the World and the Indianapolis News* (New York, 1910); and Clyde Pierce, *The Roosevelt Panama Libel Cases* (New York, 1959).

25. Oscar K. Davis, *Released for Publication* (Boston, 1925), 113–20; TR to Philander Knox, December 8, 1908; to William N. Cromwell, December 8, 1908, both in *MRL*, IV, 1414–15.

the offending line, "I took the Canal Zone and let Congress debate, and while the debate goes on the Canal does too," was misquoted as well as misunderstood. The New York *Times*, the leading American critic of Roosevelt and his speech, is also the most often cited source of the phrase that caused a congressional investigation and a new wave of Colombian diplomatic protests as well as a book using Roosevelt's phrase in its title. But Roosevelt's forty-five-hundred-word speech dealt only peripherally with Panama. He delivered it before an audience of eighty-five hundred in the Hearst Greek Theater without amplification and apparently extemporaneously. Roosevelt reached his discussion of the Panama Canal about halfway through the fourteen-page address. Roosevelt's many topics included higher education, the westward movement, the glories of applied science, and American art. The surviving final draft of his speech with the written notation "read" includes a much less aggressive version of what he said (or intended to say):

I naturally take an interest in it because I started it. There are plenty of other things I started because the time had come, but the Panama Canal wouldn't have been started if I hadn't taken hold of it. Because gentlemen if I had followed the general conservative method I should have submitted an admirable state paper, occupying a couple of hundred pages detailing the fact to Congress and asked Congress consideration of it; in which there would have been a number of excellent speeches made on the subject . . . and the debate would be proceeding at the moment with great spirit, and the beginning of the canal would be 50 years in the future.

In the field of practical achievement and in such material works as that of the Panama Canal America has done its full part and I would rather if you had one species of achievement it would be better to have that species of achievement.

Naturally the crisis came when I could begin the work unhampered. I took a trip to the Isthmus, started the canal and then left Congress not to debate the canal, but to debate me and in portions of the public press the debate still goes on as to whether or not I acted properly in getting the canal but while the debate goes on the canal does too and they are welcome to debate me as long as they wish, provided that we can go on with the canal now.[26]

26. For the variants of TR's speech and a challenge to the accuracy of the standard quotation, see James F. Vivian, "The Taking of the Panama Canal Zone: Myth and Reality," *DH*, IV (1980), 95–100. TR, "Charter Day Address at the University of California," March 23, 1911, in Reel 421, RP; New York *Times*, March 24, 1911, p. 1; March 25,

Although the Berkeley speech is almost always cited to demonstrate Roosevelt's cavalier Panama policies, its context indicates that Roosevelt was addressing the long-standing debate with Congress over the limits of executive power and that he was as much concerned with the engineering delays on the canal as with the diplomatic controversies. Roosevelt's trip to the isthmus in 1906, the first time an American president left the country, promoted his controversial decision to build a lock rather than a sea-level canal, raised the flagging morale of the canal zone workers, and began the final phase of actual construction. All of this was lost in the simplistic New York *Times* phrase that textbooks and popular histories most often use—along with the big stick—to describe Roosevelt's diplomacy and presidency.[27]

Once again, charge and countercharge followed, producing another flurry of publicity for the canal. Congressman Henry T. Rainey of Illinois, who had tried in 1908 to form a congressional committee to investigate Roosevelt, now did so. Rainey, originally a strong supporter of the Hay–Bunau-Varilla Treaty, parlayed a seven-day investigative trip to Panama in March, 1907, into a series of articles attacking graft in the Canal Zone and a popular stereopticon lecture for Chautauqua audiences. Wholly political in their motives, the Rainey hearings failed to reverse the widespread popularity of Roosevelt's policies or reveal any new disclosures. The hearings on the Rainey resolution of April 6, 1911, are a monument to the mountain of paper that Roosevelt's Panama controversies continued to produce. The Rainey resolution was never voted on, but the material gathered and later published as *The Story of Panama* included previous legal proceedings—Cromwell's brief in support of his contested legal fee and Roosevelt's *World* libel suit. The Rainey hearings made the Panama revolution once again a news story, an extraordinary phenomenon for an event that had occurred seven years previously. The regenera-

---

1911, p. 4. The most commonly cited version of Roosevelt's speech is in the New York *Times*, March 24, 1911, p. 1; a different, less harsh, version is the *University of California Chronicle*, April 9, 1911, p. 139, rpr. in part in Albert Bushnell Hart and Herbert Ronald Ferlinger, *Theodore Roosevelt Cyclopedia* (New York, 1941), 407. Colombian Minister Francisco de P. Borda, *I Took the Isthmus: Ex-President Roosevelt's Confession, Colombia's Protest and Editorial Comment by American Newspapers* (New York, 1911). See Richard, "Panama Canal in American National Consciousness," 141–42, 305–308.

27. Vivian, "Taking of the Panama Canal Zone," 95–100; Richard, "Panama Canal in American National Consciousness," 141–42, 229–35. For TR's trip to Panama as "a small luminous event that light[s] up an era," see McCullough, *Path Between the Seas*, 492–503; for the engineering delays and political problems see *ibid.*, 438–92, 502–12.

tion process continued as the Rainey hearings produced still more news stories and eventually a new event, Colombia's renewed claim for an apology and indemnity for the loss of Panama in 1903.[28]

Roosevelt did not respond immediately to the misquoted phrase or to being taken out of context, but he did work on a carefully written formal statement on his Panama policies, which the *Outlook* published as an editorial in its October 7, 1911, issue. "How the United States Acquired the Right to Dig the Panama Canal" began by emphasizing the canal as an engineering and scientific achievement: "No other great work now being carried on throughout the world is of such far-reaching and lasting importance as the Panama Canal." Roosevelt argued that a non-American canal would not be simply "bitter mortification but a genuine calamity to our people." After he defended the honesty of his diplomacy and reaffirmed the complete disclosure his administration had made, Roosevelt slipped into hyperbole that diminished the measured credibility of much of the article: "The acquisition of the Canal, and the building of the Canal, in all their details, were as free from scandal as the public acts of George Washington and Abraham Lincoln." In defining his role as president, Roosevelt wrote: "When the interest of American people imperatively demanded that a certain act should be done, and I had the power to do it, I did it unless it was specifically prohibited by law." The events of October and November, 1903,

enabled me, and which made it my highest duty to the people of the United States, to carry out the provisions of the law of Congress. I did carry them out, and the Canal is now being built because of what I thus did. It is also perfectly true that, if I had wished to shirk my responsibility, if I had been afraid of doing my duty, I could have pursued a course which would have been technically defensible, which would have prevented criticism of the kind that has been made, and which would have left the United States no nearer building the Canal at this moment than it had been for the preceding half-century.

28. For the Rainey resolution and hearings, see Lawrence O. Ealy, *Yanqui Politics and the Isthmian Canal* (University Park, Pa., 1971), 73–75; *SP*, the record of the testimony; and Robert A. Waller, *Rainey of Illinois: A Political Biography, 1903–34* (Urbana, Ill., 1977), 120–26. For examples of Rainey's political informants from Panama see Sam B. Dennis to Henry T. Rainey, December 31, 1908, January 9, 16, 1909, in Box 1, Henry T. Rainey Papers, LC. For Roosevelt's decision not to volunteer to appear before any congressional committee but to testify if summoned see TR to Nicholas Longworth, June 19, 1911, in *MRL*, VII, 290.

This was a far cry from the blustery "I took the Canal." [29]

Roosevelt defended his activist presidency: "The only thing which makes it worth while to hold a big office is taking advantage of the opportunities the office offers to do something that ought to be done and is worth doing." Roosevelt argued that paying France "a very small fraction of what it had spent" was advantageous to the United States and fair to the French, who "would have gotten absolutely nothing" without American intervention. He acknowledged that speculators probably profited but argued that many famous events encouraged speculation. Recounting the history of disorder on the isthmus, Roosevelt wrote: "On several different occasions only the attitude of the United States prevented European Powers from interfering on the Isthmus. In short, Colombia had shown itself utterly incompetent to perform the ordinary governmental duties of a civilized state; and yet it refused to permit the building of the Canal under conditions which would have perpetuated its control of the Isthmus." Roosevelt, mistaking Colombia's political turmoil for the caudillo warfare of other Latin American countries, accused Colombia of "government by a succession of baditti." Roosevelt defended American support of Panama: "The people of Panama now found themselves in a position in which their interests were identical with the interests of the United States; for the Government of Colombia with elaborate care, and with a shortsightedness equal to its iniquity, had followed out to its end the exact policy which rendered it morally impossible as well as morally improper for the United States to continue to exercise its power in the interest of Colombia, and against its own interest and the interest of Panama." [30]

Roosevelt reiterated Panama's eagerness for revolution and rejected charges that the United States aided the revolutionaries: "It was simply a case of its ceasing to be the duty of the United States to stamp on these fuses, or longer to act in the interest of those who had become the open and malignant foes of the United States—and of civilization and the world at large." In defending the American role in 1903 Roosevelt cited the precedents of the 1900, 1901, and 1902 interventions, arguing that the United States had prevented a bloody civil war in Panama without firing a shot. He called the "preceding fifty years"

29. TR, "How the United States Acquired the Right to Dig the Panama Canal," 314–18; Richard, "Panama Canal in American National Consciousness," 307–308.
30. TR, "How the United States Acquired the Right to Dig the Panama Canal," 314–17.

of Panama's history a record of unbroken "anarchic despotism," which was "inefficient, bloody, and corrupt." He had supported a monetary settlement with Colombia, "although there was not the slightest obligation on the United States to go as far as she went." Colombia no more deserved money for losing Panama than Great Britain for the loss of America in 1776. In concluding his defense, Roosevelt declared: "We not only did what was technically justifiable, but we did what was demanded by every ethical consideration, National and international." In short, Panama was another of the "many honorable chapters in [United States] history," surely a response to the accusations that most goaded him—that what he and his country had done was less than honorable.[31]

In both Colombia and Panama the revolution of 1903 became a historical milestone associated with continuing dissatisfaction with the United States. Panama resented its canal treaty, and Colombia, excited by each round of American attacks on Roosevelt's presidential policies, kept alive its historical martyrdom. Increasing American domination in the Caribbean, the obvious gulf between the undeveloped Latin American nations and the "colossus of the North," and the growing tradition of Latin American polemics against the United States in both political writing and imaginative literature made the Panama Canal episode a fertile ground for writers. In spite of the generally anti-American nature of the writing, however, there was surprisingly little unity in either Colombian or Panamanian views of the episode.[32]

In Latin American historical writing, polemics, politics, and history frequently overlap, often dramatically, as in Oscar Terán's *Del Tratado Herrán-Hay al Tratado Hay–Bunau-Varilla,* in which the historical text

31. *Ibid.*, 317–18.
32. See Gatell, "Canal in Retrospect," 23–36; Arbena, "Panama Problem in Colombian History"; Arbena, "Image of an American Imperialist," 3–20. The "colossus" image originated with Cuban writer Arango y Parreño in an address before the Cortes of Cádiz in 1811; see Juan de Onís, *The United States as Seen by Spanish-American Writers* (New York, 1952), 48. See also J. Fred Rippy, "Literary Yankeephobia in Hispanic America," *Journal of International Relations,* XII (1922), 350–71, 524–38; Rippy; "Pan-Hispanic Propaganda in Hispanic America," *Political Science Quarterly,* XXXVII (1922), 389–414; Edward Perry, "Anti-American Propaganda in Hispanic America," *HAHR,* III (1920), 17–40. For Demetrio Aguilera, *Canal Zone* (1935), an Ecuadorian's anti-American novel, and Venezuelan Rufino Blanco-Fombona, *Le americanization del mundo* (Amsterdam, 1902), which posits an Anglo-Saxon conspiracy (United States, Germany, and Great Britain) against Latin America, see John T. Reid, *Spanish American Images of the United States* (Gainesville, 1977), 159–62, 269; and Chapman, "Yankeephobia," esp. 3–4, 64–67.

coexists with gross illustrations that caricature variations on the theme of Yankee imperialism. In 1933, Ernesto J. Castillero Reyes, a prolific Panamanian historian, attacked Colombia's sovereignty argument as fiercely as the Roosevelt administration had done in 1903. Castillero Reyes argued that "the Revolution of 1903 merely cut the remaining bonds of an already debilitated Colombian sovereignty." The Panamanian historian favorably compared the revolution of 1903 with the original Bolivarian revolution against Spain in 1821. Castillero Reyes's son, also a historian, was more critical, bitterly attacking the "colossal price" Panama had paid for its independence in accepting the Hay–Bunau-Varilla Treaty. The national holiday celebrating Panamanian independence, Ernesto Castillero Pimental argued, should be changed from November 3 to November 18, commemorating the revolution against Spain and not the revolution against Colombia.[33]

Oscar Terán, a Colombian citizen living in Panama, was threatened with deportation when his detailed history of the canal diplomacy was published in 1935. Terán cited the inconsistency of Colombia's concurrent desire for American money and insistence on retaining its full sovereignty over Panama. Terán, bitter toward the United States, blamed the Yankee penchant for taking the cheapest way, although his thesis minimizes the eventual $400 million cost of building the canal. Though Latin American historiography on Roosevelt and the canal indulges in its customary Yankee-baiting, it is no more distorted than American attempts to deal with the issue. Ricardo J. Alfaro in 1959 explicitly rejected "the arbitrariness of Theodore Roosevelt" as the cause of Panama's revolution, a view supported by Panamanian historian Ricaurte Soler, who wrote in 1972 that Panama was already a nation with a national consciousness before its 1903 revolution.[34]

By 1913, Roosevelt was so infuriated with his memories of Marro-

33. Oscar Terán, Del Tratado Herrán-Hay al Tratado Hay–Bunau-Varilla (2 vols.; Panama, 1934); Ernesto J. Castillero Reyes, La causa immediata de la emancipation de Panama (Panama, 1933), 104–105; Gatell, "Canal in Retrospect," 27; Ernesto J. Castillero Reyes, Panamá: Breve historia de la república (Buenos Aires, 1939), 9; Ernesto Castillero Pimental, Panamá y los Estados Unidos (Panama, 1953), 84–85.

34. Terán, Del Tratado Herrán-Hay, I, 111, 276–77; LaFeber, Panama Canal, 26–27; Ricardo J. Alfaro, Media siglo de relaciones entre Panama y los Estados Unidos (Panama, 1959); Ricaurte Soler, Formas ideológicas de la nación Panameña (San José, Costa Rica, 1972), 125. For the view that assigning full responsibility to TR lessened antagonism to the United States see Arbena, "Image of an American Imperialist," 18–20. For the significant segment of Colombian thought that found the isthmus "a source of more harm than good" and welcomed its separation see Arbena, "Colombian Reactions to the Independence of Panama, 1903–1904," Americas, XXXIII (1976), 147.

quín that he did not even spell the Colombian's name correctly. "I did everything possible, personally and through Secretary Hay, to persuade the Colombian government to keep faith." In his 1913 *Autobiography* Roosevelt continued to play nemesis to a Marroquín he characterized as "an irresponsible dictator," "an irresponsible alien dictator," and "wicked and foolish." Roosevelt's account of his actions goes beyond simple retribution into literary metaphor. Marroquín's "Colombia had forfeited every claim to consideration. . . . Yielding to her would have meant on our part that culpable form of weakness which stands on the level of wickedness. As for me personally, if I had hesitated to act . . . I should have esteemed myself as deserving a place in Dante's inferno beside the faint-hearted cleric who was guilty of *il gran rifuto*." The sense of nemesis—the personal punishment he wished to inflict on a wicked and foolish adversary—colored Roosevelt's post-Hay-Herrán policies though he tried to keep his decisions within rational, legal, and orthodox diplomatic practice. Roosevelt viewed intervention as the only course possible for the Americans outside of surrendering hopes for a canal. "If . . . I had not acted precisely as I did . . . inaction at that crisis would have meant not only indefinite delay in building the canal, but also practical admission on our part that we were not fit to play the part on the Isthmus that we had arrogated to ourselves . . . I had no alternative, consistent with the full performance of my duty to my own people, and to the nations of mankind." [35]

The frequent argument that Roosevelt and his administration were insensitive to Colombian wishes is difficult to sustain. Three separate Colombian negotiators pushed the United States to its outer limit in demanding financial concessions. The Colombians could go to the brink of recklessness in their dealings with the Americans because Marroquín had no intention of concluding an arrangement but used the negotiations to buy time until the next American crisis or ultimatum forced him to appear to settle—at least temporarily. The highest American offer to Colombia—$10 million—grossly undervalued the eventual worth of the Panama Canal, as Colombia's diplomats during and after the negotiations persuasively argued. In 1921, Senator Henry Cabot Lodge estimated Colombia's financial loss at over $50 million. But Senator John Tyler Morgan's opposition sharply circumscribed the Roosevelt administration's ability to accommodate

35. TR, *Autobiography*, in TRWN, XX, 500, 503, 507, 508, 509, 513, 515.

Colombia's monetary demands. The combined American payment of cash and rental amounted to a lump sum equivalent to $18 million. It would have been fairer to pay $25 million, and $35 million might have made it impossible for Marroquín to continue his delaying tactics. Whether Roosevelt, Hay, or the American Senate would have considered such a sum is impossible to say. Morgan's presence, the availability of the Nicaraguan alternatives, and the considerably cheaper net cost of the Nicaraguan route made the consideration of Colombia's just demands for further compensation moot. Nicaragua remained an extremely attractive option precisely because it was relatively cheap and uncomplicated by France, the Colombian wars, or the problems of Colombia's shaky sovereignty in Panama, which relied more on artificial legal and diplomatic grounds than on organic cultural or political affinities.[36]

The only basis for a Panama canal the United States was willing to consider was an international undertaking using American capital and technology in return for Colombia's concessions in both compensation and control. When the Marroquín government first approached the United States on Panama as an alternative to Nicaragua, both Martínez Silva and Concha emphasized the international nature of the enterprise. Only after the three principals, Colombia, France, and the United States, agreed to proceed on that basis did the negotiations continue. After the complex international commitment appeared secured, Colombia intermittently reverted to arguments about the canal's actual value. Marroquín could always secure national support in these arguments because Colombia was obviously underpaid in absolute terms. But the alternative of not being paid at all was rarely mentioned either in Colombian contexts or in later diplomatic grievance proceedings. The United States remained confident that Colombia would honor its original commitment because for Roosevelt not honoring such a public and written agreement was unthinkable. Roosevelt's

36. Lodge's estimate is in the *Congressional Record*, 67th Cong., 1st Sess., Vol. LXI, p. 160; see also Frederick W. Marks III, "Morality as a Drive Wheel in the Diplomacy of Theodore Roosevelt," *DH*, II (1978), 50–55, 51, n. 28. A brief summary of Colombia's claims is in Parks, *Colombia and the United States*, 411–12. For the diplomatic difficulties of the Costa Rican part of a Nicaraguan route see Dana Munro, *Intervention and Dollar Diplomacy in the Caribbean, 1900–1921* (Princeton, 1964), 59–60. For the negotiations and eventual settlement of American-Colombian differences see Lael, *Arrogant Diplomacy*, 53–70. For the London *Times*, November 5, 1903, view of Colombian "blackmail" and "wanton procrastination" see Marks, *Velvet on Iron*, 124, n. 33.

and Hay's assumption that the United States and Colombia were natural allies was demonstrated even after the bitterness over Panama. The United States was Colombia's biggest customer for coffee and the financier and main importer of Colombia's large banana crop, an industry Reyes encouraged. Nor did the Americans imagine Rafael Uribe Uribe's sentiment of 1902 that Colombians were "happy and profoundly grateful . . . to see the work of the canal fall into the hands of a serious and strong power capable of realizing it." Uribe Uribe reiterated Concha's original promise that the canal was to be developed for civilization and not for Colombia's or anyone else's exclusive profit.[37]

Nor is Roosevelt's impatience a persuasive argument. The Americans waited out the War of the Thousand Days, satisfactorily helped settle the long war when formally invited to intercede by both Marroquín and the Liberals, and successfully fought off skillful and determined attacks by the American Senate's Nicaraguan faction led by Morgan. Sovereignty was important but much more as a symbolic than a substantive issue. Marroquín used the symbol of sovereignty to raise American financial concessions, as a domestic constitutional issue, as pure flag-waving nationalism, and as a constant red herring. Senator John Tyler Morgan was almost as effective in manipulating American nationalism with complaints about loss of American sovereignty. In 1903 the United States did not want to control a Central American country. Sovereignty was a political issue used by those opposed to the Panama Canal and has been used since 1903 in arguments accusing the United States of imperialism and aggrandizement. Roosevelt's government wanted control of a canal zone without the jurisdictional problems that were inevitable under joint sovereignty. Like the money question, sovereignty would have been a rela-

37. The most sweeping of Colombia's international statements is in José Concha to John Hay, March 31, 1903, in *House Documents*, 57th Cong., 1st Sess., No. 611, Serial 4337, pp. 2–3. For a critical view of Colombian popular opinion see Marks, *Velvet on Iron*, 15. Reyes's promotion of United Fruit's development of banana agriculture in Colombia and its eventual economic success is in Bergquist, *Coffee and Conflict in Colombia*, 236–38. For a useful account of American banana imports see Charles Morrow Wilson, *Empire in Green and Gold: The Story of the American Banana Trade* (New York, 1947). Uribe Uribe's sentiments are in Rafael Uribe Uribe, *Texto y an antecedente del Tratado de Nerlandia* (Barranquilla, Col., 1902), 6, which discusses the first of the three treaties that ended the War of the Thousand Days, quoted in Arbena, "Panama Problem in Colombian History," 52.

tively simple matter to settle had both sides been equally eager for an isthmian canal. When Roosevelt was finally convinced that Marroquín was stalling, he acted unilaterally.[38]

Marroquín—not Colombia—was the American problem. Roosevelt and Reyes were personally, politically, and intellectually congenial. Unlike Marroquín, Reyes was convinced that Colombia needed economic development to survive. When Reyes became president, he implemented his economic beliefs with a massive railroad-building program that helped transform a weak Colombian economy into a relatively healthy one. Reyes's perception of the role of the Panama Canal to help make Colombia a regional leader, stabilize its currency and politics, and encourage further development coincided with the larger American view of the canal as an international as well as a regional influence. Even while conducting his campaign to collect an indemnity from the United States, Reyes conceded that "Colombia, of all the countries of America, will probably derive proportionately the greatest advantages from the operation of the Canal, although the entire continent will be largely benefitted by the striking changes it will produce in market conditions." When Roosevelt and Reyes met at the White House on December 6, 1903, barely a month after Panama's revolution, as both nations edged toward total belligerence, Roosevelt told the Colombian leader, "If you had been President of Colombia you would have saved Panama, because you would have known how to safeguard its rights and the interests of all and would have avoided the revolution which caused its secession from Colombia." The Americans were not haggling to get the best of a less powerful country. As Roosevelt concluded in his conversation with Reyes, "My Government would have helped Colombia to be one of the richest and most prosperous countries in South America."[39]

38. See Harmodio Arias, *The Panama Canal: A Study in International Law and Diplomacy* (London, 1911), a curious abstract argument against the United States by a future president of Panama and one of the most effective of anti–United States Panamanian politicians. See LaFeber, *Panama Canal*, 81–82. See also Minger, "Panama, the Canal Zone, and Titular Sovereignty," 544–54.

39. Rafael Reyes, *The Two Americas*, trans. Leopold Grahame (London, 1921), 75; TR to Reyes, February 20, 1905, in *MRL*, IV, 1124; Bergquist, *Coffee and Conflict in Colombia*, 225–47. A more critical view of Reyes's presidency is in Malcolm Deas, "Colombia, Ecuador, and Venezuela, c. 1880–1930," in *CHLA*, V, 648–50. As the Colombians focused blame on TR rather than the United States (Arbena, "Image of an American Imperialist", 5–20), so TR blamed Marroquín more than Colombia (TR, *Autobiography*, in *TRWN*, XX, 500–515; TR to William R. Thayer, July 2, 1915, in *MRL*, VIII, 945).

Roosevelt told Reyes that the United States "so far from wronging Colombia, made every possible effort to persuade Colombia to allow herself to be benefitted." Both Reyes and Roosevelt worked hard to heal the wounds between the two nations. By 1906 amicable relations were almost restored. In a remarkable conversation with American Minister John Barrett at Reyes's private residence, the Colombian president, speaking "not so much as President Reyes, but as your old friend Reyes," told the American that "despite the Panama affair, I have always been a supporter and admirer of the United States and President Roosevelt." Reyes was seriously concerned about a rumored revolutionary movement in areas of northern Colombia, including Antioquia, Cartagena, and Cauca, that reportedly planned to merge with Panama to become a new interoceanic republic. Reyes proposed a sweeping settlement with the United States that included Colombian recognition of Panama, a new treaty of friendship with the United States to replace the Bidlack-Mallarino Treaty of 1846, and American help in negotiating a good faith settlement of existing differences between Colombia and Panama. Reyes rejected a monetary indemnity because "it would stain the national honor." Why Reyes feared a revolution in Cartagena and Cauca remains mysterious. With Panama preoccupied with its domestic elections, the American minister at Panama thought the "report incredible," and the British consul considered the supposed plot a rumor started by someone trying to prevent a pending British loan to Colombia.[40]

By August, 1906, Colombia's peace initiative so impressed the American minister that he wrote directly to Roosevelt saying that Reyes had calmed "even the most fanatical opponents of the Hay-Herrán treaty." Miguel Antonio Caro, the most dedicated of the anti-American and anti-Marroquín faction, personally assured Barrett of Colombia's friendship "and expressed regret that [he] had opposed [the Hay-Herrán Treaty]." The archbishop of Bogotá and the papal nuncio assured Barrett of the Catholic church's full support of the Reyes initiatives. Reyes expanded his already generous offer by prof-

40. TR to Rafael Reyes, February 20, 1905, in *MRL*, IV, 1124; John Barrett to ER, May 23, 1906, "Relations with Panama and Colombia"; Charles E. Magoon to ER, June 5, 1906, both in Box 27, Philander C. Knox Papers, LC. For Reyes's "stain" remarks see Parks, *Colombia and the United States*, 433, n. 36. For Barrett's role as one of the new intellectual elite in Root's expanded Pan-American policy see Donald J. Murphy, "Professors, Publicists, and Pan-Americanism, 1905–1917: A Study in the Origins of the Use of 'Experts' in the Shaping of American Foreign Policy" (Ph.D. dissertation, University of Wisconsin, 1970), 63–68.

fering the United States the use of Colombia's ports in case of an attack on the completed canal. The new friendship that Reyes proposed went far beyond the remarkable proposals of 1906. At Reyes's initiative, Barrett was invited to undertake an extensive exploration of the Colombian interior to be "the pioneer foreigner to traverse the country."[41]

Reyes's efforts eventually failed. Panama, protected by the United States, had nothing to fear from Colombia and no incentive to settle old grievances. Reyes was far more ready to forgive and forget than the many Colombians who had been subjected to unrelenting official as well as informal anti-American sentiment since 1903 and who regarded the "crime of Panama" with the same fervor as contemporary Americans felt about the Pearl Harbor attack of 1941. When Secretary Root visited Cartagena on August 17, 1906, Reyes, bowing to fierce public protests, was absent, having explained the circumstances in advance to the Americans. In spite of the appointment of a friendly Colombian diplomat in Washington, who worked closely with Root, Reyes's and Roosevelt's hopeful plans were defeated by the insuperable problems of tripartite diplomacy. Reyes's efforts to make peace with the United States eventually cost him his presidency. In 1909, when the Colombian Senate rejected his proposed treaty with the United States that recognized Panama, Reyes resigned and spent his remaining twelve years in exile. Even after Marroquín's death in 1908, his spirit triumphed over leaders as gifted and determined as Rafael Reyes and Theodore Roosevelt.[42]

Catholicism offers a useful context for viewing the American-Colombian conflict, which was but one episode in a series of wars at

41. John Barrett to TR, August 2, 1906, RP; see also Lael, *Arrogant Diplomacy,* 51–83; Parks, *Colombia and the United States,* 429–37.

42. See Philip Jessup, *Elihu Root* (2 vols.; New York, 1938), I, 521–27; Parks, *Colombia and the United States,* 429–37. The issue and TR's and Root's analyses of it are well described in Oscar Straus, Cabinet Diary, May 3, 1907, Box 22, Oscar Straus Papers, LC; see also Porthas (William Howard Taft) to Athos (ER), July 1, 1907, for a detailed discussion of the problem and American frustration, Box 166, Elihu Root Papers, LC. For Colombia's threatened alliance with Japan in 1907 during the American-Japanese crisis over California's segregation of schools see Glenn J. Kist, "The Role of Thomas C. Dawson in United States–Latin American Diplomatic Relations, 1897–1912" (Ph.D. dissertation, Loyola University of Chicago, 1971), 310–18; and Lael, *Arrogant Diplomacy,* 57–58, 62. For the American-Japanese problems see Raymond A. Esthus, *Theodore Roosevelt and Japan* (Seattle, 1966); and Thomas A. Bailey, *Theodore Roosevelt and the Japanese-American Crisis* (Gloucester, Mass., 1964). For the view that Root's plan that Colombia rejected in 1909 was superior to the ultimate settlement in 1921 see Richard Leopold, *Elihu Root and the Conservative Tradition* (Boston, 1954), 65.

the turn of the century. The American conflicts with Spanish Catholicism in Spain, Cuba, the Philippines, and Colombia shared many of the characteristics of holy wars. Although the conflicts were ostensibly caused by specific diplomatic differences, none of the issues alone was sufficient to cause war. The resort to arms occurred when older Catholic cultures refused to recognize (or accept) that American economic industrial maturity signaled a new hierarchy in the world in which the culture of technology, modernism, and Protestant materialism was about to supplant the influence of preindustrial traditional Catholic cultures. The new wealth and power of industrial Protestant capitalistic culture was the substance behind what was called Yankee imperialism. José Rodó's *Ariel* (1900) posed the classic conflict in which the spiritual Ariel (Latin America) opposed the coarse materialistic Caliban (the United States). Rubén Darío made the imagery even more explicit in his poem "To Roosevelt" (1904): "And though you have everything, you are lacking one thing: God!" José Martí suggested the contrast in 1889 with his two Americas, "whose souls differ greatly." The clash of cultural values between Protestant America and Catholic Spain and Latin America became a political problem when the United States grappled with governing its new Catholic colonies. In Spain the writers, artists, and intellectuals of the Generation of 1898 agonized over Spain's predicament and its new place in the world.[43]

In Roosevelt's last reflections on the Panama episode in 1915, he was convinced that Bunau-Varilla did start the revolution, "though of

43. José Enrique Rodó, *Ariel* (Montevideo, 1900), trans. F. J. Stimson (Boston, 1922); "To Roosevelt," in Rubén Darío, *Selected Poems of Rubén Darío*, trans. Lysander Kemp (Austin, Tex., 1965), 65–70; Martí quoted in Onís, *United States as Seen by Spanish Writers*, 198. For Rodó's influence see Martin S. Stabb, *In Quest of Identity: Patterns of the Spanish American Essay of Ideas, 1890–1960* (Chapel Hill, 1967), esp. 10–11, 38–44. For Roosevelt's sympathy with America's new Catholic colonies and his efforts to mediate between American Catholics, the church hierarchy, and American laws of separation of church and state see Frank T. Reuter, *Catholic Influence on American Colonial Policies, 1898–1904* (Austin, Tex., 1967). For the Generation of 1898 see Raymond Carr, *Spain, 1808–1939* (Oxford, 1966), 524–32. For John T. Morgan's "in a priest-ridden country like Colombia enough of the terrors of the Spanish Inquisition are still felt to paralyze the tongues of the peasantry," see *Congressional Record*, 58th Cong., 2nd Sess., p. 2259; for the influence of Morgan's well-publicized religious insults see Favell, "Antecedents," 225. See also Wilson D. Miscamble, "Catholics and American Foreign Policy from McKinley to McCarthy: A Historiographical Survey," *DH*, IV (1980), 223–40; J. Lloyd Meecham, *Church and State in Latin America: A Study of Politico-Ecclesiastical Relations* (Rev. ed.; Chapel Hill, 1966), 115–38; Lynch, "Catholic Church in Latin America," 527–95; and Frederick J. Zwierlein, *Theodore Roosevelt and Catholics* (St. Louis, 1956).

course I cannot prove it." Roosevelt insisted that the results of the Humphrey-Murphy mission and interview were "from my standpoint twenty times as important as my interviews with Bunau-Varilla and the rest put together." Cromwell "was a stage conspirator," who most impressed Hanna, who in turn was "one of those very powerful able men of limited imagination who curiously enough are sometimes easily impressed by perfectly cheap pastboard characters." Roosevelt insisted that the United States dealt honorably with responsible small nations, citing "Holland, Belgium, Switzerland, or Denmark" as examples and arguing that comparing any of them to Colombia was "a mere absurdity." Panama's revolution itself was a convenient contingency: "If they had not revolted I should have recommended to Congress to take possession of the Isthmus by force of arms." Roosevelt would have fared better if he had pursued his original plan. Had there been no revolution, and especially not one engineered by a Frenchman deeply involved in isthmian politics there would have been no change in sovereignty or questions of American complicity in a revolution to complicate the debate. The monetary award to Colombia for the American canal zone would have been set by an arbitration commission, which in bypassing both the Colombian and American Senates would have neutralized the equally baleful influence of Senators Morgan and Caro.[44]

That Roosevelt was able to do as much as he did was remarkable. Faced with the skillful opposition of José Marroquín, who should be recognized as an effective political leader as well as a determined ideologue, Roosevelt had virtually no chance for obtaining an optimal arrangement with Colombia. The only chance to outmaneuver the Colombian, by offering substantial additional money, was blocked by another effective political ideologue, Senator John Tyler Morgan. Either Morgan or Marroquín alone constituted monumental opposition. Together they were insurmountable. Roosevelt was as unfortunate in his choice of friends as he was in his opposition. Pushed by Morgan in the Senate and by Marroquín's deceptive opposition from Bogotá, Roosevelt allowed himself to be swayed by the charm, intelligence, and persuasive abilities of one of the most efficient manipulators of modern times. Once Philippe Bunau-Varilla was allowed to direct the revolution that proved a convenience as well as a disaster to the

44. TR to William R. Thayer, July 2, 1915, in *MRL*, VIII, 945–46.

Roosevelt policies, he corrupted the bold and straightforward strategy that might have circumvented both Morgan and Marroquín. Bunau-Varilla's participation made a shambles of Roosevelt's strategy. By overreacting to Morgan's obstructionist harangues, Bunau-Varilla and Hay corrupted the final canal treaty with Panama, thus adding authentic Panamanian grievances to the problems of the revolution.[45]

Although as a "penalty stockholder" Bunau-Varilla benefited from the American purchase, it is inconceivable that his motives were as venal as mere economic gain. The man who wrote on the signing of the Hay–Bunau-Varilla Treaty, "I thought of all those heroes, my comrades in the deadly battle, worthy grandsons of those Gauls who conquered the Ancient World, worthy sons of those Frenchmen who conquered the Modern World, who fell in the struggle against Nature, a smile on their lips, happy to sacrifice their lives to this work which was to render still more dazzling the glory of French genius," was as single-minded a fanatic as Morgan and Marroquín. Bunau-Varilla, who defended Dreyfus at the height of the Dreyfus Affair, who spent years engaged in futile libel suits against American newspapers that attacked him, who gave his right leg for his beloved France in the battle of Verdun, was hardly involved in Panama for anything as crass as money. Neither was Marroquín or Morgan. Roosevelt's immense political abilities were not sufficient to defeat such gifted and determined ideologues.[46]

By arguing that Roosevelt's actions were intemperate and unnecessary, that all the Americans had to do was wait while Colombia suddenly relented or Nicaragua miraculously became less prone to volcanic eruptions and earthquakes, the historiography of the Panama Canal has robbed Roosevelt of the credit for an extraordinary political

45. For Bunau-Varilla's blocking of a possible Colombian-American conciliation see *BVC*, 417–20; for other early efforts at conciliation see Lael, *Arrogant Diplomacy*, 30–32. For Morgan's continuing opposition after the Senate rejected all thirty-five of his final amendments to the Hay–Bunau-Varilla Treaty and his last "fever-laden morasses of Panama" speech see Radke, "John Tyler Morgan," 464–66; for the immediate political attacks on Bunau-Varilla see Ameringer, "Philippe Bunau-Varilla," 39.

46. For a description of the penalty stock process in which French courts required principals in the original company to subscribe to the Compagnie Nouvelle see Charles D. Ameringer, "The Panama Canal Lobby of Philippe Bunau-Varilla and William Nelson Cromwell," *AHR*, XLIII (1963), 348–49; *BVC*, 429; for Bunau-Varilla's extensive litigation see Boxes 18–19, Philippe Bunau-Varilla Papers, LC. See also Bunau-Varilla's "in spreading her protecting wings over the territory of our Republic, the American Eagle has sanctified it" letter to JH, November 7, 1903, in *BVC*, 351–52.

achievement—that of winning a partial victory in a contest with three gifted fanatics, Marroquín, Colombia's religious nationalist, Morgan, the Senate's Nicaraguan ideologue, and Bunau-Varilla, France's manipulative modern technocrat.[47]

47. A useful contemporary history and summary of the canal's achievement is Ira E. Bennett, *History of the Panama Canal: Its Construction and Builders* (Washington, D.C., 1915). For the charge that the obstruction of the canal treaty was "the work of one man [Morgan]" see *LD*, XXVI, 1903, p. 329, quoted in Richard, "Panama Canal in American National Consciousness," 158. For Morgan's charge that the "New Panama Canal Company has joined the Church party in Colombia and is bathing its filthy hands in the blood of the Liberal party," see Radke, "John Tyler Morgan," 462.

Part III

The Dominican Republic

12   The Dominican Context

At the time of its discovery by Christopher Columbus in 1492, Santo Domingo was both blessed and damned by its almost utopian natural bounty and its strategic location. Gold and sugar, Santo Domingo's earliest products, reduced its native Indian population to slavery, sickness, and death, encouraged the importation of an African slave labor force, and doomed the island to permanent colonial dependency. Isolated from the world, Santo Domingo was a classic colonial backwater, where languid colonists and their slaves raised sugar, tobacco, and cattle in a pleasant tropical environment marked by eighty- to ninety-degree days, summer and winter. The natural tranquillity was interrupted every few years by a violent Caribbean hurricane and in the nineteenth century almost constantly by insurrection and war. Rarely able to compete with neighboring French-controlled Haiti, which was more dynamic as well as more volatile, Spanish Santo Domingo reflected the diminished energy and fortunes of its mother country. The successful mercantile policies of the eighteenth-century Bourbon kings gave Santo Domingo a brief period of prosperity that ended during the Napoleonic Wars that restored French control in 1795. Following Touissant L'Ouverture's ouster of the French and a brief period of independent black rule, a devastating series of inconclusive battles reunited Santo Domingo with Spain in 1809.[1]

1. Sumner Welles, *Naboth's Vineyard: The Dominican Republic, 1844–1924* (2 vols.; New York, 1928); H. Hoetink, *The Dominican People, 1850–1900: Notes for a Historical Sociology,* trans. Stephen K. Ault (Baltimore, 1982); David MacMichael, "The United States and the Dominican Republic, 1871–1940: A Cycle in Caribbean Diplomacy" (Ph.D. dissertation, University of Oregon, 1964); Selden Rodman, *Quisqueya: A History of the Dominican Republic* (Seattle, 1964); Ian Bell, *The Dominican Republic* (Boulder, Colo., 1981); Samuel Hazard, *Santo Domingo Past and Present with a Backward Glance at Hayti* (New York, 1873); Lester D. Langley, *The Struggle for the American Mediterranean: United States–European Rivalry in the Gulf-Caribbean, 1776–1904* (Athens, Ga., 1976), 28–37.

Beset by Bolívar's revolutions, *España boba*—foolish Spain, as the Dominicans called it during its 1809–1821 rule—was a poor shield against the aggressive black Haitian revolutionaries, and in 1822 Santo Domingo reluctantly joined with Haiti. Subjection to French black rule, however, gave the occupied Dominicans a sense of their own national consciousness and an active desire for self-determination. Partial independence, encouraged by Britain and France, was achieved in 1844, when Haiti was distracted by its own revolutionary problems. Although Santo Domingo was free from Haiti and reunited in theory as a full province, rather than a colony, of Spain, the Dominicans remained in uneasy political turmoil, subject to periodic insurrection, unified mainly by fear of a world filled with larger and more powerful enemies, ranging from neighboring Haiti to distant France and Spain, as well as the emerging United States.[2]

The Dominican Republic no longer seemed like a utopia. Constant fear of Haitian domination, intermittent civil wars, and a primitive transportation system made the small nation unappealing to enterprising immigrants. A large group of Philadelphia Negro Methodists ventured to the islands in 1824, attracted by the offer of free passage and land. Other foreign groups, Arab and Cuban among the earliest and most important, also came, but because of the lack of communication and transportation the immigrant groups remained isolated, retaining their own language and churches. Dominicans themselves remained separated in twelve disparate provinces with little in common. One Dominican planter complained, "Our roads . . . are not roads: those in the neighborhoods are paths; those in the savannas are cattle trails; those denominated royal are nameless passages where absolutely no one has ever lifted a finger." Without roads, there was no national market or any possibility of entering the international economy. The only feasible development was near water transportation. In the insurrection culture of the nineteenth century, constant war further encouraged isolation. The more rural the farm, the less likely it could be found and its occupants conscripted. Since livestock transported itself, the passive enterprise of cattle raising with its reliance on grazing was the easiest way to make a living, a way of life encouraged by the old Spanish real estate system of communal lands.[3]

2. Hoetink, *Dominican People*, 185; Welles, *Naboth's Vineyard*, 63–141.

3. Hoetink, *Dominican People*, 15–18, 99, 2–3; Pedro F. Bono quoted, *ibid.*, 47. See Michael Baud, "The Origins of Capitalist Agriculture in the Dominican Republic," *Latin American Research Review*, XXII (1987), 135–53.

Guano, a natural fertilizer produced by bird droppings on uninhabited tropical islands, proved to be the commodity that attracted the outside world to the Dominican Republic in the 1850s. Extensive soil exhaustion, particularly in America's eastern seaboard farming states, created a need for an effective, abundant, and cheap fertilizer. Guano was the ideal product, available for the taking on otherwise worthless tropical islands. On August 18, 1856, the United States Congress recognized the importance of guano prospecting when it gave American businessmen who registered a guano island claim with the State Department legal ownership of the uninhabited island upon approval by the State Department and the president. By 1868 Americans had filed fifty-six guano island claims. When Captain S. R. Kimball's sailing vessel *Boston* landed at Alta Vela, near Santo Domingo, on February 23, 1860, and the ship's owners filed their guano claim with the State Department on July 16, however, they were turned down, victims of American preoccupation with the imminent Civil War and Spain's renewed interest in reestablishing control over the Dominican Republic.[4]

That the shaky Dominican Republic's main attraction had evolved from gold to guano is a more accurate reflection of its status than the sometimes exaggerated American sentiment for annexation, which was often promoted by an articulate political minority. In 1858, Sam Houston's appeal for annexation of Central America and parts of the Caribbean was firmly defeated by Congress. President James Buchanan's administration remained so indifferent that it neglected even specific limited American interests such as the claim to Alta Vela. Annexation was promoted by Dominican political leaders more than Americans in hope of maintaining their tenuous personal political power as well as seeking protection from foreign enemies, real or imagined. While the United States fought its Civil War, the Dominican Republic once again was annexed to Spain. The War of Restoration (1863–1865) not only removed Spain, it produced in Gregorio Luperón a leader who combined the virtues of caudillo, intellectual, and politician. With independence restored, the Dominicans established their first political parties. The Reds represented the Santo Domingo business classes. The Blues, led by Luperón and the heroes of the war for independence, were a mixture of liberals and nationalists,

4. Charles Callan Tansill, *The United States and Santo Domingo, 1789–1873* (Baltimore, 1938), 289–90, 323.

whose independence and disunity became a hallmark of Dominican political instability. After a customary civil war, Buenaventura Báez, an opportunistic European-educated politician, described by a friend of Senator Charles Sumner as "the worst man living of whom he has any personal knowledge," assumed the Dominican presidency for the fourth (of five) times.[5]

For Báez some affiliation with a foreign power was a necessity because he accumulated additional political enemies in each of his administrations. When the close of the American Civil War ended the legality of slavery, the United States became Báez' first choice as a protecting partner. Annexation to the United States would solve three of Báez' major problems: fear of Haitian domination, continuing Dominican poverty, and loss of personal power. The leader and the Dominican state had become one. In 1861 revolutionary caudillo Francisco Sánchez proclaimed, "I am the national flag," naturally and "without boasting," an early example of a tradition that extended into recent twentieth-century history with Rafael Trujillo.[6]

Báez courted a willing Ulysses S. Grant, who was beguiled by the promise of a black island state in the Caribbean for freed American Negroes who might want to emigrate—as long as they were as oblivious as Grant was to Santo Domingo's white origins and separate status from Haiti. Racial and national confusion were marvelously compounded when Grant's diplomatic emissary, Orville Babcock, reported that "the people are indolent and ignorant. The best class of people are the American Negroes who have come here from time to time." Lincoln's and Andrew Johnson's secretary of state, William H. Seward, coveted the Dominican Republic's Samaná Bay, a fine natural port, and Johnson included Caribbean expansion in his annual message of 1868. Báez was eager, offering both Samaná and Manzanilla bays to the Americans in return for protection and especially cash money. Samaná Bay, though a magnificent natural harbor, was not nearly as attractive a port as Haiti's Môle St. Nicolas, which Grant also pursued. All of Hispaniola's ports were peripheral to control of the Windward Passage, a strategic purpose better served by bases in

5. Dexter Perkins, *A History of the Monroe Doctrine* (Rev. ed.; Boston, 1963), 113; Tansill, *United States and Santo Domingo*, 291; Bell, *Dominican Republic*, 56–58; Sumner is quoted in Welles, *Naboth's Vineyard*, 96. Hazard, *Santo Domingo Past and Present*, 214–15, 248–52, 264–73.

6. MacMichael, "The United States and the Dominican Republic," 6–7; Hoetink, *Dominican People*, 126–27.

Cuba and Puerto Rico. The United States did not need or really want the albatross the Dominican Republic represented. The Americans could use its guano islands, make do with a coaling station at Samaná, and develop the vast uninhabited interior at great expense, but all of these advantages could be gained at less cost elsewhere. Enterprising Americans William Cazneau and Joseph W. Fabens planned to import camels to create a caravan transportation system in 1867, which reflected the difficulty of wresting an honest profit from the island.[7]

Although President Báez' plebiscite revealed only eleven Dominicans opposed to unification with America, Gregorio Luperón, the leader of the opposition liberal Blue party that had ousted Spain in 1865 only to lose the presidency to Báez, was outspoken against the idea. In two detailed letters, one to Ulysses S. Grant in 1869, the other to the United States Congress in 1870, Luperón listed the difficulties of the proposed amalgamation. A classic and unique caudillo-philosopher, Luperón thought, wrote, and fought for Dominican nationalism. He had opposed Spanish rule, not only for obvious political reasons but because he felt that being forced to carry a passport in their own country was socially demeaning to all Dominicans. He vehemently opposed the extension of executive power inherent in Báez' (and later Ulíses Heureaux's) attempts to sell Samaná Bay to the United States by evading the Dominican legislative process. Opposed to any foreign domination, Luperón rejected both the old European and the new American alternatives. Over a decade before José Martí's Pan-Hispanamerican articles began to appear in 1881, Luperón made a persuasive case against any North American intrusions.[8]

In his letter to Grant, Luperón used the United States protest against the French presence in Mexico during the Civil War as a model and compared Grant's annexation of the Dominican Republic with France's taking of Mexico. Luperón's call for the Americas to belong to themselves, free from both Europeans and Yankees, foreshadowed José Martí's later image of *Neustra America.* Luperón's belief in Dominican nationalism and his eloquent defense of it validated a sovereignty that

7. William S. McFeely, *Grant: A Biography* (New York, 1981), 333; Orville Babcock to Annie C. Babcock, July 31, 1869, *ibid.*, 339; Tansill, *United States and Santo Domingo,* 296–97, 267, 344; Alfred Thayer Mahan, *Naval Strategy* (Boston, 1911), 325–26; Mac-Michael, "The United States and the Dominican Republic," 52.

8. MacMichael, "The United States and the Dominican Republic," 8, 38; Gordon Lewis, *Main Currents in Caribbean Thought: The Historical Evolution of Caribbean Society in Its Ideological Aspects, 1492–1900* (Baltimore, 1983), 280–81; Welles, *Naboth's Vineyard,* 362.

remained almost invisible politically. In his letter to the American Congress, Luperón argued that the disparity between Dominican and North American life in social conditions, language, religion, and customs was so great that amalgamation would violate Dominican cultural sovereignty. In the attempt to bypass Dominican congressional approval, executive arrangements such as Báez proposed were politically abhorrent as well. Luperón's reasons for rejecting a Dominican-American union were echoed in the American Senate by Charles Sumner, who accused Grant of misusing executive power and argued that the Dominican climate—and race—set the island apart and made a union impossible. President Báez had already initiated an alternative scheme if his preferred American annexation plans fell through.[9]

Edward Herzberg, the first of the opportunists to finance a large Dominican loan, was a marginal businessman who found Dominican opportunities attractive. Originally a German businessman, Herzberg, who was declared a bankrupt in Paris in 1867, emigrated to London, where he changed his name to Hartmont and explored the possibilities of guano development in the Dominican Republic. President Báez and entrepreneur Hartmont were a good match. Together they began the island republic—with a total indebtedness in 1869 of $500,000—on its way to fiscal disaster. On May 1, 1869, Báez and Hartmont negotiated contracts that gave Hartmont a fifty-year concession for guano and phosphate of lime on both Alta Vela Island and the Samaná peninsula, the position of consul-general of the Dominican Republic, and the profits from a £420,000 face value loan to the Dominican Republic.[10]

Little about the Hartmont loan makes sense. Báez may well have taken Hartmont's initial cash payment with the expectation that however exorbitant the terms or consequences were, the United States would ultimately assume them. Báez lost nothing when he accepted Hartmont's initial and only cash payment of £38,095. Báez refused Hartmont's proffered additional payment of £211,100 in February, 1870, as he awaited confirmation of an anticipated annexation agreement with the United States scheduled for March 29, 1870, advising

9. Welles, *Naboth's Vineyard*, 362; Tansill, *United States and Santo Domingo*, 457, 432.
10. William H. Wynne, *State Insolvency and Foreign Bondholders: Selected Case Histories* (2 vols.; New Haven, 1951), II, 200–201; *HR* (Jacob Hollander, *Debt of Santo Domingo, Senate Documents*, 59th Cong., 1st Sess., Confidential Executive Document No. 1, p. 4; a rare book—see Chapter 15, note 1, for the bibliographical history); Wynne, *State Insolvency*, II, 200–201.

Hartmont to pay the rest of the money directly to the United States at that time. When annexation stalled, the Dominican Senate, claiming misrepresentation, formally repudiated the Hartmont loan in July, 1870. But by then the loan had assumed a life of its own. Even without its many later complications, the Hartmont loan was a bad idea. It obligated the Dominicans to pay £58,900 every year for twenty-five years, a total of £1,472,000 for a loan with net proceeds of only £320,000 (after Hartmont's commission of £100,000 was deducted). Hartmont ignored the obvious Dominican complications and issued bonds on the London market at 70 percent of face value. Only £15,000 worth of bonds were sold at retail in spite of the wildly fraudulent prospectus that promised railroad development but failed to reveal that the main purpose of the loan was government operating expenses, a euphemism for the Báez government's personal income. The unsold £136,400 of issued bonds was taken by banks and speculators at a 50 percent discount.[11]

Although Hartmont was an unprincipled scoundrel even in the context of the shady international bond market of his time, Báez was equally corrupt. During the annexation negotiations with the United States, Báez casually offered an American commercial agent immediate possession of Samaná Bay pending annexation for "say two hundred thousand dollars." President Grant, a willing game player, prepared two alternative treaties, the first calling for $1.5 million if Congress voted for annexation, and the second paying $2 million for an outright sale of Samaná Bay if Congress refused to ratify an annexation treaty. Both treaties provided an immediate $150,000 cash payment for Báez, who even shocked Orville Babcock, Grant's far from squeamish emissary. Báez hesitated to sign a treaty worded to preclude his planned bribe to Babcock, which he described as "an act of kindness." When the horrified Babcock rejected the bribe, Báez signed the treaty at once. Báez' manipulations went even further. He suggested two separate treaty drafts, one to be presented to his Senate, the other to the people. Although the Americans rejected the arrangement, Báez went ahead with his dual presentations. When the Americans raised questions concerning the Hartmont loan, Báez assured them he had taken only a "small portion" to allow his administration "to maintain itself." But even Hartmont's small advance

11. Wynne, *State Insolvency*, II, 203; Tansill, *United States and Santo Domingo*, 348–49; HR, 4, 78–82.

amounted to $260,000 when the interest to the end of 1869 was added. Secretary of State Hamilton Fish initially insisted that the Hartmont debt be canceled before the annexation treaty progressed, but in later instructions he reluctantly accepted the obligation.[12]

The Hartmont fiasco had grim consequences for the Dominican Republic. In 1872 the bonds went into default, giving Great Britain's Council of Foreign Bondholders an interest it never relinquished in Dominican finances and governing. Since the future revenues of the republic were pledged to the Hartmont bonds, the precedent of foreign representatives in Dominican customhouses was established though it was not put into practice until 1888. The well-publicized default of Hartmont's bonds in 1872 precluded further foreign loans, and the Dominican government returned to its catastrophic reliance on borrowing from local merchant-bankers at a cost that often reached 10 percent a month compounded monthly. Thus both the Dominican internal and external debt increased at an enormous rate without any improvements or development to show for it. American investors tried to make something of Samaná Bay and also to convert the Hartmont loan, but Samaná Bay was a chimera, a beautiful port that belied the dimming prospects of the nation. When the Americans could not pay further concessions, Báez' successor, President Ignacio Maria González, in 1874 canceled the original ninety-nine-year contract.[13]

Eugenio María de Hostos, a native Puerto Rican, who often was allied with Luperón politically, became one of the chief Caribbean nationalists. A Dominican intellectual who pondered the questions of dependency in the nineteenth century, Hostos was one of the world's first distinguished sociologists and an educational reformer responsible for restructuring the Dominican school system during Luperón's brief presidency. Like many nineteenth-century Latin American intellectuals, Hostos sympathized with European liberalism but rejected Comtean positivism as a possible cure for Dominican colonial, political, and economic dilemmas. Hoping for an Antillean or Caribbean union as part of a world federation that would protect small Latin states from foreign exploitation, Hostos was a cosmopolitan intellec-

---

12. Select Committee of the House of Commons on Loans to Foreign States, *British Parlimentary Papers*, 1875, XI, 134–36; J. Somers Smith to Hamilton Fish, June 22, 1869, in Tansill, *United States and Santo Domingo*, 358; *ibid.*, 363, 377, 378–79.

13. Wynne, *State Insolvency*, II, 203–206; *HR*, 150, 5; MacMichael, "The United States and the Dominican Republic," 11–12.

tual writing about world cultural problems from his specific Antillean interest. One of the first thinkers to espouse feminism, Hostos criticized the practice of teaching women to play music and read so they could spend their time reading bad novels and "dancing through life." Neither the Western civilization of Europe nor the blatantly anti-Hispanic North America fulfilled Hostos' vision of a good and just society. Hostos dreamed of a Garibaldi, a nationalist-idealist who would unite the world in an unselfish humanist order. When the Garibaldi turned out to be Theodore Roosevelt leading American soldiers in Cuba, Hostos, aware that his dream of an Antillean federation was doomed, became violently opposed to any alliance with North America.[14]

Luperón, Hostos, and Báez, for all of their differences, were painfully aware that the fate of their country depended on the policies of more powerful and prosperous foreign countries. Dominican leaders manipulated the various European interests as well as the United States fear of European domination in the Caribbean. Báez invoked German interest in Samaná Bay, a ploy that all Dominican leaders used with little real success. As long as it remained an undeveloped subsistence farming country, with only minor cash crops, the Dominican Republic could seem utopian. In 1871 its soil was so fertile that plows were neither used nor needed. A Dominican farmer could raise enough plantains, maize, potatoes, and yams to sustain a family with little effort. Tobacco was an ideal Dominican cash crop that any poor farmer could raise in six months without machines or hired labor. Credit for tobacco famers was plentiful and informal. Local shopkeepers honored a banker's credit, the half-yearly crop satisfied the debt, and tobacco farming provided a profitable, democratic, and easy market agriculture well suited to the Dominican climate and temperament.[15]

Cacao, coffee, and sugar destroyed the tranquillity of nineteenth-century Dominican agriculture and any hope of a stable, productive society. Pedro Bono, a literate planter and merchant, thought tobacco with its limited capital requirements maintained a balanced agriculture and a harmonious society and economy that avoided the great

14. Hoetink, *Dominican People*, 142–44; Lewis, *Main Currents in Caribbean Thought*, 270–72; MacMichael, "The United States and the Dominican Republic," 152; see also W. Rex Crawford, *A Century of Latin American Thought* (Cambridge, Mass., 1961), 236–46.
15. MacMichael, "The United States and the Dominican Republic," 11; *HR*, 225–26; Pedro F. Bono in Hoetink, *Dominican People*, 66–67.

windfalls of capitalistic development as well as the social gulf of large wealth. Cacao and sugar agriculture brought substantial foreign investments and a reliance on nomadic, itinerant farm labor that destroyed the stable landed peasantry. Tobacco encouraged an equitable domestic commercial economy with profits divided among the grower, broker, merchant, exporter, banker, commission agent, and manufacturer. Cacao and sugar farming, which required heavy capital investment and larger-scale operations, practically precluded domestic participation in what rapidly became the island's predominant and most profitable form of agriculture.[16]

The 1870s marked a transition decade in Dominican history. After the American annexation attempt failed, the country's chronic political instability intensified. The republic's main social strength—a rooted, landowning peasantry able to practice a shifting, above-subsistence farming—was undermined by the change to large-scale capital and labor-intensive agriculture dominated by foreign interests. In 1870, the Dominican farmer could move from one farm plot to another, selling cacao and tobacco for profit and living off sugar, rice, bananas, and meat provided by branded hogs feeding on the ample uncultivated land. There were few large landowners, almost no hired farm labor, and no real land problems. Although legal title to land was confused, the state was the chief landowner, primarily from older Haitian confiscations that remained on the Dominican books, an informal system that suited common practices and custom.[17]

Though Spain had been expelled from the Dominican Republic in the War of Restoration, 1863–1865, it remained an unsettling Caribbean presence. The bitter Ten Years' War with Cuba, 1868–1878, destroyed Cuba's sugar economy. Cuba's exiles, looking for safe havens throughout the Caribbean, ended the comparatively idyllic Dominican lifestyle when they brought Cuban sugar back to its original New World source. Juan M. Delgado, the first Cuban sugar exile, came in 1875; by 1882 thirty "cane haciendas" were built, of which four were sugar centrals using imported labor and foreign capital, mostly American and originally from Cuba. Sugar gave the Dominicans a growth industry that used foreign labor and foreign capital and produced foreign profits while providing no useful domestic benefits. Sugar eventually destroyed the Dominican social fabric. By exploiting and disrupting the local population and using imported itinerant labor, in-

16. Bono in Hoetink, *Dominican People*, 66–69.
17. Hoetink, *Dominican People*, 5–6.

creased sugar farming precluded any hope of a balanced, profitable agriculture.[18]

The Dominican custom of communal land and its informal land laws were victims of the sugar invasion. Fraud, whimsy, and arbitrary bureaucracy accompanied the redistribution of land, which changed farmland into sugar plantations with their complementary urban sugar factories. Sugar corrupted the fabric of Dominican society. The farmer turned laborer rejected the old rural economy and chicken raising in return for a salary that in a few days matched the income of weeks or months. But Hostos complained that though the state became richer, the people were poorer. Fruits, vegetables, and meat, previously raised on small farms, were now neglected and became expensive market items, often imported. Even the mainstay of the Dominican peasantry, the small sugar farmer, along with the rancher using abundant grazing lands for livestock, became victims of sugar's insatiable demand for labor, capital, and land.[19]

Sugar's labor needs at first disrupted domestic farm labor; later, as the Dominicans turned to migrant workers for sugar work, these temporary workers—mainly cheap neighboring West Indians—depressed wages, prevented normal development of an indigenous labor force, discouraged better permanent immigrants, and virtually destroyed the Dominican economy and society in the 1880s. Hostos argued that sugar carried over its slave labor origins into modern times by requiring a monopoly of capital, land, and labor which gave it a higher rate of earnings than the society or the economy could justify—16 percent in 1884. Eventually Dominican sugar production became a centrifigul industry, using imported labor and Italian and American capital, shipping the harvest to America for further refining and leaving no profit or development in return. In addition, the Dominicans were subject to the vagaries of the world market and to fierce American sugar tariff politics.[20]

18. Sidney Mintz, *Sweetness and Power: The Place of Sugar in Modern History* (New York, 1985), 32; Hoetink, *Dominican People*, 6, 68–69; MacMichael, "The United States and the Dominican Republic," 30–31; Melvin Knight, *The Americans in Santo Domingo* (New York, 1920), 25.

19. Pedro Bono to Gregorio Luperón, 1884, quoted in Hoetink, *Dominican People*, 11–12; Eugenio de Hostos, "Falsa alarma, Crisis Agrícola," *El Eco de la Opinión*, Santo Domingo, November, 1884, rpr. in Emilio Rodríguez Demorizi (ed.), *Hostos en Santo Domingo* (2 vols.; Cuidad Trujillo, 1939), I, 159–76, quoted in Hoetink, *Dominican People*, 12–14.

20. Knight, *Americans in Santo Domingo*, 25; see also Hostos on the intrinsic selfishness of sugar agriculture in Hoetink, *Dominican People*, 13–14; HR, 227; Richard

The 1882 Dominican election that elevated Ulíses Heureaux to the presidency was a watershed in Dominican politics, formally recognizing the power that Dominican outsiders had won in the War of Restoration. Commonly known as Lilís, his mother's childhood nickname for him, Heureaux was a valued protégé of Gregorio Luperón, who had willingly relinquished power after the war because he believed that dictatorship might be beneficial and necessary but tyranny was not. The 1882 election was a Dominican rarity—an honestly conducted, constitutional presidential election. Heureaux was well educated, bright, and a brilliant manipulator, consciously influenced by the nationalizing caudillo style pioneered by Antonio Guzmán Blanco in Venezuela. Heureaux proudly displayed his two favorite books on his desk, a copy of Machiavelli's *Prince* and Argentine novelist José Mármol's historical novel *Amelia*. On their first meeting in 1890, American abolitionist-diplomat Frederick Douglass was impressed with Heureaux, "a tall, slender bright-eyed man of dark complexion and well defined negro features." Heureaux, who looked younger than his stated age of forty-two, impressed Douglass with his willingness to work, his fluency in not only Spanish but French and English, and the fact that he carried his own luggage.[21]

Under Ulíses Heureaux, Dominican finances and corruption became intolerable. Although he resembled a stereotypical unregenerate Latin caudillo, Heureaux' balance sheet as a Dominican leader was mixed. Aware of the difficulties of his position and his increasing reputation as a corrupt leader, Heureaux complained to Luperón in 1887 that the country was "dominated by corruption . . . a virus that infected the masses." Dominican custom encouraged corruption. The government worked through gifts and concessions rather than regular wages, a tribute as much to the simple functions of government and poverty as to inherent greed. Heureaux tried to formalize the custom of subsidies (*asignaciones*) and make them more equitable, though still more fluid than regular wages, but as Dominican finances and government became more complex, the old system began to fail. "It has become corrupt to the point that everyone wants to live off the State. . . . The Republic has been turned topsy-turvy by others, and . . . I have come to govern, finding it in Chaos." Corruption was memorialized in

Daniel Weigle, "The Sugar Interests and American Diplomacy in Hawaii and Cuba, 1893–1903" (Ph.D. dissertation, Yale University, 1939).

21. Hoetink, *Dominican People*, 114, 161; Frederick Douglass to James G. Blaine, February 11, 1890, in Despatches from United States Ministers to the Dominican Republic, Microcopy M93, Roll 1, RG 59, NA.

popular Dominican literature. The mother in a José Ramón López short story advised her son to accept a customs inspector's job, though it offered bribes rather than wages: "Take advantage of it. God offers very few opportunities in a lifetime."[22]

Few Americans shared Elihu Root's later conviction that "the Dominicans are a proud and sensitive people." Even the sympathetic Sumner Welles, the diplomat who wrote a massive history of the republic, used a demeaning tone throughout his work, referring to Dominican leaders who had fought in revolutions (as nearly all did) as "General" instead of simply using first or last names without the consciously or unconsciously sarcastic titles. Dominicans returned the disdain. "I have always lived in distrust of Yankees," Heureaux wrote in 1882, though he would later become close friends with merchant and Republican party leader John Wanamaker and lead the Dominicans to a closer relationship with the United States, verging on annexation toward the end of his rule.[23]

The Dominican upper classes clung to identification with Europe and feared the materialistic Americans. But the "squared-off, triple-soled shoe of the Yankee speculator" was as offensive to American aristocrats such as Theodore Roosevelt as it was to Dominican leader Manuel de Jesús Galván. Indeed, the State Department made it clear that American businessmen could not expect any diplomatic support in contractual disputes with the Dominican government, a position explicitly stated in the Dominican-American Commercial Treaty of 1867 and described as "unvarying" by Assistant Secretary of State J. C. Bancroft Davis in 1882 and 1883. Davis declared, "The citizen going to a foreign country does so with his eyes open and with full knowledge of the danger . . . which he incurs." Luperón, who traveled extensively in Europe and whose brother fought as a Union soldier in the American Civil War, shared with many Latin Americans a common bond with French culture, politics, and sensibility and observed with dismay the rising influence of the United States.[24]

22. Welles is Heureaux's fiercest critic, see MacMichael, "The United States and the Dominican Republic," 136; Ulíses Heureaux to Gregorio Luperón, September 14, 1887, in Hoetink, Dominican People, 83; "Moralidad Social," ibid., 82.

23. William R. Pullham to Brigadier General Clarence E. Edwards, August 3, 1911, State Department Decimal Files, 839.51, RG 59, NA; MacMichael, "The United States and the Dominican Republic," 237; Hoetink, Dominican People, 127.

24. Manuel de Jesús Galván to Gregorio Luperón, 1888, in Hoetink, Dominican People, 164; J.C. Bancroft Davis to Henry C. C. Astwood, December 7, 1882, December 28, 1883, quoted in MacMichael, "The United States and the Dominican Republic," 18; ibid., 15, 69; Hoetink, Dominican People, 163.

The depth of the gulf between the two cultures was dramatically illustrated by journalist Eulogio Horta's list of cultural preferences that he thought fairly reflected the tastes of many educated Dominicans. Reading was the Dominican's favorite occupation, the "best culture" his main aspiration, Bolívar his preferred historical figure, and Paris "in the present" his preferred place and time. French prose writers were favored authors, financial distress his main "nightmare," and "struggle against adversity" his motto. Yet the attractions of European culture were balanced in part by the unique American political system. When the Santo Domingo *Listín* boasted that "in the whole world there were twenty-seven republics and twenty-eight monarchies," the newspaper was identifying the Dominican republican system with the New World and the United States. Many educated Dominicans remained ambivalent and wary of possible future allegiances. Poet José Joaquín Pérez reflected the growing change in Dominican preferences:

> And Europe, the ancient sterile mother
> Who needs the vigor of the other vital fluid,
> Without more faith in its conquests, will fall, faint,
> Before this new gladiator, vanquished.

In 1893 Luperón complained that Europe, preoccupied with its own "armed peace," neglected American affairs, leaving the United States free to do as it chose.[25]

The success of Guzmán Blanco's practical Latin American nationalism in Venezuela, the beginnings of José Martí's Pan-Hispanic writing, widespread distrust of both Europe and the United States, the inroads of modernism through large-scale sugar agriculture, and improved communications radically changed Dominican society. A steady influx of Cuban émigrés was attracted by cheap land, agricultural concessions, and relative peace. But small varied groups of immigrants, settling in the cities, soon created a culture closer to American pluralism than to European unity. In the 1880s, either Germans or Italians introduced the accordion, which became a classic Dominican musical instrument; and the large Arab settlement, which dominated retail business, introduced the *kipper,* an Arabian meatball, to Dominican cuisine. Hostos, who emigrated from Puerto Rico in 1875, was the country's leading intellectual.[26]

25. *Listín,* December 19, 1896, rpr. in Hoetink, *Dominican People,* 162; *ibid.,* 133, 164, 163.
26. Hoetink, *Dominican People,* 39.

In 1885 the Dominicans wanted and needed outside help. In his 1885 plea for investment and immigration, Hipolito Billini declared, "The Dominican Republic wants foreign capital, foreign enterprise, and foreign labor. She wants internal improvements, roads, railroads, telegraphs, telephones, improved harbors, etc. Her natural wealth is sufficient amply to repay any or all investments." But as Billini observed, in spite of the attractive inducements, there were few takers. Much of the immigration was exploitive, attracted by the possibilities of concessions, extraterritoriality, or other specific financial advantages. Heureaux, like Guzmán Blanco in Venezuela, was adept at dispensing concessions while reserving shares of the profits for himself. But as the concessions increased, so did the friction. As the foreigners began to absorb more and more of the profits and the resources, anarchy and bankruptcy became constant threats.[27]

In 1884 Heureaux, unwilling to relinquish the presidency, broke with Luperón and the Blue (liberal) party. After an intense political struggle for power, including a small civil war, Heureaux emerged as president in 1887, replacing the brief constitutional legitimacy of the Dominican government with an absolute and ruthless authoritarianism that continued until his assassination in 1899. Increasingly, Heureaux and the state became one, with personal and government accounts and loans intermingled. Heureaux wrote Philadelphia financier John Wanamaker in 1887 that his personal debt "has been incorporated into the Government's account," though an export loan a year later was regarded as "a deal of friend to friend rather than of government." By the time of his death in 1899, Heureaux's and the government's accounts were confused and often identical. The process reflected a financial system based on concessions and caudillo paternalism controlled by the head of government. Both Báez and Luperón had encouraged the establishment of local merchant-bankers, who advanced the government money for expenses in return for concessions and a rate of interest that varied from 2 to 10 percent a month depending on the exigencies of the moment. In 1887 Heureaux estimated the Dominican internal debt at $700,000 and the annual interest at $443,000.[28]

27. Hipolito Billini, *Present Condition of the Dominican Republic* (New York, 1885), 56, 47; MacMichael, "The United States and the Dominican Republic," 73, 72. For Guzmán Blanco see Chapter 3, note 28; for Martí see Chapter 1.

28. Welles, *Naboth's Vineyard*, 451–60; Ulíses Heureaux to John Wanamaker, February 26, 1887; to War Minister Pichardo, September 13, 1887, both in Hoetink, *Dominican People*, 80–81; Hoetink, *Dominican People*, 71.

Luperón had initiated a search for foreign money sources in 1883; though by 1887 he opposed the principle of foreign borrowing, the continuation of his initiatives under Eugenio Generoso Marchena, the Dominicans' European financial agent, led to a watershed arrangement with the Westendorp banking house of Amsterdam in August, 1888. New sources of money were essential to free the government from exorbitant local credit expenses that new tax levies had failed to alleviate. In 1887 Heureaux had tried vainly to borrow money from the United States, first offering Samaná Bay in exchange for a $4 million loan from an uninterested Cleveland administration and then failing, after negotiations reached the final stages, to secure a private loan from a group of New York investors.[29]

Although the Dominicans' Westendorp loan of August, 1888, became a catastrophe and an apparent travesty after it failed, at the time the transaction was not inherently objectionable for either party. Heureaux was freed from complete reliance on the local credit companies, and the country was able to put its finances on a more rational basis while consolidating its past unpaid debts. Westendorp made an enormous paper profit. Of the total loan of $3,850,000 of 6 percent thirty-year gold bonds, $758,300 was dedicated to paying the interior debt, $714,300 to settle the outstanding Hartmont loan at 20 percent of its face value, and $2,377,700 to be sold by Westendorp in bonds at 78 percent to provide the Dominicans with an additional $1,854,606 and Westendorp a handsome commission of $523,094, perhaps enchanced by $387,605 that remained mysteriously missing and unaccounted for.[30]

Pledged as security for the loan were all the Dominican export and import duties, which constituted the country's entire revenue. To guard against loose Dominican fiscal practices, Westendorp instituted a Caja de Recaudation, know as the "regie," through which Westendorp employees supervised customs collections, an obvious hedge against the well-known Dominican proclivity for leakages. Luperón, his followers, and the local bankers, who had been outmaneuvered, opposed an arrangement that, by allowing foreign control of the cus-

29. HR, 31, 14; Hoetink, Dominican People, 81–83, 69–72; Ulíses Heureaux to Gregorio Luperón, September 14, 1887, in Hoetink, Dominican People, 71–72; Welles, Naboth's Vineyard, 468–70, 497; HR, 5; Wynne, State Insolvency, II, 206–209.

30. HR, 5, gives the figures in pounds; I have converted them into dollars using a rough exchange of $5 to £1. A handwritten Westendorp journal with an analysis of the Dominican economy is in Box 1, Jacob Hollander Papers, RG 200, NA.

toms collections, sacrificed a substantial part of Dominican sovereignty in return for funds that were used for routine government operations. Twice a year Westendorp's regie representatives were to remit $278,270 to pay the loan, an amount representing about 24 percent of the total customs receipts and in theory well within the Dominican ability to pay. At the same time, Westendorp's regie would also pay $75,000 silver (about $52,500 in American gold dollars) each month as the Dominican government's share of the revenue, its main source of income and operating expenses. In case of a dispute, the Dutch government would act as arbiter. Almost all of the internal opposition to the Westendorp loan came from the interested local bankers, who feared that Heureaux had diminished their power and their potential profits. Heureaux's and his government's insatiable appetite for money ultimately defeated the rational theory behind the Westendorp loan. Local lending at high interest continued to flourish and, combined with additional foreign loans, including a new Westendorp bond issue in 1890, added to the rapidly accelerating Dominican public debt.[31]

The second Westendorp Dominican loan in 1890 was as sensible in what it attempted to accomplish as the first. Of the total loan of $4.5 million at 6 percent, $2.7 million was designated to build the first part of a railroad that eventually would link Puerto Plata with Santo Domingo. Although Westendorp money financed only the forty-one-mile link between Puerto Plata and Santiago, the beginnings of a Dominican transcontinental railroad promised a monumental transformation of the small country's economy and society. Even the relatively small Puerto Plata–Santiago rail link, which united two separate and previously isolated provinces, was cause for both official and popular celebration. As the governor of Santiago noted when the line opened in 1898, being able to make the trip in only four or five hours made land valuable and development possible. Hostos, a Latin American rationalist who favored railroad development, was impressed when he rode the first Dominican rail line from Sanchez to La Vega in 1887 and marveled at how railroads represented "the dragon of progress through the midst of a wild jungle that whole centuries have not been able to shake from its inertia." Continuing and increasing financial difficulties, more than railroad development, motivated the 1890

31. Wynne, State Insolvency, II, 207–208; Welles, Naboth's Vineyard, 470; Hoetink, Dominican People, 71–72.

loan. From the proceeds of that loan, Westendorp received $139,100 as a late payment on the 1888 loan and $120,000 as the first payment on the new loan, as well as $666,005 in compensation. The regie received $540,000 toward an additional payment of the internal debt as well as $150,000 to cover an expected deficit in revenues. In return for a small railroad and $184,885 in cash, the Dominican Republic agreed to pay $285,000 annually for fifty-six years, a projected total of $15,960,000. The entire scheme crashed in failure a week later when Britain's Baring Bank failed, plunging the world's financial markets into panic. Westendorp offered the bonds on the retail market in Belgium and Holland at 77 percent, but because of the depressed bond market few could be sold and Westendorp had to absorb the entire issue.[32]

As Dominican finances reeled out of control, Ulíses Heureaux increased his authority and converted the Dominican Republic into an authoritarian police state, using double agents and playing off political allies as well as enemies, as he became increasingly ruthless in his treatment of those who opposed him. The United States remained aloof from Dominican affairs. After clumsily backing the losing faction in the Haitian civil war of 1888–1889 and engaging in confused and ineffective negotiations for a naval base at Môle St. Nicolas in Haiti, the Americans appeared interested in acquiring Samaná Bay as a consolation prize. But the American desire for either Môle St. Nicolas or Samaná is often overstated. President Benjamin Harrison's secretary of state James G. Blaine seriously considered only three places worth taking for American naval expansion, Cuba, Puerto Rico, and Hawaii. He briefly considered acquiring Samaná mainly for political reasons after the American failure in Haiti became embarrassing and public. Lower-echelon American officials, especially consuls and ministers to Haiti and the Dominican Republic, encouraged Hispaniolan leaders about American interest and frequently exceeded their narrow instructions in negotiating for acquisitions they presumed were desirable. Leading American diplomats and naval intellectuals such as Blaine and Mahan seldom wavered in regarding Cuba and Puerto Rico as the only serious American strategic objectives in the Caribbean. In 1897 Mahan reiterated that Cuban and Puerto Rican bases were essential for control of the Windward Passage and argued that Samaná Bay was a liability that even an enemy would find hard to

32. Hoetink, *Dominican People*, 53; *HR*, 84–85; Wynne, *State Insolvency*, II, 210–12.

defend. Samaná Bay was one of the few unmortgaged assets Heureaux had to sell, and he misjudged how little the Americans needed it. Although Americans developed an often unreasonable fear of German Caribbean ambitions, sometimes encouraged by Heureaux, every administration resisted the pressure to take Samaná, which Heureaux offered at regular intervals.[33]

Westendorp's entry into Dominican finances complicated rather than solved the country's political and fiscal situation. Enough European citizens bought the Westendorp bonds to give their governments a pressing interest in the condition of an island republic that could not withstand any scrutiny. Belgian and Dutch investors joined the older British bondholders from the Hartmont fiasco to create increasing international pressure in the event of further fiscal failure. Though bondholders' interests became more important as Dominican finances waned, they were only a fraction of the radical changes that complicated the island's life. Since 1850 the Dominican population had tripled. Arab, European, Cuban, and Italian émigrés became merchants, technicians, planters, and financiers, joining a rising rural and urban native middle class. The large numbers of unskilled immigrant foreign laborers, mostly neighboring Caribbean blacks, put a stable, static rural society into an unstable transitional stage not sure of its identity or direction. A newspaper in 1891, commenting on the vast changes in Dominican society, observed that the former slave had turned into a señor. Immigrants such as Italian Juan B. Vicini, who made their initial fortunes in sugar, replaced the merchants as the government's principal creditors in the 1890s. Because these new creditors retained their foreign citizenship, they could take greater apparent risks and fall back on extraterritoriality when revolution or reform threatened their investments. Initially Heureaux was able to play off the foreign groups as well as the native political factions he was able to manipulate. But as the numbers of interested claimants and the amount of the debt increased, fueled by the president's increasingly lavish lifestyle and the costs of his authoritarian govern-

---

33. MacMichael, "The United States and the Dominican Republic," 61–62, 55, 65; Alice Felt Tyler, *The Foreign Policy of James G. Blaine* (Minneapolis, 1927), 91; Rayford W. Logan, *Diplomatic Relations of the United States with Haiti, 1776–1891* (Chapel Hill, 1941), 431, 456; Frederick Douglass, "Haiti and the United States: Inside History of the Negotiations for Môle St. Nicolas," *NAR*, CLIII (1891), 337–45; Welles, *Naboth's Vineyard*, 479, 494; Alfred T. Mahan, "Strategic Features of the Caribbean Sea and the Gulf of Mexico," *Harper's New Monthly Magazine*, XCV (1897), 680–91.

ment, the deepening fiscal crisis involved nations as well as individuals, and Heureaux and the Dominicans became an international problem.[34]

Although Europeans still dominated the United States economy, the rise of sugar agriculture, as well as American economic growth and ambition, gradually shifted the balance to the United States. One American businessman, embroiled in a soon to become familiar contractual dispute over the building of a bridge across the Ozama River, remained in correspondence with a reluctant State Department and in litigation for over a decade. When the 1890 Tariff Act gave the American president the right to negotiate reciprocity agreements, a new Dominican-American reciprocity treaty was negotiated to take effect on August 1, 1891. Although the treaty was an expanded version of the 1884 treaty that failed to pass Congress, the arrangement so favored the United States that the major European Dominican traders protested fiercely that their own most-favored-nation treaties precluded such favorable Dominican treatment for the United States. Heureaux used the pressure to attempt to gain a firmer commitment from the United States. But when American negotiator John W. Foster refused to indemnify Heureaux if the Germans canceled their tobacco imports or the French their cacao purchases, Heureaux backed down and the reciprocity agreement died.[35]

United States trade with the Dominican Republic was still relatively small, and American interest in the island was dwarfed by its trade with Cuba, which sent fifty times the sugar to the United States and imported two to three times the American goods. In addition, Cuba held a strategic advantage in American eyes over the Dominican Republic. But James G. Blaine cast a much wider net in the new reciprocity strategy than Dominican sugar, looking to Cuba, the larger nations of Latin American, and Germany, all of which offered many more inducements to the ambitious Americans than Ulíses Heureaux could muster. German exports of beet sugar to the United States in 1891 were almost five times the size of those from the Dominican Republic of $1,282,361. In addition, the United States saw Germany as a vast potential market for American pork. The $9 million increase in American pork exports to Germany in 1892, though far short of initial

34. See Hoetink, *Dominican People*, 178–79, 74–75; *HR*, 23–24, 12.
35. See Edgar Charles Duin, "Dominican-American Diplomatic Relations, 1895–1907" (Ph.D. dissertation, Georgetown University, 1955), 37–53; MacMichael, "The United States and the Dominican Republic," 39–41; Welles, *Naboth's Vineyard*, 481.

American expectations, easily balanced the $8 to $12 million annual export trade with the Dominican Republic.[36]

Although both reciprocity and the negotiations for leasing Samaná Bay to the Americans failed, Heureaux's manipulations eventually involved the Americans in Dominican affairs as an essential hedge against European pressure for payment of the increasing debt. By 1892, both Westendorp bond issues were in default, and Westendorp's agent C. J. Dentex Bondt tried to negotiate an American assumption of the debt, using Samaná Bay as the inducement, an offer the American consul declared was a "swindling proposition." Heureaux negotiated with his old friend John Wanamaker in Philadelphia, a group of New York lawyers who had visited Santo Domingo in 1891, and various French and German interests. Secretary of State John Foster, well aware of the Dominican situation from his experience in negotiating the reciprocity agreement of 1891, thought it would be useful if an American company, rather than a European firm, assumed Westendorp's obligations, problems, and rights. New York attorneys and businessmen Smith Mead Weed, Charles W. Wells, and Willard Brown formed the San Domingo Improvement Company (SDIC), a syndicate incorporated in New Jersey that purchased Westendorp's holdings and assumed all obligations.[37]

Heureaux, who wanted direct American government involvement, was not pleased with an American company's private participation as an additional foreign creditor. The United States, which had firmly resisted the Dominican efforts to use America as a guarantor or protector, now had a means of countering excessive European influence or pressure, at relatively small risk. But like Hartmont and Westendorp before, the Americans grievously miscalculated the ability of the Dominicans, especially Heureaux, to defeat any scheme of control or to reduce the Dominican debt. The advent of the SDIC did not mean

36. MacMichael, "The United States and the Dominican Republic," 49–51. See John L. Gignilliat, "Pigs, Politics, and Protection: The European Boycott of American Pork, 1879–1891," *Agricultural History*, XXXV (1961), 3–12.

37. MacMichael, "The United States and the Dominican Republic," 66; Welles, *Naboth's Vineyard*, 495; Wynne, *State Insolvency*, II, 213, n. 9; John Bassett Moore, "Case of the United States," February 12, 1904, SDIC Arbitration Proceedings, 7, in Boundary and Claims Commissions and Arbitrations, RG 59, NA; Dana Munro, *Intervention and Dollar Diplomacy in the Caribbean, 1900–1921* (Princeton, 1954), 7; Allan Nevins, *Grover Cleveland: A Study in Courage* (New York, 1932). The Westendorp-SDIC transaction is in query no. 4, in answers to Mr. Hollander, September 20, 1905, Box 2, Hollander Papers. J. Fred Rippy, "Antecedents of the Roosevelt Corollary of the Monroe Doctrine," *PHR* (1940), 278–79.

that the Americans had displaced the Europeans as the main foreign influence in the Dominican Republic. Rather, the SDIC's presence as a private American company made the Americans active participants in the unfolding Dominican fiscal crisis and gave the State Department a means of unofficially influencing events. The entrance of the SDIC into the Dominican Republic's economy was a precursor of the principle behind Roosevelt's Corollary to the Monroe Doctrine, which emphasized American responsibility. When the SDIC undertook to assume the European loans, it began a process of internationalization that the Roosevelt Corollary made a formal part of American policy.[38]

Westendorp's surrender of its holdings and rights to the SDIC was less a transfer from European to American control than it appeared. Already the dispersal of Dominican bonds on the European exchanges meant that Dominican affairs were matters of international concern and the main retail market for bonds remained in Europe. In spite of the generous commissions and the careful security measures, Westendorp's reign as the Dominican Republic's fiscal agent proved to be a massive failure, possibly contributing directly to Westendorp's own death. The SDIC's assumption of the transactions was more a salvage operation than the transfer of a normal business enterprise. American entrepreneurial expertise eventually proved as incapable as European banking houses at converting even the most favorable Dominican lending terms into consistent profits. The debris from Hartmont, Westendorp, and the various internal and floating debts of the little island republic seemed to assume a life of its own, overwhelming all rational efforts at control.[39]

Because the SDIC proposed to replace Westendorp as the Dominican fiscal agent, the arrangement required negotiation and ratification by the Dominican Congress. The agreement ratified by the Dominican Congress on March 24, 1893, required that the SDIC refund both Westendorp loans, including accrued interest, fund the Dominican interior floating debt, pay the Dominican government $90,000 a month in Mexican silver (about $63,000 in United States gold), administer the regie, and collect customs duties. The fourth Dominican bond issue,

38. Cesar Herrara, *Las finanzas de la Republica Dominica* (2 vols.; Ciudad Trujillo, 1955), 209–11; MacMichael, "The United States and the Dominican Republic," 67–68.

39. *HR*, 85. For the original plan to allow Westendorp to be the largest San Domingo Improvement Company stockholder and for the Americans to take Samaná Bay see John Abbott's reply to query no. 4, in answers to Mr. Hollander, September 20, 1905, in Box 2, Hollander Papers.

like the two from Westendorp before, seemed sound and sensible in theory. The first SDIC bond issue totaled $10,175,000 issued as "1893 4 per cent consolidated gold bonds of the Dominican Republic." Of the total proceeds, $3,700,000 converted the Westendorp 1888 loan at par, $3,075,000 converted the Westendorp 1890 loan at par, $730,000 was the interest in arrears, and $545,000 the expenses and profits of the conversion; the remainder of $2,125,000 replaced the unspent part of the original $2,700,000 for construction of the Puerto Plata–Santiago Railroad, already under construction by Belgian contractors. The international character of the new Dominican fiscal agency was demonstrated by the default apparatus, which provided that five nations—Holland, Belgium, Britain, France, and the United States—would each name a citizen bondholder to an international commission that would take over control of the regie from both the SDIC and the Dominican Republic and apportion collected revenues between the bondholders and the Dominican government. The entire Dominican bonded debt at the end of the first SDIC loan amounted to the face value of the loan or $10,175,000. Had the debt ended there, so would the problems.[40]

All of the Dominican lenders—Hartmont, Westendorp, Weed, Brown, and Wells of the SDIC—were attracted by the large profits that could be made at the front end from the proceeds of the bond issues. The Dominican government was likewise attracted to the immediate cash payoff, also at the front end. The institutionalization of the early profit encouraged continued borrowing, still easily rationalized by the conversion of older debts to newer ones paying less interest. The SDIC's second loan and the republic's fifth, $1,125,000 in 4 percent sixty-six-year gold bonds, followed almost simultaneously, designed to satisfy the consoliated floating indebtedness of $438,000 ($659,000 in Mexican silver), including debts of $111,300 gold to Juan Bautista Vicini, the leading domestic creditor. Dominican loan figures must be read carefully. Dominican bonds, considerably less attractive to wholesale or retail investors than those of a fiscally stable country, always sold to wholesale bond dealers at an enormous discount. Vicini took part of his settlement in the bonds issued to pay him but agreed not to sell them at less than 60 percent, which was much higher than their probable retail price. The London market price of the first SDIC issue never reached 48 percent and declined to below

40. HR, 6, 86, 6–7; the exchange rates are in HR, 7, 88.

21 percent in June, 1897, mostly selling in the high twenties and low thirties. The lender calculated the commission and the interest on the par value of the issued bonds, but the proceeds were based on the realized amounts. Thus the Dominicans exchanged a floating indebtedness of $438,000 gold for a long-term obligation of $1,250,000 plus interest. The SDIC paid out only $372,000 gold in cash, using bonds to pay the rest. In effect, the SDIC bought the bonds from the issue at 29.8 percent, making the transaction profitable for both the long and short terms. The excruciating Dominican predicament is demonstrated by the nature of the debts discharged, which included loans bearing interest at 2 percent a month plus 2 percent commission on the customs receipts used to discharge the debt, or the equivalent of 48 percent a year compounded monthly.[41]

The sixth bond issue, identical in purpose and amount with the fifth but settling other interior debts, some to the same debtors, followed in 1894. In 1894 the SDIC divided into three separate New Jersey corporations, though its operations remained unchanged. The SDIC continued as the Dominican fiscal officer administrating the regie, the San Domingo Finance Company bought and sold bonds, and the Central Dominican Railway Company continued work on the Puerto Plata-Santiago Railroad, which was completed in 1897.[42]

In spite of the international nature of the SDIC, which in effect was acting as the world's debt collector in the Dominican Republic, Europeans resisted the new American presence, "harassing Heureaux into abandoning his friendly attitude towards the United States." Spain sent a warship, Haiti threatened new hostilities, and Heureaux, possibly testing the depth of the new relationship, wanted visible American support. The Europeans had cause to be uneasy. As American Consul John Durham observed, "Though the transfer of the Westendorp loan to an American syndicate is entirely a private transaction to which the Government of the United States has given no official recognition, it promises to be a very influential agency for combatting the European commercial interests which lose no opportunity to nourish the popular prejudice against the United States." When Spain sent a warship to transport one of Heureaux's political enemies, the United States quickly responded by sending the warship *Kearsarge* to Santo Domingo. Later in the year the Germans openly courted

41. For the range of Dominican bond prices in the European market see HR, 217; HR, 88.
42. HR, 89–90, 87.

Heureaux. The most serious dispute, however, came with France when Heureaux clashed with the Banque Nationale de Saint Domingue, the republic's only bank, chartered in 1889 with the right to issue currency and coins. By 1894 Heureaux and the bank were bitterly at odds; when the president instituted a long overdue reform of the currency, the French openly rebelled.[43]

Though the dispute between France and Heureaux centered around the murder of a French national by a Dominican laborer, it also concerned the new American participation in the Dominican economy through the SDIC. Generoso Marchena, Heureaux' finance minister, who had negotiated the original Westendorp loan, pushed for a continued European financial liaison and fiercely resisted opening the bond business to Americans. Marchena openly opposed permitting the SDIC to convert the Westendorp loan, proposing instead that a six-nation European consortium convert the Westendorp obligations, develop a naval base at Samaná Bay, and operate a French national bank as the Dominican treasury. When Heureaux rejected Marchena's proposal, he allowed the French to continue to operate the Dominican national bank as a gesture of compromise to Marchena, who had originally organized the bank as part of his European economic liaison. Marchena, fearful of the new American influence, protective of his own contacts in Europe, and always anti-American, challenged Heureaux not only politically in the 1893 presidential election but personally when he encouraged the French Dominican bank to cut off Heureaux's funds. Heureaux easily defeated Marchena, who had vastly overestimated his own political power, and used him as a symbol of his increasing authoritarianism. He first denied Marchena the customary exile of defeated Dominican politicians, then incarcerated him for a year in solitary confinement before finally executing him. The battle between Heureaux and the French bank was in large part a struggle between the old European creditors and the new American interests in which both sides were willing to use naval power to consolidate the positions of their respective companies.[44]

When Heureaux placed his country on the gold standard on June 7, 1894, he was addressing a chronic currency problem, shifting the

---

43. John Durham to William Wharton, February 27, 1893; Ulíses Heureaux to Durham, February 12, 1893; Walter Gresham to Durham, March 8, 1893; Henry M. Smythe to Gresham, December 12, 1895, all in Despatches, Dominican, M93, Roll 3; *HR*, 164–65.

44. Welles, *Naboth's Vineyard*, 497–501, 503–504; Hoetink, *Dominican People*, 89–90.

monetary standard to American gold dollars with a new gold peso and openly challenging the French bank, which retained the exclusive legal right to Dominican coinage. Heureaux's actions established a legal exchange rate of $2 Mexican for $1 American and accelerated the conflict between the French, resentful of the Americans, and his own power. By pushing the French, Heureaux caused the Americans, who had previously insisted that the SDIC was wholly a private company without government sanction or support, to intervene actively for the company. The murder of a Frenchman, Noel Caccavelli, in November, 1894, dramatically ended the long negotiations between France and the Heureaux government that were near final settlement. France demanded immediate execution of the murderer, though the crime was obviously unrelated to any government matters, and when Heureaux refused to intervene, France presented an ultimatum demanding not only the immediate execution of Daniel Cott, the accused slayer, but payment of a 400,000-franc indemnity to the murdered man's family. If Heureaux refused, France threatened to blockade the country, seize the customhouses, and openly support all anti-Heureaux revolutionaries. At this point Heureaux and the SDIC asked for American intervention. Alejandro Woss y Gil, the Dominican minister to the United States, pointed out that in the customhouses France proposed seizing "all of the revenues were long since by laws and solemn contracts pledged to an American corporation." [45]

When Smith Weed of the SDIC complained to President Cleveland that the proposed French action would seriously injure the SDIC's and America's rights, Secretary of State Walter Q. Gresham immediately opened a diplomatic discourse with Paris protesting the proposed French seizure. The French were conciliatory but firm, rejecting the principle that a private company's control of Dominican finances precluded France's forcible redress of its grievances. France asked American help to bring the Dominicans "to their senses" and refused to settle until an indemnity was paid. American minister Henry Vignaud wrote Gresham that the French were not bluffing. The French foreign minister "is always very frank and means what he says." Though

45. HR, 165; see Wynne, State Insolvency, II, 217; Alejandro Woss y Gil to Walter Gresham, February 5, 1895, in FRUS, 1895, pp. 235–36; MacMichael, "The United States and the Dominican Republic," 105–13. For an overview of currency reform and the gold standard see Emily S. Rosenberg, "Foundations of United States International Financial Power: Gold Standard Diplomacy, 1900–1905," Business History Review, LIX (1985), 169–202.

Gresham was willing to intercede diplomatically to assure that an American company's rights would not be arbitrarily dismissed, basically he agreed with the French view. He cautioned Gil that the United States should not be considered an ally if the Dominicans chose, as Gil suggested, "to resist all coercive acts." The United States was a "friendly neutral," urging a peaceful settlement of the dispute, but "could not claim that the Dominican government's contract with an American company precludes France from exercising against that Government whatever means of redress are sanctioned by international law."[46]

French Foreign Minister Gabriel Hanotaux insisted, at first on moral grounds, that Heureaux must pay. Later, less outraged but still firm, Hanotaux said he would eat "the pie hot or cold" and even suggested that the SDIC ingratiate itself with the Dominicans by offering to pay the indemnity. The Americans went along with the French proposal that the SDIC pay the Caccavelli indemnity immediately and settle other French demands later. But when a French warship called on Macorís, three American warships appeared at Santo Domingo.[47]

Heureaux had won a measure of support from the Americans but was discouraged from carrying the dispute any further. He agreed to pay the French a 225,000-franc indemnity for Caccavelli, a compromise from the original 400,000 francs, and 100,000 francs for the ten-month imprisonment of a French naval officer instead of 150,000. The financial claims concerning the bank were submitted to Spanish arbitration, and French honor was assuaged by a twenty-one-gun Dominican salute and an apology when French-Dominican diplomatic relations resumed.[48]

Although Smith Weed thanked the State Department for having "defended the rights of our company—an American company and composed of American citizens"—and the Dominicans were equally effusive, the United States had in fact done very little and certainly had not prevented the French from winning everything they demanded, including the summary execution of the murderer, through gunboat diplomacy. Gresham ensured that the French were aware of

46. Walter Gresham to Henry Smythe, February 11, 1895; to J. B. Eustis, February 11, 1895; Henry Vignaud to Gresham, February 14, 1895; Alejandro Woss y Gil to Gresham, February 18, 1895; Gresham to Gil, March 1, 1895, all in FRUS, 1895, pp. 239, 397–98, 240–41.

47. Henry Vignaud to Walter Gresham, February 19, 15, 1895, in FRUS, 1895, pp. 398–400; Welles, Naboth's Vineyard, 506.

48. MacMichael, "The United States and the Dominican Republic," 113.

American interest by making the appropriate diplomatic and naval gestures, but neither the SDIC nor the Heureaux government could take as much comfort as their letters indicated from the pointedly luke-warm official American response. The SDIC, however, had more than fulfilled John Foster's original hope that an American presence might be useful. Gently, the Americans served notice that business was not quite as usual in the Caribbean and that the United States was not an entirely disinterested bystander even though in the French-Dominican crisis America supported the French more than either the Dominicans or the SDIC—which, in spite of Weed's claims, was only partly owned by American citizens.[49]

Cleveland and Gresham's Caribbean foreign policy was neither overly active nor completely passive. Balance was the main American objective, both economically and politically. American business must be able to compete, and European business should not dominate so as to exclude possible American enterprise; any use of foreign warships was matched by an American naval display. Although the Monroe Doctrine exploded onto the scene with Richard Olney's "twenty-inch gun"—Cleveland's later description of it—on July 20, 1895, Olney's corollary to the Monroe Doctrine was more a complex reaction to specific problems concerning American frustration with British policies and its long-festering border dispute with Venezuela than a realistic description of American policy. Once Olney made his dramatic restatement of the Monroe Doctrine, the principle became a subject of discussion, debate, negotiation, and policy, influencing all later American diplomatic activities. At the time, Olney's forceful statement was meant to indicate to the British American sensitivity toward the possibility of further British expansion and uncertainty about future British policies and to provide a dramatic warning not to continue treating the United States as a backward or provincial nation. Theodore Roosevelt, one of Britain's staunchest American friends, thoroughly supported Olney's establishment of a diplomatic metaphor, comparing it to the Declaration of Independence and Washington's Farewell Address. But as bellicose as the diction and style of Olney's declaration were, and Cleveland's later willingness to threaten

---

49. Smith M. Weed to Walter Gresham, March 12, April 2, 1895, in *FRUS*, 1895, pp. 402, 242; see MacMichael, "The United States and the Dominican Republic," 149, for some estimates of the extent of American ownership.

war with Britain when the British seemed unchastened, Olney's principle did not dramatically affect established diplomatic practice.[50]

While Gresham was still secretary of state, he encouraged the British to occupy Corinto, Nicaragua, on April 27, 1895. The United States made Britain aware that though the Monroe Doctrine still prohibited any permanent acquisition of territory, temporary punishment for misconduct was permissible. Likewise, the French were given wide latitude in their dispute with Heureaux. Although the Monroe Doctrine rarely produced the pyrotechnics that Olney's diction suggested, it served as a consistent American foreign policy well before Cleveland's ultimatum. Britain was continually prodded in the 1880s about American concern over the unsettled Venezuelan disputes; in 1886 Thomas Bayard specifically cited the Monroe Doctrine in one of his notes concerning Venezuela. Although American diplomatic utterances before Olney were almost always mildly phrased, the gentle tone did not prevent vigorous American diplomatic intervention if the provocation seemed severe enough, as when American citizen Charles Faray was wrongly imprisoned in a Dominican insurrection, or when Dominican courts openly ignored American contractual rights in the Ozama bridge episode. Circumspection and persuasion were usually effective; when neither availed, as with Britain's reluctance to arbitrate the Venezuelan border dispute, American diplomats and politicians were adept at stirring the diplomatic pot, stating old principles with new force, or provoking confrontations, well aware that in almost any showdown in the Caribbean the United States had an overwhelming advantage in case of war.[51]

50. Nevins, *Grover Cleveland*, 634; see Charles A. Campbell, *The Transformation of American Foreign Relations, 1865–1900* (New York, 1976); Joseph J. Mathews, "Informal Diplomacy in the Venezuela Crisis of 1896," *MVHR*, L (1963), 195–212; Walter LaFeber, "The Background of Cleveland's Venezuela Policy: A Reinterpretation," *AHR*, LXVI (1961), 947–67; Nelson Blake, "The Background of Cleveland's Venezuela Policy," *AHR*, XLVIII (1942), 259–77; George B. Young, "Intervention Under the Monroe Doctrine: The Olney Corollary," *Political Science Quarterly*, LVII (1942), 247–80; TR, "The Monroe Doctrine," *Bachelor of Arts* (March, 1896), rpr. in *TRWN*, XIII, 169; Dexter Perkins, *The Monroe Doctrine, 1867–1907* (Baltimore, 1937), 136–252; Langley, *Struggle for the American Mediterranean*, 152–63. Richard E. Welch, Jr., *The Presidency of Grover Cleveland* (Lawrence, Kan., 1988), 180–92.

51. Wilfrid H. Callcott, *The Caribbean Policy of the United States, 1890–1920* (Baltimore, 1942), 73; MacMichael, "The United States and the Dominican Republic," 114, 23–25; Duin, "Dominican-American Diplomatic Relations," 37–53; Langley, *Struggle for the American Mediterranean*, 150–52.

As much as the Americans wanted to maintain hemispheric independence from Europe, they also wanted to keep a safe distance from Latin America. The SDIC was a perfect vehicle, giving American businessmen a chance at the large profits from Caribbean banking, often more theoretical than real, and the American State Department an excuse for gently supervising American interests in a peripheral but volatile country. But the Americans were no more able than the Europeans to control the runaway Dominican economy. American investment had dramatically increased its share of the island's economy, especially in sugar production and railroads. When the SDIC undertook to buy out the French banking interests as part of the economic and diplomatic settlement following the Caccavelli dispute, Americans superficially appeared to be winning the commercial contest. They were also becoming more and more responsible for the Dominican financial mess. The seventh Dominican bond issue, the SDIC's fourth, of $1,750,000, named the "Four Percent French-American reclamation consols," transferred the control and the loans of the French bank to the SDIC. Not only did the SDIC take over all of the French claims against Heureaux, it financed the purchase of a gunboat for his government, though the vessel could have only two conceivable purposes: a weapon against domestic enemies and an expensive luxury.[52]

By now the Dominican-SDIC debt totaled a staggering $4,250,000, or twice the optimal annual Dominican income. Because of its increasing stake, the SDIC required further restrictions on Dominican expenditures and became effectively a government within a government. The Dominican Republic agreed not to reduce its customs duties without SDIC approval and also agreed that deficits in payments to service SDIC loans took precedence over government operating expenses. The arrangement was desperate and foolhardy because for all practical purposes the SDIC and the Dominican treasury were one and taking from one to pay the other was logically impossible. On January 1, 1897, the first SDIC bond issue, made in 1893, was officially in default, though it had actually failed much earlier and its payments were maintained artificially by using proceeds of later loans to keep up the pretense of fiscal responsibility. Various bondholders called for

52. Henry Smythe to Richard Olney, October 29, 1895, Despatches, Dominican, M93, Roll 3, *HR*, 7, 8.

the appointment of an international commission to take over the regie. Incredibly, the SDIC and Heureaux decided to undertake one more extravagant loan, the eighth bond issue and fifth SDIC loan, encompassing the now gargantuan total Dominican debt with all the unpaid interest and claims of $21,183,750.[53]

By now the SDIC and Heureaux were partners at cross-purposes. The government falsified its figures, underestimated its expenses and the claims against it, and had reduced the regie to a parody; by allowing an almost infinite number of exceptions and concessions, it reduced collectible Dominican revenues to a fraction of what they should have been and an even smaller fraction of the sum required to pay the astronomical debt. With eight bond issues now loose in the world, bondholder committees in open rebellion, and any semblance of order and responsibility at an end, the republic, its president, and the American company were plunged into chaos. Victims of the Dominican fiasco could be found throughout the world. Perhaps the most touching were the French peasants in the Tarn region, who had invested their life savings in the 1895 bond issue thinking that the Dominicans borrowing money were from the Catholic religious order, not the Caribbean country. The SDIC did fulfill its obligation to complete the Puerto Plata–Santiago Railroad in 1897, but with the massive default of the first SDIC loan and the questionable practices in all the succeeding issues, the country was in financial ruin. Heureaux, increasingly under pressure for payment from every quarter, disliked both for his own authoritarian rule and his association with an inept and unpopular American company, once again requested a commercial treaty with the United States and American assumption of German import purchases and made the inevitable offer of Samaná Bay. The American government was too concerned with Cuba to pay much attention to the Dominican Republic in 1897. The situation, still short of obvious crisis, simmered until the assassination of Ulíses Heureaux on July 26, 1899, plunged the Dominican Republic into political as well as financial anarchy.[54]

53. *HR*, 217, has income figures for 1900 and after; *HR*, 8.
54. *HR*, 36, 8, 13; Henry Smythe to Richard Olney, January 4, February 7, 1897, in Despatches, Dominican, M93, Roll 3; Welles, *Naboth's Vineyard*, 529–30.

13 Dominican Chaos, 1899–1904

In his last inaugural address, on February 27, 1897, Ulíses Heureaux in defending his leadership cited the "salient features" of his presidency. First on his list was the establishment of peace, which he accurately linked with maintaining local authority, both of which became scarce commodities in the troubled six years following his death. Next were railroads; improved domestic telegraph communications and international cable access to Europe and the United States; improved commerce and agriculture; and "the growth of public instruction," which included increased printing, newspapers, and libraries. Heureaux's last four points included the creation of an army and navy; a new national political system, which he claimed expanded Dominican democracy; and increased public construction. The cost of Heureaux's peace and his public improvements was prodigious. In his obsession for absolute power, he destroyed both of the Dominicans' first independent political parties, manipulating Reds and Blues until he had displaced both parties with himself, a destructive heritage that made insurrection the customary Dominican political device defined by the leader in power or trying to achieve power. *Lilistas* (followers of Heureaux), *horacistas,* followers of Horacio Vásquez, and *jimenistas,* led by Juan Isidro Jiménez, remained at war in most of the six years following Heureaux's death. Heureaux, a cruel precursor of the twentieth-century authoritarian leader, was a paradigm of the nineteenth-century Latin American caudillo. His sexual appetites and his paranoia were equally legendary; he turned the Dominican Republic into both an armed camp and a brothel with procurers, mistresses, and double agents in every settled region of the country. In his last years, he combined a degenerate's cunning with a bankrupt's recklessness, leaving his own estate with over $2 million in debts and an equal amount in claims against debtors. At the time of his death, Heureaux had substantial personal interests in twelve businesses, received part of the profits from several other businesses, and made money on loans to his own country.[1]

When Ramón Cáceres emptied his revolver at Heureaux on July 26, 1899, he eliminated both the tyrant and the political stability that held the little island in its uneasy equilibrium. With the death of Lilís, the Dominican Republic was virtually reduced to a prepolitical state of nature. The man who quoted Machiavelli and Talleyrand and boasted that he cared not what historians wrote about him had no pretensions about his own reputation. The Dominicans will "squeeze the juice out of me and throw me on the fire like bagasse." At his funeral he was laid out with a cigar in his mouth and a hat on his head before only forty mourners. Yet Heureaux, a cruel manipulator of old political allies, visited his old mentor Gregorio Luperón, dying in exile on St. Thomas in 1896, noting that "it was the first time a president had left the country to search out an enemy." Recent Dominican historians have treated Heureaux as more complex and less a complete devil than he appears in most American accounts.[2]

In spite of the obvious fiscal disaster Heureaux's various financial alliances had created, he remained hopeful that he could throw over the Americans who had replaced the Europeans and, by playing one against the other, could once again refund the entire Dominican debt and even redeem the worthless paper money that had reduced the security of the regie to a farce. Just before his death, Heureaux and the SDIC, each eager to be rid of the other, had agreed to end their relationship. Heureaux had negotiated a European buyout of the SDIC loans, the company had agreed to be replaced, and the change-over was scheduled for August 10, 1899. Heureaux and the SDIC were associated in the Dominican mind, and unfavorable feelings about either one reflected the growing distaste for the company's presence, a

1. Sumner Welles, *Naboth's Vineyard: The Dominican Republic, 1844–1924* (2 vols.; New York, 1928), 539; Selden Rodman, *Quisqueya: A History of the Dominican Republic* (Seattle, 1964), 92–93; *HR*, 4, 10, 31, 144–45. H. Hoetink, *The Dominican People, 1850–1900: Notes for a Historical Sociology*, trans. Stephen K. Ault (Baltimore, 1982), 76–77, lists businesses; *ibid.*, 73, gives loan profits. See also H. Paul Muto, "The Illusory Promise: The Dominican Republic and the Process of Economic Development, 1900–1930" (Ph.D. dissertation, University of Washington, 1976), esp. 13–18.

2. For the best account of the assassination, see David MacMichael, "The United States and the Dominican Republic, 1871–1940: A Cycle in Caribbean Diplomacy" (Ph.D. dissertation, University of Oregon, 1964), 130–33, 136; *HR*, 10; Hoetink, *Dominican People*, 131; Gordon Lewis, *Main Currents in Caribbean Thought: The Historical Evolution of Caribbean Society in Its Ideological Aspects, 1492–1900* (Baltimore, 1983), 281. The chief American detractor is Welles, *Naboth's Vineyard*.

reputation the SDIC richly deserved, even if it was unfairly blamed for all the Dominican financial problems. In September, 1899, the SDIC began to dismiss the regie's Dominican workers; by January, 1901, the regie was all American—or in Dominican eyes, foreign. But the very name of the company was offensive—whether consciously or not, the patronizing sense of an improvement company linked with the Dominican city most associated with American commerce gave the SDIC a foreign character that Dominicans came to detest. In one of his last letters Heureaux referred to it as "the New York Improvement Company of New York," possibly reflecting Dominican sensitivity to the American corporation's unfortunate choice of name.[3]

The regie, conceived by the first foreign creditor, Hartmont, in 1869, instituted by Westendorp in 1888, and continued by the SDIC in 1893, had never worked as well as intended, and by 1898 it was no longer a viable institution. When the government (or Heureaux— they were frequently the same) needed additional money it would take a loan from a merchant-importer at the going emergency rate— sometimes a stipulated principal of twice the loan's proceeds *and* 48 percent annual interest on the inflated total—and issue a credit for the inflated loan that was then directly applied to pay customs duties. In other cases exemptions from some or all duties could be purchased from the government, an especially damaging procedure when the commodity was widely used and heavily taxed, such as flour. Heureaux further devastated any system of control when he began flooding the economy with new issues totaling $5 million of paper money, thereby driving the exchange down from two to one to twenty to one; these *papelitas de Lilís* not only contributed to the regie's failure and the bond defaults but to the instability of the domestic economy as well, directly threatening the livelihood of the merchants and bankers. Heureaux, aware of the widening political disaster that threatened him, played off both the Europeans and Americans, offering the United States Samaná Bay in exchange for a protectorate, an offer the American minister eagerly accepted and Secretary of State John Hay immediately rejected. Heureaux used the first $600,000 payment from the London bankers who were to replace the SDIC to redeem debts from the most pressing Santo Domingo and San Pedro de

3. Ulíses Heureaux to Cordero y Bidó, January 17, 1899, in Hoetink, *Dominican People,* 91; John Bassett Moore, "Case of the United States," February 12, 1904, SDIC Arbitration Proceedings, 19, in Boundary and Claims Commissions and Arbitrations, RG 59, NA.

Macorís creditors. Heureaux was in the Cibao, a neglected northern tobacco-growing region gravely affected by the ruined economy, negotiating with a creditor in Moca, when Cáceres shot and killed him.[4]

The two new Dominican leaders, Horacio Vásquez and Juan Isidro Jiménez, were fundamentally honest and politically inept; both were more skilled as revolutionaries resisting tyranny than as statesmen able to govern once the tyrant had been deposed. Vásquez, a gifted soldier from an old-line Ciboan landholding family, first served with Luperón. Disillusioned by Heureaux while a colonel in his Dominican army, Vásquez had resigned to lead the young revolutionary group that eventually helped assassinate Heureaux. Like Luperón, Vásquez was a gifted general and a liberal idealist who shrank from assuming actual power. When Vásquez chose Jiménez to be president, he made as tragic a mistake as Luperón had made when he supported Heureaux in 1882. Jiménez remains an enigma, a wealthy cosmopolitan merchant, born in Santo Domingo, who directed successful businesses with branches in Monte Cristi, New York, Paris, and Hamburg. He lost his fortune and should have lost his credibility in June, 1898, when he bought and outfitted the American steamship *Fanita*, which he provisioned with enough arms and ammunition for an army. With only a score of men, Jiménez invaded Monte Cristi in a comic opera fiasco of an attempted coup. Most of his men were killed, and though Jiménez escaped to Cuba, Heureaux seized his family property to pay the cost of the aborted insurrection. On October 20, 1899, when Jiménez was elected president through the backing of Vásquez, who became vice-president, many Dominicans assumed that Jiménez would use his wealth to save his country. Unfortunately, Jiménez and his country were equally broke.[5]

Because it was associated with Heureaux as well as with the immediate Dominican economic problems, the SDIC became embroiled in domestic politics as well as continuing international dissatisfaction with its business practices. The French precipitated an immediate cri-

4. *HR*, 150, 155; Moore, "Case of the United States," 17–19; Ian Bell, *The Dominican Republic* (Boulder, Colo., 1981), 59; MacMichael, "The United States and the Dominican Republic," 130–31; William H. Wynne, *State Insolvency and Foreign Bondholders: Selected Case Histories* (2 vols.; New Haven, 1951), II, 224. For the first indication of an English syndicate bailout see WP to John Sherman, October 11, 1897, in Despatches from United States Ministers to the Dominican Republic, in Microcopy M93, Roll 3; for the treaty proposal see WP to JH, June 10, 1899, in Despatches, Dominican, M93, Roll 4, RG 59, NA.

5. Rodman, *Quisqueya*, 102–103; *HR*, 72–73; Welles, *Naboth's Vineyard*, 524–26.

sis by revealing that the SDIC was $254,000 in arrears on the Caccavelli and other claims and demanded that the Jiménez government pay at once. Jiménez pleaded with the public, and in January, when French warships arrived, the debt was miraculously paid through public subscription. During the brief interim Vásquez presidency following the death of Heureaux, negotiations had begun to sever the SDIC-Dominican tie, but except for a joint agreement between SDIC attorney and vice-president John T. Abbott and President Vásquez to make American gold coins the standard regie exchange, the unfriendly talks broke off to be resumed after Jiménez took office. When Abbott returned in December aboard the American warship *Machias*, the United States may have been prodding the Dominicans to be less unfriendly. The SDIC offered to exchange $3 million in 4 percent bonds, its interest in the bank, railway, and regie for $3.5 million, plus another $450,000 for other bonds held by SDIC "friends." The Dominicans made a counter-offer of $3 million, but the negotiations stalled when a faction in the Jiménez government headed by Finance Minister Federico Henríquez y Carvajal tried to expel the SDIC without any compensation.[6]

Jiménez began good faith negotiations either to buy out the SDIC or to modify its role as the Dominican fiscal agent, but the intermittent talks, influenced by public opinion and the political maneuverings of a divided cabinet, were unfruitful. Many Dominicans blamed the SDIC for its failure to make the agreed-upon Caccavelli payments to the French, a valid charge because the company had been collecting an import surtax for that purpose. Frustration, uncertainty, and anti-Americanism, fed by historic distrust, complicated the negotiations, already jeopardized by the Dominican debt and the difficulty of raising additional money for a buyout. The SDIC, which relied wholly on Dominican revenues, was no better off than the Dominican government and resisted obvious Dominican attempts to take its few tangible assets such as the railroad without a payment contract and some immediate cash.[7]

The State Department, which was far more comfortable when Dominican affairs could be handled indirectly by the SDIC with occasional prodding from the resident American diplomat in Haiti, began

6. Thomas Dawson's Chronology, in *FRUS*, 1906, p. 591; Welles, *Naboth's Vineyard*, 556–57, 559–60; *HR*, 109; Moore, "Case for the United States," 24–25.

7. Edgar Charles Duin, "Dominican-American Diplomatic Relations, 1895–1907" (Ph.D. dissertation, Georgetown University, 1955), 77.

to understand that the SDIC's problems increasingly involved the American government. That Secretary of State John Hay was more active in pursuing private American claims against foreign countries than previous administrations is clear from his brusque instruction to Chargé William F. Powell to recognize the Jiménez government and pursue all outstanding claims. These claims had dominated the diplomatic correspondence for several years, mainly because the Dominicans under Heureaux were masters at finding ways to postpone discussions, settlements, payments, and renegotiations and at other delays, paying only under threat of direct U.S. government intervention. With the advent of Jiménez, the deep involvement of American business in the Dominican economy—not only the SDIC but also the substantial sugar business of such men as William Bass—changed the nature of American-Dominican relations, though it was two more years before Santo Domingo was given its own resident American minister. In effect, the United States used both Chargé Powell and SDIC vice-president Abbott to deal with Dominican problems, a tactic that drew fire from both Powell and the Dominican press, which observed that when the SDIC attorney came on a United States Navy cruiser, "the 'Improvement Company' and the American Government is the same thing."[8]

After three formal proposals by the SDIC were rejected, Abbott's fourth—verbal—proposal was accepted on March 20, 1900, for a new three-year contract between the Dominican government and the SDIC to take effect April 1, 1900. Although the agreement eased the immediate SDIC-Dominican tensions, any immediate advantage ended when the Belgian bondholders rejected the SDIC's continuing as their representative, an action that removed the SDIC as the Dominican international fiscal agent and relegated the company's status to that of another foreign creditor. After the Belgian rejection three major factions emerged, the SDIC and the Americans soon joined by the British bondholders, continental Europeans (mainly Belgians and French),

8. WP to JH, December 28, 1899; JH to WP, January 5, 1900, both in *FRUS*, 1899, pp. 252–53. For examples of two protracted claims procedures, see the Ozuma bridge and the Sala claims in Duin, "Dominican-American Diplomatic Relations," 37–72. For the history of the Bass sugar concession see WP to JH, March 22, 1903, in Despatches, Dominican, M93, Roll 9. For the view that John Hay was sympathetic to American businessmen's claims, see MacMichael, "The United States and the Dominican Republic," 118–45. Powell's objection is in WP to JH, January 30, 1900, *ibid.*, Roll 4. *Listin Diario*, January 10, 1900, is quoted in Duin, "Dominican-American Diplomatic Relations," 78.

and Dominicans. The Dominicans remained divided between seeking financial and diplomatic protection from Europe or from the United States, an old division even in Heureaux's time, now made sharper by the Belgian-SDIC schism. The disorderly arrangement suited the Dominicans, who could negotiate separately with two different groups, using their ability to play off conflicting American and European interests to postpone any immediate fiscal resolution. The Belgian defection assured that the American government would be drawn more directly into the conflict because the SDIC's insecure position made it vulnerable to press and political attacks. When the government placed the SDIC-run bank into receivership, obviously for political reasons, the compromise of April, 1900, had disintegrated.[9]

When President Jiménez formally removed the SDIC from the regie in January, 1901, replacing it with an international commission, the SDIC asked the State Department to intervene in its behalf. John Hay, however, refused to negotiate directly with Foreign Minister Henríquez y Carvajal, insisting that a private settlement be negotiated, though obviously such a settlement would have to satisfy not only the SDIC but the State Department and the Belgian government as well. Henríquez negotiated separate agreements in Antwerp and Paris with the representatives of the Belgian and French bondholders, who owned two-thirds of the outstanding bonds. The Europeans agreed to a settlement that obligated the Dominican Republic to pay 15 percent of its customs revenues to the French and Belgian bondholders with a minimum payment of $25,000 a month. Henríquez' agreement with the SDIC called for disbanding the regie and submitting all other questions to international arbitration by the king of Sweden. In September, the Dominican Congress accepted the French-Belgian arrangement but rejected the SDIC agreement "in principle," a rejection based not only on anti-American sentiment but on Dominican fear of international arbitration, partly on the sound ground that big corporations and big countries were more experienced and better prepared in such proceedings. Paranoid Dominicans also feared that arbitration might permit direct intervention by the president of the United States, a legacy of the many years of annexation negotiations often undertaken at the behest of Dominican leaders.[10]

9. Duin, "Dominican-American Diplomatic Relations," 80–85. For the SDIC–Dominican Republic agreement, see *HR*, 101; Moore, "Case for the United States," 26.
10. Moore, "Case for the United States," 29.

Dominican aversion to arbitration was matched by Dominican pride, which prevented a direct discussion of the issue. The Dominicans avoided arbitration by raising technical objections to the way the SDIC had conducted its business affairs, especially repeating the persistent charge that the SDIC failed to present its accounts, an assertion that was true only because when the accounts were offered, the Dominican official in charge refused to receive them. Without the accounts, not even the preliminaries to an arbitration proceeding could begin; Abbott protested the Dominican assertions and continued to push for a resolution. Since the regie, the bank, and the activities of the SDIC were all suspended, even the minimal order of Heureaux's fiscal chaos was abandoned. The new economic mess, combined with the increasing diplomatic problems, contributed to a division between President Jiménez and Vásquez' followers in the Cibao region, traditionally a tobacco area that resisted the increasing influence of American sugar and the related rise of American commerce in the republic's capital. At the time, most Americans referred to the entire country as Santo Domingo though the capital city was only one of twelve provinces and until the 1890s a secondary city. The Dominican regional division was further exacerbated by the artificial nature of the original political liaison—Jiménez and Vásquez and their followers were united only in their hatred of Ulíses Heureaux. In temperament, self-interests, regions, and political alliances, Jiménez and Vásquez were virtual opposites, and followers of both sides prepared for an armed struggle for power.[11]

William F. Powell, the American minister to both Haiti and the Dominican Republic, was a political appointee rather than a professional diplomat and, following American diplomatic custom in the Caribbean, a Negro. Powell was an above average minor minister, who was expected to execute detailed State Department instructions in a primarily clerical function demanding small judgments that rarely involved policy decisions. During the Dominican crises, Powell worked under impossible conditions, administering Dominican affairs from Port-au-Prince, Haiti, with no effective means of communication or travel between the two cities and countries except by American naval vessel, a luxury the State Department reserved for extraordinary occasions. Dominicans resented sharing a diplomat, especially with Haiti,

11. Duin, "Dominican-American Diplomatic Relations," 90–91; Moore, "Case for the United States," 28–29.

a long-standing enemy. American foreign policy evolved as the Dominican crisis unfolded, and the State Department often dealt with new problems raised by Powell's communiqués. Powell's failure to have the right answer immediately was understandable, though Hay's frequent exasperation reflected the State Department's limited confidence in Powell's abilities. Powell, who was more amenable to Dominican suggestions of an American protectorate and a naval base at Samaná Bay than Hay, was as fond of gunboat diplomacy as some of the European diplomats, though Washington frequently chided Powell for being too gentle. Since Powell often worked without adequate instructions or the communications to get the right answer quickly, his mounting frustration was reasonable. What Powell most lacked was nuance, a devastating deficiency for someone who had to mediate between John Hay and the Dominicans, all of whom regarded Powell as a social or intellectual inferior. On one occasion Dominican Foreign Minister Manuel de J. Galván, frustrated at Powell's finger-pointing hectoring, told the man the Dominicans called the owl, "Put down the finger, señor ministero." [12]

When the SDIC informed the State Department that the contract of April 1, 1900, it had worked out with Henríquez had been repudiated by the Dominican government, John Hay agreed that the time had come for formal United States diplomatic intervention, and he instructed Powell to proceed to Santo Domingo and represent the United States and the SDIC. The Americans claimed that Henriquez' negotiations with the SDIC and the European bondholders could not be separated because the SDIC made concessions contingent on a three-way settlement. The arbitrary Dominican congressional rejection of the Henríquez-SDIC agreement rankled the Americans and caused Hay not only to intervene but to make a strong policy statement: "The United States is not disposed to pass over unheeded the equities of American companies. They have appealed to this government for protection and, in the language of their demand, ask nothing but simple justice and equity." Powell was to tell the Dominicans that "the United States is, upon principle, as well as the circumstances of this case, not disposed to acquiesce in unjust discriminations practised against its own citizens and in favor of those of other countries."

12. The problems in the Powell-Hay relationship can be seen in WP to JH, December 28, 1899; JH to WP, January 5, 1900, both in FRUS, 1899, pp. 252–55; MacMichael, "The United States and the Dominican Republic," 144; Manuel de Jesús Troncoso de la Concha, La génesis de la Convención Dominico-Americana (Santiago, D.R., 1946), 24–25.

The Dominicans stalled Powell, whose frustrations at the continuing Dominican assertion that the company refused to show its books approached open anger. Few diplomatic messages are underlined, but when Powell wrote Henríquez on March 20, 1902, he accused the Dominican government of an active disinformation campaign against the SDIC, which *"does not and has not refused* to allow an examination of its books."* Powell often applied more pressure than Hay instructed him to. Hay approved of Powell's "excellent" suggestion to urge arbitration on another Dominican claim because it "relieves the Department of any connection with or responsibility for the arbitration." But Powell had previously exceeded his instructions by proposing a settlement in the Sala claim rather than restricting his activity to mediation and arbitration.[13]

Before negotiations between Judge Abbott, Powell, and the Jiménez government produced a settlement, the simmering domestic Dominican discontent turned into a full-scale revolution on April 26 in the Cibao. When Vásquez' army reached Santo Domingo on May 2, Jiménez took exile in the French consulate and Henríquez in the American. On May 6, Horacio Vásquez, representing a region and a faction even more opposed to American interests than Jiménez, became the new Dominican president. While the Dominicans changed leaders, British bondholders allied with the SDIC rather than the French and Belgian bondholders, perhaps assuming that the Americans stood a better chance of reaching an effective settlement than the Europeans, a decision many Britons later regretted. An American warship, dispatched as a precautionary measure and a reminder of the continuing American presence, arrived at the time the hostilities ended. Powell was told to recognize the new Dominican government de facto, not to become involved in Dominican contentions, and to continue urging either private settlement or arbitration but to avoid using diction "usual in cases of direct intervention."[14]

When Vásquez favored quick settlement of all outstanding disputes, Judge Abbott and Emiliano Tejera, the new Dominican minister of foreign affairs, negotiated for five weeks. When Tejera suggested a fixed

13. Duin, "Dominican-American Diplomatic Relations," 92; JH to WP, January 20, March 11, 12, April 4, May 3, 14, 1902, in Diplomatic Instructions, Dominican Republic, M77, Roll 98, RG 59, NA; WP to Henríquez, March 20, 1902, in Despatches, Dominican, M93, Roll 5.

14. Dawson's Chronology, 592; Wynne, *State Insolvency,* II, 256; JH to WP, May 5, 1902 (2 letters), May 14, 1902; David Hill to WP, May 16, 1902, all in Instructions, Dominican, M77, Roll 98.

price for the SDIC rather than dealing with the specific claims and counterclaims of both parties, the SDIC accepted. After suggesting $11 million, the SDIC reduced its price to $6 million and then accepted Tejera's compromise offer of $4.5 million for a quick settlement. That figure may still have been higher than the SDIC's holdings were worth; they included $1.5 million in the Puerto Plata–Santiago Railroad, $923,365 in bank shares and accounts, and $4,153,270 in unsold bonds valued at 50 percent or $2,076,635, valuations that may have been generous.[15]

When the Dominicans insisted that the railroad be transferred before any payments were made, Abbott refused, left for New York, and later offered as a compromise that the railroad be turned over after five payments. When the Dominicans brusquely refused Abbott's compromise, the State Department ordered Powell to Santo Domingo with a draft of a protocol agreement and firm instructions to bring the matter to arbitration. When Powell spoke with Vásquez on November 11, the president said he feared that Theodore Roosevelt wished to annex the island but accepted Powell's assurance that nothing could be further from Roosevelt's plans. At first, the Dominicans made valid objections to continued SDIC control of the railroad, which they wanted to operate themselves with lower freight rates, a matter the Americans agreed was negotiable. Even after Vásquez had personally agreed to sign the protocol for arbitration, the Dominicans stalled, talked about the SDIC's failure to present its accounts, and again declined arbitration. A new railroad compromise was suggested and accepted, but when Tejera led the cabinet in opposition to arbitration, the issue dragged on until finally, on January 31, 1903, the two countries agreed on a price of $4.5 million with all other issues to be decided by an international arbitration commission. Until the arbitrators could decide the method and timing of payments, the Dominicans agreed to pay the SDIC $18,750 a month. The first and only payment was made in February, 1903.[16]

The protocol solved nothing. France immediately objected that the new Dominican obligations might impinge upon the French-Belgian-

15. Wynne, *State Insolvency*, II, 232; *HR*, 41.

16. See Moore, "Case for the United States," 30–33; *HR*, 110–12, 114; David Hill to WP, June 26, July 21, 1902, in Instructions, Dominican, M77, Roll 98; WP to JH, October 25, 1902; Juan Sánchez to WP, November 27, 1902; WP to Juan Sánchez, November 29, 1902, all on p. 7, in Despatches, Dominican, M93, Roll 6; Duin, "Dominican-American Diplomatic Relations," 107–12; *HR*, 114–15.

Henríquez agreement of June, 1901. When the Dominicans ended the American Clyde Steamship Company's concession, Powell was told to use "strenuous good offices" to reverse the decision. The Dominican crisis produced a number of significant American policy refinements. In the Clyde case, the Americans asked for damages for Dominican violation of American citizens' rights, not a change in the Dominican law that breached Clyde's rights, though obviously the United States was protesting the law that reduced harbor charges for Clyde's competitors. On March 6, 1903, the Dominicans withdrew the offensive law. The Americans used arbitration protocols not only for the SDIC but to settle two other long-standing Dominican claims, with the Sala Company for $394,500, an extremely complex case with political complications, and with Ernest G. Ros, a simpler contractual dispute, for $37,200.38. The protocol proved so effective as a diplomatic tool that Italy, Spain, and Germany used it to settle claims of their nationals. Although the Dominicans were easily able to defeat the terms of international arbitral awards by expedients such as requests for renegotiation, changes in terms, acting as if the decision were not binding, delay in payment, or being too broke to pay, the method suited American diplomacy by discouraging the common practice of European gunboat diplomacy as a means of collecting debts.[17]

Most of Minister Powell's time was devoted to unsuccessful attempts to entice the Dominican government to arbitrate its outstanding claims, while the Dominicans paid more attention to their own volatile political alliances, putting off the United States with "propositions . . . at times so ludicrous that they remind me of a class of children playing at government without knowing what they are doing but trying to keep up some semblance of authority; at other times they take on an air of injured innocency of a pouting child, sullen at some imaginary injury." Foreign Minister Sánchez would adopt an American request and when the cabinet was about to approve it, Finance Minister Tejera would threaten to resign, the cabinet would reject the solution, and Sánchez would reopen negotiations with the exasperated Powell.[18]

When Vásquez, a consistently weak president, was out of the capi-

17. *HR*, 115, 191–93, 130–31, 194; JH to WP, December 18, 20, 1902, in Instructions, Dominican, M77, Roll 98; Dawson's Chronology, 593; Wynne, *State Insolvency*, II, 237.
18. WP to JH, March 1, 1903, in Despatches, Dominican, M93, Roll 8.

tal, a new coalition of old Heureaux followers combined with disaffected *jimenistas* in a bitter war for control of the government that began March 23 and ended April 22 when a tired Vásquez fled to exile in Cuba and Alejandro Woss y Gil, an old *lilista,* became the new provisional president. Gil, a cosmopolitan Dominican described "as a man of more accomplishments than talent," spoke fluent English, French, and Italian, read Greek and Latin, and was knowledgeable about music, poetry, and literature. The best Gil could do was to establish a temporary siege government in Santo Domingo while his defeated enemies regrouped and a new coalition planned to unseat him. Gil's victory, though officially confirmed by elections in June, was even more fragile than the peace resulting from past Dominican revolutions. Every succeeding revolution diminished the power of the winning government, increasingly defined as temporary control of Santo Domingo City and its customhouse and an even more fragile control through temporary allies of the more important provincial customhouses. Through an anonymous emissary Gil promised a close connection with the United States, a necessity in view of the country's financial condition, which was "worse than bad." The government could not secure additional loans because it had nothing left as security. Gil's willingness for closer American relations reflected his government's extreme vulnerability to foreign claimants such as Italy, which won a guaranteed $176,000 settlement for questionable claims based on damage incurred in Gil's revolution.[19]

Although the political situation was temporarily calm, and ships laden with goods arrived weekly, by September, 1903, the Dominican situation was hopeless. The debt totaled $33 million in gold and the government was without income or the prospects of any future income to pay it. Everything was "mortgaged two or three times." Sugar, which earned $800,000 a year in export duties, had been made exempt, and cacao duties were promised to two different creditors. The aggressive Belgian-French bondholders protested the Italian settlement, the German minister was expected to make his claim for $500,000, and the government did not have enough money to pay its own workers. Woss y Gil, as expected, was incapable of governing his

19. WP to JH, April 10, May 12, 1903, in *FRUS,* 1903, pp. 390–93, vividly describes the revolution; see the last two paragraphs of his April 10, 1903, letter omitted from *FRUS,* 1903, for analysis of Dominican politics, in Despatches, Dominican, M93, Roll 8; *HR,* 75. Gil's overture and an analysis of the political situation are in Gil to WP, May 4, 5, 1903, in WP to JH, May 10, 1903, in Despatches, Dominican, M93, Roll 8; WP to JH, May 12, 1903, in *FRUS,* 1903, pp. 392–93; *HR,* 15–16.

cabinet, let alone the country. Foreign Minister Manuel Galván attempted to give Germany Samaná and Manzallino bays, but the Germans offered no encouragement, and it was clear that neither Galván nor Gil had any solutions to the Dominican problems. On September 26, 1903, Galván told Powell he did not have "five cents in the Treasury," a bad situation that got worse by October 8, when Galván declared, "we do not have one cent."[20]

Remarkably, all the principals kept up the charade of business as usual while the Dominican Republic disintegrated daily. Powell never stopped pushing the Dominicans to name an SDIC arbitrator, which they declined to do because it would be the first step toward having to (not) pay the award the arbitrators set. But claims were made continuously, arbitrators chosen, threatening letters written when the claims were not paid, even though it was apparent that there was no money, no prospects of money, no real government, and no self-generating solution. Theodore Roosevelt may have first suggested what eventually became the Roosevelt Corollary and a Dominican solution as early as April 2, 1903. In a Chicago speech mainly concerned with other matters, Roosevelt suggested that "our nation has insisted that because of its primacy in strength among the nations of the Western hemisphere it has certain duties and responsibilities which oblige it to take a leading part." Roosevelt warned, "We do not guarantee any state against punishment if it misconducts itself." Foreign Minister Galván was well aware of the Monroe Doctrine when he accused William Powell of exercising the power of a protectorate "against our will" because the United States resisted Galván's lunatic scheme of selling the Dominican bays to Germany as neutral coaling stations.[21]

Powell, who would not have been Roosevelt's choice to explain the inherent difficulties of applying the Monroe Doctrine to the Dominican default problems, defended the doctrine and the confusion by proposing that the United States take over the Dominican bays, assuring a vast influx of "American Capital." Powell only partly glimpsed the madness that had become normal in Dominican affairs, even as he compounded Galván's view of North American opportunists ready to seize the republic's $33 million in debt. Powell advised that no matter what the United States and the Dominicans agreed to, "it will not

20. Duin, "Dominican-American Diplomatic Relations," 121–25; WP to JH, September 14, 15, 17, 26, October 8, 1903, in Despatches, Dominican, M93, Roll 8.

21. Text of Chicago speech is in New York *Times*, April 3, 1903, p. 1; WP to JH, October 8, 10, 1903, in Despatches, Dominican, M93, Roll 8.

solve the question, as neither the present nor subsequent government will respect it." The State Department did not have to deal with the "interesting reading" of Powell's annexation proposition because, as State Department Solicitor Frederick Van Dyne wrote in his note to Assistant Secretary Alvey Adee regarding Powell's offer, "the attitude of the Gil government toward Samana and Manzanilla is not so important in view of the revolution which has arisen since the dispatch was written."[22]

The new Dominican revolution that began in Puerto Plata under Governor Carlos F. Morales Languasco on October 24, 1903, was almost as contradictory as its leader, once a priest, now a married man with a large family, who initially hoped to restore Juan Isidro Jiménez to the presidency but discovered as the war progressed that no one was better qualified to lead the country than himself. The common American view of the continuing Dominican revolutions, well stated by William Powell in discussing the Morales uprising, that "the main aim of all (Government officials included) is to secure possession of the Customs Revenue, which instead of being paid into the National Treasury, finds its way into the pockets of these officials," does not explain the recurring willingness of Dominican revolutionary leaders voluntarily to relinquish power, as Luperón to Heureaux, or Vásquez to Jiménez, or initially Morales, who hoped to restore Jiménez. Nor was the violent opposition between *horacista* and *jimenista* factions explicable by the simple motive of greed.[23]

While the Morales–Woss y Gil war ran its almost conventional course with troops dispatched to the various Dominican provincial cities such as Azua, described by a sympathetic American writer "as a city of three thousand inhabitants and three million goats," foreign warships descended on Dominican cities to protect their national share of the Dominican debt, and as preparations were made for the inevitable siege of the capital city, Powell, Galván, and Gil were still negotiating over SDIC arbitration. In the midst of a revolution that would inevitably unseat Gil, who was barely able to pay the wages of his remaining troops, Powell broke off diplomatic relations with the ghost of a government and finally brought Gil to agree to arbitrate the SDIC affair. Gil not only accepted the American request that he had resisted for the entire six months of his presidency, but by imme-

22. WP to JH, October 10, 1903, in Despatches, Dominican, M93, Roll 8.
23. For a brief biography of Morales see *HR*, 75; Otto Schoenrich, *Santo Domingo—A Country with a Future* (New York, 1918), 80; WP to JH, October 20, 1903, in Despatches, Dominican, M93, Roll 9.

diately naming both Dominican choices as arbitrators—Foreign Minister Galván and United States Judge George Gray—he did not use the usual Dominican ploy of accepting in principle and then delaying in execution. Powell assured Gil that the American flag Powell had taken down when he broke diplomatic relations would be restored and that American vessels converging on his capital city would salute the Dominican flag flown by his two-vessel navy. Gil left, reassured the United States would show its respect, a pathetic but proud figure in the last two weeks of his presidency, who, by naming his soon to be deposed foreign minister as one of the arbitrators, had assured consciously or unconsciously that no matter who led the next government, the SDIC arbitration issue could remain unresolved.[24]

Simple greed alone cannot explain the frequent Dominican revolutions. The Morales uprising was a surprisingly bloodless affair considering that the sixty thousand rounds of ammunition, the $700,000 cost, and the widespread destruction of property resulted in the loss of only twenty-five lives, mostly "from stray bullets and accidents." The victors gained a bankrupt country with its future resources mortgaged and constant, grating pressure from its international creditors, including the United States. With the downfall of the Gil government all of the political factions had governed and all had failed equally miserably, making it politically more difficult for any to rule as a *jimenista*, a *horacsista*, or as Woss y Gil had done as a *lilista*. Dominican politics after Heureaux had become coalition politics, involving not only groups associated with leaders but regions able to support politicians independently of weak national governments at Santo Domingo and able when the national government showed signs of excessive corruption, ineptitude, or vulnerability (or all three) to generate a revolution to replace the discredited rulers. The huge debt confounded all Dominican nationalists by intruding the specter of foreign intervention into the questions of who could govern after Heureaux and whether the small island republic could avoid the curses of Dominican political history, foreign occupation, and authoritarian tyranny. Inevitably, the foreign powers were pulled into domestic politics, and alliances became domestic as well as foreign as the Dominicans tried to find both a suitable government and a degree of national independence.[25]

24. Rodman, *Quisqueya*, 177; Dawson's Chronology, 593; WP to JH, October 20, November 6, 12, 25, 1903, in Despatches, Dominican, M93, Roll 9.
25. WP to JH, November 25, 1903, p. 6, in Despatches, Dominican, M93, Roll 9.

Though the United States acted more vigorously for the business interests of its citizens than it had in the past, it maintained its remarkably consistent continuing interest in the Dominican Republic, making it impossible for any of the European creditors to dominate while allowing the Dominican economic vicissitudes—profits and potential losses—to be shared by the various European and American competitors in an equilibrium that discouraged direct foreign intervention. When Manuel Galván objected to Powell's insistence on an arbitration protocol and insisted that he "would *never submit*" but "*would resist to the last*," Powell pointed out that the Americans had "abstained from any show of force . . . [and] had not acted in haste." American abstention encouraged European abstention, as the American practice of negotiation by protocol became universal. The protocols had prevented intervention, but they had not paid the debts, which continued to grow, fueled by prodigious arrears in compounding interest—the $50,000 the French-Belgian bondholders had offered to settle interest arrears in 1901 had grown by 1905 to $1,472,636. Increasing costs of revolution—estimated at 72 percent of its income—not only absorbed all of the Dominicans' meager resources but generated additional foreign claims.[26]

One of the first efforts to mediate international, American, and Dominican interests originated with William Bass, a maverick American industrialist, who owned an ironworks in Brooklyn and a million-dollar sugar plantation at Consuelo and enjoyed playing international sugar politics and writing verse. Bass vehemently opposed American annexation, which he thought would be disastrous for his own sugar interests as well as for the Dominicans. Bass proposed to Gil the negotiation of a new reciprocity treaty with the United States, combined with an international debt commission based on recent Greek and Egyptian models to administer, settle, and adjust the chaotic Dominican fiscal affairs. Bass wanted the United States rather than the European powers to propose the settlement, and he told Powell that Gil and his cabinet favored the idea. Powell still feared the invisible hand of Germany in Bass's international commission, even though Germany was content to send its cruiser *Vineta* at periodic intervals to add another protocol to the growing list. Bass, never one to slight his own interests, prefaced his sweeping international settlement with a cavalier proposal to "take the tax from sugar and place it on cacao

26. WP to JH, November 3, 1903, *ibid.*, HR, 18, 11.

or tobacco," a move that would produce a storm of protest from German tobacco importers as well as French and Swiss cacao interests. Eventually, Bass as well as the cacao interests would prevail and the most profitable Dominican crops would remain both foreign and untaxed, but Bass's self-interest notwithstanding, his proposal helped the United States to begin to consider possible solutions to the growing international Dominican dilemma.[27]

Even Powell was surprised by a new revolutionary outbreak, which began on December 10, 1903, and, unlike the Morales war, engulfed the entire country. When provisional President Morales was actively opposed by the *jimenistas*, who held most of the provincial governships, *horacistas* supported the president, not because they preferred Morales but as part of their continuing opposition to Jiménez. An independent revolution in Azua and Barahona, two extreme southeastern provinces, proclaimed its own leaders, who also marched on the capital. William Bass's jaundiced view that the ease of the Morales coup gave well-armed Dominican gangs the habit of revolution and plunder, as well as the determination of the three leading factions not to permit any other faction to gain power and the increasing enmity encouraged by constant fighting, contributed to the rising sense of complete anarchy. In an extraordinary meeting between Powell and provisional President Morales on December 2, 1903, Powell, ever the opportunist, proposed a virtual American protectorate to Morales in return for his "sacredly" honoring all previous agreements, allowing the United States to build lighthouses (an old peripheral American interest, revived no doubt by Panama's revolution the month before), acquire control of the usual bays, and negotiate a treaty patterned on the Cuban arrangement. Morales, who needed any support but particularly American recognition, agreed to consider Powell's proposals. William Bass's view was more practical and immediate. The present was not the time to discuss old claims or new naval bases. Bass called for immediate restoration of order to allow the government to function and customhouses to operate because they were "the only source of public income" and the main inducement to further insurrections. Bass suggested naval neutralization by the United States stationing a warship in the three major Dominican ports. Powell's and Bass's pro-

27. MacMichael, "The United States and the Dominican Republic," 209–10; William Bass to WP, December 12, 1903; WP to JH, December 14, 1903, both in Despatches, Dominican, M93, Roll 9. For the Greek debt settlement basis see Wynne, *State Insolvency,* II, 283–358; for Egypt see *ibid.,* 575–632.

posals formed the basis of the State Department's reassessment of its Dominican options in January, 1904.[28]

Other events influenced the detailed American reexamination of Dominican affairs. After the visit of three German warships on December 12, an American-German concert was negotiated that allowed the American warship *Newport* to ensure all foreign interests, making further German naval demonstrations unnecessary, another step toward an American-international mediation effort. Conflicting Dominican concessions with Vicini, the German Hamburg-American line, the Cuban line, and others all undercut the original concession, which had given the American Clyde Steamship Line a virtual monopoly in Dominican ports, an international complication that could not be addressed until the Dominicans resolved their political problems. Morales accepted the support of the *horacistas*, and together they fought an almost holy war against their former allies. With a political ticket of Morales for president and Cáceres for vice-president, the coalition had to dislodge the Jiménez forces, who controlled most of the cities but were unable to replenish their supplies and ammunition. Morales shared his military plans with Powell while negotiating a possible postrevolution settlement with the Americans. On December 30, 1903, Morales proposed a "Platt Amendment" treaty with the United States, including the customary proffer of Samaná and Manzanillo bays. Morales, as adept at diplomacy as he was in his revolutionary military strategy, followed his verbal offer with a formal treaty proposal, including a reciprocity agreement, in addition to bays, lighthouses, and coaling stations. On January 15, Morales dispatched his new foreign secretary with the title high commissioner to Washington to negotiate with John Hay, an impressive display from a provisional government fighting for its existence and as yet unrecognized by the United States.[29]

By January 14 Powell was convinced that Morales would be easier to deal with than Jiménez. Morales had already convinced Commander Albert C. Dillingham, the American naval officer commanding the cruiser *Detroit*, who arrived on the scene January 4 and quickly became one of the chief American Dominican policy makers, a role

28. William Bass to WP, December 12, 1903, in WP to JH, December 14, 1903; WP to JH, December 3, 1903, both in Despatches, Dominican, M93, Roll 9; the State Department note is bound at end of WP to JH, January 9, 1904, *ibid.*, Roll 10.

29. WP to JH December 12, 17, 21, 1903, *ibid.*, Roll 9; Morales and Cáceres statements are in Welles, *Naboth's Vineyard*, 608–609; WP to JH, December 30, 1903, January 9, 1904, in Despatches, Dominican, M93, Roll 10.

that would be formally recognized by President Theodore Roosevelt early in 1905. Puerto Plata, essential as both a political center and a port, held the key to Morales' success. When Dillingham landed troops from the *Detroit* on January 17, ostensibly to prevent street fighting, he was actually actively intervening in favor of the Morales forces: he "so arranged matters that the Jiménez party should be whipped." With control of Puerto Plata and an established friendly relationship with the United States, unlike the regimes of the immediate past, Morales was an attractive leader for the Americans to back. Morales may have won Powell completely over on January 20, when he complained of Jiménez' boast that the United States preferred a white leader (like himself) and would never recognize a mulatto like Morales. Powell was touched by the conversation and recognized Morales on the spot. "Goodbye, Mr. President," he told Morales as he left, and he later telegraphed recognition to a surprised Hay, who wrote on the cable, "ask full explanation of his action." The State Department's continuing doubt is a measure of the uncertainty in America's evolving Dominican policies. But Dillingham was sure that backing Morales "would be for the best interests of all concerned," and Powell was convinced that it would "help to solve situation."[30]

The unsigned State Department memorandum, probably written by Loomis or more likely by Adee, at the end of January (it is bound with Powell's dispatch of January 9, which was not received until January 27) noted that the precedent of the Platt Amendment in Cuba was of little help in the Dominican crisis. Customs collections, not coaling stations, were the Dominican problem, as well as some way of forbidding new debts, which would have to be "absolutely prohibited." What made a Dominican solution less daunting was the nation's relative prosperity. Minimum Dominican revenues always exceeded $2 million annually, a sum that made settlement of debts as well as "a considerable surplus" possible for "education and public

30. WP to JH, January 14, 20, in Despatches, Dominican, M93, Roll 10; J. Fred Rippy, "The Initiation of the Customs Receivership in the Dominican Republic," *HAHR*, XVII (1937), 444–45; Commander Albert C. Dillingham to Robert Bacon, January 16, 1906, in Miscellaneous Letters of the Department of State, Microcopy, M179, Roll 1276; MacMichael, "The United States and the Dominican Republic," 170, 162–63. For Dillingham's Dominican activities see Naval Records Collection, RG 45, Area 8 Files, M625, Roll 265; Santo Domingo Correspondence, RG45, entry 305, Gray, Vol. I, both in NA. Also see Richard H. Collin, "The 1904 *Detroit* Compact: U.S. Naval Diplomacy and Dominican Revolution," *Historian*, LII (May, 1990); and Richard D. Challener, *Admirals, Generals, and American Foreign Policy, 1898–1914* (Princeton, 1973), 129–34.

works," provided that war expenses were reduced. William Bass's proposal of a permanent man-of-war in each port in "his very interesting letter" suggested the American policy of sending vessels when needed, which would serve the same purpose. The memorandum's conclusion provides the core of the new American Dominican policy: "If the custom houses were removed from exclusive native control, and both the Government and its enemies were prevented from contracting debts upon the public credit, there would seem to be nothing left to fight over."[31]

As the revolutionary fighting affected Americans, President Theodore Roosevelt became more directly involved in Dominican affairs. After an American sailor from the warship *Yankee* was killed on a Santo Domingo wharf on February 1, 1904, and the *New York* was hit by insurgent fire on February 11, American warships *Newark* and *Columbia* retaliated by shelling the insurgent positions and landing troops to secure the waterfront. On February 7, Roosevelt ordered naval reinforcements to protect American citizens and property. Roosevelt, mainly occupied with the Senate battle over ratification of the Hay–Bunau-Varilla Treaty, as well as the Russo-Japanese War, which dominated the attention of Europeans and Americans, mentioned the Dominican crisis for the first time in a letter to his son on February 10. Limited practical intervention and a larger policy statement appear already connected in Roosevelt's plans: "Santo Domingo is drifting into chaos . . . most reluctantly I have been obliged to take the initial step of interference there. I hope it will be a good while before I have to go further. But sooner or later it seems to me inevitable that the United States should assume an attitude of protection and regulation in regard to all these little states in the neighborhood of the Caribbean. I hope it will be deferred as long as possible, but I fear it is inevitable."[32]

When recurrent cutting of the telegraph made communication with Santo Domingo inconsistent, Roosevelt ordered a commission of Ad-

31. Memorandum after WP to JH, January 9, 1904, in Despatches, Dominican, M93, Roll 10; this is the basis of Loomis' initialed February 9, 1904, memo cited in Rippy, "Initiation of the Customs Receivership," 441, and probably written by Adee. For Francis Loomis as the originator of the American custom receivership solution to Latin American debt default problems in his suggestions over the Venezuelan problems in 1898 see J. Fred Rippy, "Antecedents of the Roosevelt Corollary of the Monroe Doctrine," *PHR,* IX (1940), 278n.
32. Dawson's Chronology, 595; *MRL,* IV, 724n.; TR to TRJR, February 10, 1904, in *MRL,* IV, 724; see Rippy, "Initiation of the Customs Receivership," for the view that Europe's preoccupation with the Russo-Japanese War gave TR a freer hand.

mirals George Dewey and Henry C. Taylor, accompanied by Assistant Secretary of State Loomis, to "give me a full, impartial searching account of the situation as it now presents itself." Roosevelt cautioned secrecy and discretion: "I do not wish there to be any idea that your mission is official or semi-official—I want to avoid all talk about it." The State Department had dismissed the idea of annexation at the end of January, and Roosevelt had no taste for such expansionist ideas— "I have about the same desire to annex it as a gorged boa-constrictor might have to swallow a porcupine wrong-end-to." Although he discussed both parts of the sentiment that would eventually become the Roosevelt Corollary, Roosevelt was still ambivalent. "I want to do nothing but what a policeman has to do in Santo Domingo." Disturbed by the Dominican attacks on Americans, Roosevelt insisted that he wanted to do nothing, but "if it is absolutely necessary to do something, then I want to do as little as possible." Although "their government has been bedeviling us to establish some kind of protectorate over the islands, and take charge of their finances," the United States "could not possibly go into the subject now at all."[33]

Roosevelt's uncertainty reflected the difficulty of the problem, which was debated in the press by members of the American and Dominican governments, a remarkable public forum on the question of possible American expansion and the Monroe Doctrine. Further complicating Roosevelt's course was the momentous and unexpected Hague World Court arbitration decision on the Venezuelan blockade case on February 23, 1904, which, by recognizing preferential treatment for the coercing powers, lent legal encouragement to further European debt-collecting interventions in Latin America. The Hague decision, which, in the words of a "prominent State Department official," put "a premium on violence," by itself would have forced the Roosevelt administration to reexamine the major tenet of its foreign policy. When the acting president of the Hague Court, Russian Minister of Justice N. V. Muraviev, in announcing the decision, used the occasion to denounce the Japanese and invoked "the Providence which rules over battles," it was clear that the Hague Court was no longer an effective means of promoting peace. For the administration as well as the press, the Dominican question was framed in a context that included the enormous

33. See WP to JH, December 25, 1903, for a description of the process and the difficulties, in Despatches, Dominican, M93, Roll 9; TR to George Dewey, February 20, 1904; to Joseph B. Bishop, February 23, 1904, both in *MRL*, IV, 734–35. For an account of the voyage and mission see Albert C. Gleaves, Diary, 1902–1904, February 9 to March 7, 1904, entries, in Box 3, Gleaves Papers, LC.

uncertainty of the Russo-Japanese War, in which a small Asian power was challenging a major old European monarchy, the implications of the Hague decision, the continuing debate over Panama, Roosevelt's activist foreign policy as president, and the related questions of possible futher American expansion or the continued defensive use of the Monroe Doctrine. The Hague Court, by corrupting its mission of peace with propaganda for war, thereby eliminating the favored American international arbitration strategy, combined with the deteriorating conditions in the Dominican Republic to force Roosevelt to consider the Dominican problem, arbitration, and the Monroe Doctrine at the same time.[34]

The presence of Dominican Minister Juan Sánchez in Washington added to public and press interest, reflected in articles with such titles as "Do We Want Santo Domingo?" a review of public opinion on an issue the *Literary Digest* noted came up "periodically before the public." Most of the press comments reflected the administration's belief that something would have to be done, but as little as possible. Some of the most vehement antiannexation sentiment reflected American racial attitudes. The New Orleans *Times-Democrat* editorialized, "To annex the island would be to punish ourselves, not the Dominicans. That republic should stand as a monument to black government, which has made the island what it is. . . . There is no place under our flag for the blacks of Santo Domingo, for several reasons, the chief of which is, we have a sufficient black population as it is." The St. Louis *Globe Democrat* vigorously favored annexation and regretted its defeat in Grant's time because of "a few implacables in the Senate." Sánchez made his case publicly in the *Independent*, calling for American assistance, "a necessity for Santo Domingo, and possibly a convenience for both countries." Sánchez pointed out that American preferential treatment for Puerto Rican and Cuban sugar threatened American sugar investments in the Dominican Republic; that before the recent revolutions, the republic prided itself on being a safe place; and that "the idea of annexation is repulsive." Perhaps too subtly for Americans who confused the Dominicans with the black republic of Haiti, Sánchez referred to the "insubordination and lack of discipline" characteristic of the Spanish race. He offered the United States "control of the Caribbean Sea" and freedom from the threat of European bond-

34. For the Hague quote see *LD*, March 5, 1905, p. 318; see Calvin DeArmond Davis, *The United States and the Second Hague Peace Conference* (Durham, N.C., 1975), 85–90; and Dexter Perkins, *The Monroe Doctrine, 1867–1907* (Baltimore, 1937), 419–20.

holders, who might "get tired waiting." In the same issue of the *Independent*, an interview with Assistant Secretary Loomis gave the administration's view, mainly an assurance that "there is no thought or possibility of the annexation of Santo Domingo" and that "it seems probable that some such treaty as now exists with Cuba, bringing it under the Platt Amendment, or some friendly protection, may have the desired effect." Loomis also cited the desire to avoid another Venezuelan intervention crisis.[35]

Loomis' private report to the president for the Dewey-Taylor-Loomis Commission favored immediate American intervention. He cited the continuing cycle of anarchy, corruption, and destruction of property and the wish of the majority of conservative property owners, Dominican and foreign, for American intervention. Loomis emphasized the French intervention as well as the American naval communiqués indicating Jiménez' support for an American intervention along the lines of the Platt Amendment. American control of the customhouses would remove the chief incentive to revolution and the source of funds for armaments. Loomis, however, also favored accepting Samaná Bay as an American naval base. Despite sufficient press support, a foundation well set by Sánchez' public presence in Washington, a favorable report from a prestigious commission, informal support from Commander Dillingham, whose opinions the president trusted, in the last week of March Roosevelt decided against any action that might set a precedent. In his discussion with Secretary of State John Hay, Roosevelt cautiously held out hope that Dominican progress toward a political settlement should proceed without foreign intervention, but he saw "no way in which the United States could take part in the pacification of the Republic, without establishing precedents which would be equally inconvenient and undesirable for both countries." Hay informed Sánchez on March 29, who "bore his doom like a soldier and gentleman."[36]

35. *LD*, March 5, 1905, p. 319; Juan Francisco Sánchez, "The Future of Santo Domingo," *Independent*, March 3, 1904, pp. 473–76 ("prepared by his secretary who writes English"); Francis B. Loomis, "The Administration and Santo Domingo," *Independent*, March 3, 1904, p. 467.

36. Francis Loomis, "Memorandum for the Secretary of State on the Dominican Republic," in Box 6, Folder 37, No. 96, Francis Loomis Papers, Stanford University; W. H. Reeder to William Moody, March 15, 1904; Rear Admiral W. C. Wise to Moody, February 26, 28, 1904, all *ibid.*, 22–23; JH memorandum of conversation with TR, March 28, 1904, in Notes from the Dominican Legation, T-801, Roll 3, RG 59, NA; Rippy, "Initiation of the Customs Receivership," 443; JH to TR, March 30, 1904, *ibid.*, 443.

Roosevelt's decision was sound. Recognizing Morales was one thing, but sending American troops to take the customhouses might have met strong resistance from Jiménez' supporters, as well as other Dominicans who feared any foreign intervention, but especially from the United States. William Bass reported that Dominican soldiers were well armed, not with "antiquated weapons but Remingtons, Mauser-carbines and Remington-Mauser (. . . a Remington carbine carrying a regular Mauser cartridge)," eager and waiting to fight again, "flushed with the late triumph of having overthrown the Government." Haiti openly supported the anti-American *jimenistas* fighting Morales and threatened war unless Morales discontinued his negotiations with the United States. There was little Roosevelt could gain in an intervention because the mere appearance of American forces could increase hostilities and cause American casualties. Roosevelt had just won his bruising Senate battle for ratification of the Hay–Bunau-Varilla Treaty on February 23, and he was not ready to face another contest with his Senate opponents, especially in a presidential election year. Roosevelt was both bitter and explicit in his unmailed letter to Charles W. Eliot, the anti-imperialist president of Harvard University, whom he accused of "reading Rousseau in a closet." It was because of opposition from persons like Eliot that Roosevelt claimed he could not intervene in Santo Domingo: "If I acted purely in accordance with the spirit of altruistic humanitarian duty, I would grant the prayers of the best people of the island and take partial possession of it tomorrow. I do not do this, chiefly because if I did many honest people would misunderstand my purposes and motives; and so I feel obliged to put off the action until the necessity becomes so clear that even the blindest can see it."[37]

Clearly, the divided Dominicans were not going to solve their political or fiscal problems suddenly without American intervention. But Roosevelt moved carefully to improve the American position before taking formal action, taking control indirectly. Following Loomis' recommendation, he gave Commander Dillingham wide authority and command of American naval forces, a role the naval officer used to aid

37. William Bass to WP, December 12, 1903, p. 4, in WP to JH, December 14, 1903, in Despatches, Dominican, M93, Roll 9; WP to JH, March 17, 18, 1904, *ibid.;* Dana Munro, *Intervention and Dollar Diplomacy in the Caribbean, 1900–1921* (Princeton, 1964), 93; TR to Charles Eliot, April 4, 1904, in *MRL,* IV, 770 (unmailed). For Adee's assurances to Haiti that there would be no American intervention see Adee's memorandum, October 2, 1902, quoted in Brenda Plummer, *Haiti and the Great Powers, 1902–1915* (Baton Rouge, 1988), 105.

Morales, while protecting American lives and property, especially wherever *jimenistas* threatened. Dillingham had more freedom than a diplomat and did not hesitate to use the full confidence and authority Washington had given him, a pattern of American naval diplomacy well established during Colombia's War of the Thousand Days. Dillingham liked the Dominicans, though he favored a full American protectorate and later wrote that he had been "entirely responsible for the placing of Morales in power." Roosevelt also upgraded the Dominican diplomatic effort by replacing William Powell, who Loomis suggested should remain as Haiti's minister, with Thomas C. Dawson, one of the most gifted of American professional diplomats, the author of a two-volume history on Latin America, who became the first American resident minister to the Dominican Republic. Upper-class Dominicans were impressed that the United States had appointed a white man as minister. Since the agent for the United States in the pending arbitration proceedings of the SDIC and the Dominican Republic was John Bassett Moore, a key figure in the Panama controversy and the chief legal adviser to the State Department, it is likely that Roosevelt was well aware of the soon to be decided arbitration settlement that would give United States influence in Dominican affairs indisputable international legal status.[38]

William Powell, the strongest American advocate of direct American intervention and about to be replaced, was not informed of the nuances in the emerging patient American policy toward the Dominican crisis. When the Italian government insisted on a confirmatory protocol to replace an older agreement with the Gil government, Powell overreacted to Dominican concerns. Misunderstanding the recent Hague decision, Powell planned to take control of the customhouses to prevent their being seized by the Italians. Powell

38. Peter Karsten, *The Naval Aristocracy: The Golden Age of Annapolis and the Emergence of Modern American Navalism* (New York, 1972), 173–74, suggests that poor communications on land first gave rise to preference for naval officers in times of crisis; when the better-educated naval offices were more effective than the average diplomat, the successful practice became a custom. Duin, "Dominican-American Diplomatic Relations," 160; Munro, *Intervention and Dollar Diplomacy*, 94. For Loomis' recommendations to keep Dillingham and move Powell see Loomis, "Memorandum," 23, 26; Albert C. Dillingham to Robert Bacon, January 16, 1906, in Miscellaneous Letters, M179, Roll 1276; Troncoso, *Génesis de la convención*, 23–24; Thomas Cleland Dawson, *The Republics of South America* (2 vols.; New York, 1903–1904). See Glenn J. Kist, "The Role of Thomas C. Dawson in United States–Latin American Diplomatic Relations, 1897–1912" (Ph.D. dissertation, Loyola University of Chicago, 1971), 79–83; for John Bassett Moore see Richard Megaree, "The Diplomacy of John Bassett Moore: Realism in America Foreign Policy" (Ph.D. dissertation, Northwestern University, 1963).

and Dillingham were both ready to institute an extemporaneous exercise that closely resembled the *modus vivendi* of 1905. But Washington was not ready, and Hay, in gently explaining why the Hague decision was not applicable, instructed Powell not to interfere and Secretary of the Navy William H. Moody ordered Dillingham not to take any customhouses. Hay took the precaution of asking Rome about Italian intentions, a move that served a double purpose in making Italy aware of American interest and receiving assurances that Italian ambitions were limited. Morales, indebted to Dominican Italian bankers Bartolo B. Bancalari and Juan B. Vicini, settled with the Italians in a protocol that formally confirmed an earlier arrangement in the Gil presidency. The Italian protocol, announced on June 20, two days after Morales' inauguration, was immediately protested because it conflicted with arrangements previously negotiated for Belgian-French bondholders. Although no payments were made, the settlement established a legal basis for earlier questionable claims of inflated amounts.[39]

After the fall of Macorís on March 12, the Morales-*horacista* alliance controlled all of the country except Monte Cristi province, where fierce fighting continued through May. Commander Dillingham, who on May 16 had written Washington that if he could bring the revolutionaries on board "they would not leave until terms of peace had been signed," on June 3 mediated a final settlement of the revolution on the *Detroit* at Monte Cristi. Although Morales and Cáceres had been elected president and vice-president on May 30, the Dillingham peace treaties of June 3 and June 10 recognized the independence of Demetrio Rodríguez and Desiderio Arias, leaders of the revolution in Monte Cristi, who pledged "before the representative of the American Navy, who has intervened in this matter and signed the agreement," to keep peace and order in their port, free of interference from the national government in Santo Domingo, which also agreed to pay the revolutionists' war costs.[40]

39. Perkins, *The Monroe Doctrine, 1867–1907*, 423; JH to WP, May 6, 1904, in Instructions, Dominican, M77, Roll 98; Duin, "Dominican–American Diplomatic Relations," 161; Munro, *Intervention and Dollar Diplomacy* 94; HR, 126–27; Dawson's Chronology, 595. For Moody's order to Dillingham and his dispatch to the *Gloucester* to hand deliver a copy of the message see William H. Moody to *Detroit*, Moody to San Juan Naval Station, April 18, 1904, in Confidential Messages Sent, RG 45, entry 19, NA. See Collin, "The 1904 *Detroit* Compact."

40. Albert C. Dillingham to William Moody, May 16, 23, 1904, in RG 45, Area 8 Files, M625, Roll 267; Dawson's Chronology, 595; text of the treaty is in *FRUS*, 1904,

It is impossible to say with any certainty precisely what Theodore Roosevelt had in mind when he sent a letter to Secretary of War Elihu Root, to be read at a dinner celebrating the second anniversary of the republic of Cuba, although most historical accounts consider this statement the origin of the Roosevelt Corollary to the Monroe Doctrine, and many assume that Roosevelt and Root were setting the stage for their later intervention in the Dominican Republic. A more likely context for Roosevelt's letter and public statement was his campaign for reelection, in which Root was heavily involved and Roosevelt began to stress his activist foreign policy, citing Panama as "our strongest card." Cuba offered an ideal focus because Roosevelt could deflect anti-imperialist criticism of the continued American presence in the Philippines by emphasizing the American withdrawal from Cuba: "We freed Cuba from tyranny; we then stayed in the island until we had established civil order and laid the foundations for self-government and prosperity; we then made the island independent, and have since benefitted her inhabitants by making closer the commercial relations between us. I hail what we have done in Cuba not merely for its own sake, but as showing the purpose and desire of this nation toward all of the nations south of us. It is not true that the United States has any land hunger or entertains any projects as regards other nations, save such as for their welfare." [41]

The debate over the Dominican Republic, both in the administration and in the press, centered on how much control the United States might eventually exert. Powell and Loomis favored a full protectorate or annexation, citing foreign pressure and the Monroe Doctrine to support such extreme American action. Powell wrote, "It is our duty to protect these people whether we like to do so or not." Some anti-imperialist newspapers preferred no intervention. There was more public support for Roosevelt's middle ground that favored the lesser or Platt Amendment intervention that allowed the United States to clean up the mess, appear to solve the underlying problem, and get out. For Roosevelt in 1904 the Cuban strategy appeared completely successful. Cuba and Puerto Rico were Caribbean models not

---

pp. 289–90. For Sigsbee's naming of the Dillingham-Arias agreements the *Detroit* Compact see Rear Admiral Charles D. Sigsbee to Secretary of the Navy, February 13, 1905, in Santo Domingo Correspondence, Red Vol. 1, RG 45, entry 305.

41. For a critical review of the historiography see Douglas R. Gow, "How Did the Roosevelt Corollary Become Linked to the Dominican Republic?" *Mid-America*, LVIII (1976), 159–66; TR to ER, June 2, 1904, in *MRL*, IV, 810–13, lists TR's first-term achievements with comments; TR to ER, May 20, 1904, *ibid.*, 801–802.

only of political stability but of economic prosperity, often cited by both Americans and Dominicans as examples of societies benefiting from close ties to the United States in the form of favorable reciprocity agreements that helped American sugar interests and produced at least the appearance of flourishing economics. In 1904 Cuba's tranquillity offered a dramatic contrast with Dominican chaos. Roosevelt was staking the middle ground in the Cuban dinner statement, trying to reassure both the Europeans and the Latin Americans that "all we desire is to see all neighboring countries, stable, orderly, and prosperous. . . . If a nation shows that it knows how to act with decency in industrial and political matters, if it keeps order and pays its obligations, then it need fear no interference from the United States."[42]

The most controversial part of the Cuban dinner letter, in which Roosevelt declared that "brutal wrongdoing, or an impotence which results in a general loosening of the ties of civilized society, may finally require intervention by some civilized nation," expressed Roosevelt's fundamental belief in civilization as the center of modern values and lies behind his conception that civilization transcends national interest. Civilization furnished Roosevelt's motive for his Panama intervention, for his backing of Japan against Russia in the Russo-Japanese struggle, and for his support of the Hague Peace initiatives of Frederic Coudert. When Roosevelt cited duty as the reason for defending a threat to civilization, he touched another leitmotiv of his entire life, including the rejection of a possible career as a corporate lawyer, his volunteer service in the Cuban War, and many of his decisions both wise and unwise. "In the Western hemisphere," Roosevelt insisted, "the United States cannot ignore this duty," though he added the limiting phrase, "but it remains true that our interests, and those of our Southern neighbors, are in reality identical." Roosevelt meant this sincerely as he did his closing wish, "all that we ask is that they shall govern themselves well, and be prosperous and orderly," an unarguable sentiment shared no doubt by Cubans, Dominicans, and other small Caribbean nations. Roosevelt carefully avoided any discussion of how the United States would achieve this desired order, fully aware from his conflicts with the anti-imperialists that the manner of intervention would be as critical as his intent.[43]

42. But see Loomis, "Memorandum," 3, 4; WP to Francis Loomis, March 5, 1904, *ibid.*, 19; see Salvador Brau, a turn-of-the-century Puerto Rican sociologist, who claimed Puerto Rico was simply an exploited sugar factory, in Lewis, *Main Currents in Caribbean Thought*, 275.

43. TR to ER, May 20, 1904, in *MRL*, IV, 801; see Frank Ninkovich, "Theodore Roosevelt: Civilization as Ideology," *DH*, X (1986), 221–45.

How much the violent response in the press to Roosevelt's and Root's message was a reaction to its offensive tone that radiated smug American self-confidence, or its use of superficial moralistic homilies, or its absence of economic sensitivity, is impossible to say. More likely the criticism simply reflected the usual political opposition to Roosevelt as presidential candidate and Republican leader and continuing opposition from ideological and political anti-imperialists. Although Roosevelt wrote to Root, "I was rather amused at the yell about my letter," he was obviously surprised by the nature of the criticism. "What I wrote is the simplest common sense, and only the fool or coward can treat it as aught else." Roosevelt was most distressed at his critics' failure to understand his context, which was not power but responsibility, not Latin America but Europe: "If we are willing to let Germany or England act as the policeman of the Caribbean, then we can afford not to interfere when gross wrongdoing occurs. But if we intend to say 'Hands off' to the powers of Europe, then sooner or later we must keep order ourselves." In Roosevelt's view, intervention in the Dominican crisis was inevitable, and the only question was whether the United States or a concert of Europe took action. American willingness to share control with Europe through the Hague Permanent Court of Arbitration had failed miserably. But every time Roosevelt tried to reassure the anti-imperialists or the sensitive Latin Americans, he was badly rebuffed. "What a queer set of (absent-) evil-minded creatures, mixed with honest people of preposterous shortness of vision, our opponents are!"[44]

The remainder of Roosevelt's letter to Root is concerned with the political context of the imminent campaign, dealing more with Democratic enemies than with immediate crises in the Dominican Republic. Roosevelt was still formulating a policy that could justify the intervention he felt was inevitable in the Dominican crisis while at the same time reexamining the now outmoded American reliance on international arbitration to solve fiscal problems in weak neighboring countries. Europe was not a threat, immersed as it was in the complications of the Russo-Japanese War, which became a world war when the Russian fleet sailed from Europe to Asia in its vain attempt to punish the Japanese. The election, the Hague decision, the Russo-Japanese War, Panama, Venezuela, the Dominicans, and the Monroe

44. A summary of press comments is in *MRL*, IV, 801–802 n.; Gow, "How Did the Roosevelt Corollary Become Linked to the Dominican Republic?" 162; TR to ER, June 7, 1904, in *MRL*, IV, 821–22. TR's reference to "our joint letter" is probably not a reflection of joint authorship but of TR's composition and Root's delivery.

Doctrine all influenced Roosevelt's attempt to formulate an effective, moral, and limited policy, which he still hoped would solve the immediate Dominican problem.[45]

When Roosevelt wrote to British historian George Otto Treveleyan on May 28, 1904, he reflected on the vagaries of presidential politics. Our "presidential office tends to put a premium upon a man's keeping out of trouble rather than upon his accomplishing results. If a man has a very decided character, it is normally the case that he makes ardent friends and bitter enemies." Roosevelt feared his political fate: "I am not at all sure that any Democrat will vote for me because of my attitude on Panama, there are a certain number of mugwumps who will undoubtedly vote against me because of it. So as regards Cuban reciprocity. The country backed me up in the matter, but there is not a Democrat who will vote for me because I got Cuban reciprocity, while there are not a few beet sugar men who will vote against me because of it." Roosevelt sensed the looming political difficulties that would make the Dominican crisis not one of "simple common sense" but a political problem. In May, 1904, he was not looking beyond his immediate reelection campaign, nor was he setting the stage for a new leap in American foreign policy. Rather, he was seeking to become the first reelected elevated vice-president in American political history while postponing a problem that he sensed would give "mortal offense" in some unexpected way.[46]

The Dominican situation entered its final phase on July 14, 1904, when the long-awaited SDIC arbitral award was delivered. Deliberations had begun in December, 1903, by the three arbitral commissioners, Manuel de J. Galván, the designated Dominican representative, John G. Carlisle, a Cleveland Democrat named by President Roosevelt, and United States Circuit Court of Appeals Judge George Gray, chosen by the Dominicans from the pool of United States Supreme Court and appeals court justices specified by the protocol. In arbitration cases the third person named, in this instance Gray, generally acts as the umpire to cast the deciding vote if the two designated choices representing the specific contesting interests cannot agree.

45. For American diplomatic problems arising from the Russo-Japanese War, see TR to JH, Paul Morton, and Alvey Adee, August 22–24, 1904; to JH, August 20, September 19, 1904, all in *MRL*, IV, 901, 904, 913, 946. See also Raymond Esthus, *Double Eagle and Rising Sun: The Russians and Japanese at Portsmouth in 1905* (Durham, N.C., 1988); Esthus, *Theodore Roosevelt and Japan* (Seattle, 1967); and Tyler Dennett, *Roosevelt and the Russo-Japanese War* (New York, 1928).

46. TR to George O. Trevelyan, May 28, 1904, in *MRL*, IV, 806–807.

Galván, a holdover from the Woss y Gil administration, was at first contested by Morales but finally accepted when the United States, wary of further delays, refused to renegotiate his appointment. Carlisle, a Democrat originally from Kentucky, the Speaker of the House from 1883 to 1890, and secretary of the treasury in Grover Cleveland's second administration, was a founding member of the Constitution Club, a conservative Democratic political organization formed in 1904 that charged Roosevelt with governing by personal fiat rather than constitutional law. Carlisle and Smith M. Weed, the president and one of the founders of the SDIC, were active members of Cleveland's Democratic party. Gray was a respected professional arbitrator, a Gold Democrat appointed to the bench by President McKinley, who served in the Roosevelt, Taft, and Wilson administrations as a diplomatic mediator and as chairman of the Anthracite Strike Commission in 1902. In 1904 he supported Roosevelt's Democratic opponent, Judge Alton Parker, for the presidency. The arbitral commission's role was critical, not in setting the amount of the award already specified through SDIC-Dominican negotiations at $4.5 million (probably considerably more than it was worth) but in determining how it would be paid.[47]

In the arbitral decision the Dominican Republic was ordered to begin paying monthly installments of $37,500 in September, 1904, an impossible sum of $450,000 a year that would increase to $41,667 monthly or $500,000 annually after two years. As security in the likely event that no payment was made, the United States was authorized to take physical possession and control of the customhouse at Puerto Plata to administer the customs using Dominican employees limited to routine customs inspection duties. Should Puerto Plata's revenues prove insufficient to pay the monthly amount, the designated American financial agent was authorized to take control of any or all of the Sánchez, Samaná, and Monte Cristi customhouses in addition to Puerto Plata. The award set interest at 4 percent, specified the terms of delivery of SDIC bonds, the process of conversion, and the time when control of the bank, railroad, and bonds would be transferred from the SDIC to the Dominican government. The award additionally specified that old wharf concessions, other concessions for each port, and the old foreign debt took precedence over all other debts and di-

47. See *MRL*, IV, 884n.; *MRL*, III, 352n.; TR to Robert Collier, October 22, 1904, in *MRL*, IV, 991. *HR*, 41, and Wynne, *State Insolvency*, II, 232, are both critical of the SDIC settlement amount; text in *FRUS*, 1904, pp. 274–79.

rected the proper order of payment. In the event that the financial agent was obliged to take possession of Puerto Plata, he was to remain in possession of the port for six months, at which time the government could request restoration. In addition, the American financial agent was ordered to serve as paid financial adviser to the Dominican government. No provision was made for payment of other protocols to foreign governments guaranteed by the same customs receipts as the SDIC award.[48]

The Dominicans were thunderstruck by the implications of the award, which when combined with their other debts far exceeded their income. As everyone suddenly realized, the Americans had quietly gained virtually complete control of Dominican affairs without military or direct naval intervention, an event further underlined by the tour of all the Dominican ports taken by new American Resident Minister Thomas C. Dawson accompanied by Rear Admiral Charles D. Sigsbee on June 28. With the Americans about to control the largest Dominican port—no one expected the Dominicans to make even the first payment—foreign interests as well as local merchant-bankers felt equally threatened. When John Hay appointed John C. Abbott, the original SDIC attorney, the Dominicans resented the appearance of an old enemy now returning with the authority of the United States government and the legal backing of an international arbitral award. But Hay's appointment of Abbott, insensitive though it may have appeared, was consistent with American policy since the beginning of the SDIC presence in the Dominican Republic in 1893. Secretary of State John Foster wanted indirect American interest and involvement in Dominican affairs as a balance to avoid European domination. In 1904 the Roosevelt administration still resisted direct American involvement in Dominican affairs, and the appointment of Abbott may have been intended to distance the American government from direct involvement. Hay's instructions and Dawson's negotiations with the troubled Dominicans almost always cited the higher authority of the sacred arbitration commission as the source of Dominican discontent, averring that the Americans could not change an independent legal decision even if they wanted to, an argument that offended everyone and convinced no one.[49]

48. *FRUS*, 1904, pp. 274–79.
49. Dawson's Chronology, 595; Munro, *Intervention and Dollar Diplomacy*, 96; see TD to JH, September 27, 1904, last paragraph, in *FRUS*, 1904, p. 281.

Hay particularly took the high road in his instruction of October 11, 1904, indicating that the arbitral tribunal had considered all claims before making its independent finding: "The tribunal evidently proceeded upon the supposition, the just foundations of which were maintained by the United States, that, if the revenues of the Dominican Republic were properly collected, and wasteful, illegal, and hurtful expenditures done away with, the income of the Republic would be sufficient to enable it to meet all obligations and to have for legitimate purposes even more than it has ever had heretofore." Hay and the Roosevelt administration were proposing a complete transformation of a culture, of the common practices of the way it conducted business, ostensibly for the good of that society, at the behest of a higher legal authority. Poor Morales did not want to be made over; he wanted assurance that the government would receive what he considered its necessary inflated pittance or 60 percent of total revenues, a figure in contrast with the American estimate that 40 percent was sufficient, and eventually in 1905 compromised at 45 percent. Abbott rejected Dawson's suggestion that the government could be reassured with a guarantee of a minimum amount. At first, Morales, negotiating for a guaranteed monthly payment, resisted turning over Puerto Plata when John Abbott made his formal request for either payment or control on September 21.[50]

When Cáceres and the *horacistas* were infuriated both at the idea of American control and Morales' willingness to consider turning over additional customhouses for more American money, the beleaguered Dominican leader had no choice but to allow American control and accept American protection. Morales told Abbott to take possession of Puerto Plata even before discussing the matter with his divided cabinet. On October 17, the SDIC—Hay's appointment of Abbott emphasized the continuity—took possession of Puerto Plata and its $50,000 to $100,000 monthly revenues. For a week the SDIC allowed the government to use $7,500 to pay salaries in northern provinces but abruptly ended the arrangement and offered to guarantee the government $30,000 a month in exchange for control of all four northern ports. The SDIC's presence, its actions, and its demands caused deep resentment throughout the republic, and the *horacistas* threat-

50. JH to TD, October 11, 1904, in Instructions, Dominican, M77, Roll 98; TD to JH, September 27, 30, 1904, in *FRUS*, 1904, pp. 280, 283; MacMichael, "The United States and the Dominican Republic," 171.

ened Morales once again with open rebellion. As long as the other ports remained free of Abbott's control, the SDIC's complete control of Dominican revenues could be evaded by smuggling and attractive concessions, which were openly encouraged by Desiderio Arias at Monte Cristi.[51]

At first, only the Spanish diplomat speaking for his own and the German interests on August 19 protested that the award would impinge on previous claims. Most of the Europeans remained hopeful that the American initiative would eventually help all the European creditors and asked the United States, which declined, to combine in a joint initiative to make additional revolutionary claims. The Dominicans tried, unsuccessfully at first, to convince the French and Belgians to protest the award. When the Dominicans predictably failed to pay either the French and Belgian or the Italian claims on November 1, the Europeans protested vigorously, and the French threatened to seize the Santo Domingo and Macorís customhouses. When the German warship *Bremen* visited Santo Domingo City on November 30, her commanding officer conspicuously visited Dominican officials and European diplomats but pointedly avoided the Americans. The chorus of diplomatic protest increased as the situation continued unchanged. Domestic upheaval also threatened Morales' tenuous hold on the government when the American takeover resulted in widespread dismissals of Dominican employees. The government was unable to honor its customary short-term local loans against current customs.[52]

None of this surprised the Americans. By allowing the SDIC and Judge Abbott to take control, by not reassuring the Dominicans or the Europeans, and by placing responsibility for the devastated society on irresponsible Dominicans, the United States exploited the already existing pressures. Roosevelt had written in April, 1904, that he would not take action in the Dominican crisis "until the necessity becomes so clear that even the blindest can see it." The time had come. Roosevelt fully expected that the SDIC would be called upon to take over "the other three ports," on November 4, 1904, and suggested "the moral support of the presence of an American man-of-war" in a conversation with John Bassett Moore. Roosevelt was ahead of the State

51. Welles, *Naboth's Vineyard*, 617; John Abbott to TD, September 26, 1904, in *FRUS*, 1904, p. 281; Munro, *Intervention and Dollar Diplomacy*, 97.
52. Dawson's Chronology, 595–96; Munro, *Intervention and Dollar Diplomacy*, 97–98.

Department schedule. Assistant Secretary Loomis acknowledged that "Judge Abbott will have to be careful about what he does there" but cautioned that "it is not (handwritten addition: now) proposed that the *Detroit* shall assist in putting the American representative in charge of the Custom houses."[53]

Some questions remain about Roosevelt's fundamental Dominican policies in 1904. He was correct that intervention in March was premature. He was also correct that eventual American intervention was inevitable. The United States had virtually committed itself to such a policy when John Foster had first encouraged the SDIC to act as the American presence in an already troubled Caribbean situation in 1892. Obviously, Roosevelt did not want to undertake an intervention before his reelection campaign and while the Dominicans were still armed and dangerous. Roosevelt's policies are most open to question in the manner in which the Americans manipulated the Dominican crisis to ensure enough pressure to force an intervention that even Charles W. Eliot might approve—no mean task. On this count Roosevelt succeeded; by the end of 1904 the Dominicans were completely undone and Europeans threatened their own intervention, even though it was widely recognized that European diplomatic pressure on the Dominicans was really directed at the United States.[54]

Allowing John Abbott and the SDIC to become the stalking-horse for American intervention was probably Roosevelt's main miscalculation. No one was fooled by the subterfuge that a private company

53. For the navy's highly theoretical contingency plan for possible German seizure of Hispaniola see the Haiti–San Domingo Plan, in War Portfolios, General Board File 425, RG 80, NA; Challener, *Admirals, Generals, and American Foreign Policy*, 43–44, 120–22. For Lieutenant Walter S. Crosley's intelligence mission to the Dominican Republic, Vásquez' offer of Samaná Bay to the United States, and American suspicions of Vásquez' alliance with Germany, see memorandum for Admiral Taylor, May 6, 1903, in Area 8, Files M625, Roll 263, RG 45. For the Joint Army-Navy Board's attention to possible intervention see William Roger Adams, "Strategy, Diplomacy, and Isthmian Security, 1880–1917" (Ph.D. dissertation, Florida State University, 1974), 167–68. TR to Charles W. Eliot, April 4, 1904, in *MRL*, IV, 770; Francis Loomis to John Bassett Moore, November 4, 1904, Roll 4, Book 2, Loomis Papers.

54. For Europe's approval see JH to TD, December 30, 1904, in *FRUS*, 1905, p. 298. For Britain's favorable reaction see Warren G. Kneer, *Great Britain and the Caribbean, 1901–1913: A Study in Anglo-American Relations* (East Lansing, Mich., 1975), 107–109. For Roosevelt's views on Britain's debt intervention in Egypt as a possible model for the Dominican Republic, see Charles Francis Adams, "Reflex Light from Africa," *Century*, LXXII (1906), 101–11; TR to HCL, April 30, 1906, in *MRL*, V, 252; see also Kist, "Role of Thomas C. Dawson," 136–37; Howard K. Beale, *Theodore Roosevelt and the Rise of America to World Power* (Baltimore, 1956), 161–71. Perkins, *Monroe Doctrine, 1867–1907*, 419.

under an international legal arbitration award was acting independently of the United States. When the SDIC closed down the Dominican economy, it was the United States that was responsible, a move Roosevelt made for political reasons to make intervention less of a red flag to the anti-imperialists and Democrats. Roosevelt had made a similar error in Panama when he allowed Philippe Bunau-Varilla to manipulate the Panama revolution while Roosevelt publicly protested his innocence and noninvolvement. The maneuver did not work in the Dominican Republic any more than it did in Panama. Not only were Roosevelt's distancing maneuvers ineffective, they may help explain many of his contemporary credibility problems and why so many later historians distrust him. He was much more effective when he acted in a straightforward manner and did not try to hide his strong preferences behind the actions of others who were carrying out his wishes unofficially.[55]

55. For Dominican unanimity in rejecting Abbott see TD to JH, January 2, 1905, in *FRUS*, 1905, pp. 298–300. Roosevelt's postponement of the crisis to January, 1905, may have contributed to Senate suspicions of the actual intervention; see MacMichael, "The United States and the Dominican Republic," 174–75. For Abbott's appointment see John Abbott to Francis Loomis, August 4, 1904, in Miscellaneous Letters, M179, Roll 1219; Kist, "Role of Thomas C. Dawson," 85–90.

14   The Roosevelt Corollary and the *Modus Vivendi*

Ten days before the 1904 presidential election, Theodore Roosevelt tried to prepare his son Kermit for the possibility that the voters would reject the president's campaign to be reelected: "I am the first Vice-President who became President by the death of his predecessor, who has ever been nominated for the Presidential office. This is no small triumph in itself." In adding up the sure and probable states he expected to win, Roosevelt worried that he was one electoral vote short of victory and that in the remaining time a new event might "upset all calculations." We "must possess our souls in patience," he counseled. So great was Roosevelt's eventual victory that a quiet election night dinner became an impromptu celebration with visiting cabinet members and friends at Oyster Bay. The president was reelected by "majorities which astound me," comparable to McKinley's victory margin in 1900. Roosevelt admitted that "the last fortnight was nervous for both Edith and me," and though "chances favored my election [there] was a good chance of my defeat." As he had planned for some time, Roosevelt announced that "under no circumstances will I be a candidate for or accept another nomination," a controversial pronouncement that reflected his belief in an active presidency limited to two terms. Roosevelt was keenly aware of the political liabilities of his presidential style, which cost him the support of those who, though favoring his overall leadership, bitterly resented his strong stand on specific sensitive issues. In explaining his decision not to run for another term, Roosevelt wrote, "People get tired of the everlasting talk about Aristides; and moreover Aristides himself, after a certain number of years, finds that he has really delivered his message and that he has a tendency to repeat it over and over again." There is no evidence that Roosevelt, flushed with a striking election victory, mistook the landslide for a mandate to challenge the Senate, to remake the nation, or to initiate a new foreign policy.[1]

Railroad rate control and the tariff, not foreign policy, were the major political issues in Roosevelt's postelection correspondence and his Annual Message, delivered to Congress on December 4, 1904. At the start of Roosevelt's second term, domestic affairs still dominated American politics, a predilection reflected in the almost two-to-one preponderance of pages on domestic issues as opposed to foreign policy in Roosevelt's 1904 Annual Message, which made no mention of the continuing Dominican Republican crisis. To create what came to be known as the Roosevelt Corollary to the Monroe Doctrine—a phrase Elihu Root first used in a December 1, 1904, letter—Roosevelt incorported almost verbatim the text of his own letter, which Root had delivered on May 20 at the second anniversary of Cuban independence dinner. Emphasizing the principle of responsibility, Roosevelt limited the grounds for possible American intervention in Latin America. "We would interfere with them only in the last resort, and then only if it became evident that their inability or unwillingness to do justice at home and abroad had violated the rights of the United States or had invited foreign aggression to the detriment of the entire body of American nations." Although Roosevelt's principle seems to fit the Dominican situation perfectly, Venezuela may have been his primary target. Venezuela's President Cipriano Castro, a longtime antagonist of world powers (whose excessively aggressive actions may have been precipitated by an undiagnosed illness), caused serious American concern when he repudiated previous arbitration awards, confiscated foreign property, and briefly imprisoned an American businessman. At the time, Roosevelt wrote Secretary of State John Hay, "We do not want to act in the closing weeks of the campaign, but I think we should make up our minds ourselves to take the initiative and give Castro a sharp lesson, and turn the custom house over to the Belgians. This would put into deeds the policy announced in my letter read by Root at the Cuban dinner."[2]

1. TR to Kermit Roosevelt, October 16, 26, November 8, 10, 1904; to HCL, November 8, 1904; to Anna Lodge, November 10, 1904; to George O. Trevelyan, November 24, 1904, all in *MRL*, IV, 993–95, 1018, 1025–26, 1045; *ibid.*, 1021, n. 2.

2. Text of Annual Message is in *TRWN*, XV, 215–63, quote, 257–58; ER to General Thomas A. Hubbard, December 1, 1904, in Philip Jessup, *Elihu Root* (2 vols.; New York, 1938), I, 470; *TRWN*, XV, 257–58. For Castro's ill health see Judith Ewell, *Venezuela: A*

In his letter to Hay on September 2, 1904, Roosevelt connected the principle of American responsibility with the older policy of resisting armed European debt intervention with its threat of long-term occupation: "I think it will have a very healthy effect in the first place because it will do away with the foreign nations having any pretext for interference on this side of the water."By proposing Belgium as the peacekeeper, Roosevelt dramatically undercut the nationalistic character of the Monroe Doctrine, possibly for political purposes or to underline the Roosevelt Corollary's intended international purpose. Roosevelt closed his revealing letter with yet another advantage of Venezuelan intervention: "It will show those Dagos that they will have to behave decently." Roosevelt and Hay frequently referred to Latin Americans as Dagos, but only in private correspondence and conversation. In spite of his gringo diction, Roosevelt referred to Latin America's effective use of the Monroe Doctrine as a shield that allowed leaders like Castro to act as they pleased knowing that the American doctrine discouraged European retaliation. Roosevelt had previously suggested that "the Belgians, or other representatives of the Hague Court," control Castro, an indication that in spite of the unfavorable ruling on the Venezuelan blockade in February, Roosevelt still considered using the Hague arbitration and peacekeeping functions, especially in a customhouse possession, and that he viewed the corollary as part of the older American arbitration policy and not a new demonstration of American power.[3]

Both Root and Roosevelt viewed the new corollary as a limitation on American power, not an extension of it. Root specifically rejected Olney's 1895 corollary that "the United States is practically sovereign on this continent" in a December 22, 1904, speech when he declared that "we arrogate to ourselves, not sovereignty over the American continent, but only the right to protect," a limitation he correctly thought many had not understood in Roosevelt's initial statements. For Root and Roosevelt, responsibility was the keynote of the new

---

Century of Change (Stanford, 1984), 38; TR to JH September 2, 1904, in *MRL*, IV, 917. For the Venezuelan disputes see A. L. P. Dennis, *Adventures in American Diplomacy, 1896–1906* (New York, 1928), 297–301; and William M. Sullivan, "The Rise of Despotism in Venezuela: Cipriano Castro, 1899–1908" (Ph.D. dissertation, University of New Mexico, 1974), 491–528. See J. Fred Rippy, "Antecedents of the Roosevelt Corollary of the Monroe Doctrine," *PHR*, IX (1940), 267–79.

3. TR to JH, September 2, August 30, 1904, both in *MRL*, IV, 917, 914.

corollary, not an extension of diplomatic power but a reflection of the "nature of things, trade and control, and the obligation to keep order which go with them," an acknowledgment that the United States had outgrown its reliance on Europe to keep the peace in the Caribbean. Roosevelt regarded the Monroe Doctrine "as part of the inherited tradition of the country," a matter of custom that he thought might make the new American responsibilities more palatable to those reluctant for a variety of reasons to support his foreign policy. It is possible that the administration was readying the principle to defend any specific intervention actions it might take, whether in Venezuela or the Dominican Republic. Roosevelt wrote of "an opportunist foreign policy of necessity" in December, 1904, still uncertain when or whether American intervention might occur.[4]

Because the Monroe Doctrine had become a catechism of American politics, vague, mythological, and expressed but not defined, Roosevelt's pronouncements disturbed the German kaiser, who wrote, "this kind of Monroeism I cannot assent to," when informed of Root's speech. Latin Americans, historically suspicious of American intentions, were also wary. The president and the Senate had reached a significant foreign affairs stalemate when it became clear that the Senate would not approve ten identical arbitration treaties negotiated in November and December, 1904, calling for Hague Court arbitration in matters not involving the nation's vital interests. The Senate refused to allow the president to designate the limited areas of the dispute, insisting that each instance be separately approved as a treaty. In November Roosevelt had complained that "it is well nigh impossible to secure reciprocity treaties." But when Roosevelt's friend Senator Lodge proposed Senate ratification of each individual arbitration arrangement, Roosevelt objected that such a procedure relegated the treaties to "absurdities" or "the veriest shams." When the southern senators united, fearing that executive arbitration agreements might make southern states liable for previous defaulted debts, the Senate and the southern Democrats were joined in opposition to Roosevelt's policy of what some saw as executive usurpation.[5]

4. New England Society of New York Address, December 22, 1904, in Philip Jessup, *Elihu Root* (2 vols.; New York, 1938), I, 470; see Perkins, *Monroe Doctrine, 1867–1907*, 429–30; ER to Henry M. Flagler, January 3, 1905, in Jessup, *Elihu Root*, I, 471; TR to Cecil Spring Rice, December 27, 1904, in *MRL*, IV, 1084.

5. TR to Joseph Cannon, November 30, 1904; to John Spooner, January 6, 1905, both in *MRL*, IV, 1053, 1092; see *ibid.*, 1092n. W. Stull Holt, *Treaties Defeated by the Senate: A*

Roosevelt's carefully contrived policy of making an unpalatable Caribbean intervention more attractive by uniting it with the Monroe Doctrine came undone when the Senate realized that until 1905 the Monroe Doctrine and all the later corollaries were statements by the executive branch undebated or ratified by Congress. From its inception, Monroe's doctrine was heavily involved in American domestic politics. A Senate suspicious of Roosevelt's activism, sensitive of its prerogatives, embroiled in extremely sensitive debates on tariff and federal railroad control, and unwilling to approve even a relatively inoffensive arbitration arrangement was not about to ratify a Monroe Doctrine with or without a Roosevelt Corollary. When the Dominican intervention debate began, Roosevelt's tactic of tying a practical limited intervention to an attractive, if heretofore largely unquestioned, mythological statement threw doubt on the validity of either. The Dominican intervention issue plunged the president and Congress into the political debates of Roosevelt's tumultuous second term, dominated by a struggle for increased control of the government by a president seeking to extend the powers of his office with a Senate jealous of its still commanding position.[6]

Study of the Struggle Between the President and Senate over the Conduct of Foreign Relations (Baltimore, 1933), 204–12; David S. Patterson, *Toward a Warless World: The Travail of the American Peace Movement, 1887–1914* (Bloomington, Ind., 1976), 126–28. Kaiser quoted in Perkins, *Monroe Doctrine, 1867–1907*, 43. For evidence that the kaiser did accept the Roosevelt Corollary see Melvin Small, "The United States and the German Threat to the Hemisphere," *Americas*, XXVI (1972), 252–70.

6. Ernest May, *The Making of the Monroe Doctrine* (Cambridge, Mass., 1975); Samuel Flagg Bemis, *John Quincy Adams and the Foundations of American Foreign Policy* (New York, 1949); Dexter Perkins, *The Monroe Doctrine, 1823–1826* (Cambridge, Mass., 1927); Perkins, *The Monroe Doctrine, 1826–1867* (Baltimore, 1933); Perkins, *Monroe Doctrine, 1867–1907*; Perkins, *A History of the Monroe Doctrine* (Boston, 1949); Harry Ammon, "Domestic Politics or National Decision," *DH*, V (1981), 53–70; Ernest May, Response, *ibid.*, 71–72; Richard Leopold, *Growth of American Foreign Policy* (New York, 1962), 235; Charles E. Chapman, "New Corollaries of the Monroe Doctrine with Especial Reference to the Relations to the United States with Cuba," *University of California Chronicle*, XXXIII (1931), 161–89; Thomas E. Karnes, "Hiram Bingham and His Obsolete Shibboleth," *DH*, III (1979), 39–57; David Y. Thomas, "The Monroe Doctrine from Roosevelt to Roosevelt," *South Atlantic Quarterly*, XXXIV (1935), 117–35. Useful contemporary accounts include George W. Critchfield, *American Supremacy: The Rise and Progress of the Latin American Republics and Their Relations to the United States Under the Monroe Doctrine* (2 vols.; New York, 1908); Frederick Courtland Penfield, "Practical Phases of Caribbean Domination," *NAR*, CLXXVII (1904), 75–85; Walter Wellman, "Shall the Monroe Doctrine Be Modified?" *NAR*, CLXXIII (1901), 832–44; William L. Scruggs, "The Monroe Doctrine—Its Origin and Import," *NAR*, CLXXVI (1903), 185–99; Sir Alexander E. Miller, "The Monroe Doctrine from an English Standpoint," *NAR*, CLXXVI (1903), 728–33; Edward S. Rapallo and Domingo B. Castillo, "The New Monroe Doc-

On December 15, 1904, European pressure in the Dominican situation intensified sharply. Belgium insisted on resumption of payments that had remained in default since 1902. On December 15, a Belgian diplomat from Havana suggested a French-Belgian receivership in the southern ports—Santo Domingo City and Macorís—similar to the American arrangement in Puerto Plata and the north. France, traditionally the most aggressive European power in Caribbean waters, moved its warships from Martinique to Port-au-Prince, Haiti, and announced a planned visit to Santo Domingo. At the same time, the anti-Morales *jimenistas*, who were the faction most opposed to Morales' American alliance, opened negotiations with Germany to take over the Spanish, Belgian, and Italian claims and establish a European-German receivership in the southern ports. Since Finance Minister Emilio Joubert was unable to negotiate any further domestic loans or concessions, the Dominican government was virtually unable to function. On December 30, 1904, Secretary of State John Hay, seriously concerned at the "disquieting situation" and fearing that "there appears to be a concert among" the European powers, instructed Minister Thomas Dawson to "sound the President of Santo Domingo, discreetly but earnestly, and in a perfectly friendly spirit . . . whether the Government . . . would be disposed to request the United States to take charge of the collection of duties and effect an equitable distribution." Hay's note indicated that the foreign pressure was directed mainly toward the United States, since "we have grounds to think that such arrangement would satisfy the other powers."[7]

Dawson immediately entered into discussions with Morales, who

---

trine," *NAR*, CLXXX (1905), 586–601; Hiram Bingham, "Latin America and the Monroe Doctrine," *Yale Review*, III (1914), 656–72; William R. Shepherd, "New Light on the Monroe Doctrine," *Political Science Quarterly*, XXXI (1916), 578–89. For a cavalier historical treatment and the view that the Monroe Doctrine was simply an excuse for American hegemony from its inception see Kenneth M. Coleman, "The Political Mythology of the Monroe Doctrine: Reflections on the Social Psychology of Hegemony," in John D. Martz and Lars Schoultz (eds.), *Latin America, the United States, and the Inter-American System* (Boulder, Colo., 1980), 95–114. See also D. A. Graber, *Crisis Diplomacy: A History of U.S. Intervention Policies and Practices* (Washington, D.C., 1959), esp. 24–27.

7. Dawson's Chronology, in *FRUS*, 1906, p. 596; Sumner Welles, *Naboth's Vineyard: The Dominican Republic, 1824–1944* (2 vols.; New York, 1928), 620–21; JH to TD, December 30, 1904, in *FRUS*, 1905, p. 298. For previous American consideration of customhouse arrangements for debt defaults in 1872 and 1881 with Venezuela see Howard C. Hill, *Roosevelt and the Caribbean* (Chicago, 1927), 159n. For the French naval activity see Contre-Amiral Boué de Lapeyrére to Ministère de la Marine, Paris, December 20, 1904, in BB[4], 1679, Archives de la Marine, Château de Vincennes.

feared both European naval demands and an SDIC claim to the four northern ports. Although Morales favored American intervention, his cabinet was too divided to make the request for American intervention that Hay required. Morales enlisted American help to oust Desiderio Arias at Monte Cristi while taking control of its customhouse, but Dawson refused to be a pawn in Dominican politics. Both men realized that opposition to direct American involvement was intense among Dominican nationalists. Dawson negotiated with the Dominican cabinet members, persuading Foreign Minister Sánchez, already favorable to the United States, Finance Minister Joubert, inclined in that direction, and Minister of Hacienda Federico Velásquez, the least inclined to accept American supervision, to agree in principle to an American intervention. The Dominicans were concerned that they would not have sufficient money to run the government—they wanted 60 percent of customs revenues—and feared that the SDIC's John T. Abbott would gain even more power than he already had. Velásquez bargained hard to retain Dominican participation in the customs collection, not the face-saving gesture he claimed but a serious attempt to maintain a measure of Dominican sovereignty and control.[8]

On January 5, 1905, Roosevelt ordered Commander Albert C. Dillingham, with "full confidence in your ability and discretion and . . . your exceptional knowledge of the present conditions in the Dominican Republic," to join with Dawson in negotiating an American intervention to help settle the Dominican fiscal crisis. Dillingham was given sweeping discretionary powers, a naval vessel was placed at his disposal, and he was to report directly to the president through the State Department and to negotiate not only with Morales and his government but also with the revolutionary and antigovernment forces. Dillingham, a fifty-six-year-old Annapolis graduate, decorated for "gallant and conspicuous conduct" at sea in the Spanish-American War, was the only American who knew and had dealt with many aspects of Dominican politics. Roosevelt and Hay gave Dillingham a remarkable amount of maneuvering room, including leeway on the percentage of revenue available to the Dominican government, loosely indicated as "about forty percent." Dillingham was instructed to "recall to President Morales your interviews with him in the spring of 1904, and the voluntary offer he then made to you to turn over all the custom-houses . . . to the United States" and in effect indicate that

8. TD to JH, January 2, 1905, in *FRUS*, 1905, pp. 298–300.

"in view of the continued state of unrest and . . . the imminent and pressing danger" of European intervention, the United States was ready to accept the offer.[9]

Dawson and Dillingham worked well together and sympathized with the many Dominican dilemmas. A detailed instruction from Assistant Secretary Loomis on January 6 revealed why the percentage of revenue question was critical. Under Dominican customhouse management, total expected revenues were $1.85 million. With the proposed government budget of $1.3 million (over 70 percent of anticipated revenues), only $550,000 was left to pay immediate obligations of $1.7 million and interest arrears of an additional $900,000. Thus, Loomis instructed, the United States must collect all the customs revenues, prohibit changes in existing tariff laws, and only permit government expenditures "not to exceed 40 per cent" of total revenues. The United States would arrange the terms, settlement, and amortization of the entire Dominican debt. Any money left over at the end of each year would be given to the Dominican government. Dawson, who knew that Loomis' 40 percent was an impossible sticking point for the Dominicans, did not discuss the American terms with Morales but instead approached Foreign Minister Juan Sánchez, the most pro-American official in the government. Sánchez heatedly resisted, arguing that such a demand would send his government into exile. Finance Minister Joubert planned a new stringent budget in response to Dawson's pressure, but on January 14, when Dillingham arrived, the Dominicans had not yielded to the American demands. Aware that there was insufficient time to deal effectively with the *jimenistas*, the Americans concentrated on winning *horacista* support and Velásquez' agreement.[10]

On January 15, when the two Americans called on Morales, Dillingham told the president the United States desired only to help the Dominicans. Morales agreed to reorganize the government's expensive bureaucracy and asked that export duties on coffee, cacao, and tobacco, which were financially inconsequential, be removed to make an American-Dominican agreement more politically palatable to the

9. JH to Albert C. Dillingham, January 5, 1905, in *FRUS*, 1905, pp. 300–301; Dillingham, "Intervention of the United States Government in the Affairs of the Republic of Santo Domingo," in Naval Records Collection, Subject File, OH, Box 381, RG 45, NA. A summary of Dillingham's service record is in Abstracts of Service Records of Naval Officers, Vol. 6, p. 201, Microcopy M1328, Roll 4, RG 24, NA.

10. TD to JH, January 23, 1905, in *FRUS*, 1905, p. 303.

Dominican farmers. The three men were aware of the rising uneasiness in the republic, fed by rumors of impending American annexation and continued divisions within the government. Dillingham and Dawson communicated their sympathies for the Dominicans by accepting any Dominican requests they could and conducting the negotiations with gracious sensitivity. Dawson toasted "the Independence of the Dominican Republic" and Morales in Spanish, Dillingham was presented to the cabinet with full military honors (at Morales' request), and Loomis reluctantly accepted the government's request for export duty relief. Both Dillingham and Dawson, however, were aware of the "moral effect upon malcontents" of the "presence of force." Dillingham advised Hay, "I do not anticipate uprising or any great opposition, but I consider take every precaution advisable." Because the Americans negotiated rather than forced an agreement, "the public and political situation was so strained that we could not feel safe until Mr. Velásquez had affixed his signature to the completed document," a process that involved patient editing and further negotiation until the Spanish and English versions were identical in meaning.[11]

Dillingham cabled the terms of the agreement to Washington on January 21 at 10 A.M. The United States undertook to adjust all the Dominican obligations, take control of all customhouses effective February 1, and restore credit. The Dominicans received several concessions, including a guarantee of territorial integrity. The Dominican share of revenues was set at 45 rather than 40 percent, export duties could be abolished immediately, and Dillingham recommended "no appointment anyone formerly connected with Improvement Company. Such appointments objectionable." The news of the agreement was published in Santo Domingo newspapers on January 20, a political necessity to eliminate the most extreme rumors. Many of the earlier provisions had been selectively leaked "to appease the popular clamor," a process that embarrassed Washington, which received the first news of the agreement from American news reports taken from the Dominican press. The premature press disclosure that disturbed Washington had relieved Dillingham and Dawson, who, knowing the rhythms of Dominican politics, found the early "semipublicity . . . the first definite assurance" that the agreement would go through.

11. Albert C. Dillingham, Address to Carlos Morales; TD to JH, January 21, 23, 1905; Dillingham to JH, January 20, 1905, all in *FRUS*, 1905, pp. 311–12, 306.

Roosevelt's practical decision to give Dillingham and Dawson extraordinary leeway in negotiating an agreement acceptable to as many Dominicans as possible backfired when the American Senate, suspicious that Roosevelt had usurped its treaty-making function, turned the issue into a constitutional crisis and a major political confrontation.[12]

Roosevelt's original intention, much more limited than the Senate supposed, was a simple financial arrangement, basically an extension of the SDIC arbitral award backed by American naval support to maintain order. Even the sensitive Senate did not regard purely financial agreements as treaties. A plan similar to that Roosevelt originally intended was adopted in Costa Rica in July and August, 1905, whereby the New York banking house of Speyer and Company refunded the Costa Rican debt, an arrangement that caused virtually no interest on anyone's part. Roosevelt, in his concern about an efficient and equitable Dominican settlement, opened up a diplomatic and political hornet's nest by allowing his emissaries to negotiate with the Dominicans rather than impose an intervention. That Dillingham far exceeded his instructions, as Hay later admitted, was not as damaging as the early publication of the negotiations in progress. Because Dillingham yielded to Dominican sensitivity and political necessity, his concessions as well as some of his diction changed a simple financial arrangement into a more complex agreement. Ironically, when Dillingham guaranteed Dominican territorial integrity, he turned what could have been a classic case of gunboat diplomacy into an idealistic example of the national self-abnegation that Roosevelt insisted all along was part of his corollary. But Dillingham also converted his negotiation from a simple executive agreement into a protocol that required the Senate's participation. Dillingham and Dawson, dealing with sensitive Dominicans, were unaware that their term *agreement* had a different legal connotation than the State Department's *arrangement*. On January 24, senators from both parties questioned Theodore Roosevelt's new executive usurpation, even before a frustrated Acting Secretary of State Loomis received his own copy of the disputed text.[13]

12. Albert C. Dillingham to JH, January 21, 1905; text of original Dillingham proposal; text of signed agreement; TD to JH, January 23, 1905, all in *FRUS*, 1905, pp. 306, 310–12, 308; David MacMichael, "The United States and the Dominican Republic, 1871–1940: A Cycle in Caribbean Diplomacy" (Ph.D. dissertation, University of Oregon, 1964), 173–81.

13. William Merry to Alvey Adee, July 30, 1905, in Despatches from United States Ministers to Central America, Microcopy M219, Roll 93, RG 59, NA; text of agreement is in Jacob Hollander to TR, October 1, 1905, Department of State, Communications

One cannot say what changes Loomis or Roosevelt might have made in Dillingham's January 21, 1905, agreement had the Dominican press not published the text and the American Senate not begun to debate the agreement before the State Department had even received it. Once the question was raised on the Senate floor, it became, even for Senator Henry Cabot Lodge, Roosevelt's closest political friend, a matter of "very great importance and involves a great many questions of most serious gravity." The debate gave the minority Democratic party a means of politically challenging a chief executive newly elected by a landslide and about to test further his own ability to extend the powers of the presidency at the expense of the Senate. On January 9 Roosevelt had virtually predicted the Dominican confrontation when he noted the "idiotic jealousy of the Executive which tends to make the senate try to reduce the Executive to impotency." In addition, the Senate protest marked a continuation of Roosevelt's past personal and political differences, especially with Alabama Senator John Tyler Morgan, an old adversary of Roosevelt in the Panama debates, and Colorado Senator Henry M. Teller, once a Republican, who supported William Jennings Bryan in 1896 and became a Democrat in 1901. Roosevelt charged, "Senator Teller is simply trying over again what he has done with the Philippines, with Panama, with Cuba, with Porto Rico, and with every other like matter that has come up." [14]

Much of the original Senate confusion over Roosevelt's intentions occurred because the early Dominican publication of the negotiations before any American discussion led many senators, concerned with senatorial prerogatives as well as continuing domestic political con-

---

from Special Agents, Vol. 49, Microcopy M37, Roll 21, RG 59, NA; the Senate's January 24 debate is in *Congressional Record*, 58th Cong., 3rd Sess., pp. 1227, 1281–88; Mac-Michael, "The United States and the Dominican Republic," 174–77; Loomis to TD, January 24, 1905, in *FRUS*, 1905, p. 312. For Hay's immediate judgment that the agreement was a treaty that must be ratified by the Senate see JH, diary entry, January 25, 1905, Hay Papers, LC; Glenn C. Kist, "The Role of Thomas C. Dawson in United States–Latin American Relations, 1897–1912" (Ph.D. dissertation, Loyola University of Chicago, 1971), 145–50.

14. *Congressional Record*, 58th Cong., 3rd Sess., p. 1281; TR to John St. Loe Strachey, January 9, 1905, RP; Holt, *Treaties Defeated by the Senate*, 206n.; TR to Elbert Baldwin, January 26, 1905, in *MRL*, IV, 1109; Hill, *Roosevelt and the Caribbean*, 162. See Perkins, *Monroe Doctrine, 1867–1907*, 433, for the view that the Roosevelt Corollary was a revolutionary change from a policy of nonintervention to intervention and that Roosevelt's use of the doctrine was a means of making intervention politically palatable; for the view that Roosevelt's Dominican intervention was not a revolutionary change see Gordon Connell-Smith, *The United States and Latin America: An Historical Analysis of Inter-American Relations* (London, 1974), 119–20.

flicts, to assume that Roosevelt was acting in secrecy. Roosevelt's choice of an efficient naval officer cut through the difficulties of normal diplomacy so well that the results transcended not only traditional diplomatic methods but the even slower means of routine communication as well. The deal was done before even the president knew it. In defending his policy many years later, Roosevelt explained, "My whole foreign policy was based on the exercise of intelligent foresight and of decisive action sufficiently far in advance of any likely crisis to make it improbable that we would run into serious trouble." Significantly, in his autobiography, he referred to the proposed Dillingham intervention as an arrangement, probably intended to avoid complications either with the Dominicans, the European creditors, or the United States Senate.[15]

By having Dillingham negotiate the arrangement, Roosevelt hoped to avoid involved legislative struggles in either the United States or the Dominican Republic. When the press and the Senate made the intervention a constitutional as well as a political issue, the original diplomatic advantage in using Dillingham ended, as did the utility of the original simple and effective Dillingham-Morales draft of January 21. Ironically, it was with the substitute draft proposed by Acting Secretary of State Francis Loomis, acting for the intermittently ill John Hay, that the correlation between the Dominican intervention and the Roosevelt Corollary first occurred. The new Loomis revision was radically different from Dillingham's original agreement, and Roosevelt acknowledged that the arrangement was in fact a protocol that required senatorial approval. Although Loomis dismissed his changes as "not considerable," he transformed the diction, the scope, and the nature of the original agreement to a document much more concerned with placating the American Senate than Dominican sensibilities or needs. The most devastating revision for the Dominicans was the date, changed from February 1 to an indefinite limbo dependent upon legislative approval of both American and Dominican congresses, an enormous obstacle for Morales, who had never been able to control his Congress. In prose clearly intended for U.S. senators, the Loomis draft invoked "the imminent peril and urgent menace" from foreign creditors that replaced the simple financial exigency that introduced Dillingham's original. What followed was nothing less than the Roosevelt Corollary to the Monroe Doctrine coupled to Dominican inter-

15. TR, *Autobiography* (1913), rpr. in *TRWN*, XX, 497.

vention for the first time. "Viewing any attempt on the part of governments outside of this hemisphere to oppress or control the destiny of the Dominican Republic as a manifestation of an unfriendly disposition to the United States," the draft then invoked the Dominican request for American intervention. The Dominican share of 45 percent, the American guarantee of Dominican territorial integrity, and the Dominican right to abolish export duties survived intact from Dillingham's agreement.[16]

Once the early publication of the Dillingham-Morales agreement and the Senate's objections made Roosevelt's desired *fait accompli* impossible, a new solution had to be found. Loomis instructed Dawson to tell the Dominicans that the agreement they had signed was not final but "ad referendum." Morales desperately needed unequivocal American support, not an agreement conditional on approval by an American Senate, which in 1871 caused the overthrow of President Báez by failing to ratify President Grant's treaty. The continuing fiscal crisis, however, was more immediate than Morales' political future. On January 27, the Italian government, soon to emerge as the most aggressive European Dominican creditor, formally demanded a 5 percent share of the Puerto Plata customs revenues under the Italian protocol of May 1, 1904, an agreement that preceded and conflicted with the SDIC arbitral award. In Santo Domingo City financial affairs were at a standstill, awaiting resolution through an American-Dominican agreement. When it became apparent that the agreement would have to await American Senate approval, so there would be no American government assistance before approval, Dawson arranged with Santiago Michelena, a private American citizen from Puerto Rico, to loan the Dominican government $75,000 a month for operating expenses, including wages for troops, at a cost in commissions and interest of 3.5 percent a month.[17]

Roosevelt had fewer designs on the Dominicans than Francis Loomis, who on January 31 asked Dawson to remove the territorial integrity guarantee from the protocol, a request that invited Dominican

16. For Dillingham's and Dawson's defense that they had anticipated senatorial jurisdiction but had not mentioned it, see TD to JH, March 7, 1905, in *FRUS*, 1905, p. 350; for Morales, see *ibid.*, 353; MacMichael, "The United States and the Dominican Republic," 191; TR to Elbert Baldwin, January 26, 1905, in *MRL*, IV, 1109; Francis Loomis to TD, January 25, 1905, in *FRUS*, 1905, pp. 313–14.

17. Italian memo, January 27, 1905; Michelena contract; TD to JH, January 23, 1905, all in *FRUS*, 1905, pp. 315, 325, 318–20.

suspicion and which Velásquez refused to consider. Loomis had little sympathy or sensitivity to Dominican political problems. When Velásquez declined to sign Loomis' protocol omitting the original territorial guarantee, Loomis asked, "Is signature of minister of finance necessary?" Dawson replied that bypassing Velásquez would produce a *horacista* uprising in the Cibao. When neither Loomis nor Velásquez would yield, an impasse developed, which Roosevelt, who still felt like a gorged boa constrictor, resolved when he ordered Loomis to "put in anything the Dominicans want about our not annexing the Island—the stronger the better." Hay, who had more nuance and less aggressiveness than Loomis, whom he disliked, changed the diction so that the United States, "in agreeing to respect the complete territorial integrity of the Dominican Republic," disavowed any possibility of annexation or involvement in Haitian boundary disputes. Roosevelt underlined his disinclination for Dominican territory when he edited an October 12, 1905, speech that used the phrase *friendship and union*. Roosevelt crossed out *and union*. Although the Dominicans were willing to agree to an unconditional ban on increasing their debt, they objected to the phrase "without the consent of the President of the United States," which Hay and Roosevelt considered essential to American ability to reassure European creditors. That clause remained, but unconditional extraterritoriality for American employees in Dominican customhouses was removed.[18]

Although Sánchez and Velásquez still preferred the original Dillingham draft, the protocol with minor last-minute modifications was signed at 4 P.M. on February 7 and dispatched aboard the American warship *Stewart* at 4:30 P.M. to reach the San Juan mail steamer bound for New York. Reflecting on the difficult negotiation process, Thomas Dawson realized that the six weeks of hard bargaining between the United States and the Dominicans had substantially reduced Dominican distrust of American motives. Sánchez' and Morales' demands reflected Dominican political sensibilities and the need to "avoid any outbreak, which might have left an enduring hatred of the United States, even if it had been suppressed." Dawson also conceded that the majority of Dominicans—"rash and ignorant elements"—op-

18. Francis Loomis to TD, February 2, 1905; TD to JH, February 13, 1905; JH to TD, February 6, 1905, all in *FRUS*, 1905, pp. 320–23; William Loeb to Loomis, February 6, 1905, in MacMichael, "The United States and the Dominican Republic," 183; JH to TD, February 6, 1905, in *FRUS*, 1905, p. 322; draft is in Notes from the Dominican Legation, Vol. 5, Microcopy T80, Roll 3, RG 59, NA.

posed the American intervention and were held in check only by the "powerful moral effect" of the continuing American naval presence.[19]

Commander Dillingham resumed his duties as a naval officer on January 24 and with Rear Admiral Sigsbee on the warship *Newark* took control of the port of Monte Cristi under the SDIC arbitral award of July 14, 1904. The Dillingham-Arias peace agreement of June 3, 1904, guaranteed Monte Cristi independence from the Morales government. The Americans obtained control without armed resistance, by a combination of gunboat pressure and naval diplomacy. To Dawson's surprise, Morales and his government objected to giving up Monte Cristi, even though American control would eliminate Arias, one of the government's chief rivals and the remaining stronghold of *jimenista* resistance. Morales' reluctance revealed the enduring and bitter hatred all Dominicans retained for the SDIC and Judge Abbott, the continuing symbol of a hated American corporation, which explained why the Dominicans rejected Abbott's highly favorable proposals to take over Monte Cristi in October and November. Morales had no objection to surrendering Monte Cristi to the United States but would not consider such a concession, no matter how advantageous, if the hated Judge Abbott were placed in charge.[20]

Once again, delicate negotiations by Dawson with Morales in Santo Domingo and by Rear Admiral Sigsbee and Dillingham at Monte Cristi accomplished a remarkable agreement among Dominicans and a sympathetic response by the Americans, who placed Monte Cristi under the control of an American naval officer rather than the SDIC. Loomis' cable of February 4 instructed Dawson to "assure the Dominican government . . . pending arrangement . . . the Santo Domingo Improvement Company will not have possession nor control of the custom-houses. The United States itself would collect the revenues and make distribution." This marked a radical change in American policy which not only pleased the Dominicans but may have helped reassure the European creditors as well. Dillingham, who appeared to enjoy gratifying the Dominicans as well as understanding their complex political rituals, negotiated patiently with Arias, explaining that Arias' objections were both constitutional and political and that after all of the requisite visits and consultations had been completed, Arias would consent. After a tense week of disrupted communications, Ad-

19. Juan Sánchez and Federico Velásquez to TD, February 7, 1905; TD to JH, February 13, 1905, both in *FRUS*, 1905, pp. 326, 324.
20. TD to JH, February 13, 1905, in *FRUS*, 1905, p. 329.

miral Sigsbee on February 11 peacefully took control of Monte Cristi, installing American naval officer Lieutenant Commander Edwards Fayssoux Leiper as the collector. On the eve of the American Senate consideration of the arrangement, the Americans remained in temporary and uneasy diplomatic, financial, and naval control of the troubled island republic.[21]

On February 15, President Roosevelt formally submitted to the Senate the "protocol of an agreement," which was the February 7 Dawson-Sanchez-Velásquez agreement that replaced the Dillingham-Morales agreement of January 20–21, 1905. In his lengthy message Roosevelt, more than ever before, tied the proposed financial adjustment to a specifically delineated Monroe Doctrine (Roosevelt did not capitalize the "d") that both limited and expanded the old American policy. Roosevelt argued that no settlement of the Dominican debt and its attendant international diplomatic friction was possible without independent non-Dominican control of the customhouses and fiscal policies. The two customhouses at Puerto Plata and Monte Cristi were under American control, but the remaining ten remained a constant incitement to revolutionaries seeking revenue, which when seized was spent rather than applied to debt service or reduction, thus constantly exacerbating both civil disorder and the national debt. Some foreign intervention was necessary, either European, American, or through a joint group. Because control of the customhouses was a necessary part of a debt intervention, Roosevelt argued that under the Monroe Doctrine, the United States had to undertake a preemptive intervention to preclude a long-term (though temporary) European occupation of customhouses. Citing the new limitations of the Roosevelt Corollary (a term he did not use), Roosevelt declared, "The United States has not the slightest desire for territorial aggrandizement at the expense of any of its Southern neighbors." Dominican "financial rehabilitation," including payments to creditors "upon a basis of absolute equity," was the sole American motive.[22]

21. Loomis to TD, February 4, 1905; Albert C. Dillingham to TD, January 29, 1905; TD to JH, February 13, 1905, all in *FRUS*, 1905, pp. 329–33; MacMichael, "The United States and the Dominican Republic," 183–84.
22. TR, Senate Message, February 15, 1905, in *FRUS*, 1905, pp. 333–42. For the influence on Roosevelt of Britain's permanent presence in Egypt following its joint 1878 debt intervention with France, see John H. Latane, *A History of American Foreign Policy* (Garden City, N.Y., 1927), 546. For Roosevelt's rejection of the Egyptian precedent see Charles Francis Adams, "Reflex Light from Africa," *Century*, LXXII (1906), 101–11; TR to HCL, April 30, 1906, in *MRL*, V, 255–57; Howard K. Beale, *Theodore Roosevelt and the*

Roosevelt cited specific historical changes to justify both the proposed Dominican intervention and the new formulation of the Monroe Doctrine. The Hague Court's arbitration decision on the Venezuelan blockade encouraged continued European forceful intervention in Latin American debt defaults to secure preferential payment treatment, actions that would cause "a virtual sacrifice of American claims and interests in the island" because unadjusted Dominican debts far exceeded the country's present or future ability to pay. Increased commercial rivalries were producing "a growing tendency" for diplomatic intervention by governments on behalf of private business claimants. The United States, which followed a nonintervention policy, thus faced the dilemma of either sacrificing the interests of its citizens or, by intervening on behalf of business, becoming "the insurer of all the speculative risks . . . of its citizens," a policy Roosevelt opposed even more vigorously than his State Department did. Roosevelt defined American policy as limited to offers of increasingly ineffective diplomatic "good offices" except in cases of "arbitrary wrong, done or sanctioned by superior authority." Not only were "powerful influences" in the United States demanding a more active defense of American business interests abroad, but the increased revolutionary activity in the Dominican Republic had destroyed American property, including a railroad in 1904, "previously exempt from such attacks." Roosevelt suggested that European intervention would not only disrupt the Monroe Doctrine policy but would legitimize improperly made or exorbitant debts and confirm the exemptions and special privileges that had caused the fiscal mess. The president acknowledged, however, that of the $22 million European debt, "$18,000,000 is more or less formally recognized."[23]

Citing the "wise" Platt Amendment as a model, Roosevelt argued

Rise of America to World Power (Baltimore, 1956), 161–71; and Kist, "Role of Thomas C. Dawson," 136–37. For an American precedent predating the Egyptian intervention see Hill, *Roosevelt and the Caribbean*, 159 n. For the history of the Egyptian debt and its management see William H. Wynne, *State Insolvency and Foreign Bondholders: Selected Case Histories of Governmental Foreign Bond Defaults and Debt Readjustments* (2 vols.; New Haven, 1951), II, 577–632.

23. TR, Senate Message, in *FRUS*, pp. 337, 335, 340; for the Hague Court arbitration decision and its effect on the Dominican crisis see Calvin DeArmond Davis, *The United States and the Second Hague Peace Conference: American Diplomacy and International Organization, 1899–1914* (Durham, N.C., 1975), 89–90; see also Peter M. DiMeglio, "The United States and the Second Hague Peace Conference: The Extension of the Use of Arbitration" (Ph.D. dissertation, St. John's University, 1968), 16–17.

that ratification of the protocol with its 55-45 percent division of revenues would secure the republic "against over-seas aggression. This in reality entails no new obligation upon us, for the Monroe doctrine means precisely such a guaranty on our part." Refusal of the United States to intervene would constitute acquiescence in "some such action by another government." Roosevelt insisted that an effective and limited intervention would demonstrate to the world American good faith, as in Cuba, and would strengthen both the Monroe Doctrine and the cause of international justice. American self-interests would also be served, but indirectly, by making the Dominicans like "all of the communities immediately south of us . . . prosperous and stable, and therefore not merely in name, but in fact independent and self-governing." This view was consistent with Roosevelt's other statements on Latin American potential. Peace and avoidance of "increasing revolutionary violence" and "possibly embarrassing foreign complications" were the choices Roosevelt offered to the Senate as well as "a practical test of the efficiency of the United States Government in maintaining the Monroe doctrine." A memorandum by John Bassett Moore to the president with a long summary of the Dominican fiscal history as well as a self-serving account of the SDIC's role in recent Dominican affairs accompanied the message.[24]

Roosevelt's message did not fall on entirely deaf ears, but the Senate, still smarting from the original attack on its prerogatives, was more interested in debating the treaty-making process than the new Monroe Doctrine policy. The New York *Times*, a consistent anti-administration Democratic paper, at first supported the substance of Roosevelt's actions and chided the Senate: "If it appears that the President has seen his way of doing, without consulting the Senate, a patriotic and needful work, which there is every reason to believe the Senate would have obstructed if it had the opportunity, the people will rejoice." But like the *Times*, which reversed itself and accused Roosevelt of "serious violation of law and Constitution," the Senate was more interested in maintaining its prerogatives. Since three Senate seats were vacant and two senators were absent because of legal indictments, the two-thirds majority necessary to ratify a treaty was fifty-seven votes. With the support of fifty-four Republican senators assured, Roosevelt needed only three Democratic votes. Roosevelt

24. TR, Senate Message, in *FRUS*, 1905, pp. 340–42, 344–49; text of protocol, *ibid.*, 342–43.

and the Senate were already engaged in a foreign relations conflict over the ten arbitration treaties he had submitted in January. He wrote, "I dealt with the Republican Senators on my own hook and have them substantially straightened out. It is a shame if the Democratic Senators beat the treaties now." Democratic Senators Augustus O. Bacon of Georgia, Hernando de Soto Money, and John Tyler Morgan, also opponents in the Panama debate, were determined to punish Roosevelt for what they perceived as a case of executive usurpation in the original Dillingham Dominican agreement and to use their minority party legislative veto as a political weapon. Roosevelt had been willing to concede the political argument in the arbitration treaties because the main issues were abstract principles rather than specific practical policies.[25]

With the Dominican protocol, much more than abstract constitutional issues was at stake. One contemporary writer, referring only to domestic matters, compared Roosevelt's political struggle with that of Tiberius Gracchus and the Roman Senate, observing that "history shows that it is the upper branch of parliamentary bodies that the conservative interests of a State manifest their chief strength. It is in the Senate that Mr. Roosevelt will find his strongest antagonists." Southern conservative Democrats were not only waging a party fight, they were resisting the president's attempt to win more power for the executive over the still dominant Senate, a conflict involving domestic as well as foreign affairs. The Democrats were joined in the constitutional debate by Republicans torn between Senate and party loyalty. In the battle over the Hepburn railroad rate bill the *ad hoc* coalitions changed wildly from day to day, as Roosevelt and Pitchfork Ben Tillman, a southern Democrat who regularly exchanged vilifications with Roosevelt, were briefly united as allies, though they did not speak to each other. In the Dominican battle the Democratic senators had nothing to lose. Roosevelt complained about the dispute over the arbitration treaties, "The individual Senators evidently consider the prerogatives of the Senate as far more important than the welfare of the country." But no constituents clamored for a Dominican treaty, and in a struggle for power between the executive and the Senate,

25. New York *Times*, January 28, 1905, quoted in Holt, *Treaties Defeated by the Senate*, 217; New York *Times*, February 4, 1905, p. 1; TR to Lyman Abbott, January 28, 1905; TR to JH, February 6, 1905; to Shelby Cullom, February 10, 1905, all in *MRL*, IV, 1111, 1114, 1118–19.

Roosevelt seemed more vulnerable on the Dominican issue than on railroads, tariffs, Panama, or arbitration.[26]

Roosevelt's proposed protocol and Senator Bacon's resolution calling for a constitutional investigation of the administration's Dominican policy were both sent to the Senate Foreign Relations Committee for debate. On February 24 Roosevelt was not sure that the "treaty"—he no longer called it a protocol—would be reported out of committee. He did not expect its passage in the last week of the session but wanted to know "whether or not there was a chance to get it ratified at all." He sent Senator Spooner a dispatch from Dawson, who was concerned that further delay would jeopardize the Morales government. When the regular session expired, Roosevelt immediately called a special session of Congress on March 4, 1905, to deal exclusively with the Dominican treaty. Even the Republican majority on the Senate Foreign Relations Committee remained badly divided, recommending approval of the Dominican treaty with crippling amendments, a device that became a familiar part of the continuing constitutional conflict. Although most of the treaty debate took place in secret executive session, Senator John Tyler Morgan, continuing the tactics he had used in the Panama treaty debates, made some sensational but unsupported conspiracy charges that received more press attention than the issue itself. When a delegation of Republican senators told Roosevelt on March 16 that the Dominican treaty could not win approval at the special session, Roosevelt and Hay agreed that the session should adjourn without calling the treaty out of committee because disapproval by the Senate would encourage Dominican unrest or European intervention.[27]

A false report circulated by William Bass that the Senate had rejected the treaty so disquieted Santo Domingo City that Morales called Dawson every hour for official news. When an American newspaperman confirmed that the Senate had adjourned without rejecting the treaty, Morales immediately published the information to forestall further unrest. The American Senate, hopelessly divided, spent the last

26. Charles S. Dana, "Theodore Roosevelt and Tiberius Gracchus," *NAR*, CLXXX (1905), 327–34; TR to Silas McBee, February 16, 1905, in *MRL*, IV, 1121–22; Holt, *Treaties Defeated by the Senate*, 217–21. For the Hepburn battle see John M. Blum, *The Republican Roosevelt* (Cambridge, Mass., 1954).
27. TR to John Spooner, February 24, 1905, in *MRL*, IV, 1128; TD to JH, February 24, 1905, in *FRUS*, 1905, p. 352; see TR to Shelby Cullom, February 10, 1905; to Robert Bridges, March 21, 1905, both in *MRL*, 1118–19, 1142–43; Holt, *Treaties Defeated by the Senate*, 219.

day of the special session threatening to debate the Monroe Doctrine, still suspicious about Dillingham's original instructions or whether any foreign country had actually threatened the Dominicans. In short, as Senator John W. Daniel of Virginia asserted, "The Senate has its head in a complete fog."[28]

Roosevelt castigated not only the Democratic opposition but his own party leaders and the entire Senate: "The Senate is wholly incompetent to deal with foreign affairs. Creatures like Bacon, Morgan, et cetera, backed by the average yahoo among the Democratic Senators, are wholly indifferent to national honor or national welfare. . . . Unfortunately, they often receive aid and comfort from men like Spooner and Hale—one of whom invariably uses his ingenious mind to put in meticulous and usually slightly improper amendments to every treaty. . . . Both ultimately support the administration, but meanwhile they stir up opposition to it and give to Bacon, Carmack and their kind, arguments which they are too witless to develop for themselves." Roosevelt complained, "I am left to shoulder all the responsibility due to their [the Senate's] failure," forced to make "diplomatic bricks without straw." Roosevelt compared the Senate's use of amendments to presidential vetoes, arguing that both devices should be rarely used. Roosevelt, however, saw the Dominican conflict as part of the continuing domestic debate: "On the interstate commerce business next year . . . the Senate will have to give in." Senates were a problem in weak as well as powerful nations. The Dominican Congress was dissatisfied with President Morales' part in the protocol negotiations. Dawson reported that "the members were jealous of their prerogatives and were inclined to resent what they might be led to believe had been an attempt on his part to ignore and override their constitutional functions."[29]

On March 14 the sudden arrival of the Italian warship *Calabria* at Santo Domingo raised Dominican tension, even though the Italian mission eventually became a show of support for the American intervention plan. On March 23 Belgium demanded an immediate resumption of debt payments. Michelena's temporary banking arrangement met more resistance once immediate American intervention was no longer assured. Federico Velásquez, the troubled Dominican fi-

28. TD to JH, March 27, 1905, in *FRUS*, 1905, p. 356; Holt, *Treaties Defeated by the Senate*, 219; *Congressional Record*, 59th Cong., Spec., Sess., March 18, 1905.

29. TR to Joseph B. Bishop, March 23, 1905, in *MRL*, IV, 1144; TD to JH, March 7, 1905, in *FRUS*, 1905, p. 351.

nance minister, suggested "some practical *modus vivendi*" as a way out of the impasse to Thomas Dawson on March 24. Several business-men and diplomats had already considered instituting some formal arrangement short of a treaty that could operate while both senates debated the treaty. When Dawson discussed Velásquez' proposal with the foreign diplomats and other members of the Dominican government he found almost universal support for the *modus vivendi*. The Italian minister supported American intervention, as did the Belgian, French, and Spanish representatives and many Dominican creditors, though others were apprehensive about the SDIC's attitude. After conferring with Morales, Dawson cabled Hay on March 25, "Under pressure foreign creditors and domestic peril, Dominican government offers nominate a citizen of the United States receiver southern ports pending ratification protocol. . . . Forty-five per cent total to go to Dominican government, fifty-five to be deposited New York for distribution after ratification. Creditors agree to take no further steps in the meantime, and receiver to have full authority to suspend importers' preferential contracts. Italian, Spanish, German, and American creditors, except the Improvement, accept unconditionally. Belgian and French representatives will recommend acceptance." The foreign creditors did not give up either their substantive rights or their right to receive $25,000 a month, but they were willing to postpone enforcement pending ratification. "Some *modus vivendi*" was absolutely necessary, Dawson insisted.[30]

Roosevelt found a consensus for implementing Dawson's *modus vivendi* proposal both in his cabinet on Monday, March 28, and later that day with Republican Senators Joseph Foraker, Spooner, Lodge, and Philander Knox. To Roosevelt's "horror," Secretary of War William Howard Taft "genially chaffed them [the senators] about going back on their principles as to the 'usurpation of the executive.'" In addition, Roosevelt won unofficial approval from Democratic Senator Arthur Pue Gorman of Maryland, even though Gorman warned that he would publicly "condemn our action as realizing his worst forebodings." Gorman told Roosevelt privately that "he had taken it for granted that I would have to take some such action as that proposed,

30. TD to JH, March 27, 1905, in *FRUS*, 1905, p. 358; see A. E. Coulter to ER, March 13, 1906, quoted in J. Fred Rippy, "The Initiation of the Customs Receivership in the Dominican Republic," *HAHR*, XVII (1937), 456–57; TD to JH, March 25, 1905, in *FRUS*, 1905, p. 359; also TR to Alvey Adee, March 28–1905, in *MRL*, IV, 1148. See Kist, "Role of Thomas C. Dawson," 175–84.

and believed it necessary," a significant concession from the Democrat who had led the fight against Roosevelt's Panama treaty.[31]

Roosevelt's institution of the *modus vivendi*, though innovative and dramatic, was much more a response to the intensified Dominican crisis than the defiance of the Senate he later represented it to be. The *modus vivendi* worked better than anyone expected, partly because Roosevelt was able to make two brilliant appointments at the start. On March 25, even before Dawson's telegram, Roosevelt had appointed Jacob Hollander as special agent to advise him on how to deal with the Dominican debt. Hollander, a distinguished Johns Hopkins University political economist, had revised Puerto Rico's tax code in 1900, served as the treasurer of the Puerto Rican territory, and, in 1904, was special agent for taxation in the Indian Territory. The State Department had recommended Hollander as a financial consultant to the Morales government in April, 1904, but Hollander was unwilling to take academic leave for temporary and uncertain work with the Dominican government. In 1905, however, he was eager to work as an agent of the president of the United States charged with reforming the Dominican financial system. At age thirty-four, Hollander was an active progressive reformer in Baltimore, an urbane intellectual, the author of many scholarly books and articles, and the director of Johns Hopkins' first seminar in economics.[32]

If Hollander's appointment was planned before Dawson's *modus vivendi* cable, Colonel George Colton's was not. Colton, the organizer of the first American customs service at Manila, who was passing through Washington when the *modus vivendi* was implemented, was appointed as Dominican customs receiver and transferred with his existing staff from the Philippines. To make the transition less difficult, the entire administrative apparatus from the Philippines was retained so that Colton remained in the Bureau of Insular Affairs and

31. TR to JH, March 30, 1905, in *MRL*, IV, 1150; *FRUS*, 1905, p. 365.

32. See Jacob Hollander to TR, undated letter draft, in Box 1, January–February, 1905, folder, Jacob Hollander Papers, RG 200, NA; TR, *Autobiography*, in *TRWN*, XX, 500; MacMichael, "The United States and the Dominican Republic," 200–201. For the background to Hollander's appointment see Kist, "Role of Thomas C. Dawson," 189n. For Hollander's work in Puerto Rico see Hollander, "The Finances of Puerto Rico," *Political Science Quarterly*, XVI (1901), 553–79; Emily S. Rosenberg, "Foundations of United States International Financial Power: Gold Standard Diplomacy, 1900–1905," *Business History Review*, LIX (1985), esp. 174–75. For Hollander's earlier role as an academic anti-imperialist see Donald J. Murphy, "Professors, Publicists, and Pan-Americanism, 1905–1907: The Use of 'Experts' in Shaping American Foreign Policy" (Ph.D. dissertation, University of Wisconsin, 1970), 35.

reported directly to the secretary of war. Colton's thoughtful and intelligent letters to Secretary of War Taft were sensitive appraisals of Dominican affairs from an American who, like Dillingham and Hollander, remained sympathetic and supportive of the Dominicans.[33]

Considering the inherent instability of Dominican politics, the country's desperate fiscal situation, and the potential for international diplomatic friction, the early effects of the *modus vivendi* were almost miraculous. Jacob Hollander arrived on April 10 to begin his study of Dominican finances. Colonel Colton was appointed as customs collector by the Dominican government, which paid his salary and expenses, and took over the collecting of revenues at all Dominican ports on April 25. Colton retained the Dominican employees, who constituted one of the chief patronage sources of the Morales government, but used Americans as supervisors from a central office, instituted strict accounting procedures, and ended not only the practice of smuggling across the Haitian frontier but also the customary concessions and exemptions at all Dominican ports. Fifty-five percent of all revenues collected was deposited at the City National Bank of New York, unavailable to international creditors, Dominican bankers, or the government. That arrangement satisfied even the foreign bondholders whose payments were suspended because they were assured that their money was safe and that eventually the Dominican debt would be settled. Customhouses, protected by the American navy and run by American citizens, were no longer an attractive target for Dominican revolutionaries.[34]

In his report to Theodore Roosevelt on July 1, 1905, Thomas Dawson judged the post–*modus vivendi* Dominican Republic to be in an "unstable equilibrium," dependent on the eventual ratification of the February 7, 1905, treaty. The short-term effects were striking. For the first time since 1899 there was no revolution, insurrection, or even "active plotting" against the government. Agriculture flourished as the tobacco crop doubled, sugar exports increased, and livestock was replenished. Under the fiscal order imposed by George Colton's receivership, revenue collections increased to an annual $2.5 million, up from the 1904 total of $1.85 million. The end of the system of short-term loans and special concessions enabled the government, on a rare

33. MacMichael, "The United States and the Dominican Republic," 190.
34. Kist, "Role of Thomas C. Dawson," 193–95; FRUS, 1905, pp. 367–70; Dawson's Chronology, 597; for Belgian and British reaction see FRUS, 1905, pp. 371–78; TR to WHT, April 8, 1905, in MRL, IV, 1159.

cash basis, to pay its workers regularly, buy supplies for cash, and accumulate an unheard-of small surplus. Relieved of its preoccupation with financing revolutionary and foreign claims, the government replaced war chiefs with civilian urban officials, began a modest program of public construction, roads, and rebuilding a badly damaged capital city, reopening schools and courts. Assured of an eventual settlement from Colton's monthly deposits of $100,000, foreign Dominican creditors no longer applied regular pressure on the government or feared that any single foreign creditor would seize the customhouses for its own bondholders. Even in the United States the Dominican "solution has worked so well that the public is now paying no heed to the matter whatever," Roosevelt reported.[35]

When George Colton reported to Roosevelt that the SDIC's claims were questionable and that the company had inflated its value, Roosevelt acted immediately for the first time to disassociate the government from what Dominicans had long called *la nefasta compañía*. Roosevelt, mourning the death of his friend Secretary of State John Hay, was so disquieted by Colton's revelations about the SDIC that he blamed them on Hay's long illness rather than on any rational policy. Roosevelt had decided to name Elihu Root his new secretary of state, but without waiting for the appointment Roosevelt changed the government's policy toward American foreign companies: "I am always afraid of seeming to back any big company which has financial interests in one of these South American states, and can only do so under the narrowest restrictions and most sharply defined conditions." Roosevelt suggested that Hollander back the Dominicans "in refusing to pay the debt save such part of it as is just and proper." With the death of Hay, the appointment of Elihu Root, and the active involvement of George Colton and Jacob Hollander, the SDIC lost any power its American management had given it. The Americans shared the Dominican view of the SDIC, and the SDIC responded by taking an adversarial position toward American attempts to adjust the Dominican debt.[36]

35. TD to TR, July 1, 1905, in *FRUS*, 1905, pp. 378–89; TR to HCL, May 15, 1905, in *MRL*, IV, 1181.

36. Manuel de Jesús Troncoso de la Concha, *La génesis de la Convención Dominico-Americana* (Santiago, D.R., 1946), 21–22; MacMichael, "The United States and the Dominican Republic," 153; TR to Jacob Hollander, July 3, 1905; to WHT, July 3, 1905, both in *MRL*, IV, 1259–60. For Root's appointment see Jessup, *Elihu Root*, I, 447–59; for Root's role see Richard Leopold, *Elihu Root and the Conservative Tradition* (Boston, 1954), 63–64.

When Thomas Dawson pleaded with Roosevelt to ask the Senate not to wound Dominican sensibilities by insisting on extraterritoriality, he reopened the constitutional treaty debate quiescent since the *modus vivendi* had begun. New Secretary of State Root faced the major tasks of mediating the dispute between the president and the Senate and finding "some other arrangement" to replace the deadlocked treaty. Roosevelt, who later classed Spooner with the "prize idiots of the Senate," briefly tried conciliation and even charm in trying to win support for the Dominican treaty and to dissuade Spooner from the extraterritorality amendment the Senate Foreign Relations Committee had proposed adding. Roosevelt had strong words for senatorial amendments in general—"the average amendment put in I regard as merely foolish"—but this one "would probably destroy the treaty." Later in the month Roosevelt complained bitterly about the Senate's "very unsatisfactory portion of the treaty making power," especially indicting "Spooner, who in spite of his intelligence seems incapable of understanding the damage he does by striving for delay, by insisting upon meticulous amendments which may result in the absolute abandonment of the treaty, and who spends several weeks in furnishing arguments to our opponents with which to confute himself when he finally comes out on our side." [37]

In his address at Chautauqua, New York, on August 11, 1905, Roosevelt defined the differences between his corollary and the original Monroe Doctrine. Because of the United States' increased strength, the Monroe Doctrine was now recognized by more foreign powers than it had been originally. For Roosevelt, American acceptance of responsibility was the key to keeping the original doctrine from becoming "fossilized" and eventually dying. Roosevelt renounced using the doctrine as "an excuse for aggrandizement on our part at the expense of the republics to the south of us." Nor would the Latin American countries be allowed to use the doctrine "as a shield" for "misdeeds against foreign nations." He pledged to help the troubled countries "upward toward peace and order." In suggesting that the already stable Latin American powers were co-guarantors of the new doctrine

37. Dawson quoted in TR to John Spooner, July 7, 1905; TR to WHT, July 29, 1905; to John Spooner, July 3, 1905, all in *MRL*, IV, 1264, 1263, 1264. For Colton's alternate plan (rejected by Roosevelt) calling for a complex American economic intervention including full banking supervision, a railroad concession for the American bank, and Dominican transfer of land to the bank to be used by the United States as naval stations see George Colton to WHT, June 11, 1905, quoted in Kist, "Role of Thomas C. Dawson," 204–206.

("although as yet hardly consciously"), he made the Roosevelt Corollary part of the Pan-American movement. He limited the United States' responsibility by permitting punishment for "torts" Latin American nations committed against foreign citizens, providing that such punishment not include "directly or indirectly . . . territorial occupation of the offending country." Roosevelt argued that making an arrangement to ensure the payment of just debts was better than going to war to protest incidents of gunboat diplomacy. If customhouses needed to be taken over, the United States must do it rather than allowing "any foreign power" even temporary possession. In his characteristic partisan political style, Roosevelt claimed that the "only effective opposition to the treaty will probably come from dishonest creditors, *foreign and American,* and from the professional revolutionists of the island itself." He predicted that the opposition in both the American and Dominican congresses would try to kill the treaty outright or through the amendment process. In the second part of his speech Roosevelt called for greater regulation of corporations, his other major political struggle with Congress.[38]

An unusual set of alliances had emerged from the complex Dominican intervention. While Roosevelt fought the Senate, Root, at Roosevelt's urging, conciliated senators, working so closely with the Senate Foreign Relations committee that ultimately he accepted an invitation to attend all its meetings. Dawson, already sympathetic to Morales and the Dominicans, was joined by Hollander, who visited five Caribbean islands to find common problems and possible solutions before writing his report to the president on October 1, 1905. Root joined Hollander and Dawson on the side of the Dominicans; Root, Roosevelt, Dawson, and Colton broke the alliance with the SDIC; and as the explosive situation and the constitutional battle between the president and Congress evolved, so did a Dominican solution different enough from the original January 21 and February 7 protocols to satisfy many of the Senate's objections.[39]

38. Address is in TR, *Political Addresses and State Papers of Theodore Roosevelt* (4 vols.; New York, n.d.), 439–55. For the significance of Roosevelt's and Root's distinction between stable and unstable Latin American countries see Murphy, "Professors, Publicists, and Pan-Americanism," 21–22.

39. TR to WHT, July 29, 1905, in *MRL*, IV, 1291; Jessup, *Elihu Root*, 544; see Jacob Hollander to ER, January 15, 1906, in Jacob Hollander, "Notes on the West Indies," in Communications from Special Agents, M37, Roll 21.

15 Hollander's Compromise

On October 1, 1905, Jacob Hollander delivered his extraordinary report "Debt of Santo Domingo" to President Roosevelt, along with an equally remarkable confidential memorandum. Hollander, who made two trips to the Dominican Republic, reported directly to Roosevelt on May 16 just after his first seven-week stay. Judge Otto Schoenrich, an American who was a Puerto Rican municipal judge and had served on the Puerto Rican legal code commission, acted as Hollander's secretary and assistant. Schoenrich's fluent Spanish and his knowledge of and love for the Dominicans gave Hollander the freedom to become intimately acquainted with Dominicans, not just to socialize with the European elites in Santo Domingo City. While Schoenrich continued his Dominican inquiries about the debt and how to settle it, Hollander talked to Dominican creditors in New York, London, Antwerp, Paris, Rome, and Hamburg, returning for another visit to the Dominican Republic in August and an investigation of West Indian islands, "where similar problems have arisen and more or less successful solutions have been attained."[1]

Hollander's critical sympathy for the Dominican people is apparent on the first page of his report. "The population—with the exception

1. The original typescript of Hollander's report is in Communications from the Special Agents of the Department of State, Vol. 49, Microcopy M37, Roll 21, RG 59, NA. Hollander's report (Jacob Hollander, *Debt of Santo Domingo*) was printed as Confidential Executive Document, 59th Cong., 1st Sess., No. 1, marked "Confidential, Do not leave this where it can be seen," for the Senate Foreign Relations Committee, and remains extremely rare. Extant copies are at LC in the Rare Government Documents Division, the Department of State Library, and the Pan-American Union. The original in the Communications from Special Agents is essentially identical. It is cited here as *HR*, and page references are to the printed version; Jacob Hollander to ER, January 15, 1906, in Communications from Special Agents, M37, Roll 21; see Otto Schoenrich, *Santo Domingo: A Country with a Future* (New York, 1918), a loving, critical history and personal account; Hollander to TR, October 1, 1905, in *HR*, 1. For Hollander's own summary see Hollander, "The Dominican Convention and Its Lessons," *Journal of Race Relations*, IV (1914), 398–408, which also lists his other similar summary articles.

of a handful of professional malcontents—is a sturdy but inarticulate pesantry, by nature simple-minded, peace loving, and as far as any tropical people go, industrious." "Misgovernment and disorder" had produced "indirect taxes upon necessary consumption, crudely administered and long since increased beyond the point of maximum return. The taxes so wrung from the poorest classes have been wasted and stolen by successive dictator presidents." Satisfied by his Dominican and West Indian investigations that the people were more victims than lazy laggards, Hollander tried desperately, with the idealism and perhaps the naiveté of the early twentieth-century American urban progressive, to find a solution not only for the immediate debt problem but for the future of a country both he and Schoenrich had come to admire.[2]

Hollander's confidential memorandum to the president discussed the dangers, well illustrated by the SDIC's Dominican venture, of the continuing policy of American financial companies undertaking complex loans to Latin American countries under the official protection of the United States government. Citing Speyer and Company's recent loan arrangement with the government of Costa Rica for adjustment of its $15,283,551 debt, Hollander particularly objected to clauses that required copies of the agreement to be deposited with the State Department, the creation of United States gold bonds, and the designation of the president of the United States to appoint the customs receivers in the event of default. He warned that a new international syndicate based in New York (Speyer was the unnamed initiator) and working with European banks had "taken energetic measures in the past three months to acquire or control the largest part" of the funded Dominican debt (about 90 percent of the $24 million in outstanding bonds), on the assumption that a generous refunding settlement would yield a handsome profit and also to increase the chances of being chosen as the refunding and service bank, an equally profitable prospect. Hollander dismissed any real threat from the Europeans, who "after much grumbling and some threatening" would accept a debt adjustment, especially since their governments would not support their inflated claims.[3]

Hollander's view of the SDIC was critical but balanced. "Many un-

2. HR, 2.
3. "Epitome of Agreement, May 18, 1905, between the Republic of Costa Rica and Messers. Speyer and Co. of New York, Bankers," in Hollander Memorandum to TR, October 1, 1905, in Communications from Special Agents, M37, Roll 21.

worthy if not corrupt episodes" had occurred in Heureaux's era, but the company itself was "subject to blackmail and brigandage . . . . constantly menaced by spoliation and confiscation." The SDIC initially resisted the *modus vivendi*, objected to the suspension of its payments, and insisted that the amount or validity of the arbitral award could not legally be reconsidered. The SDIC backed off from its total opposition when it realized that Dominican "hostility," American "suspicion," and the unexpected success of the *modus vivendi* operation made it increasingly vulnerable and also because it shifted its tactics to work with Speyer's speculative syndicate seeking to gain control. Of all the creditors, the Dominicans themselves were the most resistant to reducing the debt, which they felt should come mostly from "the fatted foreigner and not the starved native." Hollander thought that attempts such as Senator Eugene Hale's amendment to limit United States intervention under the treaty to ten years were misguided. Since even an adjusted and reduced Dominican debt would have to be refunded, which would be possible only with guaranteed American supervision, amortizing the new bonds in only ten years placed too great a burden on the Dominican people. Hollander recommended continued United States government supervision of the customhouses with naval support rather than a policy dependent on informal private banking arrangements. Addressing only fiscal matters, not strategic or even broader economic issues, Hollander favored the "more sharply defined" responsibility of the United States for Latin American debts, which he viewed as less ambitious than backing private syndicates after trouble began. "The heretofore vague financial sponsorship for Latin-American financiering imputed to the United States causes serious misapprehension in European minds."[4]

Hollander's report, printed on December 15, 1905, for the use of the Senate Foreign Relations Committee, was an impressive work of meticulous scholarship, documenting in minute detail the hundreds of separate items that added up to create the Dominican debt of $40,269,404.83. Hollander's assessment of Dominican revolutionary politics illuminated not only the difficulties of restoring an orderly society but an intellectual North American's view of the cause and possible cure. Dominican revolutions were "not in any sense a popular uprising, wherein a mass of people, inspired by love of country or liberty, seek to overthrow or reconstruct an existing government. . . . A

4. Hollander Memorandum to TR, October 1, 1905, in Communications from Special Agents, M37, Roll 21, pp. 5, 6, 10.

Dominican revolution might be briefly defined as the attempt of a bandit guerilla to seize a custom-house. In the background, acting as a moving force, will ordinarily be found a political malcontent, ambitious to overthrow the dictator president in power and to succeed in control, to his own profit. Both the custom-house and the insurgent chief are the real keys to the situation." Because of the lack of modern roads and communications, each of the twelve provinces "has tended to become a virtually independent semifeudal principality." Order was maintained only by control of the custom-house, which supported the governing expense of each province. In an insurrection, "the governor, if he is not already active in the insurrectionist cause, either flees in defeat or awaits overtures: the army deserts to a man to the new standard, and the civil service retire to cacao farming to wait until a new turn of the political whirligig invites emergence." The same small handful of men—"no more than a dozen"—was responsible for all of the post–Heureaux revolutions from 1899 to 1905. A professional armed guerrilla group—initially "never more than a hundred ragamuffins"—would enlist with the chief seeking the customhouse,

a period of fighting follows, the issue of which is determined by the seizure of the custom-house. If the custom-house cannot be taken, the insurrectionist army melts away by desertion. . . . The "general" with a handful of devoted followers, escapes to the mountains to carry on a desultory fight until he is induced by guarantees of personal safety and the grant of an "asignacion" to lay down his arms and "come in." If . . . the custom-house can be captured and held by the insurrectionists the pockets of the bandit leaders are promptly filled by advances from local merchants until the fortnightly steamer arrives with its heavily dutiable cargo. The revolutionist army grows in numbers and in loyalty, and here again the revolution is well under way.[5]

Hollander's and Roosevelt's insistence upon the need for direct American intervention was not motivated by a desire to support American businesses competing with European rivals. Hollander was oblivious to strategic matters, and Roosevelt, sophisticated in naval policy, knew the Dominican ports were superfluous as naval bases. Hollander the intellectual and Roosevelt the aristocrat were both idealistic and paternalistic progressives who distrusted and disliked large financial groups. Hollander's constituency was

5. *HR*, 16, 48–49.

the people of Santo Domingo [who] are the victims, not the constituents of
. . . "revolutions." The average Dominican, and especially he of the countryside, is a quiet, peace loving, law-abiding, moderately hard working peasant.
In many particulars he is a typical West Indian, with his petty vices of cock-
fighting and rum drinking, inclining to be "married" but not "parsoned,"
living in a rough shack, rearing a numerous progeny, owning a few cattle,
pigs, and chickens, cultivating a little patch of communal-owned land planted
in cacao, tobacco, or plantain, and working no harder than he does because a
too bounteous nature has made it unnecessary for him to do so. He is hospitable and well-intentioned, and under ordinary conditions it is safer for a
traveler to ride by day or night alone and unarmed through even the most
remote part of the country than it would be for him in many rural districts of
the United States.

But the Dominican peasant was "plundered and pillaged" by the
revolutionary governments.

In times of peace he is crushed by a system of taxation wherein property and
incomes are exempt, and the necessary consumption of the poorest classes—
flour, beans, codfish, cotton cloth, and illuminating oil—are burdened at
least 100 per cent, often to three times their normal level. He groans under an
annual expenditure, central and local, of at least two and one-half million dollars, of which . . . the largest part goes to professional politicians and their
parasites, and much of the remainder is wasted or stolen; while roads, schools,
and public institutions are neglected. If he is wronged there is no justice to be
had. If he is sick or in want he suffers as the dogs of the town. If he is stricken
or diseased he festers by the wayside. He lives under a despotism, and as
absolutely a malevolent one as our day and generation are likely to witness.[6]

Hollander's report is one of the great muckraking documents of its
age, concerned only secondarily with foreign policy, which he viewed
as the means of meliorating the domestic social injustice perpetrated
by an armed minority on an innocent and decent majority. Peacetime
conditions were horrible, but in war life became intolerable for the
Dominican peasant, who was subject to being drafted by either a government or insurrectionist army and having his livestock seized: "His
houses may be burned, his fruit trees stripped, his fields pillaged,
and he left prostrate and terrorized." Since the American intervention, the Dominican peasant "has taken heart and enlarged his patch
of plantains, and laid out a new 'conuco' for cacao or maize," knowing that at least for the moment "he is not obliged in the literal ac-

6. *HR*, 49–50.

curacy of a Dominican phrase to 'take a gun and go into politics.'" Hollander pleaded that unless American intervention continued, the future of the Dominican Republic would be a continuing bloody struggle of outs versus ins, "in which the old, shameful story of rapine, pillage, bloodshed, and ruin are to find miserable repetition." Hollander's report remained virtually unknown in its day because of the stricture of confidentiality (so strong that the author pleaded in 1907 with Senator Lodge for a personal copy). In its sympathy for a poor Latin American peasantry, its impassioned plea for enlightened social justice, it is one of the more illuminating documents of Roosevelt's age, still little known, difficult to find, and little read except by specialist scholars. In its scope, its sympathy, its documentation, and the literary quality of its most impassioned pages, the Hollander report offers evidence of North American sympathy for Latin American problems and challenges the view that American self-interest, strategic or economic, was the major impetus for expansionist foreign policy, especially in the Dominican Republic.[7]

As idealistic and as disinterested as Roosevelt's Dominican intervention may have been when it began, once American influence was established the United States became deeply involved in Dominican domestic politics. In assuring the proper functioning of the customhouses American intervention indirectly supported the government, which, now assured of a regular source of revenue, replaced the customhouses as the main target of Dominican political dissidents. In September, Morales faced challenges from the *horacistas*, who held three of the eight Executive Council seats, controlled Congress, and were supported by Cáceres, Vásquez, the Ciboan generals, and most of the Santo Domingo City elite. When the Morales government asked the United States for naval support, Roosevelt on September 4, 1905, unequivocally ordered Rear Admiral Royal B. Bradford "to stop any revolution." Roosevelt was forthright: "I intend to keep the island in *statu quo* [sic] until the Senate has had time to act on the treaty, and I shall treat any revolutionary movement as an effort to upset the *modus vivendi*." Roosevelt had no doubt "that this is ethically right," though technically questionable. On June 9, the Dominican Congress established a rural guard, a police force based on the Cuban precedent. Later in the year, in answer to a Dominican request, Secretary of State Elihu Root assigned Lieutenant Grayson M. P. Murphy, who had car-

7. *HR*, 50–51. One of Hollander's requests for a scarce copy of his own report is in Numerical and Minor Files of the Department of State, 1906–10, Numerical File, Case 1199/297, Microcopy M862, Roll 148, RG 59, NA.

ried out Roosevelt's secret Panama mission in 1903, as an American military attaché "to undertake the organization and instruction of the proposed rural peace force of the Republic." Although Roosevelt's and Root's naval and military interventions may be seen as the precedent for future American Caribbean involvement, there were significant differences. The Morales government was not authoritarian, nor did it represent a particular ideology. The American purpose was to prevent a return to civil war, and when Morales, whom the Americans favored, fell to Cáceres, Roosevelt promptly recognized and protected the Cáceres government. Roosevelt wanted order, and he did not want war to upset the equilibrium. Whether Roosevelt's limited aims and the context of continued Dominican civil war that preceded both the Morales and Cáceres regimes constituted a precedent for later American Caribbean interventions becomes a matter of historical judgment.[8]

Root was even clearer on the need to limit the American presence. When an American employed in George Colton's customs operation was wounded by smugglers near the Haitian border, American Minister Thomas C. Dawson at first inquired about the availability of a warship, then cabled Admiral Bradford that one was not needed. Root, however, used the occasion to make an important distinction. The wounded man was not, as Dawson had wired, an "American customs official" but an American who worked for the Dominican customs service. Root, who declared the entire customs operation to be under Dominican authority, would consider using American warships only to protect American lives and property, and only if the Dominicans requested such help or were unable to provide it. Dawson acknowledged Root's decision, which further limited possible American intervention in Dominican domestic affairs. Root successfully defeated a possible Senate amendment that by allowing "the unconditional power of interference would practically destroy Dominican sovereignty, which, of course, none of us wishes to do."[9]

8. See ER to HCL, January 31, 1908, Case 1199/297, in Microcopy M862, Roll 148; Dawson's Chronology, in FRUS, 1906, pp. 597–98; TR to Charles Bonaparte, September 4, 1905, in MRL, V, 10; Emilio C. Joubert to ER, October 27, 1905, ER to Joubert, December 15, 1905, both in Notes to the Dominican Legation, Microcopy 99, Roll 59, RG 59, NA. A summary of the Dominican naval diplomacy is in Lester Langley, The Banana Wars: An Inner History of American Empire, 1900–1934 (Lexington, Ky., 1983), 27–33.

9. TD to ER, October 26, November 3, 1905; to Rear Admiral Royal B. Bradford, October 24, 26, 1905; Bradford to TD, October 26, 1905; ER to TD, October 25, 1905, all in FRUS, 1905, pp. 389–90; ER to HCL, December 7, 1905, quoted in Edgar Charles Duin, "Dominican-American Diplomatic Relations, 1895–1907" (Ph.D. dissertation, Georgetown University, 1955), 214.

On December 6, Morales' foreign minister, Juan Sánchez, fearing a *horacista* coup, warned Admiral Bradford that a revolution was imminent. When Bradford moved a shore party to an American warship in Santo Domingo's harbor, many Dominicans were sure that Morales had called on the Americans, who were about to intercede forcefully on his behalf. When a mob entered the presidential palace to kill Morales, Cáceres at Dawson's request intervened and dispersed the mob. Sánchez took exile at the American legation, the American shore parties were removed, and order was temporarily restored. Morales, outmaneuvered by the *horacistas*, secretly joined with the *jimenistas* to overthrow his own government and thereby force a reorganization that would eliminate his former allies. The bold if bizarre maneuver failed when Morales broke his leg on December 26, the second day of the self-insurrection and he was forced to remain in hiding near the capital. Serious fighting spread to Puerto Plata and Santiago, where Demetrio Rodríguez, "the ablest and most active" *jimenista*, was one of 162 soldiers killed in the battles fought on January 2, 1906. In Morales' absence, the *horacista* Congress that began impeachment proceedings on January 1 designated Vice-President Cáceres as acting president pending the outcome of the trial. On January 10 the Spanish consul discovered the injured Morales on a road seven miles from Santo Domingo and brought him to the American legation. The next day, the American, French, and Spanish diplomats negotiated his resignation and terms of exile, though at first the Dominican Congress heatedly debated whether an impeached president could legally resign. Morales, "completely sick of political life" and desiring "the peaceful tranquility of my fireside," was given safe passage and transported through Santo Domingo to his exile at San Juan, Puerto Rico, aboard the American warship *Dubuque*. The American warship *Paducah*, at the request of both sides, mediated a settlement at Samaná Bay on January 13, and on January 14 the *Nashville* carried Arias and his men to exile in San Juan. As the fighting continued, both sides used American naval vessels to exchange messages, arrange terms, and carry the losers to safe negotiated exile in Puerto Rico. The American nonintervention policy strictly followed Root's orders of December 29 that prohibited the landing of American troops.[10]

10. TD to ER, January 16, 1906; Carlos Morales to TD, January 1, 1906, both in *FRUS*, 1906, pp. 543–47; see, however, Morales' plea of January 16, 1906, to TR to save his country under the Monroe Doctrine, in Duin, "Dominican-American Diplomatic Relations," 213; see TD to ER, January 2, 16, February 2, 1906; Dawson's Chronology; ER order, all in *FRUS*, 1906, pp. 536–56, 599.

As heavy as the fighting had been, Dawson found hopeful signs that the Dominican tradition of "annual revolution"—Alvey Adee's phrase—was not as strong as it had been. The revolutionary classes were discouraged and there were fewer plundering bands because under the *modus vivendi* the custom-houses were safe and control of provincial governments was no longer decisive. On February 19, Rámon Cáceres agreed to continue serving as acting president and to work toward passage of the still pending treaty with the United States.[11]

The treaty, however, was still no closer to Senate approval. When it appeared that at least three Democrats—possibly Morgan, Isidor Rayner, Murphy J. Foster, James P. Clarke, and perhaps others—were considering voting for approval, the Democratic leadership called a caucus that bound all Democrats to its two-thirds majority vote. The treaty languished while the Senate debated the constitutional issues and the president railed against the "meanest and pettiest kind of personal partisan politics." Although even Senator Spooner fumed that "it is a sinister and ugly thing to caucus on foreign relations," and Democratic Senator Thomas M. Patterson rebuked his own party publicly for such tactics, the president and Congress were embroiled in a complex four-way political struggle (Republicans, Democrats, president, and Senate) in which the Dominican treaty played only a minor symbolic role. As long as the *modus vivendi* worked, the president and Congress had the luxury of a traditional, long, and even enjoyable debate. Roosevelt, in recounting the scene to British historian George Trevelyan, put the dispute in accurate perspective: "I am having a rough and tumble time with Congress and have been enjoying the experience of keeping my temper resolutely under every kind of provocation." Of "the four or five measures I am anxious to get through," the Dominican treaty ranked fourth behind appropriations for the Panama Canal, the railroad rate bill, and the Philippine tariff, and ahead of Oklahoma and Indian Territory statehood. "I think I shall get the first three all right (and they are the most important) and there is a chance of my getting the last two."[12]

11. Duin, "Dominican-American Diplomatic Relations," 212; TD to EH, February 2, 1906, in *FRUS*, 1906, p. 552.

12. John Spooner to Shelby Cullom, February 5, 1906, in Spooner Papers, LC; the Senate debate is described in W. Stull Holt, *Treaties Defeated by the Senate: A Study of the Struggle Between the President and Senate over the Conduct of Foreign Relations* (Baltimore, 1933), 226–27; TR to Lyman Abbott, December 14, 1905, in *MRL*, V, 112; *Congressional Record*, February 5, 1906, p. 2054, February 7, 1906, see also Democratic response, *ibid.*, February 7, 1906, pp. 2207–19; TR to George O. Trevelyan, January 22, 1906, in *MRL*, V, 137.

In the midst of his most demanding legislative struggle, Roosevelt liked to compare political problems with his British correspondents. Responding to *Spectator* editor John St. Loe Strachey's sympathy about the Senate's irresponsibility, Roosevelt answered with one of his most balanced assessments of the relative strength of the president and Senate. Roosevelt, admiring the strong Senate *esprit de corps*, observed that its traditions sprang from resistance to doctrinaire statesmen and that the system of checks reflected a time when tyranny not inefficiency was the main danger to government. "In consequence, the Senate has an immense capacity for resistance. . . . The Senators get to know one another intimately and tend to all stand together if they think any one of them is treated with discourtesy by the Executive. . . . Moreover, the Senate not unnaturally likes to take all the governmental part that it can, and now and then it is stirred by vague ambitions to do its share in initiating foreign policy." Roosevelt placed the blame (or credit) for his activist foreign policy on the Senate being "able so effectively to hold up action when they are consulted, and are so slow about it, that they force a President who has any strength to such individual action as I took in both Panama and Santo Domingo." Roosevelt enjoyed exaggeration and self-dramatization and conveniently forgot that his main plan for Panama was to call a joint session of Congress and let it decide what to do when the Panama revolution made such a policy moot. He did point out that a majority of the Senate approved both his Panama and Dominican policies but excoriated the political opposition that forced him "to try a course of some little hazard." Roosevelt, who respected the constitutional separation of powers and preferred working within them, was frustrated by the effective Democratic strategy. He justified an activism he was clearly uncomfortable about: "In any nation which amounts to anything, those in the end must govern who are willing actually to do the work of governing; and in so far as the Senate becomes a merely obstructionist body it will run the risk of seeing its power pass into other hands." But Roosevelt acknowledged that Congress generally "in the long run is apt to do what is right," and he even granted that "the extreme conservatism of the Senate" could be useful "in as purely a democratic country as ours." [13]

The *modus vivendi* worked so well that there was no real pressure

<hr />

13. John St. Loe Strachey to TR, January 29, 1906, in John St. Loe Strachey Papers, House of Lords Library, London; TR to Strachey, February 12, 1906, in *MRL*, V, 150–51. For another diatribe against the Democratic Senate opposition see TR to Lincoln Steffens, February 5, 1906, *ibid.*, 146.

for change, though thoughtful observers were constantly amazed that a temporary measure could be so effective. Both sides were aware that Dominican stability still rested on the presumption that eventually a legal treaty would be approved and consummated. Roosevelt's original idea of a simple financial arrangement, with only peripheral American support rather than outright intervention, was discarded when Dillingham granted the Dominican wish for territorial guarantees and transformed an arrangement into a treaty. Afterward, Roosevelt enlarged Dillingham's original protocol by adding his own corollary to the Monroe Doctrine. The Senate balked at the idea of a protectorate and even at the implications of the Monroe Doctrine, perhaps put off as much by Roosevelt's commandeering of the principle as by the idea itself. Root, who understood that some of the objections were not simply partisan obstructionism, tried to negotiate a compromise with the Senate. Neither Root nor Roosevelt was attached to the more sweeping claims Richard Olney had made for the Monroe Doctrine in 1895 during Cleveland's dispute with Britain. One of the advantages the Monroe Doctrine offered in times of diplomatic need was its vagueness. Never subject to a Senate debate, nor even to close analysis, the Monroe Doctrine was used to justify specific American policies. Olney's inflammatory diction—combined with circumspect diplomacy—eventually prodded the British into serious negotiations. Roosevelt's initial purposes in invoking the doctrine were already served by 1906. Europe, eager for the United States to become its Latin American debt collector, openly supported American intervention and ceased to be an active threat. Since the Senate was not swayed by the magical words, Root and Roosevelt began to disengage their Dominican strategy from the doctrine. When President Morales invoked the protection of the Monroe Doctrine to entice the United States into intervening in his behalf, Roosevelt ignored the invitation and Morales was expeditiously transported to exile on the *Dubuque*.[14]

An even more striking example of Roosevelt's unwillingness to expand the Monroe Doctrine's new powers occurred in Venezuela, which Roosevelt had wanted to chastise in 1904. When Cipriano Cas-

14. *HR*, 162; Duin, "Dominican-American Diplomatic Relations," 207; see Ernest May, *Imperial Democracy: The Emergence of America as a Great Power* (New York, 1961), 36–38; Joseph Mathews, "Informal Diplomacy in the Venezuelan Crisis," *MVHR*, L (1965), 195–212; Walter LaFeber, "The Background of Cleveland's Venezuelan Policy: A Reinterpretation," *AHR*, LXVI (1961), 947–67; and George B. Young, "Intervention Under the Monroe Doctrine: The Olney Corollary," *Political Science Quarterly*, LVII (1942), 247–80; Carlos Morales to TR, January 16, 1906, in Duin, "Dominican-American Diplomatic Relations," 213.

tro seized property owned by the French Cable Company in 1905, and persistent American and French negotiation failed to rectify the problems, both France, with five warships ready to intervene, and Venezuela sought an understanding of whether the Monroe Doctrine was an absolute shield for Venezuela in its dealings with European powers. Roosevelt and Root in a White House meeting on December 14, 1905, told French Ambassador Jean Jules Jusserand that France could temporarily occupy Venezuelan custom-houses to make its point. Roosevelt told Jusserand that "the Monroe Doctrine could certainly not be used by southern Republics to shield them from the consequences of their own torts." But Root and Roosevelt may have gotten as much as they gave by requiring a French pledge in writing that the landing and seizures were temporary and there would be no permanent occupation. The intervention did not take place, but when the French broke off diplomatic relations on January 9, 1906, the Americans took charge of French interests. In responding to Venezuela's request "to maintain and defend the Monroe Doctrine," Root formally declined to take any action.[15]

As the American Senate deadlock continued, the Dominicans, encouraged by Root, took a greater role in their own affairs. Cáceres entered office with an advantage no other Dominican leader enjoyed— sufficient money and the continued protection of the United States against revolutionary threats. A revolutionary group from Puerto Rico moved its operations to nearby St. Thomas after it was barred by the American government from shipping arms to the Dominican Republic. Root persuaded the Danish to cooperate, and the Caribbean remained closed to potential revolutionaries. The Dominican Congress was permitted by the pending treaty agreement to lower export taxes but voted instead to divert 30 percent of its export taxes to a railroad-building program under the direction of former president Horacio Vásquez, who had returned to his country in March and pledged support to Cáceres and the ratification of the American convention. With Dawson's and Colton's support, Root compromised by agreeing to the 30 percent diversion after June 1, 1906, but not to the use of funds already deposited under the *modus vivendi* in New York.[16]

15. Root's memorandum of the meeting is in Philip Jessup, *Elihu Root* (2 vols.; New York, 1938), I, 495–96; see also *ibid.*, 496–97. For the French naval plans and problems in effectively intervening against Venezuela see Contre-Amiral Boué de Lapeyrére to Ministère de la Marine, Paris, January 27, 1906, in BB⁴, 1703, Archives de la Marine, Château de Vincennes.

16. Duin, "Dominican-American Diplomatic Relations," 217–18; TD to ER, May 10, 1906; Dawson's Chronology; ER to TD, May 24, 1906, all in *FRUS*, 1906, p. 559–63, 599.

When Root found he could not budge the Senate, he looked for another solution. The public and the press had suggestions about what could be done. One that aroused Roosevelt's ire was Charles Francis Adams' suggestion that the British-Egyptian model be followed in solving Dominican and Philippine problems. Roosevelt defended his colonial policy by citing the improvements in roads as well as in self-government that he claimed would eventually make the American colonials self-governing, a policy he insisted Lord Cromer, Britain's Egyptian administrator, admired in Cuba. Although Roosevelt cited improved Dominican finances under the *modus vivendi*, it was obvious to Root, Roosevelt, and Lodge that unless the president or the Senate yielded, the treaty dispute was stalemated. Since the Dominicans as well as the Europeans were beginning to ask for an immediate division of the money on deposit, it was clear that the *modus vivendi* could not continue indefinitely. In April, Root asked Hollander "to learn informally the views of the banking syndicate who had some months before contemplated a readjustment of the island's debt, as well as the possibility of any refunding operations, independent of the pending treaty." The syndicate, headed by Speyer and Company in New York, estimated the Dominican debt at over $40 million but was unwilling to consider a refunding program unless the United States government acted as the guarantor. Hollander suggested to Root as an alternative to the pending treaty "a modified new instrument as will ensure examination and revision of the nominal debt on one hand, and faithful service by governmental authority, of the debt so revised, on the other." Hollander, however, warned against disruption of Dominican custom by instituting new reforms because even an ultimately beneficial tax structure required "civic calm and administrative security to a far greater degree than exist in San Domingo."[17]

Although the Senate's opposition owed much of its persistence to the domestic political issues that divided the Republicans and Democrats, as well as to the lingering constitutional debate over how to deal with increased American involvement in foreign affairs—and Theodore Roosevelt's more active role—Root implicitly acknowledged the

17. Charles Francis Adams, "Reflex Light from Africa," *Century*, LXXII (May, 1906), 101–11; TR to HCL, April 30, 1906, in *MRL*, V, 252; TD to ER, June 9, 1906, in *FRUS*, 1906, pp. 563–64; Jacob Hollander to ER, May 3, 1906, pp. 61, 64, in Communications from Special Agents, M37, Roll 21. For an early exchange of correspondence see Jacob Schiff to Jacob Hollander, May 22, 31, 1905, Hollander to Schiff, undated handwritten draft of a reply, in Jacob Hollander Papers, Box 2, RG 200, NA.

validity of some of the Senate's opposition to the Dominican treaty when he accepted Hollander's alternative proposal. On May 7, 1906, Root surrendered the administration's insistence on the February 7, 1905, treaty and undertook a new and radical strategy to settle the various Dominican international problems with ultimate Senate approval. Root, following Hollander, proposed that the Dominicans supervise the adjustment of their debt—a euphemism for reducing it by half—and that the United States continue as the servicing agent but not the adjuster. Root's purpose was primarily political: "We would then have a single proposition to present to the Senate; that is, the single proposition of ensuring the service of a debt already adjusted. This, perhaps might be free from some of the objections which are made to the pending treaty."[18]

Root's plan had many advantages beyond placating the Senate. Hollander, already acting as Root's and Roosevelt's special agent, would be supervising the tricky renegotiation and adjustment of the debt; though Hollander was officially acting for the Dominicans, his assumption of the adjustment role eliminated the need to choose an international commission. In his original recommendations to Roosevelt, Hollander had been wary of the creation of such a commission because of its potential political problems, and it remained a matter of concern for both the foreign creditors and the Dominicans. An equally important advantage of Hollander was his ability to work more efficiently than any committee and to represent both the Dominican and United States governments simultaneously, a role he used to pressure recalcitrant creditors to accept reduced settlements. Root had given up little of substance because Hollander, as special agent of the State Department, remained in control, able to determine the settlement before the Senate formally approved it. Ironically, Root was returning to a variation of Roosevelt's original idea, a financial arrangement backed by the measured use of regional American naval power, but with Hollander, a Johns Hopkins professor, rather than Dillingham, an American naval commander, as the administration's agent.[19]

18. ER to Jacob Hollander, May 7, 1906, in Jessup, *Elihu Root*, I, 546–47.

19. Jacob Hollander, memo to TR, October 1, 1905, in *HR*, 1. For a summary of the American naval diplomatic policy prohibiting further Dominican revolutionary activities originating in the Caribbean (especially Puerto Rico) and also prohibiting unilateral American naval intervention or insensitivity to Dominican suspicions see Commander William A. Sutherland, Senior Officer Present Commanding Naval Force in Santo Domingo Waters to Commander William F. Fullam, May 29, 1906, in William F. Fullam Papers, LC.

Hollander enthusiastically endorsed Root's new policy, which he clearly stated: "The Dominican debt should be adjusted on a fair and reasonable basis by someone acting under the authority of San Domingo, and (2) that this adjustment should be conditional upon the United States ensuring the service of the debt substantially as provided by the pending treaty." The Dominicans would support the proposed arrangement, which promised a continued flow of unencumbered revenue, relief from international pressure, and more favorable terms for the debt adjustment. Foreign creditors, who feared a "semi-judicial determination," would welcome "an amicable compromise adjustment." Hollander warned that the success of the new plan was still dependent on the treaty provisions that prohibited new indebtedness and guaranteed rigorous collection of customs duties.[20]

As part of the new Roosevelt Corollary, Elihu Root undertook an extensive South American diplomatic trip on July 4, 1906, not only to reassure Latin American governments of American good faith but to convey personally the sympathy Americans like Root, Hollander, and Roosevelt, who years later undertook an arduous Amazon River expedition, felt for South Americans. The new Dominican initiatives began with a flurry of travel arrangements. Root was off to Brazil; Hollander met with Dominican Finance Minister Velásquez in Washington on June 9 before sailing to Europe to negotiate debt adjustments with the European bondholders' representatives. Rámon Cáceres supported Hollander's new voluntary settlement plan because it called for immediate debt payments after congressional approval of the now simplified treaty arrangements. With Hollander's help, and the predisposition of Roosevelt's friend Jacob Schiff of the Kuhn, Loeb banking house, Velásquez agreed on July 20, 1906, to a sale of $20 million in gold bonds at 5 percent for fifty years with the Dominican customs as security, subject to Senate ratification of the pending treaty. The debt of $40 million still had to be adjusted to fit the Kuhn, Loeb loan of half that amount, a reduction that would be fiercely resisted by the SDIC. Hollander, supported by the French and Belgian stockholders' representative, who wrote that he had rejected a separate SDIC overture, was confident that the Europeans would be reasonable, a view reinforced by the finite amount of the refunding loan combined with the prospect of a quick cash settlement.[21]

20. Jacob Hollander to ER, May 11, 1906, in Communications from Special Agents, M37, Roll 21, pp. 66–67.
21. Root's trip is described in Jessup, *Elihu Root*, I, 468–92; Dawson's Chronology; TD to ER, June 9, 1906, both in *FRUS*, 1906, pp. 599, 563–64; Jacob Hollander to ER,

When James Speyer, the New York banker with Latin American investment interests, objected to Hollander's choice of Kuhn, Loeb and tried to get Velásquez to renegotiate the loan, Hollander rejected Speyer's charge of favoritism, insisting that J. P. Morgan had turned down the loan and that Kuhn, Loeb had taken it mainly at Jacob Schiff's behest for idealistic rather than economic reasons. Bartolo Bancalari, one of the largest "and certainly the most aggressive of the Italian creditors," began negotiations with Hollander in Baltimore, and though Hollander still considered the Italian demands excessive, he remained confident that once the Europeans had agreed, Bancalari would not "give us any further trouble." On September 11, Velásquez signed two agreements contingent on Senate ratification of the treaty and continued American supervision of customs revenues. Kuhn, Loeb would buy the $20 million in Dominican bonds at 96, the Dominicans would use the proceeds to settle in cash with the debtors, and the Morton Trust Company of New York was designated as the new fiscal agent. A full plan of adjustment, including all the major and minor debts, dated September 12, 1906, reduced most major debt claims by half, the SDIC's, protected by the legal status of its arbitral award by 10 percent, and some of the older and lesser claims by 80 or 90 percent. A deadline of December 1, 1906, was set for claims and settlement agreements to be filed with the Morton Trust Company. Payment was promised creditors within ninety days of the bond sale.[22]

Hollander left for Europe in September, where he quickly settled with the major European bondholders for 50 percent of the principal plus interest accrued since October, 1901. The more difficult negotiations to settle the interior and floating debts were often complicated by internal political considerations. When customs revenues increased a remarkable 40 percent in the last part of 1906, one Dominican enthusiastically wrote Hollander, "You really deserve the title of the Dominican Philanthrop." Prosperity underlined how costly insurrections were. One Dominican official observed that the end of the war that began in July meant "a monthly economy of $10,000 for the budget."

June 11, 1906; Kuhn, Loeb and Company to Federico Velásquez, July 20, 1906, in Hollander to Robert Bacon, July 21, 1906, in Communications from Special Agents, M37, Roll 21, pp. 68, 59.

22. Jacob Hollander to Robert Bacon, August 4, 1906, in Communications from Special Agents, M37, Roll 21, p. 73; Jessup, *Elihu Root*, I, 547–48; Dana Munro, *Intervention and Dollar Diplomacy in the Caribbean, 1900–1921* (Princeton, 1964), 120. The terms are in WHT to ER to Colton, August 7, 1906, in Communications from Special Agents, M37, Roll 21, p. 76; Adjustment plan, September 12, 1906, following Hollander to Bacon, November 27, 1906, in State Department Numerical File, Case 1199/09, M862, Roll 147.

Nonetheless, Dominican politics, complicated by the vast number of debt settlement negotiations, continued to be critical. Hollander's Dominican associate, Finance Minister Federico Velásquez, suspected not only of making money on the loan but of planning to run for president, offended close associates for Vásquez and risked Ciboan and *horacista* rebellion. But as George Colton observed, "Things go so near the edge of destruction here, and then right themselves, that I am inclined to believe a satisfactory solution will still be reached."[23]

The SDIC, though given the most liberal of all the settlements, continued to haggle, convinced that Hollander's plan would produce a small surplus, which could be better spent on an improved SDIC settlement than, as Hollander wished, on "certain imperative internal improvements" that included repair of the Central Dominican Railway, long neglected under SDIC operation. Hollander's denunciation of the American company's attitude not only rejected its claims on both moral and fiscal grounds but summarized the idealistic basis of American fiscal intervention:

The theory of "more to go round" as a principle of debt discharge, is unsound and unfair. The Dominican government is *not* now in the position of a helpless insolvent whose creditors are entitled to a full partition of all available assets. Through the moral aid and administrative support of the United States, the Dominican Government has conditionally reestablished its credit upon a very high plane, and raised a large sum of money. From out of this money it offers to adjust its indebtedness upon fair and reasonable terms. If there is a residue it should be applied to the redemption of the State from the economic ruin in which it has been permitted to fall—rather than to a larger dividend to already generously paid creditors.[24]

When the final adjustments were completed, Hollander and Velásquez had cut the original Dominican debt from $31,833,510 to $15,526,240. On February 8, 1907, a new agreement, with a new name, the Convention of 1907, to distinguish it from its stalemated predecessors, was signed by Thomas Dawson, Federico Velásquez, and Emiliano Tejera and sent to the United States Senate for ratification. Whatever the many reasons for the Senate's original opposition,

23. William H. Wynne, *State Insolvency and Foreign Bondholders: Selected Case Histories* (2 vols.; New Haven, 1951), II, 258, has the most accessible settlement figures; Julio Senior to Jacob Hollander, November 14, 1906, in Numerical File, Case 1199, M862, Roll 147; George Colton to WHT, December 10, 1906, in Numerical File, Case 1199/30, *ibid.*

24. Hollander to Bacon, November 27, 1906, in Numerical File, Case 1199/09, M862, Roll 147.

the new convention contained sufficient major differences to allow senators who measured such matters the satisfaction that in scope and diction, President Roosevelt had been forced substantially to modify many of the original agreement's provisions. All mention of the Monroe Doctrine had been eliminated, as were references to the territorial integrity of the Dominican Republic because the Senate had objected to both *guarantee* and *respect*, a word too vague for some senatorial sensibilities. The only remaining United States obligation was to continue collecting the customs revenues, not to preserve order or interfere in any other way with Dominican domestic affairs. The Dominicans were barred from incurring additional debts or changing their duties without the approval of the president of the United States. Even with these immense concessions, Root's constant lobbying, and a public that remained massively disinterested in the continuing presidential-Senate deadlock, the treaty was finally ratified 43 to 19 on February 25, 1907, a relatively close margin supplied by the three Democratic votes that Roosevelt had needed all along. Not only did nineteen Democrats vote against the treaty, but an additional nine were paired against it. Nonetheless, the final vote was a victory of sorts for Roosevelt, perhaps by attrition, since the Democrats still had the ability to deny ratification.[25]

Once the American Senate ratified the elusive treaty, the legislative battle shifted to the Dominican Republic, where ratification remained in grave doubt until the final moment. When the Dominican Congress first convened to consider the treaty, it was seven votes short of the sixteen needed for approval. The opposition, as unyielding and as vague as the American Democratic senators had been, focused on domestic issues and personalities. The Dominicans considered two separate though related bills, the Kuhn, Loeb and Company loan and the treaty with the United States. Much of the conflict centered around the loan agreement, more from its association with Velásquez than because of any specific provisions. American sugar planter William

25. David MacMichael, "The United States and the Dominican Republic, 1871–1940: A Cycle in American Diplomacy" (Ph.D. dissertation, University of Oregon, 1964), 204; Kuhn, Loeb agreement with final concessions, in Numerical File, Case 1199, M862, Roll 147; text in *FRUS*, 1907, pp. 307–309; for the disinterest see TR to WHT, August 21, 1907, in *MRL*, V, 761; Holt, *Treaties Defeated by the Senate*, 228–29. For "Treaty-Killer" John Morgan's proposal to add two amendments, including one calling for House of Representatives approval of the treaty, and Root's dissuading him see Lejune Cummins, "The Origin and Development of Elihu Root's Latin American Diplomacy" (Ph.D. dissertation, University of California, Berkeley, 1964), 223.

Bass, who opposed the treaty, muddied the waters by distributing a facsimile of a letter from Idaho Senator Weldon Heyburn claiming that he voted for the new convention as the first step to American annexation. Opposition *jimenistas* had some success in raising fears that ratification would lead not only to American annexation but to subsequent enslavement of blacks. Many Dominicans opposed the treaty in the hope that the *modus vivendi* might continue indefinitely. The opposition included Cáceres' own *horacista* party, which feared losing its main source of domestic patronage when the United States took formal control of the customhouses. Root finally refused to receive some proposed amendments, asserting that the treaty ratified by the United States Senate was final. Root pointed out that the American Senate's reluctance to approve the treaty came from its perception that "the United States derives no benefit whatever from the treaty." Root and Roosevelt did agree to accept four Dominican congressional clarifications, not as part of the treaty but as explications of its meaning with which the United States concurred. On June 18 the Dominican Congress ratified the treaty, and on June 22 Roosevelt signed it.[26]

Because of the long delay and the modifications to the loan the Dominican Congress had made in its ratification process, combined with the American financial crisis of 1907, Kuhn, Loeb and Company, legally obligated only through April 1, 1907, canceled its loan agreement, forcing renegotiation of the refunding of the debt. Root, annoyed that the Dominicans had lost the advantage of the favorable Kuhn, Loeb agreement, refused to interfere further, though he was willing to allow the Dominican bonds issued by Schiff to be regarded as American guaranteed loans, a position he had previously resisted. When Secretary of the Treasury George Cortelyou refused to back the Dominican bonds with a formal United States guarantee, Hollander had to construct a hurried rescue plan, much less advantageous than the original agreement. Since sufficient funds were on deposit from the *modus vivendi* to pay 20 percent of what was owed to the creditors in cash, Hollander offered them that amount and the remaining 80

26. George Colton to WHT, April 4, 1907, in Numerical File, Case 1199/121–22, M862, Roll 147; Jessup, *Elihu Root*, I, 549; TD to ER, April 15, 1907, in Numerical File, Case 1199/130, M862, Roll 148; see also Melvin Knight, *The Americans in Santo Domingo* (New York, 1928), 41–42; ER to TD, April 14, 1907, in Numerical File, Case 1199/130, M862, Roll 148; text in Emilio Joubert to ER, May 24, 1907, in *FRUS*, 1907, pp. 310–11; ER to Joubert, May 24, 1907, in Numerical File, Case 1199/172, M862, Roll 148.

percent in the bonds that Kuhn, Loeb had originally agreed to issue and buy. The bondholders agreed but compromised the issuing price at 98.5, taking one-half of the original banking commission themselves, rather than the original 96 or their proposed 100. On January 27, 1908, the Morton Trust Company, the Dominican fiscal agent, issued the $20 million in bonds and became the receiver for the $100,000 deposited each month to service the new debt. After the Dominican refunding was completed, the $6 million surplus was applied to public works as specified in the Hollander-inspired preamble to the Customs Treaty of 1907.[27]

After the Convention of 1907 became effective in the fiscal year beginning August 1, 1907, Dominican customs revenues reached a new high of $3,645,795, almost double the pre–*modus vivendi* level of $1,850,000 and well above the projected $2,000,000 average. The Convention of 1907 in effect ratified the *modus vivendi* procedures and continued the American-Dominican partnership with its enforced fiscal responsibility, freedom from domestic political turmoil—both a cause and an effect of the fiscal problems—and protection from European political or economic intervention. Trade with the United States increased during the *modus vivendi* to 57.8 percent of the total commercial transactions of $10,825,209; total exports exceeded imports by $2,470,941, giving the Dominicans an apparently favorable balance of trade. Despite these optimistic trade figures, there were inherent problems in the emerging Dominican prosperity. The American receiver was impressed that "the most striking feature of the year's trade is the marked increase in imports, which were considerably larger than those of any preceding year, consisting almost exclusively of staple merchandise and food supplies." Though these statistics indicated "a greatly increased purchasing power on the part of the general public," they also showed that the Dominicans were no longer able to feed themselves and were importing large amounts of food. Half of the increased trade with Germany of $382,676 was for imported rice; other imported foodstuffs included wheat flour, meat, dairy products, fish, and fish products. The tariff law of 1909, drafted with the American customs receiver's help, avoided favoring goods most frequently imported from the United States but followed the American assumption that manufactured goods would continue to be

27. Jessup, *Elihu Root,* I, 550–51; Wynne, *State Insolvency,* II, 259–61; ER, "Notes on Dominican Contracts with Bankers, August 2, 1907," in Jessup, *Elihu Root,* I, 551.

imported and that export agriculture, especially of sugar and cacao, would maintain a favorable balance of trade.[28]

Dominican prosperity during the *modus vivendi* is also misleading. In 1905, almost half of the Dominican exports consisted of $3,292,470 worth of sugar shipped to the United States, a very profitable business for machinery manufacturers and shippers like the Clyde line, but as devastating for the Dominican domestic economy as the nineteenth-century intellectuals Pedro Bono and Eugenio de Hostos had predicted. The Dominicans received almost nothing for their largest export because investment interest was paid mostly to Americans and Italians who had replaced the native local banker-merchants; even sugar labor was foreign, European or American administrators and Haitian or British West Indian farm workers. Swiss chocolate interests owned the largest cacao business, an American the largest fruit plantation. William Bass, the American sugar planter, who played a significant role before and during the *modus vivendi*, was finally able to defeat Morales' last attempt to tax sugar, passed in 1904, appealed and upheld in 1906, and finally reversed by the Dominican Congress on April 20, 1906, an event that marked the last Dominican chance to tax its exports effectively. Sugar damaged the Dominican economy in far more ways than its escape from taxation. Sugar agriculture, with its massive demands for land, capital, and labor, covered more than thirty thousand acres of the Dominican Republic's most fertile soil and precluded the more balanced farming of wheat, corn, and livestock that could have substantially diminished reliance on foreign imports for basic food staples.[29]

Much more could have been accomplished during the American intervention if not for the endless squabbling over details that were either peripheral or concerned with domestic politics and politicians in both the Dominican Republic and the United States. From the beginning Roosevelt's planned intervention was influenced as much by American domestic political considerations as by foreign policy or Dominican well-being, and the same trend continued after Roosevelt's

28. Statistics in the review of the second year of the customs receivership, March 31, 1907, in *FRUS*, 1907, pp. 345–47; Knight, *Americans in Santo Domingo*, 44; MacMichael, "The United States and the Dominican Republic," 242.

29. Knight, *Americans in Santo Domingo*, 33, 36, 38; H. Hoetink, *The Dominican People, 1850–1900: Notes for a Historical Sociology*, trans. Stephen K. Ault (Baltimore, 1982), 12, 68–69; H. Paul Muto, "The Illusory Promise: The Dominican Republic and the Process of Economic Development, 1900–1930" (Ph.D. dissertation, University of Washington, 1976), esp. 29–51.

time. The benign influence of an American presence that started when John Foster encouraged the SDIC rather than a European creditor helped the State Department maintain its interest in Dominican-European affairs, a useful insurance policy before the Spanish-American War delivered the two essential Caribbean naval bases at Guantánamo and Culebra to the United States. The informal American presence also served as a check against European economic domination. Roosevelt's main contribution, adding responsibility to Foster's benign influence and Hay's oversolicitousness to American corporate interests, has been overshadowed by seeing Roosevelt's Corollary in an entirely diplomatic context and ignoring the honorable, if paternalistic, idealism that inspired it. In defending his Dominican intervention, Roosevelt insisted that it was both limited and disinterested: "We have interfered only at the request of the Santo Domingo people. We have interfered with the hearty approval of the foreign debt holders, because our interference benefits them somewhat, although it benefits the Santo Domingo people much more. It benefits us chiefly by preventing chaos and misery in an island so near to us that its welfare must always cause us some concern." [30]

Roosevelt measured his own colonial policy against Britain's actions in Egypt: "The English are taking no steps in Egypt, and very possibly can take no steps, which would give Egypt the slightest chance of permanent betterment, if at any time during the present century the English should move out of Egypt and leave it to manage itself." Roosevelt's emphasis was on American restraint, self-abnegation, and especially making colonial peoples self-sufficient: "We are steadily endeavoring to train the Filipinos in the art of self-government, are providing them with their own legislature, are giving the control of their own municipalities into their own hands . . . as well as building cart roads." Roosevelt always emphasized not only leaving Cuba but leaving it improved. To do more in the Dominican Republic, Roosevelt argued, would have required an armed invasion that was politically impossible and practically unnecessary. For Roosevelt the main benefit to "the islands," though indirect, "chiefly by minimizing revolutionary violence and unrest, has been incalculable." [31]

Roosevelt's penchant for dramatization and oversimplification in his later writings about complex and carefully considered presidential policies contributed to the distortion of the basis and the accomplish-

30. TR to HCL, April 30, 1906, in *MRL*, V, 255.
31. *Ibid.*, 255–57.

ments of his Dominican intervention. He wrote in 1913, "after a couple of years the Senate did act, having previously made some utterly unimportant changes which I ratified and persuaded Santo Domingo to ratify," a view that dismissed not only the important constitutional and political battle with the Senate, in which the Dominican intervention was often a pawn, but also the Roosevelt administration's careful attention to Dominican sensitivities throughout the intervention. More balanced is Roosevelt's assessment of the importance of his active presidency:

While President I have *been* president, emphatically. I have used every ounce of power there was in the office and I have not cared a rap for the criticisms of those who spoke of my "usurpation of power" . . . I believe that the efficiency of this Government depends upon its possessing a strong central executive, and wherever I could establish a precedent for strength in the executive . . . as I did for instance as regards external affairs in the case of sending the fleet around the world, taking Panama, settling affairs of Santo Domingo and Cuba; or as I did in internal affairs in settling the anthracite coal strike, in keeping order in Nevada this year when the Federation of Miners threatened anarchy, or as I have done in bringing the big corporations to book—why, in all of these cases I have felt not merely that my action was right in itself, but that in showing the strength of, or in giving strength to, the executive, I was establishing a precedent of value. I believe in a strong executive; I believe in power; but I believe that responsibility should go with power and that it is not well that the strong executive should be a perpetual executive.

Roosevelt's Dominican intervention was part of a long and complex process of readjustment between the Congress and the executive that included a more active American Caribbean presence with a stronger emphasis on responsibility after limited strategic goals had been achieved. Accompanying these changes was a vast shift in emphasis in American domestic politics from complete business hegemony to shared control by business and government. The new American political order that emerged from Roosevelt's conflict with the Senate is best illustrated by the compromise Hepburn railroad rate bill of 1906, which for the first time permitted effective federal regulation of private railroad rates.[32]

32. TR, *Autobiography*, in *TRWN*, XX, 500; TR to George O. Trevelyan, June 19, 1908, in *MRL*, VI, 1087; see also TR, "Our Work in Santo Domingo," *Outlook*, CVI (March 21, 1914), 617–19. For the Hepburn bill see John M. Blum, *The Republican Roosevelt* (New York, 1954).

In April, 1907, Elihu Root, in trying to persuade the Dominicans to ratify the Convention of 1907, referred to Roosevelt's personal commitment to the Dominican intervention, which most Americans, including members of Roosevelt's administration, regarded with indifference. If a Democrat were elected in 1908, Root argued, "the whole business will be abandoned . . . unless there is a treaty preventing it." Even a Republican president would lack Roosevelt's personal interest and commitment to a policy that "received but little general support either in the United States or in Santo Domingo." Root had tired of the endless Dominican complications. When the Dominicans continued to negotiate with Kuhn, Loeb after the financial downturn in 1907, Root counseled that the Dominicans must give no excuse to Jacob Schiff "for throwing over the contract," advice they were politically unable to follow.[33]

When the financial arrangement fell apart, Jacob Hollander, like Roosevelt still a true believer, managed the salvage operation semi-independently from the American government. But Hollander unexpectedly found himself in a bitter dispute with Root. Hollander accepted not only salary and expenses of $41,769 from the State Department but a payment of $100,000—$25,000 in cash, the rest in Dominican bonds—from the Dominican government in December, 1908. Hollander insisted that Root knew about and agreed to the Dominican payment and was infuriated when his integrity was questioned by a 1911 congressional committee investigating State Department spending. Root, who may have forgotten discussing the matter or may have dismissed Bacon's informal mention, was furious that Hollander had been paid by two governments. But Hollander, aware that the New York legal firm of Stetson, Jennings, and Russell collected $250,000 for the routine drafting of the bond sale documents for Kuhn, Loeb and Company, considered his additional fee for services after the original loan fell apart entirely reasonable and hard earned.[34]

Hollander's financial adjustments of the Dominican debt were stringent but fair. The British Council of Foreign Bondholders exerted constant pressure on the British government after it became apparent that the British alliance with the SDIC in 1901 had not benefited its

---

33. ER to TD, April 24, 1907, in Numerical File Case 1199/130, M862, Roll 148; ER to Fenton McCreery, May 28, 1907, in Numerical File Case 1199/179a, *ibid.*
34. MacMichael, "The United States and the Dominican Republic," 237–41; Jessup, *Elihu Root,* I, 551–52; see Case 1199/568, 574, in M862, Roll 150; Records of the Depart-

bondholders. The British initially overpaid for their SDIC bonds, erroneously anticipating that American intervention would favor a higher settlement. British investors insisted on their right to the full value of their bonds even if American-owned SDIC bonds received only 90 percent. In 1911 a confidential British assessment of the Hollander settlement contemptuously dismissed the English bondholders' claims while expressing admiration for the settlement: "An examination of the Dominican debt is like raking in a muck-heap. There is hardly one of these transactions with which an honorable man would care to have his name associated. All the debts had their origin in the shameless exploitation of an ignorant people by corrupt leaders and rulers for whose mal-practices the funds were supplied by unscrupulous money lenders and speculators." But "for the worthless trash which the bondholders possessed, they obtained through the intervention of the United States good 5% bonds and cash to the value of 48 of the face value of the bonds . . . far above what the most sanguine bondholder could ever have expected to receive." The British diplomat concluded that the American intervention was effective and that "they abstained from intervening more than was absolutely necessary. . . . I can find nothing to criticize in the action of that government."[35]

The Dominican intervention should be measured in the context of its time. It was not a presidential defeat of the Senate's treaty-making power or an expansion of the Monroe doctrine as much as a limitation on American expansion and an affirmation of responsibility to less prosperous Caribbean peoples. In the attempt to persuade Democrats to vote for the treaty, the commercial prospects of the United States in Dominican trade were stressed. Francis Loomis predicted that "if this treaty is ratified permanent order will be established in San Domingo, capital from this country will flow there, a big market for our goods will be built up, and we shall have made a distinct forward step in our effort toward getting our share of the commerce in Latin American

---

ment of State Relating to Internal Affairs of the Dominican Republic, 1910–29, Decimal file 839.51/727, 734a, 737, and Hollander's rebuttal in 839.51/766, in Microcopy M626, Roll 48, RG 59, NA; see also the correspondence in Box 6, Hollander Papers.

35. Memorandum respecting the Santo Domingo Debt, February, 1908, Confidential Print, FO 23/106, pp. 9–10, 13, PRO; Confidential British Assessment of Dominican Settlement for English Bondholders, March 10, 1911, copy in Decimal File, 839.51/730, in M626, Roll 48. See J. Fred Rippy, "The British Bondholders and the Roosevelt Corollary to the Monroe Doctrine," *Political Science Quarterly*, XLIX (1934), 196–201.

countries." One can, of course, make Loomis' statement a forerunner of dollar diplomacy and economic dependency, but American businessmen remained indifferent to the comparatively small Dominican market.[36]

America's percentage of trade with the Dominican Republic declined after the *modus vivendi* from the high of 62.9 percent to 57.8 percent in 1911, while Germany increased its share from 16.9 to 20 percent. American Minister Fenton McCreery complained of the lack of interest in Dominican trade and wrote that only the existence of a regular shipping line maintained the 56.4 percent American share of Dominican imports. Although American sugar investments continued to increase, Jacob Hollander's legacy in the preamble of the Convention of 1907 remained the most significant American contribution. The convention set up three main goals. After providing for settlement of past debts, the Dominicans would extinguish the American "concessions and harbor monopolies, which are a burden and a hindrance to the commerce of the country." The Dominicans agreed to apply the money that remained "to the construction of certain railroads and bridges and other public improvements necessary to the industrial development of the country." Hollander and Roosevelt hoped to transplant the spirit of progressive America in the unpromising political soil of the Dominican Republic. But the gap was too great. The initial success of the American intervention had been helped by a strong Dominican government headed by Rámon Cáceres, a simple, honest strongman, who governed without a vice-president, a political organization, or any plan to pass on power. When Cáceres, Heureaux's assassin, was himself assassinated in 1911, Dominican politics once again reverted to anarchy and a bloody state of nature.[37]

Roosevelt's Dominican intervention was not the beginning of a brave new world for either the Dominicans or the Americans but rather, as Federico Velásquez argued in 1906, the only practical solution possible. Neither American political stability nor economic prosperity could be physically transported from the United States to the troubled

36. Holt, *Treaties Defeated by the Senate*, 229; Francis Loomis to George Perkins, May 19, 1906, Folder 20, Roll 5, Francis Loomis Papers, Stanford University. For the dollar diplomacy connection between Roosevelt and Taft see George H. Mowry, *The Era of Theodore Roosevelt and the Birth of Modern America, 1900–1912* (New York, 1958), 160–61.

37. MacMichael, "The United States and the Dominican Republic," 242–43, 206; text of the Convention of 1907 is in *FRUS*, 1907, pp. 307–10; Knight, *Americans in Santo Domingo*, 49.

Caribbean island. Roosevelt got the fighting stopped, restored fiscal stability, settled the debt reasonably without seriously penalizing anyone, removed the Americans as quickly as he could, and gave the Dominicans a brief interlude of surcease. The respite could not survive the end of Roosevelt's active and idealistic intervention.[38]

38. Knight, *Americans in Santo Domingo*, 41. For a view that seeks to link Roosevelt's limited Dominican objectives to a wider model of American Caribbean hegemony see David Healy, *Drive to Hegemony: The United States in the Caribbean, 1898–1917* (Madison, Wisc., 1988), 123–25. Confusing Roosevelt's political rhetoric that put the best light on his battle with the Senate and his limited restoration of order in the Dominican Republic with "an article of faith in Washington that the customs receivership had solved the Dominican problem" is not justified on the evidence of Roosevelt's, Root's, and Hollander's extremely limited objectives. An older analysis that does not try to put the Roosevelt Corollary into the more recent historiographical context of Latin American dependency is Charles E. Chapman, "New Corollaries of the Monroe Doctrine with Especial Reference to the Relations of the United States with Cuba," *University of California Chronicle*, XXXIII (1931), 161–89. Whitney Perkins, *Constraint of Empire: The United States and Caribbean Interventions* (Westport, Conn., 1981), 40–45, takes account of the changes in the Dominican situation and American policy after Roosevelt's presidency.

Part IV

Marblehead, Root, Rio, and Cuba

16   The *Marblehead* Treaty, Root, Rio, and The Hague

Unlike the crisis in the Dominican Republic, which was caused by bond defaults, difficulties in Central America were primarily political, involving wars among four of the five nations. Although all of the five republics of Central America held regular elections, authoritarianism ruled these nations. Presidents were commonly elected and then re-elected unanimously, if they survived the constant attempts to remove them through armed insurrections. Manuel Estrada Cabrera of Guatemala, Tomás Regalado of El Salvador, and José Santos Zelaya of Nicaragua dominated the politics of Central America in 1906 and were responsible for the intense rivalry among what President Porfirio Díaz of Mexico disparagingly called the "little republics." The rivalry generated a series of internecine wars encouraged by the large numbers of political exiles clustered in frontier areas awaiting the opportunity to stage counterrevolutions, frequently in alliance with a rival nation. There were no real roads connecting the nations and an almost total lack of modern communication facilities. The best way to get from one nation to another was by cumbersome ocean transport, which irregularly connected the major Pacific ports. Since the smallest outbreak could signal the beginning of conflict, major wars developed before most of the area even knew a war was being fought.[1]

1. See Dana Munro, *Intervention and Dollar Diplomacy in the Caribbean, 1900–1921* (Princeton, 1964), 142–43; for the economic difficulties see Munro, *The Five Republics of Central America: Their Political and Economic Development and Their Relations with the United States* (New York, 1918), 177, 199; Ralph L. Woodward, *Central America: A Nation Divided* (New York, 1976), 177–201; Ciro F. S. Cardoso, "Central America: The Liberal Era," in *CHLA*, V, esp. 220–27; and David Healy, "A Hinterland in Search of a Metropolis: The Mosquito Coast, 1894–1910," *International History Review*, III (1981), 20–43. See also Thomas L. Karnes, *The Failure of Union: Central America, 1824–1960* (Chapel Hill, 1961), 149–203. For Central American historiography see William Griffith, "The Historiography of Central America Since 1830," *HAHR*, XL (1960), 548–69; and Ralph Lee Woodward, Jr., "The Historiography of Modern Central America Since 1960," *HAHR*, LXVII (1987), 471–96.

In March, 1903, a small but complex war began in Honduras when Manuel Bonilla began a revolution to oust Zelaya's ally, President Terencio Sierra, who had tried to name his own successor. Bonilla's army of forty-five hundred men advanced quickly on the capital at Tegucigalpa and forced the Congress and the president to take refuge on the El Salvador frontier after they named a new president, Juan Arias, whom only Nicaragua recognized. Bonilla won the decisive victory of the war when he captured three fortified towns near the Nicaraguan border and defeated former President Sierra's forces at El Aceituno. Shortly afterward Tegucigalpa surrendered and the United States recognized the new Honduran government of President Bonilla.[2]

In 1904 El Salvador and Nicaragua cooperated in fighting President Manual Estrada Cabrera's Guatemala, a cruel and corrupt police state with no redeeming virtues. Estrada Cabrera, who could charm American diplomats to gain the support of a mostly disinterested United States, lived in constant fear that other Central American nations would allow their numerous Guatemalan exiles to organize a revolution against him. When the other four Central American republics, uniting to seek protection from Estrada Cabrera, planned a peace conference for 1904 at San José, Costa Rica, the United States was faced with its usual diplomatic dilemma—the desire to support any peace movement in Central America while maintaining "a wholly disinterested impartial manner" and avoiding "an attitude which could suggest compulsion or dictation." Although the United States was eager for a Central American peace conference, the State Department's instructions firmly warned its Central American diplomats not to issue invitations or to participate actively. The department knew that American diplomacy was viewed with apprehension regardless of its motives. A Central American treaty of November 2, 1903, negotiated at San Salvador without American help and ratified by Guatemala on April 26, 1904, pledged peace, nonintervention in the affairs of other states, and obligatory arbitration of disputes. Costa Rica, not actively involved in the conflicts or the peace conference, was urged to sign the treaty as a symbol of Central American unity. Another agreement signed at Corinto, Nicaragua, in August, 1904, pledged

2. Munro, *Five Republics,* 123; W. Heyden to Leslie Combs, March 7, 1903; Combs to JH, April 19, 24, 1903; Francis Loomis to Combs, April 24, 1903, all in *FRUS,* 1903, pp. 578–79. For the newly formed American navy's Caribbean Squadron's attempt to mediate the Honduran war see the extensive correspondence in the Naval Records Collection, Area 8, RG 45, Microcopy M625, Roll 263, NA.

the same four nations to stop allowing political exiles to stage revolutions from neutral countries.[3]

Estrada Cabrera's government was the worst in Central America. Guatemala offered no protections for life, liberty, or property and continually interfered with neighboring states, especially El Salvador. Although El Salvador's Pedro José Escalón was the most amiable of the Central American presidents, he was an interim leader chosen by the country's most powerful politician, Tomás Regalado, whose "limited intelligence," his hate of Estrada Cabrera, and his "periodical inebriation" helped precipitate the serious war of 1906 that matched El Salvador's army, "the best drilled and the most efficient in Central America," with Guatemala's much larger army and greater resources.[4]

In February, 1905, Mexico somewhat innocently became part of a worsening Central American situation. Leslie Combs, America's minister to Guatemala, was convinced that Mexico was an active instigator of unrest, primarily to counteract increasing United States influence in the region. Guatemala feared an alliance between Mexico and El Salvador that would destroy Guatemala's Central American superiority. Combs warned Secretary of State John Hay of the disruptive influence of quiet Mexican intervention and asserted that the "difficulties would disappear" if the United States requested the Mexican government to "restrain El Salvador." Hay made the request immediately. Later in the year, when Honduran political exiles threatened an invasion from bases in El Salvador and Nicaragua, Elihu Root, Hay's successor as secretary of state, further increased American involvement when he offered mediation to Honduras if needed.[5]

Hostilities broke out the following year, threatening a major conflict. In May and June, 1906, political exiles based in Mexico, El Sal-

3. Munro, *Intervention and Dollar Diplomacy*, 144; JH to William Merry, May 12, 1903, in Diplomatic Instructions, Department of State, Central America, Microcopy M77, Roll 34, RG 59, NA; Howard C. Hill, *Roosevelt and the Caribbean* (Chicago, 1927), 175–76, 182; Phillip Brown, "American Diplomacy in Central America," *American Political Science Review*, VI, *Proceedings*, Supplement, 154; texts of 1904 Central American Peace Treaty in *FRUS*, 1904, pp. 351–52, 541.

4. For the best brief account of the politics of Central America in 1906 see William L. Merry to ER, April 17, 1906, in Despatches from United States Ministers to Nicaragua, Costa Rica, and El Salvador, Microcopy M219, Roll 94, RG 59; hereafter cited as Despatches, Costa Rica, El Salvador, or other countries.

5. Leslie Combs to ER, May 30, 1906, p. 5, in Despatches, Guatemala and Honduras, Microcopy M219, Roll 72; Combs to JH, February 22, 1905, in Despatches, Guatemala, M219, Roll 71; JH to Combs, February 25, 1905; ER to Merry, November 6, 1905, both in Instructions, M77, Roll 34.

vador, and Nicaragua invaded Guatemala, and President Bonilla formally allied Honduras with El Salvador. Both El Salvador and Guatemala had massed armies of twelve thousand men along the frontier. "Neither wants war," Combs reported to Root, but "both have bluffed until it is very difficult to retreat." Combs charged that Mexico was the key to the problem for actively encouraging El Salvador. Root, disturbed by the news of Mexican involvement, immediately cabled the American minister to Mexico, David E. Thompson, of Combs's suspicions, instructing Thompson "discreetly" to call Mexican attention "to these facts." "We have a very kindly feeling" toward Guatemala, Root added. That feeling would shortly change to a view of Estrada Cabrera as a "cruel tyrant" ruling a "repulsive" government.[6]

Emigrados, the political exiles and potential revolutionaries who clustered on the Mexican-Guatemalan border, not Combs's adventuresome, opportunistic Mexico, were the main problem. *Emigrados* existed on almost every Central American frontier and encouraged unrest. Initially they sought refuge, and their numbers increased when political persecution flourished or insurrections were defeated. If encouraged by the host country, as they frequently were, they could easily become an invading army. Mexico's problem was just the opposite. The nation was so large that the federal government did not know large numbers of Guatemalan troops were on its far southern border. Mexican Foreign Minister Ignacio Masical seemed disturbed that he had not known of the military activity on the Guatemalan

6. Munro, *Intervention and Dollar Diplomacy,* 145; Leslie Combs to ER, cable, May 30, 1906; see also the long letter from Combs to ER, May 30, 1906, describing in detail the possible reasons for Mexican involvement, in Despatches, Guatemala, M219, Roll 72; Combs to ER, June 1, 1906, in *FRUS,* 1906, p. 834; Combs to ER, June 2, 1906, in Despatches, Guatemala, M219, Roll 72; ER to David Thompson, May 26, 1906, in Despatches, Mexico, M97, Roll 178; ER to Alvey Adee, July 1, 1907; ER to William I. Buchanan, March 20, 1909, both in Philip Jessup, *Elihu Root* (2 vols.; New York, 1938), I, 505, 510–11. For a critical view of Thompson's appointment as minister in 1906, his sympathy for Díaz and possible conflict of interest, and his friendship with Roosevelt see Calvin James Billman, "Backgrounds of Selected United States Diplomats to Latin America" (Ph.D. dissertation, Tulane University, 1954), 40–46. For the connection of Roosevelt and Root with Díaz and Mexico through increased American investments in Mexico see William Dirk Raat, "The Diplomacy of Suppression: *Los Revoltosos,* Mexico, and the United States, 1906–1911," *HAHR,* LVI (1976), 529–35. See Frederich Katz, *The Secret War in Mexico: Europe, the United States, and the Mexican Revolution* (Chicago, 1981), esp. 21–35; Katz, "Mexico: Restored Republic and Porfiriato," in *CHLA,* V, 62–78; a review of the recent historiography, *ibid.,* 831–45. See also Marvin D. Bernstein (ed.), *Foreign Investment in Latin America* (New York, 1966), 39–40.

border and by the accusation that Mexico was actively involved in Guatemalan affairs. Porfirio Díaz, who had ruled Mexico from 1878, was in 1906 the elder statesman of North and Central America. America's frequently stormy relations with Mexico had improved in Roosevelt's presidency when the long-standing Pious Fund dispute, a difficult border dispute, and water control problems were all settled. Díaz, aware of Guatemalan antipathy toward him, seemed surprised by its intensity. He told Thompson that when the "little republics" had asked his advice in 1898 on whether to become a single state, he encouraged them. But when he discovered that Guatemala intended to compel and dominate such a union, Díaz withdrew his support and informed El Salvador of the Guatemalan plan. Guatemala then became resentful and hostile, and El Salvador became more friendly. Mexican-Guatemalan relations were not as placid as Díaz pretended. A border dispute that verged on war had been settled through United States mediation on April 1, 1895.[7]

What Leslie Combs perceived as Mexican aggression was wholly a Guatemalan civil war. Manuel Lisandro Barillas, Guatemala's president from 1885 to 1892, who had relinquished his office and allowed "the only comparatively free election in the history of the Republic," now led a revolution to unseat Estrada Cabrera. Barillas and José Castillio, another exiled Guatemalan general, had settled quietly in Mexico City. The generals were known as Guatemalan dissidents and were warned by the Mexican government to stay away from the frontier. They evaded Mexican security by posing as American land buyers and reached Chiapas in southern Mexico. General Barillas crossed into Guatemala near Matozintia on May 27, 1906, with a force of two hundred well-armed mounted troops. On the same day General Castillio's five-hundred-man force also entered Guatemala and captured the city of Ocos, which surrendered with alacrity. Castillio was re-

7. David Thompson to ER, May 28, 1906, in Despatches, Mexico, M97, Roll 178; James Morton Callahan, *American Foreign Policy in Mexican Relations* (New York, 1932), 446–51, 439–40; conversation between Díaz and Thompson, described in Thompson to ER, June 11, 1906, in Despatches, Mexico, M97, Roll 178. For the Mexican-Guatemalan difficulties that Díaz did not mention to Thompson, see Callahan, *American Foreign Policy*, 439–40. For the long-standing disputes over a union of Central American republics see Karnes, *Failure of Union*, 148–74. For Guatemala's view of Mexico as "her own Colossus of the North" see David Healy, *Drive to Hegemony: The United States in the Caribbean, 1898–1917* (Madison, Wisc., 1988), 141. For the Mexican-American Pious Fund dispute see Calvin DeArmond Davis, *The United States and the Second Hague Peace Conference: American Diplomacy and International Organization, 1899–1914* (Durham, N.C., 1975), 58–62.

inforced by a shipload of eight thousand rifles to be used to arm the "disaffected around Ocos" and two hundred "San Francisco fighters" idled by the earthquake. Two more armies joined the simultaneous four-pronged invasion of Guatemala. The Mexico City *Herald,* an English-language newspaper, wholeheartedly approved of the Guatemalan revolutionaries and their purpose of unseating Estrada Cabrera. A "well drilled and splendidly armed" force of two thousand men, composed of Salvadorean regulars and exiles from Estrada Cabrera's Guatemala, led by General Toledo, a former Guatemalan minister of war, invaded from El Salvador, while an army under General Pineda, "a hardy old revolutionist, and one of the best Central America fighters," invaded from Belize (British Honduras). That Guatemala, suddenly beset from many directions, felt the victim of a massive conspiracy was hardly surprising, especially with the Mexican *Herald* acting as the official organ of the revolutionaries, praising the well-planned revolution with a headline that said, "Determined men marching on city of Guatemala." Barillas' manifesto, a long revolutionary statement, decried the evil of the Estrada Cabrera government and proclaimed the avenging purity of the revolutionaries. Neither the *Herald'*s enthusiasm nor its detailed information was shared by the Mexican government.[8]

Guatemala informed Mexican Foreign Minister Masical that Generals Barillas and Castillio were in Mexico and asked that they be arrested and sent to the border. Mexico ordered their arrest, but the generals evaded capture. When President Díaz offered to send Mexican troops to secure the frontier, Guatemala objected, but when Guatemala rushed troops to deal with the invasion, the Mexicans dispatched their own troops to keep order and prevent any further questions concerning Mexican integrity. Masical convinced Thompson that Mexico had no prior knowledge of the Guatemalan revolutionaries' use of Tapachula, Mexico, as their staging base. Because Estrada Cabrera had asked the Mexicans not to put troops on the border, the area was not guarded, and the revolutionaries could come and go at will. Combs's insistence on Mexican complicity was not completely inaccurate, but the culprit was not the federal government but the state government of Chiapas, which sympathized with the Guatemalan revolutionaries. Mexico, aware of the Guatemalan exiles'

8. Munro, *Five Republics,* 52. For a detailed account of the revolution see the Mexican *Herald,* May 29, 1906, copy in Despatch No. 73, David Thompson to ER, May 28, 1906, in Despatches, Mexico, M97, Roll 178.

tactic of enticing aid from Mexicans with promises of later favors, officially remained neutral. Mexico and the United States, equally indifferent to Guatemalan factions, simply wanted stability in Central
America. Díaz, "disgusted" with the Guatemalans on both sides, held
no political preference for either.[9]

Although by June 2 General Barillas was in Mexican hands and
Mexican troops had secured the border, the fighting continued because an "unsatisfactory" political atmosphere made settlement difficult. Mexico's minister to Guatemala personally offered to reimburse
the Americans for the extra cable expenses incurred because of Mexico's innocent involvement. Guatemala was willing to fight El Salvador and still feared an alliance that included Mexico. The intense
personal rivalry between Estrada Cabrera and Tomás Regalado, the
leader of the Salvadorean army and former president, complicated a
tense situation. With the Americans now convinced "of the clean
hands of Mexico," the two governments cooperated in earnest. Díaz,
who knew the complex pettiness of the little republics well, was confident that El Salvador and Costa Rica would join with the anti–
Estrada Cabrera forces. Díaz planned to dissuade El Salvador from
war, which would also neutralize Costa Rica, but he miscalculated the
determination of the little republics to continue the conflict. When the
Salvadorean government reassured Mexico of its peaceful intentions
while continuing the war, Díaz suggested that Mexico and the United
States jointly apply diplomatic pressure. Díaz warned El Salvador that
he understood its war policies, which were ill-advised, would fail,
and would "not be looked upon favorably." Díaz asked the United
States to send a similar message to El Salvador, Costa Rica, which he
was sure was allied with El Salvador (it was not), and Guatemala.
Root immediately accepted the joint initiative. He informed El Salvador "that United States fully concurs in opinion expressed by the
President of Mexico" and repeated Díaz' message verbatim. Although
President Pedro José Escalón's reply pledged peace, Díaz remained
unconvinced.[10]

9. David Thompson to ER, May 28, June 2, 6, 8, 1906, in Despatches, Mexico, M97,
Roll 178.
10. David Thompson to ER, June 2, 1906, in Despatches, Mexico, M97, Roll 178; Leslie
Combs to ER, June 4, 6, 19, 1906, in Despatches, Guatemala, M219, Roll 72; Thompson to
ER, June 4, 5, 7, 11, 1906; Robert Bacon to Thompson, June 5, 1906; Thompson to ER,
June 6, 1906, all in Despatches, Mexico, M97, Roll 178; ER to Thompson, June 9, 1906,
in Instructions, Mexico, M77, Roll 122; Thompson to ER, June 11, 1906, in Despatches,
Mexico, M97, Roll 178; see Healy, *Drive to Hegemony*, 140–41.

Although Mexico maintained only token patrols near the Mexican-Guatemalan frontier and placed its troops away from the frontier to make them less conspicuous, further fighting erupted. The border, mostly uninhabited, very long, and extremely isolated from the rest of Mexico, was more important to Guatemala, which had nearby settlements. When Guatemalan soldiers wounded a Mexican woman in a border village, however, Díaz ordered three hundred men to patrol the frontier under orders to return fire if necessary. Díaz claimed that the invasions of Guatemala from Mexico reported by Minister Combs were either caused by Guatemalan exiles who had gathered on the border or were untrue. The view in Guatemala City was far different. Estrada Cabrera's government had developed a siege mentality that influenced American Minister Leslie Combs, who persisted in making Mexico the aggressor. Combs identified two main Mexican motives, both in retrospect equally absurd. To imagine that the Mexicans wished to displace American influence in El Salvador assumed that the Americans held any influence in the first place or that it was a valuable commodity. Porfirio Díaz, who looked upon the little republics from an Olympian height, even disdained keeping soldiers on the border. Combs's arguments that Mexico could disperse Guatemalan *emigrados* "with a word" rather than an army, or that Mexico encouraged unrest because of land hunger, reflected the reality of life in Guatemala, not Mexico.[11]

Díaz, disinterested in Guatemala and its political factions and indifferent to either side, blamed Guatemala for causing a situation in which "revolution is rampant in Central America," and "advice from anyone is something not just at this time desired." The Mexicans apprehended the revolutionary General Barillas but permitted him to go as he pleased—except in the direction of Guatemala. Díaz hoped that his surveillance of Barillas would convince Guatemala of his good faith. On June 13, President Escalón confirmed that El Salvador, though "not at war with Guatemala," was actively aiding the revolutionaries in unseating President Estrada Cabrera. Asserting that the "semi-official press of Guatemala has insulted my government and those of Honduras and Nicaragua," Escalón wrote Díaz, "I am preparing for war if Cabrera does not change his attitude." Díaz replied

11. Leslie Combs to Robert Bacon, June 11, 1906, in Despatches, Guatemala, M219, Roll 72; David Thompson to ER, June 13, 15, 1906, in Despatches, Mexico, M97, Roll 178; see esp. the eight-page handwritten letter from Combs to ER, May 30, 1906, in Despatches, Guatemala, M219, Roll 72.

with sarcasm (or wistful regret) that his plea for peace "may not have agreed with your political convenience." Mediation proceeded, in the Central American style. El Salvador, Honduras, Nicaragua, and Costa Rica all indicated that they would approve any new Guatemalan president chosen by the United States and Mexico.[12]

Guatemala was the active center of political turmoil, not the innocent victim of a conspiracy. When Guatemala encouraged revolutionaries in Honduras and cut telegraphic lines to the Honduras capital, Honduras used these hostile acts as its official reason for aligning with El Salvador. The existence of large groups of *emigrados* ready to attack if encouraged was as comparable a threat to stability as the Dominican Republic's vulnerable customhouses. Minister Combs suggested on June 27, 1906, as a prerequisite for peace, that no Central American nation harbor *emigrados* from neighboring nations or interfere in any other nation's politics. Guatemala now had between thirty and forty thousand troops on the El Salvador frontier, an enormous army, especially in Central America.[13]

The joint Mexican-American peace initiative had begun to work, however, for El Salvador appealed directly to the United States for help in settling the dispute. In his letter to President Roosevelt, El Salvador's President Pedro José Escalón laid the blame for all the Central American problems on Guatemalan leader Estrada Cabrera: "The Central American Republics will be permanently perturbed by revolutionary disturbances as long as Estrada Cabrera remains in power in Guatemala; it is he who provokes the other governments. I believe that peace cannot be secured in Central America except by the removal of Estrada Cabrera from power and I myself am ready to resign the Presidency of Salvador in the cause of peace if it be deemed necessary." Roosevelt urged arbitration to settle the differences. Escalón agreed and sent a minister to Washington, at the same time ordering the troops withdrawn from the Guatemalan frontier. Guatemala's response was prompt and positive. Estrada Cabrera derided El Salvador's withdrawal of its troops, pointing out that it could easily remobilize them, whereas Guatemala's army of forty thousand men dispersed on a distant frontier was not as mobile and remained at

12. David Thompson to ER, June 14, 15, 1906; Pedro José Escalón to Porfirio Díaz, Díaz to Escalón, June 13, 1906, in Thompson to ER, June 16, all in Despatches, Mexico, M97, Roll 178.
13. W. E. Alger to Leslie Combs, June 20, 1906; Combs to ER, June 27, 1906, both in Despatches, Guatemala, M219, Roll 72.

risk. But Estrada Cabrera, eager to settle the hostilities, not only suggested that El Salvador and Guatemala accept President Roosevelt's mediation, he asked that both nations pledge—through Roosevelt—to accept arbitration in future disputes, to reduce armies and resume normal defense appropriations, and to expel *emigrados* within five days. "To make these articles effective each will name President Roosevelt to arbitrate and decide." An elated Combs was partly correct that "this offers immediate, honorable, just and lasting peace," but he was wildly overoptimistic in suggesting that "such a settlement would tend to eliminate revolution in Central America." [14]

William L. Merry, the American minister to Costa Rica, El Salvador, and Nicaragua, and the senior American diplomat in the five republics, had been hurriedly recalled from leave to deal with the diplomatic emergency. Merry first met with Combs in a neutral port so that the two American ministers could synchronize their diplomatic initiatives. When Merry arrived at San Salvador on July 5, 1906, he met with President Escalón and his new cabinet and personally conveyed Estrada Cabrera's peace proposals and Roosevelt's offer of mediation. Escalón and the cabinet agreed with the proposals but feared that General Tomás Regalado's erratic and drunken behavior prevented their openly accepting the peace settlement. Although Guatemala and most of El Salvador were ready for peace, General Tomás Regalado was not. Regalado, the commander of the Salvadorean army and the only candidate in El Salvador's next presidential election, was ready to fight anyone at any time—in his own country or another. On July 5, 1906, on one of his "periodical drunken orgies," Regalado first fired on El Salvador's presidential mansion, which the experienced President Escalón and his cabinet assiduously avoided. On the following day, still "drinking hard," Regalado with an estimated fourteen thousand troops under his command, attacked a Guatemalan town. Escalón's government could not control him, and Regalado continued his drunken foray on July 10 with several more attacks twenty miles deep in Guatemalan territory. The simultaneous end of the invasion, the major impetus for war, and Tomás Regalado occurred suddenly on July 11, when the drunken warrior was shot and killed while leading his troops in an attack on the well-entrenched Guatemalan outpost at El Sillon. Regalado's inglorious death eliminated one of the major obstacles to peace in Central America, as well as one of Central

14. Leslie Combs to ER, June 27, 29, 1906, in Despatches, Guatemala, M219, Roll 72.

America's leading anti-American politicians. Just four days before his death, Regalado, when informed of the American peace initiative, told the American consul-general John Jenkins, *"Nostros no tenemos tata"* (*tata* means father). Regalado wanted no part of North American paternalism or good offices.[15]

The weather also helped the cause of peace. In April Merry advised Root that "the advent of the rainy season now at hand ably secures the public peace of Central America for the next seven months, as these people generally revolutionize when the roads are passable." Although the efforts of Presidents Díaz and Roosevelt helped, rain was the most effective peacemaker. The swift Central American rivers were the main means of transporting troops. During the rainy season these rivers were not fordable, and the movement of men and machines was difficult or impossible. Heavy daily rain not only made the roads impassable, but troops suffered from sleeping in the mud, especially without an organized source of supplies. Tired and hungry men who lived off the land were often wracked by malaria; their families were forced to wrest a living from a difficult land without the help of the man of the family. Merry, who chafed under American early twentieth-century restraint, favored the same paternalistic intervention that Latin Americans feared and detested: "It seems a sin against humanity that the so-called sovereignty of these Republics prevents us from forbidding their periodical revolutions and wars instead of offering 'good offices' which are regarded by many of them as an evidence of our good natured political policy that regards force as the last resort." Merry, an introspective and uneasy diplomat, grappling with the problem, recalled when his intercession had prevented a war between Costa Rica and Nicaragua. Although a coffee planter appreciated that American intervention had saved him and his country from heavy financial losses, he still felt "it is a great mortification to me that the United States government can say to us 'You must not fight' and as if we were children we obey the order." Rain and diplomatic pres-

15. William Merry to ER, July 10, 1906; Merry to ER, July 15, 1906; Phillip Brown to Merry, July 11, 1906; Merry to Robert Bacon, July 12, 1906, all in Despatches, El Salvador, M219, Roll 94. For Merry's background see Munro, *Intervention and Dollar Diplomacy*, 40–41; and William Roger Adams, "Strategy, Diplomacy and Isthmian Canal Security, 1880–1917 (Ph.D. dissertation, Florida State University, 1974), 95–109. For Regalado's political career and death see Patricia Antell Andrews, "Tomás Regalado and El Salvador, 1895–1906" (M.A. thesis, Louisiana State University in New Orleans, 1972).

sure, more than enlightened self-interest, temporarily shifted the balance in Central America from war to peace.[16]

American and Mexican diplomats pursued the chance for peace. When Combs in Guatemala received Estrada Cabrera's assent, he suggested that El Salvador be approached jointly by Presidents Díaz and Roosevelt. The negotiations were proceeding smoothly when it appeared that Regalado's invasion of Guatemala might end the peace initiative. Combs's frustration was matched by his fervor: "Cannot war be yet averted? It would be inexcusable." Both American ministers recommended an American naval presence not so much to protect American interests in case of total war as for the "moral effect," a diplomatic euphemism for a show of force. "War spirit strong here," Chargé Phillip Brown reported from Guatemala on July 13, hardly surprising since the Guatemalans could not possibly yet know that the recent Salvadorean invasion was not a political statement but a drunken act. With Regalado gone, Merry could report from San Salvador that "perfect order and security exists here." American fears of possible Nicaraguan and Honduran involvement were suddenly fulfilled when Guatemala invaded Honduras and Honduras promptly announced it would fight back. When Honduras' President Bonilla announced a new alliance with El Salvador, peace suddenly seemed impossible. Still convinced that the main conflict between Guatemala and El Salvador remained the most pressing issue, Presidents Díaz and Roosevelt worked together to coordinate a joint peace effort to convince the combative and sensitive republics to settle their differences. On July 13 Roosevelt sent an identical message to Presidents Estrada Cabrera and Pedro José Escalón, "with the full concurrence of the President of Mexico," to "urge a settlement before it may be too late." Roosevelt offered "the deck of the American ship of war *Marblehead,* now on the way to the coast of Salvador, as a neutral place." President Díaz sent a similar message to the warring governments urging negotiations.[17]

16. William Merry to ER, April 17, 1906; James Bailey, chargé *ad interim,* San José, Costa Rica, to ER, June 9, 1906, both in Despatches, Costa Rica, M219, Roll 94; Merry to ER, July 15, 1906, in Despatches, Guatemala, M219, Roll 72.

17. Phillip Brown to Robert Bacon, July 10, 1906; William Merry to Brown, Brown to Merry, July 11, 1906; Merry to Robert Bacon, July 12, 1906; Brown to Merry, July 11, 1906; Merry to Brown, Alger to Brown, Brown to Bacon, July 14, 1906, all in Despatches, Guatemala, M219, Roll 72; David Thompson to ER, July 12, 1906, in *FRUS,* 1906, p. 836.

Included in the dispatch of Roosevelt's message to Guatemala was a wistful hope from Acting Secretary Robert Bacon that the new war was a "misapprehension." Roosevelt wanted it made clear that the United States would offer active mediation in addition to the presence of the *Marblehead* if the Central American nations requested it. When Honduras, El Salvador, and Guatemala all claimed that they were fighting in self-defense, the American diplomats got all three to consent to a cease-fire if the others agreed. With the cease-fire the immediate crisis passed and negotiations for the impending *Marblehead* peace conference proceeded. Assembling representatives of seven nations—Guatemala, El Salvador, Honduras, Mexico, the United States, and possibly Nicaragua and Costa Rica—without injuring any sensibilities or appearing to coerce any country was difficult. Guatemala and El Salvador agreed to a truce effective at dawn on Wednesday, July 18. President Escalón agreed to the presence of both Mexican and American diplomats and to the *Marblehead* as the site of the peace negotiations but asked that the ship remain in neutral waters. Roosevelt wrote Estrada Cabrera that he was especially pleased that Guatemala welcomed Mexican participation. Guatemala wanted peace and tolerated Mexican participation, which was essential if El Salvador was to cooperate. To underscore the American insistence on Mexican participation, Assistant Secretary of State Alvey Adee over Roosevelt's signature specified the American expectation that the Mexican minister would be accorded the same status as the American ministers and referred to President Díaz by name, an indication that the United States considered Mexican participation vital.[18]

When Leslie Combs was still in transit and Phillip Brown, the chargé acting in his absence, hesitated about Mexican participation, Acting Secretary of State Robert Bacon insisted that it was necessary. "Without the active cooperation of President of Mexico the efforts so far made might have failed, and without the continuation of his cooperation the conference may prove abortive," Bacon wrote to Brown in Guatemala City. Bacon added that if no Mexican were present, the Americans would have no excuse for attending because "the good will of Mexico is indispensable to a durable peace in Central Amer-

18. Robert Bacon to Phillip Brown, July 14, 1906; Brown to Bacon (two letters), July 14, 1906; Brown to American consul, Tegucigalpa (two letters), July 15, 1906, all in Despatches, Guatemala, M219, Roll 72.

ica." Although the diplomatic instruction was designed primarily to convince Estrada Cabrera, Washington was dismayed that its own diplomat might have missed the purpose of Mexican participation. In an unusual postscript headed "very confidential for your own information," Bacon added, "Cannot understand your evident want of appreciation of necessity including Mexican Minister and retaining cordial cooperation of President Díaz." [19]

Bacon, who could not understand the Guatemalan president's hesitation because the Mexican government had participated in all the diplomatic negotiations, was genuinely shocked to find his own delegation apparently insensitive to Mexico's importance in the peace talks. Another even stronger telegram was quickly dispatched to the beleaguered chargé with the news that "the President views with surprise and apprehension your evident want of appreciation of retaining the active cordial cooperation of President Díaz whose attitude in this matter is precisely the same as that of President Roosevelt." Brown may have been cautious, but the main problem was Washington's and Mexico City's failure to give their diplomats clear instructions about representation on the *Marblehead*. Brown reassured Bacon that he not only understood the United States position but that he "constantly emphasized" it to Estrada Cabrera. Neither El Salvador nor Guatemala had asked that a Mexican diplomat be present, and neither Mexican Minister Federico Gamboa nor the Americans had any instructions. Brown had simply assumed the oversight was a matter of policy. He added, "Cooperation of Mexico in peace conference most desirable." The State Department, nervous at intervening, fearful of missing an opportunity for peace, and justifiably wary of complex negotiations with skittish and suspicious Central American republics, verged on paranoia. Bacon feared jeopardizing a simple ending of the war by enlarging the *Marblehead* meeting into a general peace conference, although when the conference accomplished more than simply ending the war, Bacon was elated. [20]

At first, only direct negotiations between the two combatants were scheduled. Honduras, the third nation at war, was then added, and

19. Pedro José Escalón to TR, July 14, 1906; TR to Estrada Cabrera, July 15, 1906, both in *FRUS*, 1906, p. 842. See also Phillip Brown to Robert Bacon, Estrada Cabrera to TR, July 16, 1906, *ibid.*, 843; Bacon to Brown, July 17, 1906, in Instructions, M77, Roll 34. This strongly worded letter and several others are omitted from the published correspondence in *FRUS*, 1906.

20. Bacon to Phillip Brown, July 17 (No. 3), in Instructions, M77, Roll 34; Brown to Bacon, July 18, 1906, in Despatches, Guatemala, M219, Roll 72.

the American and Mexican ministers were to be present purely in an advisory capacity. Why, the State Department asked, were Costa Rica and Nicaragua represented at all? The answer, not easily phrased in a diplomatic communication, was suspicious curiosity—which in Central America verged on understandable paranoia. Once again the State Department nervously instructed its chargé, Combs, and possibly the mercurial Estrada Cabrera, of Mexico's importance in the proceedings. American minister to Mexico Thompson had sent Bacon another reassurance of Díaz' cooperation, and Bacon conveyed the strong message to the Guatemalan president as well as the American diplomats: "If Guatemalan President really has fear as to the attitude now and good intentions for the future of President Díaz he does him a very great injustice." Brown was told that Roosevelt had Díaz' permission to instruct Estrada Cabrera that the views of Díaz and Roosevelt were identical. These concerns were unnecessary because Estrada Cabrera was in one of his charming moods. When he cabled Roosevelt "Sincere felicitation," a relieved Bacon told Combs to communicate Roosevelt's deep appreciation.[21]

The two cooperating North American presidents worked out an effective division of labor. The United States supplied the warship for the peace conference and supervised the arrangements. Mexico worked out the armistice to take place at dawn on July 18. It was not easy. Estrada Cabrera cordially agreed to the Díaz armistice, then attacked El Salvador's base at Matapan in Guatemalan territory on July 17, and again agreed to an armistice. On the same day Guatemala attacked the Salvadoreans at Platanar with artillery and extra troops, before once again agreeing to the already agreed-upon armistice. Díaz thanked Estrada Cabrera for honoring "my friendly intervention" and instructed the Mexican minister in Guatemala to attend the *Marblehead* peace conference. At the time of the armistice, El Salvador occupied four fortified positions in Guatemala; Guatemala occupied one in El Salvador. In the ten days of war, El Salvador had lost nine hundred men dead and twenty-five hundred wounded.[22]

Had the already nervous State Department any idea of the bizarre

21. Robert Bacon to Brown, Bacon to Leslie Combs, July 18, 1906, in Instructions, M77, Roll 34.

22. Porfirio Díaz to Manuel Estrada Cabrera, July 17 (two letters), 18, 1906; Estrada Cabrera to Díaz, July 17, 1906; Pedro José Escalón to Díaz (two letters), July 18, 1906; Díaz to Escalón, July 18, 1906; Díaz to Federico Gamboa, July 18, 1906, all in *FRUS*, 1906, pp. 846–48; William Merry to Robert Bacon, July 22, 1906, in Despatches, El Salvador, M219, Roll 94.

scene that would unfold aboard the United States cruiser *Marblehead* off the western coast of Central America on July 19 and 20, 1906, it might have decided that the idea of holding a peace conference on the high seas among the perpetually belligerent nations of that unfortunate region was preposterous. The American ship was stationed in the Pacific Ocean roughly equidistant from the ports of the two main belligerents, San José de Guatemala and Acajutla, El Salvador. Nothing except the final and unexpectedly successful conclusion went right or as planned. Representatives of the three large nations, Federico Gamboa, the Mexican minister to Central America, William L. Merry, the American minister to El Salvador, Costa Rica, and Nicaragua, and Leslie Combs, the American minister to Guatemala, were supposed to be observers, present for moral effect, not as primary negotiators. No practice could have been further from the theory. Gamboa, Merry, and Combs became the unwieldy three-part chair of the conference when the belligerents refused to choose their own chairman. The three observers not only took part in the deliberations, they led them. Nor did the Mexicans and the Americans create a tranquil and impartial example for the Central Americans to follow. They argued as heatedly as the belligerents, becoming almost as partisan as the principal belligerents. The two American diplomats were at cross-purposes during most of the conference. The United States was far from united. Merry sided with El Salvador; Combs sided with Guatemala; Gamboa favored El Salvador. Central American belligerence seemed contagious. Perhaps by taking on the character of the countries they represented, the American diplomats became both sympathetic and extremely effective. In spite of its technical flaws, the *Marblehead* peace conference went well.[23]

The conference began early on July 19, lasted two days, and included three major sessions. There was trouble from the start. Guatemala came with four delegates, El Salvador two, and Honduras one. Oddly, the outnumbered El Salvador–Honduras party did not object, perhaps because it had brought an uninvited delegate from Nicaragua. Combs objected—mainly to Merry—and after a consultation the Nicaraguan was permitted to remain as an inactive observer. Another uninvited nonbelligerent from Costa Rica was also present. The State Department was upset that any nonbelligerents were present, possi-

23. For the best—and marvelously differing—views of the proceedings see Leslie Combs to ER, July 24, 1906, in Despatches, Guatemala, M219, Roll 72; William Merry to Robert Bacon, July 20, 22, 1906, in Despatches, El Salvador, M219, Roll 94.

bly fearing that the contagion of war might spread. Merry, who evaded the letter of his instructions by permitting the additional delegates, defended his actions by noting that the presence of other neutral observers added to the moral effect, which presumably was the reason for American-Mexican participation. The Central American neutrals, unlike those from North America, did not take an active part in the discussions.[24]

The Americans and the Mexicans both chaired and controlled the conference. Combs insisted that the problem of *emigrados* was the conference's most serious issue and argued for a strong agreement to expel them. El Salvador's constitution apparently prohibited a position as strong as Combs took—stronger than Guatemala's—and no agreement could be reached at the table though the final agreement contained a strong clause that satisfied everyone. The conferees quickly agreed to establish peace, to withdraw all invading armies within three days, and to disarm in eight days. The belligerents also agreed to a general amnesty, to exchange war prisoners, to release political prisoners, and to prevent *emigrados* from abusing the privilege of asylum. The belligerents promised to reconvene and negotiate a treaty of friendship and commerce within two months. Arbitration became the sticking point that threatened the conference.[25]

Combs suggested that the conference declare all the agreed-upon issues resolved and place the disputed matters in arbitration before representatives of the presidents of the United States and Mexico. El Salvador rejected such arbitration in principle and argued that it was politically impracticable. Combs engaged in "some pretty plain talking" to convince El Salvador to change its mind. Guatemala then proceeded to change it back by insisting that arbitration should not only include present problems but also decide who was responsible for the war. Although it was clear that neither Guatemala nor El Salvador was blameless, it was equally clear that El Salvador was the aggressor in the ten-day war and that Guatemala expected not only vindication but compensatory damages from an arbitration hearing. But El Salvador, aware of its responsibility—or that of its war minister Regalado—would never agree to an arbitration commission. Arbitration was not possible on the question of responsibility for the war because

24. William Merry to Robert Bacon, June 22, 1906, in Despatches, El Salvador, M219, Roll 94.
25. A skeleton list of peace terms is in Leslie Combs and William Merry to Robert Bacon, July 20, 1906, in *FRUS*, 1906, p. 848; text, *ibid.*, pp. 851–52.

it would violate El Salvador's vital interests and give it nothing in return. At this point both the belligerents and the supposedly peaceful observers were squabbling. Gamboa "actively" argued for El Salvador's rejection of arbitration; Combs "with equal energy" argued Guatemala's side; and Merry "in a much more moderate way" agreed with Gamboa. The idea of the North American representatives acting as impartial observers, already stretched thin, broke down completely.[26]

The deadlocked belligerents, perhaps hoping to avoid the onus of ruining the peace conference, shifted responsibility to the Mexican and American diplomats by agreeing to abide by any *unanimous* decision the three men could produce. That they eventually produced a unanimous recommendation is a testament to the art of professional diplomacy. It seemed improbable that any agreement could be reached. Gamboa informed the Americans in closed session and "extended consideration" that he had "very private information" that El Salvador would not accept the Guatemalan proposal. Merry agreed with Combs in principle but with Gamboa in practice. The diplomatic debate became more heated. Combs would be responsible for obstructing the peace conference, the Mexican charged, if he continued to hold out. Combs said he would rather hostilities resume "before I would use the influence of my government to coerce Guatemala beyond the principle of arbitration." This statement changed Merry's mind. Combs then turned the tables on Gamboa, holding him responsible for the failure of the conference. Gamboa, however, held firm and questioned how much power the three diplomats really had. The three finally agreed that they disagreed, that the question of arbitration would be dropped, and that the principals should resume discussions at the point they had been suspended. Everyone decided to adjourn for the day.[27]

Merry was pessimistic. The *Marblehead* peace conference had accomplished nothing more than a tenuous armistice. "Hopeless of results," the delegates assembled the next morning with their main goal a five-day extension of the armistice and the chance that someone in Washington or Mexico City would find inspiration or a miracle. Combs, who thought arbitration "worth all the rest of the compact," wrought a miracle. Between the evening of the nineteenth and the

26. Leslie Combs to Robert Bacon, July 24, 1906, in Despatches, Guatemala, M219, Roll 72.
27. *Ibid.*

morning of the twentieth Combs worked out the compromise that resolved the stalemate.[28]

Combs, who earlier had argued heatedly against coercing Guatemala into giving up her claims against El Salvador for beginning the
war, now undertook to convince—rather than coerce—Guatemala to
give up its claim for restitution and vindication. Combs's confidential
memorandum to the Guatemalan commissioners was the most convincing argument of the peace conference. He pointed out that even
if arbitration were agreed upon and Guatemala won, another war
would have to be fought to collect. Besides, Combs argued, arbitration commissions were unpredictable and might assign blame to both
sides. "All of the dirty linen of the two Republics for the last twenty
years would have to be washed in public," Combs pointed out, asking
whether Guatemala's best interests would be served by such a searching procedure. In the end El Salvador might not be able to give anything more than Guatemala had already won at the peace conference.
Why, Combs asked, "lose the important advantages obtained in the
articles already agreed upon"? Combs's closing argument was his
most masterful. He told the Guatemalans that he would not embar-
rass them by publicly asking them to give up their just claim, but that
privately he thought they should consider it. Would you "like me to
propose something less than what I regard and you regard as your
right to demand?"[29]

It would be hard to imagine a diplomatic resolution more satisfying
than Combs's triumph at the last session of the *Marblehead* conference. Just before the formal morning meeting, the Guatemalan commissioners told Combs: "If I would put my hand upon my heart and
advise the acceptance of the agreement as it stood, they would accept
it." Although Combs refused to advise the Guatemalans, he suggested that they would be wise to accept the Salvadorean position.
When the conference assembled for its morning session, everyone expected the deadlock to continue and the peace talks to fail. Salvador
Gallegos, the head of El Salvador's delegation, proclaimed the peace
conference a failure and laid the blame on Combs. The El Salvador
and Honduras representatives had made arrangements to leave the
Marblehead for Acajutla feeling that they could not make further concessions because of the intense war feeling in their nations. Everyone
was stunned when Guatemalan chairman Arturo Ubico dramatically

28. *Ibid.*
29. Text, *ibid.*, 5.

announced that Guatemala accepted the agreement "as it then stood." The rest of the day was spent working out the text of the treaty, and by 5 P.M. the remarkable *Marblehead* Treaty was completed and signed.[30]

The terms of the *Marblehead* agreement were impressive. El Salvador and Honduras returned to a state of peace with Guatemala, "relegating to oblivion their past differences." The armies were to withdraw by July 23 and to disarm by July 28, except for the usual city garrisons and detachments on normal police duty. Article Two provided for an exchange of prisoners, care for wounded captives, release of political prisoners, and recommendations to the three governments for a general political amnesty. The participants pledged to do better at controlling political refugees and the "machinations against the tranquility and public order" in their countries. They agreed to negotiate a general treaty of peace at San José, Costa Rica, within two months. The fifth and last article incorporated Combs's and the United States' strong wish for an arbitration procedure, specifying that failure to live up to the agreement or "new differences" could be submitted to the presidents of the United States and Mexico as arbitrators.[31]

All three of the American and Mexican diplomats exceeded their instructions by taking control of the negotiations, which were intended to be conducted directly between the active belligerents. Critics of Roosevelt's naval diplomacy suggested that "the delegates had been deliberately carried to sea in order to force them to sign an agreement they would not have signed on land." But using neutral American warships for Caribbean peace conferences was also a means of isolating delegates from the political pressures of normal diplomacy, with each point being communicated to the respective governments. American warships were also safe from pressure by insurrectionists. Neither Combs nor Merry had any delusions that these agreements were permanent. Combs's explanation of the American role is illuminating: "We had been putting all possible pressure, successfully, upon Guatemala for weeks to maintain under great provocation, a self-controlled, compromising spirit." Combs feared that Guatemala "should think I had abandoned her." Guatemala asked only, as

30. Leslie Combs to ER, *ibid.;* William Merry to Robert Bacon, June 22, 1906, in Despatches, Guatemala, M219, Roll 72.
31. Translation of final text in *FRUS,* 1906, pp. 851–52.

"President Roosevelt had suggested to President Escalón," a settlement "in accordance with the enlightened and humane spirit of the present day." Had not the Mexican diplomat so openly supported El Salvador's position, Combs would not have "been so pronounced" in his advocacy of the Guatemalan position. On reflection, Combs felt that having one American arguing for El Salvador and another for Guatemala was ultimately beneficial because it assured both countries of American support. The oldest and wisest hand at the State Department, Second Assistant Secretary Alvey Adee, who had probably written the inspiring Roosevelt letters, was seldom impressed by anything that passed through his hands. But Combs's diplomatic legerdemain moved Adee. In a memo about the unexpected Guatemalan change of heart, Adee admiringly wrote Acting Secretary of State Bacon: "Guatemala's back-down was explained by Mr. Combs. He advised it!"[32]

Costa Rica, an inactive observer at the *Marblehead* talks, hosted the formal peace conference that met on September 15, 1906, at San José to continue the peace initiatives begun on the *Marblehead* and also to celebrate the eighty-fifth anniversary of Central American independence. The Central American treaty of October 27, 1906, marked the high point of optimism and goodwill in relations between the Central American republics and the United States. Thirty-three additional articles, some of permanent value, were added to the original *Marblehead* agreement by the four attending republics. Nicaragua accepted the invitation, then declined to attend. The conference's prodigious accomplishments, though diminished by Central America's almost immediate failure to maintain the peace, signaled an impressive if short-lived peace and unity initiative. The Central American republics negotiated complex extradition arrangements, dealt firmly with the *emigrado* problem, agreed to establish a common merchant marine for trade through Panama and San Francisco, and agreed to establish what amounted to a Central American common market. Commerce was to move unimpeded by customs and duties—with several specific exceptions—and "those who have acquired a professional, literary, artistic, or industrial title in any of the contracting Republics,

---

32. Hill, *Roosevelt and the Caribbean*, 179. For a better explanation of why a ship was used—to prevent the delegates from communicating each point with their respective governments—see Brown, "American Diplomacy in Central America," 160, n. 25; for the antipathy between the two diplomats see Adee to Robert Bacon, August 14, 1906, in Despatches, Guatemala, M219, Roll 72.

shall be free to practice in any of the other countries, without any restraint whatever, their respective professions." A mutual regional copyright article was also adopted. Although the specific articles, the extradition arrangement, and the commerce union were to be effective for ten years, the peace, friendship, and arbitration agreements were "perpetual." [33]

To demonstrate the remarkable optimism and idealism following the *Marblehead* meeting, the four republics established a Central American International Bureau to be formed in Guatemala before September 15, 1907, and a Central American Pedagogical Institute in Costa Rica. The international bureau would preserve and encourage Central American interests, publish a journal, and communicate with "analogous" institutions such as the International Bureau of American Republics in Washington. Through the pedagogical institute, the formation of which was a sweeping recognition of mutual regional interests, the four republics agreed "to establish a common educational system, essentially homogeneous," and to encourage the "moral and intellectual unification of the sister countries." That the instructors and materials for the proposed twenty-five-year institute were to come from Europe was both a rejection of North American influence and an admission of Central America's intellectual poverty. Nicaragua, although not a signatory, was invited to join what may have been the last serious cultural and economic Central American movement for unity. [34]

When William Merry looked back over the successful *Marblehead* negotiations, he was not optimistic. He thought that the new American and Mexican interest might help the treaty to succeed, but he remained doubtful. The Compact of Corinto of 1902 had "maintained peace by repression in Central America for four years," Merry recalled. The present pact might last longer, but eventually "it will follow its predecessors." In words that resemble Jacob Hollander's sympathy for the victimized Dominican peasants, Merry wrote regretfully, "These international and revolutionary movements are not caused by the people of these Republics. They desire peace, but the political and military leaders strive with each other to obtain power for profit, or having both, for various reasons become bitter enemies and try to turn each other out." In 1906 the war the *Marblehead* agree-

33. William Merry to Robert Bacon, September 8, 1906, in *FRUS,* 1906, pp. 855–56; translated text, *ibid.,* 857–63.
34. Translated texts, *ibid.,* 863–66.

ment settled was caused by two such chieftains, Regalado and Estrada Cabrera. Estrada Cabrera "now has his mortal enemy under his feet in the vaults of a Guatemala church, but it will be strange if his fate is not equally tragic—it haunts him day and night." Merry thought Estrada Cabrera's crime the greater because he was better educated and had greater ability. "A Government that treats its people so cruelly and unjustly as Estrada Cabrera's has no right to exist. It is undoubtedly the worst government in Spanish America." Merry's prophecy about the fragility of the Central American peace treaties of 1906 was correct, but Estrada Cabrera ruled Guatemala until 1920, when the dictator was driven into exile and died of natural causes in 1924. The *Marblehead* agreement was hailed by the Latin American diplomats assembled at Rio de Janeiro for the Third International Conference of the American States as an effective and dramatic example of Root's and Roosevelt's new policy of peace and friendship.[35]

Although the *Marblehead* and San José treaties of 1906 appeared to fulfill the promise that Roosevelt's and Root's mediation policies would bring peace to an eager Central America, even with the success of the San José accords, the absence of Nicaragua signaled future discord. Eventually José Santos Zelaya used the new movement for a Central American union as an attempt to rule all Central America himself, precipitating a crisis that began in January, 1907, and remained unresolved despite Roosevelt's plea for mediation. After a combination of Nicaraguan troops and Honduran revolutionaries captured Tegucigalpa on March 27, Roosevelt was willing to intervene to stop further destruction, but Root limited American action to a naval presence with the *Princeton* protecting civilians from bombardment and the *Chicago* offering asylum to ousted Honduran President Bonilla. Chargé Phillip Brown, acting without instructions and on his own initiative, mediated an armistice that included an arbitration agreement between Nicaragua and El Salvador and further talks to choose a Honduran president acceptable to both Nicaragua and El Salvador.[36]

Further peace talks were held and another extended Central American peace conference convened in Washington in 1907, but Nicaraguan president José Santos Zelaya, intermittently antagonistic to the

35. William Merry to Robert Bacon, July 20, 1906, Despatches, El Salvador, in M219, Roll 94; *Senate Documents*, 59th Cong., 1st Sess., No. 365, Serial 5073, p. 24.
36. See Munro, *Intervention and Dollar Diplomacy*, 148–49, 152–53; Hill, *Roosevelt and the Caribbean*, 185–86.

United States, defeated any longer-lasting Central American peace arrangements. Although Root worked hard to make the Washington peace treaties of 1907 a success, he understood the difficulties when he asked Adee to try "a new scheme of color photography on the Central American situation, for ordinary methods" seemed hopeless. Root was also aware that the *Marblehead* liaison with Mexico had limited utility: "We can join with Mexico in urging settlement and peace but it is merely a form." As Root observed, there was no current controversy to be arbitrated: "Zelaya is bent on conquest and if driven from one pretext immediately finds another or goes on without any." The problem of Zelaya was compounded by the recurring problem of Estrada Cabrera, who, though he opposed Zelaya, was "a cruel tyrant under whom the political activity of Guatemala is confined to assassination, on both sides and all sides." Root rejected the ultimate remedy, constant armed intervention and limited American efforts to unhopeful mediation, except in Costa Rica, whose proximity to Panama made American protection essential. Central America was always able to produce a Zelaya, a Regalado, or an Estrada Cabrera at the most inappropriate time.[37]

The Central American treaties of 1907 produced a useful Permanent Court of Justice, which helped prevent some disputes from becoming wars, and an International Central American Bureau that served a needed economic and cultural function as a clearinghouse and center for Central American activities. But even in the relatively passive intervention during the April, 1907, conflict, American naval forces clashed with revolutionaries, creating bad feelings, ill will, and frustration. Roosevelt, who acknowledged that Root was responsible "during the last three years [for] the bulk of the most important work . . . with the South and Central American States," was proud that "we have done more as regards these States than ever before in the history of the State Department." Root would not go further than "patience and a few years of the right kind of treatment" to give the United States "the only kind of hegemony we need to seek or ought to want." A policy that depended on a partnership with Porfirio Díaz, about to be expelled from his presidency in a tumultuous Mexican revolution, was not likely to succeed without active help from Central America. Roosevelt's and Root's Central American policy, symbolized

37. ER to Alvey Adee, July 1, 1907, in Jessup, *Elihu Root,* I, 505.

by the diplomatic serendipity of the *Marblehead* peace conference, was more notable for its effort than for its ultimate success.[38]

In 1912 Phillip Brown, a participant in the *Marblehead* negotiations as Combs's chargé in Guatemala and the diplomat who arranged the armistice in the Nicaragua-Honduras war in 1907, reflected on Central American problems. "Their ways are not our ways," Brown wrote, comparing the Spanish culture of Central America to the Anglo-Saxon temper of the United States. In spite of the historic Spanish-American aversion for Yankees, Brown remained cautiously hopeful: "Diplomacy, by rigidly square dealing and by encouraging a friendly appreciation of all that is admirable in both races, is able to do much to lessen this natural antipathy." Brown reflected the working American diplomat's distaste for American entrepreneurial adventurers—*caballaros de industria*—a widespread antipathy often overlooked by critics who see business as the main motive of the American Latin American interventions. Brown's American capitalist was the original ugly American, whom he considered largely responsible for the Latin American antipathy to and suspicion of the United States because these "social derelicts" were the only North Americans many Latin Americans ever met. Brown tried to put the best possible face on Roosevelt and Root's policy of constructive paternalism: "Though the republics of Central America are under no specific tutelage and naturally resent being treated as children, they cannot object to being considered as our younger brothers whom we hold in affection and desire earnestly and disinterestedly to help." Brown made a sharp distinction, however, between the Roosevelt and Root policy of "simple mediation and scrupulous non-intervention" and "a policy of active, direct interventions in their internal affairs."[39]

38. Munro, *Five Republics*, 225; Hill, *Roosevelt and the Caribbean*, 193; Munro, *Intervention and Dollar Diplomacy*, 149–50; TR to Andrew Carnegie, February 26, 1909, in *MRL*, VI, 1539; ER to Albert Shaw, January 3, 1908, in Jessup, *Elihu Root*, I, 513. Correspondence, proceedings, and treaty texts are in *FRUS*, 1907, pp. 634–727. See Lejeune Cummins, "The Origin and Development of Elihu Root's Latin American Diplomacy" (Ph.D. dissertation, University of California, Berkeley, 1964), 247–53.

39. Brown, "American Diplomacy," 159, 162. For the contrast between Roosevelt's policy and Taft's dollar diplomacy, see Eugene Trani, "Dollar Diplomacy," in Alexander DeConde (ed.), *Encyclopedia of American Foreign Policy* (3 vols.; New York, 1978), I, 268–74; D. W. Dinwoodie, "Dollar Diplomacy in the Light of the Guatemalan Loan Project, 1909–1913," *Americas*, XXVI (1970), 237–53; Walter Scholes and Marie Scholes, "United States and Ecuador, 1909–1913," *Americas*, XIX (1963), 237–53; Seward B. Livermore, "Battleship Diplomacy in South America, 1905–1925," *Journal of Modern History*, XVI

"How has your constitution stood the sweet champagne of Our Sister Republics?" Theodore Roosevelt asked his secretary of state, Elihu Root, in the third month of Root's monumental goodwill tour of South America. Root had undertaken this tour not only to dispel the widespread Latin American fear of United States annexation or protectorate ambitions but to bridge a cultural gulf that hindered normal diplomacy and trade. Root summed up the part of the problem that he thought could be changed: "The South Americans now hate us largely because they think we despise them and try to bully them. I really like them and I intend to show it." Root hated "banquets, and receptions, and ceremonial calls and drinking warm, sweet champagne in the middle of the day," but he felt that only by graciously meeting Latin Americans on their social terms could he begin to reverse their feeling that all North Americans despised them. To court Latin American diplomats Root sent twelve thousand engraved invitations from Tiffany, kept a supply of Havana cigars and imported wines on board the *Charleston,* and issued instructions to American diplomats to make long and careful guest lists for social functions. Root worked hard to undo the habitual North American disdain exemplified by his predecessor John Hay's remark, "They were mostly dagoes and chargés at the diplomatic reception." Root explained his purpose: "If you want to make a man your friend, it does not pay to treat him like a yellow dog."[40]

The Root family visited Uruguay, Argentina, Chile, Peru, Panama, and Colombia on their way to and from the Third International Ameri-

---

(1944), 31–48; and Cummins, "Origins and Development of Elihu Root's Latin American Diplomacy," 211–13. For the view that dollar diplomacy was much more inclusive see Robert Freeman Smith, "Cuba: Laboratory for Dollar Diplomacy, 1898–1917," *Historian,* XXVIII (1966), 586–609; for the view that dollar diplomacy was a change in emphasis rather than a radical change of policy see Healy, *Drive to Hegemony,* 145–51; for the connection between Root and Roosevelt with Taft's later dollar diplomacy see George E. Mowry, *The Era of Theodore Roosevelt and the Birth of Modern America, 1900–1912* (New York, 1962), 160–61.

40. TR to ER, September 4, 1906, in *MRL,* V, 396; TR, Annual Message, 1906, in *TRWN,* XV, 393; A. Curtis Wilgus, "The Third International American Conference at Rio de Janeiro, 1906," *HAHR,* XII (1932), 441; ER to Benjamin Tillman, December 13, 1905; to William J. Wallace, June 22, 1906, both in Jessup, *Elihu Root,* I, 469, 475–77, 468; Tyler Dennett, *John Hay: From Poetry to Politics* (New York, 1934), 264. See Edwin A. Muth, "Elihu Root: His Role and Concepts Pertaining to United States Policies of Intervention" (Ph.D. dissertation, Georgetown University, 1966), 41–61; and Robert Neal Seidel, "Progressive Pan-Americanism: Development and United States Policy Toward South America, 1906–1931" (Ph.D. dissertation, Cornell University, 1973), 22–38. For the view that Root's Latin American initiatives were designed to deemphasize the

can Conference at Rio de Janeiro, July 26 to August 26, 1906. Root's message throughout his trip echoed his main speech on July 31 at Rio: "We wish for no victories but those of peace; for no territory except our own; for no sovereignty except the sovereignty over ourselves. We deem the independence and equal rights of the smallest and weakest member of the family of nations entitled to as much respect as those of the greatest empire, and we deem the observance of that respect the chief guarantee of the weak against the oppression of the strong." Root's performance under the eyes of a wary Latin American audience, especially the press, proved a spectacular diplomatic success, "one of the most notable political events that has taken place in our relations with Central and South America." The extremely critical opposition newspaper *Jornal do Brasil* reflected the universal acclaim of a speech "that never failed to hit the mark aimed at, and never overshot it. . . . Never an unsuitable or unapt word."[41]

The success of the Rio conference, as of Root's entire South American odyssey, resulted in part from the meticulous planning and careful organization by the two largest nations, Brazil and the United States, each of which wished to achieve specific political and diplomatic purposes. Both nations were aware of the transitional nature of a decade in which North America first challenged Europe's dominant influence in South American affairs. Brazil, the largest and most powerful Latin American nation, the only one that spoke Portuguese, was regarded with almost as much suspicion by smaller Spanish-speaking Latin American nations as was the United States. Root's earliest Latin American friend was Joaquim Nabuco, Brazil's first-ranked ambassador, a writer and cosmopolitan diplomat, who had previously served as minister to Britain. In the year before the Rio confer-

---

Monroe Doctrine, combine Blaine's older economic Pan-Americanism with an appeal to increasingly anti-American Latin American intellectuals, and win greater acceptance for Roosevelt's policies from American intellectuals see Donald J. Murphy, "Professors, Publicists, and Pan-Americanism, 1905–1917: A Study in the Origins of the Use of 'Experts' in Shaping American Foreign Policy" (Ph.D. dissertation, University of Wisconsin, 1970), 53–63.

41. "Report of the Delegates of the United States to the Third International Conference of the American States," in *Senate Documents*, 59th Cong., 2nd Sess., No. 365, Serial 5073, p. 73; Wilgus, "Third International American Conference," 420–56; James Brown Scott (ed.), *The International Conferences of American States, 1889–1928* (New York, 1931), 113–50. TR, Annual Message, in *TRWN*, XV, 392–97; Jessup, *Elihu Root*, I, 477–83, 481–82. For the favorable impression Roosevelt's mediation of the Russo-Japanese War made on Latin America see Murphy, "Professors, Publicists, and Pan-Americanism," 62.

ence, Root began his friendship campaign by forging closer social ties with Latin American diplomats in Washington, reversing the customary Washington practice of ignoring Latin American diplomatic dinners. Root urged cabinet members and other well-known members of government such as Admiral Dewey and Senator Lodge to accept Nabuco's dinner invitations. Root took his family on his Latin American journey, making the trip both social and diplomatic and strengthening the social ties he had cultivated in Washington.[42]

That Latin America's sympathies and main cultural and trade connections lay with Europe was apparent in a comparison of "the constant coming and going of the splendid passenger ships that ply between the South Atlantic ports and those of England, Germany, France, Spain, and Italy" with the two passenger ships a month from the United States. Brazil looked to Europe for its cultural inspiration. The redesign of Rio's main street, the Avenida Central, in 1903–1905, was inspired by Baron Haussmann's Paris boulevards; Brazil's new architecture was a recreation of French Second Empire style. But the beginnings of United States influence were apparent in the resplendent new conference building, a replica of Brazil's building at the Louisiana Purchase Exposition in 1904 at St. Louis and named the Monroe Palace in response to American gestures of friendship. Root well understood that he and the United States were competing with Europe for Latin American commerce as well as affection.[43]

The world's press reports captured the transitional character of the Third Conference (as it was known). The meeting of the two Americas was not an anti-European concert as such, but rather a new recognition of Latin American demands for "equality by international law, and that sovereignty of the people should be as that of European nations." The main commercial purpose of Root's visit was to encourage the entry of American commerce, a notion the Paris *Journal des Débats*

42. Jessup, *Elihu Root,* I, 471–74; ER to TR, August 2, 1906, *ibid.,* 475. See Frederick William Ganzert, "The Baron Do Rio-Branco, Joaquim Nabuco, and the Growth of Brazilian-American Friendship, 1900–1910," *HAHR,* XXII (1942), 432–51; and E. Bradford Burns, *The Unwritten Alliance: Rio-Branco and Brazilian-American Relations* (New York, 1966), 97–114. French Ambassador Jean Jules Jusserand was impressed by Root taking his family. See Jusserand to MAE, March 21, April 5, 1906, in N.S., Etats-Unis, 15, AMAE.

43. "Report of the Delegates of the United States," 26, 3; Norma Evenson, *Two Brazilian Capitals: Architecture and Expansion in Rio de Janeiro and Brasília* (New Haven, 1973), 38–39; Elihu Root, "Reasons Why the United States in Particular Should Encourage the Pan-American Conference," *National Geographic,* August, 1906, 479–80; Wilgus, "Third International American Conference," 453.

compared to "tilting at windmills." A Russian paper saw the conference as a North American attempt to wrest hegemony from Europe, and the London *Times* understood the affinity of both parts of the New World for impressive displays and the practice of democratic principles in the conference procedures. Putting the conference into a European perspective, the Swiss *Journal de Genève* wrote, "We have had Pan-Germanism, Pan-Slavism, Pan-Islamism, etc., and finally Pan-Americanism which for some time has been making more noise than all the other 'Pans' put together." The Rio conference's relative success owed to the careful planning of the committee structures. By dealing with specific problems such as sanitation, the coffee industry, and patents, the participants avoided grandiose expectations. The conference did not "attempt radical changes" but sought to make limited structural and administrative changes, a necessity given the impossibility of any agreement among the diverse separate states of both Americas. Gestures more than substance marked the accomplishments of the Rio conference, of which the Pan-American Union building and association in Washington, completed on May 10, 1910, were the most striking and lasting.[44]

Since the Roosevelt Corollary had effectively ended Europe's practice of intervention to collect debts, Argentine diplomat and scholar Luis M. Drago's doctrine had become more a matter of symbol than substance. Drago's doctrine, formally proposed in a letter to Secretary of State John Hay on December 29, 1902, and directed at the Anglo-German intervention in Venezuela, formulated the principle that "the public debt can not occasion armed intervention nor even the actual occupation of territory of American nations by a European power." Drago recognized and referred to the Monroe Doctrine's prohibition against European colonization, but like Roosevelt feared that a temporary action to collect a debt might lead to a permanent occupation. Both the Drago and Monroe doctrines were directed against Europe, and they partly merged, not only in the Venezuelan blockade crisis but in the Dominican receivership intervention. The Dominican crisis proved a better example of Drago's principle because Germany (os-

---

44. Rio de Janeiro *Journal de Commercio*, December 11, 1905; *LD*, September 1, 1906; *Review of Reviews*, March, 1907, p. 360; Paul S. Reinsch (editor of the *American Political Science Review*) quote, all in Wilgus, "Third International American Conference," esp. 446, 451; for the origins of the pan movements see Thomas L. Karnes, "Pan-Americanism," in DeConde (ed.), *Encyclopedia of American Foreign Policy*, III, 730; see Clifford B. Casey, "The Creation and Development of the Pan-American Union," *HAHR*, XIII (1933), 437–56.

tensibly) and Britain had intervened against Venezuela not to collect private debts but because of international friction—what the British called "outrages"—which included sinking of vessels, jailing of citizens, and Cipriano Castro's refusal to follow the customary diplomatic conventions. Drago's doctrine was an outgrowth of a long-standing Latin American contractual convention, the Calvo Clause, a legal argument originated by Argentine diplomat Carlos Calvo that denied extraterritoriality to alien businessmen in foreign countries. Calvo insisted that aliens should have no diplomatic protection when doing business in Latin America and that all contractual disputes should be resolved in local courts and not through recourse to international jurisdiction that transcended local laws.[45]

Although Calvo's purpose—to eliminate the universal practice of gunboat diplomacy in Latin American countries—was admirable, his self-serving doctrine offered no relief for injustice to foreign businessmen at the hands of local courts. Since local courts often substituted political standards for legal judgment, both Europe and the United States rejected Calvo in favor of international arbitration, a preference that the developed nations defended as fair and just and Latin Americans resisted as an impingement of both sovereignty and honor. Napoleon III's occupation of Mexico in 1861–1862, the classic European debt intervention, led to Maximilian's extended occupation that lasted until the end of the American Civil War and created the long tradition of Latin American legal writing and national resentment that coalesced when the United States displaced Europe as the dominant Caribbean power during Roosevelt's presidency. Part of the purpose of Root's Rio diplomacy was to set Latin American fears over Calvo, Drago, and big sticks to rest.[46]

---

45. Text of Drago's message in *FRUS*, 1903, pp. 1–5; Donald Shea, *The Calvo Clause: A Problem of Inter-American and International Law and Diplomacy* (Minneapolis, 1955), 16–21; Luis M. Drago, "State Loans in Their Relation to International Policy," *American Journal of International Law*, I (1907), 692–726; Amos S. Hershey, "The Calvo and Drago Doctrines," *American Journal of International Law*, I (1907), 26–45. For the need to modify international law to include uniquely Latin American circumstances see Alejandro Alvarez, "Latin America and International Law," *American Journal of International Law*, III (1909), 269–353; for Alvarez' long involvement with the questions posed by the Monroe Doctrine for Latin America see Frederick B. Pike, *Chile and the United States, 1880–1962* (South Bend, Ind., 1963), 220–26, 399–401.

46. Shea, *Calvo Clause*, 20; for the legal dispute see *ibid.*, 12; Thomas F. McGann, *Argentina, the United States, and the Inter-American System, 1880–1914* (Cambridge, Mass., 1957), 240–56; and Pike, *Chile and the United States*, 131–34.

One of the most dramatic moments in Root's long trip occurred when he and Luis Drago together addressed an audience at the Buenos Aires Opera House on August 17, 1906. Root was unequivocal in his statement of American policy against armed debt intervention, though he fell short of entirely endorsing Drago's principle:

The United States of America has never deemed it to be suitable that she should use her army and navy for the collection of ordinary contract debts of foreign governments to her citizens. For more than a century . . . [it] has refused to take such action, and that has become the settled policy of our country. We deem it to be inconsistent with that respect for the sovereignty of weaker powers which is essential to their protection against the aggression of the strong. We deem the use of force for the collection of ordinary contract debts to be an invitation to abuses, in their necessary results far worse, far more baleful to humanity than that the debts contracted by any nation should go unpaid. We consider that the use of the army and navy of a great power to compel a weaker power to answer to a contract with a private individual, is both an invitation to speculation upon the necessities of weak and struggling countries and an infringement upon the sovereignties of those countries, and we are now, as we have always been, opposed to it.[47]

Drago, satisfied with the practical support the American Monroe Doctrine policy gave to his doctrine, directed his main remarks toward Europe. Though acknowledging Latin America's intellectual debts to Europe, he insisted that "the genius and tendency of our democratic communities be respected. They are advancing slowly, it is true; struggling at times and occasionally making a pause," while succeeding "at what may be called the most considerable trial mankind has ever made of the republican system of government." Root invited Drago to come to the United States as a guest of the American government and lecture at Harvard University, but he declined for personal reasons.[48]

Root, Roosevelt, and Drago were in fundamental agreement that Europe could no longer be permitted to intervene either for political reasons, the principle of the original Monroe Doctrine, or to collect debts, the focus of Roosevelt's Corollary. The area of disagreement,

47. Elihu Root, *Latin America and the United States* (Cambridge, Mass., 1917), 98.
48. *Ibid.*, 96; Arthur P. Whitaker, *The Western Hemisphere Idea: Its Rise and Decline* (Ithaca, N.Y., 1954), 104.

however, remained essentially unbridgeable because the United States, like Europe before, insisted that contracted debts must be paid or settled. For the United States, international arbitration seemed the ideal solution, precluding naval force to collect debts and guarding investors against willful default protected by local law or changes in national governments through revolution that conveniently repudiated past debts. Drago's principle, which he came closest to stating explicitly in his speech with Root at Buenos Aires, asked the capitalist or developed countries to forgo their customary contractual rights and allow Latin American nations to work out their obligations internally, trusting that forbearance would eventually produce either the requisite payment or gradually bring developing Latin American nations into the mainstream of international capitalism. Latin American diplomats frequently pointed to Louisiana and Mississippi in the 1830s and 1840s as examples of states whose defaulted debts remained unpunished. Why should Latin America be singled out for enforced collection, a point further underlined by Theodore Roosevelt's "chronic wrongdoing" phrase? Drago's doctrine was better suited to the larger Latin American nations, Argentina, Brazil, and Chile, but in the hands of an unprincipled opportunist such as Cipriano Castro, it could serve as a shield, like the Monroe Doctrine, to promote personal political and economic aggrandizement. Castro's Venezuela shared almost no common ground with Drago's elitist, Europeanized Argentina. Roosevelt's Corollary was by necessity a temporary measure; its initial success in discouraging European intervention could easily be subverted, making the United States a convenient debt collector for Europe in Latin America. The United States moved away from both Drago's universal principle and Roosevelt's unilateral policy, toward a preference for using the international justice courts of The Hague.[49]

Though Root's Latin American policy changed American attitudes toward Latin America, it was unable to bridge the gap between Drago's idealized Pan-Hispanicism and North American reverence for contractual rights and capital development. As shrewd and sympa-

49. Drago, "State Loans in Their Relation to International Policy," 719–26; Hershey, "Calvo and Drago Doctrines," 26–31, 44–45; ER, *The United States and Latin America,* 96; Whitaker, *Western Hemisphere Idea,* 106. For the flaws in the arbitration system and Root's efforts to reform it at the Second Hague Peace Conference see David S. Patterson, *Toward a Warless World: The Travail of the American Peace Movement, 1887–1914* (Bloomington, Ind., 1976), 155–64.

thetic as Root was, the gulf between the Americas was too great for politics and diplomacy to bridge. But as part of Root's continuing diplomatic offensive, he persuaded Russia to postpone its convening of the Second Hague Peace Conference for a year, to avoid a conflict with the Rio conference. He supported the presence of a large Latin American contingent. When the Hague Peace Conference convened in 1907, Luis M. Drago represented Argentina, and all the Latin American republics were invited, a marked difference from 1899, when only Mexico and Brazil were present. Roosevelt, who had supported the Hague arbitration principle and the World Court throughout his presidency, was not enthusiastic about a peace conference that required unanimous consent to carry proposals. Roosevelt feared that public hopes from such a widely promoted forum would be raised to unrealistic levels. Andrew Carnegie, the chief private sponsor of the international peace movement, exasperated both Roosevelt and Kaiser Wilhelm, who angrily wrote to Roosevelt of Carnegie's "foul and filthy lies" and conceded his lack of enthusiasm for the Hague conference. Root, who wanted a unified American endorsement of the Drago Doctrine, feared that Europe would find such a policy too radical and would also object to its self-serving denial of creditors' rights. Root, looking for a compromise on a difficult matter, may not have understood how dedicated Drago was to his principle. The Americans, however, were determined to win some affirmation of Drago's principle because Root was convinced that speculators, assured of enforced debt collection, encouraged arms sales and revolutions in Latin America. Both the revolutions and the ensuing defaults threatened the Monroe Doctrine and added to Latin American instability.[50]

When as a compromise Root proposed arbitration as a necessary prerequisite to ultimate intervention he bitterly disappointed Drago, who thought the Americans had agreed to the conditional use of force, even if it was avoided until after arbitration failed. General Horace Porter, the American delegate, compromised the compromise by

---

50. TR to ER, September 14, 1905, in *MRL*, V, 25–26; Root, *Latin America and the United States*, 3. For the Hague diplomatic correspondence see James B. Scott (ed.), *The Reports to the Hague Conferences of 1899 and 1907* (Oxford, 1916), 180–94; see TR to Andrew Carnegie, April 5, 1907; Kaiser Wilhelm II to TR, n.d.; TR to Whitelaw Reid, January 10, 1907; to Cecil Spring Rice, July 1, 1907, all in *MRL*, V, 638–42, 544n., 543–44, 698–99; Davis, *The United States and the Second Hague Peace Conference*, 170; Jessup, *Elihu Root*, II, 67–82. For Carnegie's complex leadership of the peace movement see Joseph Wall, *Andrew Carnegie* (New York, 1970), esp. 886–940.

making the Hague resolution a pledge not to use force for contract debts unless the debtor prevented arbitration or failed to pay an international award. Porter, a legendary American cosmopolitan, had served as Grant's aide at Appomattox, became a railroad businessman, spoke fluent French and served with social distinction for eight years as ambassador to France, was honored as the first American recipient of the French Legion of Honor, and was best known for discovering the body of John Paul Jones in a Paris cemetery. Porter's argument for his compromise was so convincing that except for Switzerland, the objections anticipated from European countries failed to materialize:

Expeditions undertaken for the purpose of recovering debts have seldom been successful. The principle of non-intervention by force would be of inestimable benefit to all the interested parties.

Recognition of this principle would be a real relief to neutrals; for blockades and hostilities seriously threaten their commerce by interrupting all trade. It would also be a warning to a certain class of persons, who are too much disposed to speculate on the needs of a weak and embarrassed Government, and count on the authorities of their own country to assure the success of their operations.

Debtor states would find it to their advantage, for thereafter moneylenders could only count on the good faith of the Government, the national credit, the justice of local courts, and the economical administration of public affairs, to answer for the success of their transactions.

Arbitration, moreover, would give guarantees to genuine creditors, who would prefer it to the employment of arms.[51]

When Germany and Britain accepted Porter's compromise without reservation, the Americans had won a surprising and unexpected victory, only to be disappointed by Drago's reservations and a mixed, though mostly favorable, Latin American response. Argentina voted for the American proposal with two reservations that limited arbitration to private debts as a last resort and denied the use of force under any circumstances. Brazil vehemently rejected Drago's proposal of immunity for public debts, insisting that national borrowing was a civil, not a political act, and praised the ultimate resort to force that Porter proposed. When only ·Switzerland rejected Porter's proposal

---

51. Davis, *The United States and the Second Hague Peace Conference,* 127; Scott (ed.), *Reports to the Hague Conferences of 1899 and 1907,* 491–92.

completely, a compromise was adopted that pledged the powers not to use force to collect debts except when arbitration was not offered or an arbitration award was not honored. Drago indicated his willingness to accept a naval demonstration but resisted "the employment of armed force" or hard-to-regulate "coercive measures." [52]

Root, disappointed at winning his point in Europe at the cost of Latin American support, complained that the Latin Americans "pursue every line of thought to a strict, logical conclusion and are unwilling to stop and achieve a practical benefit as the Anglo Saxons do." Yet Drago was right in objecting not only on ideal grounds but also in practical terms. The Porter Convention, like the Roosevelt Corollary, was only as strong as an administration's intentions. Although Roosevelt and Root were genuinely horrified at the prospect of armed intervention for trivial reasons, neither Europe nor the United States was willing to grant Latin Americans the assumption of good faith, which was the underlying idea behind both the Calvo and Drago doctrines. The American delegation worked hard to win support for a compromise Root considered acceptable between the opposing camps of creditors and debtors, and Europe and Latin America, with the United States standing in both camps. In the end, the American efforts won acceptance with thirty-seven favorable votes; six nations abstained, and Argentina, Colombia, and Ecuador approved the convention while making their reservations public. When the plenary session approved the vote, Porter's amendment to the Drago Doctrine was promulgated as the Convention Respecting the Limitation of the Employment of Force for the Recovery of Contract Debts, the second convention of the 1907 Hague Peace Conference. [53]

Roosevelt remained indifferent, almost antagonistic to the Hague proceedings, offended both by Andrew Carnegie's active involvement and Britain's refusal to consider limitations on its naval superiority. Although Root's policy of involving Latin America directly in international diplomacy failed on several counts, most conspicuously in

52. Scott (ed.), *Reports to the Hague Conferences of 1899 and 1907,* 492, 496–97; Davis, *The United States and the Second Hague Peace Conference,* 278–86; for the Argentine division see William Haggard to Sir Edward Grey, August 22, 1906, in FO 420/237, p. 29, PRO.

53. ER to Elbert F. Baldwin, November 1, 1907, in Jessup, *Elihu Root,* II, 74; *ibid.* gives specific examples of practical failings of Porter's compromise; Whitaker, *Western Hemisphere Idea,* 107; see Davis, *The United States and the Second Hague Peace Conference,* 257–58, for the debate; for the text see Scott (ed.), *The Reports to the Hague Conferences of 1899 and 1907,* 489–90.

Brazil's attempts to include itself and Mexico on an unwieldy world court organization, the effort to find a meeting ground between new Latin American nationalism, new American interests, and established European power was a notable change from the complete indifference to Latin American sensibilities of the past. Roosevelt and Root called the Porter resolution "a very great" advance, culminating the work at the Third American Conference at Rio. When Roosevelt, recalling the Dominican intervention, wrote in 1914 that "the Drago Doctrine (by which governments are withheld from applying force to the collection of private debts) had not yet gone into effect," his remarks suggested that he felt that Porter's compromise did not negate Drago's original doctrine. North American peacekeeping attempts, however well meant, could not keep the peace in Central America. Latin America and Central America were both too diverse to be mollified by any single American policy or by the series of initiatives that Roosevelt and Root undertook in 1906 and after. Root's obvious courting of Latin America has often been contrasted with Roosevelt's apparently aggressive policies, though the two men worked closely together to try to bridge the vast gulf that separated the unified colossus from the heterogeneous Latin American republics. When the journal *Advocate of Peace* praised the part of Roosevelt's Annual Message taken from Root's report of the Hague proceedings and criticized Roosevelt's call for a larger army and navy, Root wrote on the clipping to Roosevelt, "Your name which is mud / I am an angel."[54]

54. TR to ER, July 2, 1907, in *MRL,* V, 700; see Jessup, *Elihu Root,* II, 77–78, 82; TR, Annual Message, in *TRWN,* XV, 479; TR, "Our Work in Santo Domingo," *Outlook,* CVI (March 21, 1914), 618. For an example of how Root's and Roosevelt's policies are still regarded as interventionist see Brenda G. Plummer, *Haiti and the Great Powers, 1902–1915* (Baton Rouge, 1988), 81, in which to support Root's and Roosevelt's "interventionist Haitian policy" in 1904, Root's December, 1908, letter is quoted to show Root waiting for the "psychological moment" to establish closer relations with Haiti. But the quote omits the key phrase "we could be of material help to them." For the original source and correct version see Jessup, *Elihu Root,* I, 555. For Root's absolute noninterventionist policy toward Haiti see his handwritten draft cabled to American Minister Henry Watson Furniss, December 4, 1908: "The United States has no intention of intervening in Haiti," quoted in Muth, "Elihu Root," 65. For Root's objections to interventionist tactics and for a balanced account of how Roosevelt and Root complemented each other see Healy, *Drive to Hegemony,* 139–40, 143–44. For Roosevelt's later peace initiatives see William Clinton Olson, "Theodore Roosevelt's Conception of an International League," *World Affairs Quarterly,* XXIX (1959), 329–53.

17 Cuba *Libre*, Cuba *Triste*

In 1823 Secretary of State John Quincy Adams, attempting to dissuade Spain from ceding Cuba to Great Britain, wrote that as surely as "an apple severed by the tempest from its native tree, cannot choose to fall to the ground, Cuba, forcibly disjointed from its own unnatural connection with Spain, and incapable of self-support, can gravitate only toward the North American Union, which by the same law of nature cannot cast her off from its bosom." North American concern for "the Turkey of transatlantic politics" was understandable since the island "almost in sight of our shores" controlled both entrances to the Gulf of Mexico and Havana offered an ambitious European power "ports as impregnable as the rock of Gibraltar." Spanish control suited American purposes by neutralizing Cuba until it could be annexed by the United States, an assumption many American statesmen shared with Adams. American ambivalence toward Cuba matched its concern. Race and slavery in both Cuba and the United States made union politically impractical, and when in 1898 Cuba was separated from Spain, it fell not as naturally as John Quincy Adams' wind-driven apple but in a process closer to a cesarean section followed by severe postoperative complications. Alfred T. Mahan in 1897 underlined the strategic importance of Cuba: "Great Britain, if at war with a state possessing Cuba, is shut out of the Windward Passage by Guantánamo, and from the Gulf of Mexico by Havana. The Mona Passage, also, though not necessarily closed, will be too dangerous to be relied upon. . . . The possessor of Cuba . . . has all the resources of the United States at his disposal." If benevolent and neutral Spanish control was no longer possible, American strategic interests had to be conserved, as President William McKinley wisely understood, even in the heady moments following the Spanish defeat when annexation and independence defined the political polarities of American debate over the fate of Cuba.[1]

Cane sugar, slavery, and Spain, three declining nineteenth-century institutions, contributed to Cuban unrest. Cuba's Ten Years' War (1868–1878) with Spain physically destroyed the island's sugar agriculture, requiring a rebuilding process that was both expansive and of questionable economic utility. Rising sugar consumption in the early nineteenth century led to the first French experiments in the 1840s of extracting sugar from beets to free Europe from its dependence on foreign sources. By 1852 Britain was using a billion pounds annually. In the United States sugar consumption rose from 12.1 pounds per person in 1800 to 65.2 pounds in 1900, a rise compounded by the threefold increase in American population. When Cuba emancipated its slaves in 1884, it had to contend not only with the difficult transition from slave to free labor but also with competition from beet sugar, which held 53.7 percent of the world market. In 1884 France, Austria, and Germany were the world's largest sugar suppliers. Since Hawaii and much of Latin America also produced large amounts of cane sugar, the market price dropped from 11 to 8 cents a pound (eventually to 3.2 cents in 1894). At the same time Cuba's postwar taxation system virtually destroyed the economic foundations of the old planter class.[2]

The peace of Zanjón that ended the Ten Years' War in 1878 was only a respite in Cuba's thirty-year war for political freedom and racial emancipation, a bitter civil war that destroyed almost all of Cuba's existing institutions. When it became obvious that slave and oxen power could not compete with the new technologies of world sugar

1. John Quincy Adams to Hugh Nelson, Instructions, April 28, 1823, in Russell H. Fitzgibbon, *Cuba and the United States, 1900–1935* (Menosha, Wisc., 1935), 265; London *Courier*, 1825, and Daniel Webster to Campbell, January 14, 1843, in Leland H. Jenks, *Our Cuban Colony: A Study in Sugar* (New York, 1928), 10–11; Alfred T. Mahan, "Strategic Features of the Caribbean Sea and the Gulf of Mexico," *Harper's New Monthly Magazine*, XCV (1897), 680–91, rpr. in Alfred T. Mahan, *Mahan on Naval Warfare* (Boston, 1918), 105; Charles E. Chapman, *A History of the Cuban Republic* (New York, 1927), 126; James M. Callahan, *Cuba and International Relations* (Baltimore, 1899), esp. 140.

2. Louis A. Pérez, Jr., "Vagrants, Beggars, and Bandits: Social Origins of Cuban Separatism, 1878–1895," *AHR*, XC (1985), 1093–94; Jenks, *Our Cuban Colony*, 27; Sidney W. Mintz, *Sweetness and Power: The Place of Sugar in Modern History* (New York, 1985), 143; Richard Daniel Weigle, "The Sugar Interests and American Diplomacy in Hawaii and Cuba, 1893–1903" (Ph.D. dissertation, Yale University, 1939), 25. For the dependence of sugar on slavery see Hugh Thomas, *Cuba* (New York, 1971), 30–31; Weigle, "Sugar Interests," 165; Jenks, *Our Cuban Colony*, 26–27; Fernando Ortiz, *Cuban Counterpoint: Tobacco and Sugar* (New York, 1947).

production, the *centrale* system, derived from French innovations in Martinique and later used in British Guiana and Brazil, replaced the old sugar plantation system based on slave labor. Sugar *centrales* separated the agricultural from the manufacturing process and replaced slaves with *colono* labor. The *colonos*, who harvested the sugar and sold it to the mills, were paid in sugar, thereby becoming members of a new social class, far removed from the old slave labor class but exposed to the risk of world market prices and capitalism. By 1887 the *colono* system accounted for 35 to 40 percent of Cuban sugar production and transformed Cuba's prewar sugar culture. The *centrale* used railroads, cheap land and labor, and sophisticated technology, and it required a large capital investment. The old sugar plantation with its varied subsistence agriculture was replaced by the modern latifundium, in reality an agricultural factory in which workers supplanted peasants and the former landowning class became a landless rural proletariat. The United States supplied capital, railroad engineers, and an intermittent market.[3]

Several influential American political groups opposed U.S. involvement in the Cuban sugar economy. Four American sugar constituencies—Louisiana Gulf Coast cane growers, Hawaii sugar planters, the midwestern beet sugar industry, and the Sugar Trust—were responsible for protectionist American tariffs that had grave consequences for Cuba. The price paid for sugar was determined by the world market, not by American tariffs. The sugar industry's—and Cuba's—problem in the late nineteenth century was how to make a profit on a crop that cost about a cent and a quarter a pound to grow and manufacture and sold for two and a quarter cents. All expenses and a profit had to come out of a penny a pound. Improved sugar technology and an increasingly competitive world market helped destroy Cuban society after both the dissolution of traditional sugar agriculture and the chaos of Cuba's civil wars.[4]

3. Allan Reed Millet, *Politics of Intervention: The Military Occupation of Cuba, 1906–1909* (Columbus, Ohio, 1968), 22; Jenks, *Our Cuban Colony,* 31–33; Pérez, "Vagrants, Beggars, and Bandits," 1099–1102; Weigle, "Sugar Interests," 179. For late nineteenth-century sugar investments see David Healy, *Drive to Hegemony: The United States in the Caribbean, 1898–1917* (Madison, Wisc., 1988), 15–18; see also Edwin Atkins, *Sixty Years in Cuba* (Cambridge, Mass., 1926); and Robert B. Hoernel, "Sugar and Social Change in Oriente, Cuba, 1898–1916," *Journal of Latin American Studies,* VIII (1976), 215–49. Robert Freeman Smith (ed.), *Background to Revolution: Development of Modern Cuba* (New York, 1966), is a useful historiographical collection.

4. For the worldwide social upheavals caused by technological change see Joel Migdal, "Capitalist Penetration in the Nineteenth Century: Creating Conditions for Social

When American industrialist Henry Oxnard imported the latest beet sugar technology, which required substantial government subsidies, from Europe to the American Midwest in 1888, and, almost simultaneously, Harry and Theodore Havemeyer merged fifteen independent refineries with their old family company to form the Sugar Trust in 1887, Cuba faced serious new challenges to its already diminished role in the world sugar market. In spite of increasing American capital investment, U.S. protectionist tariffs had already devastated Cuba's sugar economy. Cuban exports to the United States following the tariff of 1883 fell from $70 million in 1882 to $42 million in 1885. Since midwestern beet sugar producers made a 12 percent investment return from their government subsidies alone, a strong and growing anti-Cuban constituency in the Midwest opposed any ties—from reciprocity to annexation—that might endanger beet sugar profits. The reciprocity provisions of the McKinley Tariff of 1890 gave the Cuban sugar industry a brief respite before enactment of the Wilson-Gorman Tariff of 1894, which favored refined over raw sugar and eliminated the special reciprocity privileges, thereby virtually wiping out the Cuban sugar industry and helping precipitate a new civil war with Spain. Although American sugar politics continually played havoc with Cuba's fragile social and political structure, the enormous diversity of American sugar interests precluded any possibility of unity. These different interests were suspicious of each other, worked at cross-purposes, and, indeed, because of heavy European investments, were only partly American.[5]

Cuba's second war for independence against Spain began on February 24, 1895, and gathered momentum in April, when workers freed after the sugar harvest joined the insurgency as many exiled leaders of the independence movement returned to the island. When José Martí, the intellectual revolutionary leader, now major general in the Liberation Army, was killed in Oriente Province on May 19, 1895, *Cuba Libre* died a cruel premature death. Martí's genius lay not so much in the idea of Cuban independence, a dedication he shared with many other Cuban leaders, but in his metaphysical vision of unification after military victory. Martí's "redemptive revolution," directed against

---

Control," in Robert P. Weller and Scott E. Guggenheim (eds.), *Power and Protest in the Countryside* (Durham, N.C., 1982), 60–61; Weigle, "Sugar Interests," 2–3; Thomas, *Cuba,* 457.

5. Weigle, "Sugar Interests," 2–3, 19, 179; Fitzgibbon, *Cuba and the United States,* 14; Jenks, *Our Cuban Colony,* 40.

both Spain and Cuba's colonial situation, was a forceful and revolutionary poetic metaphor that transformed the bleak economic and political prospects of a ruined island into a magnificent political work of art. Martí made the insurrection into a revolution. Had he lived, Cuba's fate might have been far different. Martí's understanding of the international context of Cuba's problems suggests that a military victory over Spain might have been the beginning rather than the end of Martí's and Cuba's thirty-year revolution. "I called up the war. My responsibility begins rather than ends with it," Martí wrote two months before his death. Martí's death was a historical catastrophe that led first to the grisly irony of Theodore Roosevelt's charge up San Juan Hill—the main historical metaphor of Cuba freed—and the passing of Cuba's revolutionary leadership to Tomás Estrada Palma, a man who might have been better suited as a president of the United States than as the leader of an independent post-revolutionary Cuba.[6]

Cuba's second war for independence produced an entirely new political elite—*políticos*—independent of the existing major classes of landowners, peasants, and workers. By relying on *personalissmo* and xenophobia, political metaphors useful during a revolution, *políticos* made guerrilla warfare Cuba's most enduring political heritage and failed to deal with the postrevolutionary problem of achieving political independence from the United States or cultural freedom from Spain. Many Americans, though uneasy at the visible and rapid disintegration of Cuba's society and the end of the system of benign Spanish control the United States favored and relied on, hoped that direct

6. A useful Martí chronology is in José Martí, *On Art and Literature: Critical Writings,* ed. Philip Foner (New York, 1982), 342; Louis A. Perez Jr., *Cuba Between Empires, 1878–1902* (Pittsburgh, 1983), 108–10, 385–86; José Martí to Federico Henríquez y Carvajal, March 25, 1895, *ibid.,* 90; Chapman, *History of the Cuban Republic,* 159; John M. Kirk, "José Martí and the United States: A Further Interpretation," *Journal of Latin American Studies,* IX (1977), 275–90; Kirk, *José Martí: Mentor of the Cuban Nation* (Tampa, 1983); Manuel Pedro Gonzales, *José Martí: Epic Chronicler of the United States in the Eighties* (Chapel Hill, 1953); Roberta Day Corbitt, "This Colossal Theater: The United States Interpreted by José Martí" (Ph.D. dissertation, University of Kentucky, 1955); Robert Roland Anderson, *Spanish American Modernism: A Selected Bibliography* (Tucson, 1970), 107–28. For Cuba's separation from Spain see Gerald E. Poyo, "Evolution of Cuban Separatist Thought in the Emigré Communities of the United States, 1848–1895," *HAHR,* LXVI (1986), 486–507. For a useful historiographical summary see Duvon C. Corbitt, "Cuban Revisionist Interpretations of Cuba's Struggle for Independence," *HAHR,* XLIII (1963), 395–404. Though often exasperating, Philip S. Foner, *The Spanish-Cuban-American War and the Birth of American Imperialism, 1895–1902* (2 vols.; New York, 1972) is the most comprehensive history of the war. For a perceptive analysis of Martí's role and later Protestant-Catholic cultural friction see C. A. M. Hennessy, "The Roots of Cuban Nationalism," *International Affairs,* XXXIX (1963), esp. 345–53.

intervention could be avoided. Theodore Roosevelt's feelings about war are more complex than his eagerly bellicose letters suggest. Roosevelt, like Martí, believed that fighting in wars was the responsibility of all classes, not just the young or the poor. As an early advocate of American intervention, Roosevelt felt that the price of his advocacy was participation in the war, especially risking his life. Fighting and even dying were not only terrible risks, they were inconvenient interruptions of life, for politicians, intellectuals, and businessmen alike. Martí's fate was Roosevelt's risk, and both men were fully aware of the stakes and the threat to their personal credibility (to themselves as much as to the public) if they evaded the call to duty. Whether Roosevelt enjoyed the fighting is irrelevant. The ebullience and bravado of the warrior and revolutionary is an essential ingredient of the heroic process. Sensible and rational men do not court war or death and rarely become heroes. For Roosevelt heroism was a part of an aristocratic sense of duty, a motivation that made his wartime volunteer service profoundly anti-heroic. Even more impressive was the miracle that enabled the Rough Rider to elude the storm of bullets that should have killed or wounded him as he charged up the Cuban hill in face of a murderous Spanish fusillade.[7]

On March 19, 1895, though Roosevelt thought a war with Spain was "very improbable," he formally applied to Governor Levi Morton for "a commission in the [New York militia] force that goes to Cuba." In a resolution passed on April 6, 1896, the Senate urged recognition of Cuban independence, in effect urging a war with Spain; President Grover Cleveland proclaimed American neutrality when he formally recognized the rebellion's existence. Roosevelt, still New York City police commissioner, and Henry Cabot Lodge, two major proponents of American intervention, favored Cuban independence over continued Spanish misrule. Roosevelt wanted "to really interfere in Cuba" and "drive the Spaniards out" and also to establish as an American policy "the ultimate removal of all European powers from the colonies they hold in the Western hemisphere." At the end of 1896, Roosevelt,

7. Millet, *Politics of Intervention*, 22–23; for Roosevelt see Richard H. Collin, *Theodore Roosevelt, Culture, Diplomacy, and Expansion* (Baton Rouge, 1985), 132–34; and Gerald F. Lindermann, *The Mirror of War: American Society and the Spanish-American War* (Ann Arbor, 1974), 91–113; and see esp. TR to William Sturges Bigelow, March 29, 1898, in *MRL*, II, 803; John P. Mallan, "Roosevelt, Brooks Adams, and Lea: The Warrior Critique of the Business Civilization," *AQ*, VIII (1956), 216–30. A stirring and useful account of the battle of San Juan Hill is in Edmund Morris, *The Rise of Theodore Roosevelt* (New York, 1979), 632–61.

who described himself as "a quietly rampant 'Cuba Libre' man," doubted Cuban abilities in self-government but thought "anything would be better than the continuance of Spanish rule." Roosevelt thought that Cleveland should send the fleet, recognize Cuban independence, and accept the losses that "would be thrice over repaid by the ultimate results of our action." War with Spain, he argued, would neither strain the nation nor dampen prosperity. By the end of 1897, Roosevelt, now assistant secretary of the navy under President McKinley, was more measured. "Not sure" that Spain could pacify Cuba, Roosevelt thought "interfering"—his customary word—was inevitable "if the insurrection goes on much longer." But Germany, not Spain, had become Roosevelt's main concern.[8]

Unlike Lodge, Roosevelt never wavered in his support of Cuban independence regardless of whether the United States intervened: "There is absolutely but one possible solution of a permanent nature to that affair, and that is Cuban independence. The sooner we make up our minds to this the better. If we can attain our object peacefully, of course we should try to do so." By March, 1898, Roosevelt felt "so deeply that it is with great difficulty I can restrain myself." Convinced that the *Maine* was destroyed "by an act of dirty treachery on the part of the Spaniards," Roosevelt wanted McKinley "to order the fleet to Havana tomorrow." Roosevelt's frustration was compounded by the attitude of senators who argued that the surest way to prevent battleships from being sunk was not to have any battleships.[9]

Spanish, Cuban, and American domestic politics all affected the ebb and flow of crisis and calm that preceded American intervention against Spain in Cuba. The idea that Spain might sell either Cuba or Cuba's independence to the United States was considered, then rejected. German activities in Asia and the Caribbean underlined both Cuba's strategic significance and its vulnerability. Whereas McKinley tried to win a Spanish-Cuban-American settlement through painstaking and patient diplomacy, Roosevelt saw advantages to a war that

8. TR to Levi Morton, March 19, 1895; to Anna Cowles, March 30, 1896, January 2, 1897; to William Cowles, April 5, 1896; to HCL, December 4, 1896; to William Wirt Kimball, December 17, 1897, all in *MRL*, I, 436, 522, 573–74, 524, 567, 743; see also *ibid.*, 504 n.; see HCL to Moreton Frewen, March 11, 1896, in John Garraty, *Henry Cabot Lodge* (New York, 1953), 181.

9. TR to Henry White, March 9, 1898; to Benjamin Dribble, February 16, 1898; to John Long, February 19, 1898, all in *MRL*, I, 791, 775, 780; for Lodge's "acquiring of additional territory," see HCL to Moreton Frewen, March 11, 1896, in Garraty, *Henry Cabot Lodge*, 181.

would give the United States "both St. Thomas and Hawaii," as well as a "moral lift." Only an unconditional Spanish acknowledgment of Cuban independence "within twenty-four hours" would satisfy Roosevelt on April 4, 1898. He was concerned that Spain had improved its navy and that fighting would occur during the "unhealthy season." Spain must make "the only amends possible for the loss of the *Maine* by at once leaving the western world." It was not possible "to higgle and barter and submit to arbitration." For Roosevelt, Spain's unwelcome European presence in Cuba and the *Maine*'s sinking coalesced into an almost revolutionary fervor. "The independence of Cuba and the driving of the Spaniard from American soil" were the only acceptable forms of Spanish "atonement," Roosevelt declared, railing against businessmen, who were concerned only that "the business situation be not disturbed." Actual and effective fighting, not merely serving, remained Roosevelt's goal. "If there is no serious land war I (of course) shall have to continue in my present place, because I shall be useless on a ship, and have no desire to form part of a garrison in a fort." When the war came, Roosevelt refused a command offered him by Secretary of War Russell A. Alger because he felt he did not know enough to command. Instead, he accepted a lieutenant colonel's commission with Colonel Leonard Wood's volunteer regiment of Rough Riders, which he hoped would get to fight in Cuba before the navy ended the war.[10]

Even during April, 1898, when war became more likely, President McKinley's diplomatic efforts to avoid intervention continued. McKinley, not the press or minor officials such as Theodore Roosevelt, was in full command of his government's foreign policy, but to prevent war he needed more cooperation from Spain and Cuba than either was politically able to offer. As a foreign war, a unique event, almost unthinkable for many Americans, seemed increasingly likely, Congress and the president grappled with the new importance of foreign policy in American government and how it would affect political

10. Lewis L. Gould, *The Presidency of William McKinley* (Lawrence, Kan., 1980), 75–77, 71; Alfred L. P. Dennis, *Adventures in American Diplomacy, 1896–1926* (New York, 1928), 63–100; TR to William Frye, March 31, 1898, in *MRL*, II, 806; see Walter LaFeber, *The New Empire: An Interpretation of American Expansion, 1860–1898* (Ithaca, N.Y., 1964), 354–406; John A. S. Grenville and George Berkeley Young, *Politics, Strategy, and American Diplomacy: Studies in Foreign Policy, 1873–1917* (New Haven, 1966), 257–60; TR to Benjamin F. Tracy, April 4, 1898; to Robert Bacon, April 5, 1898, both in *MRL*, II, 810–12; Henry Pringle, *Theodore Roosevelt: A Biography* (New York, 1931), 183–200; TR, *Autobiography* (1913), in *TRWN*, XX, 223–61.

power. A struggle between the president and Congress began in earnest over the war with Spain and lasted throughout Roosevelt's presidency. Henry M. Teller's amendment to guarantee Cuban independence and prohibit American annexation was a complex temporary political compromise between Congress and the president, in spite of its diction of idealism and self-denial. The Teller Amendment not only satisfied Teller's Colorado beet sugar constituency that wanted no part of Cuban sugar but reflected midwestern rural fears that Cuban annexation, directed by the chief executive as part of American foreign policy, might indirectly defeat the protective tariff in Cuba, a domestic issue of enormous weight for farming interests. Thus foreign policy, a relatively new political force in the United States, could be exploited by the chief executive and his party to upset the domestic political balance of power between eastern industrial capital and midwestern agriculture. Teller's amendment helped maintain the balance, and by precluding annexation, it protected the tariff and the beet sugar industry and reassured the large political constituency that feared amalgamation with Cuba's large Negro population. The Teller Amendment was a compromise that allowed the president to go to war but denied him a blank check.[11]

The United States did indeed have a "large policy" in 1898, but it was incremental and episodic, a result of the failure to find an accommodation with Spain, not the cause of the war. Had Spain met the American demands, there would have been no opportunities and no larger policy, at least for the moment. Cuba would have been spared being freed by North American intervention, the question of Hawaii as well as the Philippines would have remained part of the long-standing American debate between expansionists and those opposed, and Henry Cabot Lodge would not have had the occasion to reassure Roosevelt, fighting in Cuba, that "Porto Rico is not forgotten and we mean to have it." Roosevelt's demands were "Cuba being independent, Porto Rico ours and the Philippines taken away from Spain."

11. See Lewis Gould, "Chocolate Eclair or Mandarin Manipulator? William McKinley, the Spanish-American War, and the Philippines: A Review Essay," *Ohio History,* XCIV (1985), 183–84, 187; Joseph A. Fry, "William McKinley and the Coming of the Spanish-American War: A Study of the Besmirching and Redemption of an Historical Image," *DH,* III (1979), 77–98; John Offner, "President McKinley's Final Attempt to Avoid War with Spain," *Ohio History,* XCIV (1985), 125–38; Lester Langley, *The Cuban Policy of the United States: A Brief History* (New York, 1968), 109; Jules Robert Benjamin, *The United States and Cuba: Hegemony and Dependent Development, 1880–1934* (Pittsburgh, 1977), p. 194, n. 31.

The larger policy was not a policy at all until the war with Spain pushed a reluctant president into a world war that made Roosevelt's and Lodge's expansionist and activist foreign policy feasible. James Bryce, the British writer and diplomat, summed up the serendipity of the new large policy: "How stupendous a change in the world these six months have brought. Six months ago you no more thought of annexing the Philippine Isles and Porto Rico than you think of annexing Spitzbergen today." [12]

Cuba was in ruins. Towns were sacked, livestock was purposely slain and left to rot to deprive survivors of food and to spread disease, and cisterns were maliciously filled with manure by departing Spanish soldiers. The three-year revolution cost Cuba three hundred thousand lives directly and indirectly. In addition to the immense immediate wartime economic losses, the island was left with a staggering $500 million debt. Sixty percent of Cuba's surviving population was illiterate, and only 1 percent was college-educated. Havana, better off than the countryside, suffered fewer war losses and enjoyed a literacy rate of about 67 percent. During the process of its reluctant "relinquishment," Spain urged the United States to annex an island that it virtually assured was incapable of survival, let alone self-government. As 1898 closed, the only active force in Cuba was American troops under the command of newly promoted General Leonard Wood in Oriente province, where the doctor-general worked to institute basic sanitation, stop the spread of disease and starvation, and establish a rudimentary structure of government. On January 1, 1899, General John R. Brooke, an honest but unimaginative professional army administrator, became governor-general of Cuba. [13]

Cuba's problems in 1899 were sufficient to test the mettle of a man more gifted than General Brooke, who was approaching retirement

12. HCL to TR, May 24, 1898, in *Selections from the Correspondence of Theodore Roosevelt and Henry Cabot Lodge, 1884–1918* (2 vols.; New York, 1925), I, 299–300; Julius Pratt, "The 'Large Policy' of 1898," *MVHR*, XIX (1932), 219–42. On the acquisition of Hawaii see Gould, *Presidency of William McKinley*, 48–50, 98–99; HCL to TR, June 15, 1898, in Lodge (ed.), *Selections*, I, 311; TR to HCL, May 25, 1898, in *MRL*, II, 833; James Bryce to TR, September 12, 1898, in Joseph B. Bishop, *Theodore Roosevelt and His Times* (2 vols.; New York, 1920), I, 106. See Louis A. Pérez, Jr., "Insurrection, Intervention, and the Transformation of the Land Tenure Systems in Cuba, 1895–1902," *HAHR*, LXV (1985), 229–54.

13. Thomas, *Cuba*, 410; *ibid.*, 423, uses the three hundred thousand figure for losses from death and wartime unborn; Langley, *Cuban Policy of the United States*, 116; Thomas, *Cuba*, 432; Chapman, *History of the Cuban Republic*, 95–97; David Lockmiller, *Magoon in Cuba: A History of the Second Intervention, 1906–1909* (Westport, Conn., 1969), 6–7.

and ill equipped in intellect or sensitivity to deal with the massive cultural and political changes accompanying Cuba's transition from Spanish to North American governance. Brooke, an honest man, who maintained enough of the old Spanish and Cuban laws and bureaucrats to make the transition less radical, was reasonably successful in cleaning up the devastated country and alleviating some of the appalling postwar conditions. But Brooke gave too much power to the new Cuban *políticos* and did not supply enough initiative at a time when Cuba desperately needed inspired leadership. Theodore Roosevelt was "uneasy at the way things are going." Unlike Cuba, Puerto Rico had not suffered as a Spanish colony, and many Puerto Ricans regretted Spain's displacement by the United States. Roosevelt, then governor of New York, in a long letter dealing with American colonial policy, wrote Secretary of State John Hay that though Puerto Rico presented no danger to the United States through armed rebellion, it was still incumbent upon the Americans "to give it the best type of government." Cubans, Roosevelt counseled, must be handled "with a proper mixture of firmness, courtesy, and tact." He urged that Leonard Wood, then military governor at Santiago, who frequently clashed with Brooke, was "the ideal of a military administrator"—"a born diplomat, just as he is a born soldier." Roosevelt admired Wood's "peculiar facility for getting on with the Spaniards and Cubans," who, "like him, trust him, and down in their hearts are afraid of him." Wood, Roosevelt wrote, paid attention to "their sensitiveness and their spirit of punctilio," without sacrificing his firmness or leadership ability. McKinley, however, was still satisfied with Brooke, and in spite of Roosevelt's "long talk with the President," McKinley still believed "that things in Cuba are satisfactory." [14]

In July, 1899, McKinley made a brilliant appointment when he named Elihu Root his new secretary of war. Root, a corporation lawyer with no experience in foreign policy, told McKinley, "I know nothing about the army." Congressman Lemuel E. Quigg, McKinley's emissary, told Root, "He has got to have a lawyer to direct the government of these Spanish islands, and you are the lawyer he wants." Roosevelt was disappointed because the president chose a lawyer

14. See Fitzgibbon, *Cuba and the United States,* 32; Lockmiller, *Magoon in Cuba,* 6–7; Langley, *Cuban Policy of the United States,* 119; TR to JH, July 1, 1899; to Leonard Wood, July 10, 1899, both in *MRL,* II, 1025–28, 1032. See Lejune Cummins, "The Origin and Development of Elihu Root's Latin American Diplomacy" (Ph.D. dissertation, University of California, Berkeley, 1964).

over a general, passing over James Wilson, Roosevelt's preference for the post, and also because McKinley still believed that "General Brooke is the right man." Roosevelt urged McKinley and Root separately to promote Wood and give him control of Cuba. On December 13, 1899, when Root appointed Wood military governor of Cuba, Wood instituted a program of constructive paternalism that, as even most Cuban critics of American intervention concede, gave Cuba the best government it ever had.[15]

Although Wood's efforts to transform "a race that has been steadily going downhill for a hundred years" into an ideal progressive middle-class American society were doomed, his policies provided Cuba with substantial immediate material gains. Although mistaken for an American annexationist, Wood opposed annexation and favored Cuban independence but feared that Cuba was not ready for self-government. Wood's self-professed goal, "the building up of a republic, by Anglo-Saxons, in a Latin country," could not transform a transitional Cuban society, caught between Spain and North America, the nineteenth and twentieth centuries, and its emergence from colonialism to semi-independence. Yet Wood's introduction of American energy and efficiency may have helped the difficult transition from colony to state. A Cuban verse parody of Wood's "Rules of the Office" captured the interaction of sensibilities:

> Don't eat, don't spit;
> Don't scratch, don't smoke;
> Arrive very early;
> Depart almost by night.
> There is no time for lunch
> Nor anything other than working;
> He who wishes to work here
> Is he who wishes to die.

Wood, more a medical missionary than a soldier, eradicated yellow fever, imposed strict sanitation procedures, by force when necessary, and lowered the military mortality rate in Cuba from 67.94 per thousand in 1898 to 1.76 per thousand in 1902. Wood also reformed the

15. Philip Jessup, *Elihu Root* (2 vols.; New York, 1938), I, 216–26, 286–87; TR to James Wilson, July 25, August 21, 1899; to Leonard Wood, August 28, September 4, 1899; to ER, September 2, 4, 1899, all in *MRL,* II, 1041, 1061–62, 1066; Langley, *Cuban Policy of the United States,* 115, uses the term *progressive paternalism;* Lockmiller, *Magoon in Cuba,* 9; see ER to Charles W. Eliot, May 4, 1900, in Jessup, *Elihu Root,* I, 287–88.

legal system; introduced an educational system in a country where not a single schoolhouse existed after the revolution; built public works, including buildings, roads, railroads, and harbor improvements; restocked Cuba's depleted livestock; and even founded a national library. A colonial administrator compared to Britain's renowned Lord Curzon and France's Louis Lyautey, Wood was admiringly described by an American congressman as the man "who found Cuba a den of filth and disease and left it a sewer system."[16]

Wood's autocratic rule was based on the American presumption that economic development produced political stability and that law and order generated prosperity and civilization. But in the process of trying to make Cuba a progressive North American society, the Americans unwittingly clashed not only with Hispanic and Hispanic-American culture but, in both the Philippines and Cuba, with an established Catholic church. One of Theodore Roosevelt's most unusual roles was his service as sympathetic mediator in the cultural conflicts involving traditional unestablished American Protestantism, the unique and highly fragmented American Catholic church, and the anticlerical established Catholicism of the Spanish islands. Questions about Cuba's marriage law caused the first conflict, mostly from cultural misunderstanding among Catholics. Cubans, who widely practiced consensual marriage to avoid the expense of an ecclesiastical ceremony, approved General Brooke's May 31, 1899, order that made civil marriage in Cuba legal, as it was in the United States. Cuba's Catholic hierarchy objected, and the newly awakened American Catholic church assumed that Brooke's order was an anti-Catholic intervention by a Protestant-inspired military government. Until the new American civil responsibilities in the Spanish Catholic islands made the unique character of American Catholicism impossible for the Vatican to continue to ignore, the American Catholic church was a prime

16. Leonard Wood to William McKinley, April 12, 1900, in Thomas, *Cuba*, 445; see Jack C. Lane, *Armed Progressive: General Leonard Wood* (San Rafael, Calif., 1978), 102–13, 100; James H. Hitchman, "The Platt Amendment Revisited: A Bibliographical Survey," *Americas*, XXXIII (1967), 366–67; Leonard Wood, "Civil Report for 1902," pt. I, 217, quoted in Thomas, *Cuba*, 415; see Leo S. Rowe, "The Reorganization of Local Government in Cuba," *Annals of the American Academy of Political and Social Science*, C (May, 1905), 100; Fitzgibbon, *Cuba and the United States*, 31 n., 30–66; Langley, *Cuban Policy of the United States*, 120. For Wood's impressive accomplishments in Oriente, see Thomas, *Cuba*, 411; Indiana Congressman Charles Scott (praising Wood) in "Civil Report of General Wood, 1900," p. 9, quoted in Lane, *Armed Progressive*, 100. See Lester D. Langley, *The Banana Wars: An Inner History of American Empire, 1900–1934* (Lexington, Ky., 1983), 11–19.

example of exceptionalism, easier for the Vatican to tolerate than to try to change. American governance over the Catholic Spanish islands presented the United States and the Catholic church with a vexing series of dilemmas. Through his many Catholic correspondents, including leading members of the American clergy, Roosevelt was able to help newly aware American Catholics cope with the anticlericalism of America's new Catholic protectorates.[17]

Both McKinley and Roosevelt were extremely sensitive to these religious problems, and eventually the Americans made peace, more easily with the Catholic islanders than with the American Catholic establishment. When Roosevelt told one of his Catholic correspondents that "the chance for bettering the Catholic inhabitants of the tropic islands lies by bringing them up to the highest standard of American catholicism," he was offering a sensitive means of allowing Spanish Catholics to adapt to their new competitive, progressive, and unestablished Protestant culture. Until the occupation of the Spanish islands, a fractionalized American Catholicism, reflecting its mixed ethnic background, was more aware of its national origins than its religious commonality. When established Spanish Catholicism seemingly confronted Protestant missionary zeal, the American Catholic press suddenly became the watchdog of world Catholicism without comprehending the vast differences between the unorthodox American church and its anticlerical formerly Spanish counterparts. Roosevelt urged Wood to repeal the marriage law, acknowledging it to be "very delicate and arduous work." On August 8, Wood satisfied the Cubans as well as the American Catholics by providing that marriages could be either civil or ecclesiastical.[18]

Wood wisely decided against recruiting American teachers to rebuild Cuba's educational structure and instead sent 1,300 Cuban schoolteachers and 125 professors, mostly from the University of Havana, on five transports for a six-week summer study program at Harvard University. This admirable exercise in efficient sensibility almost came undone when Boston and Cambridge temperance so-

17. Langley, *Cuban Policy of the United States*, 121; Frank T. Reuter, *Catholic Influence on American Colonial Policies, 1898–1904* (Austin, Tex., 1967), esp. 22–27. For Latin American anticlericalism see J. Lloyd Mecham, *Church and State in Latin America* (rev. ed.; Chapel Hill, 1966), 416–28; Fitzgibbon, *Cuba and the United States*, 35–36.

18. Reuter, *Catholic Influence on American Colonial Policies*, 54; TR to Maria Storer, May 18, 1900, to Leonard Wood, August 3, 29, 1900; see TR to William McKinley, July 27, 1900; to William M. Byrne, August 1, 1900, all in *MRL*, II, 1298, 1367, 1369–72; Fitzgibbon, *Cuba and the United States*, 36.

cieties objected to the drinking habits of the Cuban teachers. Roosevelt thanked Harvard president Charles W. Eliot, who had raised $70,000 to entertain the Cuban guests and who defended them against the temperance objecters. When Bishop Donatus Sbaretti, an Italian, who became the head of the Cuban Catholic church, objected to the American termination of payments from church lands deeded to the Spanish crown, Wood in June, 1902, arranged for the Cubans to buy the lands at a reasonable price. The dispute was amicably settled when the United States paid the rent arrears recommended by Wood's specially convened commission.[19]

On July 25, 1900, when Wood ordered an election of delegates to frame a new constitution, many Cubans thought his action was motivated as much by the desire to keep the Cuban issue out of the 1900 American presidential election as it was to give Cuba an independent government. Cuban political groups, still rudimentary and uncertain of their future role or share of power, were as ambivalent as most American politicians about the country's future. Havana Nationalists favored a centralized republic, Santa Clara Republicans a states'-rights program, and Havana Union Democrats, compromised by their advocacy of home rule under Spain rather than outright independence, remained autonomists who felt that "Cuba is not well prepared for absolute independence." Cuban autonomists, whose views resembled some middle-road American opinion, believed "it is necessary to establish the government of the country in a way to bring about the preservation of order and peace through conservative and evolutionary processes." Even within the separate political groups, opinion was divided. Some autonomists favored annexation, others an American protectorate. While the Cuban constitutional convention debated its options, the American government began to consider how to implement its Cuban colonial policy. After extensive cabinet consultation, Elihu Root, in his memorandum to Secretary of State John Hay on January 11, 1901, first formulated what soon became the Platt Amendment. Although the Platt Amendment, the single most important definition of the evolving United States Caribbean policy, was debated for only two hours, and was amended and passed after only a one-hour Senate debate, by the time it reached the Senate floor, it was a well-honed, carefully modulated instrument that limited

19. Fitzgibbon, *Cuba and the United States* 48, 36–37; TR to Charles W. Eliot, July 14, 1900; to William McKinley, November 10, 1900; to Mark Hanna, November 10, 1900, all in *MRL*, II, 1355, 1413–14; *ibid.*, 1414n.

American expansion, accepted responsibility, and compromised the political extremes between altruism and annexation.[20]

Although both Root and Wood favored American withdrawal from Cuba, Root wanted it to happen faster than Wood, who feared the Cubans were unprepared for self-government. Root wanted to resolve "the question of the ultimate relations of this country to Cuba" so that a permanent Cuban government could take control from the withdrawing American military authorities. Root's formulation reserved for the United States the right of intervention, continued superintendence of Cuba's treaty-making powers, provision for an unspecified number of naval stations, and Cuban ratification of laws enacted under the American military governorship. In a separate letter to Wood of January 9 attached to a memorandum, Root revealed the motivation for his carefully structured policy when he warned that "in international affairs the existence of a right recognized by international law is of the utmost importance." Although Root was eager to give Cuba its independence, he made it clear that Cuba would not be permitted to deal away America's binding responsibility to guarantee Cuban independence, a right and a duty that legally originated from Spain's relinquishment of sovereignty in the Treaty of Paris. The American Cuban obligation, Root believed, "should never be terminated, but should be continued with a reservation, with the consent of the Cuban people, at the time when the authority which we now exercise is placed in their hands."[21]

Root worried about possible German interference if Cuba were left completely independent. "You cannot understand the Platt Amendment unless you know something about the character of Kaiser Wilhelm the Second," he wrote years later. Aware that "the Monroe Doctrine is not a part of international law and has never been recognized by European nations," Root wanted to avoid a "war in support of that doctrine" should a European power challenge it. To view the Platt Amendment as a simple American expediency for expansion or as a

20. Lockmiller, *Magoon in Cuba*, 12; David Healy, *The United States in Cuba, 1898–1902* (Madison, Wisc., 1963), 164–67, 214; Chapman, *History of the Cuban Republic*, 130–31; quote from *El Nuevo Pais, ibid.*, 131; Dennis, *Adventures in American Diplomacy*, 261; Gould, *Presidency of William McKinley*, 237; Jessup, *Elihu Root*, I, 308–309. Lejune Cummins, "The Formulation of the 'Platt' Amendment," *Americas*, XXXIII (1967), 370–89, is the most detailed treatment of the Platt drafts.

21. ER to JH, January 11, 1901; to Leonard Wood, January 9, 1901, both in Elihu Root Papers, LC; Hitchman, "Platt Amendment Revisited," 367; Dennis, *Adventures in Diplomacy*, 262.

retreat from the idealism of the Teller Amendment ignores Root's other concerns that included foreclosing the possibility of future American annexation and protecting the Spanish who chose to remain in Cuba but feared Cuban retaliation when the United States left. The Cuban constitutional convention that began on November 5, 1900, in Havana, worked undisturbed by General Wood to prepare a constitution that separated church and state and provided for universal suffrage, provisions the Cubans expected the Americans to reject as too radical. Although Root did not like many of the Cuban provisions, he did not object to those the Cubans had already decided on but made it clear that the United States' rights as "guarantors of Cuban independence and . . . stable and orderly government protecting life and property in that island" must be preserved in the constitution.[22]

Root, the lawyer William McKinley chose specifically to establish American colonial policy, insisted that the United States' Cuban policy—the Platt Amendment—be made of legal cement. To make the amendment virtually irrevocable, Root designed a tripartiate arrangement in which it was embedded in the Cuban constitution, enacted in United States law, and ratified as a United States–Cuban treaty. To make his policy work, Root had to win acceptance not only from the American Senate but from the Cuban constitutional convention, two bodies that viewed treaties originating in the executive branch of the American government with almost equal suspicion. After Senator Orville H. Platt convened the Republican members of his Senate Cuban Relations Committee on February 3, President McKinley approved the text produced by Senators Platt and John Coit Spooner on February 8. The next day Root sent Wood the agreement that the president and Senate Republican leaders approved, in substance Root's five original points with stylistic changes. Because Root and McKinley had already established a consensus in the Senate, the Platt Amendment, attached to a routine appropriations bill, passed with little debate.[23]

22. ER to Philip Jessup, December 20, 1934, in Jessup, *Elihu Root*, I, 314–15; ER to Leonard Wood, January 9, 1901, in Root Papers; Chapman, *History of the Cuban Republic*, 134–35; ER to Wood, February 9, 1901, in Elihu Root, *The Military and Colonial Policy of the United States* (Cambridge, Mass., 1916), 210. See William Roger Adams, "Strategy, Diplomacy, and Isthmian Canal Security, 1880–1917" (Ph.D. dissertation, Florida State University, 1974), 257–58.

23. Lockmiller, *Magoon in Cuba*, 14; Gould, *Presidency of William McKinley*, 238–39.

The Platt Amendment was controversial in both the United States and Cuba, and a bitter battle occurred over its inclusion in the new Cuban constitution. The main Cuban objections centered on Article III, the American "right to intervene for the preservation of Cuban independence, the maintenance of a government adequate for the protection of life, property, and individual liberty." When the Platt Amendment was first presented, the Cuban constitutional convention rejected it by a vote of twenty-four to two and sent a committee to Washington to negotiate the differences.[24]

The main differences centered on questions of Cuban sovereignty. Cubans felt Platt limited their sovereignty; Root insisted that it was intended to do just the opposite. Domestic Cuban politics accounted for some of the appearance of resistance to Platt. Since sentiment for complete independence remained popular, radicals could always challenge any arrangement with the United States. Because the Platt Amendment did limit Cuban sovereignty, some opposition delegates told Wood that they favored it but had to oppose it publicly for political reasons. Some Cubans were willing to vote for Platt if the United States demanded that they do so but were afraid to seem too complaisant. How much the "extreme element" or the American agitators contributed to the demonstrations and protest resolutions in Cuba during the Platt debate is impossible to say. Root saw the main danger not in Cuban rejection of Platt but in the convention dissolving without voting on the amendment or continuing negotiation, a distinct possibility in the volatile political climate of the debate in Cuba.[25]

Root reassured the Cubans that the United States had no intention of "intermeddling or interference" in their affairs. The Platt Amendment "gives to the United States no right which she does not already possess and which she would not exercise, but it gives her, for the benefit of Cuba, a standing as between herself and foreign nations in the exercise of that right which may be of immense value in enabling the United States to protect the independence of Cuba." Root agreed to other modifications the Cubans desired, and on April 25 and 26 he met with the five members of the committee sent by the constitutional convention. Wood had advised Root that the committee would accept Platt, but "this must not even be intimated." Root insisted that Article

24. See Hitchman, "Platt Amendment Revisited," 344; Chapman, *History of the Cuban Republic,* 139–43.
25. Jessup, *Elihu Root,* I, 316; Leonard Wood to ER, March 2, 1901, in Root Papers; Healy, *United States in Cuba,* 168–69.

III as well as Article VII, which established American naval coaling stations, were not intended for selfish American purposes or to facilitate intervention in Cuban affairs but to protect American waters from foreign attack. Senator Platt, in an extraordinary personal appearance, assured the Cuban committee that he and the Senate had not intended to establish a protectorate or suzerainty over Cuba and that the amendment's "well defined purpose is to secure and safeguard Cuban independence."[26]

When the Cuban constitutional convention voted on inclusion of the Platt Amendment in the new constitution, it approved a substantially modified draft by a narrow fifteen to fourteen vote. Although Root did not object to the meaning of explanatory phrases the Cubans added to the version of the Platt Amendment to be incorporated in the Cuban constitution, he feared that any differences raised future legal problems of interpretation. What often appears as American intransigence, not only with Cuba but in the Panama negotiations as well, was instead an awareness of how fragile executive-Senate agreements could be and of the political problems involved in renegotiating American Senate reapproval of any changes—in diction or substance—made by a foreign government. McKinley, well aware of senatorial prerogatives, rights, and sensitivity, told Root that any changes "should be submitted in advance of its adoption to senators Platt and Spooner." Wood at first accepted the addition of Cuban interpretations. Root, dissatisfied with "the cloud of words," was annoyed that the Cubans had included as part of their text of the law not only Root's informal assurances and interpretations, which were inappropriate, but serious substantive changes that made the coaling stations dependent on a new reciprocity agreement and claimed the Isle of Pines for Cuba, rather than allowing it to be negotiated separately as previously agreed. Although the Cubans held political demonstrations against the Platt Amendment, which Wood tried to minimize, the Cuban proposals that Root rejected reflected Cuban domestic politics as much as they did a serious rejection of the Platt Amendment. The Platt issue was largely ignored in the peaceful Cuban municipal elections of June 1, 1901.[27]

---

26. ER to Leonard Wood, March 29, 1901; Wood to ER, April 15, 1901; Orville Platt to ER, April 26, 1901, all in Jessup, *Elihu Root*, I, 316–20.

27. Chapman, *History of the Cuban Republic*, 142; Leonard Wood to ER, ER to Wood, May 17, 1901; William McKinley to ER, May 19, 1901, all in Jessup, *Elihu Root*, I, 321–23; Healy, *United States in Cuba*, 168–69.

Root reassured a concerned Theodore Roosevelt and placed the dispute in its correct political perspective. When the Cuban committee was in Washington, it had been ready to accept Platt "without any substantial amendment," but afterward, "for the purpose of getting votes, they loaded it down with a great variety of explanations, which really changed the meaning, and they also did a very improper thing in putting into their resolutions a lot of statements which they claim to have been made by me, which I object to chiefly because they make me appear to say stupid and foolish things." Root was frustrated by the Cuban failure to understand that he could not change any part of a law already passed by Congress. Root's explanations and glosses on the meaning and intention of the law were meant to assure the Cubans of American good faith and to limit future less benign American readings of Platt, not to reopen the issue with the American Senate. The problem intensified on June 6, when Wood, fearful that Root's detailed explanations of his rejection might encourage further debate, submitted only selected passages to the Cuban convention. The Cubans, pressured by American insistence on the exact American wording, and probably assuaged by the assurance of a future reciprocity agreement, finally adopted an unchanged Platt Amendment on June 12 by a sixteen to eleven vote. The treaty incorporating the Platt Amendment, which Root had insisted upon to eliminate any loopholes or unilateral modifications, was not finally ratified until June 25, 1904.[28]

In spite of its mixed historical reception, the Platt Amendment was a complex, uniquely American colonial compromise, meant to encourage Cuban independence while preserving American strategic interests. Since the United States and especially its Congress were severely divided on how Cuba would best serve American economic interests, economics was not a primary consideration in the genesis or initial negotiations of the Platt Amendment. Nor was Cuba as utterly opposed to Platt as the debate and the quibbling made it appear. The heated Cuban debate demonstrated the American good faith that allowed the Cubans full freedom to write a constitution and establish their own government. There was little chance that any Cuban political group or constitutional convention would reject an American accord because a constant and vocal minority favoring annexation re-

28. TR to ER, June 1, 1901, in *MRL,* III, 85; ER to TR, June 4, 1901; to Leonard Wood, May 28, 1901, both in Jessup, *Elihu Root,* I, 322–23; Fitzgibbon, *Cuba and the United States,* 84–85; Healy, *United States in Cuba,* 172–73.

mained active and influential enough to prevent complete rejection of an American arrangement.[29]

Cuban moderates and conservatives controlled enough votes in the constitutional convention to prevent an outright rejection of Platt. When the Cuban convention sent its committee to Washington, only six of the thirty-one delegates opposed an American arrangement. McKinley, Wood, Root, and Platt were willing to negotiate patiently with the Cubans. Annoyance at Cuban political maneuvers did not dilute American acceptance of Cuban political equality and independence. The Cuban constitutional convention was no more stormy than American state conventions of the time, especially Arizona's radical double constitutional convention of 1912. Platt was not a cure-all for Cuba's basic problems, which were rooted in an unsound sugar economy that no American alliance, Platt or reciprocity, could cure. The Platt Amendment, as it was intended to do, gave Cuba breathing space, allowed it to form a transition government, and prevented an immediate threat to life, liberty, and property "by the quarrels of political factions." Both nations accommodated to their political traditions. As political factionalism contributed to Cuba's divisive society in the early 1900s, so the tradition of guarantees of security for industrial and commercial development influenced North American preferences in relations with Cuba.[30]

Although the Platt Amendment preserved a measure of Cuban sovereignty by giving it "quasi-independence" and represented a marked improvement over Europe's previous colonial policies, it also fastened a permanent psychological dependency on Cuba, which was exacerbated by the "capricious interpretations" of later American governments. In a remarkable prediction of the course of future American intervention, Senator Joseph Foraker objected that Article III would "invite intervention," rather than prevent it: "Suppose they have an election. One party or the other will be defeated. The party that is out

29. See Pérez, *Cuba Between Empires*, 350–51, for a summary of the economic conspiracy view. For an example of how Roosevelt's economic arguments to win congressional support ("it is eminently for our interests to control the Cuban market") is cited as evidence of the primacy of his economic motives in Cuba see Luis Aguilar, "Cuba, c. 1870–1940," *CHLA*, V, 245.

30. Philip G. Wright, *The Cuban Situation and Our Treaty Relations* (Washington, D.C., 1932), 31; Pedro Capó Rodríguez, "The Platt Amendment," *American Journal of International Law*, XVII (1923), 761–65; Gay Calbó, "Génesis de la enmienda Platt," *Cuba Contemporánea*, XL (May, 1926), 47–63, all in Hitchman, "Platt Amendment Revisited," 365 n., 365, 362, 351.

is liable to complain . . . by making trouble they would make a condition that would lead to an intervention of the United States." Foraker, however, did not propose that the United States give up the right of intervention but only that the diction allowing intervention be modified, an amendment the Senate rejected.[31]

Although the Platt Amendment gave the United States a continuing sense of its obligation to protect Cuba, disagreements continued on what and when to protect. Many Cubans hoped Platt would be used as a cure after trouble began, whereas Americans invoked it as a preventive measure before trouble actually occurred. Some Cubans thought the United States policy reflected misguided altruism. "You handed us a loaded pistol, knowing we would shoot ourselves," one Cuban complained in 1902. The Platt Amendment, a complex compromise that satisfied American anti-imperialists, Root, and McKinley and provided the United States, in Platt's words, with "a sufficiently effective position in Cuba," went as far as Cuba would allow without American coercion. The result of a political process in both the United States Senate and the Cuban constitutional convention, the Platt Amendment was a political compromise that fully satisfied almost no one and proved minimally acceptable to Cubans and Americans alike.[32]

The Platt Amendment's limitation on Cuban independence confirmed Cuba's political fate. Spain's expulsion from Cuba marked the culmination of Cuban revolutionary politics, not the beginning of an independent Cuba. After Spain's defeat, Cuban political unity disintegrated, as the United States, its ally in the expulsion of Spain, became a major distraction in Cuban domestic politics. The militancy that flourished during the thirty-year war produced a society in which political toleration was neither valued, practiced, nor understood. When Wood and the Americans left on May 20, 1902, neither the American occupation nor the withdrawal could be considered a complete success or an utter failure. Wood's efficient autocracy established a fundamental operating government in Cuba but no political basis on which to build, leading some Cubans to suggest that Wood might have made an ideal Cuban president. Wood had left Cuba's Spanish culture intact, ended the danger of yellow fever, instituted

31. Parker Moon, *Imperialism and World Politics* (New York, 1936), 419–20; Fitzgibbon, *Cuba and the United States,* 93; Joseph B. Foraker, *Notes of a Busy Life* (2 vols.; Cincinnati, 1916), II, 54–55; Langley, *Cuban Policy of the United States,* 123.

32. Lockmiller, *Magoon in Cuba,* 14; Hitchman, "Platt Amendment Revisited," 359; Healy, *United States in Cuba,* 167.

the protections of due process and *habeas corpus*, and, in leaving, astonished a skeptical world unused to the voluntary relinquishment of power. Cuba had survived, but it could not thrive. There could be no ideal solutions for the devastated island's attempt to comply with the North American vision of an ordered economic and political life, realistically impossible in a Third World society utterly dependent on trade with developed nations in a competitive world market.[33]

Cuba had won freedom from Spain, but though it was encouraged by American political idealism, Wood's impressive accomplishments, and Cuba's own romantic revolutionary fervor, complete economic or political independence was not a realistic possibility. James Bryce, the British diplomat and political writer, understood the difficulties Cuba faced: "Debts beyond the power of Cuba to pay may be incurred. Sanitation may be neglected. . . . There may be civil strife, or disorders . . . the Executive cannot suppress. . . . The judiciary [may] . . . fail to protect the rights of property." Although it was not on Bryce's formidable list of dangers, Cuban fresh fruit was exported to United States markets while Cubans ate imported American canned fruit, canned tomatoes, and even canned milk. The world context, not just the United States, contributed to the dire economic prospects that diminished Cuba's political and social hope. Both European and American beet sugar manufacturers, encouraged by the removal of Cuban sugarcane crops during the war with Spain, had increased their beet sugar capacity. Between 1896 and 1902, new American investment of $21 million produced thirty-five new American beet sugar factories. Cuba's contribution to the world sugar market, already diminished by war, dropped from about 13 percent to 3.5 percent. Competition with a beet sugar industry that was subsidized by bounties and protectionism kept sugar prices so low that Cuba's cane sugar traditions and its memories of past prosperity provided a false hope for future economic salvation.[34]

Tomás Estrada Palma, a distinguished Cuban revolutionary with strong American ties and sympathies, was elected the first president of the new Cuban republic without organized political opposition. Estrada Palma, who assumed leadership of the Partido Revolucionario

33. Perez, *Cuba Between Empires*, 376; Rafael Martínez Ortiz, *Cuba, los prieros años de independencia* (2 vols., 3rd ed.; Paris, 1929), 288–91; Hitchman, "Platt Amendment Revisited," 349; Chapman, *History of the Cuban Republic*, 148; Thomas, *Cuba*, 461.

34. James Bryce, "Some Reflections on the State of Cuba," *NAR*, CLXXIV (1902), 445–46; Thomas, *Cuba*, 503, 438; Jenks, *Our Cuban Colony*, 129.

Cubano (PRC) after Martí's death, radically changed Cuban revolutionary strategy from Martí's insistence on Cuban primacy to alliance with and dependence on the United States. Estrada Palma predicated his strategy on using United States intervention to put enough pressure on Spain to force it to give up its Cuban fight, a complete departure from Martí's insistence that Cuba's independence must be achieved by Cuban arms with only limited and secondary American help. Although he was an authentic and effective Cuban patriot, Estrada Palma represented the polar opposite from Martí's passionate Cuban nationalism and his radical revolutionary genius. A naturalized American citizen, who taught school in upstate New York in the 1880s and 1890s, he acquired his diplomatic preferences for alliance with the United States while leading the New York junta after Martí's death. When he assumed the Cuban presidency, Estrada Palma was "more plattish than Platt himself." [35]

Cuba's first president, known affectionately as Don Tomás, was a conservative who favored eventual American annexation after an initial ten-year period of independence. Although he was a genuine political independent, Estrada Palma installed a coalition cabinet and relied heavily on conservative support. By no means an American puppet, though Roosevelt and Root regarded him as a model president, the Cuban leader managed to dissuade the Americans from their initial plan for four naval stations to two and eventually to an enlarged single naval base at Guantánamo. Estrada Palma husbanded Cuba's scarce resources, budgeted 25 percent of government expenditures for education, and resolutely refused to trade a treasury surplus, painstakingly accumulated, for the safeguard of an army, probably his most damaging mistake. Estrada Palma's benign, independent, though partisan, style of government led to a severe political factionalization in Congress and eventually resulted in the stalemate and paralysis of a government that was as inflexible and stubborn as its leader. [36]

Domestic politics, not an expansionist foreign policy, was at the center of Theodore Roosevelt's struggle with Congress over the pro-

35. Perez, *Cuba Between Empires,* 110–11; Benjamin, *United States and Cuba,* 199, n. 34. For the view that Estrada Palma fulfilled Martí's promise and that Martí's martyrdom helped rather than hindered the Cuban cause, see Chapman, *History of the Cuban Republic,* 77; Luis Araquistain, *La Agonia Antillana* (Madrid, 1928), 234; Fitzgibbon, *Cuba and the United States,* 112.

36. Chapman, *History of the Cuban Republic,* 166, 159, 161; Fitzgibbon, *Cuba and the United States,* 108, 112, 105; Lockmiller, *Magoon in Cuba,* 38, 26–27.

posed American-Cuban reciprocity treaty. The Cuban reciprocity debate offers a classic demonstration of the complicated intertwining of
Cuban and American domestic politics. Reciprocity, the favored treatment of Cuban sugar imports and American manufactured exports,
originated in Cuban public demands and became a bargaining issue
in American negotiations with the Cuban constitutional convention.
Eventually the effects of the reciprocity agreement stifled the Cuban
economy by making it completely dependent on the United States,
discouraging not only competitive trade with Europe but any possibility of a varied Cuban agriculture or domestic industrial development. Sugar more than the United States was the cause of Cuba's
problem. Although American sugar consumption had increased as-
tronomically by 1902, the new world sugar technology made Cuba's
cane sugar economically obsolete. Europe's subsidized beet sugar had
so depressed the world market price that Cuba's first postwar sugar
crop in 1902, though it doubled the 1901 harvest, earned two cents a
pound less than the already low 1901 price. Recovery of Cuba's sugar
production was not self-generated but mainly produced by American
investors, concerned over Cuba's plight and genuinely sympathetic,
who poured their money into the Cuban sugar economy to restore
what appeared to be the only viable Cuban source of income. Neither
sugar nor American economic subsidies could cure Cuban economic
malaise, but Cubans and Americans alike earnestly sought immediate
relief through reciprocity.[37]

Theodore Roosevelt, though a staunch agricultural protectionist,
not only felt that the United States was obligated to Cuba but that he
was also committed to McKinley's and Root's implied promises of
trade concessions that they had made in return for Cuba's approval of
the Platt Amendment. Roosevelt's advocacy, at the behest of Root and
Wood, was beneficient, though he often appealed to economic self-
interest to sway a stubborn Congress, heavily influenced by Henry
Oxnard's American Beet Sugar Association as well as extensive cane
sugar interests in Louisiana, Hawaii, and Puerto Rico. "I wish that
Cuba grew steel and glass," Roosevelt complained, in referring to his
antipathy to reducing duties on agricultural products. In Cuba's "particular case of reciprocity a moral question is involved," an uncomfortable Roosevelt explained. "There are great moral and economic

37. Healy, *United States in Cuba,* 215; see Langley, *Cuban Policy of the United States,*
137–39; Weigle, "Sugar Interests," 25, 260–61.

issues of a national kind involved. . . . The attitude of those who have been against us is wholly wrong; but it is difficult to convince a man of this when his immediate interests are the other way." Roosevelt's temporary political ally, the American Sugar Refining Company—the Sugar Trust—complicated rather than helped Roosevelt's beneficent arguments since the Sugar Trust, adding to its Cuban investments, used bad economic conditions in Cuba to promote its own business interests.[38]

Roosevelt faced immense political opposition to a Cuban reciprocity agreement. Republicans barely managed to get the reciprocity bill to the House floor for bitter debate even though poorly organized Cuban reciprocity interests spread a rumor that Estrada Palma might decline to assume the presidency in May, 1902, if a reciprocity agreement was not concluded. Although the House passed a measure calling for a 20 percent reduction of duties on Cuban sugar, any chance for Senate passage was lost when Henry Teller charged Leonard Wood with using War Department funds to pay for Sugar Trust propaganda supporting reciprocity. Roosevelt called a special session for June 13, 1902, but the political deadlock continued. Reciprocity also became a Cuban domestic issue. The Cuban Congress, not enamored with American paternalism and inexperienced in complex negotiations between nations, tried to link reciprocity with approval of a Platt Amendment treaty and the leasing of American coaling stations. Roosevelt would not permit the issues to be connected. He wrote John Hay "to let the Cubans know at once and definitely that whatever is done about reciprocity the naval stations are to be ceded and in the near future. There is no intention of placing a naval station at Havana or at Santiago; but the question itself is not a matter open to discussion by the Cubans. It is already contained in their constitution, and no discussion concerning it will be entertained."[39]

Roosevelt, though firm in his instructions to his secretary of state, was gracious and conciliatory when he explained his actions to Es-

38. TR to Nicholas M. Butler, February 4, May 27, 1902; to Le Grand Bouton Cannon, September 19, 1903, all in *MRL,* III, 226–28, 265–66, 603; *ibid.,* 196 n.; TR, Annual Message to Congress, 1902, in *TRWN,* XV, 150; Fitzgibbon, *Cuba and the United States,* 208–209. For the Sugar Trust see Joe A. Fisher, "The Knight Case Revisited," *Historian* XXXV (1973), 365–83; Mark Schmitz, "The Transformation of the Southern Sugar Cane Sector 1860–1930," *Agricultural History,* LIII (1979), 270–84. For TR's antitrust policies see Hans B. Thorelli, *The Federal Antitrust Policy: Origination of an American Tradition* (Baltimore, 1953), 445–48, 586–609.

39. Fitzgibbon, *Cuba and the United States, MRL,* III, 271 n.; Dennis, *Adventures in American Diplomacy,* 268–69; TR to JH, October 23, 1902, in *MRL,* III, 367.

trada Palma. Calling the Cubans "friends and equals," Roosevelt connected Cuban resentment over the continued presence of American artillerymen to the ongoing negotiations over coaling stations. Roosevelt agreed to remove the troops employed in Cuban coastal defenses, but only to the proposed naval stations, not back to the United States. Since the United States did not want or plan for a naval base at Havana, Roosevelt, in a partial compromise, agreed to remove American troops from the capital immediately. Although Roosevelt refused to allow the Cubans to connect reciprocity with the negotiations over naval stations, he attempted without success to relate the two issues in the American Congress. After another regular and special session also failed to win approval of reciprocity, Roosevelt finally prevailed in November, 1903, only because the Havemeyer Sugar Trust bought 50 percent of the beet sugar trust, thereby ending organized opposition to Cuban reciprocity. The Cuban reciprocity agreements passed the House on November 19 and the Senate on December 16 by large majorities.[40]

Reciprocity represented a tragic short-term victory for the Cuban economy. By tying Cuban sugar into the enormous American Sugar Trust, reciprocity ensured that Cuba as a supplier of raw materials for refining in the United States would become dependent on the American sugar industry but would receive no long-term benefit from this relationship. Since reciprocity also gave American manufacturers useful concessions in Cuba, all effective foreign competition for Cuban markets was eliminated. Sugar dependency, more than any other development, profoundly clashed with Martí's romantic revolutionary vision that had inspired the original Cuban revolution, a serious dichotomy that became clearer after the initial stabilizing benefits had passed, and contributed to deep and continuing psychological friction between the United States and Cuba. For Roosevelt, reciprocity culminated his bitter personal struggle to redeem the American good faith promises from the initial intervention in the Cuban revolution and later during Root's and McKinley's negotiations of a Platt Amendment compromise. Roosevelt also related the struggle over Cuban reciprocity to his conflict with domestic interest groups connected with "the trust issue and the Northern Securities suit." As poorly as reciprocity worked for Cuba, it would have taken an immense intel-

40. TR to Tomás Estrada Palma, October 27, 1902; TR to John Dalzell, February 24, 1903, both in *MRL*, III, 369–70, 423; Weigle, "Sugar Interests," 347; Fitzgibbon, *Cuba and the United States*, 212.

lectual leap in 1902 to understand that sugar was Cuba's curse and not its salvation.[41]

Estrada Palma, who was determined that Cuba should have more teachers than soldiers, devoted a fourth of Cuba's budget to education but almost none to establishing an army. By 1905 the frugal Estrada Palma had accumulated enough of a surplus in Cuba's treasury to tempt the professional *políticos.* Surplus money with no military establishment to protect it encouraged instability. As long as the appearance of political tranquillity was maintained, the United States was content to treat Cuba as if it were an independent nation. Although Roosevelt in 1904 had warned Cuba that the Platt Amendment prohibited any increase in indebtedness "save for genuine necessity," he exercised almost no supervision over Cuban affairs, an attitude reflected by Estrada Palma's independent reciprocity diplomacy. In 1902 the Cubans pursued possible alternative reciprocity arrangements with Britain, France, and Germany when the Cuban-American reciprocity treaty remained deadlocked, but also afterward in 1903 and 1905.[42]

Except for relatively minor diplomatic problems caused by American Minister Herbert G. Squiers, a tactless annexationist, who was replaced by Edwin V. Morgan, a professional career diplomat, on November 29, 1905, Cuba under Estrada Palma and the Platt Amendment seemed tranquil. When Root, speaking for Roosevelt, addressed the celebrants at the second anniversary of the Republic of Cuba in New York on May 20, 1904, he summed up the American government's feeling of pride about its Cuba policy: "We freed Cuba from tyranny; we then stayed in the island until we had established civil order and laid the foundations for self-government and prosperity; we then made the island independent, and have since benefitted her inhabitants by making closer the commercial relations between us. I hail what had been done in Cuba not merely for its own sake, but as showing the purpose and desire of this nation toward all the nations south of us." Roosevelt, who used the Cuba policy as the model of American Caribbean policy and to forestall criticism of possible American intervention under the Roosevelt Corollary, was aware that Cuban independence was limited. "We have not given independence in the

41. See Lockmiller, *Magoon in Cuba,* 21; Benjamin, *United States and Cuba,* 12; TR to HCL, September 30, 1903, in *MRL,* III, 608.
42. Carlos Trelles, "The Progress of Cuba (1902 to 1905)," in Chapman, *History of the Cuban Republic,* 161; *ibid.,* 162; Fitzgibbon, *Cuba and the United States,* 108–109.

full sense to Cuba," Roosevelt confided in September, 1904; earlier he had referred to the establishment of "a kind of protectorate over Cuba." Roosevelt, however, often cited his beneficient foreign policy that "put an end to bloody misrule and bloody civil strife in Cuba." [43]

The Cuban revolution of 1906 was rooted in a flawed political system further complicated by Estrada Palma's olympian political independence. For the 1904 elections the main political parties changed their names to Conservative Republicans and National Liberals, and they competed vigorously and fraudulently for votes in what Cuban critics regarded as a farcical political exercise. Cuba's increasing political combativeness and instability began at the municipal level and spread to national politics when the National Liberal party boycotted the April, 1904, Congress, depriving the government of the two-thirds quorum required by the constitution. Cuban government was paralyzed until conservatives adopted the "quorum Dolz" rule that held that the two-thirds attendance was required only at the start of a legislative term. Estrada Palma, who regarded anyone who questioned his policies or disagreed with him as an enemy, did nothing to calm the political unrest. Congress remained so factionalized and Estrada Palma so stubborn that the frustrated leader was reluctant to run for reelection. Only the hope of preserving the treasury surplus he had lovingly accumulated induced Don Tomás to consider serving again. [44]

But Cuba's political parties were so badly split that institutionalized partisanship and fraud quickly led to insurrection, Cuba's characteristic political tradition. As new presidential elections approached, Conservative Republicans divided into new Moderate and Liberal parties. The Moderates convinced Estrada Palma, frustrated at his inability to persuade Congress to pass his recommended legislation, to end his political independence, use the Moderate party to get his programs passed, and reluctantly run for reelection. Estrada Palma, who understood and admired the American political system, may have agreed to stand for reelection because of the American tradition of two presidential terms. Critical of his country's political development, he complained, "In Cuba we have a republic, but no citizens." But when

43. TR to ER, May 20, 1904; to Henry Waters Taft, September 28, 1904; to Theodore E. Burton, February 23, 1904, all in *MRL*, IV, 801, 957, 736–37.

44. The main source for the Cuban crisis of 1906 is the "Taft-Bacon Report," in *House Documents*, 59th Cong., 2nd Sess., No. 2, Serial 5105 (TBR), 444–542; *ibid.* 451; TBR, see 451; Chapman, *History of the Cuban Republic*, 170–73.

Estrada Palma gave up his political independence to become the partisan leader of the Moderate party, his inappropriate political appointments, especially in his Gabinete de Combate, composed of war veterans and politicians willing to win at any cost, pushed Cuba closer to its familiar politics of insurrection.[45]

William Howard Taft, Robert Bacon, and Cuban historian Martínez Ortiz all agreed that Estrada Palma and the Moderates would have won an honest presidential election in 1905. But Moderates, unwilling to risk an honest election with "dishonest" Liberals, used the executive power to politicize almost every government position, including rural schoolteachers. When their ruthless success convinced Liberals that victory was impossible, the Liberals withdrew from active participation in the election and began to plan the overthrow of the government. By the September preliminary election, Cuban politics was both polarized and vicious as Moderates referred to Liberals as tartars, and they in turn called Moderates cossacks. José Miguel Gómez, the Liberal presidential candidate, traveled to New York in September to demand United States intervention, which he preferred to life under Moderate despotism. Both sides were equally frenetic. In defending the addition of 150,000 non-existent names to the voting registry, an inept inflation of Cuba's voting population of 300,000, General Freyre Andrade said "it was impossible to hold an election in Cuba without fraud."[46]

Joseph Foraker's 1902 prediction that the United States would be drawn into Cuban domestic politics was fulfilled by the end of 1905. Liberals, eliminated from the political process, terrorized the nation to force American intervention. Estrada Palma, convinced that he had American backing to put down any rebellion, also looked to the United States as his ultimate political ally. Reliance on eventual American intervention encouraged both Estrada Palma's obduracy and the Liberals' recklessness. The Cuban *campesino's* antiauthoritarian tradition, the familiar rituals of revolution, as much Spanish as Latin-American, and the fascination with guerrilla life that provided the excitement of living off the country, the adulation and respect the rural poor and uneducated directed toward insurrectionists, and the promise of political prominence after a war all drew recruits to insurrectionary adventures that had little to do with principles or political divisions.

45. Chapman, *History of the Cuban Republic* 171–74; TBR, 452.
46. See WHT to TR, September 21, 1906, in TBR, 470; Lockmiller, *Magoon in Cuba,* 30–32; TBR, 454–55.

Cuba *Libre,* Cuba *Triste*   531

Both sides were equally aggrieved to start, and as the insurrection gathered momentum, they could cite specific additional atrocities.[47]

The Cubans were well aware that the United States was so anxious for a peaceful Cuba that American intervention seemed not only virtually inevitable but preferable to living under a Cuban Liberal or Moderate government. Since virtually all of Cuba's wealth was owned by foreign investors, the $70 million worth of sugar mills and fields served as a substantial property hostage. Estrada Palma's army of three hundred artillerymen and three thousand rural guards was obviously unable to protect Havana, the sugar fields, or any part of Cuba from insurrectionist armies, which by September 19 surrounded and virtually besieged Havana, purposefully waiting for the American intervention.[48]

On September 1, 1906, a committee of the veterans of the war of independence intervened as a neutral group to mediate the conflict and avoid United States intervention. General Mario García Menocal, a forty-year-old graduate of Cornell University's engineering school and manager of the world's largest sugar estate, proposed a compromise to cancel the 1905 elections, retain in office only Estrada Palma and his vice-president, reform the election law, institute broad reforms including an independent judiciary and municipal and civil service structures, and finally hold new elections under the new laws. Although Estrada Palma, who may have resented the late timing of Menocal's veterans' support, did not reject the plan, which later became the starting point of the American intervention negotiations, he probably had already decided that an American Platt intervention better suited his political purposes than a Cuban compromise.[49]

At this critical moment the United States suffered from two serious diplomatic deficiencies. Secretary of State Elihu Root, the architect of the Platt Amendment and the new American peace offensive in Latin America, was in Chile, and the experienced American minister in Havana, Edwin V. Morgan, was on vacation in Europe. Jacob Sleeper, the legation secretary in charge during Morgan's absence, was young, inexperienced, and unprepared, as his reported telegram to Roosevelt, "Revolution spreading, everything quiet," amusingly demonstrated. Morgan's absence and Sleeper's youth gave effective Ameri-

47. Foraker, *Notes of a Busy Life,* II, 54; Millet, *Politics of Intervention,* 68–69, 106; TR to Charles W. Eliot, September 13, 1906, in *MRL,* IV, 410; Thomas, *Cuba,* 474–75; TBR, 458.
48. TBR, 456–57.
49. Chapman, *History of the Cuban Republic,* 198; Millet, *Politics of Intervention,* 70–71.

can power and influence to Frank Maximilian Steinhart, the American consul-general, an extraordinary figure, who began as Wood's chief clerk and later became an official of the Havana Electric Railway Company, a well-respected American businessman in Cuba, and a friend of President Estrada Palma. When Steinhart indirectly wrote to Roosevelt on September 5, he reported that Estrada Palma was despondent and fearful, the Cuban economy was close to collapse, the army was incapable of controlling the insurrection, Jacob Sleeper was "an ass," and American intervention was likely within a month.[50]

Even Steinhart was overly optimistic on how long Cuba could continue, for on September 8 Estrada Palma requested immediate American intervention. Steinhart cabled Roosevelt asking for "two vessels—one to Habana, other to Ciénfuegos. They must come at once. Government forces are unable to quell rebellion. The Government is unable to protect life and property." Roosevelt immediately dispatched the vessels, though he realized that the Americans were being manipulated: "These people have had for four years a decent, respectable government of their own. They are not suffering from any grievance whatsoever. Yet they have deliberately plunged the country into a civil war . . . I am by no means certain that it will be possible to prop him up and I expect to do some tall thinking in the effort to . . . put an end to anarchy without necessitating a reoccupation of the island by our troops."[51]

United States involvement in a Cuban guerrilla war was unthinkable. Brigadier General James F. Bell, Roosevelt's army chief of staff, a veteran of the Philippine-American war, advised the president that a Cuban operation "would be one of the most difficult operations in the world" because the Americans would have "to completely disarm a hostile population as skillful in the arts of concealment and deception as is the Latin Race." Cuban troops were not as ineffective as the Americans who fought in Cuba assumed. Brigadier General Frederick Funston, a veteran of Cuba and the Philippines, warned Bell that the Cuban insurgent army had not only defeated the Spanish, it was skilled in guerrilla and ambush tactics, and an enormous American army would be required to control it. As Secretary of War William

---

50. The Sleeper tale is an apocryphal story, reported in the New York *World* but denied by Sleeper and unsupported by State Department files; Frank Steinhart to William Loeb, September 5, 1906, in Numerical and Minor Files of the Department of State, 1906–10, Case 244/310, Microcopy M862, Roll 37, RG 59, NA; Millet, *Politics of Intervention,* 72, 85–86, n. 46.

51. TR to Charles W. Eliot, September 13, 1906, in *MRL,* V, 410.

Howard Taft observed, "Spain had 200,000 men in Cuba, and yet the guerrilla warfare went on." Taft estimated that forceful pacification would take at least a year and "cost much blood and money." Roosevelt needed no convincing. Intervention was so repugnant to him that even when the United States did intervene, Roosevelt refused to use the word or permit Taft to use it.[52]

Yet each side in Cuba was convinced that its political salvation lay in American intervention. Estrada Palma was certain that Roosevelt would intervene under the Platt Amendment to save his government because the rebels' carefully modulated escalation campaign threatened wholesale destruction of foreign property if the United States did not intervene. On September 11, Roosevelt felt "active intervention to be out of the question." Acting Secretary of State Robert Bacon's plan to warn the Cubans emphatically of American intervention "unless the people of Cuba, for the sake of their country, find some way to settle their difficulties, irrespective of personalities, cease their contentions, and live in peace" was an exercise in American fantasy. In a strange way the Cubans were already working together, not to settle their differences peacefully but to force a reluctant United States to intervene. When Steinhart reported that three sugar plantations had been destroyed, Ciénfuegos was undefended, and Estrada Palma was determined to resign as president with no one to replace him and no possibility of a congressional session, the only choice the Cubans left to the United States was the degree and duration of intervention.[53]

On September 14, 1906, Roosevelt, who had hoped that Secretary of State Elihu Root would return from his Latin American goodwill trip before the Cuban crisis escalated, sent Secretary of War Taft and Acting Secretary of State Robert Bacon to Havana to attempt to find a solution short of outright intervention. He explained both his actions and his passionate commitment to Cuban independence in a letter to Gonzalo de Quesada, the Cuban minister in Washington. By September 15, Taft had arranged for as many as eighteen thousand American troops to be dispatched to Cuba as needed. Acting on a request from Taft and Roosevelt, the Justice Department issued a formal ruling that

52. James F. Bell to TR, August 30, 1906; Frederick Funston to Bell, August 28, 1906, both in Millet, *Politics of Intervention*, 66–67; TBR, 458; Fitzgibbon, *Cuba and the United States*, 120.
53. Millet, *Politics of Intervention*, 72, 77, 68–69; Robert Bacon to Frederick Steinhart, September 11, 1906; Steinhart to Bacon, September 13, 14, 1906, all in TBR, 446–47.

intervention to maintain law and order and protect property was not an act of war requiring congressional approval, an issue already raised by William Jennings Bryan, who accused Roosevelt of "reckless militarism," Joseph Foraker, who made the charges "with the deliberate desire to be mischievous," and the press.[54]

Taft and Bacon arrived in Havana on Wednesday, September 19, as Cuban crowds cheered the Americans with "viva Taft y Bacon," and "viva Mis'tah Roo——velt." Both sides had instituted a cease-fire while awaiting the American peace mission. Taft and Bacon immediately went to the presidential palace for a dispiriting audience with Estrada Palma, who talked mainly of his futile efforts to impart to Cubans the wisdom of his experience in self-government from his twenty years in the United States and regret at his countrymen's lack of gratitude and patriotism. He referred discussion of all problems to the political parties.[55]

Taft and Bacon established themselves in Edwin Morgan's residence, nine miles from Havana, politically situated "between the lines" with the insurgents only a thousand yards away. American naval power had already prevented the possibility of an uncontrolled rebellion as three battleships and four cruisers with six thousand bluejackets assembled in Havana harbor. The insurgents agreed to allow Alfredo Zayas, the head of the Liberal party, to act as their spokesman, and Taft adopted Mario Menocal's compromise proposal of September 4 as the basis for negotiation. On September 21 Taft reported to Roosevelt that the Estrada Palma government "cannot maintain itself." Because the government lacked "moral support of large majority of the people . . . we cannot maintain the Palma government except by forcible intervention against the whole weight of public opinion in the island." Taft proposed trying to keep Estrada Palma as a functioning chief executive, though he doubted that either the president or the insurgents would agree. He proposed fresh elections under a new election law, followed by a call for disarmament of the insurgents. Taft sought political support from the Cuban people for a fair compromise that would make continued insurgency less popular. If intervention was still necessary, Taft reported that the United States would "do its duty." After warning the insurgents that

54. TR to Gonzalo de Quesada, September 14, 1906; to HCL, September 27, 1906, both in *MRL,* V, 411–12, 428; WHT to TR, September 15, 1906; George B. Davis to WHT, September 15, 1906, both in TBR, 492–95; TBR, 459.
55. Quoted in Millet, *Politics of Intervention,* 94; TBR, 448–49.

American troops would oppose any further encroachment on Havana, Taft reported that "they at once withdrew to a proper distance."[56]

Although Roosevelt cabled Taft, "I approve entirely your plan," he asked him to "avoid the use of the word 'intervention,' " and if landing troops proved necessary, "simply state that they are landed to save life and property in Havana." Roosevelt advised Taft to act quickly on his own if he needed to, but "if possible . . . communicate with me before taking such final steps as will irrevocably commit us to intervention." Taft and especially Bacon held hope that Estrada Palma could be retained, mainly because there was no one of his stature in either party with the necessary leadership qualities to assume control, but Roosevelt gave up that hope. Conscious of his potential domestic political opposition, Roosevelt urged Taft to refrain from making ultimatums, to try to find counterproposals if the insurgents rejected the American plan, and to "make it plain that we are exhausting every effort to come to an agreement before we intervene." Taft managed to get the Moderates to agree to resign from the government if the Liberals agreed to disarm, but Estrada Palma "absolutely declines to help us secure a compromise with the Liberals by remaining in office." Estrada Palma refused to remain as a political convenience while his Moderate allies in Congress resigned as part of a political compromise until new elections and election laws were instituted. Taft advised that more ships should be sent as a precaution.[57]

Roosevelt had little hope that Estrada Palma would listen, but to make the most convincing case for American restraint, Roosevelt pleaded "for the sake of your own fair fame not so to conduct yourself that the responsibility if such there be for the death of your republic can be put at your door." Roosevelt sent his message to Estrada Palma through Taft with instructions to deliver it or "vary the phraseology" at Taft's discretion. Roosevelt also instructed Taft to tell the insurgents "not to forever stand as people [who] . . . by their own wicked act reduced [Cuba] to a condition of dependence."[58]

When Estrada Palma remained adamant about leaving the presidency to satisfy "his dignity and honor," Roosevelt, furious at his

56. TBR, 449, 459–60; WHT to TR, September 21, 1906 (two cables), in TBR, 470–71.

57. TR to WHT, September 21, 1906, in TBR, 471, and *MRL*, V, 418; WHT to TR, September 22, 23, 24 (two cables), 1906; TR to WHT, September 22, 1906 (two cables), all in TBR, 472–73.

58. TR to Tomás Estrada Palma in TR to WHT, September 25, 1906, in TBR, 473–74, and *MRL*, V, 423–24.

stubbornness and his refusal to honor the political requirements of a national leader, suggested punishing the president and his Moderate party by turning the government over to the insurgent Liberal party. But this idea deeply troubled Taft, who preferred to intervene and disarm the insurgents, fearing they might regard the United States as their next enemy. A massively reluctant Roosevelt still refused to consider intervention. "I do not understand how conditions have changed so completely," Roosevelt argued, pushing for "substituting the hitherto insurrectionary party as the government *de facto.*" Roosevelt, stung by Estrada Palma's refusal to do what Roosevelt considered his political duty, wanted to punish him while at the same time avoiding American intervention. "I do not believe we should, simply because Palma has turned sulky and will not act like a patriot, put ourselves in the place of his unpopular government and face all the likelihood of a long drawn out and very destructive guerrilla warfare." How could the insurgents have changed their minds in forty-eight hours, Roosevelt asked, incredulous at the politics of abdication that Cubans appeared to be playing. But though Roosevelt could not comprehend such a situation, neither the Liberals nor the Moderates wanted power, especially if it involved compromise; both were still convinced that their best course was to step aside and force American intervention.[59]

Taft was just as contemptuous of Estrada Palma's Moderates, who "will now take away their dolls and not play." To Taft, however, Roosevelt's idea of turning over the government to the Liberals and the insurgents "makes me shiver at the consequences." The poor and uneducated insurgents, not the "men of ability and substance" in the Liberal party, would eventually gain political control of any *de facto* government because anti-authoritarian insurgency itself, not any political ideology, commanded the main Cuban popular allegiance. Roosevelt conceded that a Cuban political solution was beyond reach, but he instructed Taft to "avoid the use of the word 'intervention'" while "emphasizing the temporary character of the landing . . . for a short time until a permanent government has been formed." The United States, Roosevelt cautioned, "must simply put ourselves for the time being in Palma's place, land a sufficient force to insure order" until a new Cuban government was installed.[60]

59. TR to WHT, September 25, 1906 (three cables); WHT to TR, September 25, 1906, in *MRL,* V, 423; WHT to TR, September 28, 1906, in TBR, 474–75, 482.
60. WHT to TR, September 26, 1906 (two cables); TR to WHT, September 26, 1906 (three cables), all in TBR, 475–78.

Europe was content to allow the Americans considerable latitude in dealing with the Cuban crisis. Estrada Palma's cabinet may even have considered using troops to destroy British and German property to force European governments to exert additional pressure on the United States. On September 17, Spain proposed a European concert of England, France, and Spain, but France feared "complications with the United States" and the possible inclusion of Germany. Britain's Foreign Minister Sir Edward Grey was appalled at the Spanish proposal and warned, "we must not be drawn into intervention in Cuba." Lord Acton's reports of the crisis confirmed the American opposition to annexation and placed annexationist sentiment wholly in Cuba, though Acton also noted that a majority of Cubans "were satisfied with the present relation of the Island to the United States." Acton advised London that many Americans feared annexation because it "would mean the admission of an alien race into the Commonwealth and the presence of Spaniards in Congress with an indirect share in the Government," with no offsetting material advantages. The Foreign Office was impressed that "Taft appears . . . to have plumped for the revolutionists." Acton understood Roosevelt's view that "the use of Cuban ports as naval bases had practically given to America all that she desired." He accurately reported that Roosevelt would support the present government "without regard to the question of its legality or incorruptibility."[61]

Roosevelt still worried about "phraseology" that would place insurgents in revolt against the United States. He told Taft to base his "action upon the ground that organized government had disappeared and that order must be kept," a succinct and accurate statement of what happened in Cuba and the American response. Matters in Cuba were "kaleidoscopic" and efforts by Taft to establish a Cuban provisional government collapsed. But the substantial political and temperamental differences between Taft and Roosevelt, amplified when Taft became president in 1909, were evident in the last stages of the Taft mission. Taft worried about the legal and constitutional questions, and Roosevelt, genuinely puzzled by Taft's concern, replied, "I do not see that two revolutions would be in any way more objectionable than one." Roosevelt wanted an effective and efficient solution,

---

61. Millet, *Politics of Intervention,* 98; Lord Acton to Sir Edward Grey, September 17, 1906; Acton to Grey No. 31949, September 22, 1906, Acton to Grey, September 24, 1906, No. 32573; situation paper, No. 32753, September 27, 1906; Acton to Grey, September 24, 1906, all in FO 371/56, PRO.

preferably with Cubans—any Cubans—in charge. "Upon my word, I do not see that with Cuba in the position it is we need bother our heads much about the exact way in which Cubans observe or do not observe so much of their own constitution."[62]

Roosevelt cautioned Taft that the United States must demonstrate that it had "exhausted every method . . . to obtain peace and the perpetuation of the government with some show of order prior to our taking control ourselves." When Taft managed to get the Liberals to agree to a new Cuban government, the Moderates balked, "and many are strongly in favor of intervention and indeed annexation." Taft summed up the futility: "We have been very patient . . . but have failed." On September 28, 1906, Roosevelt agreed: "All right; land forces . . . but emphasize the fact that you are landing only at Palma's request and because there is no government left. . . . Also tell them that the government you form is only provisional and temporary until the Cubans can form one for themselves." Taft surrounded the treasury with American troops, tried once more to form a Cuban government, failed, and proclaimed a provisional American military government that was promptly approved by both the revolutionary committee and President Estrada Palma. Roosevelt still worried: "If any bloodshed occurs it should be between Cubans and Cubans, not between Americans and Cubans." Roosevelt need not have fretted. The Cubans had won what both warring sides had wanted, a second American intervention and an imposed political peace that denied victory to any Cuban political party.[63]

Roosevelt had more difficulties in keeping the Cuban crisis from becoming a political problem and, like the Philippines or Panama, impinging upon domestic politics or further jeopardizing the ultimate passage of his stalled treaty with the Dominican Republic. Roosevelt recounted that Indiana Senator Albert Beveridge, the most influential American expansionist, advised the president "at once" to "take the island—advice about as rational as requests . . . at the time of the anthracite coal strike, to 'take the coal barons by the throat.'" At the other extreme, Ohio Senator Joseph B. Foraker told Roosevelt not to

62. TR to WHT, September 26, 1906, in TBR, 478, and in *MRL,* V, 425; TR to WHT, September 26, 28, 1906, in TBR, 479, 481.

63. TR to WHT, September 28, October 2, 1906; WHT to TR, September 28, 1906, all in TBR, 480, 487, 483–84. For a useful description of the naval intervention see Lieutenant Christopher A. Abel, "Controlling the Big Stick: Theodore Roosevelt and the Cuban Crisis of 1906," *Naval War College Review,* XL (Summer, 1987), 88–98.

intervene because it was a matter for Congress, not the president, and "anyhow, Palma was all right." Bryan wanted Roosevelt to pledge in advance not to use armed force. Roosevelt felt that "the Buchanan-like course of summoning Congress for a six weeks debate," more political than useful, would have reduced Cuba to "a welter of blood." Specifically linking opposition to his domestic policies with foreign affairs, Roosevelt called Foraker "one of the most unblushing servers and beneficiaries of corporate wealth," who would have made the Republican party "an appanage to Wall Street." Because Roosevelt (in his own view) had "helped rescue the Republican party and therefore the country from ruin . . . he intends hereafter to fight me on every point, good or bad." When he wrote to Foraker, however, Roosevelt was charming and persuasive in setting forth his main purpose in the Cuban intervention: "All I ask of the Cubans is that they shall be prosperous and happy; and they cannot be prosperous and happy unless they have a reasonable degree of order and of protection of life and property."[64]

Roosevelt, aware that Congress could exert substantial pressure on any presidential decisions on Cuba because it controlled appropriations under the Platt Amendment, conciliated his main protagonists such as Foraker and Eugene Hale and assured senators that he felt "it was very unwise to summon Congress now." He took a firmer tone on Beveridge's objection "to keep on setting up one Cuban government after another," reminding him that it would take Congress and at least twenty-five thousand troops "to conquer the island." He reminded the senator that only "*one* Cuban government has been tumbled over. It would come perilously near bad faith if we do what would amount to seizing this excuse immediately to conquer the island."[65]

The proclamation issued by William Howard Taft as "Secretary of War of the United States" and "Provisional Governor of Cuba" on September 29, 1906, pledged a Cuban government under Cuban courts, the Cuban constitution, and the Cuban flag. Taft supervised the initial disbanding of the Cuban insurgent forces and turned the administration of the island over to Charles E. Magoon, who served from October 13, 1906, until January 28, 1909, a date chosen not only

64. TR to HCL, September 27, 1906; to Joseph B. Foraker, September 28, 1906, both in *MRL,* V, 427–30.
65. TR to HCL, September 27, October 1, 1906; to Joseph B. Foraker, October 5, 1906, all in *MRL,* V, 428, 436–37, 444.

to fulfill Theodore Roosevelt's determination to leave the presidency with Cuba restored but appropriately because it was José Martí's birthday.[66]

Seldom has an intervention been undertaken with as much reluctance and distaste as America's second Cuban intervention. When Elihu Root returned from his arduous South American goodwill mission on September 29, 1906, the same day that Taft proclaimed an American provisional government in Cuba, both Bacon and Taft were aware of the ironic juxtaposition that intervention and goodwill placed upon American policy. Acting Secretary Bacon, in Cuba and unable to greet Root in person, cabled his "great disappointment not to be on hand to welcome you home . . . and what a terrible disappointment and real sorrow it has been . . . [not] . . . to prevent or delay the failure of the Constitutional Government of Cuba." Taft wrote, "This has been the greatest crisis I ever passed through. . . . I am anxious to get away from here out of this atmosphere which is only of disappointment, intrigues, and discouragement. . . . I sincerely hope that this Cuban business will not interfere with the success of your South American trip."[67]

Charles E. Magoon was not Leonard Wood, and Cuba in 1906 under Magoon was no longer the land with a dream of an unlimited independent future it had been in 1900. Roosevelt, aware of Magoon's assets and liabilities, wrote that "Magoon gets on beautifully with the Cubans; he has done his work well, but he is not a man of masterful type or, indeed, of great force, and he shrinks from following any course to which he thinks any considerable number of Cubans would object, whether rightly or wrongly." Unlike Wood, who was a general and a physician, Magoon was a bureaucrat, who reported to Taft, with extremely limited imagination or power, constrained by his very limited administrative mandate rooted in the American determination to keep Cuba as unfettered by American intervention as possible. Root likened the second intervention in Cuba to a situation in which the National Guard was called in to an American state; sovereignty continues and laws "remain in abeyance until the military authority ends." Roosevelt refused to consider a permanent American presence, though he was aware that "the best, most intelligent, and most

66. Text of proclamation in TBR, 486; Chapman, *History of the Cuban Republic,* 264.
67. Robert Bacon to ER, October 1, 1906; WHT to ER, October 4, 1906, both in Jessup, *Elihu Root,* I, 535.

thrifty and industrious Cubans wish us to stay." Roosevelt insisted that "the Cubans are entitled to at least one more trial for their independent republic." Lord Acton, reporting a conversation with an American diplomat, wrote of the close bonds that still existed in 1906 between Cuba and Spain: "Whatever the ultimate political settlement, the ties of sentiment and affection between Cuba and Spain would always remain of a closer kind than those between the Island and her political protectors."[68]

Root summed up the American ambivalence: "We do not want Cuba ourselves, we cannot permit any other power to get possession of her, and to prevent the necessity of one and the possibility of the other of those results, we want her to govern herself decently and in order." Roosevelt remarked on his satisfaction with his Cuban policy: "In international affairs we have in the past six years measurably realized our ideal; we have shown our ability to hold our own against the strong; while no nation has ever behaved towards the weak with quite the disinterestedness and sanity combined which we have shown as regards Cuba and the Philippines." Of the two major aims of American Cuban policy in McKinley's and Roosevelt's administrations, only one, the establishment of "the main naval base of the United States to the Caribbean Sea and the principal guard of the Atlantic entrance of the Panama Canal," at Guantánamo was accomplished. Neither Wood, the beloved proconsul, Magoon, the self-effacing bureaucrat, nor Estrada Palma, the Cuban patriot with a love of the American political system but not the ability to bring the art of compromise to his homeland, was able to teach Cubans self-government. Nor could Cuba produce the economic self-sufficiency that more than any other single element might have given the island the prosperity necessary for the luxury of intelligent self-government.[69]

Roosevelt, who wanted to transform a Latin America that he knew was different from both the United States and Europe, hoped that politics and some intelligent economic help might make the difference. In November, 1906, on his return from a visit to the Panama Ca-

68. Fitzgibbon, *Cuba and the United States*, 143–44; TR to ER, July 20, 1908, in *MRL*, VI, 1137; ER to A. K. McClure, October 26, 1906, in Jessup, *Elihu Root*, I, 537; TR to William C. Lane, April 15, 1907, in *MRL*, V, 648; Lord Acton to Sir Edward Grey, September 24, 1906, in FO 371/56, PRO.
69. ER to Henry Watterson, March 5, 1908, in Jessup, *Elihu Root*, I, 538; TR to Grafton Dulany Cushing, February 27, 1908; to Charles W. Fairbanks, February 21, 1908, both in *MRL*, VI, 955, 951.

nal site, Roosevelt was struck by the natural beauty and political simplicity of the Puerto Ricans:

There were vines with masses of brilliant purple and pink flowers, and others with masses of little white flowers, which at nighttime smell deliciously. There were trees studded over with huge white flowers, and others, the flamboyants, which as I saw in the campaign at Santiago are a mass of large scarlet blossoms in June, but which now had shed them. I thought the tree ferns especially beautiful. The towns were just as you saw in Cuba, quaint, brilliantly colored, with the old church or cathedral fronting the plaza, and the plaza always full of flowers. Of course the towns are dirty, but they are not nearly as dirty and offensive of those of Italy; and there is something pathetic and childlike about the people. We are giving them a good government and the island is prospering.[70]

Roosevelt was proud to have promised that the United States would leave Cuba and to have fulfilled that promise: "When the promise was made, I doubt if there was a single ruler or diplomat in Europe who believed that it would be kept." Roosevelt remained aware of the fragility of Cuban independence and its reliance on American support. In his last message to Congress (and Cuba) in 1908, he warned that "the only way a people can permanently avoid being governed from without is to show that they both can and will govern themselves from within." The Americans left Cuba's Spanish culture intact. The main American legacy, 608 kilometers of new roads under Magoon in the second intervention, a fair and orderly political election in 1908, and an extraordinary restoration of the Cuban government in 1909, fulfilled Roosevelt's most ambitious Caribbean goals but without emancipating Cuba from its dependence on a sugar export agriculture or from its cultural preference for Spanish rather than American politics.[71]

70. TR to Kermit Roosevelt, November 23, 1906, in *MRL,* V, 501.
71. TR, *Autobiography,* in *TRWN,* XX, 493; *TRWN,* 539; Thomas, *Cuba,* 493. For a balanced analysis of American influence and Cuban weakness see Healy, *Drive to Hegemony,* 203–18; see also Langley, *Banana Republics,* 43–50.

Part V

Conclusion

18   Roosevelt's Diplomacy in the Context of His Time

When Lieutenant Colonel Theodore Roosevelt and his Rough Riders took San Juan Hill on July 1, 1898, America's world—north as well as south—radically changed. The United States became a global power with possessions in Asia as well as the Caribbean, Spain was ousted from the New World, and an aristocrat from New York City became the most famous man in America. Roosevelt returned to the United States to become governor of New York, then vice-president, and finally on September 14, 1901, at the age of forty-two, the youngest president of the United States. Although one could argue that the United States had been a world power since 1776 and John Bassett Moore had published a chapter titled "The United States as a World Power" in the *Cambridge Modern History* in 1903, the process that had tentatively begun with William McKinley's war with Spain in 1898 matured in the seven and a half years of Theodore Roosevelt's presidency. Roosevelt, who had begun the era with his legendary charge at San Juan, ended his presidency with the United States as protector of Spain's Asian and Caribbean islands; a canal at Panama; a Nobel Peace Prize for settling a world war between Russia and Japan; a twenty-two-battleship navy, second only to Great Britain's, dramatically displayed to the world when the Great White Fleet steamed to Japan; and the Roosevelt Corollary to the Monroe Doctrine, a new formal policy toward Latin America and Europe. Roosevelt disengaged the United States from its second Cuban intervention, pledged no further American expansion, settled with and recognized Japan's growing power and influence, and continued his vast naval building program with seven battleships in progress.[1]

1. TR's main attack was actually up a hill adjoining San Juan named Kettle Hill for the Spanish sugar kettles found there after the Americans had won the Battle of San Juan. See Edmund Morris, *The Rise of Theodore Roosevelt* (New York, 1979), 651–65. For America's new role see Thomas Bailey, "America's Emergence as a World Power: The

Yet the impression of Theodore Roosevelt as diplomatic whirlwind and the United States embarked on a new era of activism or expansion is more an American than a European perception. In Britain's diplomatic correspondence there is almost no mention of American influence, even in Latin America. In his confidential annual report for 1908, Roosevelt's last year as president, British Ambassador James Bryce observed, "In the sphere of foreign policy the action of the United States is, it need hardly be said, very limited compared to that of the great States of Europe, for the principle of avoiding interference with matters relating to the Old World is adhered to with a strictness which has been little affected even by the acquisition of the new transmarine possessions." Bryce's summation speaks to the core of the historiographical enigma of Theodore Roosevelt's presidency. The man who won a Nobel Peace Prize for settling the difficult Russo-Japanese War, often spoke and wrote as a jingo before he became president, exemplified the big stick as president—in image if not in substance—and later compounded his warlike image by exhorting Democratic President Woodrow Wilson to intervene in World War I on the side of the Allies. Historians remain divided on the effectiveness of Roosevelt's foreign policy, on whether he was a man of peace or war, and are especially and almost universally critical of his Panama and Caribbean policies. Because of the multiplicity of the problem, it is useful to consider the various facets of Roosevelt's diplomacy separately before attempting an overall conclusion.[2]

Myth and the Verity," *PHR*, XXIX (1961), 1–16; Richard Leopold, "The Emergence of America as a World Power: Some Second Thoughts," in John Braeman, Robert H. Bremmer, and Everett Walters (eds.), *Change and Continuity in Twentieth-Century America* (Columbus, Ohio, 1964), 4; Frank Freidel, *The Splendid Little War* (Boston, 1958), 143; James Bryce to Sir Edward Grey, April 30, 1908, Confidential Print, United States, in FO 881/9265, p. 33, PRO; James R. Reckner, *Teddy Roosevelt's Great White Fleet* (Annapolis, 1988). See also Seward W. Livermore, "The American Navy as a Factor in World Politics," *AHR*, LXIII (1958), 863–79.

2. James Bryce to Sir Edward Grey, April 30, 1908, in FO 881/9265, p. 30, PRO; Jerald A. Combs, *American Diplomatic History: Two Centuries of Changing Interpretations* (Berkeley, 1983), 182–96; Ernest R. May, "Emergence to World Power," in John Higham (ed.), *The Reconstruction of American History* (New York, 1962), 180–96; William C. Widenor, *Henry Cabot Lodge and the Search for an American Foreign Policy* (Berkeley, 1980), 121–70; Eugene P. Trani, "Cautious Warrior: Theodore Roosevelt and the Diplomacy of Activism," in Frank J. Merli and Theodore A. Wilson (eds.), *Makers of American Diplomacy from Benjamin Franklin to Henry Kissinger* (New York, 1974), 305–31, are thoughtful analytical summaries; Frederick W. Marks III, *Velvet on Iron: The Diplomacy of Theodore Roosevelt* (Lincoln, 1979), is a significant revision; see also Richard H. Collin, *Theodore Roose-*

Context

Context still remains one of the main problems in Roosevelt historiography. Roosevelt's age was far different from our own and radically different from the two administrations that followed. President William Howard Taft and Secretary of State Philander Knox purposefully and radically changed Roosevelt's emphasis on power, responsibility, and especially altruism—the key to Roosevelt's Latin American foreign policies and their essential meliorating ingredient. Taft and Knox placed a far greater emphasis on American self-interest, including a conscious effort to impose American political and economic settlements upon weaker Latin American nations, a practice Roosevelt and Secretary of State Elihu Root assiduously avoided. Although dollar diplomacy radically changed Roosevelt's emphasis on beneficient paternalism, it was World War I, the transcendent event of the early twentieth century, that overwhelmed and virtually obliterated Roosevelt's limited, narrow, transitional policies and made Roosevelt's era anachronistic. World War I changed the nature of warfare, discredited Europe's claims to political and cultural leadership, transformed the United States from Europe's debtor to its creditor, and marked a monumental sea change in world history that dwarfed in significance all the changes in Roosevelt's presidency. In an age when charging up a hill in Cuba and surviving was still possible, Roosevelt could play the heroic figure. There could be no San Juan Hills in Europe's trenches in 1915; the machine gun, the tank, and the airplane transformed the nature of warfare.[3]

---

velt, *Culture, Diplomacy, and Expansion* (Baton Rouge, 1985). For the historiographical imbalance, especially in high school textbooks, see Frederick W. Marks III, "Theodore Roosevelt and the Righting of History," *TRAJ*, XII (Winter, 1986), 8–12. For the view that the big stick was the voice of progressivism, not jingoism, see Lloyd C. Gardner, *Safe for Democracy: The Anglo-American Response to Revolution, 1913–1923* (New York, 1984), 33. The most recent historiographical assessment is William Tilchin, "The Rising Star of Theodore Roosevelt's Diplomacy: Major Studies from Beale to the Present," *TRAJ*, XV (Summer, 1989), 2–24.

3. Marks, *Velvet on Iron*, 1; Frank Ninkovich, "Theodore Roosevelt: Civilization as Ideology," *DH*, X (1986), 228; D. H. Dinwoodie, "Dollar Diplomacy in the Light of the Guatemalan Loan Project, 1909–1913," *Americas*, XXVI (1970), 237–38; Seward Livermore, "Battleship Diplomacy in South America, 1905–1925," *Journal of Modern History*, XVI (1944), 31–48; Eugene P. Trani, "Dollar Diplomacy," in Alexander DeConde (ed.), *Encyclopedia of American Foreign Policy* (3 vols.; New York, 1978), II, 268–74. For a fictional portrait of the age that uses the leitmotiv of transitional ragtime music as its unifying metaphor, see E. L. Doctorow, *Ragtime* (New York, 1975). The Armory Art Exhibi-

Lost in the diplomatic and economic American transcendence following World War I was the still struggling America of Roosevelt's era, a land of unlimited potential but still painfully dependent on European culture, economics, and naval power. Roosevelt's main accomplishment as president was to disengage the United States—and Latin America—from European domination through diplomacy, not belligerence, an accomplishment more readily acknowledged by Europeans, who awarded Roosevelt a Nobel Peace Prize in 1906 and recognized the role of the United States as the world's essential peacemaker in Roosevelt's presidency. Roosevelt's America led the international arbitration movement, was an original participant in the Hague peace movement of 1899, an effective early supporter of the Hague World Court, and an active conciliator in Europe's political quarrels. These activities were later overshadowed by the political and historical debate over Woodrow Wilson's war and peace policies. Roosevelt may have been painfully aware that Wilson's war crisis presidency almost automatically secured for him a more important historical standing than Roosevelt's, regardless of their relative effectiveness as diplomats.[4]

Insularity

Senator Henry Cabot Lodge observed that isolation in pre-Roosevelt America was a habit, not a policy. Roosevelt, well aware of the funda-

---

tion and the sinking of the *Titanic* in 1913 are important watersheds that also tend to isolate Roosevelt's time from the more complicated America that followed. See also John Ellis, *The Social History of the Machine Gun* (1976; rpr. Baltimore, 1985). For American changes in World War I, see John Milton Cooper, *The Warrior and the Priest: Woodrow Wilson and Theodore Roosevelt* (Cambridge, Mass., 1983); and David M. Kennedy, *Over Here: The First World War and American Society* (New York, 1980). For World War I as a watershed see Modrus Eksteins, *Rites of Spring: The Great War and the Birth of the Modern Age* (Boston, 1988).

4. Combs, *American Diplomatic History*, 191; Tyler Dennett, *Americans in Eastern Asia* (New York, 1922), 626, 631, 634; Colville Barclay to Sir Edward Grey, August 8, 1906, Confidential Print, South America, in FO 420/237, PRO; William Stead, *The Americanisation of the World* (London, 1902), 95; Calvin DeArmond Davis, *The United States and the Second Hague Peace Conference: American Diplomacy and International Organization, 1899–1914* (Durham, N.C., 1975); Eugene N. Anderson, *The First Moroccan Crisis, 1904–1906* (Chicago, 1930); Peter Larsen, "Theodore Roosevelt and the Moroccan Crisis, 1904–1906" (Ph.D. dissertation, Princeton University, 1984). For the settling of the Russo-Japanese War see Eugene P. Trani, *The Treaty of Portsmouth: An Adventure in American Diplomacy* (Lexington, Ky., 1969); and Raymond Esthus, *Double Eagle and Rising Sun: The Russians and Japanese at Portsmouth in 1905* (Durham, N.C., 1988). For a critical summary of TR's role as a European diplomatist see Esthus, *Theodore Roosevelt*

mental skepticism of even sympathetic Europeans such as Alexis de Tocqueville to the effective conduct of foreign affairs in a democratic society, countered the problem by confronting it politically in moralistic language. Roosevelt labored with a Congress and an electorate in which domestic matters consistently overshadowed foreign affairs; most Americans could not imagine their country as an active force in world affairs. As foreign and domestic matters increasingly overlapped, especially in tariffs affecting Cuba and the Philippines, the president and Congress established a new balance of shared power within the American government, a political struggle that began in McKinley's presidency over the war with Spain and reached its apogee with the conflict over Roosevelt's Dominican intervention in 1905. Roosevelt firmly believed in democracy, constitutional government, and working within the system. He marveled at the extent of American public disinterest, even in the near West Indian islands. Roosevelt insisted that the president, not the people, must adapt, and he relied on the president's ability to use publicity to change American resistance to greater participation in world affairs. Roosevelt's speeches rarely contained close reasoning or even detailed factual information. James Bryce observed: "They deal entirely in general moral principles set forth in popular, forcible style, sometimes assisted by the purple adjective, of which Mr. Roosevelt is a master." Presidential messages, Bryce reported, were so numerous that newspaper cartoons pictured "Roosevelt's private secretaries as tumbling over one another in their haste to get from the White House to the Capitol . . . or Members of Congress hurrying away . . . to escape from a hail of Presidential lectures." But the newness of foreign policy and Roosevelt's belief in the democratic system impelled him to put as many facts before the people as he could.[5]

---

and the International Rivalries (Waltham, Mass., 1970). For Henry Adams' description of TR as "the best herder of Emperors since Napoleon" and his request for "your views about the relative docility of Kings, Presidents of South American Republics, Railway Presidents, and Senators," see Adams to TR, November 6, 1905, in RP; for a comparison of TR with Garibaldi see William Morton Fullerton, *Problems of Power: A Study of International Politics from Sadowa to Kirk-Kilissé* (New York, 1913), esp. 23–25, 302–303; for the view that "he played the game of Realpolitik as if he were a monarch of divine right, but he played it well and for the peace of the world," see Arthur S. Link, "Theodore Roosevelt in His Letters," *Yale Review*, XLIII (1954), 597. For the Roosevelt-Wilson debate see Cooper, *The Warrior and the Priest*.

5. Widenor, *Henry Cabot Lodge*, 122, 125, 110, 147–50, 157; Elihu Root, "Roosevelt's Conduct of Foreign Affairs," in *TRWN*, XVI, xiii, xii; Marks, *Velvet on Iron*, 3; Howard Beale, *Theodore Roosevelt and the Rise of America to World Power* (Baltimore, 1956), 453–55;

Roosevelt's theatricality helped establish the new American world presence of "active participation and beneficent influence" in which power was used in concert with Europe as a legitimate international force for peace. Roosevelt did not shrink from the use of force, but he insisted that it be used judiciously with wisdom and justice; he regarded force as a form of self-mastery, an important limitation on his use of power as president. He was able to overcome the theoretical Tocquevillian limitations on democratic power through his partial transcendence of the American political tradition that tended to limit power to more ordinary people. As an aristocrat with established social status and economic security, Roosevelt had enormous freedom to pursue his program of deprovincializing the American people. He dealt with European leaders as social and political equals and scorned the limited self-interests of the economic man, whom he despised. Economics were never directly a part of Roosevelt's programs or interests, though he reluctantly added economic arguments to sway Congress. Roosevelt's vision of the interdependence of society was closer to Lincoln's than to either Bismarck's or Napoleon's; he saw society in constant flux and attempted to reorder American and world society to prserve it. In his extensive political speaking tours as president, he consistently related both domestic and foreign issues through a moral diction that reflected his view that international affairs were not isolated matters but part of a national course of conduct through which he tried to move the American people from a traditional materialistic individualism to a more beneficent altruism, though able to defend itself if necessary.[6]

Race, Darwin, and Lamarck

In the political and cultural conflicts with Latin America, race remains one of the critical early twentieth-century issues. Roosevelt, stung in

---

TR to WHT, August 21, 1907, in *MRL*, V, 761–62; James Bryce to Sir Edward Grey, April 30, 1908, in FO 881/9265, p. 5. PRO. For the primacy of domestic over foreign policy see Ernest May, *Imperial Democracy: The Emergence of America as a Great Power* (New York, 1961), 269–70. See also David Healy, *US Expansionism: The Imperialist Urge in the 1890s* (Madison, Wisc., 1970), 126; and Paul Holbo, "Economics, Emotion, and Expansion: An Emerging Foreign Policy," in H. Wayne Morgan (ed.), *Gilded Age* (Rev. ed.; Syracuse, 1970), 199–221, 315–19.

6. John Dewey, "Theodore Roosevelt," *Dial*, February 8, 1919, pp. 115–16; Henry Cabot Lodge's phrase "active participation" is quoted in Widenor, *Henry Cabot Lodge*, 134; John M. Blum, *The Republican Roosevelt* (Cambridge, Mass., 1954), 133; David H. Burton, *Theodore Roosevelt and His English Correspondents: A Special Relationship of Friends*

his first term by controversies over black patronage in the South and his social relationship with Booker T. Washington, was much more cautious in his second term, courting the South's whites even though privately he railed against their racial mores. No more striking example of racial colonialism exists than at the Panama Canal site, where the imported black West Indians who built the canal were paid lower wages from the segregated or "silver" payroll while American whites enjoyed the benefits of a "gold" payroll that paid 25 percent higher salaries than comparable jobs in the United States. As president, Roosevelt consistently acted as a pragmatic diplomat and practical domestic politician, not a crusader. Panama's labor structure reflected Roosevelt's ability to adapt and compromise to achieve his highest priority, in this case building an isthmian canal.[7]

Roosevelt, however, was not a racist. Sharing many of the common contemporary confusions of both social scientists and politicians, Roosevelt used race interchangeably with national, historical, ethnic, and color matters—or as a vague concept with very broad limits. Nor was Roosevelt a Social Darwinist; he agreed with Darwin's biological theories but regarded the sociobiological applications as "irritating delusions." Roosevelt's racial beliefs followed fairly traditional turn-of-the-century opinion. As a neo-Lamarckian, Roosevelt differed from conventional contemporary Social Darwinists such as William Graham Sumner and Herbert Spencer. Especially relevant to his optimism about Latin American development were Roosevelt's Lamarckian beliefs in the efficacy of reform and change, the inheritance of acquired characteristics, and the conviction that peoples, societies, or races (the three designations were often used interchangeably) could

(Philadelphia, 1973), 34; Beale, *Theodore Roosevelt*, 453, 449–50; deprovincialization is H. Stuart Hughes's term cited by John Patrick Diggins, Review of Lewis A. Coser, *Refugee Scholars in America, JAH*, LXXII (1985), 188; David H. Burton, *Theodore Roosevelt: Confident Imperialist* (Philadelphia, 1968), 93; William H. Harbaugh (ed.), *The Writings of Theodore Roosevelt* (Indianapolis, 1967), xxvii; Root, "Roosevelt's Conduct of Foreign Affairs," p. xiii; Trani, "Cautious Warrior," esp. 305–306. For French admiration of TR see Jean-Baptiste Duroselle, *France and the United States: From the Beginning to the Present Day*, trans. Derek Coltman (Chicago, 1976), 77; and Abbe Felix Klien, *Au pays de la vie intense* (Paris, 1904).

7. Willard B. Gatewood, Jr., *Theodore Roosevelt and the Art of Controversy* (Baton Rouge, 1970), 32–134; Owen Wister, *Roosevelt: The Story of a Friendship, 1880–1919* (New York, 1930), 117–19; Milton L. Conniff, *Black Labor on a White Canal: Panama, 1904–1981* (Pittsburgh, 1985), 4–5; Esthus, *Theodore Roosevelt and the International Rivalries*, 3; Thomas G. Dyer, *Theodore Roosevelt and the Idea of Race* (Baton Rouge, 1980), 42, 43, 29, 31, 35–39.

be improved through acquired characteristics passed on to future generations.[8]

For Roosevelt, societies, like the world itself, were in flux; developed societies could regress from their civilized state, and lesser people could move up, beliefs consonant with classic Lamarckianism. Roosevelt's Lamarckian attitudes might explain his constant exhortations directed not only toward wrongdoing Latin American leaders but also toward materialistic American businessmen or weak congressmen, who, in Roosevelt's view, placed the United States in grave danger of moral and practical backsliding. Roosevelt was always instructing public opinion, much to the delight of the populace and the dismay of Congress, which resented his didactic and at times apparently dictatorial tone. Roosevelt's speeches were more important in explaining the ideas behind them than in promoting specific policies. Roosevelt believed that his most important domestic and foreign programs were united as exemplars of a proper moral civilization, which he explained in terms of a federal authority that expressed national aspirations for equality, a central unifying belief in American political thought.[9]

James Bryce, the British ambassador and keen scholar of American politics, found Roosevelt's methods illuminating. None of the president's four speeches on his October, 1907, trip to the Midwest and South was notable in itself, but each "represents an exposition of the leading principle of the Roosevelt policy." At Canton, the theme was "introducing industrial democracy, i.e. equalization of opportunity for all," at Keokuk, "national responsibility for . . . enjoyment of natural resources," at St. Louis, "national responsibility for regulating railways and public utilities," at Cairo, Illinois, "equalization of opportunity between America and foreign interests by means of a strong naval and colonial policy." Although the unity of Roosevelt's common purpose was obscured by "local and topical considerations," his underlying theme throughout his presidency, well illustrated by his midwestern speaking trip, was the use of federal authority to achieve equality—what he once called the Square Deal. In the best democratic sense, Roosevelt considered educating the people one of his essential

8. Ninkovich, "Theodore Roosevelt," 227; TR, "Social Evolution," in TRWN, XIII, 223–41; TR, "National Life and Character," ibid., 200–222; Ernest May, American Imperialism: A Speculative Essay (New York, 1968), 228–29.

9. Dyer, Theodore Roosevelt, 43–44; James Bryce to Sir Edward Grey, October 14, 1907, in FO 414/195, No. 34, p. 69; Sir Mortimer Durand to Grey, January 2, 1906, in FO 414/189, p. 48, both in PRO.

duties as president. In Roosevelt's hierarchy of values, hard work and duty were the essential prerequisites of power and order, necessary attributes for civilization and national survival, his two highest political priorities.[10]

The Politics of Controversy

Roosevelt was a product of his time, which he both reflected and effectively led. The seeming modernity of Roosevelt's *realpolitik* is startlingly balanced by his anachronistic appeals to moralism delivered with fervor and in strenuous language. Although both Roosevelt's goals and his achievements were substantial, they were much more limited than his own exaggerated historical accounts of them. Roosevelt consistently overstated his own role, although the chief example of such overstatement was the New York *Times* misquote "I took the canal zone in 1911." When he finally came to terms with the Senate's objections to his original Dominican treaty, Roosevelt claimed a total political victory for what was instead a profound political and constitutional compromise. Most of Roosevelt's policies were continuations of initiatives first taken by William McKinley, who was the first president to deal with modernism, the new relationship between Congress and the chief executive, and the beginning of American colonialism. Both of Roosevelt's secretaries of state, John Hay and Elihu Root, were originally McKinley's appointees.[11]

Roosevelt's genius was his style of government. Like Woodrow Wilson, who was instructed and inspired by Roosevelt's transformation of the presidency, Roosevelt was a political intellectual as well as an artist of power. He used his confrontational style to dramatize the presidency, his policies, and life itself in his equal relish for thought and action. The confrontational style produced in Roosevelt's presidency a politics of controversy that often made caution seem audacious and clothed conservative tradition with the appearance of innovative modernity. Roosevelt could be impulsive in his private conversations and his sometimes violent personal letters because he

10. James Bryce to Sir Edward Grey, October 14, 1907, in FO 414/195, p. 69, PRO; Blum, *Republican Roosevelt*, 106; Ninkovich, "Theodore Roosevelt."

11. Dewey, "Theodore Roosevelt"; Blum, *Republican Roosevelt*, 132; the Panama Canal speech is cited in New York *Times*, March 24, 1911, p. 1; for the correct text and the historical issue see Chapter 11, note 26; TR to Eugene Hale, December 3, 1908; to Sydney Brooks, December 28, 1908, both in *MRL*, VI, 1408, 1445; May, "Emergence to World Power," 185; Lewis L. Gould, *The Presidency of William McKinley* (Lawrence, Kan., 1980), 252–53.

knew the difference between what he wanted to do and what was morally and politically possible. His indigenous political realism, his ability to adapt an ideal policy to the political realities of a democratic society, allowed him to weigh carefully the best ways of achieving a desired goal.[12]

Woodrow Wilson may well have been the warrior and Theodore Roosevelt the priest of early twentieth-century American presidents. Wilson fought in more wars and intervened in more Latin American countries than Roosevelt. But the relationship between the two prodigious American leaders still reveals much about the United States of their time. Personally and intellectually congenial, they fought constantly after 1907 when it became apparent that they were political rivals. Although Theodore Roosevelt first suggested a world peace organization when he accepted his Nobel Peace Prize in 1910, when Wilson proposed a League of Nations, Roosevelt, reacting as a member of the political opposition, treated an idea that may originally have been his own as rank heresy or nonsense. In 1912 the two leading diplomatic leaders of the early twentieth century engaged in a direct political contest for the presidency in which foreign policy was hardly mentioned. In 1912 the United States was much more concerned with its own domestic politics—controlling the corporations, tariffs, and labor—than with foreign or world affairs.[13]

There could be no continuity in American foreign policy because power always passed from one party to another, and even when power was maintained in the same party, radical changes would occur, as when William Howard Taft succeeded Theodore Roosevelt in 1909. Traditionally, before, during, and after Roosevelt's presidency, American opposition party politics was more opportunistic than con-

12. Cooper, *The Warrior and the Priest,* 134; Gatewood, *Theodore Roosevelt,* 26–31; Edward Wagenknecht, *The Seven Worlds of Theodore Roosevelt* (New York, 1958), 1; Ninkovich, "Theodore Roosevelt," 235; Widenor, *Henry Cabot Lodge,* 159.
13. Robert Endicott Osgood, *Ideals and Self-Interest in America's Foreign Relations* (Chicago, 1955), 144–45; Cooper, *The Warrior and the Priest;* TR, "International Peace" (May 5, 1910), in *TRWN,* XVI, 305–309; William Clinton Olson, "Theodore Roosevelt's Conception of an International League," *World Affairs Quarterly,* XXIX (1959), 329–53. For TR's opposition to Wilson and his League of Nations see TR to James Bryce, November 19, 1918, and to Rudyard Kipling, November 30, 1918, both in *MRL,* VIII, 1400–1401, 1409–10; for a summary of Roosevelt's arguments, see Albert Bushnell Hart and Herbert Ronald Ferleger, *Theodore Roosevelt Cyclopedia* (New York, 1941), 304–307. For the election campaign of 1912 see John Allen Gable, *The Bull Moose Years* (Port Washington, N.Y., 1968), 111–30; and Arthur S. Link, *Wilson: The Road to the White House* (Princeton, 1947), 467–528.

structive. Much of what remains controversial in Roosevelt's foreign policy comes not from his policies or his supposedly impulsive personality but from an inherent and insurmountable political tension in American society. The Philippines ceased being a complex foreign policy matter when it became a politicized issue in the presidential election of 1900, a party conflict between the Republican ins and the Democratic outs, not simply an ideological imperialist versus anti-imperialist debate. Roosevelt's controversial diplomatic policies were often affected as much by domestic American politics as by foreign affairs. Critics of Roosevelt's Panama policies conveniently overlook the power of the minority Democratic party led by the determined John Tyler Morgan, a much narrower nationalist than Roosevelt, who blocked any possibility of a larger cash settlement to Colombia that might have averted the problems of Panama's separation.[14]

Europe

The relationships of Germany and Britain to American Caribbean diplomacy have been extensively treated, but France's critical role in Latin American intellectual affairs as well as foreign relations is often overlooked. French influence on Latin American thought began with Auguste Comte's positivism, accelerated through a carefully nurtured pan-Latinism that coincided with the French occupation of Mexico in the early 1860s, and extended to Ferdinand de Lesseps' effort to build an interoceanic canal at Panama. France was actually the key to Roosevelt's policy of extricating both Americas from European influence or domination through diplomatic agreement that avoided belligerency. Britain reluctantly but gradually acceded to American wishes on the Monroe Doctrine, Germany remained resistant, and France, an active Caribbean presence, became the decisive European power. The United States cautiously nurtured French pride in the Dominican Republic even before Roosevelt became president. Roosevelt, through his personal relationship with Ambassador Jean Jules Jusserand, carefully courted the French, avoiding conflict in the Dominican Republic, Guatemala, Venezuela, and especially Panama. French acquiescence in a Panama canal settlement was a necessary prerequisite to French

14. On the discontinuity of American diplomacy see TR, *Autobiography* (1913), in *TRWN*, XX, 523; and ER to Thomas Dawson, April 24, 1907, in Numerical and Minor Files of the Department of State, 1906–1910, Case 1199/130, Microcopy M862, Roll 148, RG 59, NA; Widenor, *Henry Cabot Lodge*, 125; Frank Reuter, *Catholic Influence on American Colonial Policies, 1898–1904* (Austin, Tex., 1967), 102.

concurrence in the new American Caribbean hegemony. When both Britain and France were mollified by the limited American policies and ambitions, Germany and Spain were more inclined to accept the new American hegemony in the Caribbean and northern Latin America without serious reservation.[15]

Roosevelt's Corollary to the Monroe Doctrine ended the historic ideological breach between the United States and Europe, substituting a global relationship that was closer to reality and more useful. Roosevelt did cut corners in his Panama diplomacy, but his actions in freeing Panama from its forced subjection to Colombia appeared to him morally defensible. Had Roosevelt pursued the policy suggested by many of his critics, he might have lost France's acquiescence in the removal of Europe, including Germany and Britain, from Latin America, while at the same time continuing to support Colombia's forceful subjection of an unwilling Panama. Roosevelt made some errors of judgment in his Panama policies, especially in allowing Phillipe Bunau-Varilla too much influence, but the intense moral tone of much of the historiography on Roosevelt's Panama policies is unjustified and consistently understates the critical importance of France while concentrating on ephemeral Latin American public opinion. Although Europe was effectively neutralized by Roosevelt's careful handling of Britain and France and his firmer dealing with Germany, the European powers still considered a formal concert against the United States proposed by Spain in September, 1906, when the Cuban crisis began. Europe's divided interests as well as Roosevelt's carefully delimited American policy made such European intervention unnecessary as well as impractical.[16]

15. Burton, *Theodore Roosevelt*, 38–42, Collin, *Theodore Roosevelt*, 158–72; for French-Dominican conflict see *FRUS*, 1895, pp. 235–42, 397–402; for France and Guatemala see *FRUS*, 1902, p. 569, and Warren G. Kneer, *Great Britain and the Caribbean, 1901–1913* (East Lansing, Mich., 1975), 15–16; for France and Venezuela in 1905 see Philip Jessup, *Elihu Root* (2 vols.; New York, 1938), I, 495–99; Jean Jules Jusserand, *What Me Befell* (London, 1933), 219–26, 260–346; Ninkovich, "Theodore Roosevelt," 234. For French approval of American Panama policies and a thoughtful assessment of the growth of American power see Jean Jules Jusserand to MAE, November 9, 1903, N.S., Colombie, 5; for French concern about Roosevelt's Monroe Doctrine policy see Jusserand to MAE, August 12, December 4, 1905, in N.S. Etats-Unis, 15, all in AMAE.

16. Robert A. Friedlander, "A Reassessment of Roosevelt's Role in the Panamanian Revolution of 1903," *Western Political Quarterly*, XIV (1961), 535–43; for French opposition see Lucien N. B. Wyse, *Le Rapt de Panama: L'Abandon du canal aux Etats-Unis* (Toulon, 1904); on Latin American public opinion see John Patterson, "Latin American Reaction to the Panama Revolution of 1903," *HAHR*, XXIV (1944), 342–51; Louis E. Van Norman, "Latin-American Views of Panama and the Canal," *American Review of Re-*

Latin America

Roosevelt remained optimistic that Latin America would experience the "extraordinary development" and political stability that would make it independent of American "guardianship." Roosevelt, who had no ulterior motives in establishing the Dominican receivership, hoped that the Panama Canal would revitalize the Caribbean and northern Latin America and that limited amounts of American economic and political aid might move Latin America's smaller nations into the world mainstream. Roosevelt's and Root's Central American peace initiatives in 1906 and 1907 sought to unify the small states and change the system that made nations the private fiefs of the political leaders James Bryce called "selfish adventurers." [17]

Latin America's clash with the new power of North America came at a bad time in Latin American development both economically and culturally. After Auguste Comte's positivism provided a transforming influence in Brazil, Chile, and Mexico, incipient Latin American nationalism in the 1850s was further encouraged by literary romanticism. But Spanish America, already divided in its heritage between its nativist and colonial traditions, was overwhelmed in its most receptive stage in the mid–nineteenth century by European culture, mainly French influences, which had little relevance to New World society. Juan B. Terán proclaimed that "[Latin] America was the satellite of Europe," an ironic and inappropriate foundation for a Latin American nationalism based almost wholly on European literary romanticism. France particularly courted Latin America, adopting a pan-Latinism that eventually inspired José Rodó's Ariel-Calaban metaphor of the early twentieth century, a division between North American materialism and Latin American sensitivity that oversimplified and romanticized the differences between a developed, unified North America and an undeveloped, disunited Latin America. In the

---

views, March, 1904, p. 335; Marks, Velvet on Iron, 97–105. For one example of a severely critical analysis see George E. Mowry, The Era of Theodore Roosevelt and the Birth of Modern America, 1900–1912 (New York, 1962), 154–55; Lord Acton to Sir Edward Grey, September 17, 1906, Cuba, in FO 371/56, PRO. For European-American economic rivalry in Mexico see Frederich Katz, The Secret War in Mexico: Europe, The United States, and the Mexican Revolution (Chicago, 1981), 21–27.

17. TR, "The Republics of the South" (May 11, 1908), in TRWN, XVI, 280; TR, "The United States and the South American Republics" (October 3, 1913), ibid., 299; Lester D. Langley, The United States and the Caribbean (rev. ed.; Athens, Ga., 1985), 29; James Bryce to Sir Edward Grey, April 30, 1908, in FO 881/9265, p. 31, PRO.

1890s, encouraged by Spanish political propaganda directed at the coming conflict with the United States, Latin America made a cultural rapprochement with Spain, no longer a serious direct political threat. Latin America's schizophrenia was best exemplified by Leopold Zea's observation that pre-Columbian culture had nothing in common with the new Europeanized modern Latin America.[18]

At the beginning of the twentieth century, Latin America remained deeply frightened by and breathtakingly ignorant of the fully developed colossus to the north. In 1902, William Stead, a British writer convinced that the world was becoming totally Americanized, observed that Latin America had almost completely escaped the North American cultural invasion. While the United States had been Americanizing Europe, Britain had been anglicizing Latin America, the Monroe Doctrine notwithstanding. Stead observed that New York and Chicago had more influence in London than in Santiago.[19]

Part of Roosevelt's problem with Latin America was to convince skeptical Latin Americans that the United States was not an ugly, coarse colossus looking for additional territory, new colonies for Negro slaves, or other unimaginable devil theories spread equally by Europeans resisting new American influence, American senators resisting the new power of the executive in foreign affairs, and the press, technologically able to produce newspapers cheaply and willing to sensationalize for partisan—mainly domestic—political motives or to sell more papers. Roosevelt only partly succeeded in allaying Latin American fears. The sense of North American betrayal, however, owes as much to Latin American disappointment in its inability to match North American political and economic success as to the foreign policies of Roosevelt's presidency.[20]

18. Eugenio Pereira Salas, "Cultural Emancipation of America," in UNESCO, *Old World and New World* (Berne, Switzerland, 1956), 102, 104–105, 107, 109. Leopoldo Zea, *The Latin American Mind*, trans. James H. Abbott and Lowell Dunham (Norman, 1963); and Zea, *Latin America and the World*, trans. Frances K. Hendricks and Beatrice Berler (Norman, 1969), 27–31.

19. Mary Patricia Chapman, "Yankeephobia: An Analysis of the Anti-United States Bias of Certain Spanish South American Intellectuals, 1898–1928" (Ph.D. dissertation, Stanford University, 1950); J. Fred Rippy, "Literary Yankeephobia in Hispanic America," *Journal of International Relations*, XII (1922), 350–71, 524–38; Clemente Pereda, *Rodó's Main Sources* (San Juan, P.R., 1941), 107–109; Stead, *Americanisation of the World*, 83, 85.

20. John Reid, *Spanish American Images of the United States* (Gainesville, 1977), 260; Samuel Shapiro, "A Common History of the Americas?" in Shapiro (ed.), *Cultural Factors in Inter-American Relations* (South Bend, Ind., 1968), 39–66; Chapman, "Yankeephobia," 19–30.

The major tragic failure of Roosevelt's Caribbean policies stemmed from the catastrophic vacuum left by the death of José Martí, Latin America's charismatic intellectual and patriot, who at the time of his death in 1895 had already begun to evoke a new revolutionary American nationalism divorced from Europe and independent of the other, northern America. Martí not only led the Cuban revolution from Spain, he had formulated the basis for a post-Spanish Cuba based on freedom from Western colonialism, an activist *criollo* role, free from elitist, Europeanized culture. Martí's death deprived the Caribbean of its only political and intellectual leader with the ability to lead and inspire a new Latin American nationalism. In Martí's absence, Theodore Roosevelt played the role of the archetypal hero freeing Cuba from Spain, and Theodore Roosevelt presided over the new Caribbean order, not nearly as dreadful as Latin American nationalists proclaim but hardly what Martí would have wanted. Although Martí and Roosevelt would have made fierce rivals, they shared some affinities, including fragile physical health, the belief that an intellectual and political leader must be able to fight and die, and a charismatic ability to inspire huge masses of people. Martí, like Roosevelt, a man whose whole life was a moral sermon, believed that he could lead a moral regeneration of Cuba. Both North and South America might have been better served if José Martí, not Theodore Roosevelt, had freed Cuba and become the intellectual and political leader of a new independent Caribbean nationalism.[21]

One can only speculate what José Martí's Caribbean and his Cuba might have been like. Martí and Roosevelt both believed that sugar was Cuba's strength and salvation; whether Martí could have instituted an alternative economy based on something other than extractive agriculture is speculative. But with the death of young Martí in 1895, and to a lesser extent of the older Gregorio Luperón in 1896, there were no Latin American leaders capable of inspiring or speaking for Latin American nationalism; there were virtually no Latin American leaders at all. The United States looked to Porfirio Díaz in Mexico for help, not because Díaz was malleable but because he had become an elder statesman by default. Venezuela's Cipriano Castro and the Dominican Republic's Ulíses Heureaux were hardly inspiring Latin

21. John M. Kirk, *José Martí: Mentor of the Cuban Nation* (Tampa, Fla., 1983), 155; C. A. M. Hennessy, "The Roots of Cuban Nationalism," *International Affairs*, XXXIX (1963), 348–52; Gordon K. Lewis, *Main Currents in Caribbean Thought: The Historical Evolution of Caribbean Society in Its Ideological Aspects, 1492–1900* (Baltimore, 1983), 297–303.

American leaders though both followed the example of Venezuela's Antonio Guzmán Blanco in using nationalism as a political device to maintain power. José Marroquín was too parochial, Guatemala's Estrada Cabrera and Nicaragua's José Zelaya too self-serving, and Colombia's Rafael Reyes too politically ineffective, even in post-Marroquín Colombia, to offer any hope of an indigenous Latin American political solution. Tomás Estrada Palma is a grim reminder of what all Latin America and especially Cuba lost with the death of Martí.[22]

In the vacuum that followed Martí's death, Americans vainly searched for an indigenous Latin American leader or leaders. The American-inspired governments that were installed were mainly vehicles of convenience instituted reluctantly and by default. Cuba and the Dominican Republic were two striking examples of American efforts to disengage from colonial entanglements. In Panama Roosevelt turned to a Frenchman, Phillipe Bunau-Varilla, to avoid the difficulties of working with local Latin American politicians. Root and Roosevelt hoped Porfirio Díaz might prove to be the American intermediary in Central America, but Díaz was obviously a temporary solution. Roosevelt's interest in Latin America declined sharply in his second term, as he devoted more of his energies to European matters and the settlement of the Russo-Japanese War.

Root, too, began to lose interest and became discouraged as he perceived that even the most patient and intelligent diplomacy might prove unavailing in a still divided Latin America, where national rivalries and domestic instabilities, even within the larger nations, made any overall settlement unlikely. Even in Argentina, where Luis Drago pursued his doctrine of nonintervention, his own government, though it openly supported his position, secretly opposed and undermined him. In 1907 Assistant Secretary of State Alvey Adee, in an effort to unify the five increasingly volatile Central American republics, worked at the only tactic that seemed open to the United States, a new coalition with Mexico's Díaz, a hopeless policy that revealed the limits of Roosevelt's and Root's Central American diplomacy. Roosevelt, like McKinley before, extremely sensitive to the cultural prob-

---

22. Kirk, *José Martí*, 155; Hennessy, "Roots of Cuban Nationalism," 348–52; Lewis, *Main Currents in Caribbean Thought*, 297–303. For a detailed American analysis of the Central American political leaders and their governments see "Preparations for Secretary Knox's Central American Trip, 1912," Box 33, Philander Knox Papers, LC. See also A. Curtis Wilgus (ed.), *South American Dictators During the First Century of Independence* (Washington, D.C., 1937).

lems of Protestant democracy in Catholic colonial dependencies, supported retention of Catholic educational and legal systems, while avoiding interference with local customs, though Cuban and Filipino anti-clericalism made such meliorating practices politically difficult.[23]

Roosevelt's preference for noneconomic international policies, though praiseworthy, by purposefully neglecting American business interests may have tempted the next administration to reverse Roosevelt's policy of beneficent altruism in favor of a cruder dollar diplomacy. Roosevelt was satisfied with his political settlement with Britain, which left British economic influence intact in the most profitable Latin American areas, creating problems, especially in Mexico, for Wilson's administration. Egypt, India, and South Africa constituted the sum of contemporary considerations about colonialism, which still revolved around primitive political issues and rudimentary, mostly short-term, economic solutions. The Third World existed, as the American-Philippine war and frequent Caribbean unrest demonstrated, but the immediate problems, especially of race, religion, and acquiring coal for new naval technology, were too pressing for questions of the Third World and development capitalism to be considered by intellectuals, let alone politicians.[24]

Conclusion

Roosevelt moved the United States closer to Europe, won Europe's assent to the Monroe Doctrine, made peace and a realistic diplomatic understanding with Japan, and tried to temper American power in the Caribbean with a genuine understanding of Latin American sensitivities, political disappointment, and suspicions. There were no clearly superior choices in Latin America. Backing Columbia over Panama was no more correct than choosing Panama. Making peace in Central America included "the retention in power of President Estrada Cabrera," which meant "the old regime of assassination, torture, robbery, and corruption will now continue unchecked." In Cuba Roosevelt tried without success to put the insurgents in power

23. William Haggard to Sir Edward Grey, August 22, 1906, in FO 420/237, p. 29, PRO; Adee's plan is in Case 7805, M862, Roll 582, RG 59, NA; Reuter, *Catholic Influence on American Colonial Policies*, 102; May, *Imperial Democracy*, 269–70.

24. Kendrick A. Clements, "Woodrow Wilson's Mexican Policy," *DH*, IV (1980), 120, 125; see, for example, Charles Francis Adams, "Reflex Light from Africa," *Century*, LXXII (May, 1906), 101–11; problems of colonialism are discussed throughout the TR-Cecil Spring Rice correspondence; see TR's Romanes Lecture at Oxford University, June 7, 1910, "Biological Analogies in History," in *TRWN*, XII, 25–60.

in 1906, an attempt that impressed and astonished the British but failed to establish an indigenous Cuban government. In the Dominican Republic, Roosevelt's choices were to allow a European struggle for a share of the debt or intervene and impose an orderly apportionment, an effort applauded by Europeans and most Americans, contested by the Senate on domestic and party grounds, and finally compromised to everyone's short-term satisfaction.[25]

But the energies that might have gone to thinking more constructively about the real Latin American dilemmas were spent in trying to get the smallest arrangement approved by a suspicious Congress. Not much was possible in Roosevelt's time; he was a master at getting what he could, and what he did get was not the beginning of a new American imperial age but the limited success of a small transitional period between early American geographical isolation and the Armageddon of total world war. World War I transformed the world and the Americas and created new international relationships that owed little to Roosevelt's intelligent efforts or to his brief, colorful age of transition.[26]

25. H. A. R. Hervey to Sir Edward Grey, September 4, 1906, in FO 420/237, p. 31, PRO.

26. For the limitations of Roosevelt's goals see Robert H. Weibe, *The Search for Order, 1877–1920* (New York, 1967), 252. For the transforming character of World War I see Eksteins, *Rites of Spring;* Eric Hobsbawm, *The Age of Empire, 1875–1914* (New York, 1987), 329–34; and Frank Costigliola, *Awkward Dominion: American Political, Economic, and Cultural Relations with Europe, 1919–1933* (Ithaca, N.Y., 1984), 15–26. For the flux in the Roosevelt administration's relationship to business see William H. Becker, *The Dynamics of Business-Government Relations: Industry and Exports, 1893–1921* (Chicago, 1981), esp. 114–15, see also Burton I. Kaufman, "The Organizational Dimension of United States Economic Foreign Policy, 1900–1920," *Business History Review,* XLVI (1972), 17–44. The corporatist synthesis may offer a more promising historiography than the economic determinism or dependency theories of the 1970s. See John Lewis Gaddis, "The Corporatist Synthesis: A Skeptical View," and Michael J. Hogan, "Corporatism: A Positive Appraisal," both in *DH,* X (1986), 357–62, 363–72. Most of the corporatist emphasis is the on post-Roosevelt and post-World War I eras. My main historiographical concern is the tacking on of Roosevelt and his times to paradigms more concerned with the later twentieth century, when America's economy was fully developed and the world diplomatic context was far different. For a more nuanced awareness of how historical circumstances in the United States and the individual Caribbean and Central American countries changed the degree and nature of American involvement see Whitney T. Perkins, *Constraint of Empire: The United States and Caribbean Interventions* (Westport, Conn., 1981).

Bibliographical Essay

Theodore Roosevelt

Central to TR scholarship are the massive Theodore Roosevelt Papers at LC, part of the microfilmed Presidential Papers Series (485 reels); Elting E. Morison (ed.), *The Letters of Theodore Roosevelt* (8 vols.; Cambridge, Mass., 1951–54); and *The Works of Theodore Roosevelt* (Memorial Edition, 24 vols.; New York, 1923–26; National Edition, 20 vols., New York, 1926). A valuable reference work based on the two sets is Albert Bushnell Hart and Herbert Ronald Ferleger, *Theodore Roosevelt Cyclopedia* (1941; rev. ed.; New York, 1988), with a new bibliographical essay by John A. Gable, which updates Roosevelt scholarship. The Harvard University *Theodore Roosevelt Collection: Dictionary Catalog and Shelflist* (5 vols.; Cambridge, Mass., 1970) is the basic bibliographical guide; the new *Supplement* (Cambridge, Mass., 1986) offers a one-volume updating of the material since 1950. Two older but still useful compilations of letters are Joseph B. Bishop, *Theodore Roosevelt and His Time* (2 vols.; New York, 1920), and *Selected Correspondence of Theodore Roosevelt and Henry Cabot Lodge, 1884–1918* (New York, 1925).

The basic biography, Henry Pringle, *Theodore Roosevelt: A Biography* (New York, 1931), though seriously flawed, has not been superseded. The best of the interpretive biographies is William Harbaugh, *Power and Responsibility: The Life and Times of Theodore Roosevelt* (New York, 1961), revised as *The Life and Times of Theodore Roosevelt* (New York, 1963). Edmund Morris, *The Rise of Theodore Roosevelt* (New York, 1979), the first volume of a multivolume biography, ends with the vice-presidency.

There is no consensus on how to replace Pringle's original portrayal. Some recent treatments of note include Frederick W. Marks III, *Velvet on Iron: The Diplomacy of Theodore Roosevelt* (Lincoln, Neb., 1979), and Richard H. Collin, *Theodore Roosevelt, Culture, Diplomacy, and Expansion* (Baton Rouge, 1985), both sympathetic studies of Roosevelt's diplomacy. William C. Widenor, *Henry Cabot Lodge and the Search for an American Foreign Policy* (Berkeley, 1980), deals extensively with Roosevelt's diplomacy. John Milton Cooper, *The Warrior and the Priest: Woodrow Wilson and Theodore Roosevelt* (Cambridge, Mass., 1983), is an important comparative study focusing mainly on the post-presidential

Roosevelt; see also Frank Ninkovich, "Theodore Roosevelt: Civilization as Ideology," *DH*, X (1986), 221–45, a combination of intellectual and diplomatic history. Eugene P. Trani, "Cautious Warrior: Theodore Roosevelt and the Diplomacy of Activism," in Frank J. Merli and Theodore A. Wilson (eds.), *Makers of American Diplomacy from Benjamin Franklin to Henry Kissinger* (New York, 1974), 305–31, is an especially judicious assessment. G. Wallace Chessman, *Theodore Roosevelt and the Politics of Power* (Boston, 1969), is a useful short biography; George E. Mowry, *The Era of Theodore Roosevelt and the Birth of Modern America, 1900–1912* (New York, 1958), is a good basic history.

Some older works that are still essential include Howard K. Beale, *Theodore Roosevelt and the Rise of America to World Power* (Baltimore, 1956); Alfred L. P. Dennis, *Adventures in American Diplomacy, 1896–1906* (New York, 1928); John M. Blum, *The Republican Roosevelt* (Cambridge, Mass., 1954); and John Dewey, "Theodore Roosevelt," *Dial*, February 8, 1919, pp. 115–16.

Changes in American diplomacy are well covered in Charles S. Campbell, *The Transformation of American Foreign Relations, 1865–1900* (New York, 1976); Ernest May, *Imperial Democracy: The Emergence of America as a World Power* (New York, 1961); May, *American Imperialism: A Speculative Essay* (New York, 1968); Walter LaFeber, *The New Empire: An Interpretation of American Expansion, 1860–1898* (Ithaca, N.Y., 1963); Robert Endicott Osgood, *Ideals and Self-Interest in America's Foreign Relations* (Chicago, 1955); and Raymond Esthus, *Theodore Roosevelt and the International Rivalries* (Waltham, Mass., 1970), a suggestive interpretive essay. For Roosevelt's significant relations with Japan see Esthus, *Theodore Roosevelt and Japan* (Seattle, 1966); Esthus, *Double Eagle and Rising Sun: The Russians and Japanese at Portsmouth in 1905* (Durham, N.C., 1988); and Charles Neu, *An Uncertain Friendship: Theodore Roosevelt and Japan, 1906–1909* (Cambridge, Mass., 1967).

For Latin American relations essential works include David Healy, *Drive to Hegemony: The United States in the Caribbean, 1898–1917* (Madison, Wisc., 1988); Healy, *US Expansionism: The Imperialist Urge in the 1890s* (Madison, Wisc., 1970); Lester D. Langley, *The Banana Wars: An Inner History of American Empire, 1900–1934* (Lexington, Ky., 1983); Dana G. Munro, *Intervention and Dollar Diplomacy in the Caribbean, 1900–1921* (Princeton, 1964); and Whitney Perkins, *Constraint of Empire: The United States and Caribbean Interventions* (Westport, Conn., 1981), though it concentrates on post–Roosevelt diplomacy.

For the diplomatic historiography of Roosevelt's era see Hugh de Santis, "Imperialist Impulse and American Innocence," and Paolo E. Coletta, "The Diplomacy of Theodore Roosevelt and William Howard Taft," in Gerald K. Haines and J. Samuel Walker (eds.), *American Foreign Relations: A Historiographical Review* (Westport, Conn., 1981); and Richard Dean Burns (ed.), *Guide to American Foreign Relations Since 1700* (Santa Barbara, Calif., 1983), 401–50.

Naval history is central to Roosevelt's time. The two most comprehensive treatments are Richard D. Challener, *Admirals, Generals, and American Foreign*

Policy (Princeton, 1973); and William Reynolds Braisted, *The United States Navy in the Pacific, 1897–1909* (Austin, Tex., 1958). Also useful are Ronald Spector, *Admiral of the New Empire: The Life and Career of George Dewey* (Baton Rouge, 1974); Peter Karsten, *The Naval Aristocracy: The Golden Age of Annapolis and the Emergence of Modern Navalism* (New York, 1972). Richard W. Turk, *The Ambiguous Relationship: Theodore Roosevelt and Alfred Thayer Mahan* (Westport, Conn., 1987), reprints the Roosevelt-Mahan correspondence. James B. Reckner, *Teddy Roosevelt's Great White Fleet* (Annapolis, 1988), summarizes the new naval technology and Roosevelt's use of the navy as a diplomatic tool. Two useful doctoral dissertations should be consulted: Daniel J. Costello, "Planning for War: A History of the General Board of the Navy, 1900–1914" (Ph.D. dissertation, Fletcher School of Law and Diplomacy, 1958); and Albert C. Stillson, "The Development and Maintenance of the American Naval Establishment, 1901–1909" (Ph.D. dissertation, Columbia University, 1959). J. A. S. Grenville and George Berkeley Young, *Politics, Strategy, and American Diplomacy: Studies in Foreign Policy, 1873–1917* (New Haven, 1966), is an especially useful combination of naval, strategic, and diplomatic research.

Other useful monographs include Willard B. Gatewood, Jr., *Theodore Roosevelt and the Art of Controversy* (Baton Rouge, 1970); David H. Burton, *Theodore Roosevelt and His English Correspondents: A Special Relationship of Friends* (Philadelphia, 1973); Burton, *Theodore Roosevelt: Confident Imperialist* (Philadelphia, 1968); Thomas G. Dyer, *Theodore Roosevelt and the Idea of Race* (Baton Rouge, 1980); Edward Wagenknecht, *The Seven Worlds of Theodore Roosevelt* (New York, 1958); and John Allen Gable, *The Bull Moose Years* (Port Washington, N.Y., 1968).

Europe

The rich historiography on the changing European diplomatic relationships at the turn of the century includes Charles S. Campbell, *Anglo-American Understanding, 1898–1903* (Baltimore, 1957); R. G. Neale, *Great Britain and the United States, 1898–1900* (East Lansing, Mich., 1966), especially the overview of British diplomatic options in 1898, xiii–xxii; George Monger, *The End of Isolation* (London, 1963); Paul Kennedy, *The Rise of the Anglo-German Antagonism, 1860–1914* (London, 1980); William L. Langer, *The Diplomacy of Imperialism* (New York, 1935); Lionel Gelber, *The Rise of Anglo-American Friendship: A Study in World Politics, 1898–1906* (London, 1938); H. C. Allen, *Great Britain and the United States: A History of Anglo-American Relations, 1783–1952* (New York, 1955); A. E. Campbell, *Great Britain and the United States, 1895–1905* (London, 1960); and Bradford Perkins, *The Great Rapprochement: England and the United States, 1895–1914* (London, 1969).

Warren G. Kneer, *Great Britain and the Caribbean, 1901–1913* (East Lansing, Mich., 1975), is extremely useful. Kenneth Bourne, *The Balance of Power in North America* (Berkeley, 1967), is essential for both the diplomatic and naval changes. Also see Arthur J. Marder, *Anatomy of British Sea Power* (New York, 1940); and E. L. Woodward, *Great Britain and the German Navy* (London, 1935). Paul Kennedy, *The Rise and Fall of the Great Powers: Economic Change and Military Conflict from 1500 to 2000* (New York, 1987), is a sweeping multidimensional synthesis. See also Kennedy, *Strategy and Diplomacy, 1870–1945* (London, 1983), which reprints several useful studies of the Anglo-German naval rivalry; and Franklyn Arthur Johnson, *Defence by Committee: The British Committee of Imperial Defence, 1885–1959* (London, 1960).

Manfred Jonas, *The United States and Germany: A Diplomatic History* (Ithaca, N.Y., 1984); and Ivo Nikolai Lambi, *The Navy and German Power Politics* (London, 1984), are recent and thorough. Holger H. Herwig, *Politics of Frustration: The United States in German Naval Planning, 1889–1941* (Boston, 1976), and Challener, *Admirals, Generals, and American Foreign Policy*, must be consulted.

The German-American diplomatic effects of the Spanish-American War are covered in Lester Shippee, "Germany and the Spanish-American War," *AHR*, XXX (1925), 754–77; J. Fred Rippy, "The European Powers and the Spanish-American War," *James Sprunt Historical Studies* (1927), No. 2, pp. 22–52; Thomas Bailey, "Dewey and the Germans at Manila Bay," *AHR*, XLV (1939), 59–81. Also see John Gary Clifford, "Admiral Dewey and the Germans, 1903: A New Perspective," *Mid-America*, XLIX (1967), 214–20.

Venezuela and the Anglo-German Blockade

Although a great deal of the diplomatic correspondence has been printed in *FRUS*, 1903, it is still necessary to use the Despatches from American Ministers files in RG 59, NA. Venezuela Despatches are in Microcopy M79, Roll 56, and the British Despatches are in M30, Roll 193. The most important British Foreign Office Papers are in the Venezuela Confidential Print, FO 420/206, PRO. Many British documents have been unexpectedly reprinted as the "British Blue Book No. 1, 1903," in *Senate Documents*, 58th Cong., 3rd Sess., No. 119, Serial 4769, papers relating to the blockade and the Hague Court hearings. Herbert Bowen's Correspondence is in *Senate Documents*, 58th Cong., 2nd Sess., No. 316, Serial 4620.

On the question of debt Herbert Feis, *Europe: The World's Banker, 1870–1914* (New Haven, 1930), is an indispensable guide for European involvement and competition in a world context. Equally valuable is William H. Wynne and Edwin Borchard, *State Insolvency and Foreign Bondholders* (2 vols.; New Haven, 1951). Borchard treats the general legal principles of nineteenth- and early twentieth-century national debt default; Wynne in the second volume offers detailed case studies of the major debt defaults and their consequences. D. C. M. Platt, *Latin America and British Trade, 1806–1914* (London, 1972); "British Bondholders in Nineteenth Century Latin America—Injury and Remedy," *Inter-American Economic Affairs*, XIV (Winter, 1960), 9–44; and "The Allied Coercion of Venezuela, 1902–3—A Reassessment," *Inter-American Economic Affairs*, XV (Spring, 1962), 3–28, are essential.

For Venezuela see especially Judith Ewell, *Venezuela: A Century of Change* (Stanford, 1984), a sensitive political and cultural history; and Miriam Hood, *Gunboat Diplomacy, 1895–1905: Great Power Pressure in Venezuela* (London, 1983). The best Venezuelan histories include John V. Lombardi, *Venezuela: The Search for Order, the Dream of Progress* (New York, 1982); and Guillermo Moron, *A History of Venezuela*, ed. and trans. John Street (London, 1963). Also see George S. Wise, *Caudillo: A Portrait of Antonio Guzmán Blanco* (Columbia, Mo., 1951). Two doctoral dissertations are indispensable: William M. Sullivan, "The Rise of Despotism in Venezuela: Cipriano Castro, 1899–1908" (Ph.D. dissertation, University of New Mexico, 1974), an encyclopedic examination of Venezuela's domestic and foreign affairs; and Wayne Lee Guthrie, "The Anglo-German Intervention in Venezuela, 1902–03" (Ph.D. dissertation, University of California, San Diego, 1983), a compelling account of the Anglo-German diplomatic difficulties.

American-German relations are thoroughly explored in Alfred Vagts, *Deutschland und die Vereinigten Staaten in Der Weltpolitik* (2 vols.; New York, 1935); and Vagts, "Hopes and Fears of an American-German War, 1870–1915," *Political Science Quarterly*, LIV (1939), 514–35, LV (1940), 53–76. For full treatments of the developing German-American rivalry see Jeanette L. Keim, *Forty Years of German-American Political Relations* (Philadelphia, 1919); Clara Eve Schieber, *The Transformation of American Sentiment Toward Germany* (Boston, 1923); and Charles C. Tansill, *The Purchase of the Danish West Indies* (Baltimore, 1932). Holger H. Herwig's works on Germany, the United States, and Venezuela are especially helpful, including *Politics of Frustration: The United States in German Naval Planning, 1889–1941* (Boston, 1976); *Germany's Vision of Empire in Venezuela, 1871–1914* (Princeton, 1986); and Herwig and J. Leon Helguera, *Alemania y el bloqueo internacional de Venezuela* (Caracas, 1977), in English and Spanish, especially useful for the German naval intervention. Maurizio Vernassa, *Emigrazione, diplomazia e cannoniero l'inteventi Italiano in Venezuela, 1902–1903* (Leghorn, 1980), covers the Italian participation.

For the controversy over TR's ultimatum to Germany see Howard K. Beale, *Theodore Roosevelt and the Rise of America to World Power* (Baltimore, 1956), 399–431; and Frederick Marks III, *Velvet on Iron: The Diplomacy of Theodore Roosevelt* (Lincoln, Neb., 1979), 38–53, 70–77. A summary of how the historiographical debate developed is in Edward D. Parsons, "The German-American Crisis of 1902–1903," *Historian*, XXXIII (1971), 436–52. See also Paul S. Holbo, "Perilous Obscurity: Public Diplomacy and the Press in the Venezuela Crisis, 1902–1903," *Historian*, XXXII (1970), 428–48. A thorough reconstruction of the events and Roosevelt's account of his ultimatum are in Edmund Morris, "'A Few Pregnant Days': Theodore Roosevelt and the Venezuelan Crisis of 1902," *TRAJ*, XV (Winter, 1989), 2–13. For TR's naval diplomacy, Seward W. Livermore, "Theodore Roosevelt, the American Navy, and the Venezuelan Crisis of 1902–1903," *AHR*, LI (1946), 452–71, is essential.

Calvin DeArmond Davis, *The United States and the First Hague Peace Confer-

ence (Ithaca, N.Y., 1962); and Davis, *The United States and the Second Hague Peace Conference: American Diplomacy and International Organization, 1899–1914* (Durham, N.C., 1975), deal with the arbitration movement, Roosevelt's support of arbitration and the Hague World Court, and the consequences of the Hague Court rulings. Also see Margaret Robinson, *Arbitration and the Hague Peace Conferences, 1899 and 1907* (Philadelphia, 1936). Allan Nevins, *Henry White: Thirty Years of American Diplomacy* (New York, 1930), is useful on the Anglo-American diplomacy.

Panama

Many of the most useful primary sources are printed. Because of the political controversies concerning Panama and the canal, virtually all of the official American diplomatic and naval correspondence is available in American government documents. Two useful guides to the enormous document bibliography are in Gerstle Mack, *The Land Divided: A History of the Panama Canal and Other Isthmian Canal Projects* (New York, 1944), 598–607; and Miles P. DuVal, Jr., *Cadiz to Cathay: The Story of the Long Diplomatic Struggle for the Panama Canal* (Stanford, 1940), 522–29. Besides the TR, John Hay, and Elihu Root Papers at LC, the Tomás Herrán Papers, Special Collections Division, Georgetown University Library, are invaluable, especially since Captain Miles Duval, Jr., translated the Herrán correspondence used in his books. Lewis Haupt's Papers at LC are a full source of canal commission and canal route politics. See also the John G. Walker Papers and the Albert C. Gleaves Papers in the Naval Historical Foundation Manuscript Collection in LC. The John Bassett Moore Papers, LC, are a varied and rich collection, especially the Panama folders in Box 134, the bound and unbound scrapbooks, and the memoir segments recalling specific events. The Francis B. Loomis Papers, Stanford University, are essential for the background and the diplomacy of American involvement. The usual diplomatic and naval correspondence in the Despatches and naval records for Panama are less illuminating since much of the archival material was printed in the myriad government documents produced by the countless debates and investigations. The Area 8 and the Subject Files (especially VI) in RG 45, Naval Records Collection of the Naval Records and Library, NA, are well worth consulting. Copies of the naval correspondence are preserved in the Panama Correspondence, RG 45, entry 304, NA. Also useful is the correspondence in Records of Naval Operating Forces, Caribbean Squadron, RG 313, NA, though some of it is duplicated in other naval records collections. American naval strategic concerns are treated in William Roger Adams, "Strategy, Diplomacy, and Isthmian Canal Security, 1880–1917" (Ph.D. dissertation, Florida State University, 1974).

The most useful of the government document collections include the Isthmian Canal Commission Reports in *Senate Documents* 58th Cong., 2nd Sess., No. 222, Serial 4609; *Complete Correspondence of the New Company and the United*

States in *Senate Documents*, 57th Cong., 2nd Sess., No. 34, Serial 4417; *Diplomatic History of the Panama Canal* in *Senate Documents*, 63rd Cong., 2nd Sess., No. 474, Serial 6582; and *The Use of Military Force in Colombia* in *Senate Documents*, 58th Cong., 2nd Sess., No. 143, Serial 4589. For the other relevant government documents see the footnote citations and the DuVal and Mack bibliographies.

One enormous source bears special attention and caution, *The Story of Panama: Hearings on the Rainey Resolution Before the Committee of Foreign Affairs of the House of Representatives* (Washington, D.C., 1913). *SP* contains much that is useful, including good translations of Colombian diplomatic correspondence and Roosevelt's messages to Congress, as well as much that is speculative, including William Nelson Cromwell's legal brief prepared to support his large bill for legal services to the Compagnie Nouvelle. *SP* is an extremely useful hodgepodge but must be used with caution. The same caveat applies to Philippe Bunau-Varilla, *Panama, the Creation, Destruction, and Resurrection* (London, 1913), an autobiographical account that serves to justify its author. John Major, "Who Wrote the Hay–Bunau-Varilla Convention?" *DH*, VIII (1984), 115–23, persuasively demonstrates that Bunau-Varilla's account of his key role in drafting the treaty was utterly false. Although most of the material in Bunau-Varilla's colorful account is essential, much of what he writes is necessarily suspect. Both the Philippe Bunau-Varilla Papers, and the John Tyler Morgan Papers at LC are useful but ultimately disappointing. George S. Morison's Papers at the Smithsonian Museum of American History are of some interest though marred by the absence of the critical 1902 letterbooks. George Abbott Morison, *George Shattuck Morison, 1842–1903: A Memoir* (Peterborough, N.H., 1942), is an important account of the key second Walker Commission engineer.

Although Colombia's diplomatic documents concerning its Panamanian diplomacy, in *Libro azul, documentos diplomáticos sobre el canal y la rebellion del Istmo de Panamá* (Bogotá, 1904), are extensive, the collection was edited by Rafael Reyes and is not complete.

The most useful overall histories of Panama and the canal are Miles P. DuVal, Jr., *Cadiz to Cathay: The Story of the Long Diplomatic Struggle for the Panama Canal* (Stanford, 1940); DuVal, *And the Mountains Will Move: The Story of the Building of the Panama Canal* (Stanford, 1947); Gerstle Mack, *The Land Divided: A History of the Panama Canal and Other Isthmian Canal Projects* (New York, 1944); Dwight Carroll Miner, *The Fight for the Panama Route: The Story of the Spooner Act and the Hay-Herrán Treaty* (New York, 1940); and David McCullough, *The Path Between the Seas: The Creation of the Panama Canal, 1870–1914* (New York, 1977); see also Alex Perez-Venero, *Before the Five Frontiers: Panama from 1821–1903* (New York, 1978); and Gustave Anguizola, *Philippe Bunau-Varilla: The Man Behind the Panama Canal* (Chicago, 1980), a very sympathetic account of Bunau-Varilla. Charles D. Ameringer, "The Panama

Canal Lobby of Philippe Bunau-Varilla and William Nelson Cromwell, *AHR*, LXVIII (1963), 346–63; and "Philippe Bunau-Varilla: New Light on the Panama Canal Treaty," *AHR*, XLVI (1966), 28–52, are detailed and useful. Alfred Charles Richard, "The Panama Canal in American National Consciousness, 1870–1922" (Ph.D. dissertation, Boston University, 1969), is a valuable compilation of the changing public image of the canal from projection to after its completion. James F. Vivian, "The Taking of the Panama Canal Zone: Myth and Reality," *DH*, IV (1980), 95–100, argues persuasively that TR never said, "I took the canal zone," in his March, 1911, Berkeley speech and that the main historiographical attack on Roosevelt's arrogance is based on a New York *Times* misquotation. Roosevelt's own reading draft of the speech is in RP, Reel 421; his version and defense of his canal policies is in TR, "How the United States Acquired the Right to Dig the Panama Canal," *Outlook*, XCIX (October 7, 1911), 314–18.

E. Taylor Parks, *Colombia and the United States, 1760–1934* (Durham, N.C., 1935), is basic and balanced; Thomas R. Favell, "The Antecedents of Panama's Separation from Colombia" (Ph.D. dissertation, Fletcher School of Law and Diplomacy, 1951), is invaluable in relating the Colombian civil war to the diplomatic dispute with America and in translating much of the Colombian correspondence; Charles W. Bergquist, *Coffee and Conflict in Colombia, 1886–1910* (Durham, N.C., 1978), is much broader than its title might suggest, ranging through Colombian culture, politics, economics, and the War of the Thousand Days; Helen Delpar, *Red Against Blue: The Liberal Party in Colombian Politics, 1863–1899* (University, Ala., 1981), treats Colombia's central political and ideological dispute that ended in war; James William Park, *Rafael Núñez and the Politics of Colombian Regionalism, 1863–1886* (Baton Rouge, 1985), is a useful history of the Regeneration and Núñez' leadership. Vincent Baillie Dunlap, "Tragedy of a Colombian Martyr: Rafael Uribe Uribe in the Liberal Party, 1896–1914" (Ph.D. dissertation, University of North Carolina, 1979), is useful for the political and military struggle.

Joseph Arbena, "The Panama Problem in Colombian History" (Ph.D. dissertation, University of Virginia, 1970), is a comprehensive treatment of Colombia's relationship to Panama before the revolution and to the United States afterward. A valuable overview and analysis of Panama Canal historiography in Spanish is in Frank Otto Gatell, "The Canal in Retrospect," *Americas*, XV (July, 1958), 23–36. Useful works in Spanish include Luis Martinez Delgado, *Historia cambio de gobierno* (Bogotá, 1958); Ernesto J. Castillero Reyes, *La causa immediata de la empancipa de Panama* (Panama City, 1933); Oscar Terán, *Del Tratado Herrán-Hay al Tratado Hay–Bunau-Varilla* (2 vols.; Panama, 1934); Ernesto J. Castillero Reyes, *Panamá: Breve historia de la república* (Buenos Aires, 1939); Ernesto Castillero Pimental, *Panamá y los Estados Unidos* (Panama, 1953); Ricardo J. Alfaro, *Media siglo de relaciones entre Panama y los Estados Unidos* (Panama, 1959); Ricaurte Soler, *Formas ideológicas de la nación Pan-*

ameña (San José, C.R., 1972); and Eduardo Lemaitre, *Panama y su separacion de Colombia* (Bogotá, 1971).

Useful works in English from Spanish-American sources include G. A. Mellender, *The United States in Panamanian Politics: The Intriguing Formative Years* (Danville, Ill., 1971); Richard L. Lael, *Arrogant Diplomacy: U.S. Foreign Policy Toward Colombia, 1903–1922* (Wilmington, Del., 1987); and three articles by Joseph L. Arbena, "The Image of an American Imperialist: Colombian Views of Theodore Roosevelt," *West Georgia College Studies in the Social Sciences*, VI (June, 1967), 3–20; "Colombian Interpretations of the Role of the United States in the Independence of Panama," *North Dakota Quarterly* (Spring, 1973), 29–42; and "Colombian Reactions to the Independence of Panama," *Americas*, XXXIII (1976), 130–48, all based on his dissertation. For the War of the Thousand Days see the memoirs by Victor M. Salazar, *Memorias de la guerra (1899–1902)* (Bogotá, 1943); Lucas Caballaro, *Memorias de la guerra de los mil días* (Bogotá, 1939); and Malcolm Deas, "A Colombian Coffee Estate: Santa Bárbara, Cudinamarca, 1870–1912," in Kenneth Duncan and Ian Rutledge (eds.), *Land and Labour in Latin America* (Cambridge, Eng., 1977), 285–98.

Walter LaFeber's *The Panama Canal: The Crisis in Historical Perspective* (Rev. ed.; New York, 1979), is a curious mixture, part history, part polemic, written as part of the 1978 debate on the new Panama Canal treaties. William McCain, *The United States and the Republic of Panama* (Durham, N.C., 1937), is a good basic history. See also Lawrence O. Ealy, *Yanqui Politics and the Isthmian Canal* (University Park, Pa., 1971).

Useful major articles include J. A. S. Grenville, "Great Britain and the Isthmian Canal, 1898–1901," *AHR*, LXI (1955), 48–69; John Major, "Who Wrote the Hay-Bunau Varilla Convention?" *DH*, VIII (1984), 115–23; Robert A. Friedlander, "A Reassessment of Roosevelt's Role in the Panamanian Revolution of 1903," *Western Political Quarterly*, XIV (1961), 535–43; John Patterson, "Latin American Reaction to the Panama Revolution of 1903," *HAHR*, XXIV (1944), 342–51; Louis E. Van Norman, "Latin-American Views of Panama and the Canal," *American Review of Reviews*, March, 1904, pp. 334–37; E. Bradford Burns, "The Recognition of Panama by the Major Latin American States," *Americas*, XXVI (1969), 3–14; Frederick Marks III, "Morality as a Drive Wheel in the Diplomacy of Theodore Roosevelt," *DH*, II (1978), 43–62; Alfred D. Chandler, "Theodore Roosevelt and the Panama Canal: A Study in Administration," in *MRL*, VI, 1547–57; and Ralph Eldin Minger, "Panama, the Canal Zone, and Titular Sovereignty," *Western Political Quarterly*, XIV (1961), 544–54.

For American interventions from 1856 to 1903, Milton Offutt, *The Protection of Citizens Abroad by Armed Forces of the United States* (Baltimore, 1928), offers good summaries; *Use of Military Force in Colombia* (*Senate Documents*, 58th Cong., 2nd Sess., No. 143) gives the naval correspondence. For the earlier diplomatic correspondence see William Manning (ed.), *Diplomatic Correspondence of the United States: Inter-American Affairs* (12 vols.; Washington, D.C., 1935). For the 1885 intervention see Daniel H. Wicks, "Dress Rehearsal: United States Intervention on the Isthmus of Panama, 1885," *PHR*, XLIX (1980), 581–605. See also Richard W. Turk, "The United States Navy and the 'Taking' of Panama, 1901–1903," *Military Affairs*, XXXVIII (1974), 92–96.

Jesús María Henao and Gerardo Arrubla, *History of Colombia*, trans. and ed. J. Fred Rippy (Chapel Hill, 1938), is a basic history of pre-twentieth-century Colombia. Joseph Lockey, *Essays in Pan-Americanism* (Berkeley, 1939); and Lockey, *Pan-Americanism: The Beginnings* (New York, 1920), are useful histories of the Pan-American movement; James Brown Scott (ed.), *The International Conferences of American States, 1889–1928* (London, 1931), has a useful introduction and selected documents of the major Pan-American meetings, especially the first at Panama in 1826.

Useful treatments of early British-American diplomacy are in Robert Naylor, "The British Role in Central America Prior to the Clayton-Bulwer Treaty of 1850," *HAHR*, XL (1960), 361–82; J. Fred Rippy, *Rivalry of the United States and Great Britain* (Baltimore, 1929); Mary W. Williams, *Anglo-Isthmian Diplomacy, 1815–1915* (Washington, D.C., 1916); David Pletcher, *The Diplomacy of Annexation: Texas, Oregon, and the Mexican War* (Columbia, Mo., 1973); Richard W. Van Alstyne, "The Central American Policy of Lord Palmerston, 1846–1848," *HAHR*, XVI (1936), 339–59; Joseph B. Lockey, "A Neglected Aspect of Isthmian Diplomacy," *AHR*, XLI (1936), 295–305; Richard W. Van Alstyne, "British Diplomacy and the Clayton-Bulwer Treaty, 1850–1860," *Journal of Modern History*, XI (1939), 149–83; Mark Van Aken, "British Policy Considerations in Central America Before 1850," *HAHR*, XLII (1962), 54–59; Kenneth Bourne, "The Clayton-Bulwer Treaty and the Decline of British Opposition to the Territorial Expansion of the United States, 1857–1860," *Journal of Modern History*, XXXIII (1961), 287–91; and Joseph Smith, *Illusions of Conflict: Anglo American Diplomacy Toward Latin America, 1865–1896* (Pittsburgh, 1979).

For Colombia's Conservative-Liberal conflict see Joseph L. Helguera, "The First Mosquera Administration in New Granada" (Ph.D. dissertation, University of North Carolina, 1958); Helguera, "The Problem of Liberalism Versus Conservatism in Colombia, 1849–85," in Frederick B. Pike (ed.), *Latin American History: Select Problems, Identity, Integration, and Nationhood* (New York, 1969); Helen Delpar, "Aspects of Liberal Factionalism in Colombia, 1875–1885," *HAHR*, LI (1971), 250–74; for the historiography of Colombian Liberalism see Delpar, "The Liberal Record and Colombian Historiography," *Revista Americana de Bibliografia*, XXXI (1981), 524–37. Other useful works on nineteenth-century Colombia include Frank Safford, "Foreign and National Enterprise in Nineteenth-Century Colombia," *Business History Review*, XXXIX (1965), 503–26; Safford, *The Ideal of the Practical: Colombia's Struggle to Form a*

Technical Elite (Austin, Tex., 1976); Marco Palacios, *Coffee in Colombia, 1850–1970* (Cambridge, Eng., 1980); Malcolm Deas, "The Fiscal Problems of Nineteenth-Century Colombia," *Journal of Latin American Studies,* XIV (1982), 287–328; Deas, "Colombia, Ecuador, and Venezuela," in *CHLA,* V, 644–62; William Paul McGreevey, *An Economic History of Colombia, 1845–1930* (Cambridge, Eng., 1971); Hernán Horna, "Transportation, Modernization, and Entrepreneurship in Nineteenth-Century Colombia," *Journal of Latin American Studies,* XIV (1982), 33–54; David Bushnell, "Two Stages in Colombian Tariff Policy: The Radical Era and the Return to Protection (1865–1885)," *Inter-American Economic Affairs,* IX (1956), 3–23; J. Fred Rippy, "Dawn of the Railway Era in Colombia," *HAHR,* XXXIII (1943), 650–63; Jane Meyer Loy, "Primary Education During the Colombian Federation: The School Reform of 1870," *HAHR,* LI (1971), 275–94; and Jonathan C. Brown, "The Genteel Tradition of Nineteenth Century Colombian Culture," *Americas,* XXXVI (1980), 445–64.

For the history of the Panama route see John Haskell Kemble, *The Panama Route, 1848–1869* (Berkeley, 1943); for the Nicaragua route and Walker's filibusters see David I. Folkman, Jr., *The Nicaragua Route* (Salt Lake City, 1972). A useful overview of the idea of a Central American canal is in Ira E. Bennett, *History of the Panama Canal: Its Construction and Builders* (Washington, D.C., 1915); for a comparative history of the Suez and Panama canals see André Siegfried, *Suez and Panama,* trans. H. H. Heming and Doris Heming (New York, 1940).

For later nineteenth-century American interest in a Central American canal see Jackson Crowell, "The United States and a Central American Canal, 1869–1877," *HAHR,* XLIX (1969), 27–52; Roscoe R. Hill, "The Nicaraguan Canal Idea to 1913," *HAHR,* XXVII (1948), 197–211; Paul J. Scheips, "United States Commercial Pressures for a Nicaraguan Canal in the 1890's," *Americas,* XX (1964), 333–58; Lawrence A. Clayton, "The Nicaraguan Canal in the Nineteenth Century: Prelude to American Empire in the Caribbean," *Journal of Latin American Studies,* XIX (1987), 333–52; David M. Pletcher, *The Awkward Years: American Foreign Relations Under Garfield and Arthur* (Columbia, Mo., 1962), 278–83; and Kenneth J. Hagan, *American Gunboat Diplomacy and the Old Navy, 1877–1889* (Westport, Conn., 1973), 143–59.

Useful works on Panama include Donald Lee DeWitt, "Social and Educational Thought in the Development of the Republic of Panama, 1903–1946" (Ph.D. dissertation, University of Arizona, 1972); Arnold M. Freedman, "The Independence of Panama and Its Incorporation in Gran Colombia, 1820–1830" (Ph.D. dissertation, University of Florida, 1978); Louis E. Guzmán, *Farming and Farmlands in Panama* (Chicago, 1956); Ramon Valdes, "The Independence of the Isthmus of Panama—Its History, Causes, and Justification," trans. U.S. State Department, in *FRUS,* 1903, pp. 319–33; and Perez-Venero, *Before the Five Frontiers.*

Until Joseph Fry's study of John Tyler Morgan is published, the most useful

works include August C. Radke, "John Tyler Morgan: An Expansionist Sena-
tor, 1877–1907" (Ph.D. dissertation, University of Washington, 1953); Radke,
"Senator Morgan and the Nicaragua Canal," *Alabama Review*, XII (1959),
5–34; A. L. Venable, "John T. Morgan, Father of the Inter-Oceanic Canal,"
Southwestern Social Science Quarterly, XIX (1939), 376–87; O. Lawrence
Burnette, Jr., "John Tyler Morgan and Expansionist Sentiment in the New
South," *Alabama Review*, XVIII (1965), 163–82; Tennant S. McWilliams, "The
Lure of Empire: Southern Interest in the Caribbean, 1877–1900," *Mississippi
Quarterly*, XXIX (1975–76), 43–63; McWilliams, *The New South Faces the World:
Foreign Affairs and the Southern Sense of Self, 1877–1950* (Baton Rouge, 1988);
and Joseph A. Fry, "John Tyler Morgan's Southern Expansionism," *DH*, 9
(1985), 329–46.

A contemporary summary of opposition to Roosevelt's canal policies is in
George L. Fox, *President Roosevelt's Coup d'Etat: The Panama Affair in a Nutshell*
(New Haven, 1904), copy in Panama Affair Folder, Box 134, John Bassett
Moore Papers, LC.

Dominican Republic

The major primary diplomatic sources for American-Dominican relations are
the Despatches from United States Ministers to the Dominican Republic,
1883–1906, M93, Rolls 1–15, RG 59, NA. Much of the more significant diplomatic correspondence is reprinted in *FRUS*, especially in the 1905–1907 period, but the omissions are often illogical and unpredictable. American Minister Thomas C. Dawson's "Chronology of Political Events in Santo Domingo,"
October 18, 1906, in *FRUS*, 1906, pp. 572–600, remains the best single source
of Dominican history in English. After June 1906, Dominican diplomatic correspondence is in Numerical and Minor Files of the Department of State,
1906–10, Numerical File 1199, M862, Rolls 147–50, RG 59, NA. In the Decimal File instituted in 1910 Dominican affairs are in Records of the Department
of State Relating to Internal Affairs of the Dominican Republic, 1910–29, Files
839.00 to 839.9251 in M626, Rolls 1–79, RG 59, NA. Often disappointing but
still useful are Notes from the Legation of the Dominican Republic to the
United States, T801, Roll 3; and Notes to the Legation of the Dominican Republic, M99, Roll 59. The three Dominican series of consular despatches,
Puerto Plata, T662, Roll 3; Samaná, T670, Roll 2; and Santo Domingo, T56,
Rolls 15–19, all RG 59, NA, are of marginal use because the few significant
messages are duplicated in the diplomatic Despatches series. Other useful
collections include Diplomatic Instructions of the Department of State, M77,
Roll 98, RG 59, NA; and Miscellaneous Letters of the Department of State,
M179, Rolls 1195–1310, RG 59, NA, which contain extremely scattered but
relevant material, especially communications from William T. Bass, the American sugar planter who frequently offered advice to the State Department.

Jacob Hollander's basic work is found in Communications from Special

Agents of the Department of State, Vol. 49, Microcopy M37, Roll 21, RG 59, NA. Included in this collection are not only Hollander's letters to the president and State Department but the typescripts of his "Report on the Debt of Santo Domingo"; "Notes on the West Indies"; and Hollander's long confidential memorandum to Roosevelt that supplements his printed letter to Roosevelt issued with the debt report. A printed version of *Debt of Santo Domingo* is in *Senate Confidential Executive Documents,* 59th Cong., 1st Sess., No. 1 (or 1A), an extremely rare government document still uncataloged in the printed government document guides. It was printed (but not published) for the exclusive use of the Senate Foreign Relations Committee and remained a secret document until after the Convention of 1907 was ratified. A few extant copies have survived, in the rare government documents collection at LC, the Department of State Library, and the Pan-American Union. A virtually identical typescript, from which the printed copy was composed, in Communications from Special Agents, M37, Roll 21, is possibly a more accessible source. Jacob Hollander's Papers constitute a rare National Archives manuscript collection (RG 200, Department of State) and illuminate his dealings with individual Dominicans, his dispute with Congress and the State Department over the additional Dominican payment of $100,000 in 1908, and personal matters.

Valuable naval correspondence is in Santo Domingo Correspondence, RG 45, entry 305, and in Area File 8, M625, Rolls 256–71, RG 45, Naval Records Collection of the Office of Naval Records and Library, NA. Much of the SDIC history is in John Bassett Moore, "Case of the United States," February 12, 1904, SDIC Arbitration Proceedings, RG 59, Boundary Claims, Commissions, and Arbitrations, NA.

For Dominican history, H. Hoetink, *The Dominican People, 1850–1900: Notes for a Historical Sociology,* trans. Stephen K. Ault (Baltimore, 1982), is an essential guide to Dominican life and thought in the nineteenth century; Gordon K. Lewis, *Caribbean Nationalism: The Historical Evolution of Caribbean Society in Its Ideological Aspects, 1492–1900* (Baltimore, 1983), is a thorough guide to Caribbean nationalism and literature.

Sumner Welles, *Naboth's Vineyard: Dominican Republic, 1844–1924* (2 vols.; New York, 1928) is a deeply flawed but essential source. Welles, frequently sloppy as well as needlessly condescending, tried to write as both a historian and a diplomat with predictable confusion. The single best historical treatment of American-Dominican relations is David Charles MacMichael, "The United States and the Dominican Republic, 1871–1940: A Cycle in Caribbean Diplomacy" (Ph.D. dissertation, University of Oregon, 1964). MacMichael's magesterial thesis has none of the tentativeness of a cautious dissertation; it is critical, exhaustive, and usually persuasive in examining both American and Dominican policies and motives. See also Glenn Joseph Kist, "The Role of Thomas C. Dawson in United States–Latin American Diplomatic Relations, 1897–1912" (Ph.D. dissertation, Loyola University of Chicago, 1971); and H.

Paul Muto, "The Illusory Promise: The Dominican Republic and the Process of Economic Development, 1900–1930" (Ph.D. dissertation, University of Washington, 1976). See also Michael Baud, "The Origins of Capitalist Agriculture in the Dominican Republic," *Latin American Research Review*, XXII (1987), 135–53. Edgar Charles Duin, "Dominican-American Diplomatic Relations, 1895–1907" (Ph.D. dissertation, Georgetown University, 1955), is useful mainly as a guide to the American diplomatic sources, which it quotes at great length. Melvin Knight, *The Americans in Santo Domingo* (New York, 1928), is one of the best of the Studies in American Imperialism under the general editorship of Harry Elmer Barnes and the economic support of one of the first American political foundations, the American Fund for Public Service. Knight, a professional economic historian, has written a critical account of American involvement in Dominican affairs. William H. Wynne, *State Insolvency and Foreign Bondholders: Selected Case Histories* (New Haven, 1951), is an invaluable history of the Dominican debt placed in the essential context of nineteenth-century international bond disputes. See also Lester D. Langley, *The Struggle for the American Mediterranean: United States–European Rivalry in the Gulf-Caribbean, 1776–1904* (Athens, Ga., 1976); David Healy, *Drive to Hegemony: The United States in the Caribbean, 1898–1917* (Madison, Wisc., 1988); and Wilfrid H. Callcott, *The Caribbean Policy of the United States, 1890–1920* (Baltimore, 1942). Of ancillary interest are Brenda Plummer, *Haiti and the Great Powers, 1902–1915* (Baton Rouge, 1988); and Sir Harold Mitchell, *Europe in the Caribbean: The Policies of Great Britain, France, and the Netherlands Toward Their West Indian Territories in the Twentieth Century* (Stanford, 1963).

Useful general Dominican histories include Selden Rodman, *Quisqueya: A History of the Dominican Republic* (Seattle, 1964); and Ian Bell, *The Dominican Republic* (Boulder, Colo., 1981). Otto Schoenrich, a distinguished American jurist, who served as Hollander's secretary in 1905–1907 and helped write Puerto Rico's new legal code, in his *Santo Domingo: A Country with a Future* (New York, 1918), partly memoir, history, and travel guide, offers a valuable book that serves as one American's love ode to a nation's tragic destiny. An older history, still of some interest, is Samuel Hazard, *Santo Domingo Past and Present with a Backward Glance at Hayti* (New York, 1873).

Useful Spanish sources include Manuel de Jesús Troncoso de la Concha, *La genesis de la Convención Dominico-America* (Santiago, D.R., 1946); and César Herrera, *Las finanzas de la República Dominicana* (2 vols.; Ciudad Trujillo, D.R., 1955), more a documentary compilation than a critical analysis.

Philip Jessup, *Elihu Root* (2 vols.; New York, 1938), offers an essential reading of Secretary of State Elihu Root's role through the primary State Department sources. J. Fred Rippy's many works bear heavily on American-Dominican relations; Rippy is both useful and uneven. See especially "The Initiation of the Customs Receivership in the Dominican Republic," *HAHR*, XVII (1937), 419–57. For the Grant administration's attempts at annexation see Charles Callan Tansill, *The United States and Santo Domingo, 1798–1893* (Baltimore, 1938). On the political and constitutional conflict, W. Stull Holt, *Treaties Defeated by the Senate* (Baltimore, 1933), is indispensable.

The Monroe Doctrine

Dexter Perkins, *A History of the Monroe Doctrine* (Boston, 1963); Perkins, *The Monroe Doctrine, 1823–1826* (Cambridge, Mass., 1927); Perkins, *The Monroe Doctrine, 1826–1867* (Baltimore, 1933); and Perkins, *The Monroe Doctrine, 1867–1907* (Baltimore, 1937), are the standard works. For the European and American political contexts see Ernest May, *The Making of the Monroe Doctrine* (Cambridge, Mass., 1975); Samuel Flagg Bemis, *John Quincy Adams and the Foundations of American Foreign Policy* (New York, 1949); Harry Ammon, "The Monroe Doctrine: Domestic Politics or National Decision?" *DH*, V (1981), 53–70; and Ernest May, "Response to Harry Ammon," *ibid.*, 71–72.

Useful articles include J. Fred Rippy, "Antecedents of the Roosevelt Corollary of the Monroe Doctrine," *PHR*, IX (1940), 267–79; Charles E. Chapman, "New Corollaries of the Monroe Doctrine with Especial Reference to the Relations of the United States with Cuba," *University of California Chronicle*, XXXIII (1931), 161–89; Thomas E. Karnes, "Hiram Bingham and His Obsolete Shibboleth," *DH*, III (1979), 39–57; David Y. Thomas, "The Monroe Doctrine from Roosevelt to Roosevelt," *South Atlantic Quarterly*, XXXIV (1935), 117–35. Useful contemporary accounts include George W. Critchfield, *American Supremacy: The Rise and Progress of the Latin American Republics and Their Relations to the United States Under the Monroe Doctrine* (2 vols.; New York, 1908); Frederick Courtland Penfield, "Practical Phases of Caribbean Domination," *NAR*, CLXXVII (1904), 75–85; Walter Wellman, "Shall the Monroe Doctrine Be Modified?" *NAR*, CLXXIII (1901), 832–44; William L. Scruggs, "The Monroe Doctrine—Its Origin and Import," *NAR*, CLXXVI (1903), 185–99; Sir Alexander E. Miller, "The Monroe Doctrine from an English Standpoint," *NAR*, CLXXVI (1903), 728–33; Edward S. Rapallo and Domingo B. Castillo, "The New Monroe Doctrine," *NAR*, CLXXX (1905), 586–601; Hiram Bingham, "Latin America and the Monroe Doctrine," *Yale Review*, III (1914), 656–72; William R. Shepherd, "New Light on the Monroe Doctrine," *Political Science Quarterly*, XXXI (1916), 578–89. Kenneth M. Coleman, "The Political Mythology of the Monroe Doctrine: Reflections on the Social Psychology of Hegemony," in John D. Martz and Lars Schoultz (eds.), *Latin America, the United States, and the Inter-American System* (Boulder, Colo., 1980), 95–114, is political science model making that ignores history.

Central America and the Peace Conferences

The basic archival materials, still relatively untapped, are in the standard National Archives diplomatic collections: Despatches from United States Ministers to Nicaragua, Costa Rica, and El Salvador, M219, Rolls 87–94, RG 59,

NA; Despatches from American Ministers to Guatemala and Honduras, M219, Rolls 63–72; Despatches from American Ministers to Mexico, M97, Rolls 158–179. Diplomatic Instructions are in M77, Roll 34 (Central America) and 122 (Mexico) all in RG 59, NA. Notes to Central American Legations are in M99, Roll 11, and Notes from Central American Legations are in T34, Roll 10.

The most comprehensive diplomatic history is Dana Munro, *Intervention and Dollar Diplomacy in the Caribbean, 1900–1921* (Princeton, 1964). The best general history is Ralph L. Woodward, *Central America: A Nation Divided* (Rev. ed.; New York, 1985). A sympathetic account of Central American economic difficulties is in Dana Munro, *The Five Republics of Central America: Their Political and Economic Development and Their Relations with the United States* (New York, 1918). Thomas L. Karnes, *The Failure of Union: Central America, 1824–1960* (Chapel Hill, 1961), traces the failure of political unification. Still useful though old and spotty is Howard C. Hill, *Roosevelt and the Caribbean* (Chicago, 1927); Phillip Brown, "American Diplomacy in Central America," *American Political Science Review*, VI (1912), *Proceedings*, 151–61, is a good firsthand account by a practicing diplomat. James Morton Callahan, *American Foreign Policy in Mexican Relations* (New York, 1932), is the standard account.

William Griffith, "The Historiography of Central America Since 1830," *HAHR*, XL (1960), 548–69; and Ralph Lee Woodward, Jr., "The Historiography of Modern Central America Since 1960," *HAHR*, LXVII (1987), 471–96, are comprehensive. See David Healy, "A Hinterland in Search of a Metropolis: The Mosquito Coast, 1894–1910," *International History Review*, III (1981), 20–43. Frederich Katz, *The Secret War in Mexico: Europe, the United States, and the Mexican Revolution* (Chicago, 1981), examines the decline of the Porfiriato and American economic rivalry with Europe.

Donald Shea, *The Calvo Clause: A Problem of Inter-American and International Law and Diplomacy* (Minneapolis, 1955), is a good account of the history of the Calvo and Drago doctrines. The text of the Drago message is in *FRUS*, 1903, pp. 1–5; see also Luis M. Drago, "State Loans in Their Relation to International Policy," *American Journal of International Law*, I (1907), 692–726; and Amos S. Hershey, "The Calvo and Drago Doctrines," *American Journal of International Law*, I (1907), 26–45. Elihu Root, *Latin America and the United States* (Cambridge, Mass., 1917), collects Root's major diplomatic addresses. Arthur P. Whitaker, *The Western Hemisphere Idea: Its Rise and Decline* (Ithaca, N.Y., 1954), is useful though polemical.

For the Rio Conference of 1906 see A. Curtis Wilgus, "The Third International American Conference at Rio de Janeiro, 1906," *HAHR*, XII (1932), 420–56; "Report of the Delegates of the United States to the Third International Conference of the American States," in *Senate Documents*, 59th Cong., 2nd Sess., No. 365, Serial 5073; Clifford B. Casey, "The Creation and Development of the Pan American Union," *HAHR*, XIII (1933), 437–56. For the Hague diplomatic correspondence see James B. Scott (ed.), *The Reports to the Hague Conferences of 1899 and 1907* (Oxford, 1916); Calvin DeArmond Davis, *The United States and the Second Hague Peace Conference: American Diplomacy and International Organization, 1899–1914* (Durham, N.C., 1975), is the standard account. Philip Jessup, *Elihu Root* (2 vols.; New York, 1938), is essential for both conferences. Joseph Wall, *Andrew Carnegie* (New York, 1970), 886–940, should be consulted.

The most useful doctoral dissertations include Lejune Cummins, "The Origin and Development of Elihu Root's Latin American Diplomacy" (Ph.D. dissertation, University of California, Berkeley, 1964); Donald J. Murphy, "Professors, Publicists, and Pan-Americanism, 1905–1917: A Study in the Origins of the Use of Experts in Shaping American Foreign Policy" (Ph.D. dissertation, University of Wisconsin, 1970); Robert Neal Seidel, "Progressive Pan-Americanism, 1905–1917: Development and United States Policy Toward South America, 1906–1931" (Ph.D. dissertation, Cornell University, 1973); Edwin A. Muth, "Elihu Root: His Role and Concepts Pertaining to United States Policies of Intervention" (Ph.D. dissertation, Georgetown University, 1966); Richard Megargee, "The Diplomacy of John Bassett Moore: Realism in American Foreign Policy" (Ph.D. dissertation, Northwestern University, 1963); and Peter M. DiMeglio, "The United States and the Second Hague Peace Conference: The Extension of the Use of Arbitration" (Ph.D. dissertation, St. John's University, 1968).

See also E. Bradford Burns, *The Unwritten Alliance: Rio-Branco and Brazilian-American Relations* (New York, 1966); Thomas F. McGann, *Argentina, the United States, and the Inter-American System, 1880–1914* (Cambridge, Mass., 1957); Frederick B. Pike, *Chile and the United States, 1880–1962* (South Bend, Ind., 1963); and Frederick William Ganzert, "The Baron Do Rio-Branco, Joaquim Nabuco, and the Growth of Brazilian-American Friendship, 1900–1910," *HAHR*, XXII (1942), 432–51. David S. Patterson, *Toward a Warless World: The Travail of the American Peace Movement, 1887–1914* (Bloomington, Ind., 1976), is helpful.

Cuba

The basic source for the second American intervention is the "Taft-Bacon Report," in *House Documents*, 59th Cong., 2nd Sess., No. 2, Serial 5105, pp. 444–542, which reprints most of the Taft-Roosevelt correspondence. Cuba historiography is rich and distinguished. The major treatments include Russell H. Fitzgibbon, *Cuba and the United States, 1900–1935* (Menosha, Wisc., 1935); Leland H. Jenks, *Our Cuban Colony: A Study in Sugar* (New York, 1928); Allan Reed Millet, *Politics of Intervention: The Military Occupation of Cuba, 1906–1909* (Columbus, Ohio, 1968); Lester D. Langley, *The Cuban Policy of the United States: A Brief History* (New York, 1968); Jules Robert Benjamin, *The United States and Cuba: Hegemony and Dependent Development, 1880–1934* (Pittsburgh,

1977); Lewis L. Gould, *The Presidency of William McKinley* (Lawrence, Kan., 1980); David Healy, *The United States in Cuba, 1898–1902* (Madison, Wisc., 1963). Philip S. Foner, *The Spanish-Cuban-American War and the Birth of American Imperialism, 1895–1902* (2 vols.; New York, 1972), is full and informative in spite of its polemics. David F. Trask, *The War with Spain in 1898* (New York, 1981), is the best history of the war. A thorough historiographical survey is Duvon C. Corbitt, "Cuban Revisionist Interpretations of Cuba's Struggle for Independence," *HAHR*, XLIII (1963), 395–404.

For Cuban history, Charles E. Chapman, *A History of the Cuban Republic* (New York, 1927), is intelligent and sensitive; Hugh Thomas, *Cuba* (New York, 1971), is encylopedic; Louis A. Pérez, Jr., *Cuba Between Empires, 1878–1902* (Pittsburgh, 1983), is very useful though occasionally marred by its obsession with North American economic motives; Pérez, "Vagrants, Beggars, and Bandits: Social Origins of Cuban Separatism, 1878–1895," *AHR*, XC (1985), 1093–94, is excellent. See also Gerald E. Poyo, "Evolution of Cuban Separatist Thought in the Emigré Communities of the United States, 1848–1895," *HAHR*, LXVI (1986), 486–507.

On the importance of sugar see Sidney W. Mintz, *Sweetness and Power: The Place of Sugar in Modern History* (New York, 1985); Richard Daniel Weigle, "The Sugar Interests and American Diplomacy in Hawaii and Cuba, 1893–1903" (Ph.D. dissertation, Yale University, 1939), is exhaustive. See also Fernando Ortiz, *Cuban Counterpoint: Tobacco and Sugar* (New York, 1947); and Robert B. Hoernel, "Sugar and Change in Oriente, Cuba," *Journal of Latin American Studies*, VIII (1976), 215–49. Roosevelt's anti-trust policies and the legal history of the Sugar Trust are in Hans Thorelli, *The Federal Antitrust Policy: Origination of an American Tradition* (Baltimore, 1953), 586–609, 445–48. See also Joe A. Fisher, "The Knight Case Revisited," *Historian*, XXXV (1973), 365–83. Mark Schmitz, "The Transformation of the Southern Sugar Cane Sector, 1860–1930," *Agricultural History*, LIII (1979), 270–84, traces the changes in the American sugar market.

A valuable overview of both the American and Cuban Platt Amendment historiography is in James H. Hitchman, "The Platt Amendment Revisited: A Bibliographical Survey," *Americas*, XXXIII (1967), 343–69. See also Lejune Cummins, "The Formulation of the 'Platt' Amendment," *Americas*, XXIII (1967), 370–89. Phillip Jessup, *Elihu Root* (2 vols.; New York, 1938), is especially useful on the Platt Amendment and American Cuban ambitions. Other important articles include Lewis Gould, "Chocolate Eclair or Mandarin Manipulator? William McKinley, the Spanish-American War, and the Philippines: A Review Essay," *Ohio History*, XCIV (1985), 182–87; Joseph A. Fry, "William McKinley and the Coming of the Spanish-American War: A Study of the Besmirching and Redemption of an Historical Image," *DH*, III (1979), 77–98; John Offner, "President McKinley's Final Attempt to Avoid War with Spain," *Ohio History*, XCIV (1985), 125–38; Alfred T. Mahan, "Strategic Features of the Caribbean Sea and Gulf of Mexico," *Harper's New Monthly Magazine*, XCV (October, 1897), 680–91, rpr. in Alfred T. Mahan, *Mahan on Naval Warfare* (Boston, 1918), is most helpful in explaining the limits of American strategic ambitions.

For Leonard Wood see the extensive Leonard Wood Papers and the Elihu Root Papers at LC. Hermann Hagedorn, *Leonard Wood* (New York, 1931), is still useful. See also Jack C. Lane, *Armed Progressive: General Leonard Wood* (San Rafael, Calif., 1978); and James H. Hitchman, *Leonard Wood and Cuban Independence, 1898–1902* (The Hague, 1971).

For the Catholic influence on American colonial policies see Frank T. Reuter, *Catholic Influence on American Colonial Policies, 1898–1904* (Austin, Tex., 1967); for Latin American anticlericalism see J. Lloyd Mecham, *Church and State in Latin America* (Rev. ed.; Chapel Hill, 1966). C. A. M. Hennessy, "The Roots of Cuban Nationalism," *International Affairs*, XXXIX (1963), 345–59, is especially perceptive on Martí's role and the cultural conflict between Protestantism and Catholicism.

Latin American Culture

For the best overview see Gerald Martin, "The Literature, Music, and Art of Latin America, 1870–1930," an admirable synthesis in Leslie Bethell, *The Cambridge History of Latin America*, Vol. IV (Cambridge, Eng., 1986), 445–526, 643–56.

English translations of Martí and Darío include José Martí, *Inside the Monster: Writings on the United States and American Imperialism*, ed. Philip S. Foner, trans. Elinor Randall (New York, 1975); José Martí, *Our America: Writings on Latin America and the Struggle for Cuban Independence*, ed. Philip S. Foner, trans. Elinor Randall (New York, 1977); José Martí, *On Art and Literature: Critical Writings*, ed. Philip S. Foner, trans. Elinor Randall (New York, 1982); and Rubén Darío, *Selected Poems of Rubén Darío*, trans. Lysander Kemp (Austin, Tex., 1965).

Juan de Onis, *The United States as Seen by Spanish American Writers, 1776–1890* (New York, 1952); Gordon K. Lewis, *Main Currents in Caribbean Thought: The Historical Evolution of Caribbean Society in Its Ideological Aspects, 1492–1900* (Baltimore, 1983); John Reid, *Spanish American Images of the United States* (Gainesville, 1977); and Eugenio Pereira Salas, "Cultural Emancipation of America," in UNESCO, *Old World and New World* (Berne, Switzerland, 1956), are essential; see also E. Bradford Burns, *The Poverty of Progress: Latin America in the Nineteenth Century* (Berkeley, 1980); R. A. Humphreys, "The Caudillo Tradition," in R. A. Humphreys, *Tradition and Revolt in Latin America and Other Essays* (New York, 1969); and John A. Crow, *The Epic of Latin America* (3rd ed.; Berkeley, 1980).

For Martí's life see Manuel Pedro Gonzales, *José Martí: Epic Chronicler of the United States in the Eighties* (Chapel Hill, 1953); Richard Butler Gray, *José Martí:*

Cuban Patriot (Gainesville, 1962); and John M. Kirk, *José Martí: Mentor of the Cuban Nation* (Tampa, 1983). For Martí's writing in New York see Roberta Day Corbitt, "This Colossal Theater: The United States Interpreted by José Martí" (Ph.D. dissertation, University of Kentucky, 1955); see Robert Roland Anderson, *Spanish American Modernism: A Selected Bibliography* (Tucson, 1970), for bibliographies of Martí, Rodó, and Darío. Clemente Pereda, *Rodó's Main Sources* (San Juan, P.R., 1941); Keith Ellis, *Critical Approaches to Rubén Darío* (Toronto, 1974); and Isaac Goldberg, *Studies in Spanish-American Literature* (New York, 1920), are useful literary studies.

Postindependence Latin American cultural and intellectual life are well treated in A. Owen Aldridge, "The Concept of the Ibero-American Enlightenment," in Aldridge, *The Ibero-American Enlightenment* (Urbana, 1971), 3–20; Arthur P. Whitaker, "Changing and Unchanging Interpretations of the Enlightenment in Spanish America," *ibid.*, 21–57; Russell P. Sebold, "Enlightenment Philosophy and the Emergence of Spanish Romanticism," *ibid.*, 111–40; Arthur P. Whitaker, *The United States and the Independence of Latin America, 1800–1830* (Baltimore, 1941); and Whitaker, *The Western Hemisphere Idea: Its Rise and Decline* (Ithaca, N.Y., 1954). For the influence of positivism in Latin America see Ralph Lee Woodward, Jr. (ed.), *Positivism in Latin America: 1850–1900* (Lexington, Mass., 1971). For the controversy about Herbert E. Bolton's thesis of a commonality between the two Americas see Lewis Hanke (ed.), *Do the Americas Have a Common History? A Critique of the Bolton Theory* (New York, 1964); see also Harry Bernstein, *Making an Inter-American Mind* (Gainesville, 1961); Bernstein, *Origins of Inter-American Interest, 1700–1812* (Washington, D.C., 1945); Samuel Shapiro, "A Common History of the Americas," in Shapiro (ed.), *Cultural Factors in Inter-American Relations* (South Bend, Ind., 1968); Leopoldo Zea, *The Latin American Mind*, trans. James H. Abbott and Lowell Dunham (Norman, Okla., 1963); Zea, *Latin America and the World*, trans. Frances K. Hendrichs and Beatrice Becker (Norman, Okla., 1969); Martin S. Stabb, *In Quest of Identity: Patterns in the Spanish-American Essay of Ideas, 1890–1960* (Chapel Hill, 1967); Jean Franco, *The Modern Culture of Latin America: Society and Artist* (New York, 1967); W. Rex Crawford, *A Century of Latin American Thought* (Cambridge, Mass., 1961); José Agustín Balseiro, *The Americas Look at Each Other*, trans. Muna Muñoz Lee (Coral Gables, Fla., 1969); and Glen Caudill Dealy, *The Public Man: An Interpretation of Latin American and Other Catholic Countries* (Amherst, Mass., 1977).

For Simón Bolívar see John Lynch, "Bolívar and the Caudillos," *HAHR,* LXIII (1983), 3–35; Simon Collier, "Nationality, Nationalism, and Supranationalism in the Writings of Simón Bolívar," *HAHR,* LXIII (1983), 37–64; and David Bushnell, "The Last Dictatorship: Betrayal or Consummation?" *HAHR,* LXIII (1983), 65–105. Older useful treatments include William R. Shephard, "Bolívar and the United States," *HAHR,* I (1918), 270–98; Víctor Andrés Belaúnde, *Bolívar and the Political Thought of the Spanish American Revolution*

(Baltimore, 1938); David Bushnell (ed.), *The Liberator, Simón Bolívar: Man and Image* (New York, 1970); Gerhard Masur, *Simón Bolívar* (Rev. ed.; Albuquerque, 1969); R. A. Humphreys and John Lynch (eds.), *The Origins of the Latin American Revolutions, 1808–1826* (New York, 1964); Joseph B. Lockey, "Bolívar, After a Century," in Lockey, *Essays in Pan-Americanism* (Berkeley, 1939), 135–42.

For literary and historical analyses of anti-American writing by Latin Americans see Mary Patricia Chapman, "Yankeephobia: An Analysis of the Anti-United States Bias of Certain South American Intellectuals, 1898–1928" (Ph.D. dissertation, Stanford University, 1950); and J. Fred Rippy, "Literary Yankeephobia in Hispanic America," *Journal of International Relations,* XII (1922), 350–71, 524–38.

For a summary of modernization theory see Cyril E. Black (ed.), *Comparative Modernization: A Reader* (New York, 1976), esp. James O'Connell, "The Concept of Modernization," *ibid.,* 13–14; and Donald R. Headrick, *The Tools of Empire: Technology and European Imperialism in the Nineteenth Century* (New York, 1981). For a critical view of dependency theory see David Ray, "The Dependency Model of Latin American Underdevelopment: Three Basic Fallacies," *Journal of Inter-American Studies and World Affairs,* XV (1973), 4–20. Syntheses of the historiographical debate are in William Glade, "Latin America and the International Economy, 1870–1914," in *CHLA,* IV, 46–56; and Thomas F. O'Brien, "Dependency Revisited: A Review Essay," *Business History Review,* LIV (1985), 663–70. For some of the debates over imperialism see Richard Koebner and H. D. Schmidt, *Imperialism: The Story and Significance of a Political Word, 1840–1960* (Cambridge, Eng., 1964); David Healy, *Modern Imperialism: Changing Styles in Historical Interpretation* (Washington, D.C., 1967); and Hugh de Santis, "Imperialist Impulse and American Innocence," in Gerald K. Haines and J. Samuel Walker (eds.), *American Foreign Relations: A Historiographical Review* (Westport, Conn., 1981), 65–90. See also Louis A. Pérez, Jr., "Intervention, Hegemony, and Dependency: The United States in the circum-Caribbean, 1898–1980," *PHR,* LI (1982), 165–82.

For a summary of the recent criticism of William Appleman Williams' views on American economic expansionism see J. A. Thompson, "William Appleman Williams and the 'American Empire,'" *Journal of American Studies* (Great Britain), VII (1973), 91–104; David M. Pletcher, "1861–1898: Economic Growth and Diplomatic Adjustment," in William H. Becker and Samuel Wells, Jr. (eds.), *Economics and World Power: An Assessment of American Diplomacy Since 1789* (Westport, Conn., 1984), 125–31; Pletcher, "Rhetoric and Results: A Pragmatic View of American Economic Expansion, 1865–98," *DH,* V (1981), 93–108. For the rejection of the Williams school's connection between American business and government see William H. Becker, *The Dynamics of Business-Government Relations, 1893–1921* (Chicago, 1981); Mira Wilkins, *The Emergence of Multinational Enterprise: American Business Abroad from the Colonial*

Era to 1914 (Cambridge, Mass., 1970); and Paul S. Holbo, "Economics, Emotion, and Expansion: An Emerging Foreign Policy," in H. Wayne Morgan (ed.), *The Gilded Age* (Rev. ed.; Syracuse, N.Y., 1970), 199–221; 315–19. See also Joel Migdal, "Capitalist Penetration in the Nineteenth Century: Creating Conditions for Social Control," in Robert P. Weller and Scott E. Guggenheim (eds.), *Power and Protest in the Countryside* (Durham, N.C., 1982), 57–74; and L. W. Pye (ed.), *Communications and Political Development* (Princeton, 1963), 3–21, 149–51.

D. A. Graber, *Crisis Diplomacy: A History of U.S. Intervention Policies and Practices* (Washington, D.C., 1959); and Marvin D. Bernstein, *Foreign Investment in Latin America* (New York, 1966), are useful reference works. See also Burton I. Kaufman, "The Organizational Dimension of United States Economic Foreign Policy, 1900–1920," *Business History Review*, XLVI (1972), 17–44; and Emily S. Rosenberg, "Foundations of United States International Financial Power: Gold Standard Diplomacy," *Business History Review*, LIX (1985), 169–202. For recent corporatist historiography see John Lewis Gaddis, "The Corporatist Synthesis: A Skeptical View," and Michael J. Hogan, "Corporatism: A Positive Appraisal," both in *DH*, X (1986), 357–62, 363–72.

Other useful overviews include J. Fred Rippy, *Latin America in World Politics* (New York, 1928); J. Lloyd Meecham, *The United States and Inter-American Security, 1889–1960* (Austin, Tex., 1961); Graham A. Stuart, *Latin America and the United States* (New York, 1955); Samuel Flagg Bemis, *The Latin American Policy of the United States* (New York, 1967); and Hubert Herring, *A History of Latin America* (New York, 1957). Leslie Bethel (ed.), *The Cambridge History of Latin America* (5 vols.; Cambridge, Eng., 1984–86), offers the most recent scholarship on Latin America; its interpretive overviews and excellent bibliographies are the starting point for research concerning Latin America. Robert J. Alexander (ed.), *Biographical Dictionary of Latin America and Caribbean Political Leaders* (Westport, Conn., 1988) is useful if curiously selective.

Index